# THE REAL LITTLE ULTIMATE BROADWAY FAKE BOOK

Over 720 Songs

from over 240 Shows

For Piano, Vocal, Guitar, Electronic Keyboards

and all "C" Instruments

2   Index of Songs

5   Index of Shows

10   Index of Composers & Lyricists

17   About the Shows

69   Music

Fourth Edition

D1260978

ISBN 0-7935-8246-6

## HAL•LEONARD®
### CORPORATION
7777 W. BLUEMOUND RD. P.O. BOX 13819 MILWAUKEE, WI 53213

For all works contained herein:
Unauthorized copying, arranging, adapting, recording or public performance is an infringement of copyright.
Infringers are liable under the law.

Technicolor® is the registered trademark of the Technicolor group of companies.

Visit Hal Leonard Online at
**www.halleonard.com**

# INDEX OF SONGS

## A

363 Ace In The Hole
152 Ad-dressing Of Cats, The
242 Adelaide's Lament
449 After You've Gone
220 Ah, Paris!
74 Ain't Misbehavin'
486 All At Once You Love Her
432 All Er Nothin'
260 All For The Best
262 All Good Gifts
468 All I Ask Of You
278 All I Need Is The Girl
526 All Of You
583 All The Things You Are
137 Allez-Vous-En, Go Away
306 Almost
116 Alone Too Long
338 Always True To You In My Fashion
202 Anatevka
172 And All That Jazz
472 Angel Of Music
164 Another Hundred People
336 Another Op'nin', Another Show
194 Another Suitcase In Another Hall
141 Anthem
322 Any Dream Will Do
549 Any Place I Hang My Hat Is Home
90 Anyone Can Whistle
184 Anyone Would Love You
84 Anything You Can Do
253 Are You Havin' Any Fun?
570 Artificial Flowers
622 As If We Never Said Goodbye
440 As Long As He Needs Me
500 As Once I Loved You
602 At Long Last Love
173 At The Ballet

## B

540 Bali Ha'i
567 Ballad Of Sweeney Todd, The
426 Ballad Of The Sad Young Men, The
566 Be A Santa
399 Be Happy
196 Be Kind To Your Parents
91 Beautiful, Beautiful World
98 Beauty And The Beast
273 Beauty School Dropout
288 Before The Parade Passes By
166 Being Alive
520 Believe
100 Bells Are Ringing
490 Bess, You Is My Woman
343 Best Of Times, The
268 Best Things In Life Are Free, The
461 Bewitched
393 Beyond My Wildest Dreams
453 Big Beat, The
408 Big D
522 Bill
386 Black
73 Black And Blue,
    (What Did I Do To Be So)
541 Bloody Mary
258 Blue Room, The
99 Blue Skies
159 Boys And Girls Like You And Me
354 Bring Him Home
222 Broadway Baby
300 Brotherhood Of Man
336 Brush Up Your Shakespeare
104 Buckle Down, Winsocki
191 Buenos Aires
241 Bushel And A Peck, A
154 Bustopher Jones: The Cat About Town
232 Button Up Your Overcoat
264 By My Side
104 By Myself
525 By Strauss

## C

138 C'est Magnifique
123 Cabaret
130 Camelot
523 Can't Help Lovin' Dat Man
292 Can't You Just See Yourself?
508 Capped Teeth And Caesar Salad
530 Caravan
353 Castle On A Cloud
455 Charlie's Place
452 Cherry Pies Ought To Be You
72 City Lights
79 Civilization (Bongo, Bongo, Bongo)
533 Climb Ev'ry Mountain
582 Close As Pages In A Book
323 Close Every Door
542 Cock-Eyed Optimist, A
314 Cocoanut Sweet
442 Come Back To Me
508 Come Back With The Same Look In
    Your Eyes
550 Come Rain Or Come Shine
239 Comedy Tonight
166 Company
440 Consider Yourself
225 Could I Leave You

## D

517 Dance Only With Me
176 Dance: Ten; Looks: Three
499 Dancing On The Ceiling
576 Darn It, Baby, That's Love
259 Day By Day
182 Dear World
542 Dites-Moi (Tell Me Why)
184 Do I Hear A Waltz?
160 Do I Love You Because You're Beautiful?
356 Do You Hear The People Sing?
200 Do You Love Me?
534 Do-Re-Mi
193 Don't Cry For Me Argentina
565 Don't Ever Leave Me
298 Don't Like Goodbyes
218 Don't Marry Me
234 Don't Rain On My Parade
483 Down In The Depths (On The Ninetieth
    Floor)
297 Down With Love
387 Dream Babies
353 Drink With Me (To Days Gone By)
371 Dulcinea

## E

70 Easter Parade
80 Easy Street
537 Edelweiss
359 Empty Chairs At Empty Tables
552 Engine Of Love
518 Ev'ry Time We Say Goodbye
117 Ev'rything I've Got
112 Evelina
487 Everybody's Got A Home But Me
318 Everything's Alright
278 Everything's Coming Up Roses

## F

572 Fallin'
115 Falling In Love With Love
195 Fanny
202 Far From The Home I Love
438 Farmer And The Cowman, The
527 Fated To Be Mated
502 Feeling Good
77 Fellow Needs A Girl, A
201 Fiddler On The Roof
607 First Time, The
135 Follow Me
294 Forever And A Day
252 Forty-five Minutes From Broadway
520 Freedom
190 Friendship
451 From This Moment On
246 Fugue For Tinhorns

## G

78 Gentleman Is A Dope, The
213 Gentleman Jimmy
416 Get Me To The Church On Time
351 Get Out Of Town
427 Getting Tall
331 Getting To Know You
254 Gigi
250 Give My Regards To Broadway
447 Glad To Be Unhappy
224 God-Why-Don't-You-Love-Me Blues, Th
560 Gonna Build A Mountain
270 Good News
395 Good Thing Going
411 Goodnight My Someone
232 Got A Date With An Angel
369 Green-Up Time
258 Guess I'll Hang My Tears Out To Dry
242 Guys And Dolls

## H

283 Half A Sixpence
75 Handful Of Keys
605 Happy Birthday To Me
544 Happy Talk
285 Happy Time, The
250 Harrigan
310 Haunted Heart
308 Have You Met Miss Jones?
391 He Who Knows The Way
333 He's In Love
71 Heat Wave
151 Heaven Help My Heart
287 Hello, Dolly!
327 Hello, Young Lovers
615 Here Comes The Morning
370 Here I'll Stay
588 Hey, Look Me Over
548 Honey Bun
76 Honeysuckle Rose
320 Hosanna
298 House Of Flowers
210 How Are Things In Glocca Morra
534 How Can Love Survive
286 How Do You Speak To An Angel?
580 How High The Moon
389 How I Feel
102 How Laughable It Is
132 How To Handle A Woman
216 Hundred Million Miracles, A

## I

572 I Ain't Down Yet
606 I Am Free
138 I Am In Love
452 I Am Loved
557 I Am The Starlight
302 I Believe In You
432 I Cain't Say No!
175 I Can Do That
500 I Can Dream, Can't I?
390 I Can Make It Happen
603 I Can't Get Started With You
111 I Can't Give You Anything But Love
418 I Could Have Danced All Night
462 I Could Write A Book
577 I Didn't Know What Time It Was
580 I Do Not Know A Day I Did Not Love You
319 I Don't Know How To Love Him
182 I Don't Want To Know
352 I Dreamed A Dream
219 I Enjoy Being A Girl
584 I Gave My Love A Cherry
494 I Got Plenty O' Nuttin'
306 I Had A Ball
337 I Hate Men
329 I Have Dreamed
196 I Have To Tell You
142 I Know Him So Well
584 I Know Where I'm Going
563 I Love A Piano
304 I Love My Wife

| | |
|---|---|
| 136 | I Love Paris |
| 397 | I Love You (Mexican Hayride) |
| 528 | I Love You (Song of Norway) |
| 31 | I Loved You Once In Silence |
| 88 | I Loves You Porgy |
| 16 | I Only Want To Say (Gethsemane) |
| 254 | I Remember It Well |
| 106 | I See Your Face Before Me |
| 340 | I Sing Of Love |
| 74 | I Still Believe In Love |
| 92 | I Still Get Jealous |
| 60 | I Still See Elisa |
| 458 | I Talk To The Trees |
| 330 | I Whistle A Happy Tune |
| 92 | I Wish I Were In Love Again |
| 166 | I Won't Grow Up |
| 574 | I Won't Send Roses |
| 170 | I Wonder What It's Like |
| 33 | I Wonder What The King Is Doing Tonight |
| 590 | I Wrote The Book |
| 439 | I'd Do Anything |
| 107 | I'd Rather Be Right |
| 01 | I'll Be Seeing You |
| 80 | I'll Follow My Secret Heart |
| 243 | I'll Know |
| 481 | I'll Never Be Lonely Again |
| 571 | I'll Never Say No |
| 698 | I'm All Smiles |
| 465 | I'm Flying |
| 256 | I'm Glad I'm Not Young Anymore |
| 75 | I'm Gonna Sit Right Down And Write Myself A Letter |
| 546 | I'm Gonna Wash That Man Right Outa My Hair |
| 228 | I'm Still Here |
| 238 | I'm The Greatest Star |
| 365 | I've Got Your Number |
| 466 | I've Gotta Crow |
| 417 | I've Grown Accustomed To Her Face |
| 244 | I've Never Been In Love Before |
| 36 | If A Girl Isn't Pretty |
| 34 | If Ever I Would Leave You |
| 376 | If He Walked Into My Life |
| 96 | If I Can't Love Her |
| 597 | If I Could've Been |
| 293 | If I Gave You… |
| 139 | If I Loved You |
| 482 | If I Ruled The World |
| 244 | If I Were A Bell |
| 630 | If I Were A Man |
| 201 | If I Were A Rich Man |
| 116 | If I Were The Man |
| 208 | If This Isn't Love |
| 26 | If You Could See Her |
| 515 | If You Let Me Make Love To You Then Why Can't I Touch You? |
| 575 | If You Really Knew Me |
| 160 | Impossible |
| 372 | Impossible Dream (The Quest), The |
| 310 | In A Simple Way I Love You |
| 221 | In Buddy's Eyes (Buddy's There) |
| 354 | In My Life |
| 159 | In My Own Little Corner |
| 312 | Irma La Douce |
| 188 | Is You Is, Or Is You Ain't (Ma' Baby) |
| 492 | It Ain't Necessarily So |
| 630 | It Don't Mean A Thing (If It Ain't Got That Swing) |
| 560 | It Might As Well Be Spring |
| 295 | It Never Entered My Mind |
| 341 | It Never Was You |
| 288 | It Only Takes A Moment |
| 187 | It Takes A Whole Lot Of Human Feeling |
| 189 | It Was Written In The Stars |
| 559 | It's A Grand Night For Singing |
| 129 | It's A Lovely Day Today |
| 36 | It's All Right With Me |
| 484 | It's De-Lovely |
| 31 | It's The Hard-Knock Life |

**J**

| | |
|---|---|
| 406 | Jacques D'Iraque |
| 519 | Jailhouse Rock |
| 508 | Joey, Joey, Joey |
| 569 | Johanna |
| 92 | Johnny One Note |
| 76 | Joint Is Jumpin', The |
| 502 | Joker, The |
| 755 | Journey To The Heavyside Layer, The |

| | |
|---|---|
| 558 | Juke Box Saturday Night |
| 140 | June Is Bustin' Out All Over |
| 574 | Just For Tonight |
| 181 | Just Go To The Movies |
| 101 | Just In Time |
| 514 | Just One Person |
| 418 | Just You Wait |

**K**

| | |
|---|---|
| 434 | Kansas City |
| 620 | Kansas City |
| 120 | Kids! |
| 600 | Kind Of Man A Woman Needs, The |
| 320 | King Herod's Song |
| 183 | Kiss Her Now |

**L**

| | |
|---|---|
| 344 | La Cage Aux Folles |
| 94 | Lady Is A Tramp, The |
| 380 | Lambeth Walk |
| 400 | Last Night Of The World, The |
| 268 | Lazy Afternoon |
| 381 | Leaning On A Lamp-Post |
| 259 | Learn Your Lessons Well |
| 387 | Let Me Come In |
| 280 | Let Me Entertain You |
| 464 | Let's Be Buddies |
| 194 | Let's Have Another Cup O' Coffee |
| 362 | Let's Not Talk About Love |
| 412 | Lida Rose |
| 252 | Life Is Just A Bowl Of Cherries |
| 214 | Life Without Her, A |
| 553 | Light At The End Of The Tunnel |
| 264 | Light Of The World |
| 388 | Light Sings |
| 360 | Little Fall Of Rain, A |
| 325 | Little Girl Blue |
| 80 | Little Girls |
| 90 | Little Hands |
| 281 | Little Lamb |
| 364 | Little Mary Sunshine |
| 367 | Little Night Music, A |
| 526 | Little Old Lady |
| 168 | Little Things You Do Together, The |
| 627 | Living In The Shadows |
| 536 | Lonely Goatherd, The |
| 102 | Long Before I Knew You |
| 103 | Look For Small Pleasures |
| 517 | Look For The Silver Lining |
| 208 | Look To The Rainbow |
| 74 | Lookin' Good But Feelin' Bad |
| 230 | Losing My Mind |
| 368 | Lost In The Stars |
| 120 | Lot Of Livin' To Do, A |
| 87 | Love Changes Everything |
| 382 | Love Makes The World Go Round |
| 290 | Love, Come Take Me Again |
| 216 | Love, Look Away |
| 621 | Love Potion Number 9 |
| 587 | Lovelier Than Ever |
| 240 | Lovely |
| 162 | Lovely Night, A |
| 596 | Lovin' Al |
| 241 | Luck Be A Lady |
| 269 | Lucky In Love |
| 134 | Lusty Month Of May, The |

**M**

| | |
|---|---|
| 594 | Mad About The Boy |
| 524 | Make Believe |
| 186 | Make Someone Happy |
| 551 | Make Up My Heart |
| 588 | Makin' Whoopee! |
| 399 | Mama, A Rainbow |
| 378 | Maman |
| 375 | Mame |
| 373 | Man Of La Mancha (I, Don Quixote) |
| 249 | Manhattan |
| 436 | Many A New Day |
| 328 | March Of The Siamese Children, The |
| 535 | Maria |
| 379 | Marriage Type Love |
| 123 | Married (Heiraten) |
| 250 | Mary's A Grand Old Name |
| 478 | Masquerade |
| 356 | Master Of The House |
| 205 | Matchmaker |
| 82 | Maybe |
| 383 | Me And My Girl |

| | |
|---|---|
| 126 | Mein Herr |
| 156 | Memory |
| 398 | Milk And Honey |
| 203 | Miracle Of Miracles |
| 302 | Miss Marmelstein |
| 334 | Mon Ami, My Friend |
| 531 | Mood Indigo |
| 564 | Moon-Faced, Starry-Eyed |
| 246 | More I Cannot Wish You |
| 324 | Most Beautiful Girl In The World, The |
| 248 | Mountain Greenery |
| 156 | Mr. Mistoffelees |
| 405 | Mr. Wonderful |
| 108 | Muddy Water |
| 276 | Music Of Home, The |
| 467 | Music Of The Night, The |
| 233 | Music That Makes Me Dance, The |
| 95 | Must It Be Love? |
| 284 | Mutual Admiration Society |
| 377 | My Best Girl (My Best Beau) |
| 304 | My Cup Runneth Over |
| 586 | My Darling, My Darling |
| 454 | My Dream For Tomorrow |
| 536 | My Favorite Things |
| 95 | My Funny Valentine |
| 350 | My Heart Belongs To Daddy |
| 178 | My Heart Stood Still |
| 180 | My Little Dog Has Ego |
| 448 | My Man Blues |
| 497 | My Man's Gone Now |
| 571 | My Miss Mary |
| 464 | My Mother Would Love You |
| 170 | My Own Best Friend |
| 325 | My Romance |
| 348 | My Ship |
| 290 | My Wish |

**N**

| | |
|---|---|
| 82 | N.Y.C. |
| 465 | Never Never Land |
| 276 | Never Will I Marry |
| 585 | New Ashmolean Marching Society And Students Conservatory Band, The |
| 610 | New Life, A |
| 626 | New Ways To Dream |
| 255 | Night They Invented Champagne, The |
| 458 | No Goodbyes |
| 379 | No Other Love |
| 430 | No Strings |
| 396 | Not A Day Goes By |
| 567 | Not While I'm Around |
| 504 | Nothing Can Stop Me Now! |

**O**

| | |
|---|---|
| 262 | O Bless The Lord, My Soul |
| 436 | Oh, What A Beautiful Mornin' |
| 595 | Ohio |
| 434 | Oklahoma |
| 524 | Ol' Man River |
| 153 | Old Deuteronomy |
| 207 | Old Devil Moon |
| 308 | Old Friend |
| 158 | Old Gumbie Cat, The |
| 442 | On A Clear Day (You Can See Forever) |
| 621 | On Broadway |
| 361 | On My Own |
| 366 | On The Other Side Of The Tracks |
| 424 | On The Street Where You Live |
| 263 | On The Willows |
| 446 | On Your Toes |
| 364 | Once In A Blue Moon |
| 561 | Once In A Lifetime |
| 586 | Once In Love With Amy |
| 384 | Once You Lose Your Heart |
| 177 | One |
| 121 | One Boy |
| 230 | One More Kiss |
| 144 | One Night In Bangkok |
| 592 | One Of The Girls |
| 632 | One Song Glory |
| 583 | Only A Rose |
| 605 | Only Love |
| 555 | Only You |
| 533 | Ordinary Couple, An |
| 88 | Other Pleasures |
| 312 | Our Language Of Love |
| 433 | Out Of My Dreams |
| 601 | Out Of This World |
| 456 | Over Here! |

**P** _____

628  Paris By Night
528  Paris Loves Lovers
100  Party's Over, The
270  Pass That Peace Pipe
238  People
435  People Will Say We're In Love
470  Phantom Of The Opera, The
317  Pilate's Dream
291  Pine Cones And Holly Berries
146  Pity The Child
197  Plant A Radish
473  Point Of No Return, The
212  Politics And Poker
265  Prepare Ye (The Way Of The Lord)
608  Pretty Girl Is Like A Melody, A
569  Pretty Women
475  Prima Donna
231  Prologue (Beautiful Girls)
313  Push De Button
122  Put On A Happy Face
289  Put On Your Sunday Clothes

**Q** _____

446  Quiet Night

**R** _____

420  Rain In Spain, The
171  Razzle Dazzle
347  Real American Folk Song (Is A Rag), The
365  Real Live Girl
578  Real Slow Drag, A
368  Remember?
638  Rent
311  Rhode Island Is Famous For You
287  Ribbons Down My Back
485  Ridin' High
113  Right As The Rain
107  River In The Rain
512  Rock-A-Bye Your Baby
     With A Dixie Melody
581  Room With A View, A
122  Rosie

**S** _____

206  Sabbath Prayer
235  Sadie, Sadie
348  Saga Of Jenny, The
332  Sands Of Time
392  Satan Rules
532  Satin Doll
260  Save The People
634  Seasons Of Love
300  Secretary Is Not A Toy, A
89   Seeing Is Believing
286  Seeing Things
367  Send In The Clowns
248  Sentimental Me
342  September Song
410  Seventy Six Trombones
329  Shall We Dance?
398  Shalom
179  She (He) Touched Me
424  Show Me
165  Side By Side By Side
428  Simple
132  Simple Joys Of Maidenhood, The
448  Simple Little Things
456  Since You're Not Around
114  Sing For Your Supper
486  Sing Me A Song With Social Significance
215  Sing Me Not A Ballad
245  Sit Down You're Rockin' The Boat
538  Sixteen Going On Seventeen
444  Slaughter On Tenth Avenue
299  Sleepin' Bee, A
282  Small World
506  Smoke Gets In Your Eyes
78   So Far
338  So In Love
538  So Long, Farewell
511  So Much To Do In New York
548  Some Enchanted Evening
280  Some People
498  Someday I'll Find You
618  Someone
150  Someone Else's Story
167  Someone Is Waiting
185  Someone Like You
609  Someone Like You
562  Someone Nice Like You
512  Something For The Boys

394  Something More
210  Something Sort Of Grandish
593  Something To Do With Spring
328  Something Wonderful
592  Sometimes A Day Goes By
410  Song Is You, The
346  Song On The Sand (La Da Da Da)
198  Soon It's Gonna Rain
532  Sophisticated Lady
163  Sorry-Grateful
539  Sound Of Music, The
450  Speak Low
409  Standing On The Corner
556  Starlight Express
161  Stepsisters' Lament
529  Strange Music
332  Stranger In Paradise
274  Summer Nights
493  Summertime
277  Summertime Love
404  Sun And Moon
384  Sun Has Got His Hat On (He's Coming
     Out Today), The
218  Sunday
271  Sunny Side Up
204  Sunrise, Sunset
314  Superstar
69   Supper Time
625  Surrender
437  Surrey With The Fringe On Top, The
326  Sweet Danger
430  Sweetest Sounds, The

**T** _____

247  Take Back Your Mink
612  Take Me As I Am
636  Take Me Or Leave Me
118  Telephone Hour, The
507  Tell Me On A Sunday
616  Tell Me To Go
499  Ten Cents A Dance
162  Ten Minutes Ago
256  Thank Heaven For Little Girls
186  Thank Heaven For You
211  That Great Come And Get It Day
275  There Are Worse Things I Could Do
544  There Is Nothin' Like A Dame
494  There's A Boat Dat's Leavin' Soon For
     New York
296  There's A Great Day Coming Mañana
447  There's A Small Hotel
85   There's No Business Like Show Business
460  They Call The Wind Maria
257  They Didn't Believe Me
86   They Say It's Wonderful
199  They Were You
573  They're Playing My Song
480  Think Of Me
115  This Can't Be Love
350  This Is New
612  This Is The Moment
547  This Nearly Was Mine
322  Those Canaan Days
178  Thou Swell
253  Thrill Is Gone, The
431  Till The Clouds Roll By
412  Till There Was You
213  'Til Tomorrow
374  Time Heals Everything
206  To Life
269  Together
305  Together Forever
282  Together Wherever We Go
83   Tomorrow
124  Tomorrow Belongs To Me
516  Tomorrow Is The First Day Of The Rest
     Of My Life
407  Too Close For Comfort
340  Too Darn Hot
222  Too Many Mornings
204  Tradition
105  Triplets
198  Try To Remember
267  Turn Back, O Man
541  Twin Soliloquies  (This Is How It Feels)
326  Two Cigarettes In The Dark
124  Two Ladies

**U** _____

510  Unexpected Song
429  Unusual Way (In A Very Unusual Way)

**V** _____

272  Varsity Drag, The
397  Vilia
522  Violets And Silverbells

**W** _____

118  Wait Till You See Her
109  Waitin' For The Light To Shine
224  Waiting For The Girls Upstairs
459  Wand'rin' Star
266  We Beseech Thee
272  We Go Together
394  We Haven't Fought A Battle In Years
330  We Kiss In A Shadow
521  We Make A Beautiful Pair
377  We Need A Little Christmas
602  We're Gonna Have A Good Time
190  Well, Did You Evah?
416  Wells Fargo Wagon, The
443  What Did I Have That I Don't Have?
564  What Good Would The Moon Be?
177  What I Did For Love
562  What Kind Of Fool Am I?
407  What'll I Do?
214  When Did I Fall In Love
209  When I'm Not Near The Girl I Love
614  When Will Somone Hear?
457  Where Did The Good Times Go?
212  Where Do I Go From Here
439  Where Is Love?
94   Where Or When
565  Who?
358  Who Am I?
504  Who Can I Turn To (When Nobody
     Needs Me)
577  Who Is Silvia?
441  Who Will Buy?
227  Who's That Woman?
422  Why Can't The English?
335  Why Can't You Behave
599  Why Did I Choose You?
525  Why Do I Love You?
402  Why God Why?
363  Will We Ever Know Each Other
127  Willkommen
590  Wish You Were Here
477  Wishing You Were Somehow Here Again
420  With A Little Bit Of Luck
550  With A Song In My Heart
624  With One Look
284  Without Me
421  Without You
640  Without You
496  Woman Is A Sometime Thing, A
503  Wonderful Day Like Today, A
543  Wonderful Guy, A
110  Worlds Apart
423  Wouldn't It Be Lovely
594  Wrong Note Rag, The
339  Wunderbar

**Y** _____

413  Ya Got Trouble
251  Yankee Doodle Dandy, (I'm A)
519  Yes
506  Yesterdays
148  You And I
220  You Are Beautiful
237  You Are Woman, I Am Man
425  You Better Go Now
168  You Could Drive A Person Crazy
513  You Fell Out Of The Sky
518  You For Me
462  You Mustn't Kick It Around
498  You Took Advantage Of Me
294  You'd Better Love Me
279  You'll Never Get Away From Me
140  You'll Never Walk Alone
251  You're A Grand Old Flag
114  You're Blasé
128  You're Just In Love, (I Wonder Why?)
83   You're Never Fully Dressed Without A
     Smile
296  You're The Cream In My Coffee
589  You've Come Home
484  You've Got Something
545  You've Got To Be Carefully Taught
488  Young And Foolish
546  Younger Than Springtime

**Z** _____

463  Zip
604  Zorba Theme (Life Is)

4

# INDEX OF SHOWS

## A

**THE ACT**
72 City Lights

**AIN'T MISBEHAVIN'**
74 Ain't Misbehavin'
73 Black And Blue, (What Did I Do To Be So)
75 Handful Of Keys
76 Honeysuckle Rose
75 I'm Gonna Sit Right Down And Write Myself A Letter
76 Joint Is Jumpin', The
74 Lookin' Good But Feelin' Bad

**ALLEGRO**
77 Fellow Needs A Girl, A
78 Gentleman Is A Dope, The
78 So Far

**ANGEL IN THE WINGS**
79 Civilization (Bongo, Bongo, Bongo)

**ANNIE**
80 Easy Street
81 It's The Hard-Knock Life
80 Little Girls
82 Maybe
82 N.Y.C.
83 Tomorrow
83 You're Never Fully Dressed Without A Smile

**ANNIE GET YOUR GUN**
84 Anything You Can Do
85 There's No Business Like Show Business
86 They Say It's Wonderful

**ANYA (Based on themes of S. Rachmaninoff)**
90 Little Hands

**ANYONE CAN WHISTLE**
90 Anyone Can Whistle

**THE APPLE TREE**
91 Beautiful, Beautiful World

**AS THOUSANDS CHEER**
70 Easter Parade
71 Heat Wave
69 Supper Time

**ASPECTS OF LOVE**
87 Love Changes Everything
88 Other Pleasures
89 Seeing Is Believing

## B

**BABES IN ARMS**
92 I Wish I Were In Love Again
92 Johnny One Note
94 Lady Is A Tramp, The
95 My Funny Valentine
94 Where Or When

**BAJOUR**
95 Must It Be Love?

**BEAUTY AND THE BEAST: A NEW MUSICAL**
98 Beauty And The Beast
06 If I Can't Love Her

**BELLS ARE RINGING**
100 Bells Are Ringing
101 Just In Time
102 Long Before I Knew You
00 Party's Over, The

**BEN FRANKLIN IN PARIS**
102 How Laughable It Is
103 Look For Small Pleasures

**BEST FOOT FORWARD**
104 Buckle Down, Winsocki

**BETSY**
99 Blue Skies

**BETWEEN THE DEVIL**
104 By Myself
106 I See Your Face Before Me
105 Triplets

**BIG RIVER**
108 Muddy Water
107 River In The Rain
109 Waitin' For The Light To Shine
110 Worlds Apart

**BLACKBIRDS OF 1928**
111 I Can't Give You Anything But Love

**BLOOMER GIRL**
112 Evelina
113 Right As The Rain

**BOW BELLS**
114 You're Blasé

**THE BOYS FROM SYRACUSE**
115 Falling In Love With Love
114 Sing For Your Supper
115 This Can't Be Love

**BRAVO GIOVANNI**
116 If I Were The Man

**BY JUPITER**
117 Ev'rything I've Got
118 Wait Till You See Her

**BY THE BEAUTIFUL SEA**
116 Alone Too Long

**BYE BYE BIRDIE**
120 Kids!
120 Lot Of Livin' To Do, A
121 One Boy
122 Put On A Happy Face
122 Rosie
118 Telephone Hour, The

## C

**CABARET**
123 Cabaret
126 If You Could See Her
123 Married (Heiraten)
126 Mein Herr
124 Tomorrow Belongs To Me
124 Two Ladies
127 Willkommen

**CALL ME MADAM**
129 It's A Lovely Day Today
128 You're Just In Love, (I Wonder Why?)

**CAMELOT**
130 Camelot
135 Follow Me
132 How To Handle A Woman
131 I Loved You Once In Silence
133 I Wonder What The King Is Doing Tonight
134 If Ever I Would Leave You
134 Lusty Month Of May, The
132 Simple Joys Of Maidenhood, The

**CAN-CAN**
137 Allez-Vous-En, Go Away
138 C'est Magnifique
138 I Am In Love
136 I Love Paris
136 It's All Right With Me

**CAROUSEL**
139 If I Loved You
140 June Is Bustin' Out All Over
140 You'll Never Walk Alone

**CATS**
152 Ad-dressing Of Cats, The
154 Bustopher Jones: The Cat About Town
155 Journey To The Heavyside Layer, The
156 Memory
156 Mr. Mistoffelees
153 Old Deuteronomy
158 Old Gumbie Cat, The

**CHESS**
141 Anthem
151 Heaven Help My Heart
142 I Know Him So Well
144 One Night In Bangkok
146 Pity The Child
150 Someone Else's Story
148 You And I

**CHICAGO**
172 And All That Jazz
170 My Own Best Friend
171 Razzle Dazzle

**A CHORUS LINE**
173 At The Ballet
176 Dance: Ten; Looks: Three
175 I Can Do That
177 One
177 What I Did For Love

**CINDERELLA**
159 Boys And Girls Like You And Me
160 Do I Love You Because You're Beautiful?
160 Impossible
159 In My Own Little Corner
162 Lovely Night, A
161 Stepsisters' Lament
162 Ten Minutes Ago

**COMPANY**
164 Another Hundred People
166 Being Alive
166 Company
168 Little Things You Do Together, The
165 Side By Side By Side
167 Someone Is Waiting
163 Sorry-Grateful
168 You Could Drive A Person Crazy

**A CONNECTICUT YANKEE**
178 My Heart Stood Still
178 Thou Swell

**CONVERSATION PIECE**
180 I'll Follow My Secret Heart

## D

**DANCE ME A SONG**
180 My Little Dog Has Ego

**A DAY IN HOLLYWOOD/A NIGHT IN THE UKRAINE**
181 Just Go To The Movies

**DEAR WORLD**
182 Dear World
182 I Don't Want To Know
183 Kiss Her Now

**DESTRY RIDES AGAIN**
184 Anyone Would Love You

**DO I HEAR A WALTZ?**
184 Do I Hear A Waltz?
185 Someone Like You

**DO RE MI**
186 Make Someone Happy

**DON'T BOTHER ME, I CAN'T COPE**
187 It Takes A Whole Lot Of Human Feeling
186 Thank Heaven For You

**DRAT! THE CAT!**
179 She (He) Touched Me

**DUBARRY WAS A LADY**
190 Friendship
189 It Was Written In The Stars
190 Well, Did You Evah?

**E** _____

**EVITA**
194 Another Suitcase In Another Hall
191 Buenos Aires
193 Don't Cry For Me Argentina

**F** _____

**FACE THE MUSIC**
194 Let's Have Another Cup O' Coffee

**FANNY**
196 Be Kind To Your Parents
195 Fanny
196 I Have To Tell You

**THE FANTASTICKS**
197 Plant A Radish
198 Soon It's Gonna Rain
199 They Were You
198 Try To Remember

**FASHION**
214 Life Without Her, A

**FIDDLER ON THE ROOF**
202 Anatevka
200 Do You Love Me?
202 Far From The Home I Love
201 Fiddler On The Roof
201 If I Were A Rich Man
205 Matchmaker
203 Miracle Of Miracles
206 Sabbath Prayer
204 Sunrise, Sunset
206 To Life
204 Tradition

**FINIAN'S RAINBOW**
210 How Are Things In Glocca Morra
208 If This Isn't Love
208 Look To The Rainbow
207 Old Devil Moon
210 Something Sort Of Grandish
211 That Great Come And Get It Day
209 When I'm Not Near The Girl I Love

**FIORELLO!**
213 Gentleman Jimmy
212 Politics And Poker
213 'Til Tomorrow
214 When Did I Fall In Love
212 Where Do I Go From Here

**FIREBRAND OF FLORENCE**
215 Sing Me Not A Ballad

**THE FIRST**
363 Will We Ever Know Each Other

**FIVE GUYS NAMED MOE**
188 Is You Is, Or Is You Ain't (Ma' Baby)

**FLOWER DRUM SONG**
218 Don't Marry Me
216 Hundred Million Miracles, A
219 I Enjoy Being A Girl
216 Love, Look Away
218 Sunday
220 You Are Beautiful

**FOLLIES**
220 Ah, Paris!
222 Broadway Baby
225 Could I Leave You
224 God-Why-Don't-You-Love-Me Blues, The
228 I'm Still Here
221 In Buddy's Eyes (Buddy's There)
230 Losing My Mind
230 One More Kiss
231 Prologue (Beautiful Girls)
222 Too Many Mornings
224 Waiting For The Girls Upstairs
227 Who's That Woman?

**FOLLOW THRU**
232 Button Up Your Overcoat

**FOR THE LOVE OF MIKE**
232 Got A Date With An Angel

**FUNNY GIRL**
234 Don't Rain On My Parade
238 I'm The Greatest Star
236 If A Girl Isn't Pretty
233 Music That Makes Me Dance, The
238 People
235 Sadie, Sadie
237 You Are Woman, I Am Man

**A FUNNY THING HAPPENED ON THE WAY TO THE FORUM**
239 Comedy Tonight
240 Lovely

**G** _____

**GARRICK GAIETIES**
249 Manhattan
248 Mountain Greenery
248 Sentimental Me

**GEORGE M!**
252 Forty-five Minutes From Broadway
250 Give My Regards To Broadway
250 Harrigan
250 Mary's A Grand Old Name
251 Yankee Doodle Dandy, (I'm A)
251 You're A Grand Old Flag

**GEORGE WHITE'S SCANDALS (1931 Edition)**
252 Life Is Just A Bowl Of Cherries
253 Thrill Is Gone, The

**GEORGE WHITE'S SCANDALS (1939 Edition)**
253 Are You Havin' Any Fun?

**GIGI**
254 Gigi
254 I Remember It Well
256 I'm Glad I'm Not Young Anymore
255 Night They Invented Champagne, The
256 Thank Heaven For Little Girls

**THE GIRL FRIEND**
258 Blue Room, The

**THE GIRL FROM UTAH**
257 They Didn't Believe Me

**GLAD TO SEE YOU**
258 Guess I'll Hang My Tears Out To Dry

**GODSPELL**
260 All For The Best
262 All Good Gifts
264 By My Side
259 Day By Day
259 Learn Your Lessons Well
264 Light Of The World
262 O Bless The Lord, My Soul
263 On The Willows
265 Prepare Ye (The Way Of The Lord)
260 Save The People
267 Turn Back, O Man
266 We Beseech Thee

**THE GOLDEN APPLE**
268 Lazy Afternoon

**GOOD NEWS**
268 Best Things In Life Are Free, The
270 Good News
269 Lucky In Love
270 Pass That Peace Pipe
271 Sunny Side Up
269 Together
272 Varsity Drag, The

**GREASE**
273 Beauty School Dropout
274 Summer Nights
275 There Are Worse Things I Could Do
272 We Go Together

**GREENWILLOW**
276 Music Of Home, The
276 Never Will I Marry
277 Summertime Love

**GUYS AND DOLLS**
242 Adelaide's Lament
241 Bushel And A Peck, A
246 Fugue For Tinhorns
242 Guys And Dolls
243 I'll Know
244 I've Never Been In Love Before
244 If I Were A Bell
241 Luck Be A Lady
246 More I Cannot Wish You
245 Sit Down You're Rockin' The Boat
247 Take Back Your Mink

**GYPSY**
278 All I Need Is The Girl
278 Everything's Coming Up Roses
280 Let Me Entertain You
281 Little Lamb
282 Small World
280 Some People
282 Together Wherever We Go
279 You'll Never Get Away From Me

**H** _____

**HALF A SIXPENCE**
283 Half A Sixpence

**HAPPY HUNTING**
284 Mutual Admiration Society

**THE HAPPY TIME**
285 Happy Time, The
286 Seeing Things
284 Without Me

**HAZEL FLAGG**
286 How Do You Speak To An Angel?

**HELLO, DOLLY!**
288 Before The Parade Passes By
287 Hello, Dolly!
288 It Only Takes A Moment
289 Put On Your Sunday Clothes
287 Ribbons Down My Back

**HERE'S LOVE**
290 Love, Come Take Me Again
290 My Wish
291 Pine Cones And Holly Berries

**HIGH BUTTON SHOES**
292 Can't You Just See Yourself?
292 I Still Get Jealous

**HIGH SPIRITS**
294 Forever And A Day
293 If I Gave You...
294 You'd Better Love Me

**HIGHER AND HIGHER**
295 It Never Entered My Mind

**HOLD EVERYTHING**
296 You're The Cream In My Coffee

**HOLD ON TO YOUR HATS**
296 There's A Great Day Coming Mañana

**HOORAY FOR WHAT**
297 Down With Love

**HOUSE OF FLOWERS**
298 Don't Like Goodbyes
298 House Of Flowers
299 Sleepin' Bee, A

**HOW TO SUCCEED IN BUSINESS WITHOUT REALLY TRYING**
300 Brotherhood Of Man
302 I Believe In You
300 Secretary Is Not A Toy, A

**I CAN GET IT FOR YOU WHOLESALE**
302 Miss Marmelstein

**I DO! I DO!**
304 I Love My Wife
304 My Cup Runneth Over
305 Together Forever

**I HAD A BALL**
306 Almost
306 I Had A Ball

**I'D RATHER BE RIGHT**
308 Have You Met Miss Jones?
307 I'd Rather Be Right

**I'M GETTING MY ACT TOGETHER AND TAKING IT ON THE ROAD**
310 In A Simple Way I Love You
308 Old Friend

**INSIDE U.S.A.**
310 Haunted Heart
311 Rhode Island Is Famous For You

**IRMA LA DOUCE**
312 Irma La Douce
312 Our Language Of Love

**J** _____

**JAMAICA**
314 Cocoanut Sweet
313 Push De Button

**JEKYLL & HYDE**
310 A New Life
309 Someone Like You
312 Take Me As I Am
312 This Is The Moment

**JESUS CHRIST SUPERSTAR**
318 Everything's Alright
320 Hosanna
319 I Don't Know How To Love Him
316 I Only Want To Say (Gethsemane)
320 King Herod's Song
317 Pilate's Dream
314 Superstar

**JOHNNY JOHNSON**
334 Mon Ami, My Friend

**JOSEPH AND THE AMAZING TECHNICOLOR® DREAMCOAT**
322 Any Dream Will Do
323 Close Every Door
322 Those Canaan Days

**JUMBO**
325 Little Girl Blue
324 Most Beautiful Girl In The World, The
325 My Romance

**K** _____

**KEAN**
326 Sweet Danger

**KILL THAT STORY**
326 Two Cigarettes In The Dark

**THE KING AND I**
331 Getting To Know You
327 Hello, Young Lovers
329 I Have Dreamed
330 I Whistle A Happy Tune
328 March Of The Siamese Children, The
329 Shall We Dance?
328 Something Wonderful
330 We Kiss In A Shadow

**KISMET**
333 He's In Love
332 Sands Of Time
332 Stranger In Paradise

**KISS ME, KATE**
338 Always True To You In My Fashion
336 Another Op'nin', Another Show
336 Brush Up Your Shakespeare
337 I Hate Men
340 I Sing Of Love
338 So In Love
340 Too Darn Hot
335 Why Can't You Behave
339 Wunderbar

**KNICKERBOCKER HOLIDAY**
341 It Never Was You
342 September Song

**L** _____

**LA CAGE AUX FOLLES**
343 Best Of Times, The
344 La Cage Aux Folles
346 Song On The Sand (La Da Da Da)

**LADIES FIRST**
347 Real American Folk Song (Is A Rag), The

**LADY IN THE DARK**
348 My Ship
348 Saga Of Jenny, The
350 This Is New

**LEAVE IT TO ME**
351 Get Out Of Town
350 My Heart Belongs To Daddy

**LES MISÉRABLES**
354 Bring Him Home
353 Castle On A Cloud
356 Do You Hear The People Sing?
353 Drink With Me (To Days Gone By)
359 Empty Chairs At Empty Tables
352 I Dreamed A Dream
354 In My Life
360 Little Fall Of Rain, A
356 Master Of The House
361 On My Own
358 Who Am I?

**LET'S FACE IT**
363 Ace In The Hole
362 Let's Not Talk About Love

**LITTLE MARY SUNSHINE**
364 Little Mary Sunshine
364 Once In A Blue Moon

**LITTLE ME**
365 I've Got Your Number
366 On The Other Side Of The Tracks
365 Real Live Girl

**A LITTLE NIGHT MUSIC**
367 Little Night Music, A
368 Remember?
367 Send In The Clowns

**LOST IN THE STARS**
368 Lost In The Stars

**LOVE LIFE**
369 Green-Up Time
370 Here I'll Stay

**M** _____

**MACK AND MABEL**
374 I Won't Send Roses
374 Time Heals Everything

**MAME**
376 If He Walked Into My Life
375 Mame
377 My Best Girl (My Best Beau)
377 We Need A Little Christmas

**MAN OF LA MANCHA**
371 Dulcinea
372 Impossible Dream (The Quest), The
373 Man Of La Mancha (I, Don Quixote)

**MARTIN GUERRE**
615 Here Comes The Morning
618 Someone
616 Tell Me To Go
614 When Will Someone Hear?

**MATA HARI**
378 Maman

**ME AND JULIET**
379 Marriage Type Love
379 No Other Love

**ME AND MY GIRL**
380 Lambeth Walk
381 Leaning On A Lamp-Post
382 Love Makes The World Go Round
383 Me And My Girl
384 Once You Lose Your Heart
384 Sun Has Got His Hat On (He's Coming Out Today), The

**THE ME NOBODY KNOWS**
386 Black
387 Dream Babies
389 How I Feel
387 Let Me Come In
388 Light Sings

**MERLIN**
393 Beyond My Wildest Dreams
391 He Who Knows The Way
390 I Can Make It Happen
392 Satan Rules
394 Something More
394 We Haven't Fought A Battle In Years

**MERRILY WE ROLL ALONG**
395 Good Thing Going
396 Not A Day Goes By

**THE MERRY WIDOW**
397 Vilia

**MEXICAN HAYRIDE**
397 I Love You

**MILK AND HONEY**
398 Milk And Honey
398 Shalom

**MINNIE'S BOYS**
399 Be Happy
399 Mama, A Rainbow

**MISS SAIGON**
400 Last Night Of The World, The
404 Sun And Moon
402 Why God Why?

**THE MOST HAPPY FELLA**
408 Big D
408 Joey, Joey, Joey
409 Standing On The Corner

**MR. WONDERFUL**
406 Jacques D'Iraque
405 Mr. Wonderful
407 Too Close For Comfort

**MUSIC BOX REVUE OF 1924**
407 What'll I Do?

**MUSIC IN THE AIR**
410 Song Is You, The

## THE MUSIC MAN
411  Goodnight My Someone
412  Lida Rose
410  Seventy Six Trombones
412  Till There Was You
416  Wells Fargo Wagon, The
413  Ya Got Trouble

## MY FAIR LADY
416  Get Me To The Church On Time
418  I Could Have Danced All Night
417  I've Grown Accustomed To Her Face
418  Just You Wait
424  On The Street Where You Live
420  Rain In Spain, The
424  Show Me
422  Why Can't The English?
420  With A Little Bit Of Luck
421  Without You
423  Wouldn't It Be Loverly

## N _____

## THE NERVOUS SET
426  Ballad Of The Sad Young Men, The

## NEW FACES OF 1936
425  You Better Go Now

## NINE
427  Getting Tall
428  Simple
429  Unusual Way (In A Very Unusual Way)

## NO STRINGS
430  No Strings
430  Sweetest Sounds, The

## O _____

## OH BOY!
431  Till The Clouds Roll By

## OKLAHOMA!
432  All Er Nothin'
438  Farmer And The Cowman, The
432  I Cain't Say No!
434  Kansas City
436  Many A New Day
436  Oh, What A Beautiful Mornin'
434  Oklahoma
433  Out Of My Dreams
435  People Will Say We're In Love
437  Surrey With The Fringe On Top, The

## OLIVER!
440  As Long As He Needs Me
440  Consider Yourself
439  I'd Do Anything
439  Where Is Love?
441  Who Will Buy?

## ON A CLEAR DAY YOU CAN SEE FOREVER
442  Come Back To Me
442  On A Clear Day (You Can See Forever)
443  What Did I Have That I Don't Have?

## ON YOUR TOES
447  Glad To Be Unhappy
446  On Your Toes
446  Quiet Night
444  Slaughter On Tenth Avenue
447  There's A Small Hotel

## 110 IN THE SHADE
448  Simple Little Things

## ONE MO' TIME
449  After You've Gone
448  My Man Blues

## ONE TOUCH OF VENUS
450  Speak Low

## OUT OF THIS WORLD
452  Cherry Pies Ought To Be You
451  From This Moment On
452  I Am Loved

## OVER HERE!
453  Big Beat, The
455  Charlie's Place

454  My Dream For Tomorrow
458  No Goodbyes
456  Over Here!
456  Since You're Not Around
457  Where Did The Good Times Go?

## P _____

## PAINT YOUR WAGON
460  I Still See Elisa
458  I Talk To The Trees
460  They Call The Wind Maria
459  Wand'rin' Star

## PAL JOEY
461  Bewitched
462  I Could Write A Book
462  You Mustn't Kick It Around
463  Zip

## PANAMA HATTIE
464  Let's Be Buddies
464  My Mother Would Love You

## PETER PAN
466  I Won't Grow Up
465  I'm Flying
466  I've Gotta Crow
465  Never Never Land

## THE PHANTOM OF THE OPERA
468  All I Ask Of You
472  Angel Of Music
478  Masquerade
467  Music Of The Night, The
470  Phantom Of The Opera, The
473  Point Of No Return, The
475  Prima Donna
480  Think Of Me
477  Wishing You Were Somehow Here Again

## PICKWICK
481  I'll Never Be Lonely Again
482  If I Ruled The World

## PINS AND NEEDLES
486  Sing Me A Song With Social Significance

## PIPE DREAM
486  All At Once You Love Her
487  Everybody's Got A Home But Me

## PLAIN AND FANCY
488  Young And Foolish

## PORGY AND BESS
490  Bess, You Is My Woman
494  I Got Plenty O' Nuttin'
488  I Loves You Porgy
492  It Ain't Necessarily So
497  My Man's Gone Now
493  Summertime
494  There's A Boat Dat's Leavin' Soon For New York
496  Woman Is A Sometime Thing, A

## PRESENT ARMS
498  You Took Advantage Of Me

## PRIVATE LIVES
498  Someday I'll Find You

## R _____

## RED, HOT AND BLUE!
483  Down In The Depths (On The Ninetieth Floor)
484  It's De-Lovely
485  Ridin' High
484  You've Got Something

## RENT
632  One Song Glory
638  Rent
634  Seasons Of Love
636  Take Me Or Leave Me
640  Without You

## REX
500  As Once I Loved You

## RIGHT THIS WAY
500  I Can Dream, Can't I?
501  I'll Be Seeing You

## THE ROAR OF THE GREASEPAINT - THE SMELL OF THE CROWD
502  Feeling Good
502  Joker, The
504  Nothing Can Stop Me Now!
504  Who Can I Turn To (When Nobody Needs Me)
503  Wonderful Day Like Today, A

## ROBERTA
506  Smoke Gets In Your Eyes
506  Yesterdays

## S _____

## SALLY
517  Look For The Silver Lining

## SALVATION
515  If You Let Me Make Love To You Then Why Can't I Touch You?
516  Tomorrow Is The First Day Of The Rest Of My Life

## SARATOGA
518  You For Me

## SAY, DARLING
517  Dance Only With Me

## SEVEN LIVELY ARTS
518  Ev'ry Time We Say Goodbye

## 70, GIRLS, 70
520  Believe
519  Yes

## SHENANDOAH
520  Freedom
522  Violets And Silverbells
521  We Make A Beautiful Pair

## SHOW BOAT
522  Bill
523  Can't Help Lovin' Dat Man
524  Make Believe
524  Ol' Man River
525  Why Do I Love You?

## THE SHOW IS ON
525  By Strauss
526  Little Old Lady

## SILK STOCKINGS
526  All Of You
527  Fated To Be Mated
528  Paris Loves Lovers

## SIMPLE SIMON
499  Dancing On The Ceiling
499  Ten Cents A Dance

## SINBAD
512  Rock-A-Bye Your Baby With A Dixie Melody

## SMOKEY JOE'S CAFE
619  Jailhouse Rock
620  Kansas City
621  Love Potion Number 9
621  On Broadway

## SNOOPY
514  Just One Person

## SOMETHING FOR THE BOYS
512  Something For The Boys

## SOMETHING'S AFOOT
513  You Fell Out Of The Sky

## SONG & DANCE
508  Capped Teeth And Caesar Salad
508  Come Back With The Same Look In Your Eyes
511  So Much To Do In New York
507  Tell Me On A Sunday
510  Unexpected Song

## SONG OF NORWAY
528  I Love You
529  Strange Music

**PHISTICATED LADIES**
) Caravan
) It Don't Mean A Thing (If It Ain't Got That Swing)
◄ Mood Indigo
2 Satin Doll
2 Sophisticated Lady

**E SOUND OF MUSIC**
3 Climb Ev'ry Mountain
4 Do-Re-Mi
7 Edelweiss
4 How Can Love Survive
5 Lonely Goatherd, The
5 Maria
5 My Favorite Things
3 Ordinary Couple, An
3 Sixteen Going On Seventeen
3 So Long, Farewell
9 Sound Of Music, The

**UTH PACIFIC**
) Bali Ha'i
1 Bloody Mary
2 Cock-Eyed Optimist, A
2 Dites-Moi (Tell Me Why)
4 Happy Talk
8 Honey Bun
6 I'm Gonna Wash That Man Right Outa My Hair
8 Some Enchanted Evening
4 There Is Nothin' Like A Dame
7 This Nearly Was Mine
1 Twin Soliloquies (This Is How It Feels)
3 Wonderful Guy, A
5 You've Got To Be Carefully Taught
6 Younger Than Springtime

**'RING IS HERE**
0 With A Song In My Heart

**'. LOUIS WOMAN**
9 Any Place I Hang My Hat Is Home
0 Come Rain Or Come Shine

**'ARLIGHT EXPRESS**
2 Engine Of Love
7 I Am The Starlight
3 Light At The End Of The Tunnel
1 Make Up My Heart
5 Only You
6 Starlight Express

**'ARS ON ICE**
8 Juke Box Saturday Night

**'ATE FAIR**
'0 It Might As Well Be Spring
9 It's A Grand Night For Singing

**'OP THE WORLD - I WANT ) GET OFF**
0 Gonna Build A Mountain
1 Once In A Lifetime
2 Someone Nice Like You
2 What Kind Of Fool Am I?

**'OP! LOOK! LISTEN!**
3 I Love A Piano

**'REET SCENE**
14 Moon-Faced, Starry-Eyed
14 What Good Would The Moon Be?

**JBWAYS ARE FOR SLEEPING**
6 Be A Santa

**UNNY**
5 Who?

**UNSET BOULEVARD**
22 As If We Never Said Goodbye
26 New Ways To Dream
25 Surrender
24 With One Look

**SWEENEY TODD, THE DEMON BARBER OF FLEET STREET**
567 Ballad Of Sweeney Todd, The
569 Johanna
567 Not While I'm Around
569 Pretty Women

**SWEET ADELINE**
565 Don't Ever Leave Me

**T** _____
**TENDERLOIN**
570 Artificial Flowers
570 I Wonder What It's Like
571 My Miss Mary

**THEY'RE PLAYING OUR SONG**
572 Fallin'
574 I Still Believe In Love
575 If You Really Knew Me
574 Just For Tonight
573 They're Playing My Song

**THIS YEAR OF GRACE**
581 Room With A View, A

**TICKETS, PLEASE!**
576 Darn It, Baby, That's Love

**TOO MANY GIRLS**
577 I Didn't Know What Time It Was

**TREEMONISHA**
578 Real Slow Drag, A

**TWO BY TWO**
580 I Do Not Know A Day I Did Not Love You

**TWO FOR THE SHOW**
580 How High The Moon

**TWO GENTLEMEN OF VERONA**
577 Who Is Silvia?

**U** _____
**THE UNSINKABLE MOLLY BROWN**
572 I Ain't Down Yet
571 I'll Never Say No

**UP IN CENTRAL PARK**
582 Close As Pages In A Book

**V** _____
**THE VAGABOND KING**
583 Only A Rose

**VERY WARM FOR MAY**
583 All The Things You Are

**VICTOR/VICTORIA**
630 If I Were A Man
627 Living In The Shadows
628 Paris By Night

**W** _____
**WAIT A MINIM!**
584 I Gave My Love A Cherry
584 I Know Where I'm Going

**WHERE'S CHARLEY?**
587 Lovelier Than Ever
586 My Darling, My Darling
585 New Ashmolean Marching Society And Students Conservatory Band, The
586 Once In Love With Amy

**WHOOPEE!**
588 Makin' Whoopee!

**WILDCAT**
588 Hey, Look Me Over
589 You've Come Home

**WISH YOU WERE HERE**
590 Wish You Were Here

**WOMAN OF THE YEAR**
590 I Wrote The Book
592 One Of The Girls
592 Sometimes A Day Goes By

**WONDERFUL TOWN**
595 Ohio
594 Wrong Note Rag, The

**WORDS AND MUSIC**
594 Mad About The Boy
593 Something To Do With Spring

**WORKING**
597 If I Could've Been
596 Lovin' Al

**Y** _____
**THE YEARLING**
598 I'm All Smiles
600 Kind Of Man A Woman Needs, The
599 Why Did I Choose You?

**YOU NEVER KNOW**
602 At Long Last Love

**YOUR ARMS TOO SHORT TO BOX WITH GOD**
602 We're Gonna Have A Good Time

**Z** _____
**ZIEGFELD FOLLIES OF 1919**
608 Pretty Girl Is Like A Melody, A

**ZIEGFELD FOLLIES OF 1936**
603 I Can't Get Started With You

**ZORBA**
607 First Time, The
605 Happy Birthday To Me
606 I Am Free
605 Only Love
604 Zorba Theme (Life Is)

**THE ZULU AND THE ZAYDA**
601 Out Of This World

# INDEX OF COMPOSERS & LYRICISTS

## A

**LEE ADAMS**
Kids!, p.120
Lot Of Livin' To Do, A, p.120
One Boy, p.121
Put On A Happy Face, p.122
Rosie, p.122
Telephone Hour, The, p.118

**STANLEY ADAMS**
Little Old Lady, p.526

**FRED E. AHLERT**
I'm Gonna Sit Right Down And Write Myself A Letter, p.75

**BENNY ANDERSSON**
Someone Else's Story, p.150

**MAXWELL ANDERSON**
It Never Was You, p.341
Lost In The Stars, p.368
September Song, p.342

**HAROLD ARLEN**
Any Place I Hang My Hat Is Home, p.549
Cocoanut Sweet, p.314
Come Rain Or Come Shine, p.550
Don't Like Goodbyes, p.298
Down With Love, p.297
Evelina, p.112
House Of Flowers, p.298
Push De Button, p.313
Right As The Rain, p.113
Sleepin' Bee, A, p.299
You For Me, p.518

**HOWARD ASHMAN**
Beauty And The Beast, p.98
If I Can't Love Her, p.96

**BILLY AUSTIN**
Is You Is, Or Is You Ain't (Ma' Baby), p.188

## B

**MIKE BAIT**
Phantom Of The Opera, The, p.470

**LIONEL BART**
As Long As He Needs Me, p.440
Consider Yourself, p.440
I'd Do Anything, p.439
Where Is Love?, p.439
Who Will Buy?, p.441

**IRVING BERLIN**
Anything You Can Do, p.84
Blue Skies, p.99
Easter Parade, p.70
Heat Wave, p.71
I Love A Piano, p.563
It's A Lovely Day Today, p.129
Let's Have Another Cup O' Coffee, p.194
Pretty Girl Is Like A Melody, A, p.608
Supper Time, p.69
There's No Business Like Show Business, p.85
They Say It's Wonderful, p.86
What'll I Do?, p.407
You're Just In Love, (I Wonder Why?), p.128

**ELMER BERNSTEIN**
Beyond My Wildest Dreams, p.393
He Who Knows The Way, p.391
I Can Make It Happen, p.390
Satan Rules, p.392
Something More, p.394
We Haven't Fought A Battle In Years, p.394

**LEONARD BERNSTEIN**
Ohio, p.595
Wrong Note Rag, The, p.594

**RICK BESOYAN**
Little Mary Sunshine, p.364
Once In A Blue Moon, p.364

**ALBANY BIGARD**
Mood Indigo, p.531

**DON BLACK**
As If We Never Said Goodbye, p. 622
Beyond My Wildest Dreams, p.393
Capped Teeth And Caesar Salad p.508
Come Back With The Same Look In Your Eyes, p.508
He Who Knows The Way, p.391
I Can Make It Happen, p.390
New Ways To Dream, p. 626
Satan Rules, p.392
So Much To Do In New York, p.511
Something More, p.394
Surrender, p. 625
Tell Me On A Sunday, p.507
Unexpected Song, p.510
We Haven't Fought A Battle In Years, p.394
With One Look, p. 624

**RALPH BLANE**
Buckle Down, Winsocki, p.104
Pass That Peace Pipe, p.270

**JERRY BOCK**
Anatevka, p.202
Artificial Flowers, p.570
Beautiful, Beautiful World, p.91
Do You Love Me?, p.200
Far From The Home I Love, p.202
Fiddler On The Roof, p.201
Gentleman Jimmy, p.213
I Wonder What It's Like, p.570
If I Were A Rich Man, p.201
Jacques D'Iraque, p.406
Matchmaker, p.205
Miracle Of Miracles, p.203
Mr. Wonderful, p.405
My Miss Mary, p.571
Politics And Poker, p.212
Sabbath Prayer, p.206
Sunrise, Sunset, p.204
'Til Tomorrow, p.213
To Life, p.206
Too Close For Comfort, p.407
Tradition, p.204
When Did I Fall In Love, p.214
Where Do I Go From Here, p.212

**ALAIN BOUBLIL**
Bring Him Home, p.354
Castle On A Cloud, p.353
Do You Hear The People Sing?, p.356
Drink With Me (To Days Gone By), p.353
Empty Chairs At Empty Tables, p.359
Here Comes The Morning, p. 615
I Dreamed A Dream, p.352
In My Life, p.354
Little Fall Of Rain, A, p.360
Master Of The House, p.356
On My Own, p.361
Someone, p. 618
Tell Me To Go, p. 616
When Will Someone Hear, p. 614
Who Am I?, p.358

**ALEXANDER BREFFORT**
Our Language Of Love, p.312

**LESLIE BRICUSSE**
Feeling Good, p.502
Gonna Build A Mountain, p.560
I'll Never Be Lonely Again, p.481
If I Ruled The World, p.482
If I Were A Man, p.630
Joker, The, p.502
Living In The Shadows, p. 627
A New Life, p.610
Nothing Can Stop Me Now!, p.504

Once In A Lifetime, p.561
Paris By Night, p. 628
Someone Like You, p. 609
Someone Nice Like You, p.562
Take Me As I Am, p. 612
This Is The Moment, p. 612
What Kind Of Fool Am I?, p.562
Who Can I Turn To (When Nobody Needs Me) p.504
Wonderful Day Like Today, A, p.503

**HARRY BROOKS**
Ain't Misbehavin', p.74
(What Did I Do To Be So) Black And Blue, p.73

**LEW BROWN**
Best Things In Life Are Free, The, p.268
Button Up Your Overcoat, p.232
Good News, p.270
Life Is Just A Bowl Of Cherries, p.252
Lucky In Love, p.269
Sunny Side Up, p.271
Thrill Is Gone, The, p.253
Together, p.269
Varsity Drag, The, p.272
You're The Cream In My Coffee, p.296

**STEVE BROWN**
Life Without Her, A, p.214

**BOB BRUSH**
Will We Ever Know Each Other, p.363

**RALPH BUTLER**
Sun Has Got His Hat On, The, p.384

## C

**SAMMY CAHN**
Can't You Just See Yourself?, p.292
Guess I'll Hang My Tears Out To Dry, p.258
I Still Get Jealous, p.292

**JOHN CAIRD**
On My Own, p.361

**TRUMAN CAPOTE**
Don't Like Goodbyes, p.298
House Of Flowers, p.298
Sleepin' Bee, A, p.299

**HOAGY CARMICHAEL**
Little Old Lady, p.526

**WARREN CASEY**
Beauty School Dropout, p.273
Summer Nights, p.274
There Are Worse Things I Could Do, p.275
We Go Together, p.272

**MARK CHARLAP**
I Won't Grow Up, p.466
I'm Flying, p.465
I've Gotta Crow, p.466

**MARTIN CHARNIN**
Easy Street, p.80
I Do Not Know A Day I Did Not Love You, p.580
It's The Hard-Knock Life, p.81
Little Girls, p.80
Maman, p.378
Maybe, p.82
N.Y.C., p.82
Tomorrow, p.83
Will We Ever Know Each Other, p.363
You're Never Fully Dressed Without A Smile, p.83

**STEPHEN CLARK**
Here Comes The Morning, p. 615
Someone, p. 618
Tell Me To Go, p. 616
When Will Someone Hear, p. 614

**EORGE M. COHAN**
rty-Five Minutes From Broadway, p.252
ve My Regards To Broadway, p.250
arrigan, p.250
m A) Yankee Doodle Dandy, p.251
ou're A Grand Old Flag, p.251

**IARY COHAN**
orty-Five Minutes From Broadway, p.252

**V COLEMAN**
ey, Look Me Over, p.588
ve Got Your Number, p.365
n The Other Side Of The Tracks, p.366
eal Live Girl, p.365
ou've Come Home, p.589

**ETTY COMDEN**
e A Santa, p.566
ells Are Ringing, p.100
ance Only With Me, p.517
ust In Time, p.101
ong Before I Knew You, p.102
lake Someone Happy, p.186
ever Never Land, p.465
hio, p.595
arty's Over, The, p.100
rong Note Rag, The, p.594

**.C. COURTNEY**
You Let Me Make Love To You Then
Vhy Can't I Touch You?, p.515
omorrow Is The First Day Of The Rest Of
My Life, p.516

**OEL COWARD**
ll Follow My Secret Heart, p.180
lad About The Boy, p.594
oom With A View, A, p.581
omeday I'll Find You, p.498
omething To Do With Spring, p.593

**REAMER & LAYTON**
fter You've Gone, p.449

**RETCHEN CRYER**
n A Simple Way I Love You, p.310
)ld Friend, p.308

**D** _____

**.G. DeSYLVA**
est Things In Life Are Free, The, p.268
utton Up Your Overcoat, p.232
ood News, p.270
ook For The Silver Lining, p.517
ucky In Love, p.269
unny Side Up, p.271
ogether, p.269
/arsity Drag, The, p.272
ou're The Cream In My Coffee, p.296

**HOWARD DIETZ**
3y Myself, p.104
Haunted Heart, p.310
 See Your Face Before Me, p.106
Rhode Island Is Famous For You, p.311
Triplets, p.105

**WALTER DONALDSON**
Makin' Whoopee!, p.588

**MATT DUBEY**
Mutual Admiration Society, p.284

**LYN DUDDY**
)arn it Baby, That's Love, p.576

**JERNON DUKE**
Can't Get Started With You, p.603

**E** _____

**RED EBB**
nd All That Jazz, p.172
elieve, p.520
abaret, p.123
ity Lights, p.72

First Time, The, p.607
Happy Birthday To Me, p.605
Happy Time, The, p.285
I Am Free, p.606
I Wrote The Book, p.590
If You Could See Her, p.126
Married (Heiraten), p.123
Mein Herr, p.126
My Own Best Friend, p.170
One Of The Girls, p.592
Only Love, p.605
Razzle Dazzle, p.171
Seeing Things, p.286
Sometimes A Day Goes By, p.592
Tomorrow Belongs To Me, p.124
Two Ladies, p.124
Willkommen, p.127
Without Me, p.284
Yes, p.519
Zorba Theme (Life Is), p.604

**ROGER EDENS**
Pass That Peace Pipe, p.270

**JOAN EDWARDS**
Darn It, Baby, That's Love, p.576

**T.S. ELIOT**
Ad-dressing Of Cats, The, p.152
Bustopher Jones: The Cat About Town, p.154
Journey To The Heaviside Layer, The, p.155
Mr. Mistoffelees, p.156
Old Deuteronomy, p.153
Old Gumbie Cat, The, p.158

**DUKE ELLINGTON**
Caravan, p.530
It Don't Mean A Thing (If It Ain't Got That
   Swing), p.530
Mood Indigo, p.531
Satin Doll, p.532
Sophisticated Lady, p.532

**F** _____

**SAMMY FAIN**
Are You Havin' Any Fun?, p.253
I Can Dream, Can't I?, p.500
I'll Be Seeing You, p.501

**DOROTHY FIELDS**
Alone Too Long, p.116
Close As Pages In A Book, p.582
I Can't Give You Anything But Love, p.111

**NANCY FORD**
In A Simple Way I Love You, p.310
Old Friend, p.308

**GEORGE FORREST**
He's In Love, p.333
I Love You (Song Of Norway), p.528
Little Hands, p.90
Sands Of Time, p.332
Strange Music, p.529
Stranger In Paradise, p.332
Sweet Danger, p.326

**STAN FREEMAN**
Almost, p.306
I Had A Ball, p.306

**GARY WILLIAM FRIEDMAN**
Black, p.386
Dream Babies, p.387
How I Feel, p.389
Let Me Come In, p.387
Light Sings, p.388

**RUDOLF FRIML**
Only A Rose, p.583

**DOUGLAS FURBER**
Lambeth Walk, The, p.380
Me And My Girl, p.383

**G** _____

**NOEL GAY**
Lambeth Walk, The, p.380
Leaning On A Lamp-Post, p.381
Love Makes The World Go Round, p.382
Me And My Girl, p.383
Once You Lose Your Heart, p.384
Sun Has Got His Hat On, The, p.384

**GARY GELD**
Violets And Silverbells, p.522
We Make A Beautiful Pair, p.521

**ROBERT GERLACH**
You Fell Out Of The Sky, p.513

**GEORGE GERSHWIN**
Bess, You Is My Woman, p.490
By Strauss, p.525
I Got Plenty O' Nuttin', p.494
I Loves You Porgy, p.488
It Ain't Necessarily So, p.492
My Man's Gone Now, p.497
Real American Folk Song
   (Is A Rag), The, p.347
Summertime, p.493
There's A Boat Dat's Leavin Soon For New
   York, p.494
Woman Is A Sometime Thing, A, p.496

**IRA GERSHWIN**
Bess, You Is My Woman, p.490
By Strauss, p.525
I Can t Get Started With You, p.603
I Got Plenty O Nuttin, p.494
I Loves You Porgy, p.488
It Ain't Necessarily So, p.492
My Ship, p.348
Real American Folk Song (Is A Rag), The,
   p.347
Sing Me Not A Ballad, p.215
This Is New, p.350

**PEGGY GORDON**
By My Side, p.264

**ROBERT GRAHAM**
You Better Go Now, p.425

**RONNY GRAHAM**
If I Were The Man, p.116

**MICKI GRANT**
If I Could've Been, p.597
It Takes A Whole Lot Of Human Feeling,
   p.187
Lovin' Al, p.596
Thank Heaven For You, p.186
We're Gonna Have A Good Time, p.602

**TIMOTHY GRAY**
Forever And A Day, p.294
If I Gave You..., p.293
You'd Better Love Me, p.294

**ADOLPH GREEN**
Be A Santa, p.566
Bells Are Ringing, p.100
Dance Only With Me, p.517
Just In Time, p.101
Long Before I Knew You, p.102
Make Someone Happy, p.186
Never Never Land, p.465
Ohio, p.595
Party s Over, The, p.100
Wrong Note Rag, The, p.594

**PAUL GREEN**
Mon Ami, My Friend, p.334

**CLIFFORD GREY**
Got A Date With An Angel, p.232

**EDVARD GRIEG**
I Love You (Song Of Norway), p.528
Strange Music, p.529

**LARRY GROSSMAN**
Be Happy, p.399
Just One Person, p.514
Mama, A Rainbow, p.399

# H _____

**HAL HACKADY**
Be Happy, p.399
Just One Person, p.514
Mama, A Rainbow, p.399

**ALBERT HAGUE**
Young And Foolish, p.488

**OTTO HARBACH**
Smoke Gets In Your Eyes, p.506
Who?, p.565
Yesterdays, p.506

**EDWARD HARDY**
Here Comes The Morning, p. 615
Someone, p. 618
Tell Me To Go, p. 616

**JAY HAMBURGER**
By My Side, p.264

**NANCY HAMILTON**
How High The Moon, p.580

**ORD HAMILTON**
You're Blasé, p.114

**MARVIN HAMLISCH**
At The Ballet, p.173
Dance: Ten; Looks: Three, p.176
Fallin', p.572
I Can Do That, p.175
I Still Believe In Love, p.574
If You Really Knew Me, p.575
Just For Tonight, p.574
One, p.177
They're Playing My Song, p.573
What I Did For Love, p.177

**OSCAR HAMMERSTEIN II**
All Er Nothin', p.432
All At Once You Love Her, p.486
All The Things You Are, p.583
Bali Ha'i, p.540
Bill, p.522
Bloody Mary, p.541
Boys And Girls Like You And Me, p.159
Can't Help Lovin' Dat Man, p.523
Climb Ev'ry Mountain, p.533
Cock-Eyed Optimist, A, p.542
Dites-Moi (Tell Me Why), p.542
Do I Love You Because You're Beautiful?, p.160
Do-Re-Mi, p.534
Don't Ever Leave Me, p.565
Don't Marry Me, p.218
Edelweiss, p.537
Everybody's Got A Home But Me, p.487
Farmer And The Cowman, The, p.438
Fellow Needs A Girl, A, p.77
Gentleman Is A Dope, The, p.78
Getting To Know You, p.331
Happy Talk, p.544
Hello, Young Lovers, p.327
Honey Bun, p.548
How Can Love Survive, p.534
Hundred Million Miracles, A, p.216
I Cain't Say No!, p.432
I Enjoy Being A Girl, p.219
I Have Dreamed, p.329
I Whistle A Happy Tune, p.330
I'm Gonna Wash That Man Right Outa My Hair, p.546
If I Loved You, p.139
Impossible, p.160
In My Own Little Corner, p.159
It Might As Well Be Spring, p.560
It's A Grand Night For Singing, p.559
June Is Bustin' Out All Over, p.140
Kansas City, p.434

Lonely Goatherd, The, p.536
Love, Look Away, p.216
Lovely Night, A, p.162
Make Believe, p.524
Many A New Day, p.436
March Of The Siamese Children, The, p.328
Maria, p.535
Marriage Type Love, p.379
My Favorite Things, p.536
No Other Love, p.379
Oh, What A Beautiful Mornin', p.436
Oklahoma, p.434
Ol' Man River, p.524
Ordinary Couple, An, p.533
Out Of My Dreams, p.433
People Will Say We're In Love, p.435
Shall We Dance?, p.329
Sixteen Going On Seventeen, p.538
So Far, p.78
So Long, Farewell, p.538
Some Enchanted Evening, p.548
Something Wonderful, p.328
Song Is You, The, p.410
Sound Of Music, The, p.539
Stepsisters' Lament, p.161
Sunday, p.218
Surrey With The Fringe On Top, The, p.437
Ten Minutes Ago, p.162
There Is Nothin' Like A Dame, p.544
This Nearly Was Mine, p.547
Twin Soliloquies (This Is How It Feels), p.541
We Kiss In A Shadow, p.330
Who?, p.565
Why Do I Love You?, p.525
Wonderful Guy, A, p.543
You Are Beautiful, p.220
You'll Never Walk Alone, p.140
You've Got To Be Carefully Taught, p.545
Younger Than Springtime, p.546

**CHRISTOPHER HAMPTON**
As If We Never Said Goodbye, p. 622
New Ways To Dream, p. 626
Surrender, p. 625
With One Look, p. 624

**E.Y. HARBURG**
Cocoanut Sweet, p.314
Down With Love, p.297
Evelina, p.112
How Are Things In Glocca Morra, p.210
If This Isn't Love, p.208
Look To The Rainbow, p.208
Old Devil Moon, p.207
Push De Button, p.313
Right As The Rain, p.113
Something Sort Of Grandish, p.210
That Great Come And Get It Day, p.211
There's A Great Day Coming Mañana, p.296
When I'm Not Near The Girl I Love, p.209

**SHELDON HARNICK**
Anatevka, p.202
Artificial Flowers, p.570
As Once I Loved You, p.500
Beautiful, Beautiful World, p.91
Do You Love Me?, p.200
Far From The Home I Love, p.202
Fiddler On The Roof, p.201
Gentleman Jimmy, p.213
I Wonder What It's Like, p.570
If I Were A Rich Man, p.201
Matchmaker, p.205
Miracle Of Miracles, p.203
My Miss Mary, p.571
Politics And Poker, p.212
Sabbath Prayer, p.206
Sunrise, Sunset, p.204
'Til Tomorrow, p.213
To Life, p.206
Tradition, p.204
When Did I Fall In Love, p.214
Where Do I Go From Here, p.212

**CHARLES HART**
All I Ask Of You, p.468
Angel Of Music, p.472
Masquerade, p.478
Music Of The Night, The, p.467
Phantom Of The Opera, The, p.470
Point Of No Return, The, p.473
Prima Donna, p.475
Think Of Me, p.480
Wishing You Were Somehow Here Again, p.477

**LORENZ HART**
Bewitched, p.461
Blue Room, The, p.258
Dancing On The Ceiling, p.499
Ev'rything I've Got, p.117
Falling In Love With Love, p.115
Glad To Be Unhappy, p.447
Have You Met Miss Jones?, p.308
I Could Write A Book, p.462
I Didn't Know What Time It Was, p.577
I Wish I Were In Love Again, p.92
I'd Rather Be Right, p.307
It Never Entered My Mind, p.295
Johnny One Note, p.92
Lady Is A Tramp, The, p.94
Little Girl Blue, p.325
Manhattan, p.249
Most Beautiful Girl In The World, The, p.32
Mountain Greenery, p.248
My Funny Valentine, p.95
My Heart Stood Still, p.178
My Romance, p.325
On Your Toes, p.446
Quiet Night, p.446
Sentimental Me, p.248
Sing For Your Supper, p.114
Ten Cents A Dance, p.499
There's A Small Hotel, p.447
This Can't Be Love, p.115
Thou Swell, p.178
Wait Till You See Her, p.118
With A Song In My Heart, p.550
Where Or When, p.94
You Mustn't Kick It Around, p.462
You Took Advantage Of Me, p.498
Zip, p.463

**RAY HENDERSON**
Best Things In Life Are Free, The, p.268
Button Up Your Overcoat, p.232
Good News, p.270
Life Is Just A Bowl Of Cherries, p.252
Lucky In Love, p.269
Sunny Side Up, p.271
Thrill Is Gone, The, p.253
Together, p.269
Varsity Drag, The, p.272
You're The Cream In My Coffee, p.296

**DAVID HENEKER**
Half A Sixpence, p.283
Irma La Douce, p.312
Our Language Of Love, p.312

**JERRY HERMAN**
Before The Parade Passes By, p.288
Best Of Times, The, p.343
Dear World, p.182
Hello, Dolly!, p.287
I Don't Want To Know, p.182
I Won't Send Roses, p. 374
If He Walked Into My Life, p.376
It Only Takes A Moment, p.288
Just Go To The Movies, p.181
Kiss Her Now, p.183
La Cage Aux Folles, p.344
Mame, p.375
Milk And Honey, p.398
My Best Girl (My Best Beau), p.377
Put On Your Sunday Clothes, p.289
Ribbons Down My Back, p.287
Shalom, p.398
Song On The Sand, p.346
Time Heals Everything, p.374
We Need A Little Christmas, p.377

**DuBOSE HEYWARD**
Bess, You Is My Woman, p.490
I Got Plenty O' Nuttin', p.494
Loves You Porgy, p.488
My Man's Gone Now, p.497
Summertime, p.493
There's A Boat Dat's Leavin' Soon For
New York, p.494
Woman Is A Sometime Thing, A, p.496

**BOB HILLIARD**
Civilization (Bongo, Bongo, Bongo), p.79
How Do You Speak To An Angel?, p.286

**LARRY HOLOFCENER**
Jacques D'Iraque, p.406
Mr. Wonderful, p.405
Too Close For Comfort, p.407

**WILL HOLT**
Black, p.386
How I Feel, p.389
Let Me Come In, p.387
Night Sings, p.388

**BRIAN HOOKER**
Only A Rose, p.583

**ARNOLD HORWITT**
Young And Foolish, p.488

**LANGSTON HUGHES**
Moon-Faced, Starry-Eyed, p.564
What Good Would The Moon Be?, p.564

**HERMAN HUPFELD**
My Little Dog Has Ego, p.180

**J** _____
**JIM JACOBS**
Beauty School Dropout, p.273
Summer Nights, p.274
There Are Worse Things I Could Do, p.275
We Go Together, p.272

**J.C. JOHNSON**
Joint Is Jumpin', The, p.76

**TOM JONES**
Love My Wife, p.304
My Cup Runneth Over, p.304
Want A Radish, p.197
Simple Little Things, p.448
Soon It's Gonna Rain, p.198
They Were You, p.199
Together Forever, p.305
Try To Remember, p.198

**SCOTT JOPLIN**
Real Slow Drag, A, p.578

**LOUIS JORDAN**
Is You Is, Or Is You Ain't (Ma' Baby), p.188

**K** _____
**IRVING KAHAL**
Can Dream, Can't I?, p.500
I'll Be Seeing You, p.501

**GUS KAHN**
Makin' Whoopee!, p.588

**JOHN KANDER**
And All That Jazz, p.172
Believe, p.520
Cabaret, p.123
City Lights, p.72
First Time, The, p.607
Happy Birthday To Me, p.605
Happy Time, The, p.285
I Am Free, p.606
I Wrote The Book, p.590
If You Could See Her, p.126
Married (Heiraten), p.123
Mein Herr, p.126
My Own Best Friend, p.170

One Of The Girls, p.592
Only Love, p.605
Razzle Dazzle, p.171
Seeing Things, p.286
Sometimes A Day Goes By, p.592
Tomorrow Belongs To Me, p.124
Two Ladies, p.124
Willkommen, p.127
Without Me, p.284
Yes, p.519
Zorba Theme (Life Is), p.604

**HAROLD KARR**
Mutual Admiration Society, p.284

**JEROME KERN**
All The Things You Are, p.583
Bill, p.522
Can't Help Lovin' Dat Man, p.523
Don't Ever Leave Me, p.565
Look For The Silver Lining, p.517
Make Believe, p.524
Ol' Man River, p.524
Smoke Gets In Your Eyes, p.506
Song Is You, The, p.410
Till The Clouds Roll By, p.431
Who?, p.565
Why Do I Love You?, p.525
Yesterdays, p.506

**EDWARD KLEBAN**
At The Ballet, p.173
Dance: Ten; Looks: Three, p.176
I Can Do That, p.175
One, p.177
What I Did For Love, p.177

**HERBERT KRETZMER**
Bring Him Home, p.354
Castle On A Cloud, p.353
Do You Hear The People Sing?, p.356
Drink With Me (To Days Gone By), p.353
Empty Chairs At Empty Tables, p.359
Here Comes The Morning, p. 615
I Dreamed A Dream, p.352
In My Life, p.354
Little Fall Of Rain, A, p.360
Master Of The House, p.356
On My Own, p.361
Who Am I?, p.358

**L** _____
**FRAN LANDESMAN**
Ballad Of The Sad Young Men, The, p.426

**BURTON LANE**
Come Back To Me, p.442
How Are Things In Glocca Morra, p.210
If This Isn't Love, p.208
Look To The Rainbow, p.208
Old Devil Moon, p.207
On A Clear Day (You Can See Forever), p.442
Something Sort Of Grandish, p.210
That Great Come And Get It Day, p.211
There's A Great Day Coming Mañana, p.296
What Did I Have That I Don't Have?, p.443
When I'm Not Near The Girl I Love, p.209

**JONATHAN LARSON**
One Song Glory, p. 632
Rent, p. 638
Seasons Of Love, p. 634
Take Me Or Leave Me, p. 636
Without You, p. 640

**JOHN LaTOUCHE**
Lazy Afternoon, p.268

**JACK LAWRENCE**
Almost, p.306
I Had A Ball, p.306

**FRANZ LEHAR**
Vilia, p.397

**JERRY LEIBER**
Jailhouse Rock, p. 619
Kansas City, p. 620
Love Potion Number 9, p. 621
On Broadway, p. 621

**CAROLYN LEIGH**
Hey, Look Me Over, p.588
I Won't Grow Up, p.466
I'm Flying, p.465
I've Got Your Number, p.365
I've Gotta Crow, p.466
On The Other Side Of The Tracks, p.366
Real Live Girl, p.365
You've Come Home, p.589

**MICHAEL LEONARD**
I'm All Smiles, p.598
Kind Of Man A Woman Needs, The, p.600
Why Did I Choose You?, p.599

**ALAN JAY LERNER**
Camelot, p.130
Come Back To Me, p.442
Follow Me, p.135
Get Me To The Church On Time, p.416
Gigi, p.254
Green-Up Time, p.369
Here I'll Stay, p.370
How To Handle A Woman, p. 132
I Cold Have Danced All Night, p.418
I Loved You Once In Silence, p.131
I Remember It Well, p.254
I Still See Elisa, p.460
I Talk To The Trees, p.458
I Wonder What The King Is Doing
Tonight, p.133
I'm Glad I'm Not Young Anymore, p.256
I've Grown Accustomed To Her Face, p.417
If Ever I Would Leave You, p.134
Just You Wait, p.418
Lusty Month Of May, The, p.134
Night They Invented Champagne, The,
p.255
On A Clear Day (You Can See Forever),
p.442
On The Street Where You Live, p.424
Rain In Spain, The, p.420
Show Me, p.424
Simple Joys Of Maidenhood, The, p.132
Thank Heaven For Little Girls, p.256
They Call The Wind Maria, p.460
Wand'rin' Star, p.459
What Did I Have That I Don't Have?, p.443
Why Can't The English?, p.422
With A Little Bit Of Luck, p.420
Without You, p.421
Wouldn't It Be Loverly, p.423

**IRA LEVIN**
She (He) Touched Me, p.179

**MORGAN LEWIS**
How High The Moon, p.580

**ED LINDERMAN**
You Fell Out Of The Sky, p.513

**PETER LINK**
If You Let Me Make Love To You Then
Why Can't I Touch You?, p.515
Tomorrow Is The First Day Of The Rest Of
My Life, p.516

**ANDREW LLOYD WEBBER**
Ad-dressing Of Cats, The, p.152
All I Ask Of You, p.468
Angel Of Music, p.472
Another Suitcase In Another Hall, p.194
Any Dream Will Do, p.322
As If We Never Said Goodbye, p. 622
Buenos Aries, p.191
Bustopher Jones: The Cat About Town,
p.154
Capped Teeth And Caesar Salad, p.508
Close Every Door, p.323
Come Back With The Same Look In Your
Eyes, p.508
Don't Cry For Me Argentina, p.193
Engine Of Love, p.552
Everything's Alright, p.318
Hosanna, p.320
I Am The Starlight, p.557

13

I Don't Know How To Love Him, p.319
I Only Want To Say (Gethsemane), p.316
Journey To The Heavyside Layer, The, p.155
King Herod's Song, p.320
Light At The End Of The Tunnel, p.553
Make Up My Heart, p.551
Masquerade, p.478
Mr. Mistoffelees, p.156
Music Of The Night, The, p.467
New Ways To Dream, p. 626
Old Deuteronomy, p.153
Old Gumbie Cat, The, p.158
Only You, p.555
Phantom Of The Opera, The, p.470
Pilate's Dream, p.317
Point Of No Return, The, p.473
Prima Donna, p.475
So Much To Do In New York, p.511
Starlight Express, p.556
Superstar, p.314
Surrender, p. 625
Tell Me On A Sunday, p.507
Think Of Me, p.480
Those Canaan Days, p.322
Unexpected Song, p.510
Wishing You Were Somehow Here Again,
    p.477
With One Look, p. 624

**FRANK LOESSER**
Adelaide's Lament, p.242
Big D, p.408
Brotherhood Of Man, p.300
Bushel And A Peck, A, p.241
Fugue For Tinhorns, p.246
Guys And Dolls, p.242
I Believe In You, p.302
I'll Know, p.243
I've Never Been In Love Before, p.244
If I Were A Bell, p.244
Joey, Joey, Joey, p.408
Lovelier Than Ever, p.587
Luck Be A Lady, p.241
More I Cannot Wish You, p.246
Music Of Home, The, p.276
My Darling, My Darling, p.586
Never Will I Marry, p.276
New Ashmolean Marching Society And
    Students Conservatory Band, The, p.585
Once In Love With Amy, p.586
Secretary Is Not A Toy, A, p.300
Sit Down You're Rockin' The Boat, p.245
Standing On The Corner, p.409
Summertime Love, p.277
Take Back Your Mink, p.247

**FREDERICK LOEWE**
Camelot, p.130
Follow Me, p.135
Get Me To The Church On Time, p.416
Gigi, p.254
How To Handle A Woman, p.132
I Could Have Danced All Night, p.418
I Loved You Once In Silence, p.131
I Remember It Well, p.254
I Still See Elisa, p.460
I Talk To The Trees, p.458
I Wonder What The King Is Doing
    Tonight, p.133
I'm Glad I'm Not Young Anymore, p.256
I've Grown Accustomed To Her Face, p.417
If Ever I Would Leave You, p.134
Just You Wait, p.418
Lusty Month Of May, The, p.134
Night They Invented Champagne, The, p.255
On The Street Where You Live, p.424
Rain In Spain, The, p.420
Show Me, p.424
Simple Joys Of Maidenhood, The, p.132
Thank Heaven For Little Girls, p.256
They Call The Wind Maria, p.460
Wand'rin' Star, p.459

Why Can't The English?, p.422
With A Little Bit Of Luck, p.420
Without You, p.421
Wouldn't It Be Loverly, p.423

**M** _____

**JIMMY McHUGH**
I Can't Give You Anything But Love, p.111

**RICHARD MALTBY, JR.**
So Much To Do In New York, p.511

**HENRY MANCINI**
If I Were A Man, p. 630
Paris By Night, p. 628

**WALTER MARKS**
Must It Be Love?, p.95

**HERBERT MARTIN**
I'm All Smiles, p.598
Kind Of Man A Woman Needs, The, p.600
Why Did I Choose You?, p.599

**HUGH MARTIN**
Buckle Down, Winsocki, p.104
Forever And A Day, p.294
If I Gave You…, p.293
Pass That Peace Pipe, p.270
You'd Better Love Me, p.294

**GALT McDERMOT**
Who Is Silvia?, p.577

**JAMES McDONALD**
You Fell Out Of The Sky, p.513

**PAUL McGRANE**
Juke Box Saturday Night, p.558

**ALAN MENKEN**
Beauty And The Beast, p.98
If I Can't Love Her, p.96

**JOHNNY MERCER**
Any Place I Hang My Hat Is Home, p.549
Come Rain Or Come Shine, p.550
Satin Doll, p.532
You For Me, p.518

**BOB MERRILL**
Don't Rain On My Parade, p.234
I'm The Greatest Star, p.238
If A Girl Isn't Pretty, p.236
Music That Makes Me Dance, The, p.233
People, p.238
Sadie, Sadie, p.235
You Are Woman, I Am Man, p.237

**SIDNEY MICHAELS**
How Laughable It Is, p.102
Look For Small Pleasures, p.103

**ROGER MILLER**
Muddy Water, p.108
River In The Rain, p.107
Waitin' For The Light To Shine, p.109
Worlds Apart, p.110

**SONNY MILLER**
Got A Date With An Angel, p.232

**IRVING MILLS**
Caravan, p.530
It Don't Mean A Thing (If It Ain't Got That
    Swing), p.530
Mood Indigo, p.531
Sophisticated Lady, p.532

**MARGUERITE MONNOT**
Irma La Douce, p.312
Our Language Of Love, p.312

**JULIAN MORE**
Irma La Douce, p.312
Our Language Of Love, p.312

**JEROME MOROSS**
Lazy Afternoon, p.268

**OGDEN NASH**
Speak Low, p.450

**JEAN-MARC NATEL**
Castle On A Cloud, p.353
Do You Hear The People Sing?, p.356
I Dreamed A Dream, p.352
In My Life, p.354
Little Fall Of Rain, A, p.360
Master Of The House, p.356
On My Own, p.361
Who Am I?, p.358

**ANTHONY NEWLEY**
Feeling Good, p.502
Gonna Build A Mountain, p.560
Joker, The, p.502
Nothing Can Stop Me Now!, p.504
Once In A Lifetime, p.561
Someone Nice Like You, p.562
What Kind Of Fool Am I?, p.562
Who Can I Turn To (When Nobody
    Needs Me), p.504
Wonderful Day Like Today, A, p.503

**MONTY NORMAN**
Irma La Douce, p.312
Our Language Of Love, p.312

**TREVOR NUNN**
Memory, p.156
On My Own, p.361

**O** _____

**CYRIL ORNADEL**
If I Ruled The World, p.482

**P** _____

**DON PIPPIN**
Life Without Her, A, p.214

**GARY PIPPIN**
Freedom, p.520

**LEW POLLACK**
Two Cigarettes In The Dark, p.326

**COLE PORTER**
Ace In The Hole, p.363
All Of You, p.526
Allez-vous-en, Go Away, p.137
Always True To You In My Fashion, p.338
Another Op'nin', Another Show, p.336
At Long Last Love, p.526
Brush Up Your Shakespeare, p.336
C'est Magnifique, p.138
Cherry Pies Ought To Be You, p.452
Down In The Depths (On The Ninetieth
    Floor), p.483
Ev'ry Time We Say Goodbye, p.518
Fated To Be Mated, p.527
Friendship, p.190
From This Moment On, p.451
Get Out Of Town, p.351
I Am In Love, p.138
I Am Loved, p.452
I Hate Men, p.337
I Love Paris, p.136
I Love You (Mexican Hayride), p.397
I Sing Of Love, p.340
It Was Written In The Stars, p.189
It's All Right With Me, p.136
It's De-Lovely, p.484
Let's Be Buddies, p.464
Let's Not Talk About Love, p.362
My Heart Belongs To Daddy, p.350
My Mother Would Love You, p.464
Paris Loves Lovers, p.528
Ridin' High, p.485
So In Love, p.338
Something For The Boys, p.512
Too Darn Hot, p.340
Well, Did You Evah?, p.190
Why Can t You Behave, p.335
Wunderbar, p.339
You've Got Something, p.484

**DY RAZAF**
n't Misbehavin', p.74
neysuckle Rose, p.76
nt Is Jumpin', The, p.76
hat Did I Do To Be So) Black And Blue, p.73

**CKLEY REICHNER**
u Better Go Now, p. 425

**M RICE**
other Suitcase In Another Hall, p.194
y Dream Will Do, p.322
enos Aires, p.191
ose Every Door, p.323
n't Cry For Me Argentina, p.193
erything's Alright, p.318
osanna, p.320
on't Know How To Love Him, p.319
nly Want To Say (Gethsemane), p.316
ng Herod's Song, p.320
ate's Dream, p.317
meone Else's Story, p.150
perstar, p.314
ose Canaan Days, p.322

**CHARD RODGERS**
Er Nothin', p.432
At Once You Love Her, p.486
s Once I Loved You, p.500
ali Ha'i, p.540
witched, p.461
oody Mary, p.541
ue Room, The, p.258
ys And Girls Like You And Me, p.159
mb Ev'ry Mountain, p.533
ock-Eyed Optimist, A, p.542
ncing On The Ceiling, p.499
tes-Moi (Tell Me Why), p.542
o I Hear A Waltz?, p.184
o I Love You Because You're Beautiful?,
p.160
o-Re-Mi, p.534
on't Marry Me, p.218
delweiss, p.537
v'rything I've Got, p.117
verybody's Got A Home But Me, p.487
alling In Love With Love, p.115
armer And The Cowman, The, p.438
ellow Needs A Girl, A, p.77
entleman Is A Dope, The, p.78
etting To Know You, p.331
ad To Be Unhappy, p.447
appy Talk, p.544
ave You Met Miss Jones?, p.308
ello, Young Lovers, p.327
oney Bun, p.548
ow Can Love Survive, p.534
undred Million Miracles, A, p.216
Cain't Say No!, p.432
Could Write A Book, p.462
Didn't Know What Time It Was, p.577
Do Not Know A Day I Did Not Love You,
p.580
Enjoy Being A Girl, p.219
Have Dreamed, p.329
Whistle A Happy Tune, p.330
Wish I Were In Love Again, p.92
d Rather Be Right, p.307
m Gonna Wash That Man Right Outta
My Hair, p.546
I Loved You, p.139
npossible, p.160
My Own Little Corner, p.159
Might As Well Be Spring, p.560
Never Entered My Mind, p.295
s A Grand Night For Singing, p.559
ohnny One Note, p.92
une Is Bustin' Out All Over, p.140
ansas City, p.434
ady Is A Tramp, The, p.94
ttle Girl Blue, p.325

Lonely Goatherd, The, p.536
Love, Look Away, p.216
Lovely Night, A, p.162
Manhattan, p.249
Many A New Day, p.436
March Of The Siamese Children, The, p.328
Maria, p.535
Marriage Type Love, p.379
Most Beautiful Girl In The World, The, p.324
Mountain Greenery, p.248
My Favorite Things, p.536
My Funny Valentine, p.95
My Heart Stood Still, p.178
My Romance, p.325
No Other Love, p.379
No Strings, p.430
Oh, What A Beautiful Mornin', p.436
Oklahoma, p.434
On Your Toes, p.446
Ordinary Couple, An, p.533
Out Of My Dreams, p.433
People Will Say We're In Love, p.435
Quiet Night, p.446
Sentimental Me, p.248
Shall We Dance?, p.329
Sing For Your Supper, p.114
Sixteen Going On Seventeen, p.538
Slaughter On Tenth Avenue, p.444
So Far, p.78
So Long, Farewell, p.538
Some Enchanted Evening, p.548
Someone Like You, p.185
Something Wonderful, p.328
Sound Of Music, The, p.539
Stepsisters' Lament, p.161
Sunday, p.218
Surrey With The Fringe On Top, The, p.437
Sweetest Sounds, The, p.430
Ten Cents A Dance, p.499
Ten Minutes Ago, p.162
There Is Nothin' Like A Dame, p.544
This Can't Be Love, p.115
This Nearly Was Mine, p.547
Thou Swell, p.178
Twin Soliloquies (This Is How It Feels),    p.541
Wait Till You See Her, p.118
We Kiss In A Shadow, p.330
Where Or When, p.94
With A Song In My Heart, p.550
Wonderful Guy, A, p.543
You Are Beautiful, p.220
You Mustn't Kick It Around, p.462
You Took Advantage Of Me, p.498
You'll Never Walk Alone, p.140
You've Got To Be Carefully Taught, p.545
Younger Than Springtime, p.546
Zip, p.463

**SIGMUND ROMBERG**
Close As Pages In A Book, p.582

**HAROLD ROME**
Anyone Would Love You, p.184
Be Kind To Your Parents, p.196
Fanny, p.195
I Have To Tell You, p.196
Miss Marmelstein, p.302
Out Of This World, p.601
Sing Me A Song With Social Significance,
p.486
Wish You Were Here, p.590

**ADRIAN ROSS**
Villa, p.397

**S** _____

**CAROLE BAYER SAGER**
Fallin', p.572
I Still Believe In Love, p.574
If You Really Knew Me, p.575
Just For Tonight, p.574
They're Playing My Song, p.573

**MARK SANDRICH JR.**
How Laughable It Is, p.102
Look For Small Pleasures, p.103

**LESTER A. SANTLEY**
Lookin' Good But Feelin' Bad, p.74

**MILTON SCHAFER**
If I Were The Man, p.116
She (He) Touched Me, p.179

**HERB SCHAPIRO**
Dream Babies, p.387

**HARVEY SCHMIDT**
I Love My Wife, p.304
My Cup Runneth Over, p.304
Plant A Radish, p.197
Simple Little Things, p.448
Soon It's Gonna Rain, p.198
They Were You, p.199
Together Forever, p.305
Try To Remember, p.198

**CLAUDE-MICHEL SCHÖNBERG**
Bring Him Home, p.354
Castle On A Cloud, p.353
Do You Hear The People Sing?, p.356
Drink With Me (To Days Gone By), p.353
Empty Chairs At Empty Tables, p.359
Here Comes The Morning, p. 615
I Dreamed A Dream, p.352
In My Life, p.354
Little Fall Of Rain, A, p.360
Master Of The House, p.356
On My Own, p.361
Someone, p. 618
Tell Me To Go, p. 616
When Will Someone Hear, p. 614
Who Am I?, p.358

**ARTHUR SCHWARTZ**
Alone Too Long, p.116
By Myself, p.104
Haunted Heart, p.310
I See Your Face Before Me, p.106
Rhode Island Is Famous For You, p.311
Triplets, p.105

**STEPHEN SCHWARTZ**
All For The Best, p.260
All Good Gifts, p.262
Day By Day, p.259
Learn Your Lessons Well, p.259
Light Of The World, p.264
O Bless The Lord, My Soul, p.262
On The Willows, p.263
Prepare Ye (The Way Of The Lord), p.265
Save The People, p.260
Turn Back, O Man, p.267
We Beseech Thee, p.266

**WILLIAM SHAKESPEARE**
Who Is Silvia?, p.577

**RICHARD M. SHERMAN**
Big Beat, The, p.453
Charlie's Place, p.455
My Dream For Tomorrow, p.454
No Goodbyes, p.458
Over Here!, p.456
Since You're Not Around, p.456
Where Did The Good Times Go?, p.457

**ROBERT B. SHERMAN**
Big Beat, The, p.453
Charlie's Place, p.455
My Dream For Tomorrow, p.454
No Goodbyes, p.458
Over Here!, p.456
Since You're Not Around, p.456
Where Did The Good Times Go?, p.457

**BRUCE SIEVIER**
You're Blasé, p.114

**CARL SIGMAN**
Civilization (Bongo, Bongo, Bongo), p.79

**BESSIE SMITH**
My Man Blues, p.448

**STEPHEN SONDHEIM**
Ah, Paris!, p.220
All I Need Is The Girl, p.278
Another Hundred People, p.164
Anyone Can Whistle, p.90
Ballad Of Sweeney Todd, The, p.567
Being Alive, p.166
Broadway Baby, p.222
Comedy Tonight, p.239
Company, p.166
Could I Leave You, p.225
Do I Hear A Waltz?, p.184
Everything's Coming Up Roses, p.278
God-Why-Don't-You-Love-Me Blues, The, p.224
Good Thing Going, p.395
I'm Still Here, p.228
In Buddy's Eyes (Buddy's There), p.221
Johanna, p.569
Let Me Entertain You, p.280
Little Lamb, p.281
Little Night Music, A, p.367
Little Things You Do Together, The, p.168
Losing My Mind, p.230
Lovely, p.240
Not A Day Goes By, p.396
Not While I'm Around, p.567
One More Kiss, p.230
Pretty Women, p.569
Prologue (Beautiful Girls), p.231
Remember?, p.368
Send In The Clowns, p.367
Side By Side By Side, p.165
Small World, p.282
Some People, p.280
Someone Is Waiting, p.167
Someone Like You, p.185
Sorry-Grateful, p.163
Together Wherever We Go, p.282
Too Many Mornings, p.222
Waiting For The Girls Upstairs, p.224
Who's That Woman?, p.227
You Could Drive A Person Crazy, p.168
You'll Never Get Away From Me, p.279

**RICHARD STILGOE**
All I Ask Of You, p.468
Angel Of Music, p.472
Engine Of Love, p.552
I Am The Starlight, p.557
Light At The End Of The Tunnel, p.553
Make Up My Heart, p.551
Masquerade, p.478
Music Of The Night, The, p.467
Only You, p.555
Phantom Of The Opera, The, p.470
Point Of No Return, The, p.473
Prima Donna, p.475
Starlight Express, p.556
Think Of Me, p.480
Wishing You Were Somehow Here Again, p.477

**AL STILLMAN**
Juke Box Saturday Night, p.558

**MIKE STOLLER**
Jailhouse Rock, p. 619
Kansas City, p. 620
Love Potion Number 9, p. 621
On Broadway, p. 621

**BILLY STRAYHORN**
Satin Doll, p.532

**CHARLES STROUSE**
Easy Street, p.80
It's The Hard-Knock Life, p.81
Kids!, p.120
Little Girls, p.80
Lot Of Livin' To Do, A, p.120
Maybe, p.82
N.Y.C., p.82
One Boy, p.121
Put On A Happy Face, p.122
Rosie, p.122
Telephone Hour, The, p.118
Tomorrow, p.83
You're Never Fully Dressed With A
Smile, p.83

**JULE STYNE**
All I Need Is The Girl, p.278
Be A Santa, p.566
Bells Are Ringing, p.100
Can't You Just See Yourself?, p.292
Dance Only With Me, p.517
Don't Rain On My Parade, p.234
Everything's Coming Up Roses, p.278
Guess I'll Hang My Tears Out To Dry, p.258
How Do You Speak To An Angel?, p.286
I Still Get Jealous, p.292
I'm The Greatest Star, p.238
If A Girl Isn't Pretty, p.236
Just In Time, p.101
Let Me Entertain You, p.280
Little Lamb, p.281
Long Before I Knew You, p.102
Make Someone Happy, p.186
Music That Makes Me Dance, The, p.233
Never Never Land, p.465
Party's Over, The, p.100
People, p.238
Sadie, Sadie, p.235
Small World, p.282
Some People, p.280
Together Wherever We Go, p.282
You Are Woman, I Am Man, p.237
You'll Never Get Away, From Me, p.279

**T**

**EDWARD THOMAS**
Maman, p.378

**JUAN TIZOL**
Caravan, p.530

**ANDREW TRACEY**
I Gave My Love A Cherry, p.584
I Know Where I'm Going, p.584

**PAUL TRACEY**
I Gave My Love A Cherry, p.584
I Know Where I'm Going, p.584

**JOSEPH TURNBRIDGE**
Got A Date With An Angel, p.232

**U**

**PETER UDELL**
Freedom, p.520
Violets And Silverbells, p.522
We Make A Beautiful Pair, p.521

**BJORN ULVAEUS**
Someone Else's Story, p.150

**V**

**DAVID VOS**
You Fell Out Of The Sky, p.513

**W**

**JACK WALLER**
Got A Date With An Angel, p.232

**THOMAS "FATS" WALLER**
Ain't Misbehavin', p.74
(What Did I Do To Be So) Black And Blue, p.7
Handful Of Keys, A, p.75
Honeysuckle Rose, p.76
Joint Is Jumpin, The, p.76
Lookin Good But Feelin Bad, p.74

**PAUL FRANCIS WEBSTER**
Two Cigarettes In The Dark, p.326

**KURT WEILL**
Green-up Time, p.369
Here I'll Stay, p.370
It Never Was You, p.341
Lost In The Stars, p.368
Mon Ami, My Friend, p.334
Moon-Faced, Starry-Eyed, p.564
My Ship, p.348
September Song, p.342
Sing Me Not A Ballad, p.215
Speak Low, p.450
This Is New, p.350
What Good Would The Moon Be?, p.564

**GEORGE WEISS**
Jacques D'Iraque, p.406
Mr. Wonderful, p.405
Too Close For Comfort, p.407

**FRANK WILDHORN**
Living In The Shadows, p. 627
A New Life, p. 610
Someone Like You, p. 609
Take Me As I Am, p. 612
This Is The Moment, p. 612

**MEREDITH WILLSON**
Goodnight, My Someone, p.411
I Ain't Down Yet, p.572
I'll Never Say No, p.571
Lida Rose, p.412
Love, Come Take Me Again, p.290
My Wish, p.290
Pine Cones And Holly Berries, p.291
Seventy Six Trombones, p.410
Till There Was You, p.412
Wells Fargo Wagon, The, p.416
Ya Got Trouble, p.413

**P.G. WODEHOUSE**
Bill, p.522
Till The Clouds Roll By, p.431

**TOMMY WOLF**
Ballad Of The Sad Young Men, The, p.426

**ROBERT WRIGHT**
He's In Love, p.333
I Love You (Song Of Norway), p.528
Little Hands, p.90
Sands Of Time, p.332
Strange Music, p.529
Stranger In Paradise, p.332
Sweet Danger, p.326

**Y**

**JACK YELLEN**
Are You Havin' Any Fun, p.253

**JOE YOUNG**
I'm Gonna Sit Right Down And Write
Myself A Letter, p.75

# ABOUT THE SHOWS...

## THE ACT
MUSIC AND LYRICS: John Kander and Fred Ebb
BOOK: George Furth  PRODUCER: Shubert Organization, Cy Feuer and Ernest Martin
DIRECTOR: Martin Scorsese, Gower Champion (uncredited)  CHOREOGRAPHER: Ron Lewis
MAJOR PERFORMERS: Liza Minnelli, Barry Nelson, Arnold Soboloff, Gayle Crofoot, Roger Minami, Wayne Cilento
OPENED: 10/29/77        THEATER: Majestic        PERFORMANCES: 233

Initially it was the intention of film director Martin Scorsese and songwriters John Kander and Fred Ebb to create a stage musical for Liza Minnelli—tried out as *Shine It On*—that took the same basic character she had played in the movie, *New York, New York* and focused on how she was affected by success. By the time the musical reached Broadway—under the title of *The Act*—Scorsese had been succeeded by Gower Champion, about half the songs were replaced, and the show was now primarily a supercharged Las Vegas presentation with an incidental story line about the problems of combining a career with a personal life.

## AIN'T MISBEHAVIN'
MUSIC AND LYRICS: Mostly by Fats Waller
BOOK: Based on an idea by Murray Horwitz & Richard Maltby, Jr.
PRODUCER: Emanuel Azenberg, Dasha Epstein, The Shubert Organization, Jane Gaynor and Ron Dante
DIRECTOR: Richard Maltby, Jr.  CHOREOGRAPHER: Arthur Faria
MAJOR PERFORMERS: Nell Carter, Andre DeShields, Armelia McQueen, Ken Page and Charlaine Woodard
OPENED: 5/9/78        THEATER: Longacre        PERFORMANCES: 1,604

*Ain't Misbehavin'* made no pretense of being a book musical. It was simply a jubilant celebration of the songs written by (or, in some cases, recorded by) Fats Waller. There have been tributes of this type before and since *Ain't Misbehavin'* but few have shown such a high degree of originality, professionalism and continous high spirits from beginning to end.

## ALLEGRO
MUSIC AND LYRICS: Richard Rodgers and Oscar Hammerstein II
BOOK: Oscar Hammerstein II  PRODUCER: Theatre Guild  DIRECTOR: Agnes de Mille
CHOREOGRAPHER: Agnes de Mille
MAJOR PERFORMERS: John Battles, Roberta Jonay, John Conte, Kathryn Lee, Annamary Dickey, William Ching, Muriel O'Malley, Lisa Kirk
OPENED: 10/10/47        THEATER: Majestic        PERFORMANCES: 315

*Allegro* was the third Rodgers and Hammerstein musical on Broadway and the first with a story that had not been based on a previous source. It was a particularly ambitious undertaking, with its theme of the corrupting effect of big institutions told through the life of a doctor, Joseph Taylor, Jr. (John Battles), from his birth in a small American town to his thirty-fifth year. Joe grows up, goes to school, marries a local belle (Roberta Jonay), joins the staff of a large Chicago hospital that panders to wealthy patients, discovers that his wife is unfaithful, and, in the end, returns to his home town with his adoring nurse (Lisa Kirk) to dedicate himself to healing the sick and helping the needy. One innovation in the musical was the use of a Greek chorus to comment on the action and to sing directly to the actors and the audience.

## ANGEL IN THE WINGS
MUSIC AND LYRICS: Bob Hilliard & Carl Sigman
BOOK: Sketches by Hank Ladd, Ted Luce & The Hartmans  PRODUCER: Majorie and Sherman Ewing
DIRECTOR: John Kennedy  CHOREOGRAPHER: Edward Noll
MAJOR PERFORMERS: Paul and Grace Hartman (The Hartmans), Hank Ladd, Elaine Stritch
OPENED: 12/11/47        THEATER: Coronet        PERFORMANCES: 308

Comprised of singing, dancing and comedy sketches, *Angel in the Wings* was a vaudeville-like revue of a type no longer seen on Broadway, due largely to the competition television eventually provided for this type of entertainment. Among the shows outstanding moments was Elaine Stritch's singing of "Civilization (Bongo, Bongo, Bongo)."

## ANNIE
MUSIC AND LYRICS: Music by Charles Strouse Lyrics by Martin Charnin
BOOK: Thomas Meehan  PRODUCER: Mike Nichols, Irwin Meyer, Stephen R. Friedman and Lewis Allen  DIRECTOR: Martin Charnin
CHOREOGRAPHER: Peter Gennaro
MAJOR PERFORMERS: Andrea McArdle, Reid Shelton, Dorothy Louden, Sandy Faison, Robert Fitch and Sandy the Dog
OPENED: 4/21/77        THEATER: Alvin Theatre        PERFORMANCES: 2,377

Once in a while comes an idea which seems so simple and natural that an occasional "I could have thought of that" can be heard among the countless shouts of "Bravo!" and "Encore!" *Annie* is such an idea. An orphan girl and her dog searching for the warmth and comfort of a real home served as the basis for this gigantic hit musical, inspired by a popular comic strip. With the help of Charles Strouse's tuneful score, including "Tomorrow," *Annie* now ranks with such all time family favorites as *Peter Pan* and *The Wizard of Oz*. A new production opened on Broadway in 1997.

Consultant for this section: Stanley Green, author of *The World of Musical Comedy* and *Broadway Musicals: Show By Show*.

## ANNIE GET YOUR GUN

MUSIC & LYRICS: Irving Berlin BOOK: Herbert & Dorothy Fields.
PRODUCERS: Richard Rodgers & Oscar Hammerstein DIRECTOR: Josh Logan
CHOREOGRAPHER: Helen Tamiris
MAJOR PERFORMERS: Ethel Merman, Ray Middleton, Marty May, Kenny Bowers, Lea Penman, Betty Anne Nyman
OPENED: 5/16/46          THEATER: Imperial          PERFORMANCES: 1,147

The story goes that Herbert and Dorothy Fields pitched the idea in one sentence to Rodgers & Hammerstein: Ethel Merman as Annie Oakley. Rodgers and Hammerstein were at the height of their activity, and decided the project wasn't suitable for them to write, but they were to be producers. With Dorothy Fields as the lyric writer, they sought and won Jerome Kern for writing the music. Kern's death shortly after forced a search for a way to save the concept. Berlin was approached, and at first declined, saying he didn't feel confident about writing songs for a book-show integrated musical. He was persuaded to try it, and a few days later came in with 5 songs and a confidence that he could take on the job. The show is clearly built around it's star, one of "La Merman's" 3 biggest triumphs on Broadway (the others are *Girl Crazy* and *Gypsy*).

## ANYA

MUSIC AND LYRICS: Robert Wright and George Forrest based on themes of S. Rachmaninoff
BOOK: George Abbott and Guy Bolton based on *Anastasia* by Marcell Maurette and Guy Bolton
PRODUCER: Fred R. Fehlhaber DIRECTOR: George Abbott CHOREOGRAPHER: Hanya Holm
MAJOR PERORMERS: Constance Towers, Michael Kermoyan, Lillian Gish and Irra Petina
OPENED: 11/29/65          THEATER: Ziegfeld          PERFORMANCES: 16

Adapted from the successful play, *Anastasia*, this musical told the story of a young woman surfacing in Berlin in the mid-twenties, professing to be the sole survivor of Czar Nicholas' supposedly slaughtered family. Adapting the music of a well-known composer, a method which had served them well in *Kismet* and *Song of Norway*, Wright and Forrest produced a richly melodic score.

## ANYONE CAN WHISTLE

MUSIC AND LYRICS: Stephen Sondheim BOOK: Arthur Laurents
PRODUCER: Kermit Bloomgarden and Diana Krasny DIRECTOR: Arthur Laurents CHOREOGRAPHER: Herbert Ross
MAJOR PERFORMERS: Lee Remick, Angela Lansbury, Harry Guardino, Gabriel Dell
OPENED: 4/4/64          THEATER: Majestic          PERFORMANCES: 9

Something of a "cult" musical, *Anyone Can Whistle* was an allegorical satire in which Angela Lansbury (in her first Broadway musical) played a corrupt mayor of a bankrupt town who comes up with a scheme to attract tourists: a fake miracle in which a stream of water appears to spout out of a solid rock. The town soon becomes a mecca for the gullible and the pious, but the hoax is exposed when the inmates of a mental institution called the Cookie Jar get mixed up with the pilgrims. Harry Guardino played a candidate for the booby hatch mistaken for the new doctor, and Lee Remick was the head nurse, so inhibited, she was unable to whistle.

## THE APPLE TREE

MUSIC AND LYRICS: Jerry Bock and Sheldon Harnick
BOOK: Sheldon Hamick, Jerry Bock, and Jerome Coopersmith PRODUCER: Stuart Ostrow
DIRECTOR Mike Nichols CHOREOGRAPHER: Lee Theodore and Herbert Ross
MAJOR PERFORMERS: Barbara Harris, Alan Alda, Larry Blyden. Carmen Alvarez, Marc Jordan
OPENED: 10/18/66          THEATER: Shubert          PERFORMANCES: 463

Here was a new concept for Broadway —one musical containing three separate one act musicals. Though the stories in *The Apple Tree* had nothing in common and, in fact, could be played separately, they were tied together by interrelated musical themes and by the whimsical reference to the color brown. The first act was based on Mark Twain's *The Diary of Adam and Eve* (whence came "Beautiful, Beautiful World") and dealt with the dawn of humanity and innocence: the second act was based on Frank R. Stockton's celebrated *The Lady or the Tiger?* in which a warrior's fate, unresolved in the story, was determined by the choice of door he enters: and the third act was based on Jules Feiffer's *Passionella*, a fantasy about a poor chimney sweep who became a movie star.

## AS THOUSANDS CHEER

MUSIC & LYRICS: Irving Berlin SKETCHES: Moss Hart PRODUCER: Sam H. Harris
DIRECTOR: Hassard Short CHOREOGRAPHER: Charles Weidman
MAJOR PERFORMERS: Marilyn Miller, Clifton Webb, Helen Broderick, Ethel Waters, Hal Forde, Jerome Cowan, Harry Stockwell, Jose Limon
OPENED: 9/30/33          THEATER: Music Box          PERFORMANCES: 400

One of the most successful and sophisticated revues of its time, *As Thousands Cheer* dealt satirically with current topics of the day, with the show presented in the form of a newspaper, with headlines before each number. There was society news, hard news, weather (introducing the song "Heat Wave"), sports, a personal advice column, etc. The tone was light except for Ethel Waters; singing "Supper Time," a song about a woman whose man has been murdered in a lynching. Celebrities of the day were parodied and impersonated throughout the evening.

## ASPECTS OF LOVE

MUSIC: Andrew Lloyd Webber  LYRICS: Don Black & Charles Hart
BOOK: Andrew Lloyd Webber
PRODUCER: The Really Useful Theatre Company  DIRECTOR: Trevor Nunn  CHOREOGRAPHER: Gillian Lynne
MAJOR PERFORMERS: Ann Crumb, Michael Ball, Kevin Colson, Walter Charles, Kathleen Rowe McAllen, Deanna DuClos, Daniel CuClos
OPENED: 4/8/90          THEATER: Broadhurst          PERFORMANCES: 377

The musical is based on David Garnett's autobiographical novel, and follows a group of characters over a 17 year period. The plot is quite emotionally complex, as are the characters' relationships. David Garnett was a nephew of Virginia Woolf. Though certainly not an outright failure by any standard, it is the least successful show of Andrew Lloyd Webber's shows to play on Broadway (as of this writing, 6/94). There is an intimate production style, and orchestrations that throw out the brass and stick to a chamber music sound.


## BABES IN ARMS

MUSIC AND LYRICS: Richard Rodgers and Lorenz Hart  BOOK: Richard Rodgers and Lorenz Hart
PRODUCER: Dwight Deere Wiman  DIRECTOR: Robert Sinclair  CHOREOGRAPHER: George Balanchine
MAJOR PERFORMERS: Mitzi Green, Wynn Murray, Ray Heatherton, Duke McHale, Alfred Drake, Ray McDonald, Grace McDonald, Harold and Fayard Nicholas, Rolly Pickert, Dan Dailey
OPENED: 4/14/37          THEATER: Shubert          PERFORMANCES: 289

With such songs as "I Wish I Were In Love Again," "Johnny One Note," "The Lady Is A Tramp," "My Funny Valentine," and "Where Or When," *Babes in Arms* boasted more hits than any of Rodgers and Hart's twenty-nine stage musicals. In the high-spirited, youthful show, a group of youngsters, whose parents are out-of-work vaudevillians, stage a revue to keep from being sent to a work farm. Unfortunately, the show is not a success. Later, when a transatlantic French flyer lands nearby, they attract enough publicity to put on a successful show and have their own youth center. Among the cast's babes in arms were such future stars as Alfred Drake and Dan Dailey, both appearing in their first Broadway roles. MGM's 1939 film version, starring Mickey Rooney and Judy Garland, retained only two of the Rodgers and Hart songs. The director was Busby Berkeley. The show was revised in 1959, with a new plot and newly named characters (it's the revision that appears in the vocal score).


## BAJOUR

MUSIC AND LYRICS: Walter Marks
BOOK: Ernest Kinoy  PRODUCER: Edward Padula, Carroli and Harris Masterson
DIRECTOR: Lawrence Kasha and Norman Twain  CHOREOGRAPHER: Peter Gennaro
MAJOR PERFORMERS: Chita Rivera, Nancy Dussault, Herschel Bernardi, Robert Burr, Mae Questel, Gus Trikonis & Herb Edelman
OPENED: 11/23/64          THEATER: Shubert          PERFORMANCES: 218

Unlike operettas romanticizing nineteenth century Austro-Hungarian gypsies, *Bajour* is the story of a pretty, young anthropologist studying the customs of a twentieth century tribe moving in on New York City to pull off a grand swindle—the big bajour! Among the show's assets were the fiery performance of Chita Rivera and Walter Marks' melodic score and witty lyrics.


## BEAUTY AND THE BEAST: A NEW MUSICAL

MUSIC: Alan Mencken  LYRICS: Howard Ashman & Tim Rice  BOOK: Linda Woolverton
PRODUCER: Walt Disney Productions  DIRECTOR: Robert Jess Roth  CHOREOGRAPHER: Matt West
MAJOR PERFORMERS: Susan Egan, Terrence Mann, Burke Moses, Tom Bosley, Beth Fowler, Gary Beach,
OPENED: 4/18/94          THEATER: Palace          PERFORMANCES: (still running 6/1/97)

The mega-hit Disney movie on stage. Tim Rice was called upon to write lyrics for added material for the stage version with composer Alan Menken. New songs written for the stage are "No Matter What," "Me," "Home," "How Long Must This Go On?," "If I Can't Love Her," "Maison des Lunes," "Transformation." These are added to the well known songs from the movie, "Beauty and the Beast," "Gaston," "Be Our Guest," and 6 others. It used to be that movies were based on musicals, but times have changed.


## BELLS ARE RINGING

MUSIC AND LYRICS: Jule Styne, Betty Comden and Adolph Green  BOOK: Betty Comden and Adolph Green
PRODUCER: Theatre Guild  DIRECTOR: Jerome Robbins  CHOREOGRAPHER: Jerome Robbins and Bob Fosse
MAJOR PERFORMERS: Judy Holliday, Sydney Chaplin, Jean Stapleton, Eddie Lawrence, Peter Gennaro, Bernie West, Frank Aletter
OPENED: 11/29/56          THEATER: Shubert          PERFORMANCES: 924

Ever since appearing together in a night-club revue, Betty Comden and Adolph Green had wanted to write a musical for their friend, Judy Holliday. The idea they eventually hit upon was to cast Miss Holliday as a meddlesome operator at a telephone answering service who gets involved with her clients lives. She is in fact so helpful to one, a playwright in need of inspiration, that they meet, fall in love, dance and sing in the subway, and entertain fellow New Yorkers in Central Park. In addition to being Comden and Green's longest-running Broadway hit, *Bells Are Ringing* introduced no less than three standards—"Just In Time," "Long Before I Knew You," and "The Party's Over." For the 1960 MGM movie version, Miss Holliday was co-starred with Dean Martin in a production directed by Vincente Minnelli.

## BEN FRANKLIN IN PARIS

MUSIC: Mark Sandrich Jr. LYRICS: Sidney Michaels
BOOK: Sidney Michaels PRODUCER: George W. George and Frank Granat DIRECTOR: Michael Kidd
CHOREOGRAPHER: Michael Kidd MAJOR PERFORMERS: Robert Preston, Ulla Sallert, Susan Watson
OPENED: 10/27/64    THEATER: Lunt-Fontanne PERFORMANCES: 215

*Ben Franklin in Paris* was a romantic account of a period in Franklin's later life. Among the show's strengths were a vibrant performance by Robert Preston, a gentle and charming score, and Oliver Smith's production design which included the ascension of Franklin and his lady-friend in a hot-air balloon.


## BEST FOOT FORWARD

MUSIC AND LYRICS: Hugh Martin and Ralph Blane BOOK: John Cecil Holm
PRODUCER: George Abbott and Richard Rodgers (uncredited) DIRECTOR: George Abbott
CHOREOGRAPHER: Gene Kelly
MAJOR PERFORMERS: Rosemary Lane, Marty May, Gil Stratton Jr., Maureen Cannon, Nancy Walker, June Allyson, Kenneth Bowers, Victoria Schools, Tommy Dix
OPENED: 10/1/41    THEATER: Ethel Barrymore    PERFORMANCES: 326

After having directed five musicals with songs by Richard Rodgers and Lorenz Hart, George Abbott was joined by Rodgers as an uncredited co-sponsor of a show introducing the talents of a new song-writing team, Hugh Martin and Ralph Blane. Taking place at a Pennsylvania prep school named Winsocki, *Best Foot Forward* is concerned with the activities attending the school's annual prom. The one unexpected complication is the arrival of movie glamour girl Gale Joy (Rosemary Lane) who, as a publicity stunt, has accepted the invitation of Bud Hooper (Gil Stratton Jr.) to be his date. This provokes jealousy and hurt feelings on the part of Bud's steady girl, Helen Schlessinger (Maureen Cannon), and a near-riot when souvenir hungry prom-trotters strip the movie star down to her essentials. The rousing "Buckle Down, Winsocki" became the best known song in the show, which was also the first to reveal the talents of Nancy Walker and June Allyson. In 1963, an Off Broadway revival of *Best Foot Forward* performed a similar function for seventeen year old Liza Minnelli. MGM's movie version, made in 1943, featured Lucille Ball, William Gaxton, Nancy Walker, and June Allyson. Edward Buzzell was the director.


## BETSY

MUSIC: Richard Rodgers LYRICS: Lorenz Hart (with one added song, music & lyrics by Irving Berlin)
BOOK: Irving Caesar & David Freedman, Rev. William Anthony McGuire PRODUCER: Florenz Ziegfeld
DIRECTOR: William Anthony McGuire CHOREOGRAPHER: Sammy Lee
MAJOR PERFORMERS: Bobie Perkins, Belle Baker, Pauline Hoffman, Madeline Cameron, Allen Kearns
OPENED: 12/28/26    THEATER: New Amsterdam    PERFORMANCES: 39

This Ziegfeld creation for vaudeville star Belle Barker was one of the most unhappy projects that Rodgers & Hart ever took on. By all accounts, Ziegfeld was very interested in lavish sets, but had no interest in the book, or the songs in particular. The result was a classic example of an overproduced fiasco. As Rodgers tells the story in his autobiography, the worst sting of all was sitting in the audience on opening night and, without warning, hearing Irving Berlin's "Blue Skies" thrown in the show. Berlin had written the number the day before at either Ziegfeld or Barker's request. The song became widely known, and was included in the first musical on film, *The Jazz Singer*.


## BETWEEN THE DEVIL

MUSIC AND LYRICS: Arthur Schwartz and Howard Dietz BOOK: Howard Dietz PRODUCER: Messrs. Shubert
DIRECTOR: Hassard Short and John Hayden CHOREOGRAPHER: Robert Alton
MAJOR PERFORMERS: Jack Buchanan, Evelyn Laye, Adele Dixon, Charles Walters, Velma Ebsen, William Kendall
OPENED: 12/22/37    THEATER: Imperial    PERFORMANCES: 93

In this sophisticated continental farce, Jack Buchanan played Peter Anthony, an Englishman who is known as Pierre Antoine whenever he spends time in Paris. Believing that his French wife Claudette (Adele Dixon) has been lost in a shipwreck, Peter weds London socialite Natalie (Evelyn Laye), only to have Claudette show up in great shape and voice. Enjoying his bigamous condition, Peter-Pierre hops between London and Paris, dodging both police (while singing "By Myself") and jealous wives (to whom he sings "I See Your Face Before Me"). Since librettist Howard Dietz could find no satisfactory resolution to the dilemma, the musical ends with the chorus simply advising the audience to make up its own conclusion.


## BIG RIVER

MUSIC & LYRICS: Roger Miller BOOK: William Hauptman
PRODUCER: Rocco Landesman, Heidi Landesman, Rick Steiner, M. Anthony Fisher, Dodger Productions
DIRECTOR: Des McAnuff CHOREOGRAPHER: JANET WATSON
MAJOR PERFORMERS: Daniel H. Jenkins, Ron Richardson, Rene Auberjonois, Reathal Bean, Susan Browning, Patti Cohenour, Gordon Connell, Bob Bunton
OPENED: 4/25/85    THEATER: Eugene O'Neill    PERFORMANCES: 1,005

The show is based on Twain's *The Adventures of Huckleberry Finn*, and featured a score from country songwriter Roger Miller. The large novel is represented mainly in the relationship between Huck and Jim, the runaway slave, as they encounter life on the Mississippi. The set invoked the river as constantly present, almost as a character behind the entire play.

## BLACKBIRDS OF 1928

MUSIC: Jimmy McHugh  LYRICS:  Dorothy Fields
SKETCHES: Uncredited  PRODUCER/DIRECTOR: Lew Leslie
MAJOR PERFORMERS: Adelaide Hall, Bill Robinson, Aida Ward, Tim Moore, Elizabeth Welch, Mantan Moreland, Cecil Mack, the Hall
Johnson Choir
OPENED: 5/9/28          THEATER: Liberty          PERFORMANCES: 518

Fashionable Manhattan society spent many evenings in the Harlem clubs in the 1920s. The "Blackbirds" show was a successful attempt to bring
a black revue to Broadway. (The idea had been tried out in London in 1926). The show produced the hit "I Can't Give You Anything But
Love." Interestingly, there was a musicalized version of Dubose Heyward's play *Porgy*. Subsequent editions of "Blackbirds" opened in 1930,
1933, and 1939, but none achieved the success of the original.


## BLOOMER GIRL

MUSIC AND LYRICS: Harold Arlen and E.Y. Harburg  BOOK: Sig Herzig and Fred Saidy
PRODUCER: John C. Wilson and Nat Goldstone  DIRECTOR: E.Y. Harburg and William Schorr
CHOREOGRAPHER: Agnes de Mille
MAJOR PERFORMERS: Celeste Holm, David Brooks, Joan McCracken, Margaret Douglass, Dooley Wilson, Richard Huey, Matt Briggs
OPENED: 10/5/44          THEATER: Shubert          PERFORMANCES: 654

Although founded on a play by Lillith and Dan James that dealt with the introduction of bloomers during the Civil War, *Bloomer Girl* expanded
the story to cover other aspects of the women's reform movement and also the struggle for civil rights. Set in Cicero Falls, New York, in 1861, it
tells of the rebellion of Evelina Applegate (Celeste Holm) against her father (Matt Briggs), a manufacturer of hoopskirts, who wants her to marry
one of his salesmen. Evelina is so provoked that she joins her aunt, Dolly Bloomer (Margaret Douglass), in her crusade for more practical
clothing for women and also in her abolitionist activities. But Evelina's convictions get a severe test when she falls in love with Jefferson Calhoun
(David Brooks), a Southern slaveholder, particularly when they join voices in their romantic duet, "Right As The Rain." Bloomer Girl, which
made a star of Celeste Holm, was also noted for Agnes de Mille's "Civil War Ballet," a depiction of the anguish felt by women who must remain
at home while their men are off fighting.


## BOW BELLS

MUSIC AND LYRICS: Henry Sullivan and Desmond Carter; Ord Hamilton and Bruce Sievier
BOOK: Sketches by Dion Titheradge, Ronald Jeans, John Murray Anderson
PRODUCER: Moss Empires Ltd.  DIRECTOR: John Murray Anderson  CHOREOGRAPHER: Ninette de Valois, Seymour Felix
MAJOR PERFORMERS: Robert Hale, Binnie Hale, Nelson Keys, Harriet Hoctor, Max Wall, Billy Milton
OPENED: 1/4/32          THEATER: London Hippodrome          PERFORMANCES: 232

John Murray Anderson, one of Broadway's most esteemed directors of revues, was responsible for an artistically innovative London show, *Bow
Bells* which had no front curtain, changed all the settings in full view of the audience, and used a double treadmill, one for the scenery and one
for the performers. Two of the West End's star attractions, Robert Hale and his daughter, Binnie Hale, were featured in the entertainment, with
Miss Hale introducing the interpolated "You're Blasé" (by Ord Hamilton and Bruce Sievier), sung to the most world-weary individual ever to
inspire a popular song.


## THE BOYS FROM SYRACUSE

MUSIC AND LYRICS: Richard Rodgers and Lorenz Hart  BOOK: George Abbott  PRODUCER: George Abbott
DIRECTOR: George Abbott  CHOREOGRAPHER: George Balanchine
MAJOR PERFORMERS: Jimmy Savo, Teddy Hart, Eddie Albert, Wynn Murray, Ronald Graham, Muriel Angelus, Marcy Wescott, Betty Bruce
OPENED: 11/23/38          THEATER: Alvin          PERFORMANCES: 235

The idea for *The Boys from Syracuse* began when Rodgers and Hart, while working on another show, were discussing the fact that no one had yet
done a musical based on a play by Shakespeare. Their obvious choice was *The Comedy of Errors* chiefly because Lorenz Hart's brother Teddy Hart
was always being confused with another comic actor, Jimmy Savo. Set in Ephesus in ancient Asia Minor, the ribald tale concerns the efforts of
two boys from Syracuse, Antipholus and his servant Dromio (Eddie Albert and Jimmy Savo) to find their long-lost twins, also named
Antipholus and Dromio (Ronald Graham and Teddy Hart). Complications arise when the wives of the Ephesians, Adriana (Muriel Angelus) and
her servant Luce (Wynn Murray), mistake the two strangers for their husbands. A highly successful Off Broadway revival of *The Boys from
Syracuse* was presented in 1963 and ran for 502 performances. The movie version, which RKO-Radio released in 1940, starred Allan Jones and
Joe Penner (both in dual roles). It was directed by A. Edward Sutherland.


## BRAVO GIOVANNI

MUSIC AND LYRICS: Milton Schafer and Ronny Graham
BOOK: A.J. Russell (from the novel by Howard Shaw)  PRODUCER: Philip Rose  DIRECTOR: Stanley Prager
CHOREOGRAPHER: Carol Haney
MAJOR PERFORMERS: Cesare Siepi, Michele Lee, David Opatoshu, George S. Irving and Maria Karnilova
OPENED: 5/19/62          THEATER: Broadhurst          PERFORMANCES: 76

Opera star Cesare Siepi made his musical comedy debut as restaurant-owner Giovanni Venturi, who schemes to beat the fast-food tourist trap
next door to his charming establishment in modern-day Rome by tunnelling from his own kitchen to his competitor's dumbwaiter and stealing
his food. Along the way, he unearths an Etruscan tomb and falls in love with his partner's young niece.

## BY JUPITER

MUSIC AND LYRICS: Richard Rodgers and Lorenz Hart  BOOK: Richard Rodgers and Lorenz Hart
PRODUCER: Dwight Deere Wiman and Richard Rodgers  DIRECTOR: Joshua Logan  CHOREOGRAPHER: Robert Alton  MAJOR
PERFORMERS: Ray Bolger, Constance Moore, Benay Venuta, Ronald Graham, Ralph Dumke, Bertha Belmore
OPENED: 6/2/42          THEATER: Shubert          PERFORMANCES: 427

Because of its ancient Greek characters and its Asia Minor setting, *By Jupiter* was something of a successor to the previous Rodgers and Hart hit,
*The Boys from Syracuse*. The new work, which tried out under the title *All's Fair*, was based on Julian Thompson's play, *The Warrior's Husband* in
which Katharine Hepburn had first attracted notice. The musical deals with the conflict between the Greeks and the legendary warrior women
called Amazons, who live in a female dominated land ruled by Queen Hippolyta (Benay Venuta). As one of his labors, Hercules (Ralph Dumke)
has arrived with a Greek army led by Theseus (Ronald Graham) to wrest the queens magical girdle of Diana, which is the source of her strength.
But when Hippolyta's sister Antiope (Constance Moore) sees Theseus, it isn't long before she's laid down her spear for love, an example her sister
warriors soon follow.

*By Jupiter* had the longest Broadway run of any Rodgers and Hart musical during the team's partnership. It could, in fact, have run longer had
not Ray Bolger (in his first starring role as Sapiens, the queen's husband) quit the cast to entertain American troops in the Far East. One curious
aspect of the show's score is that "Wait Till You See Her," which has since become its best-known song, was dropped from the production about
a month after the Broadway opening. In 1967 an Off Broadway revival of *By Jupiter* ran for 118 performances.

## BY THE BEAUTIFUL SEA

MUSIC AND LYRICS: Arthur Schwartz and Dorothy Fields
BOOK: Herbert & Dorothy Fields  PRODUCER: Robert Fryer and Lawrence Carr
DIRECTOR: Michael Jamison  CHOREOGRAPHER: Helen Tamiris
MAJOR PERFORMERS: Shirley Booth, Wilbur Evans, Cameron Prud'homme, Richard France & Mae Barnes
OPENED: 4/8/54          THEATER: Majestic          PERFORMANCES: 270

Following her triumphant performance in the Fields and Schwartz musical *A Tree Grows in Brooklyn*, Shirley Booth returned to Broadway in this
colorful show by the same songwriting team. Set in turn-of-the-century Coney Island, the show boasted period sets and costumes and a lively
and spirited score, although it is most often noted for the haunting ballad, "Alone Too Long."

## BYE BYE BIRDIE

MUSIC AND LYRICS: Music by Charles Strouse Lyrics by Lee Adams  BOOK: Michael Stewart
PRODUCER: Edward Padula and L. Slade Brown  DIRECTOR: Gower Champion  CHOREOGRAPHER: Gower Champion
MAJOR PERFORMERS: Chita Rivera, Dick van Dyke, Kay Medford, Paul Lynde, Dick Gautier, Michael J. Pollard, Susan Watson
OPENED: 4/14/60          THEATER: Martin Beck          PERFORMANCES: 607

The young songwriting team of Lee Adams and Charles Strouse struck gold on their first outing with this strictly-for-laughs look at the drafting
of a Presley-like rock star and the devastating effect it had on his songwriter-agent—and the entire country. Gower Champion's fresh and
imaginative choreography, combined with expert performances, helped make this an immediate success, but the show's fun-filled book and lively
score have made it a lasting favorite with theater groups around the world.

## CABARET

MUSIC AND LYRICS: John Kander and Fred Ebb  BOOK: Joe Masteroff  PRODUCER: Harold Prince
DIRECTOR: Harold Prince  CHOREOGRAPHER: Ron Field
MAJOR PERFORMERS: Jill Haworth, Jack Gilford, Bert Convy, Lotte Lenya, Joel Grey, Peg Murray, Edward Winter
OPENED: 11/20/66          THEATER: Broadhurst          PERFORMANCES: 1,165

Adapted from Christopher Isherwood's *Berlin Stories* and John van Druten's dramatization, *I Am a Camera*, *Cabaret* used a sleazy Berlin night
club as a metaphor for the decadent world of pre-Hitler Germany. Though the story focused on Sally Bowles (Jill Haworth), a hedonistic British
expatriate, and her ill-fated affair with Clifford Bradshaw (Bert Convy), an American writer, the symbolism of the show was conveyed through
an epicene Master of Ceremonies (Joel Grey) who recreated the tawdry atmosphere of the early thirties through a series of musical numbers at
the Kit Kat Club. Adding to the mood of the evening was a score that was purposely reminiscent of Kurt Weill, and included such evocative
pieces as "Willkommen," "Cabaret," and "Married."  In 1972, Bob Fosse directed a successful movie version for Allied Artists using a somewhat
different story. Joel Grey repeated his original role, and others in the film were Liza Minnelli, Michael York, and Marisa Berenson. Seven of the
songs written for the stage production were retained, with "Maybe This Time," "Mein Herr," and "Money, Money" added.

## CALL ME MADAM

MUISC & LYRICS: Irving Berlin  BOOK: Howard Lindsay & Russel Crouse
PRODUCER: Leland Hayward  DIRECTOR: George Abbott  CHOREOGRAPHER: Jerome Robbins
MAJOR PERFORMERS: Ethel Merman, Paul Lukas, Russell Nype, Galina Talva, Pat Harringtom, Alan Hewitt, Tommy Rall, Nathaniel Frey
OPENED: 10/12/50          THEATER: Imperial          PERFORMANCES: 644

This tale of a former Washington party-giver named ambassador to a tiny European country ("Lichtenburg"), was actually based on fact.
Truman had named Perle Mesta ambassador to Luxembourg 2 years before.  Merman's very American directness and informality plays against
European propriety.  Other characters are Sally's (Merman) young aide, who falls in love with the princess.  A little-seen film version of the
musical was released in 1953, also starring Ethel Merman (and at this writing is not on video cassette).

# CAMELOT

MUSIC AND LYRICS: Frederick Loewe and Alan Jay Lerner  BOOK: Alan Jay Lerner
PRODUCER: Alan Jay Lerner, Frederick Loewe, and Moss Hart  DIRECTOR: Moss Hart  CHOREOGRAPHER: Hanya Holm
MAJOR PERFORMERS: Richard Burton, Julie Andrews, Robert Goulet, Robert Coote, Roddy McDowall, M'el Dowd, John Cullum
OPENED: 12/3/60          THEATER: Majestic          PERFORMANCES: 873

Lerner and Loewe's first Broadway production following their spectacular hit *My Fair Lady*, was another musical based on a highly esteemed work of British fiction, T. H. White's novel, *The Once and Future King*. Again, too, they were joined by fair lady Julie Andrews and director Moss Hart for an opulently mounted retelling of the Arthurian legend, with its high-minded knights of the round table and its tragic, romantic triangle involving King Arthur, his queen Guenevere, and his trusted knight, Sir Lancelot. Helped by a huge advance ticket sale, *Camelot* easily surmounted a divided press to become something of a Broadway legend itself.

In 1980, during a tour headed by Richard Burton, the original King Arthur, *Camelot* returned to New York to play the New York State Theatre for 56 performances. After Burton was succeeded on the road by Richard Harris, the musical came back again, this time to the Winter Garden for an additional 48 performances. Mr. Harris also starred in the film version with Vanessa Redgrave, which Joshua Logan directed for Warner Bros. in 1967.

# CAN-CAN

MUSIC AND LYRICS: Cole Porter  BOOK: Abe Burrows  PRODUCER: Cy Feuer and Ernest Martin
DIRECTOR: Abe Burrows  CHOREOGRAPHER: Michael Kidd
MAJOR PERFORMERS: Lilo, Peter Cookson, Hans Conried, Erik Rhodes, Gwen Verdon
OPENED: 5/7/53          THEATER: Shubert          PERFORMANCES: 892

Next to *Kiss Me, Kate*, *Can-Can* was Cole Porter's most successful Broadway musical. To make sure that his script would be grounded on the origins of the scandalous dance known as the Can-Can, librettist Abe Burrows traveled to Paris where he studied the records of the courts, the police, and the Chamber of Deputies. In Burrows' story, set in 1893, La Mome Pistache, owner of the Bal du Paradis, is distressed about the investigation of her establishment because of the Can-Can. She uses her wiles to attract the stern Judge Aristide Forestier, who has been appointed to investigate, but eventually they fall in love and Forestier himself takes over the defense and wins acquittal. The musical, originally intended for Carol Channing, starred the French actress Lilo (who sang the hit ballad, "I Love Paris"), but most of the kudos were for dancer Gwen Verdon in her first major Broadway role. A film version with a much altered story was made by Twentieth Century-Fox in 1960. Walter Lang directed, and the cast was headed by Frank Sinatra, Shirley MacLaine, Maurice Chevalier, and Louis Jourdan.

# CAROUSEL

MUSIC: Richard Rodgers  LYRICS & BOOK: Oscar Hammerstein II  PRODUCER: Theatre Guild
DIRECTOR: Rouben Mamoulian  CHOREOGRAPHER: Agnes De Mille
MAJOR PERFORMERS: John Raitt, Jan Clayton, Murvyn Vye, Jean Darling, Christine Johnson, Eric Mattson, Bambi Linn, Peter Birch, Pearl Lang
OPENED: 4/19/45          THEATER: Majestic          PERFORMANCES: 890

Based on Ferenc Molnar's 1921 play *Liliom*, *Carousel* was the second of the collaborations between Rodgers and Hammerstein, following their revolutionary successful *Oklahoma!* The writers changed the locale from Budapest, in the original play, to 19th-century New England. Billy Bigelow, a carousel barker, meets and marries Julie Jordan, a worker at the local mill. This is not all sunshine and flowers. Billy is abusive and rough, and Julie suffers for it, buoyed only by her love and understanding of her husband. Billy is talked into a robbery attempt, and is killed in the skirmish, leaving Julie with a baby to raise alone. In secondary roles are Carrie Pipperidge, Julie's friend and co-worker, who is engaged to Mr. Enoch Snow (his only glaring fault is that he can't seem to lose the smell of fish), and also Julie's cousin Nettie, who adds a maternal touch to her watchful eye over her young relative. It's worth noting that Rodgers always considered this his very best work for the stage. A successful revival opened in New York in 1994.

# CATS

MUSIC AND LYRICS: Andrew Lloyd Webber and T.S. Eliot
PRODUCER: Cameron Mackintosh, The Really Useful Co. Ltd., Shubert Organization
DIRECTOR: Trevor Nunn David Geffen, The  CHOREOGRAPHER: Gillian Lynne
MAJOR PERFORMERS: Betty Buckley, Ken Page, Terry Mann, Stephen Hanan, Harry Groener, Rene Clemente, Timothy Scott
OPENED: 10/7/82          THEATER: Winter Garden          PERFORMANCES: over 6,000 (still running 6/1/97)

*Cats* opened at the New London Theatre in London, on May 11, 1981, and, at this writing, is still playing there. Charged with energy, flair and imagination, this feline fantasy has proven to be equally successful on Broadway, where it is even more of an environmental experience than in the West End. With the entire Winter Garden theatre transformed into one enormous junkyard, a theatre-goer is confronted with such unexpected sights as outsized garbage objects spilling into the audience, the elimination of the proscenium arch, and a ceiling that has been lowered and transformed into a twinkling canopy suggesting both cats' eyes and stars. Adapted from T.S. Eliot's collection of poems, *Old Possum's Book of Practical Cats*, the song-and-dance spectacle introduces such whimsical characters as the mysterious Mr. Mistoffelees, the patriarchal Old Deuteronomy, Skimbleshanks the Railway Cat, and Jennyanydots, the Old Gumbie Cat who sits all day and becomes active only at night. The musical's song hit, "Memory," is sung by Grizabella, the faded Glamour Cat, who, at the evening's end, ascends to the cats' heaven known as the Heavyside Layer.

## CHESS

MUSIC: Benny Andersson & Bjorn Ulvaeus  LYRICS: Tim Rice  BOOK: Richard Nelson (based on an idea by Tim Rice)
PRODUCERS: Shubert Organization, 3 Knights Ltd, Robert Fox Ltd.  DIRECTOR: Trevor Nunn
CHOREOGRAPHER: Lynne Taylor-Corbett
MAJOR PERFORMERS: Judy Kun, David Carroll, Philip Casnoff, Dennis Parlato, Marcia Mitzman, Paul Harman, Harry Goz, Ann Crumb
OPENED: 4/28/88          THEATER: Imperial          PERFORMANCES: 68

*Chess* is quite possibly the last of the cold war musicals (earlier stories on stage were *Leave it to Me* and *Silk Stockings*). Rice at first wanted his previous partner Andrew Lloyd Webber to write the show with him, but failing that, turned to writers from the Swedish group Abba. *Chess* was a successful album before it hit the stage (like *Evita* and *Jesus Christ Superstar*). The story is of an international chess match between an American and Russian, and a woman in between them. Though the show ran for 3 years in London, it never made back the initial investment. In New York it lost $6 million. The song "Someone Else's Story" was added for the New York production.

## CHICAGO

MUSIC AND LYRICS: John Kander and Fred Ebb  BOOK: Fred Ebb and Bob Fosse
PRODUCER: Robert Fryer and James Cresson  DIRECTOR: Bob Fosse  CHOREOGRAPHER: Bob Fosse
MAJOR PERFORMERS: Gwen Verdon, Chita Rivera, Jerry Orbach, Barney Martin, Mary McCarty, Graciela Daniele
OPENED: 6/3/75          THEATER: 46th Street          PERFORMANCES: 923

*Chicago* had a lengthy gestation period. In the mid-Fifties, director Bob Fosse tried to secure the rights to Maurine Dallas Watkins' 1926 play of the same name, but it was not until thirteen years later that the way was cleared for him to turn it into a musical for Gwen Verdon. The saga of murderess Roxie Hart, and the way she manages not only to avoid going to prison but also to become a vaudeville headliner, was adapted into a sardonic commentary on American huckstering, vulgarity and decadence. With the tale performed as a show-business vaudeville show, the songs were able to capture the required showbusiness tawdriness through numbers such as "And All That Jazz" and "Razzle-Dazzle." Shortly after the Broadway opening of *Chicago*, Miss Verdon was hospitalized and was replaced for six weeks by Liza Minnelli. A major Broadway revival opened in 1997.

## A CHORUS LINE

MUSIC AND LYRICS: Music by Marvin Hamlisch Lyrics by Edward Kleban
BOOK: James Kirkwood and Nicholas Dante  PRODUCER: NY Shakespeare Festival (Joseph Papp)
DIRECTOR: Michael Bennett  CHOREOGRAPHER: Michael Bennett (and Bob Avian)
MAJOR PERFORMERS: Carole Bishop, Pamela Blair, Wayne Cilento, Kay Cole, Priscilla Lopez, Donna McKechnie & Sammy Wiliams
OPENED: 4/15/75          THEATER: Shubert          PERFORMANCES: 6,137

Beginning with the deceptively simple premise of an audition for chorus dancers, *A Chorus Line* eventually proves to be a serious and absorbing examination of the dancer's mentality, interpreted in universal themes through a series of monologues, dialogues and musical sequences. Created as a workshop production in Joseph Papp's Public Theatre, the show pointed the way to a production process now as common to new musicals as the once mandatory out-of-town tryout. In 1983, *A Chorus Line* became the longest-running musical in Broadway history.

## CINDERELLA

MUSIC AND LYRICS: Richard Rodgers and Oscar Hammerstein II  BOOK: Oscar Hammerstein II
PRODUCER: Richard Lewine for CBS-TV  DIRECTOR: Ralph Nelson  CHOREOGRAPHER: Jonathan Lucas
MAJOR PERFORMERS: Julie Andrews, Howard Lindsay, Dorothy Stickney, Ilka Chase Kaye Ballard, Alice Ghostley, Edith Adams, Jon Cypher
AIR DATE: 3/31/57

When CBS-TV decided to mount a musical version of *Cinderella*, the network was fortunate in securing the services of Julie Andrews, fresh from her engagement as the Cinderella-like heroine of *My Fair Lady*, as well as the Broadway theatre's most illustrious writing team Richard Rodgers and Oscar Hammerstein II. In adapting the children's fairy tale, Hammerstein was careful not to alter or update the familiar story. It was still about the put-upon drudge (Julie Andrews), her wicked Stepmother (Ilka Chase) and Stepsisters (Kaye Ballard and Alice Ghostley), her Fairy godmother (Edith Adams), the ball that the King and Queen (Howard Lindsay and Dorothy Stickney) give for their son (Jon Cypher), the love that blossoms when Cinderella and Prince meet, Cinderella's loss of a glass slipper, and the Prince's discovery that the foot that belongs to the slipper also belongs to his inamorata. Because the production was filmed live and could not be preserved except in black-and-white kinescope, a new production was filmed on tape in 1965, and has since been repeated eight times. Heading the cast were Lesley Ann Warren (Cinderella), Stuart Damon (The Prince), Celeste Holm (Fairy Godmother), Walter Pidgeon (King), and Ginger Rogers (Queen). The stage adaptation (which includes the song "Boys and Girls Like You and Me," originally intended for *Oklahoma!*), has been produced frequently throughout the United States. A prominent stage production appeared in New York in 1993 by the New York City Opera.

## COMPANY

MUSIC AND LYRICS: Stephen Sondheim  BOOK: George Furth  PRODUCER: Harold Prince
DIRECTOR: Harold Prince  CHOREOGRAPHER: Michael Bennett
MAJOR PERFORMERS: Dean Jones, Elaine Stritch, Barbara Barrie, Donna McKechnie, Susan Browning, Beth Howland, Pamela Myers, George Coe, John Cunningham, Charles Braswell
OPENED: 4/26/70          THEATER: Alvin          PERFORMANCES: 706

*Company* was the first of six Stephen Sondheim musicals that, to date, have been directed by Harold Prince. The musical was concerned with five affluent couples living in a Manhattan apartment house and their excessively protective feeling about a bachelor named Bobby (Dean Jones), whom they are anxious to see married. In the end, as he sings "Being Alive," Bobby is ready to take the plunge. Music and lyrics were used throughout the story to express often ambivalent or caustic attitudes of sophisticated New Yorkers in such songs as "Sorry-Grateful," "The Little Things You Do Together," and "Another Hundred People." Dean Jones played the part of Bobby for only one month, after which he was succeeded by Larry Kert. A Broadway revival ran briefly in 1995.


## A CONNECTICUT YANKEE

MUSIC: Richard Rodgers  LYRICS: Lorenz Hart  BOOK: Herbert Fields  PRODUCERS: Lew Fields & Lyle Andrews
DIRECTOR: Alexander Leftwich  CHOREOGRAPHER: Busby Berkeley
MAJOR PERFORMERS: William Gaxton, Constance Carpenter, Nana Bryant, June Cochrane, William Norris, Jack Thompson
OPENED: 11/3/27          THEATER: Vanderbilt          PERFORMANCES: 418

The show is based on Mark Twain's *A Connecticut Yankee in King Arthur's Court*. A modern day Martin gets hit on the head by his fiancée, and dreams of being as he is but in Arthur's Court of Medieval England. The time warp shows up in clever Hart touches such as the song "Thou Swell." When Martin comes to, he gets his life straightened out by marrying someone else (he recognizes her from the dream). Happiness follows. A revival in 1943 added 5 new songs by Rodgers & Hart, their last work together. Hart died a few days after the revival opened. One of the score's standout songs, "My Heart Stood Still," was written for a London show from 1927 called *One Dam Thing After Another*. Since the song had not been heard in New York, the songwriters interpolated it into their next Broadway musical.


## CONVERSATION PIECE

MUSIC AND LYRICS: Noel Coward  BOOK: Noel Coward
PRODUCER: Arch Selwyn and Harold B. Franklin  DIRECTOR: Noel Coward
MAJOR PERFORMERS: Yvonne Printemps, Pierre Fresnay, Irene Browne, Athole Stewart, Moya Nugent, Sylvia Leslie, George Sanders
OPENED: 10/23/34          THEATER: 44th Street          PERFORMANCES: 55

In *Conversation Piece*, theatre-goers were transported back to the fashionable seaside resort of Brighton during the Regency period in England. The stylish operetta was concerned with an impoverished French duke and his attempts to find a suitably wealthy husband for his ward, though eventually the two follow their secret hearts and confess their love for each other. The musical was written expressly for Yvonne Printemps by the multi-talented Noel Coward, who also played the part of the duke when *Conversation Piece* first opened at His Majesty's Theatre in London early in 1934. That run lasted 177 performances. Most of the original cast was recruited for the New York engagement, except for the substitution of Pierre Fresnay (Mlle. Printemps husband) for Mr. Coward.


## DANCE ME A SONG

MUSIC AND LYRICS: Herman Hupfeld, James Shelton, Albert Hague and Maurice Valency, etc.
BOOK: Sketches by Jimmy Kirkwood and Lee Goodman, Wally Cox, Robert Anderson, Marya Mannes, etc.
PRODUCER: Dwight Deere Wiman  DIRECTOR: James Shelton  CHOREOGRAPHER: Robert Sidney
MAJOR PERFORMERS: Joan McCracken, Ann Thomas, Marion Lorne, Wally Cox, Jimmy Kirkwood and Lee Goodman, Bob Fosse, Donald Saddler, Erik Rhodes, Bob Scheerer
OPENED: 1/20/50          THEATER: Royale          PERFORMANCES: 35

Poking sly fun at such targets as Hollywood gossip columnists, the rivalry between Alfred Lunt and Lynn Fontanne (in a sketch by playwright Robert Anderson), and folksy film documentaries, *Dance Me a Song* was a modest revue that had a modest run. Other pleasures included Bob Scheerer's song and dance number with a dog ("My Little Dog Has Ego") and the goofy monologues by Wally Cox, soon to become a television favorite in the *Mr. Peepers* series.


## A DAY IN HOLLYWOOD/A NIGHT IN THE UKRAINE

MUSIC AND LYRICS: Frank Lazarus and David Vosburgh, Jerry Herman, etc.  BOOK: David Vosburgh
PRODUCER: Alexander H. Cohen and Hildy Parks  DIRECTOR: Tommy Tune
CHOREOGRAPHER: Tommy Tune and Thommie Walsh
MAJOR PERFORMERS: Priscilla Lopez, Frank Lazarus, David Garrison
OPENED: 5/1/80          THEATER: John Golden          PERFORMANCES: 588

For their satirical but affectionate view of Hollywood movies, the authors divided the entertainment into two parts. The first, *A Day in Hollywood*, was composed of a series of songs and dances poking fun at the movie capitol's past, ending with a medley of songs written by Richard A. Whiting. The second, *A Night in the Ukraine*, was a slambang spoof of a typical Marx Brothers comedy. The show marked the first Broadway musical directed by Tommy Tune, whose later-works included *Nine* and *My One and Only*.

## DEAR WORLD

MUSIC AND LYRICS: Jerry Herman
BOOK: Jerome Lawrence & Robert E. Lee (based on *The Madwoman Of Chaillot* by Jean Giraudoux as adapted by Maurice Valency)
PRODUCER: Alexander H. Cohen  DIRECTOR: Joe Layton  CHOREOGRAPHER: Joe Layton
MAJOR PERFORMERS: Angela Lansbury, Milo O'Shea, Jane Connell, Carmen Mathews, Kurt Peterson & Pamela Hall
OPENED: 2/6/69          THEATER: Mark Hellinger          PERFORMANCES: 132

Although *Dear World* contains one of Jerry Herman's best scores, it did not enjoy the success of his previous Broadway efforts. Angela Lansbury received the Tony Award for her portrayal of the eccentric Countess Aurelia, determined to rid the world of corruption and evil in the course of a single afternoon. Unfortunately the lavish production overwhelmed the original play's charms and, despite a first rate cast and Oliver Smith's enchanting stage design, *Dear World* lasted only four months.

## DESTRY RIDES AGAIN

MUSIC AND LYRICS: Harold Rome  BOOK: Leonard Gershe  PRODUCER: David Merrick
DIRECTOR: Michael Kidd  CHOREOGRAPHER: Michael Kidd
MAJOR PERFORMERS: Andy Griffith, Dolores Gray, Scott Brady, Swen Swenson, Marc Breaux, Jack Prince
OPENED: 4/23/59          THEATER: Imperia          PERFORMANCES: 473

Max Brand's classic Western tale, *Destry Rides Again* had been filmed three times (most notably in 1939 with Marlene Dietrich and James Stewart) when producer David Merrick got the idea to turn this durable sagebrush saga into a Broadway musical. The lively, whip-cracking show, set in the town of Bottleneck just before the turn of the century, starred Andy Griffith as the violence-hating sheriff and Dolores Gray as Frenchie the frontier saloon entertainer who beat the bad guys, led by Scott Brady, who gets the girl.

## DO I HEAR A WALTZ?

MUSIC AND LYRICS: Richard Rodgers and Stephen Sondheim  BOOK: Arthur Laurents
PRODUCER: Richard Rodgers  DIRECTOR: John Dexter  CHOREOGRAPHER: Herbert Ross
MAJOR PERFORMERS: Elizabeth Allen, Sergio Franchi, Carol Bruce, Stuart Damon, Julienne Marie
OPENED: 3/18/65          THEATER: 46th Street          PERFORMANCES: 220

Since Stephen Sondheim was something of a protege of Oscar Hammerstein II, it was almost inevitable that Richard Rodgers would team up with the younger man after his partner's death. Their joint effort resulted in *Do I Hear A Waltz?*, which Arthur Laurents adapted from his own play, *The Time of the Cuckoo*. Taking place in Venice, the tale concerns an attractive American tourist (Ellzabeth Allen) who meets and has an intense but foredoomed affair with a married Italian shopkeeper (Sergio Franchi). Though initially there was to be no dancing in the musical, the authors soon felt that the rueful story needed a lift and choreographer Herbert Ross was called in to heighten the dramatic quality of some of the key scenes. This was most apparent in the scene in which the heroine, certain that true love will be hers if she hears an imaginary waitz, hears it, sings about it, and dances to it. The production became notorious for the feud that began, and later accelerated, between Rodgers and Sondheim.

## DO RE MI

MUSIC AND LYRICS: Juie Styne, Betty Comden and Adolph Green  BOOK: Garson Kanin
PRODUCER: David Merrick  DIRECTOR: Garson Kanin  CHOREOGRAPHER: Marc Breaux and Deedee Wood
MAJOR PERFORMERS: Phil Silvers, Nancy Walker, John Reardon, Nancy Dussault, David Burns, George Mathews, George Givot
OPENED: 12/26/60          THEATER: St. James          PERFORMANCES: 400

A wild satire on the ways in which the underworld muscled in on the jukebox business, *Do Re Mi* was adapted by Garson Kanin from his own novel. With characters reminiscent of the raffish denizens of *Guys and Dolls*, the show offered two outstanding clowns in Phil Silvers, as a fast-talking, would-be bigshot, and Nancy Walker as his long-suffering spouse. It was also fitting that a musical about the making of song hits would have one of its own, the altruistic prescription for romantic bliss called "Make Someone Happy."

## DON'T BOTHER ME, I CAN'T COPE

MUSIC AND LYRICS: Micki Grant  BOOK: Conceived by Vinnette Carroll
PRODUCER: Edward Padula and Arch Lustberg  DIRECTOR: Vinnette Carroll
CHOREOGRAPHER: George Faison  MAJOR PERFORMERS: Alex Bradford, Hope Clarke, Micki Grant, Bobby Hill, Arnold Wilkerson
OPENED: 4/19/72          THEATER: Playhouse          PERFORMANCES: 1,065

A generally good-humored look at the social problems faced by black people today, *Don't Bother Me, I Can't Cope* was essentially a procession of numbers based on gospel, rock, and folk music. The show originated as a workshop project of Vinnette Carroll's Urban Arts Corps Theatre, after which it made appearances in Washington, D.C., Philadelphia, and Detroit before opening in New York. The lack of bitterness in the material and its affirmative view of life helped the musical achieve a two and one-half year stay on Broadway.

## DRAT! THE CAT!

MUSIC AND LYRICS: Milton Schafer and Ira Levin  BOOK: Ira Levin
PRODUCER: Jerry Adler and Norman Rosemont  DIRECTOR: Joe Layton  CHOREOGRAPHER: Joe Layton
MAJOR PERFORMERS: Elliott Gould, Lesley Ann Warren, Charles Durning, Jane Connell, Jack Fletcher
OPENED: 10/10/65          THEATER: Martin Beck          PERFORMANCES: 8

If it is recalled at all, *Drat! The Cat!* is remembered today mainly for two reasons: it marked Elliott Gould's last appearance on the Broadway stage (as of the present at least), and it was the show in which the song, "She Touched Me" (changed to "He Touched Me" when the girl sings it), was first introduced. A spoof of cops-and-robbers melodrama, the musical was concerned with an oddball romance between a bumbling policeman (Mr. Gould) and a larcenous madcap heiress (Lesley Ann Warren) in New York in the late 1800s. Barbra Streisand, Gould's wife at the time, made a recording of "He Touched Me" that will always make the show at least a footnote in popular culture.

## DuBARRY WAS A LADY

MUSIC AND LYRICS: Cole Porter  BOOK: Herbert Fields and B.G. DeSylva  PRODUCER: B.G. DeSylva
DIRECTOR: Edgar MacGregor  CHOREOGRAPHER: Robert Alton
MAJOR PERFORMERS: Ethel Merman, Bert Lahr, Betty Grable, Charles Walters, Benny Baker, Ronald Graham
OPENED: 12/6/39          THEATER: 46th Street          PERFORMANCES: 408

One of Broadway's biggest hits of the thirties, *DuBarry Was a Lady* evolved through the merging of two ideas: co-librettist Herbert Fields wanted to write a musical with Mae West as DuBarry, and co-librettist producer B.G. DeSylva wanted to do one about a night-club washroom attendant who is smitten by a glamorous debutante. Both concepts were combined by having a washroom attendant named Louis Blore infatuated with May Daly, the flashy star of a swank New York night spot. Then, after winning $75,000 in the Irish Sweepstakes, Louis mistakenly takes a mickey finn and dreams that he is King Louis XV and May is his unaccommodating concubine, Mme. DuBarry. When Mae West proved unavailable, the logical choice for DuBarry was Broadway's queen of musicals, Ethel Merman, with Bert Lahr as the French sovereign. The show also offered Broadway its only chance to see Betty Grable before she attained Hollywood stardom. In the Cole Porter score was the showstopping "Friendship" (for Merman and Lahr) and "Well, Did You Evah?" (for Grable and future MGM director Charles Walters). The film version was made by MGM in 1943, with Roy Del Ruth directing, and Lucille Ball, Gene Kelly, and Red Skelton heading the cast.

## EVITA

MUSIC AND LYRICS: Andrew Lloyd Webber and Tim Rice  BOOK: Tim Rice
PRODUCER: Robert Stigwood and David Land  DIRECTOR: Harold Prince  CHOREOGRAPHER: Larry Fuller
MAJOR PERFORMERS: Patti LuPone, Bob Gunton, Mandy Patinkin
OPENED: 9/25/79          THEATER: Broadway          PERFORMANCES: 1,567

Because of its great success in London (where it opened at the Prince Edward Theatre on June 32, 1978, and is at this writing, still playing), *Evita* was a practically pre-sold hit when it began its run on Broadway. Based on events in the life of Argentina's strong-willed leader, Eva Peron, the musical—with Patti LuPone in the title role—traced her rise from struggling actress to wife of dictator Juan Peron (Bob Gunton), and virtual co-ruler of the country. Though the plot was told entirely through song, and had originally been conceived as a project for records, the razzle-dazzle staging of Harold Prince turned *Evita* into an exciting theatrical concept that has been hailed throughout the world. Of no little help, of course, has been the universal popularity of the haunting melody, "Don't Cry For Me, Argentina." The film version, starring Madonna, was released in December of 1996.

## FACE THE MUSIC

MUSIC & LYRICS: Irving Berlin  BOOK: Moss Hart  PRODUCER: Sam H. Harris
DIRECTORS: Hassard Short, George S. Kaufman  CHOREOGRAPHER: Albertina Rasch
MAJOR PERFORMERS: Mary Boland, Harold Murray, Andrew Tombes, Hugh O'Connell, Katherine Carrington, David Burns
OPENED: 2/17/32          THEATER: New Amsterdam          PERFORMANCES: 165

Like the Gershwin musicals *Of Thee I Sing*, *Strike Up the Band* and *Let 'Em Eat Cake*, *Face the Music* was a satirical musical that came from the country's mood during the years of economic depression. The Berlin show had former millionaires reduced to pedestrian simple pleasures ("Let's Have Another Cup O' Coffee"), corrupt and vapid politicians and policemen, and the crazy world of backing a musical (the backer actually wants to lose money by backing a tasteless show, which turns out to be a hit, naturally).

## FANNY

MUSIC AND LYRICS: Harold Rorne  BOOK: S.N. Behrman and Joshua Logan  PRODUCER: David Merrick and Joshua Logan
DIRECTOR: Joshua Logan  CHOREOGRAPHER: Helen Tamiris
MAJOR PERFORMERS: Ezio Pinza, Walter Slezak, Florence Henderson, William Tabbert, Gerald Price
OPENED: 11/4/54          THEATER: Majestic          PERFORMANCES: 888

*Fanny* takes us to the colorful, bustling port of Marseilles "not so long ago" for a musical version of Marcel Pagnol's French film trilogy, *Marius, Fanny and Cesar*. Compressed into an evening's entertainment, the action-packed story concerns Marius (William Tabbert), who yearns to go to sea; his father, Cesar (Ezio Pinza), the local cafe owner; Panisse (Walter Slezak), a prosperous middle-aged sail-maker; and Fanny (Florence Henderson) the girl beloved by both Marius and Panisse. Though Fanny has a child with Marius just before he ships off, Panisse marries her and brings up the boy as his own. When Marius returns demanding both Fanny and his son, Cesar convinces him that Panisse has the more rightful claim. Years later, however, the dying Panisse dictates a letter to Marius offering him Fanny's hand in marriage. During the Broadway run, former Metropolitan Opera star Ezio Pinza was succeeded by another former Met singer, Lawrence Tibbett, and Walter Slezak was replaced by Billy Gilbert. All of the songs were eliminated for the Warner Bros. 1960 film version, which had a cast headed by Leslie Caron, Maurice Chevalier, and Charles Boyer. Joshua Logan again directed.

## THE FANTASTICKS

MUSIC AND LYRICS: Harvey Schmidt and Tom Jones  BOOK: Tom Jones
PRODUCER: Lore Noto  DIRECTOR: Word Baker
MAJOR PERFORMERS: Jerry Orbach, Kenneth Nelson, Rita Gardner, William Larson, Hugh Thomas, Thomas Bruce (Tom Jones)
OPENED: 5/3/60          THEATER: Sullivan St. Playhouse          PERFORMANCES: over 15,000; still running 6/1/97

The statistics alone are, well, fantastic. Since *The Fantasticks* opened over thirty-four years ago at a tiny Greenwich Village theater, there have been, to date, 9,000 productions in the United States, fifteen touring companies, over 500 productions in 66 foreign countries, and the backers have received more than an 8,000% profit on their initial investment of $16,500. No other production, on or off Broadway, has ever enjoyed such a lengthy run, and there is still no end in sight. Curiously, the initial reviews were either mixed or negative, and producer Lore Noto seriously considered closing the show after its first discouraging week. But an Off-Broadway award, the popularity of the song "Try To Remember," and, most important, word of mouth, all helped to turn the show's fortunes around. The fragile fantasy is concerned with the theme of seasonal rebirth, or the paradox of "why Spring is born out of Winter's laboring pain." In the story, adapted from Edmond Rostand's play, *Les Ramanesques*, the fathers of two youthful lovers, Luisa and Matt, feel they must show parental disapproval to make sure that their progenies remain together. When this deception is revealed, the lovers quarrel and Matt goes off to seek adventure. At the end, after a number of degrading experiences, he returns to Luisa's waiting arms.

## FASHION

MUSIC AND LYRICS: Don Pippin and Steve Brown  BOOK: Anthony Stimac  PRODUCER: R. Scott Lucas
DIRECTOR: Anthony Stimac  MAJOR PERFORMERS: Sydney Blake, Mary Jo Catlett, Ty McConnell, Henrietta Valor
OPENED: 2/17/74          THEATER: McAlpin Rooftop          PERFORMANCES: 94

Based on a play by Anna Cora Mowatt written in 1845—credited as the first dramatic work by an American woman—the musical updated the plot to 1973 for its campy view of the members of the Long Island Masque and Wig Society, an organization devoted to preserving early American drama. The story poked most of its fun at cultural snobs, social-climbing suburban matrons, and phony European royalty, and derived much of its humor by casting women in male as well as female roles.

## FIDDLER ON THE ROOF

MUSIC AND LYRICS: Jerry Bock and Sheldon Harnick BOOK: Joseph Stein  PRODUCER: Harold Prince
DIRECTOR: Jerome Robbins  CHOREOGRAPHER: Jerome Robbins
MAJOR PERFORMERS: Zero Mostel, Maria Karnilova, Beatrice Arthur, Joanna Merlin, Austin Pendleton, Bert Convy, Julia Migenes
OPENED: 9/22/64          THEATER: Imperial          PERFORMANCES: 3,242

An undeniable classic of the Broadway theatre, *Fiddler on the Roof* took a compassionate view of a Jewish community in Czarist Russia where the people struggled to maintain their traditions and identity in the face of persecution. Despite a story that some thought had limited appeal (it was based on tales by Sholom Aleichem, including "Tevye's Daughters"), the theme struck such a universal response that the Fiddler was perched precariously on his roof for a record run of over seven years, nine months. The plot is set in the village of Anatevka in 1905, and deals mainly with the efforts of Tevye (Zero Mostel), a dairyman, his wife Golde (Maria Karnilova), and their five daughters to cope with their harsh existence. At the play's end, when a Cossack pogrom has forced everyone out of the village, Tevye and what is left of his family look forward to a new life in America. Because of the musical's lengthy run, Zero Mostel was succeeded after a year by Luther Adler, followed by Herschel Bernardi, Harry Goz, Paul Lipson, and Jan Peerce. Others who took over roles during the Broadway engagement were Pia Zadora and Bette Midler, playing two of the daughters. *Fiddler on the Roof* was revived on Broadway at the Winter Garden in 1976, with Zero Mostel again in the lead, and at the New York State Theatre in 1981 with Herschel Bernardi and Maria Karnilova. The United Artists film version, directed by Norman Jewison, opened in 1971 with Topol (who had played Tevye in London), Norma Crane and Molly Picon. Isaac Stern was the violin soloist heard on the soundtrack.

## FINIAN'S RAINBOW

MUSIC AND LYRICS: Burton Lane and E.Y. Harburg BOOK: E.Y. Harburg and Fred Saidy
PRODUCER: Lee Sabinson and William Katzell  DIRECTOR: Bretaigne Windust
CHOREOGRAPHER: Michael Kidd          MAJOR PERFORMERS: Ella Logan, Albert Sharpe, Donald Richards, David Wayne, Anita Alvarez, Robert Pitkin
OPENED: 1/10/47 THEATER: 46th Street          PERFORMANCES: 725

*Finian's Rainbow* evolved out of co-librettist E.Y. Harburg's desire to satirize an economic system that requires gold reserves to be buried in the ground at Fort Knox. This led to the idea of leprechauns and their crock of gold that, according to legend, could grant three wishes. The story takes place in Rainbow Valley, Missitucky, and involves Finian McLonergan (Albert Sharpe), an Irish immigrant, and his efforts to bury a crock of gold which, he is sure, will grow and make him rich. Also involved are Og (David Wayne), a leprechaun from whom the crock has been stolen, Finian's daughter, Sharon (Ella Logan), who dreams wistfully of Glocca Morra, and Woody Mahoney (Donald Richards), a labor organizer who blames that "Old Devil Moon" for the way he feels about Sharon.  In the 1968 Warner Bros. adaptation, Fred Astaire played Finian, Petula Clark was his daughter, and Tommy Steele was the leprechaun. The director was Francis Coppola.

# FIORELLO!

MUSIC AND LYRICS: Jerry Bock and Sheldon Harnick  BOOK: Jerome Weidman and George Abbott
PRODUCER: Robert Griffith and Harold Prince  DIRECTOR: George Abbott  CHOREOGRAPHER: Peter Gennaro
MAJOR PERFORMERS: Tom Bosley, Patricia Wilson, Ellen Hanley, Howard DaSilva, Mark Dawson, Pat Stanley, Eileen Rodgers, Nathaniel Frey
OPENED: 11/23/59       THEATER: Broadhurst       PERFORMANCES: 795

New York's favorite mayor, Fiorello LaGuardia, was a peppery, pugnacious reformer whose larger-than life personality readily lent itself to depiction on the musical stage. With Tom Bosley making an auspicious Broadway debut in the title role, *Fiorello!* covered the ten year period in LaGuardia's life before he became mayor. It begins with his surprise election to congress prior to World War I and includes such events as his enlistment in the Air Force, his first race for mayor and his defeat by James J. Walker, the death of his first wife, and, finally, the preparations for his successful campaign as a Fusion candidate for mayor in 1933. Among the musical numbers: the spirited "Gentleman Jimmy" (about Walker), the cynical "Politics and Poker," and the nostalgic "'Til Tomorrow." *Fiorello!* had the distinction of being the third musical to win the Pulitzer Prize in drama (the previous two had been *Of Thee I Sing* and *South Pacific*).


# FIREBRAND OF FLORENCE

MUSIC AND LYRICS: Kurt Weill and Ira Gershwin  BOOK: Edwin Justus Mayer
PRODUCER: Max Gordon  DIRECTOR: John Murray Anderson and John Haggott
CHOREOGRAPHER: Catherine Littlefield
MAJOR PERFORMERS: Earl Wrightson, Lotte Lenya, Melville Cooper, Beverly Tyler, Ferdi Hoffman
OPENED: 3/22/45       THEATER: Alvin       PERFORMANCES: 43

Kurt Weill's rich score embellished Ira Gershwin and Edwin Justus Mayer's adaptation of Mayer's 1924 hit play *Firebrand*, a comic romance about the adventures of Benvenuto Cellini, the celebrated Italian Renaissance sculptor and goldsmith. In the story, Cellini (Earl Wrightson) not only must outwit his patron, the bumbling Duke of Florence (Melville Cooper), who lusts after Angela, Cellini's model (Beverly Tyler), but also the Duchess (Lotte Lenya, Kurt Weill's wife), who lusts after Cellini.


# THE FIRST

MUSIC AND LYRICS: Bob Brush and Martin Charnin  BOOK: Joel Siegel and Martin Charnin
PRODUCER: Zev Bufman and Neil Bogart, Michael Harvey and Peter A. Bobley
DIRECTOR: Martin Charnin  CHOREOGRAPHER: Alan Johnson
MAJOR PERFORMERS: David Alan Grier, David Huddleston, Lonette McKee, Clent Bowers
OPENED: 10/17/81       THEATER: Martin Beck       PERFORMANCES: 37

*The First* was a celebration of the achievements of Jackie Robinson (played by David Alan Grier in his Broadway debut), the first black player to be admitted to major-league baseball. Covering events between 1945 and 1947, the story takes in the decision of Branch Rickey (David Huddleston), the owner of the Brooklyn Dodgers, to sign Robinson, Robinson's bitter experiences with the antagonism of both teammates and fans, and the ballplayer's final acceptance when his efforts enable the Dodgers to win the 1947 National League pennant.


# FIVE GUYS NAMED MOE

MUSIC & LYRICS: Various writers  BOOK: Clarke Peters  PRODUCER: Cameron Mackintosh
DIRECTOR-CHOREOGRAPHER: Charles Augins
MAJOR PERFORMERS: Jerry Dixon, Doug Eskew, Milton Craig Nealy, Kevin Ramsey, Jeffrey D. Sams, Glen Turner
OPENED: 4/8/92       THEATER: Eugene O'Neill       PERFORMANCES: 445

The show was basically a revue of songs associated with musician Louis Jordan, strung together with the barest bit of plot. Five guys named Moe jump from a jukebox to coach Nomax on keeping his girlfriend. The style of the production aimed at that of a British Music Hall. The audience was involved in sing-alongs, and the actors formed a conga line down the aisles at intermission to go to the lobby.


# FLOWER DRUM SONG

MUSIC AND LYRICS: Richard Rodgers and Oscar Hammerstein II  BOOK: Oscar Hammerstein II and Joseph Fields
PRODUCER: Richard Rodgers and Oscar Hammerstein II  DIRECTOR: Gene Kelly  CHOREOGRAPHER: Carol Haney
MAJOR PERFORMERS: Miyoshi Umeki, Pat Suzuki, Larry Blyden, Juanita Hall, Ed Kenney, Keye Luke
OPENED: 12/1/58       THEATER: St. James       PERFORMANCES: 600

It was librettist Joseph Fields who first secured the rights to C.Y. Lee's novel and then approached Rodgers and Hammerstein to join him as collaborators. To dramatize the conflict between the traditionalist, older Chinese-Americans living in San Francisco and their thoroughly Americanized offsprings, the musical tells the story of Mei Li (Miyoshi Umeki), a timid "picture bride" from China, who arrives to fulfill her contract to marry night-club owner Sammy Fong (Larry Blyden). Sammy, however, prefers dancer Linda Low (Pat Suzuki), who obviously enjoys being a girl, and the problem is resolved when Sammy's friend Wang Ta (Ed Kenney) discovers that Mei Li is really the bride for him. *Flower Drum Song* marked the only Broadway musical directed by Gene Kelly. In Universal's 1961 movie version, the cast was headed by Miyoshi Umeki, Nancy Kwan, and James Shigeta. Henry Koster was the director.

## FOLLIES

MUSIC AND LYRICS: Stephen Sondheim  BOOK: James Goldman  PRODUCER: Harold Prince
DIRECTOR: Harold Prince and Michael Bennett  CHOREOGRAPHER: Michael Bennett
MAJOR PERFORMERS: Alexis Smith, Dorothy Collins, Gene Nelson, John McMartin, Yvonne DeCarlo, Mary McCarty, Fifi D'Orsay,
Ethel Barrymore Colt, Ethel Shutta, Arnold Moss
OPENED: 4/4/71          THEATER: Winter Garden          PERFORMANCES: S22

Taking place at a reunion of former *Ziegfeld Follies*-type showgirls, the musical dealt with the reality of life as contrasted with the unreality of the theatre, a theme it explored through the lives of two couples, the upper-class, unhappy Phyllis and Benjamin Stone (Alexis Smith and John McMartin) and the middle-class, unhappy Sally and Buddy Plummer (Dorothy Collins and Gene Nelson). *Follies* also depicted these couples as they were in their youth, a flashback device that prompted Stephen Sondheim to come up with songs purposely reminiscent of the styles of some of the theatre's great composers and lyricists of the past.

## FOLLOW THRU

MUSIC AND LYRICS: Ray Henderson, B.G. DeSylva and Lew Brown
BOOK: Laurence Schwab and B.G. DeSylva  PRODUCER: Laurence Schwab and Frank Mandel
DIRECTOR: Edgar MacGregor  CHOREOGRAPHER: Bobby Connolly
MAJOR PERFORMERS: Jack Haley, Irene Delroy, Zelma O'Neal, John Barker, Eleanor Powell
OPENED: 1/9/29          THEATER: 46th Street          PERFORMANCES: 403

After DeSylva, Brown and Henderson had collaborated on musicals about football (*Good News!*) and boxing (*Hold Everything!*), they followed them up with a musical about golf. Subtitled "*A Musical Slice of Country Club Life,*" *Follow Thru* was a fittingly fast-paced successor to the previous sporty musicals, with another hummable score (including "Button Up Your Overcoat"), some funny situations for comedian Jack Haley (in his first major Broadway role), and a not-too-taxing plot about female rivalry for both the club championship and the golf pro.  Jack Haley repeated his role in the 1930 Paramount screen version, in which he was joined by Nancy Carroll and Charles "Buddy" Rogers. Laurence Schwab and Lloyd Corrigan were co-directors.

## FOR THE LOVE OF MIKE

MUSIC AND LYRICS: Jack Waller, Joseph Tunbridge, Clifford Grey, and Sonny Miller  BOOK: Clifford Grey
PRODUCER: Jack Waller  DIRECTOR: H.F. Maltby and Campbell Gullan  CHOREOGRAPHER: Fred Leslie
MAJOR PERFORMERS: Bobby Howes, Arthur Riscoe, Alfred Drayton, Olga Lindo, Peggy Cartwright, Viola Tree
OPENED: 10/8/31          THEATER: Saville, London          PERFORMANCES: 239

Anyone who lived through the big-band era must surely recall the whispery voice of Skinnay Ennis singing "Got A Date With An Angel" accompanied by the Hal Kemp Orchestra. What will doubtlessly come as a surprise is that the ballad was written for a long-forgotten London musical, *For the Love of Mike*, in which it was introduced by the popular British comedian, Bobby Howes. Howes, whose daughter, Sally Ann Howes, later appeared on Broadway and in films, sang it to Peggy Cartwright, the "Mike" of the title, in the premiere attraction at the newly built Saville Theatre.

## FUNNY GIRL

MUSIC AND LYRICS: Jule Styne and Bob Merrill  BOOK: Isabel Lennart  PRODUCER: Ray Stark
DIRECTOR: Garson Kanin and Jerome Robbins  CHOREOGRAPHER: Carol Haney
MAJOR PERFORMERS: Barbra Streisand, Sydney Chaplin, Danny Meehan, Jean Stapleton, Kay Medford
OPENED: 3/26/64          THEATER: Winter Garden          PERFORMANCES: 1,348

The funny girl of the title refers to Fanny Brice, one of Broadway's legendary clowns, and the story, told mostly in flashback, covers her discovery by impresario Florenz Zeigfeld, her triumphs in the Ziegfeld Follies, her stormy marriage to smooth-talking con man Nick Arnstein, and the breakup of her marriage after Nick has served time for stock swindling. Film producer Ray Stark, Miss Brice's son-in-law, had long wanted to make a movie based on the Fanny Brice story, but the original screenplay convinced him that it should first be done on the stage. At one time or another Mary Martin, Carol Burnett, and Anne Bancroft were announced for the leading role, but the assignment went to 21-year-old Barbra Streisand, whose only other Broadway experience had been in a supporting part in *I Can Get It For You Wholesale*. Miss Streisand succeeded so well—her recording of "People" was a hit even before *Funny Girl* opened—that she soon became an even bigger star than the woman she portrayed.  The 1968 Columbia movie version, in which the song "Funny Girl" was introduced, also starred Miss Streisand. It was directed by William Wyler and Herbert Ross.

## A FUNNY THING HAPPENED ON THE WAY TO THE FORUM

MUSIC AND LYRICS: Stephen Sondheim  BOOK: Burt Shevelove and Larry Gelbart  PRODUCER: Harold Prince
DIRECTOR: George Abbott, Jerome Robbins (uncredited)  CHOREOGRAPHER: Jack Cole
MAJOR PERFORMERS: Zero Mostel, Jack Gilford, David Burns, Raymond Walburn, John Carradine, Ruth Kobart, Brian Davies,
Preshy Marker, Ronald Holgate
OPENED: 5/8/62          THEATER: Alvin          PERFORMANCES: 964

Full of sight gags, pratfalls, mistaken identity, leggy girls, and other familiar vaudeville ingredients, this was a bawdy, farcical, pellmell musical whose likes have seldom been seen on Broadway. Originally intended as a vehicle first for Phil Silvers and then for Milton Berle, *A Funny Thing Happened on the Way to the Forum* opened on Broadway with Zero Mostel as Pseudolus the slave, who is forced to go through a series of madcap adventures before being allowed his freedom. Though the show was a hit, things had not looked very promising during the pre-Broadway tryout, and director Jerome Robbins was called in. The most important change beginning the musical with the song "Comedy Tonight," which set the right mood for the wacky doings that followed. To come up with a script, the librettists researched all twenty-one surviving comedies by the Roman playwright Plautus (254 BC -184 BC), then wrote an original book incorporating such typical Plautus characters as the conniving servants, the lascivious master, the domineering mistress, the officious warrior, the simple-minded hero (called Hero), and the senile old man. One situation, regarding the senile old man who is kept from entering his house because he believes it haunted, was, in truth, originally discovered in a play titled Mostellaria. In 1972, Phil Silvers at last got his chance to appear as Pseudolus in a well-received revival whose run was curtailed by the star's illness. Both Mostel (as Pseudolus) and Silvers (as Marcus Lycus) were in the 1966 United Artists screen version, along with Jack Gilford and Buster Keaton. Richard Lester was the director. The Broadway revival starring Nathan Lane opened in 1996. Whoopi Goldberg replaced Lane in 1997.


## THE GARRICK GAIETIES

MUSIC: Richard Rodgers  LYRICS: Lorenz Hart  SKETCHES: Various writers  PRODUCERS: Theatre Guild
DIRECTOR: Philip Loeb  CHOREOGRAPHER: Herbert Fields
MAJOR PERFORMERS: Sterling Holloway, Romney Brent, Betty Starbuck, Libby Holman, June Cochrane, Edith Meiser, Philip Loeb,
Sanford Meisner, Lee Strasberg
OPENED: 6/8/25          THEATER: Garrick          PERFORMANCES: 211

The revue began as a benefit production presented by the Theatre Guild, but the results were so successful that a professional run was arranged. "Manhattan" was the song that launched the career of Rodgers and Hart. Though they had been writing together a few years and had had songs on Broadway, "Manhattan" was their first hit. After *The Garrick Gaieties* the team never looked back, with production upon production until their partnership ended in 1943. A second *Garrick Gaieties* followed the next year, producing the hit "Mountain Greenery."


## GEORGE M!

MUSIC AND LYRICS: George M. Cohan  BOOK: Michael Stewart, John and Fran Pascal
PRODUCER: David Black, Konrad Matthaei, and Lorin E. Price
DIRECTOR: Joe Layton  CHOREOGRAPHER: Joe Layton
MAJOR PERFORMERS: Joel Grey, Betty Ann Grove, Jerry Dodge, Jill O'Hara, Bernadette Peters, Loni Ackerman
OPENED: 4/10/68          THEATER: Palace          PERFORMANCES: 435

George M. Cohan was a composer, lyricist, librettist, director, producer, actor, and song-and-dance man who wrote twenty-one musicals between 1901 and 1928, and who made his last major stage appearance playing President Franklin D. Roosevelt in the 1937 Rodgers and Hart show, *I'd Rather Be Right*. No other figure in the American musical theatre was so talented in so many areas, and with Joel Grey as Cohan, the biographical musical *George M!* paid fitting tribute to Broadway's dancing, prancing Yankee Doodle Boy. The score spotlighted a multitude of Cohan hits, including "Give My Regards To Broadway" (from *Little Johnny Jones*, 1904), "Forty-five Minutes From Broadway" and "Mary's a Grand Old Name" (from *Forty-five Minutes From Broadway*, 1906), "You're a Grand Old Flag" (from *George Washington, Jr.*, 1906) and "Harrigan ' (from *Fifty Miles From Boston*, 1908).


## GEORGE WHITE'S SCANDALS (1931 EDITION)

MUSIC AND LYRICS: Ray Henderson and Lew Brown
BOOK: Sketches by George White, Lew Brown, Irving Caesar, Harry Conn
PRODUCER: George White  DIRECTOR: George White  CHOREOGRAPHER: George White
MAJOR PERFORMERS: Rudy Vallee, Willie and Eugene Howard, Ethel Merman, Ray Bolger, Everett Marshall, Gale Quadruplets,
Ethel Barrymore Colt, Alice Faye
OPENED: 9/14/31          THEATER: Apollo          PERFORMANCES: 202

The success of the *Ziegfeld Follies* naturally encouraged other showmen to offer their own series of successive revues. The ones that came closest to the Follies in audience favor and prestige were the *George Whites Scandals*, which went through thirteen editions between 1919 and 1939. White produced, directed, choreographed, and wrote sketches for all these youthful, fast-paced, high-stepping shows that made up in talent and spirit what they may have lacked in Ziegfeldian glamour. In the eleventh edition, in 1931, the *Scandals* even provided a musical antidote to the Depression in " Life Is Just a Bowl of Cherries," which Ethel Merman trumpeted clear up to the second balcony. In addition, theatregoers could enjoy crooning heartthrob Rudy Vallee, the fleetfooted Ray Bolger, and Willie and Eugene Howard in their classic sketch, "Pay The Two Dollars."

## GEORGE WHITE'S SCANDALS (1939 EDITION)

MUSIC AND LYRICS: Sammy Fain and Jack Yellen BOOK: Sketches by Matt Brooks, Eddie Davis, George White
PRODUCER: George White DIRECTOR: George White CHOREOGRAPHER: George White
MAJOR PERFORMERS: Willie and Eugene Howard, Ella Logan, Ray Middleton, Ann Miller, The Three Stooges, Ben Blue
OPENED: 8/28/39          THEATER: Alvin          PERFORMANCES: 120

Opening about the same time that World War II began, the thirteenth and final edition of the George White's Scandals was a raucous revue, much influenced by the slapstick humor of *Hellzapoppin*, which tried countering the enveloping gloom with a cheery case for getting the most out of life, "Are You Having Any Fun?," sung by Ella Logan. The cast also included veteran comics Willie and Eugene Howard (it was their sixth appearance in a *Scandals*) and a dark-haired, sixteen-year-old, tap dancer named Ann Miller (who would not return to Broadway until *Sugar Babies* in 1979).


## GIGI

MUSIC AND LYRICS: Frederick Loewe and Alan Jay Lerner BOOK: Alan Jay Lerner PRODUCER: Saint-Subber
DIRECTOR: Joseph Hardy CHOREOGRAPHER: Onna White
MAJOR PERFORMERS: Alfred Drake, Daniel Massey, Maria Karnilova, Agnes Moorehead, Karin Wolfe
OPENED: 11/13/73          THEATER: Uris          PERFORMANCES: 103

*Gigi* had the distinction of being the first Broadway version of a Hollywood musical to use virtually the entire original score—including "I Remember It Well," "Thank Heaven For Little Girls," and "The Night They Invented Champagne." Set in Paris, the fin-de-siecle tale was concerned with a French girl who shocks her grandmother and aunt, two elegant coquettes, by her determination to get the dashing but bored Gaston Lachailles to propose marriage. Eventually, of course, he does. The story originated in a 60-page novel by Colette, which was then turned into a 1950 French film (with Danielle Delorme) and a 1954 Broadway play (with Audrey Hepburn). For the 1973 stage production, roles created in the 1958 MGM film musical by Leslie Caron, Louis Jourdan, Maurice Chevalier, and Hermione Gingold were played, respectively, by Karin Wolfe, Daniel Massey, Alfred Drake, and Maria Karnilova.


## THE GIRL FRIEND

MUSIC: Richard Rodgers LYRICS: Lorenz Hart BOOK: Herbert Fields
PRODUCER: Lew Fields DIRECTOR: John Harwood CHOREOGRAPHER: Jack Haskell
MAJOR PERFORMERS: Eva Condon, Dorothy Barber, Eva Puck, Sammy White, Evelyn Cavanaugh, June Cochrane
OPENED: 3/17/26          THEATER: Vanderbilt          PERFORMANCES: 301

Like most of the musical comedies of the 1920s, this one has a light, unobtrusive plot, presenting amusing and carefree characters in romantic situations. In this show, Leonard is a dairyman on Long Island. He aspires to be a great bicycle racer, with his girlfriend Mollie as his trainer and promoter. A rival promoter tries to lure Leonard away, but he sticks with his girl. The show is notable for its one lasting standard song, "The Blue Room."


## THE GIRL FROM UTAH

MUSIC: Jerome Kern and others LYRICS: Harry B. Smith and others
BOOK: James Tanner, Harry B. Smith PRODUCER: Charles Frohman DIRECTOR: J. A. E. Malone
MAJOR PERFORMERS: Julia Sanderson, Donald Brian, Joseph Cawthorn, Queenie Vassar, Venita Fitzhugh
OPENED: 8/24/14          THEATER: Knickerbocker          PERFORMANCES: 120

The show originated in London, which was the custom at the time. And, as was the custom, the score was revised in New York, creating a new pastiche. In this case, Jerome Kern added 7 new songs, with one surviving to lasting fame, "They Didn't Believe Me." The story is about a girl named Una who has fled to London to avoid marriying a bigamist from Utah. Una falls in love with a hoofer. The musical didn't have the freshness nor the book or unity that those very soon to come would have (meaning the "Princess" musicals of 1915-1917), but there were hints here of an emerging American style of musical comedy.


## GLAD TO SEE YOU

MUSIC AND LYRICS: Jule Styne and Sammy Cahn BOOK: Eddie Davis and Fred Thompson
PRODUCER: David Wolper DIRECTOR: Busby Berkeley CHOREOGRAPHER: Valerie Bettis
MAJOR PERFORMERS: Eddie Davis, Jane Withers, June Knight, Kenny Bowers, Gene Barry
OPENED: 11/13/44          THEATER: Shubert, Philadelphia          PERFORMANCES: None on Broadway

Hollywood songwriters Jule Styne and Sammy Cahn were to have made their mainstream debuts with the score for *Glad To See You*, originally intended as a vehicle for comedian Phil Silvers (whose "Gladdaseeya !" was then a popular catch phrase). Silvers, however, proved unavailable, and the role—that of a night-club entertainer who tours USO bases in the Pacific during World War II—went to Eddie Davis, a night-club entertainer usually seen at his own 52nd Street spot, Leon and Eddie's. Following the show's poorly received tryout opening in Philadelphia, Davis had to quit because of an automobile accident, and his role was temporarily takenover by lyricist Cahn (who at least knew the songs). By the time the musical opened in Boston, Eddie Foy Jr. had been rushed in as replacement, but audiences still did not reciprocate the sentiment of the show's cheery title, and New York never did get to see *Glad to See You*.

## GODSPELL

MUSIC AND LYRICS: Stephen Schwartz  BOOK: John-Michael Tebelak
PRODUCER: Edgar Lansbury, Stuart Duncan, Joseph Beruh  DIRECTOR: John-Michael Tebelak
MAJOR PERFORMERS: Stephen Nathan, David Haskell, Lamar Alford, Robin Lamont
OPENED: 5/17/71        THEATER: Cherry Lane (Off Broadway)        PERFORMANCES: 2,124 (Off Broadway)
                       Broadhurst (Broadway)                                    527 (Broadway)

With its rock-flavored score, *Godspell* was a contemporary, flower-children view of the Gospel according to St. Matthew, containing dramatized parables of the Prodigal Son, the Good Samaritan, and the Pharisee and the Tax Collector, and with Christ depicted as a clown-faced innocent with a Superman "S" on his shirt. The work originated as a nonmusical play and was first presented at the experimental Cafe La Mama: after Stephen Schwartz added words and music, the show began its Off-Broadway run at the Cherry Lane Theatre in Greenwich Village, then transferred to the Promenade Theatre where it remained for over five years. Beginning in June 1976, it also had a healthy Broadway run at the Broadhurst Theatre. The show's success launched Schwartz's career, which was also boosted when one of the songs, "Day By Day," became a pop hit. *Godspell* was filmed by Columbia in 1973 (David Greene directing), with Victor Garber (Jesus) and David Haskell (Judas) in the cast.


## THE GOLDEN APPLE

MUSIC AND LYRICS: Jerome Moross and John Latouche  BOOK: John Latouche
PRODUCER: T. Edward Hambleton and Norris Houghton
DIRECTOR: Norman Lloyd  CHOREOGRAPHER: Hanya Holm
MAJOR PERFORMERS: Stephen Douglass, Priscilla Gillette, Kaye Ballard, Jack Whiting, Bibi Osterwald, Jonathan Lucas, Portia Nelson
OPENED: 3/11/54        THEATER: Phoenix        PERFORMANCES: 125

Based on Homer's Odyssey and Iliad, *The Golden Apple* updated the epic sagas to the period between 1900 and 1910 and relocated the action in the state of Washington. With dialogue cut to a minimum, the story is told through the musical numbers (including the standard, "Lazy Afternoon"), and relates the consternation caused when a salesman named Paris (Jonathan Lucas) abducts Menelaus' all-too-willing wife, Helen (Kaye Ballard), thus compelling the duty-bound Ulysses (Stephen Douglass) to go off to fetch her back. It takes him ten years, during which time he resists temptations, beats Paris in a bare-knuckle fight, and finally returns to his incredibly patient spouse, Penelope (Priscilla Gillette). Following its successful Off Broadway opening, The Golden Apple was moved uptown to the Alvin Theatre, where it had a disappointing, short run.


## GOOD NEWS

MUSIC AND LYRICS: Ray Henderson, B.G. DeSylva and Lew Brown
BOOK: B.G. DeSylva and Laurence Schwab  PRODUCER: Laurence Schwab and Frank Mandel
DIRECTOR: Edgar MacGregor  CHOREOGRAPHER: Bobby Connolly
MAJOR PERFORMERS: Mary Lawlor, Gus Shy, John Price Jones, Inez Courtney, Shirley Vernon, Zelma O'Neal, George Olsen Orchestra
OPENED: 9/6/27        THEATER: 46th Street        PERFORMANCES: 557

*Good News* inaugurated a series of bright and breezy DeSylva, Brown and Henderson musical comedies that captured the fast-paced spirit of America's flaming youth. In this collegiate caper, the setting is Tait College where the student body is composed of flappers and sheiks, and where the biggest issue is whether the school's football hero will be allowed to play in the big game against Colton despite his failing grade in astronomy. Of the songs represented in this collection, "Sunny Side Up" and "Together" were first sung on Broadway in the unsuccessful 1974 revival, starring Alice Faye and Gene Nelson, and "Pass That Peace Pipe" (by Roger Edens, Hugh Martin and Ralph Blane) was written for the 1947 MGM film version starring June Allyson and Peter Lawford, and directed by Charles Walters.


## GREASE

MUSIC AND LYRICS: Warren Casey & Jim Jacobs  BOOK: Warren Casey & Jim Jacobs
PRODUCER: Kenneth Waissman and Maxine Fox  DIRECTOR: Tom Moore and Anthony D'Amato  CHOREOGRAPHER: Patricia Birch
MAJOR PERFORMERS: Barry Bostwick. Carole Demas, Adrienne Barbeau, Garn Stephens, Timothy Meyers and Don Billett
OPENED: 2/14/72        THEATER: Royale        PERFORMANCES: 3,388

The story of hip Danny Duke and his wholesome, girl Sandy Dumbrowski, serves as an excuse for this light-hearted recreation of the rock 'n' rolling '50s. It's a romp with the conformity required to be cool, and the show is mostly about virginity's lack of appeal. After a highly successful Broadway engagement, Grease became one of the biggest film musicals in recent history with John Travolta and Olivia Newton John in the leads. For a time, until being overtaken by *A Chorus Line*, *Grease* was the longest running show in Broadway history. A major Broadway revival opened in 1994, and has starred many celebrities.


## GREENWILLOW

MUSIC AND LYRICS: Frank Loesser  BOOK: Lesser Samuels and Frank Loesser
PRODUCER: Robert A Willey, in association with Frank Productions
DIRECTOR: George Roy Hill  CHOREOGRAPHER: Joe Layton
MAJOR PERFORMERS: Anthony Perkins, Cecil Kellaway, Pert Kelton, Ellen McCown, William Chapman, Lee Cass & Grover Dale
OPENED: 3/8/60        THEATER: Alvin        PERFORMANCES: 95

Anthony Perkins made a rare musical comedy appearance as a young man with a fear of his own wanderlust in this uneasy blend of folk humor and Broadway musical comedy. Although *Greenwillow* had the shortest run of any Frank Loesser show to open on Broadway, it provided the musical theatre with another charming Loesser score, including the popular "Never Will I Marry."

## GUYS AND DOLLS

MUSIC AND LYRICS: Frank Loesser  BOOK: Abe Burrows and Jo Swerling  PRODUCER: Cy Feuer and Ernest Martin
DIRECTOR: George S. Kaufman  CHOREOGRAPHER: Michael Kidd
MAJOR PERFORMERS: Robert Alda, Vivian Blaine, Sam Levene, Isabel Bigley, Pat Rooney, Stubby Kaye, B.S. Pully, Tom Pedi, Johnny Silver, Peter Gennaro, Onna White
OPENED: 11/24/50        THEATER: 46th Street        PERFORMANCES: 1,200

Populated by the hard-shelled but soft-centered characters who inhabit the world of writer Damon Runyon, this "Musical Fable of Broadway" tells the tale of how Miss Sarah Brown (Isabel Bigley), of the Save-a-Soul Mission, saves the souls of assorted Times Square riffraff while losing her heart to the smooth-talking gambler, Sky Masterson (Robert Alda). A more comic romance involves Nathan Detroit (Sam Levene), who runs the "oldest established permanent floating crap game in New York," and Miss Adelaide (Vivian Blaine), the star of the Hot Box night club, to whom he has been engaged for fourteen years.  A number of writers originally worked on the book of *Guys And Dolls* (based on Runyon's short story, "The Idyll Of Miss Sarah Brown") before Abe Burrows was engaged to submit an entirely new libretto, his first for Broadway. Burrows' story fitted Frank Loesser's already written score so perfectly that the musical is an accepted theatrical classic.  In 1976, an all-black version was mounted on Broadway with Robert Guillaume (Nathan), James Randolph (Sky), Ernestine Jackson (Sarah), and Norma Donaldson (Adelaide) heading the cast. It ran for 239 performances. The Samuel Goldwyn film version, released in 1955, starred Marlon Brando, Frank Sinatra, Jean Simmons, and Vivian Blaine, with Joseph Mankiewicz directing.  A highly successful revival opened on Broadway in 1992, with Peter Gallagher, Josie de Guzman, Faith Prince, and Nathan Lane.

## GYPSY

MUSIC AND LYRICS: Jule Styne and Stephen Sondheim  BOOK: Arthur Laurents
PRODUCER: David Merrick and Leland Hayward  DIRECTOR: Jerome Robbins
CHOREOGRAPHER: Jerome Robbins
MAJOR PERFORMERS: Ethel Merman, Jack Klugman, Sandra Church, Karen Moore, Lane Bradbury, Maria Karnilova, Faith Dane, Chotzi Foley, Paul Wallace, Jacqueline Mayro
OPENED: 5/21/59        THEATER: Broadway        PERFORMANCES: 702

With Ethel Merman giving the performance of her career as Gypsy Rose Lee's ruthless, domineering mother, *Gypsy* was one of the musical theatre's most memorable achievements. The idea for the musical began with producer David Merrick, who needed to read only one chapter in Miss Lee's autobiography to convince him of its stage potential. Originally, Stephen Sondheim was to have supplied the music as well as the lyrics, but Miss Merman felt that a more experienced composer was needed and Jule Styne was brought in. The Styne-Sondheim team created an impressive collection of songs for Miss Merman, from such nerve-tingling expressions of raw ambition as "Some People" and "Everything's Coming Up Roses" to the softer sentiments of "Small World" and "You'll Never Get Away From Me." In the story, Mama Rose is determined to escape from her humdrum life by pushing the vaudeville career of her daughter June; after June runs away to get married, she focuses all her attention on her other daugher, Louise. Eventually, Louise turns into the celebrated burlesque stripper Gypsy Rose Lee, and Rose suffers a breakdown when she realizes that she is no longer needed in her daughter's career.  *Gypsy* also enjoyed a successful London engagement in 1973 with Angela Lansbury as Rose. This production opened in New York the following year and ran for 120 performances. A film version was made by Warner Bros. in 1962, with Mervyn LeRoy directing, and Rosalind Russell, Natalie Wood, and Karl Malden in the cast.  A 1989 revival, starring Tyne Daley as Mama Rose, was a success in New York and on tour.  Bette Midler starred in a television film of the show, first aired in 1994.

## HALF A SIXPENCE

MUSIC AND LYRICS: David Hieneker  BOOK: Beverly Cross  PRODUCER: Allen-Hodgdon, Stevens Productions, Harold Fielding
DIRECTOR: Gene Saks  CHOREOGRAPHER: Onna White
MAJOR PERFORMERS: Tommy Steele, Polly James, Carrie Nye, Grover Dale, Will Mackenzie, John Cleese, James Grout
OPENED: 4/25/65        THEATER: Broadhurst        PERFORMANCES: 512

H.G. Wells' novel, *Kipps*, supplied the story for this period musical in which Tommy Steele (for whom it was written) starred in London, in New York and on film. *Half a Sixpence* is about Arthur Kipps, an orphan who becomes a draper's apprentice in Folkestone, England, at the turn of the century. Arthur inherits a fortune, gets engaged to high-born Helen Walsingham (Carrie Nye), breaks off the engagement, loses his money, and ends happily with faithful Ann Pornick (Polly James). The original London production opened at the Cambridge Theatre on March 1, 1953, and ran for 677 performances. There were some changes in the score for Broadway, where the show was hailed for its rousing dance numbers.  The film version, which also starred Cyril Ritchard, was made by Paramount in 1967 with George Sidney directing.

## HAPPY HUNTING

MUSIC AND LYRICS: Harold Karr and Matt Dubey  BOOK: Howard Lindsay and Russel Crouse
PRODUCER: Jo Mielziner  DIRECTOR: Abe Burrows  CHOREOGRAPHER: Alex Romero and Bob Herget
MAJOR PERFORMERS: Ethel Merman, Fernando Lamas, Virginia Gibson, Gordon Polk, Mary Finney, Leon Belasco, Estelle Parsons
OPENED: 12/6/56        THEATER: Majestic        PERFORMANCES: 408

*Happy Hunting* was the vehicle in which the dynamic Ethel Merman returned to Broadway after a four-and-a-half-year retirement. It tells of a wealthy Philadelphia widow, Liz Livingstone (Miss Merman), and her daughter Beth (Virginia Gibson), who are in Monaco for the wedding of Grace Kelly and Prince Rainier even though they do not have an invitation. Miffed at the slight, Liz vows to get even by having Beth marry the Duke of Granada (Fernando Lamas), a penniless pretender to the Spanish throne. Back in Philadelphia, the duke admits that it's the mother not the daughter whom he loves, which seems to straighten things out for everyone.

# THE HAPPY TIME

MUSIC AND LYRICS: John Kander and Fred Ebb  BOOK: N. Richard Nash  PRODUCER: David Merrick
DIRECTOR: Gower Champion  CHOREOGRAPHER: Gower Champion
MAJOR PERFORMERS: Robert Goulet, David Wayne, Julie Gregg, Mike Rupert, George S. Irving
OPENED: 1/18/68          THEATER: Broadway          PERFORMANCES: 286

A gentle, nostalgic look at a French-Canadian family in a small town, *The Happy Time* was adapted from the novel by Robert Fontaine and the play by Samuel Taylor, which Rodgers and Hammerstein had produced in 1950. The musical was primarily concerned with the coming of age of a young member of the Bonnard family (played by Mike Rupert) and his desire to see the world with his uncle Jacques (Robert Goulet), a footloose photographer who has returned to his family for a brief visit. The use of film projections to establish the mood for the various scenes was one of the highly effective touches introduced by director Gower Champion.

# HAZEL FLAGG

MUSIC AND LYRICS: Jule Styne and Bob Hilliard  BOOK: Ben Hecht
PRGDUCER: Jule Styne and Anthony Brady Farrell
DIRECTOR: David Alexander  CHOREOGRAPHER: Robert Alton
MAJOR PERFORMERS: Helen Gallagher, Thomas Mitchell, Benay Venuta, John Howard, Jack Whiting, Sheree North
OPENED: 2/11/53          THEATER: Mark Hellinger          PERFORMANCES: 190

With its Ben Hecht libretto based on his own screenplay for the 1937 movie, *Nothing Sacred* the musical took a jaundiced look at the power of publicity to influence a gullible public. Hazel Flagg (Helen Gallagher), supposedly dying of radium poisoning in a Vermont town, is brought to New York by *Everywhere Magazine* and immediately becomes the darling of the city. When the diagnosis is found to be incorrect, Hazel is just as quickly abandoned by all her admirers with the exception ot Wallace Cook (John Howard), the magazine writer assigned to her story. The show did much to revive the career of Jack Whiting, playing a jaunty New York mayor and to help launch the popular ballad, "How Do You Speak To An Angel?" In 1954, Jerry Lewis (as Homer Flagg) and Dean Martin made a screen version which Paramount retitled *Living It Up*. The director was Norrnan Taurog.

# HELLO, DOLLY!

MUSIC AND LYRICS: Jerry Herman  BOOK: Michael Stewart  PRODUCER: David Merrick
DIRECTOR: Gower Champion  CHOREOGRAPHER: Gower Champion
MAJOR PERFORMERS: Carol Channing, David Burns, Eileen Brennan, Sondra Lee, Charles Nelson Reilly, Jerry Dodge
OPENED: 1/16/64          THEATER: St. James          PERFORMANCES: 2,844

Under the expert direction of Gower Champion, this stylish production, based on Thornton Wilder's play *The Matchmaker*, proved not only a triumph for its original star, but a successful vehicle for a multitude of actresses: on the screen, around the country (Dorothy Lamour and Eve Arden), and around the world (Mary Martin), as well as on Broadway where Carol Channing was succeeded by Ginger Rogers, Martha Raye, Betty Grable, Phyllis Diller, Pearl Bailey (heading an all-black cast) and finally Ethel Merman, who had turned down the role when it was offered to her almost ten years earlier. The show returned to Broadway with Channing twice, in 1978 and 1995.

# HERE'S LOVE

MUSIC AND LYRICS: Meredith Willson  BOOK: Meredith Willson  PRODUCER: Stuart Ostrow
DIRECTOR: Stuart Ostrow  CHOREOGRAPHER: Michael Kidd
MAJOR PERFORMERS: Janis Paige, Craig Stevens, Laurence Naismith, Paul Reed and Valerie Lee
OPENED: 10/3/63          THEATER: Shubert          PERFORMANCES: 334

A cynical young mother and her precocious daughter are caught up in the confusion when a department store Santa Claus announces that he is the genuine article. This musicalization of *Miracle On 34th Street* boasted a lively score including the holiday standard, "It's Beginning To Look Like Christmas".

# HIGH BUTTON SHOES

MUSIC AND LYRICS: Music by Jule Styne Lyrics by Sammy Cahn
BOOK: Stephen Longstreet (based on the book *The Sisters Liked Them Handsome* by Stephen Longstreet)
PRODUCER: Monte Proser and Joseph Kipness  DIRECTOR: George Abbott  CHOREOGRAPHER: Jerome Robbins
MAJOR PERFORMERS: Phil Silvers, Nanette Fabray, Jack McCauley, Mark Dawson, Joey Faye, Lois Lee, Helen Gallagher
OPENED: 10/9/47          THEATER: New Century          PERFORMANCES: 77

Phil Silvers and Nanette Fabray were crowd-pleasers in this early Broadway effort by songwriters Jule Styne and Sammy Cahn, who had collaborated with great success on several film scores. Silvers found his share of laughs as a man whose attempts at making a fast dollar continually land him in hot water. Of course all was well by the final curtain, and along the way the audience had been introduced to a melodic score, including "I Still Get Jealous" and "You're My Girl".

## HIGH SPIRITS

MUSIC AND LYRICS: Hugh Martin and Timothy Gray  BOOK: Hugh Martin and Timothy Gray
PRODUCER: Lester Osterman, Robert Fletcher  DIRECTOR Noel Coward, and Richard Horner Gower Champion (uncredited)
CHOREOGRAPHER: Danny Daniels  MAJOR PERFORMERS: Beatrice Lillie, Tammy Grimes, Louise Troy, Edward Woodward
OPENED: 4/7/64          THEATER: Alvin          PERFORMANCES: 375

Hugh Martin and Timothy Gray adapted *High Spirits* from Noel Coward's play, *Blithe Spirit*. In the story, Beatrice Lillie brilliantly portrayed the irrepressible and mischievous spiritualist, Madam Arcati, who disrupts the second marriage of a writer named Charles Condomine (Edward Woodward) by bringing his first wife, Elvira (Tammy Grimes), back from the dead. In an attempt to take her former husband with her to the spirit world, Elvira accidently causes the death of the second wife (Louise Troy) who then takes revenge by playing some ghostly tricks of her own. Though as director, Noel Coward made sure that the musical was in the proper blithe spirit of his play, he took ill in Philadelphia and agreed to let Gower Champion take over the reins.


## HIGHER AND HIGHER

MUSIC AND LYRICS: Richard Rodgers and Lorenz Hart  BOOK: Gladys Hurlbut and Joshua Logan
PRODUCER: Dwight Deere Wiman  DIRECTOR: Joshua Logan  CHOREOGRAPHER: Robert Alton
MAJOR PERFORMERS: Jack Haley, Marta Eggert, Shirley Ross, Leif Erickson, Lee Dixon, Hollace Shaw
OPENED: 4/4/40          THEATER: SHUBERT          PERFORMANCES: 104

One of the lesser-known Rodgers and Hart endeavors, *Higher And Higher* was originally conceived with Norwegian ballet dancer Vera Zorina in the leading female role. When she proved unavailable, her part was rewritten for the Hungarian operetta diva, Marta Eggert. In the story, a group of servants, facing unemployment because of the bankruptcy of their employer, pass off one of the maids as a debutante so that she might marry a rich man. Though the show boasted such talented people as comedian Jack Haley and singer Shirley Ross (she introduced the durable ballad, "It Never Entered My Mind"), most of the attention of the audience was directed at the antics of a trained seal named Sharkey. Or as Richard Rodgers once put it, "If a trained seal steals your show, you don't have a show."

Frank Sinatra made his acting debut in RKO's 1943 screen version. The cast also included Michele Morgan and Jack Haley, the director was Tim Whelen, and only one Rodgers and Hart song was retained.


## HOLD EVERYTHING

MUSIC AND LYRICS: Ray Henderson, B.G. DeSylva, and Lew Brown  BOOK: B.G. DeSylva and Jack McGowan
PRODUCER: Alex A. Aarons and Vinton Freedley  DIRECTOR: uncredited
CHOREOGRAPHER: Sam Rose and Jack Haskell
MAJOR PERFORMERS: Jack Whiting, Ona Munson, Bert Lahr, Betty Compton, Victor Moore, Nina Olivette
OPENED: 10/10/28          THEATER: Broadhurst          PERFORMANCES: 413

Despite a title suggesting a tale about wrestling, *Hold Everything* was all about boxing, with a story dealing with Sunny Jim Brooks (Jack Whiting), a welterweight challenger, and his girl, Sue Burke (Ona Munson), who is the cream in his coffee. Sunny Jim becomes temporarily distracted by debutante Norine Lloyd (Betty Compton) who advises him to use his boxing skill rather than try to slug it out for the championship. But when our hero finds out that the champ has insulted Sue, his killer instincts are aroused and he wins both his crown and his beloved. The major attraction of the show, however, turned out to be the uninhibited buffoon, Bert Lahr, who scored an overnight sensation as a punch-drunk pug. A Warner Bros. movie version was made in 1930. It was directed by Roy Del Ruth, featured Joe E. Brown and Winnie Lightner, and had new songs by Joe Burke and Al Dubin.


## HOLD ON TO YOUR HATS

MUSIC AND LYRICS: Burton Lane and E.Y. Harburg  BOOK: Guy Bolton, Matt Brooks, and Eddie Davis
PRODUCER: Al Jolson and George Hale  DIRECTOR: Edgar MacGregor  CHOREOGRAPHER: Catherine Littlefield
MAIOR PERFORMERS: Al Jolson, Martha Raye, Bert Gordon, Jack Whiting, Arnold Moss, Gil Lamb, Eunice Healey, Jinx Falkenburg
OPENED: 9/11/40          THEATER: Shubert          PERFORMANCES: 158

One of the theatre's greatest entertainers, Al Jolson, had been away from Broadway for over nine years when he returned in *Hold on to Your Hats*. The show had a loosely written book about a timid actor celebrated for his role as the fearless Lone Rider in a radio series. Somehow the actor is persuaded to go West to capture a notorious Mexican bandit and, somehow, after a couple of narrow escapes, he does. The story, however, counted for little as Al traded gags with Martha Raye and Bert Gordon ("The Mad Russian"), socked across numbers like "There's A Great Day Coming Mañana," and ended the evening with a medley of his old favorites.  Part of Jolson's motivation in doing the musical was that he saw it as a means through which he could win back his divorced wife, Ruby Keeler, who was originally in the cast. Miss Keeler, however, walked out when Jolson, during a performance, inserted a discussion of their marital problems in the middle of a scene. The run of the show, which marked Jolson's last appearance on Broadway, was cut short when the star was hospitalized for pneumonia.

## HOORAY FOR WHAT

MUSIC AND LYRICS: Harold Arlen and E.Y. Harburg  BOOK: Howard Lindsay and Russel Crouse
PRODUCER: Messrs. Shubert  DIRECTOR: Vincente Minnelli and Howard Lindsay
CHOREOGRAPHER: Robert Alton, Agnes de Mille
MAJOR PERFORMERS: Ed Wynn, Jack Whiting, June Clyde, Vivian Vance, Paul Haakon, Leo Chalzel, Ruthanna Boris
OPENED: 12/1/37          THEATER: Winter Garden          PERFORMANCES: 200

Although it starred the zany clown, Ed Wynn, and even made room for his vaudeville specialties, *Hooray for What* was primarily concerned with such weighty and timely matters as poison gas, munitions, diplomatic duplicity, espionage, and actual warfare. In the satirical plot, Chuckles, a horticulturist, invents a gas to kill worms but then discovers that it can also kill humans. Chuckles' invention sets off an arms race among the European powers who meet at a so-called Peace conference in Geneva, where spies try to steal the formula from Chuckle's room at the Hotel del' Espionage. When, using a mirror, a seductive spy copies the formula backwards, the gas turns out to be harmless and war is miraculously averted. *Hooray for What* marked Agnes de Mille's first efforts as a Broadway choreographer, though most of her work was cut by the time the show reached New York.

## HOUSE OF FLOWERS

MUSIC: Harold Arlen  LYRICS: Harold Arlen and Truman Capote  BOOK: Truman Capote
PRODUCER: Saint Subber  DIRECTOR: Peter Brook  CHOREOGRAPHER: Herbert Ross
MAJOR PERFORMERS: Pearl Bailey, Diahann Carroll, J uanita Hall, Ray Walston and Geoffrey Holder
OPENED: 12/20/54          THEATER: Alvin          PERFORMANCES: 165

This "musical Mardi gras" provided a showcase for the talents of Pearl Bailey as Madame Fleur, a Carribean island madame whose "house of flowers" competed with the house of Madame Tango (Juanita Hall) for the patronage of visiting sailors. Complications result when the girl Violet displays a preference for marrying her sweetheart to being sold to one of Fleur's wealthy clients. The song ''A Sleepin' Bee'' typifies the sweet and gentle charms of the show's score.

## HOW TO SUCCEED IN BUSINESS WITHOUT REALLY TRYING

MUSIC AND LYRICS: Frank Loesser  BOOK: Abe Burrows, Jack Weinstock and Willie Gilbert (based on the book by Shepherd Mead)
PRODUCER: Cy Feuer and Ernest Martin  DIRECTOR: Abe Burrows  CHOREOGRAPHER: Bob Fosse and Hugh Lambert
MAJOR PERFORMERS: Robert Morse, Rudy Vallee, Bonnie Scott, Virginia Martin, Charles Nelson Reilly and Ruth Kobart
OPENED: 10/14/61          THEATER: 46th Street          PERFORMANCES: 1,417

*How to Succeed in Business Without Really Trying* traces the career of J. Pierpont Finch (Robert Morse) as he climbs to the top of the business world, not by hard work, but by the teachings of a book called *How to Succeed in Business Without Really Trying*. Finch's charming but ruthless character is summed up neatly as he sings the show's hit song "I Believe In You" to his own reflection in the mirror of the Executive Washroom. The teaming of Loesser and Burrows, who shared an earthy and slightly cynical sense of humor, resulted in a hard-edged, but hilarious, look at the world of big business. A 1995 Broadway revival starred Matthew Broderick as Finch.

## I CAN GET IT FOR YOU WHOLESALE

MUSIC AND LYRICS: Harold Rome  BOOK: Jerome Weidman  PRODUCER: David Merrick
DIRECTOR: Arthur Laurents  CHOREOGRAPHER: Herbert Ross
MAJOR PERFORMERS: Elliott Gould, Lillian Roth, Sheree North, Harold Lang, Jack Kruschen, Ken LeRoy, Marilyn Cooper, Barbra Streisand, Bambi Linn
OPENED: 3/22/62          THEATER: Shubert          PERFORMANCES: 300

Harry Bogen, the leading character in *I Can Get It For You Wholesale*, is an unscrupulous conniver who uses and misuses people on his way to the top. Based on Jerome Weidman s best-selling novel, which Weidman himself adapted, the musical also helped two young people on their way to the top: Elliott Gould, who played Harry, and Barbra Streisand, who played the overworked, unappreciated Miss Marmelstein. The production is set in New York's Garment District in the Thirties, where Harry rises in the business world through a series of shady deals until he finally outsmarts himself. At the end, though, there is a hint of redemption when he gets a new job and his estranged sweetheart comes back to him.

## I DO! I DO!

MUSIC AND LYRICS: Harvey Schmidt and Tom Jones  BOOK: Tom Jones  PRODUCER: David Merrick
DIRECTOR: Gower Champion  MAJOR PERFORMERS: Mary Martin, Robert Preston
OPENED: 12/5/66          THEATER: 46th Street          PERFORMANCES: 584

*I Do! I Do!* was the first Broadway musical ever to have a cast consisting of only two characters. But since the parts were played by two of the theatre's most luminous stars, Mary Martin and Robert Preston, no one could possibly feel the need of anyone else on the stage. In all other ways, however, *I Do! I Do!* (adapted from Jan de Hartog's play, *The Fourposter*) was an ambitious undertaking, covering fifty years in the life of a married couple, Agnes and Michael, from their wedding to the day they move out of their house. In between, they bring up a family, quarrel, threaten to break up, have a reconciliation, reminisce about the past, plan for a life without children in the house, and express their deep feelings for each other through such pieces as "I Love My Wife," "My Cup Runneth Over," and "Together Forever."

## I HAD A BALL

MUSIC AND LYRICS Jack Lawrence and Stan Freeman  BOOK: Jerome Chodorov
PRODUCER: Joseph Kipness  DIRECTOR: Lloyd Richards  CHOREOGRAPHER: Onna White
MAJOR PERFORMERS: Buddy Hackett, Richard Kiley, Karen Morrow, and Rosetta LeNoire
OPENED: 12/15/64          THEATER: Martin Beck          PERFORMANCES: 184

In a show tailored to his talents, Buddy Hackett portrayed Garside, a Coney Island con man (with a crystal ball named Sam) who decides to play matchmaker. Complications ensue when Sam is revealed to have genuine powers and Garside's bungled forecasts result in the collision of mismatched couples, crooks and an ex-hustler. The bright score helps an unruly plot move toward the "Tunnel Of Love" chase at the climax.


## I'D RATHER BE RIGHT

MUSIC AND LYRICS: Richard Rodgers and Lorenz Hart  BOOK: George S. Kaufman and Moss Hart
PRODUCER: Sam H. Harris  DIRECTOR: George S. Kaufman  CHOREOCRAPHER: Charles Weidman, Ned McGurn
MAJOR PERFORMERS: George M. Cohan, Taylor Holmes, Joy Hodges, Austin Marshall, Marion Green, Mary Jan Walsh, Georgie Tapps
OPENED: 11/2/37          THEATER: Alvin          PERFORMANCES: 290

The reasons that *I'd Rather Be Right* was such an eagerly anticipated production are not hard to find. One was that its central character was President Franklin D. Roosevelt, not only depicted by name but shown as a figure of fun and the butt of jokes. The other was that the part was being played by the legendary George M. Cohan, marking his return to the musical stage for the first time in ten years (and his only appearance in a song-and-dance show that he did not write himself). The musical's locale is New York's Central Park and the date is the Fourth of July. Peggy (Joy Hodges) and Phil (Austin Marshall) hope to get married but Phil's boss won't give him a raise until Roosevelt balances the budget. Phil falls asleep and dreams that they meet F.D.R. strolling through the park. After Phil explains the couple's dilemma, Roosevelt promises to help, which is only an excuse for some genial ribbing at the expense of Cabinet members, the Supreme Court, the P.W.A., a Fireside Chat, Alf Landon, and Roosevelt's decision to seek a third term.


## I'M GETTING MY ACT TOGETHER AND TAKING IT ON THE ROAD

MUSIC AND LYRICS: Nancy Ford and Gretchen Cryer  BOOK: Gretchen Cryer
PRODUCER: New York Shakespeare Festival  DIRECTOR: Word Baker
MAJOR PERFORMERS: Gretchen Cryer, Betty Aberlin, Don Scardino
OPENED: 6/14/78          THEATER: Public          PERFORMANCES: 1,165

In all of their work to date, Nancy Ford and Gretchen Cryer have been preeminently identified as feminist writers. *I'm Getting My Act Together And Taking It On The Road*, by far their most personal expression, even had the central role, that of a divorced 39-year-old pop singer attempting a comeback, played by Gretchen Cryer herself. Through songs she auditions for her manager, the singer gradually becomes the embodiment of the outspoken, totally liberated woman who knows who she is and where she is going.


## INSIDE U.S.A.

MUSIC AND LYRICS: Arthur Schwartz and Howard Dietz  BOOK: Sketches by Arnold Auerbach, Moss Hart and Arnold B. Horwitt
PRODUCER: Arthur Schwartz  DIRECTOR: Robert H. Gordon
CHOREOGRAPHER: Helen Tamiris
MAJOR PERFORMERS: Beatrice Lillie, Jack Haley, Valerie Bettis, John Tyers, Estelle Loring, Thelma Carpenter, Herb Shriner, Carl Reiner, Louis Nye
OPENED: 4/30/48          THEATER: New Century          PERFORMANCES: 399

Using the title of the celebrated sociological study by John Gunther as an excuse to visit a variety of locales within the United States, *Inside U.S.A.* was a revue in which songs, dances and sketches were presented in scenes from all over the country. Among stops in the itinerary: Pittsburgh (to deride industrial pollution), the Kentucky Derby, Rhode Island (to offer "Rhode Island Is Famous For You"), San Francisco (to present the haunting "Haunted Heart" in a waterfront setting), a Wisconsin state fair, the New Orleans Mardi Gras, a Wyoming rodeo, and Albuquerque, New Mexico (where two Indians, Beatrice Lillie and Jack Haley resolutely refuse to take the country back). Inside U.S.A. was the last of seven revues written by the team of Howard Dietz and Arthur Schwartz (among the others were *Three's a Crowd* and *The Band Wagon*).


## IRMA LA DOUCE

MUSIC AND LYRICS: Marguerite Monnot; Julian More, Monty Norman, and David Heneker
BOOK: Julian More, Monty Norman, and David Henker
PRODUCER: David Merrick  DIRECTOR: Peter Brook  CHOREOGRAPHER: Onna White
MAJOR PERFORMERS: Elizabeth Seal, Keith Michell, Clive Revill, Fred Gwynne, George S. Irving, Stuart Damon, Elliott Gould
OPENED: 9/29/60          THEATER: Plymouth          PERFORMANCES: 524

*Irma La Douce*, with book and lyrics by Alexandre Breffort, originated in Paris in 1956 and ran for four years. The English-language version opened two years later in London at the Lyric Theatre and ran 1,512 performances. With Elizabeth Seal, Keith Michell, and Clive Revill recreating their roles in New York (Miss Seal was the only female member of the cast), the production was a virtual carbon of the West End original. Set in a dingy quarter of Paris, the plot revolves around the romance between Irma, a pure-at-heart prostitute, and Nestor, a poor student. Anxious to have Irma all to himself, Nestor disguises himself as the imaginary Oscar, supposedly wealthy enough to be the lady's only provider. But the student grows jealous of Oscar, "kills" him, and is sent to Devil's Island. After escaping, he proves his innocence and is happily reunited with Irma as they reprise the show's chief romantic duet, "Our Language Of Love." All the songs were cut from Billy Wilder's 1963 film version, which was released by United Artists and starred Shirley MacLaine and Jack Lemmon.

## JAMAICA

MUSIC AND LYRICS: Harold Arlen and E.Y. Harburg  BOOK: E.Y. Harburg and Fred Saidy
PRODUCER: David Merrick  DIRECTOR: Robert Lewis  CHOREOGRAPHER: Jack Cole
MAJOR PERFORMERS: Lena Horne, Ricardo Montalban, Josephine Premice, Adelaide Hall, Ossie Davis and Erik Rhodes
OPENED: 10/31/57          THEATER: Imperial          PERFORMANCES: 558

Although the show featured a score by Harold Arlen and the energetic choreography of Jack Cole, Lena Horne, in her first Broadway role, was the special attraction that kept *Jamaica* running for over a year. Set in the paradise of Pigeon's Island off Jamaica's coast, it told the story of a poor fisherman's love for the beautiful Savannah, who longs to live in New York. The simple story line allowed for many musical numbers, more than half of which featured Miss Horne.


## JEKYLL & HYDE

MUSIC: Frank Wildhorn LYRICS & BOOK: Leslie Bricusse
OPENED: At this writing the Broadway opening is announced for 4/28/97
PRODUCERS: Pace Theatrical Group, Fox Theatricals  DIRECTOR: Robin Phillips
MAJOR PERFORMERS: Robert Cuccioli, Linda Eder, Christina Noll, George Merritt, Barrie Ingham
OPENED: 4/28/97          THEATER: Plymouth          PERFORMANCES: (still running 6/1/97)

The show has been a thirteen-year saga on its way to Broadway. It began in 1984 with Steve Cuden as lyricist, replaced a few years later by Leslie Bricusse. The musical debuted at the Alley Theatre in Houson in 1990. A recording of the show became a runaway hit. After revisions and rewrites and added material a new production opened again in Houston in 1995. A national tour followed. The story, based on Robert Louis Stevenson's novel, takes place in London, 1888. Henry Jekyll is a doctor and scientist who believes he has discovered the way to separate good and evil in human nature. His research proposal is rejected by the hospital, and he runs his experiments on himself, using the formula he's concocted, which ultimately leads to his being consumed by the evil "Edward Hyde."


## JESUS CHRIST SUPERSTAR

MUSIC AND LYRICS: Andrew Lloyd Webber and Tim Rice  BOOK: Tom O'Horgan
PRODUCER: Robert Stigwood  DIRECTOR: Tom O'Horgan
MAJOR PERFORMERS: Jeff Fenholt, Yvonne Elliman, Ben Vereen, Barry Dennen
OPENED: 10/12/71          THEATER: Mark Hellinger          PERFORMANCES: 711

First it was a pop hit single called "Superstar." Then the song was expanded into a full score which was recorded and became a Gold-Record album. Then the album became the basis for a series of well-attended concert tours. Eventually, the concert version was developed into a self-described "rock opera" that retold the last seven days of Christ in such a flamboyant, campy, and mind-blowing fashion that it became a media hype and a runaway hit.  A film version was made by Universal in 1973. It was directed by Norman Jewison, and had a cast headed by Ted Neeley and Carl Anderson.


## JOHNNY JOHNSON

MUSIC AND LYRICS: Kurt Weill and Paul Green  BOOK: Paul Green
PRODUCER: The Group Theatre  DIRECTOR: Lee Strasberg
MAJOR PERFORMERS: Russell Collins, Roman Bohnen, Phoebe Brand, Sanford Meisner, Robert Lewis, Lee J. Cobb, Albert Van Dekker, Elia Kazan, Luther Adler, Jules (John) Garfield, Morris Carnovsky.
OPENED: 11/19/36          THEATER: 44th Street          PERFORMANCES: 68

Like *The Threepenny Opera*, Kurt Weill's first musical written in the United States uses the grotesquery of caricature to soften its angry barbs at irresponsible national leaders, industrialists, phony psychiatrists, and other charlatans. The Group Theatre, a politically sensitive repertory company founded in the mid-thirties and dedicated to introducing new works by promising writers, invited Weill to collaborate with Pulitzer Prize-winning playwright Paul Green on *Johnny Johnson*. Written as a parable, the play follows the history of a pacifist stonecutter. Johnny Johnson (Russell Collins) creates a stone Monument to Peace, but shortly after the dedication, he is drafted into service in World War I. After being wounded, he momentarily disrupts the war by spraying the Allied high command with laughing gas and is promptly committed to a mental institution. Johnny and his fellow inmates assume the roles of world statesmen, establishing a League of World republics. As they play ends, the stonecutter is released and returns home to peddle nonmilitary toys in a town where everyone else is whooping it up for war.


## JOSEPH AND THE AMAZING TECHNICOLOR DREAMCOAT

MUSIC: Andrew Lloyd Webber  LYRICS: Tim Rice  PRODUCERS: Zev Bufman & Susan Rose
DIRECTOR-CHOREOGRAPHER: Tony Tanner
MAJOR PERFORMERS: Bill Hutton, Laurie Beechman, David Ardeo, Tom Carder
OPENED: 11/18/81          THEATER: Entermedia          PERFORMANCES: 824

The show was 15 minutes in its original form, written for a school in London and first performed in 1968.  It was first expanded to 40 minutes, then 90 minutes, and then to closer to 2 hours.  The story is of Jacob and his 12 sons.  Joseph, the favorite son, receives a beautiful coat as a present from his father, and the jealous brothers sell him into slavery. While captive in Egypt, Joseph impresses the Pharoah with his ability to interpret dreams and is elevated to a position of prestige and honor.  The professional production history is complex.  First produced in the West End in 1973, on Broadway in 1981; a new version and production opened in London in 1990, in Toronto in 1991. The Toronto company toured, giving long runs in major cities, Chicago most notably.  On Broadway again, "Joseph" opened in 1993.  There have been 4 different cast recordings.

## JUMBO

MUSIC: Richard Rodgers  LYRICS: Lorenz Hart  BOOK: Ben Hecht & Charles MacArthur
PRODUCER: Billy Rose  DIRECTORS: John Murray Anderson, George Abbott  CHOREOGRAPHER: Allan K. Foster
MAJOR PERFORMERS: Jimmy Durante, Paul Whiteman Orchestra, Donald Novis, Gloria Grafton, A. P. Kaye, A. Robins,
Poodles Hanneford, Big Rosie, Tilda Getze
OPENED: 11/16/35        THEATER: Hippodrome        PERFORMANCES: 233

The circus comes to Broadway.  The huge Hippodrome Theater was rebuilt to house this unusual show, with a circular revolving stage and
"grandstand" seating sloping up around it.  It was the most expensive show ever to open in New York up to that time, costing $340,000.
Rehearsals lasted 6 months.  The thin plot served as a framework for specialty acts.  In his autobiography Richard Rodgers complains that the
show would have been more successful had Billy Rose not forbidden that any of the songs in the score be broadcast or recorded during the run.

## KEAN

MUSIC AND LYRICS: Robert Wright and George Forrest
BOOK: Peter Stone (From a comedy by Jean-Paul Sartre, based on the play by Alexander Dumas)
PRODUCER: Robert Lantz  DIRECTOR: Jack Cole  CHOREOGRAPHER: Jack Cole
MAJOR PERFORMERS: Alfred Drake, Lee Venora, Oliver Gray, Joan Weldon, Roderick Cook and Patricia Cutts
OPENED: 11/2/61        THEATER: Broadhurst        PERFORMANCES: 92

The great Shakespearean actor, Edmund Kean, was the subject of this musical, noted by the critics for its lavish production and the powerful
performance of Alfred Drake in the title role. Amid the elegance and festivity of early nineteenth-century London, we glimpse Kean's amorous
escapades, his yearning to be accepted in society and the confusion of identity which plagued him throughout his career.

## KILL THAT STORY

MUSIC AND LYRICS: Lew Pollack and Paul Francis Webster  BOOK: Play by Harry Madden and Philip Dunning
PRODUCER: George Abbott and Philip Dunning  DIRECTOR: George Abbott
MAJOR PERFORMERS: James Bell, Matt Briggs, Emily Lowry, Wyrley Birch, Gloria Grafton
OPENED: 8/29/34        THEATER: Booth        PERFORMANCES: 117

*Kill That Story* was a non-musical play taking place at a convention hotel where a newspaper reporter, falsely accused of responsibility in a young
woman's death, clears his name, wins back his former wife, and brings the guilty party to justice. The interpolated song, "Two Cigarettes In The
Dark," was sung in a party scene by Gloria Grafton.

## THE KING AND I

MUSIC AND LYRICS: Richard Rodgers and Oscar Hammerstein II  BOOK: Oscar Hammerstein II
PRODUCER: Richard Rodgers and Oscar Hammerstein II
DIRECTOR: John van Druten  CHOREOGRAPHER: Jerome Robbins
MAJOR PERFORMERS: Gertrude Lawrence, Yul Brynner, Dorothy Sarnoff, Larry Douglas, Doretta Morrow
OPENED: 3/29/51        THEATER: St. James        PERFORMANCES: 1 ,246

The idea of turning Margaret Landon's Novel, *Anna and the King of Siam*, into a musical first occurred to Gertrude Lawrence who saw it as a
suitable vehicle for her return to the Broadway musical stage. Based on the diaries of an adventurous Englishwoman, the story is set in Bangkok
in the early 1860s. Anna Leonowens, who has accepted the post of schoolteacher to the Siamese king's children, has frequent clashes with the
monarch but eventually comes to exert great influence on him, particularly in creating a more democratic society for his people. The show
marked the fifth collaboration between Richard Rodgers and Oscar Hammerstein II, and their third to run over one thousand performances.
Cast opposite Miss Lawrence (who died in 1952 during the run of the play) was the then little-known Yul Brynner. Since the original
production, Brynner has virtually made the King his personal property. In 1956, he co-starred with Deborah Kerr in the Fox movie version
directed by Walter Lang. Twenty years later, by now solo starred, he began touring in a new stage production which played New York in 1977
with Constance Towers as Anna, and London in 1979 with Virginia McKenna as Anna. Brynner resumed touring in 1981 and, by the time of
his death had given over 4,000 performances as King Rama IV. A critically acclaimed new Broadway production opened in 1996.

## KISMET

MUSIC AND LYRICS: Robert Wright and George Forrest based on music by Alexander Borodin
BOOK: Charles Lederer and Luther Davis  PRODUCER: Charles Lederer  DIRECTOR: Albert Marre
CHOREOGRAPHER: Jack Cole  MAJOR PERFORMERS: Alfred Drake, Doretta Morrow, Joan Diener, Richard Kiley, Beatrice Kraft
OPENED: 12/3/53        THEATER: Ziegfeld        PERFORMANCES: 583

The story of *Kismet* was adapted from Edward Knoblock's play first presented in New York in 1911 as a vehicle for Otis Skinner. The music of
*Kismet* was adapted from themes by Alexander Borodin first heard in such works as the "Polovtsian Dances" ("He's In Love," "Stranger In
Paradise") and "In The Steppes Of Central Asia" ("Sands Of Time"). In the musical, the action occurs within a twenty-four-hour period from
dawn to dawn in and around ancient Baghdad, where a Public Poet (Alfred Drake) assumes the identity of Hajj the beggar and gets into all sorts
of Arabian Nights adventures. At the end of the day, he is elevated to the position of Emir of Baghdad and his daughter Marsinah (Doretta
Morrow) weds the handsome young Caliph (Richard Kiley).  The film version was made by MGM in 1955, with Howard Keel as the Poet, Ann
Blyth as Marsinah, and Vic Damone as the Caliph. Vincente Minnelli directed.

## KISS ME, KATE

MUSIC AND LYRICS: Cole Porter  BOOK: Samuel and Bella Spewack  PRODUCER: Saint Subber and Lemuel Ayers
DIRECTOR: John C. Wilson  CHOREOGRAPHER: Hanya Holm
MAJOR PERFORMERS: Alfred Drake, Patricia Morison, Lisa Kirk. Harold Lang, Jack Diamond, Harry Clark, Annabelle Hill
OPENED: 12/30/48       THEATER: NewCentury       PERFORMANCES: 1,077

The genesis of Cole Porter's longest-running musical occurred in 1935 when producer Saint Subber, then a stagehand for the Theatre Guild's production of Shakespeare's *Taming Of The Shrew*, became aware that its stars Alfred Lunt and Lynn Fontanne, quarreled almost as much in private as did the characters in the play. Years later he offered this parallel story as the basis for a musical comedy to the same writing trio, Porter and the Spewacks, who had already worked on the successful show, *Leave It To Me!* The entire action of Kiss Me, Kate occurs backstage and onstage at Ford's Theatre, Baltimore, during a tryout of a musical version of *The Taming Of The Shrew*. The main plot concerns the egotistical actor-producer Fred Graham (Alfred Drake) and his temperamental ex-wife Lili Vanessi (Patricia Morison) who—like Shakespeare's Petruchio and Kate—fight and make up and eventually demonstrate their enduring affection for each other.  One of the chief features of the score is the skillful way Cole Porter combined his own musical world (in "So In Love," "Too Darn Hot," and "Why Can't You Behave?") with Shakespeare's world ("I Hate Men"), while also tossing off a Viennese waltz parody ("Wunderbar") and a comic view of the Bard's plays ("Brush Up Your Shakespeare"). MGM's 1953 screen version, under George Sidney's direction, had a cast headed by Howard Keel, Kathryn Grayson, and Ann Miller.

## KNICKERBOCKER HOLIDAY

MUSIC AND LYRICS: Kurt Weill and Maxwell Anderson  BOOK: Maxwell Anderson  PRODUCER: The Playwrights' Company
DIRECTOR: Joshua Logan  CHOREOGRAPHER: Carl Randall and Edwin Denby
MAJOR PERFORMERS: Walter Huston, Ray Middleton, Jeanne Madden, Richard Kollmar
OPENED: 10/19/38       THEATER: Ethel Barrymore       PERFORMANCES: 168

In spite of its relatively short run, *Knickerbocker Holiday* is considered a significant milestone in the development of American Musical Theatre. In one of the first musicals to use an historical subject to comment on contemporary political problems, its anti-fascist theme pitted democracy against totalitarianism in its retelling of the reign of Gov. Stuyvesant in New Amsterdam in 1647. The story tells how Gov. Stuyvesant (Walter Huston) intervenes on behalf of an independent and troublesome knife sharpener, Brom Broeck (Richard Kollmar) who has been arbitrarily selected by the council to be executed on a trumped up charge, mainly because they had no one to hang. When the father of Tina, (Jeanne Madden), Brom's true love, offers his daughter's hand in marriage to the governor, Stuyvesant reveals his feelings about love and growing old in the touching "September Song." The reactionary governor proceeds to abolish whatever freedoms the town had previously enjoyed, and when Brom protests, throws him in jail. But Brom, the freedom loving "first American" escapes and steals the Governor's intended bride.  Nelson Eddy and Charles Coburn starred in the 1944 UA film version, which Harry Joe Brown directed.

## LA CAGE AUX FOLLES

MUSIC AND LYRICS: Jerry Herman  BOOK: Harvey Fierstein  PRODUCER: Allan Carr, Kenneth Greenblatt, Marvin Krauss,
DIRECTOR: Arthur Laurents Steward Lane, James M. Nederlander, Martin Richards  CHOREOGRAPHER: Scott Salmon
MAJOR PERFORMERS: George Hearn, Gene Barry, Elizabeth Parrish, Jay Garner, William Thomas Jr.
OPENED: 8/21/83       THEATER: Palace       PERFORMANCES: 1,761

The successful French play and film, about Georges, the owner of a gay night club in Cannes and Albin, his chief attraction, spawned Broadway's first musical dealing with a homosexual relationship. The book's conflict arises, when the impresario's son (the result of a youthful indiscretion) wants his father to meet his fiancee and her straightlaced parents, and Georges is faced with the dilemma of what to do with Albin. With such songs as "The Best Of Times," "La Cage Aux Folles," and "Song on the Sand," the show revived the career of composer-lyricist Jerry Herman (his last hit had been *Mame*, seventeen years before) and won acclaim for its stars, George Hearn (Albin) and Gene Barry (Georges).

## LADIES FIRST

MUSIC AND LYRICS: A. Baldwin Sloane and Harry B. Smith; George and Ira Gershwin  BOOK: Harry B. Smith
PRODUCER: H.H. Frazee  DIRECTOR: Frank Smithson
MAJOR PERFORMERS: Nora Bayes, William Kent, Irving Fisher, Clarence Nordstrom
OPENED: 10/24/18       THEATER: Broadhurst       PERFORMANCES: 164

"The Real American Folk Song (Is a Rag)" was the first George and Ira Gershwin collaboration to be sung in a Broadway musical. George, then primarily a pianist, had been signed to accompany Nora Bayes in a scene in *Ladies First* and, during the try out in Trenton, New Jersey, he managed to convince the singer to include the song in her performance. Gershwin did not remain in the show, but "The Real American Folk Song" did, at least through the first eight weeks of the Broadway run. It was largely forgotten until 1959 when Ella Fitzgerald recorded it in an album of Gershwin songs.

## LADY IN THE DARK

MUSIC AND LYRICS: Kurt Weill and Ira Gershwin  BOOK: Moss Hart  PRODUCER: Sam H. Harris
DIRECTOR: Hassard Short and Moss Hart  CHOREOGRAPHER: Albertina Rasch
MAJOR PERFORMERS: Gertrude Lawrence, Bert Lytell, MacDonald Carey, Victor Mature, Danny Kaye
OPENED: 1/23/41       THEATER: Alvin       PERFORMANCES: 467

Although dreams had long been employed as a theatrical device, Moss Hart was the first to write a musical play dealing with their psychoanalytic implications. An austere and businesslike Liza Elliot (Gertrude Lawrence), editor of a successful fashion magazine, has been bothered by her dreams and visits a psychoanalyst. Her four haunting dreams revolve around four men: Kendall Nesbitt (Bert Lytell), her married lover who aided her rise to editor; Randy Curtis (Victor Mature), a glamorous but shallow Hollywood star; Russell Paxton (Danny Kaye), the magazine's effeminate and zany photographer; and most importantly, Charlie Johnson (MacDonald Carey), the magazine's crusty advertising manager. In relating her dreams, Liza finally comes to understand that all her decisions in life were made because of her father's rejection. With the exception of "My Ship", the musical numbers were sung only during the elaborate dream sequences Liza describes to her doctor.  Ginger Rogers and Ray Milland starred in the 1944 Paramount film version under the director of Mitchell Leisen.

## LEAVE IT TO ME

MUSIC AND LYRICS: Cole Porter  BOOK: Bella and Samuel Spewack  PRODUCER: Vinton Freedley
DIRECTOR: Samuel Spewack  CHOREOGRAPHER: Robert Alton
MAJOR PERFORMERS: William Gaxton, Victor Moore, Sophie Tucker, Mary Martin Edward H. Robins, George Tobias, Gene Kelly
OPENED: 11/9/38        THEATER: Imperial       PERFORMANCES: 291

With a book loosely related to their own play, Clear All Wires, Bella and Samuel Spewack came up with a spoof of Communism and U.S. diplomacy that provided comedian Victor Moore with one of his meatiest roles and introduced Broadway to the showstopping charms of Mary Martin (singing Cole Porter's "My Heart Belongs To Daddy"). Moore's part was that of mild-mannered Alonzo P. "Stinky" Goodhue, who is unwillingly appointed Ambassador to the Soviet Union because his ambitious wife (Sophie Tucker) has contributed handsomely to President Roosevelt's re-election campaign. With the aid of foreign correspondent Buckley Joyce Thomas (William Gaxton), Goodhue does everything he can to be recalled, but all of his blunders only succeed in making him a hero. Finally he introduces a plan to ensure world peace, which no one wants, and Stinky is soon happily on his way back to Kansas.

## LES MISÉRABLES

MUSIC: Claude-Michel Schönberg  LYRICS: Herbert Kretzmer  CONCEPTION: Alain Boublil & Claude-Michel Schönberg
ORIGINAL FRENCH TEXT: Alain Boublil & Jean-Marc Natel  ADAPATION: Trevor Nunn & John Caird
PRODUCER: Cameron Mackintosh  DIRECTOR: Trevor Nunn & John Caird  CHOREOGRAPHER: Kate Flatt
MAJOR PERFORMERS: Colm Wilkinson, Terrence Mann, Randy Graff, Michale Maguire, Leo Burmester, Frances Ruggelle, David Bryant, Judy Kuhn, Jennifer Butt, Braden Danner
OPENED: 3/12/87        THEATER: Broadway       PERFORMANCES: over 4,100 (still running 6/1/97)

Victor Hugo's monumental romantic novel is the basis of the show of the same name.  The epic story presents the downtrodden and their struggle to survive in 19th-century France against the obstacles inherent in a class structured society.  The show was originally written in 1979 and presented in Paris on a relatively small scale.  Reconceived and blown into a full-fledged pop opera, it opened in Lonodon in 1985.  As unlikely a route as it was (the last musical of French origin had been Irma la Douce in 1960), the show became one of the most phenomenal successes in Broadway history, with extensive international touring.  It also inaugurated an international approach to production that had before that time not been seen, with companies opening  in different languages around the world.

## LET'S FACE IT

MUSIC AND LYRICS: Cole Porter  BOOK: Herbert and Dorothy Fields  PRODUCER: Vinton Freedley
DIRECTOR: Edgar MacGregor  CHOREOGRAPHER: Charles Walters
MA.JOR PERFORMERS: Danny Kaye, Eve Arden, Vivian Vance, Mary Jane Walsh, Benny Baker, Nanette Fabray, Edith Meiser, Sunnie O'Dea, Jack Williams
OPENED: 10/29/41       THEATER: Imperial       PERFORMANCES: 547

Producer Vinton Freedley got the idea for Let's Face It when he read a newspaper account about a number of patriotic ladies who, anxious to improve the morale of World War II draftees, had written to army camps requesting permission to entertain the men in their homes. Using the rough outline of the Russell Medcraft-Norma Mitchell play, The Cradle Snatchers, as foundation, the musical was about three Southampton matrons, having grown suspicious of their husbands' frequent hunting trips, hire three rookies from a local army camp for an evening of fun. Comic complications arise when the husbands and their girls—as well as the soldiers' neglected girlfriends—show up at the party. After Milton Berle and Martha Raye turned down leading roles, their parts went to Danny Kaye (his first time as a Broadway star) and Eve Arden. Miss Arden repeated her role in the 1943 Paramount film version with Bob Hope and Betty Hutton. Sidney Lanfield directed.

## LITTLE MARY SUNSHINE

MUSIC AND LYRICS: Rick Besoyan  BOOK: Rick Besoyan  PRODUCER: Howard Barker, Cynthia Baer, Robert Chambers
DIRECTOR: Ray I larrison and Rick Besoyan  CHOREOGRAPHER: Ray Harrison
MAJOR PERFORMERS: Eileen Brennan, William Graham, John McMartin, Elizabeth Parrish
OPENED: 11/18/59       THEATER: Orpheum       PERFORMANCES: 1,143

*Little Mary Sunshine*, a witty, melodious takeoff of the *Naughty Marietta-Rose-Marie* school of operetta, was initially presented at a night club some three years before the long-running production opened Off Broadway. The story is set in the Colorado Rockies early in the century, and deals with the romance between the mincing heroine (played by Eileen Brennan) and stalwart Capt. Big Jim Warrington (William Graham), who saves his beloved from the clutches of a treacherous Indian just in time for their "Colorado Love Call" duet. The musical marked the professional debut of composer-lyricist-librettist Rick Besoyan, who died in 1970 at the age of 45.


## LITTLE ME

MUSIC AND LYRICS: Cy Coleman and Carolyn Leigh
BOOK: Neil Simon (based on the novel by Patrick Dennis)  PRODUCER: Cy Feuer and Ernest Martin
DIRECTOR: Cy Feuer and Ernest Martin  CHOREOGRAPHER: Bob Fosse
MA JOR PERFORMERS: Sid Caesar, Virginia Martin, Nancy Andrews and Swen Swenson
OPENED: 1/17/62       THEATER: Lunt-Fontanne       PERFORMANCES: 257

A hilarious parody of star autobiographies, *Little Me* follows the rise to stardom of actress Belle Poitrine through a series of comic affairs with suspiciously convenient endings. Although often noted for the gimmick of having several characters portrayed by one actor, the show's witty book and lyrics, combined with a sparkling score, compare favorably with the best of Broadway's musical comedies—and make the show as fresh today as when it was first presented.


## A LITTLE NIGHT MUSIC

MUSIC AND LYRICS: Stephen Sondheim  BOOK: Hugh Wheeler
PRODUCER: Harold Prince  DIRECTOR: Harold Prince  CHOREOGRAPHER: Patricia Birch
MAJOR PERFORMERS: Glynis Johns, Len Cariou, Hermione Gingold, Victoria Mallory, Laurence Guittard, Patricia Elliott, D. Jamin-Bartlett
OPENED: 2/25/73       THEATER: Shubert       PERFORMANCES: 601

Based on Ingmar Bergman's 1955 film, *Smiles of a Summer Night*, *A Little Night Music* could claim two musical distinctions: the entire Stephen Sondheim score was composed in 3/4 time (or multiples thereof) and it contained, in "Send In The Clowns," the biggest song hit that Sondheim ever wrote. The musical took a somewhat jaded look at a group of well-to-do Swedes at the turn of the century, among them a lawyer, Fredrik Egerman (Len Cariou), his virginal child bride, Anne (Victoria Mallory), his former mistress, the actress Desiree Armfeldt (Glynis Johns), Desiree's current lover, the aristocratic Count Carl-Magnus Malcolm (Laurence Guittard), and the count's suicidal wife, Charlotte (Patricia Elliott). Eventually, the proper partners are sorted out at a weekend at the country house of Desiree's brother, a former concubine of European nobility (Hermione Gingold). A film version was released by New World Pictures in 1978, with Elizabeth Taylor (Desiree), Len Cariou, Diana Rigg (Charlotte), and Hermione Gingold. The director was Harold Prince and the locale was switched to Vienna.


## LOST IN THE STARS

MUSIC AND LYRICS: Kurt Weill and Maxwell Anderson BOOK: Maxwell Anderson
PRODUCER: The Playwrights' Company  DIRECTOR: Rouben Mamoulian
MAJOR PERFORMERS: Todd Duncan, Leslie Banks, Inez Matthews, Warren Coleman, Sheila Guyse, Herbert Coleman
OPENED: 10/30/49       THEATER: Music Box       PERFORMANCES: 281

Kurt Weill's last Broadway musical (his second in collaboration with Maxwell Anderson) was written to convey "a message of hope that people, through a personal approach, will solve whatever racial problems exist." In the story, adapted from Alan Paton's novel, *Cry, The Beloved Country*, the action is set in and around Johannesburg, South Africa. Absalom Kumalo, the errant son of a black minister, Stephen Kumalo, accidentally kills a white man in a robbery attempt and is condemned to hang. The tragedy, however, leads to a sympathetic bond between Stephen and James Jarvis, the dead man's father, which gives some indication that understanding between the races can be achieved in the land of apartheid. A screen version, presented by Ely Landau's American Film Theatre, was shown in 1974 with a cast headed by Brock Peters and Melba Moore. It was directed by Daniel Mann.


## LOVE LIFE

MUSIC AND LYRICS: Kurt Weill and Alan Jay Lerner BOOK: Alan Jay Lerner
PRODUCER: Cheryl Crawford  DIRECTOR: Elia Kazan
CHOREOGRAPHER: Michael Kidd  MAJOR PERFORMERS: Nanette Fabray, Ray Middleton
OPENED: 10/7/48       THEATER: 46th Street       PERFORMANCES: 252

Temporarily disassociated from his partnership with Frederick Loewe, Alan Jay Lerner collaborated with Kurt Weill on this musical allegory. Love Life, termed by its authors as simply "a vaudeville," chronicled the fluctuations of a single marriage through 150 years of American History, showing how tensions of modern life made it increasingly difficult for the couple to maintain their matrimonial equilibrium. The two most enduring songs in the score were "Green-Up Time" and "Here I'll Stay."

## MACK AND MABEL

MUSIC AND LYRICS: Jerry Herman  BOOK: Michael Stewart  PRODUCER: David Merrick
DIRECTOR: Gower Champion  CHOREOGRAPHER: Gower Champion
MAJOR PERFORMERS: Robert Preston, Bernadette Peters, Lisa Kirk, James Mitchell and Jerry Dodge
OPENED: 10/6/74        THEATER: Majestic            PERFORMANCES: 65

Robert Preston and Bernadette Peters gave expert performances in this musical based on the romance of Mack Sennett and Mabel Normand, who Sennett transformed from Brooklyn waitress to film star. The show was characterized by the sort of clever and imaginative production numbers which were Gower Champion's trademark. The ballads, "I Won't Send Roses" and "Time Heals Everything" were standouts in one of Jerry Herman's best scores.


## MAME

MUSIC AND LYRICS: Jerry Herman  BOOK: Jerome Lawrence and Robert E. Lee
PRODUCER: Robert Fryer, Lawrence Carr, Sylvia and Joseph Harris  DIRECTOR: Gene Sachs  CHOREOGRAPHER: Onna White
MAJOR PERFORMERS: Angela Lansbury, Beatrice Arthur, Jane Connell, Willard Waterman, Frankie Michaels and Jerry Lanning
OPENED: 5/24/66        THEATER: Winter Garden        PERFORMANCES: 1,508

Ten years after premiering their hilarious comedy based on Patrick Dennis' fictional account of his free-wheeling Auntie Mame, playwrights Lawrence & Lee joined forces with songwriter Jerry Herman to transform their play into a lively hit musical. Angela Lansbury, after years of first-rate stage and screen performances, finally achieved her long-deserved stardom in the title role, and went on to become the first lady of Broadway musical theatre. A film version, starring Lucille Ball and Robert Preston, was released in 1974.


## MAN OF LA MANCHA

MUSIC: Mitch Leigh  LYRICS: Joe Darion  BOOK: Dale Wasserman
PRODUCERS: Albert Selden & Hal James  DIRECTOR: Albert Marre  CHOREOGRAPHER: Jack Cole
MAJOR PERFORMERS: Richard Kiley, Joan Diener, Irving Jacobson, Ray Middleton, Robert Rounseville, Jon Cypher, Gerrianne Raphael
OPENED: 11/22/65        THEATER: ANTA Washington Square        PERFORMANCES: 2,328

Based on Dale Wasserman's television play, I, Don Quixote, the musical was one of the surprise hits of the 1960s. After playing Off-Broadway for a year and a half, it successfully transferred to the Martin Beck, and ran another 4 years.  The title character is Cervantes' great, demented knight, and his pursuit of the ideals of outdated chivalry.  He places on a pedestal the servant girl Aldonza, calling her his Dulcinea, and though she first finds him foolish, is moved and won over by his sincerity.  The show produced the classic song "The Impossible Dream." A film version, largely unseen by the public, was released in 1972 starring Peter O'Toole and Sophia Loren.


## MARTIN GUERRE

MUSIC: Claude-Michel Schönberg  LYRICS: Edward Hardy & Stephen Clark; additional lyrics by Herbert Kretzmer & Alain Boublil
BOOK: Alain Boublil & Claude-Michel Schönberg
OPENED: London, 1996; at this writing the show, though intended for Broadway, has not yet run in New York

The basic true story dates from 1560 in Toulouse, actually based on a court case. There have been several accounts of the tale in the form of published histories, novels, and operas. The two most prominent previous treatments of the tale are the 1941 novel by Janet Louis The Wife of Martin Guerre, and the 1982 film Le Retour de Martin Guerre (The Return of Martin Guerre). The musical takes place in 16th century France, torn apart by the warring of the Catholics and Protestants. The complex story involves one man being mistaken for another who has been gone for seven years.


## MATA HARI

MUSIC AND LYRICS: Edward Thomas and Martin Charnin  BOOK: Jerome Coopersmith
PRODUCER: David Merrick  DIRECTOR: Vincente Minnelli  CHOREOGRAPHER: Jack Cole
MAJOR PERFORMERS: Marisa Mell, Parnell Roberts, Martha Schlamme, Blythe Danner
OPENED: 11/18/67        THEATER: National, Washington        PERFORMANCES: Never opened on Broadway

The alluring dancer, Mata Hari, whose sultry charms made strong men weak and who was executed as a German spy in World War I, won certified immortality when Greta Garbo played her part in the 1931 MGM talkie. Cast in the role in the musical was the Austrian actress-singer Marisa Mell, with Parnell Roberts (of television's Bonanza) playing opposite as the romantic interest. Vincente Minnelli, who had been away from Broadway for almost thirty years, was the director. The work, however, suffered from differing viewpoints (the writers wanted it to be an anti-war polemic, the director did not), and it was withdrawn before reaching New York. Late in 1968, retitled Ballad for a Firing Squad, the musical was remounted on a more modest scale, with Renata Vaselle and James Hurst in the leading roles. Still unable to find an audience, it lasted a week at Greenwich Village's Theatre de Lys.

## ME AND JULIET

MUSIC AND LYRICS: Richard Rodgers and Oscar Hammerstein II  BOOK: Oscar Hammerstein II
PRODUCER: Richard Rodgers and Oscar Hammerstein II  DIRECTOR: George Abbott  CHOREOGRAPHER: Robert Alton
MAJOR PERFORMERS: Bill Hayes, Isabel Bigley, Mark Dawson, Ray Walston, Joan McCracken, George S. Irving
OPENED: 5/28/53          THEATER: Majestic          PERFORMANCES: 358

*Me and Juliet* was Rodgers and Hammerstein's Valentine to show business, with its action—in *Kiss Me, Kate* fashion—taking place both backstage in a theatre and onstage during the performance of a play. Here the tale concerns a romance between a singer in the chorus (Isabel Bigley) and the assistant stage manager (Bill Hayes) whose newfound bliss is seriously threatened by the jealous electrician (Mark Dawson). A comic romantic subplot involves the stage manager (Ray Walston) and the principal dancer (Joan McCracken). The melody of the show's best-remembered song, "No Other Love," had previously been composed by Rodgers as background music for the "Beneath the Southern Cross" episode in the NBC-TV documentary series, *Victory at Sea*.

## ME AND MY GIRL

MUSIC: Noel Gay  LYRICS: Douglas Furber and others  BOOK: Arthur Rose & Douglas Furber, revised by Stephen Fry
PRODUCER: Richard Armitage, Terry Allen Kramer, James Nederlander, Stage Promotions Ltd.
DIRECTOR: Mike Ockrent  CHOREOGRAPHER: Gillian Gregory
MAJOR PERFORMERS: Robert Lindsay, Maryann Plunkett, George S. Irving, Jane Connell, Jane Summerhays, Nick Ullett, Timothy Jerome, Thomas Toner, Justine Jonston, Elizabeth Larner
OPENED: 8/10/86          THEATER: Marquis          PERFORMANCES: 1,412

This charming, light-weight English musical comedy dates from the 1930s, and opened in 1985 to great success in London in revival. Though some worried that it was just too English to succeed on Broadway, succeed it did., opening the brand new Marquis Theater. Robert Lindsay scored a triumph as the singing-dancing comedian with a light touch in the role of Bill Snibson. The character had originated in a 1935 show *Twenty to One*. In 1937, enamoured of the charcter, the writers and the actor who played him (Lupino Lane) built a new show around Snibson, which was *Me and My Girl*. The highlights of the show were the "Lambeth Walk" and "Leaning on a Lamp-Post."

## THE ME NOBODY KNOWS

MUSIC AND LYRICS: Gary William Friedman and Will Holt  BOOK: Edited by Stephen M. Joseph  PRODUCER: Jeff Britton
DIRECTOR: Robert H. Livingston  CHOREOGRAPHER: Patricia Birch
MAJOR PERFORMERS: Hattie Winston, Northern Calloway, Paul Mace, Carl Thoma
OPENED: 5/18/70          THEATER: Orpheum (Off Broadway) Helen Hayes (Broadway)
PERFORMANCES: 208 (Off Broadway) 378 (Broadway)

Essentially a compilation of songs, *The Me Nobody Knows* was based on a book of the same title containing writings by young people between the ages of seven and eighteen who live in the underprivileged sections of New York. With the writings converted into songs by Gary William Friedman and Will Holt, the evening offered a multitude of voices expressing the fears, frustrations, and loneliness of alienated children living in an affluent world. After its Off-Broadway engagement, *The Me Nobody Knows* was transferred to Broadway on December 18, 1970, and achieved an even longer run.

## MERLIN

MUSIC AND LYRICS: Elmer Bernstein and Don Black  BOOK: Richard Levinson and William Link
PRODUCER: Ivan Reitman, Columbia Pictures Stage  DIRECTOR: Ivan Reitman Productions Inc., Marvin Krauss, James M. Nederlander
CHOREOGRAPHER: Christopher Chadman, Billy Wilson
MAJOR PERFORMERS: Doug Henning, Chita Rivera, Edmund Lyndeck, Rebecca Wright
OPENED: 2/13/83          THEATER: Mark Hellinger          PERFORMANCES: 199

After a lengthy and successful engagement in the intimate musical, *The Magic Show*, illusionist Doug Henning returned to Broadway in a lavish musical *Merlin* in which he played the legendary sorcerer in the days just before the Arthurian age. Though the show proved that bigger did not necessarily make better, it again enabled Henning to demonstrate his incredible skill in a production that was one of the few legitimate entertainments of the season with special appeal to children.

## MERRILY WE ROLL ALONG

MUSIC AND LYRICS: Stephen Sondheim  BOOK: George Furth  PRODUCER: Lord Grade, Martin Starger.
DIRECTOR: Harold Prince  Robert Fryer, Harold Prince  CHOREOGRAPHER: Larry Fuller
MAJOR PERFORMERS: Jim Walton, Ann Morrison, Lonny Price
OPENED: 11/16/81          THEATER: Alvin          PERFORMANCES: 16

Founded on the George S. Kaufman-Moss Hart play of the same name, *Merrily We Roll Along* had a highly innovative concept: it told its tale backwards—or from the present when Franklln Shepard (Jim Walton) is a rich, famous, but morally compromised film producer and composer to his idealistic youth when he graduated from high school. Though daring and original, *Merrily We Roll Along* proved too much of a musical morality play, and represented the only out-and-out commercial failure with which composer/lyricist Sondheim and director Prince were associated together. The score remains alive, however, and there are productions of the musical from time to time; a new production opened in New York in 1994.

## THE MERRY WIDOW

MUSIC AND LYRICS: Franz Lehar and Adrian Ross  BOOK: Basil Hood  PRODUCER: Henry W. Savage  DIRECTOR: George Marion
MAJOR PERFORMERS: Ethel Jackson, Donald Brian, Lois Ewell, R.E. Graham, William Weedon, Fred Frear
OPENED: 10/21/07          THEATER: New Amsterdam          PERFORMANCES: 416

The epitome of the swirling, melodious, romantic Viennese operetta, *The Merry Widow* was first performed in 1905 under the title *Die Lustige Witwe*, with a libretto by Victor Leon and Leo Stein. Its initial English-language version opened at Daly's Theatre, London, where it ran for 778 performances. This was the text that was used for the New York production, which was so acclaimed that it even prompted the introduction of Merry Widow hats, gowns, corsets, and cigarettes. The story, based on a French play *L'Attaché d'Ambassade*, is set in Paris and concerns the efforts of the ambassador of the imaginary kingdom of Marsovia to get his attache, Prince Danilo, to marry the wealthy widow, Sonya Sadoya, so that she might contribute to the country's dwindling finances. Though he balks at being a fortune-hunter, Danilo finds himself falling in love and he eventually proposes marriage—but only after Sonya has led him to believe she is penniless. The most successful Broadway revival was shown in 1943, with Jan Keipura and Marta Eggerth. It played the Majestic Theatre for 322 performances. Three Hollywood screen versions were made, all at MGM. In 1925, it was filmed as a silent directed by Erich Von Stroheim, with John Gilbert and Mae Murray in the leads. In 1934, with new lyrics by Lorenz Hart, it was remade by director Ernst Lubisch and co-starred Jeanette MacDonald and Maurice Chevalier. The third version, in 1952, had lyrics by Paul Francis Webster, and a cast headed by Lana Turner and Fernando Lamas. Curtis Bernhardt was the director.


## MEXICAN HAYRIDE

MUSIC AND LYRICS: Cole Porter  BOOK: Herbert and Dorothy Fields
PRODUCER: Michael Todd  DIRECTOR: Hassard Short, John Kennedy  CHOREOGRAPHER: Paul Haakon
MAJOR PERFORMERS: Bobby Clark, June Havoc, George Givot, Wilbur Evans, Luba Malina, Corinna Mura, Paul Haakon,
Edith Meiser, Bill Callahan
OPENED: 1/28/44          THEATER: Winter Garden          PERFORMANCES: 481

One of Broadway's biggest wartime attractions, *Mexican Hayride* owed its success largely to its appealing Latin-flavored score by Cole Porter (including the hit ballad, "I Love You"), its eye-dazzling decor, its rows of long-stemmed show girls, and the antics of a mad mountebank named Bobby Clark. As Joe Bascom, alias Humphrey Fish, Clark played a numbers racketeer on the lam in Mexico where, at a bull fight, he is mistakenly selected as the good-will ambassador for a week. Alternately hailed by the populace and trailed by the police, Bascom must assume a number of loony disguises, including that of a mariachi flute player and a tortilla-vending, cigar-chomping Indian squaw. Abbott and Costello were co-starred in the 1948 Universal movie version, directed by Charles Barton, in which nary a note of Cole Porter music was heard.


## MILK AND HONEY

MUSIC AND LYRICS: Jerry Herman  BOOK: Don Appell
PRODUCER: Gerard Oestreicher  DIRECTOR: Albert Marre  CHOREOGRAPHER: Donald Saddler
MAJOR PERFORMERS: Robert Weede, Mimi Benzell, Molly Picon & Tommy Rall
OPENED: 10/10/61          THEATER: Martin Beck          PERFORMANCES: 543

*Milk and Honey* was composer/lyricist Jerry Herman's first Broadway show and his first Broadway hit. Relating the ill-fated romance of a middle-aged businessman and a younger woman who cannot overcome her qualms about a liaison with a married man, the show was carried less by its plot than by the spirit and exhuberance of the people of Israel. Molly Picon made an important contribution as the leader of a group of American widows on a husband-hunting tour of Europe. The show was given a new production in New York in 1994.


## MINNIE'S BOYS

MUSIC AND LYRICS: Larry Grossman and Hal Hackaday  BOOK: Arthur Marx and Robert Fisher
PRODUCER: Arthur Whitelaw, Max J. Brown, Byron Goldman  DIRECTOR: Stanley Prager  CHOREOGRAPHER: Marc Breaux
MAJOR PERFORMERS: Shelley Winters, Amy Freeman, Mort Marshall, Lewis J. Stadlen, Roland Winters, Daniel Fortus,
Irwin Pearl, Alvin Kupperman
OPENED: 3/26/70          THEATER: Imperial          PERFORMANCES: 80

Minnie's boys were the Marx Brothers—Groucho, Harpo, Chico, Zeppo, and the quickly eliminated Gummo—and the musical was concerned with the ways Mama Marx (Shelley Winters) pushed and shoved her brood into show business. The musical ended with the team, after many false starts, finally assuming the charcteristic trade marks (Groucho's mustache and cigar, Harpo's wig and "dumb" act, Chico's cone-shaped hat and Italian dialect) that would later help win them immortality on the screen. The book was co-authored by Groucho's son, Arthur, and Groucho himself served as consultant.

## MISS SAIGON

MUSIC: Claude-Michel Schönberg
LYRICS: Richard Maltby, Jr. & Alain Boublil, adapted from the original French lyrics by Alain Boublil, additional material by Richard Maltby, Jr.
PRODUCER: Cameron Mackintosh DIRECTOR: Nicholas Hytner MUSICAL STAGING: Bob Avian
MAJOR PERFORMERS: Jonathan Pryce, Lea Salonga, Hinton Battle, Willy Falk, Barry K. Bernal, Liz Callaway, Kam Cheeng
OPENED: 4/11/91          THEATER: Broadway          PERFORMANCES; over 2,500 (still running 6/1/97)

The team that brought us *Les Misérables* were back on the boards with *Miss Saigon*, loosely adapted from the *Madame Butterfly* story but updated to Saigon during the Viet-man war. The story has an American soldier falling in love with Kim, a Vietnamese native. The soldier is sent home, and Kim is left pregnant. The soldier goes home and marries, but is tormented by the memories. A few years later he returns to find Kim, who want s him to take their son back to the U.S. with him. She abandons the boy by committing suicide, forcing Chris to take him. The production is famous for a lifesize helicopter that rescues Chris as Saigon is falling to the communists. Before it opened, there was a highly publicized controversy between Actors Equity and the production, the union insisting on Asian actors representing Asian characters on stage. Eventually, after polling its members, the union backed down, and the show, which had threatened not to open in the face of the labor challenges, went ahead as scheduled.

## THE MOST HAPPY FELLA

MUSIC AND LYRICS: Frank Loesser BOOK: Frank Loesser PRODUCER: Kermit Bloomgarden and Lynn Loesser
DIRECTOR: Joseph Arlthony CHOREOGRAPHER: Dania Krupska
MAJOR PERFORMERS: Robert Weede, Jo Sullivan, Art Lund, Susan Johnson, Shorty Long
OPENED: 5/3/56          THEATER: Imperial          PERFORMANCES: 676

Adapted from Sidney Howard's Pulitzer Prize-winning play, *They Knew What They Wanted*, *The Most Happy Fella* was a particularly ambitious work for the Broadway theatre, with over thirty separate musical numbers including arias, duets, trios, quartets, choral pieces, and recitatives. Robust, emotional expressions (such as "Joey, Joey, Joey") were interspersed with more traditional specialty numbers (such as "Big 'D' and "Standing on the Corner"), though in the manner of an opera, the program credits did not list individual selections. In the story, set in California's Napa Valley, an aging vinyard owner (played by opera singer Robert Weede, in his first Broadway role) proposes to a waitress, Rosabella (Jo Sullivan), by mail and she accepts. Rosabella is so upset to find Tony old and fat that, on their wedding night, she allows herself to be seduced by Joe, the handsome ranch foreman (Art Lund). Once he discovers that his wife is to have another man's child, Tony threatens to kill Joe, but there is a reconciliation and the vintner even offers to raise the child as his own. A revival of *The Most Happy Fella* played on Broadway in 1979, with Giorgio Tozzi in the leading role. It ran 52 performances. Another Broadway revival opened in 1992, running for 229 performances.

## MR. WONDERFUL

MUSIC AND LYRICS: Jerry Bock, Larry Holofcener and George Weiss BOOK: Joseph Stein and Will Glickman
PRODUCER: Jule Styne and George Gilbert DIRECTOR: Jack Donohue CHOREOGRAPHER: Jack Donohue
MAJOR PERFORMERS: Sammy Davis Jr., Jack Carter, Pat Marshall, Olga James, Chita Rivera, Sammy Davis Sr., Will Mastin
OPENED: 3/22/56          THEATER: Broadway          PERFORMANCES: 383

The first book musical with a score by composer Jerry Bock (who would later write music for *Fiorello!* and *Fiddler On The Roof*), *Mr. Wonderful* was little more than a showcase for the multiple talents of Sammy Davis Jr., here appearing with his father and uncle as lead member of the Will Mastin Trio. Boasting two substantial song hits—the title song and "Too Close For Comfort"—the show spotlighted the career of Charlie Welch from appearances in small-time night spots to his overnight smash at the Palm Club in Miami Beach.

## MUSIC BOX REVUE

MUSIC & LYRICS: Irving Berlin SKETCHES: Miscellaneous writers PRODUCER: Sam H. Harris
DIRECTORS: Hassard Short, William Collier CHOREOGRAPHERS: Bert French, I. Tarasoff
MAJOR PERFORMERS: William Collier, Wilda Bennett, Paul Frawley, Sam Bernard, Ivy Sawyer, Joseph Santley, Florence Moore, Brox Sisters, Chester Hale, Irving Berlin, Miriam Hopkins
OPENED: 9/22/21          THEATER: Music Box          PERFORMANCES: 440

With new editions in 1922, 1923 and 1924, *Music Box Revue* was the only show of its kind designed to feature the work of one songwriter. The series opened the new theater by the same name. The first edition was lavishly produced; subsequent editions became more modest, though certainly successful. At the time the revues at the *Music Box* seemed a tasteful yet lively alternative to the *Ziegfeld Follies*. This was one of Berlin's richest periods as a theater composer, and the Music Box Revues featured such new material as "Everybody Step," "Say It With Music," "Lady of the Evening," "What'll I Do?", and "All Alone."

## MUSIC IN THE AIR

MUSIC: Jerome Kern LYRICS & BOOK: Oscar Hammerstein II
PRODUCER: Peggy Fears (A.C. Blumenthal uncredited) DIRECTORS: Jerome Kern & Oscar Hammerstein II
MAJOR PERFORMERS: Reinald Werrenrath, Natalie Hall, Tullio Carminati, Katherine Carrington, Al Shean, Walter Slezak, Nicholas Joy, Marjorie Main
OPENED: 11/8/32          THEATER: Alvin          PERFORMANCES: 342

A follow up to the graceful musical-operetta *The Cat and the Fiddle* (with lyrics by Otto Harbach), *Music in the Air* was also set in Europe, with a story about producing an operetta. And like its predecessor, the show integrates character and song in a charming manner. Set in Germany, the story is of two Bavarian youths (Sieglinde and Karl) who hike to Munich to help Sieglinde's father try to get his new song published. They meet an operetta star and become involved in a theatrical production. The diva walks out and Sieglinde takes over—and flops! (this is not *42nd Street*). The star comes back and Sieglinde returns to her mountain village with her dreams shattered. The score is highly regarded as a neglected masterwork of its genre, showing Kern at his best (along with *Show Boat* and *The Cat and the Fiddle*).

## THE MUSIC MAN

MUSIC, LYRICS & BOOK: Meredith Willson  PRODUCER: Kermit Bloomgarden
DIRECTOR: Morton Da Costa  CHOREOGRAPHER: Onna White
MAJOR PERFORMERS: Robert Preston, Barbara Cook, David Burns, Pert Kelton, Iggie Wolfington, The Buffalo Bills,
Helen Raymond, Eddie Hodges
OPENED: 12/19/57          THEATER: Majestic          PERFORMANCES: 1,375

With *The Music Man*, composer-lyricist-librettist Meredith Willson recaptured the innocent charm of the middle America he knew growing up in an Iowa town. It is the Fourth of July, 1912, in River City, Iowa, and "Professor" Harold Hill, a traveling salesman of musical instruments, has arrived to con the citizens into believing that he can teach the town's children how to play in a marching band. But instead of skipping town before the instruments are to arrive, Hill is persuaded to remain because of the love of a good woman, librarian Marian Paroo. The story ends with the children, though barely able to produce any kind of a recognizable musical sound, being hailed by their proud parents. The show. which took eight years and over thirty rewrites before it was produced on Broadway, marked Willson's auspicious debut in the theatre. It was also the first musical-stage appearance of Robet Preston, playing the role of Harold Hill, who went on to repeat his dynamic performance in the 1962 Warner Bros. screen version. Shirley Jones and Hermione Gingold were also in the movie, which was directed by the original stage director, Morton Da Costa.

## MY FAIR LADY

MUSIC AND LYRICS: Frederick Loewe and Alan Jay Lerner  BOOK: Alan Jay Lerner
PRODUCER: Herman Levin  DIRECTOR: Moss Hart  CHOREOGRAPHER: Hanya Holm
MAJOR PERFORMERS: Rex Harrison, Julie Andrews, Stanley Holloway, Robert Coote, Cathleen Nesbitt, John Michael King,
Christopher Hewett
OPENED: 3/15/56          THEATER: Mark Hellinger          PERFORMANCES: 2,717

The most celebrated musical of the 1950s began as an idea of Hungarian film producer Garbiel Pascal, who devoted the last two years of his life trying to find writers to adapt George Bernard Shaw's play, *Pygmalion*, into a stage musical. The team of Lerner and Loewe also saw the possibilities, particularly when they realized that they could use most of the original dialogue and simply expand the action to include scenes at the Ascot Races and the Embassy Ball. They were also scrupulous in maintaining the Shavian flavor in their songs, most apparent in such pieces as "Get Me To The Church On Time," "Just You Wait," "Why Can't The English?," "Show Me," and "Without You."

Shaw's concern with class distinction and his belief that barriers would fall if all Englishmen would learn to speak properly was conveyed through a story about Eliza Doolittle, (Julie Andrews) a scruffy flower seller in Covent Garden. who takes speech lessons from Prof. Henry Higgins (Rex Harrison) so that she might qualify for the position of a florist in a shop. Eliza succeeds so well that she outgrows her social station and—in a development added by librettist Lerner—even makes Higgins fall in love with her. Though the record was subsequently broken, *My Fair Lady* became the longest running production in Broadway history, remaining for over six and a half years. Two major revivals were mounted in New York. In 1976, the musical ran for 377 performances with Ian Richardson and Christine Andreas as Higgins and Eliza; in 1981, it lasted 119 performances with Rex Harrison, in his original role, and Nancy Ringham. Harrison and Audrey Hepburn (whose singing was dubbed by Marni Nixon) were costarred in the 1964 Warner Bros. movie version, which was directed by George Cukor. A new revival opened on Broadway in 1993, starring Richard Chamberlain.

## THE NERVOUS SET

MUSIC: Tommy Wolf  LYRICS: Fran Landesman
BOOK: Jay Landesman and Theodore J. Flicker (based on the novel by Jay Landesman)
PRODUCER: Robert Lantz  DIRECTOR: Theodore J. Flicker
MAJOR PERFORMERS: Richard Hayes, Tani Seitz, Larry Hagman, Del Close, Gerald Hiken and Thomas Aldredge
OPENED: 5/12/59          THEATER: Henry Miller          PERFORMANCES: 23

*The Nervous Set* offered a '50's Broadway version of that segment of '50's society known as "the beat generation". Unlike the carefree kids of *Grease*, these young adults were shown to have felt opressed and alienated by the rules of American society. Despite its initial success, *The Nervous Set* is very much a product of its time and is rarely revived, although "The Ballad Of The Sad Young Men" is still heard frequently.

## NEW FACES OF 1936

MUSIC AND LYRICS: Miscellaneous writers  BOOK: Sketches by miscellaneous writers
PRODUCER: Leonard Sillman  DIRECTORS: Leonard Sillman, Anton Bundsmann  CHOREOGRAPHER: Ned McGurn
MAJOR PERFORMERS: Imogene Coca, Jack Smart, Helen Craig, Marion Pearce, Billie Haywood, Nancy Noland, Ralph Blane, George Byron
OPENED: 5/19/36          THEATER: Vanderbilt          PERFORMANCES: 193

*New Faces of 1936* was the second of seven talent shows assembled by Leonard Sillman bearing the "New Faces" rubric. As usual with these ventures, the producer had trouble raising the required money—in this case $15,000. His chief backer, Martin Jones, also owned the Vanderbilt Theatre in which the revue was playing, and within three months after the opening he was able to take over artistic control of the show. Trying to hype business, Jones even brought in the veteran Duncan Sisters who had been Broadway headliners since 1924. In addition to this edition, there were versions in 1934, 1942, 1952, 1956, 1962, and 1968. Among faces first seen in these shows were those of Henry Fonda, John Lund, Ronny Graham, Eartha Kitt, Paul Lynde, Carol Lawrence, Maggie Smith, Robert Klein, and Madeline Kahn.

## NINE

MUSIC & LYRICS: Maury Yeston  BOOK: Arthur Kopit, Mario Fratti
PRODUCER: Michel Stuart, Harvey Klaris, Roger Berlin, and others  DIRECTOR: Tommy Tune
CHOREOGRAPHERS: Tommy Tune, Thommie Walsh
MAJOR PERFORMERS: Raul Julia, Karen Akers, Sheely Burch, Taina Elg, Anita Morris, Lilianne Montevecchi, Kathi Moss
OPENED: 5/9/82          THEATER: 46th Street          PERFORMANCES: 732

Tommy Tune's stylized, visually stunning production of *Nine* also revealed a major composer-lyricist in Maury Yeston. The musical is based on Federico Fellini's semi-autobiographical 1963 film *8 1/2*. Guido Contini is an Italian movie director in a mid-life crisis, and is torn between the several women in his life. There are flashbacks to Guido's childhood. Eventually, the 10 year old Guido advises the 40 year old Guido on how to get on with his life. A London production opened in 1997.

## NO STRINGS

MUSIC AND LYRICS: Richard Rodgers  BOOK: Samuel Taylor  PRODUCER: Richard Rodgers
DIRECTOR: Joe Layton  CHOREOGRAPHER: Joe Layton
MAJOR PERFORMERS: Diahann Carroll, Richard Kiley, Bernice Massi, Polly Rowles, Noelle Adam, Alvin Epstein
OPENED: 3/15/62          THEATER: 54th Street          PERFORMANCES: 580

Richard Rodgers' first musical after the death of his partner, Oscar Hammerstein II, and the only Broadway production for which the composer also served as his own lyricist, *No Strings* offered such innovations as hiding the orchestra backstage, featuring instrumentalists onstage to accompany the singers, having the principals and chorus move scenery and props in full view of the audience, and—to conform to the play's title—eliminating the orchestra's string section. Dealing with the first interracial romance in a musical since *Show Boat*, the libretto tells of a love affair between a fashion model living in Paris (Diahann Carroll) and a former Pulitzer Prize-winning novelist now a "Europe bum" (Richard Kiley). In the end, after enjoying the good life in Monte Carlo, Honfleur, Deauville, and St. Tropez, the writer, with no strings attached, returns home to the United States to resume his career. In this interracial romance race was never mentioned in the script.

## OH, BOY!

MUSIC: Jerome Kern  LYRICS: P.G. Wodehouse  BOOK: Guy Bolton & P.G. Wodehouse
PRODUCERS: William Elliott & F. Ray Comstock  DIRECTORS: Edward Royce, Robert Milton  CHOREOGRAPHER: Edward Royce
MAJOR PERFORMERS: Marie Carroll, Tom Powers, Anna Wheaton, Hal Forde, Edna May Oliver, Marion Davies, Justine Joyhnstone, Dorothy Dickson, Carl Hyson
OPENED: 2/20/17          THEATER: Princess          PERFORMANCES: 463

*Oh, Boy!* is one of the pieces by Kern/Wodehouse/Bolton that defined for the first time an American style of musical comedy. These Princess theater shows came about because a presenter was having a hard time filling the small, intimate theater. They hit on the plan of small scale musicals, minus the dozens of chorus members. Rather than operetta-like stories in exotic locales, the Princess shows were of modern-day middle and upper class Americans in light romantic and comic situations. The plot of *Oh, Boy!* involves a Long Island couple's mistaken suspicion of romantic infidelity. There are unlikely pairings and narrow escapes, and all ends happily when the central couple is reunited in a festive scene at the Meadowsides Country Club.

## OKLAHOMA!

MUSIC AND LYRICS: Richard Rodgers and Oscar Hammerstein II  BOOK: Oscar Hammerstein II
PRODUCER: Theatre Guild  DIRECTOR: Rouben Mamoulian  CHOREOGRAPHER: Agnes de Mille
MAJOR PERFORMERS: Betty Garde, Alfred Drake, Joan Roberts, Howard Da Silva, Celeste Holm, Joseph Buloff, Lee Dixon
OPENED: 3/31/43          THEATER: St. James          PERFORMANCES: 2,212

There are many reasons why *Oklahoma!* is a recognized landmark in the history of the American musical theatre. In the initial collaboration between Richard Rodgers and Oscar Hammerstein II, it not only expertly fused the major elements in the production—story, songs and dances—it also utilized dream ballets to reveal hidden desires and fears of the principals. In addition, the musical, based on Lynn Riggs' play, *Green Grow The Lilacs*, was the first with a book that honestly depicted the kind of rugged pioneers who had once tilled the land and tended the cattle. Set in Indian Territory soon after the turn of the century, *Oklahoma!* spins a simple tale mostly concerned with whether the decent Curly (Alfred Drake) or the menacing Jud (Howard Da Silva) gets to take Laurey (Joan Roberts) to the box social. Though she chooses Jud in a fit of pique, Laurey really loves Curly and they soon make plans to marry. At their wedding they join in celebrating Oklahoma's impending statehood, then—after Jud is accidentally killed in a fight with Curly—the couple ride off in their surrey with the fringe on top. With its Broadway run of five years, nine months, *Oklahoma!* established a long-run record that it held for fifteen years. It also toured the United States and Canada for over a decade. In 1979, the musical was revived on Broadway with a cast headed by Laurence Guittard and Christine Andreas, and ran for 293 performances. The film version, the first to Todd-AO, was released by Magna in 1955. Gordon MacRae, Shirley Jones and Charlotte Greenwood were in it, and the director was Fred Zinnemann.

## OLIVER!

MUSIC AND LYRICS: Lionel Bart  BOOK: Lionel Bart
PRODUCER: David Merrick and Donald Albery  DIRECTOR: Peter Coe
MAJOR PERFORMERS: Clive Revill, Georgia Brown, Bruce Prochnik, Willoughby Goddard, Hope Jackman, Danny Sewell, Geoffrey Lumb, David Jones, Barry Humphries
OPENED: 1/6/63          THEATER: Imperial          PERFORMANCES: 744

*Oliver!* established Lionel Bart as Britain's outstanding musical-theatre talent of the 60's when the musical opened at the New Theatre, London, on June 30, 1960, where it had a run of 2,618 performances. Until overtaken by *Jesus Christ Superstar*, this set the record as the longest running musical in British history. Based on Charles Dickens' novel about the orphan Oliver Twist and his adventures as one of Fagin's pickpocketing crew, *Oliver!* also had the longest run of any British musical presented in New York. In 1968, it was made into an Academy Award winning movie produced by Columbia, directed by Carol Reed, and starring Ron Moody, Harry Secombe and Shani Wallis. In 1984, a new stage production opened on Broadway with Ron Moody and Patti LuPone.

## ON A CLEAR DAY YOU CAN SEE FOREVER

MUSIC AND LYRICS: Burton Lane and Alan Jay Lerner  BOOK: Alan Jay Lerner
PRODUCER: Alan Jay Lerner  DIRECTOR: Robert Lewis  CHOREOGRAPHER: Herbert Ross
MAJOR PERFORMERS: Barbara Harris, John Cullum, Titos Vandis, William Daniels, Clifford David
OPENED: 10/17/65          THEATER: Mark Hellinger          PERFORMANCES: 280

Alan Jay Lerner's fascination with the phenomenon of extrasensory perception (ESP) led to his teaming with composer Richard Rodgers in 1962 to write a musical to be called *I Picked a Daisy*. When that didn't work out, Lerner turned to composer Burton Lane. Their musical, now called *On A Clear Day You Can See Forever* was concerned with Daisy Gamble (Barbara Harris) who can predict the future and, when hypnotized by Dr. Mark Bruckner (John Cullum), is also able to recall her life as Melinda Wells in 18th Century London. Mark's infatuation with Melinda makes her something of a rival to the real-life Daisy, and she leaves him. In the end, however, his plea "Come Back To Me" is so compelling that it reunites the couple. Barbra Streisand and Yves Montand starred in the 1970 Paramount film version, which was directed by Vincente Minnelli.

## ON YOUR TOES

MUSIC AND LYRICS: Richard Rodgers and Lorenz Hart  BOOK: George Abbott, Richard Rodgers and Lorenz Hart
PRODUCER: Dwight Deere Wiman  DIRECTOR: Worthington Miner,  George Abbott (uncredited)
CHOREOGRAPHER: George Balanchine
MAJOR PERFORMERS: Ray Bolger, Tamara Geva, Monty Woolley, Doris Carson, David Morris, Luella Gear, Robert Sidney, Demetrios Vilan
OPENED: 4/11/36          THEATER: Imperial          PERFORMANCES: 315

*On Your Toes* scored a major theatrical breakthrough as the first Broadway entertainment to combine musical comedy and ballet. The story tells of how Junior Dolan (Ray Bolger), an ex-vaudevillian now a music teacher in New York, persuades a classical ballet company to perform a modern work, "Slaughter On Tenth Avenue," and then assumes the leading male role himself. Because he has also become involved with the company's chief ballerina, Vera Barnova (Tamara Geva), Vera's jealous lover and dancing partner hires two thugs to kill Junior during a performance of the ballet. To avoid being a target, Junior keeps dancing after the ballet is over; after the police have arrested the gunmen, he falls exhausted to the floor. The musical offered Ray Bolger his first major role and it also marked the first time that the ballet choreographer, George Balanchine, was engaged to create dances for a book musical.

Rodgers and Hart had originally conceived the musical as a screen vehicle for Fred Astaire, but the dancer turned it down because it did not give him the chance to wear top hat, white tie and tails. Though George Abbott, the book's co-author, was to have directed the production, repeated delays forced him to withdraw; he did, however, return to the show when it was having problems during the Boston tryout. *On Your Toes* has had two major Broadway revivals. In 1954, Abbott and Balanchine put together a production starring Bobby Van, Vera Zorina, and Elaine Stritch, which had a run of 64 performances. A more successful Broadway revival was mounted in 1983, again with Abbott directing and with choreography by Donald Saddler and Peter Martens based on Balanchine's original work. The cast was headed by Natalia Makarova (Vera) and Lara Teeter (Junior). With Eddie Albert and Vera Zorina in the leads (and the music used only as background), *On Your Toes* was filmed by Warner Bros. in 1939. Ray Enright directed.

## 110 IN THE SHADE

MUSIC: Harvey Schmidt  LYRICS: Tom Jones  BOOK: N. Richard Nash
PRODUCER: David Merrick  DIRECTOR: Joseph Anthony  CHOREOGRAPHER: Agnes de Mille
MAJOR PERFORMERS: Robert Horton, Inga Swenson, Stephen Douglass, Will Geer, Steve Roland, Anthony Teague, Lesley Ann Warrren, Gretchen Cryer
OPENED: 10/24/63          THEATER: Broadhurst          PERFORMANCES: 330

The show is adapted from Nash's play *The Rainmaker* (made into a memorable movie starring Katharine Hepburn and Burt Lancaster). The story is of Lizzie, a potential spinster taking care of her bachelor brothers and widowed father on a drought stricken range in the west. A "rainmaker" comes to town, and sweeps Lizzie off her feet. Her own personal drought ends, though she choses a local suitor instead of the flashy con man. The musical entered the repetory of the New York City Opera in 1993.

## ONE MO' TIME

MUSIC AND LYRICS: Miscellaneous writers  BOOK: Conceived by Vernel Bagneris
PRODUCER: Art D'Lugoff, Burt D'Lugoff, Jerry Wexler  DIRECTOR: Vernel Bagneris
MAJOR PERFORMERS: Vernel Bagneris, Sylvia "Kuumba" Williams, Thais Clark, Topsy Chapman
OPENED: 10/22/79        THEATER: Village Gate Downstairs        PERFORMANCES: 1,372

One Mo' Time was a tribute to the Lyric Theatre, New Orleans, once the mecca of black vaudeville, which burned down in 1927. Little more than a procession of songs and dances featuring pop music of the Twenties, the show had an infectious spirit and style that gave it the atmosphere of an authentic bill of the period, and succeeded so well in giving everyone a hot time in the old town that it became one of Off Broadway's longest running hits.


## ONE TOUCH OF VENUS

MUSIC AND LYRICS: Kurt Weill and Ogden Nash  BOOK: S. J. Perelman and Ogden Nash
PRODUCER: Cheryl Crawford and John Wildberg  DIRECTOR: Elia Kazan  CHOREOGRAPHER: Agnes de Mille
MAJOR PERFORMERS: Mary Martin, Kenny Baker, John Boles, Paul Laurence, Teddy Hart, Sono Osato, Harry Clark
OPENED: 10/7/43        THEATER: Imperial        PERFORMANCES: 567

Composer Kurt Weill's longest running Broadway musical, on which he worked with two of America's foremost humorists, poet Ogden Nash and short-story writer S.J. Perelman, was a fantasy about a statue of Venus at a New York museum who comes to life after barber Rodney Hatch (Kenny Baker) places a ring on her finger. There is much confusion when Venus falls in love with the barber, but after dreaming of life with him in Ozone Heights, she realizes that it would be a pretty humdrum existence and back to marble she turns. Happily, Rodney meets a girl who looks just like the statue and loves living in Ozone Heights. Though first intended as a vehicle for Marlene Dietrich, One Touch Of Venus (suggested by a story, "The Tinted Venus," by F. Anstey) provided Mary Martin with her first starring role on Broadway and the chance to sing the dreamy ballad "Speak Low". William A. Seiter directed the 1948 Universal screen version, which starred Ava Gardner, Robert Walker, and Dick Haymes.


## OUT OF THIS WORLD

MUSIC AND LYRICS: Cole Porter  BOOK: Dwight Taylor and Reginald Lawrence  PRODUCER: Saint Subber and Lemuel Ayers
DIRECTOR: Anges de Mille, George Abbott (uncredited)  CHOREOGRAPHER: Hanya Holm
MAJOR PERFORMERS: Charlotte Greenwood, William Eythe, David Burns, Priscilla Gillette, William Redfield, Barbara Ashley, Janet Collins, George Jongeyans
OPENED: 2/21/50        THEATER: New Century        PERFORMANCES: 157

With the Amphitryon legend providing the basis for its story, Out Of This World served to bring long-legged comedienne Charlotte Greenwood back to Broadway after an absence of twenty-three years. Miss Greenwood played the goddess Juno, wife of god Jupiter (George Jongeyans), who descends from Mount Olympus to follow her philandering husband to Greece where, in disguise, he enjoys a rapturous night with a beautiful mortal. Cole Porter's attractive score, by turns soulfully melodic ("I Am Loved") and comical ("Cherry Pies Ought To Be You"), would have been even stronger had not George Abbott, who took over as director during the Philadelphia tryout, insisted that "From This Moment On" had to be dropped from the show.


## OVER HERE!

MUSIC AND LYRICS: Richard M. Sherman and Robert B. Sherman  BOOK: Will Holt
PRODUCER: Ken Waissman and Maxine Fox  DIRECTOR: Tom Moore  CHOREOGRAPHER: Patricia Birch
MAJOR PERFORMERS: Patti and Maxene Andrews, Janie Sell, Douglass Watson, April Shawhan, Samuel Wright, John Travolta, Treat Williams, Ann Reinking
OPENED: 3/6/74        THEATER: Shubert        PERFORMANCES: 341

Recapturing the swingband sound of the World War II years, Over Here starred two genuine swinging attractions of the period, Patti and Maxene Andrews (the third member of the original trio, La Verne, died in 1967). The show, however, used a completely new score by movieland's Sherman brothers (best known for their Mary Poppins songs), though its intention was to suggest such Andrews Sisters' standards as "Juke Box Saturday Night," "Boogie Woogie Bugle Boy," "The Victory Polka," and the rest. In the story, a sister act, Pauline and Paulette de Paul, are wartime entertainers on a cross-country train where they form a trio with another singer (Janie Sell)—only to discover that she is a Nazi spy. Also along for the ride were two future Hollywood stars, John Travolta and Treat Williams.


## PAINT YOUR WAGON

MUSIC AND LYRICS: Frederick Loewe and Alan Jay Lerner  BOOK: Alan Jay Lerner
PRODUCER: Cheryl Crawford  DIRECTOR: Daniel Mann  CHOREOGRAPHER: Agnes de Mille
MAJOR PERFORMERS: James Barton, Olga San Juan, Tony Bavaar, James Mitchell, Kay Medford
OPENED: 11/12/51        THEATER: Shubert        PERFORMANCES: 289

Filling their musical play with authentic incidents and backgrounds, Lerner and Loewe struck it rich both musically and dramatically with a work that captured all the flavor of the roistering, robust California gold prospectors of 1853. James Barton, returning to the musical stage for the first time in twenty years, took the part of Ben Rumson, a grizzled prospector whose daughter Jennifer (Olga San Juan) discovers gold near their camp. Word of the strike quickly spreads and before long there are over 4,000 inhabitants in the new town of Rumson. Jennifer, who has fallen in love with Julio, a Mexican (Tony Bavaar), goes East to school but returns to Julio when the gold strike peters out. Rumson is virtually a ghost town, and Ben is left with nothing but his hopes and dreams. Paramount's 1969 screen version used a different story. In the leading roles were Clint Eastwood, Lee Marvin, and Jean Seberg, and Joshua Logan was the director.

## PAL JOEY

MUSIC AND LYRICS: Richard Rodgers and Lorenz Hart  BOOK: John O'Hara
PRODUCER: George Abbott  DIRECTOR: George Abbott  CHOREOGRAPHER: Robert Alton
MAJOR PERFORMERS: Vivienne Segal, Gene Kelly, June Havoc, Jack Durant, Leila Ernst, Jean Casto, Van Johnson
OPENED: 12/25/40        THEATER: Ethel Barrymore        PERFORMANCES: 374

With its heel for a hero, its smoky night-club atmosphere, and its true-to-life characters, *Pal Joey* was a major breakthrough in bringing about a more adult form of musical theatre. Adapted by John O'Hara from his own *New Yorker* short stories, the show is about Joey Evans, an entertainer at a small Chicago night club, who is attracted to the innocent Linda English, but drops her in favor of wealthy, middle-aged Vera Simpson. Vera builds a glittering night club, the Chez Joey, for her paramour but she soon grows tired of him and Joey, at the end, is on his way to other conquests. In his only major Broadway role, Gene Kelly got the chance to sing "I Could Write a Book," and Vivienne Segal, as Vera, introduced "Bewitched." Though it had a respectable run, *Pal Joey* was considered somewhat ahead of its time when it was first produced. A 1952 Broadway revival, with Miss Segal repeating her original role and Harold Lang as Joey, received a more appreciative reception and went on to a run of 542 performances. In 1957, Columbia made a film version, with George Sidney directing, which starred Frank Sinatra, Kim Novak, and Rita Hayworth.

## PANAMA HATTIE

MUSIC AND LYRICS: Cole Porter  BOOK: Herbert Fields and B.G. DeSylva
PRODUCER: B.G. DeSylva  DIRECTOR: Edgar MacGregor  CHOREOGRAPHER: Robert Alton
MAJOR PERFORMERS: Ethel Merman, James Dunn, Arthur Treacher, Betty Hutton, Rags Ragland, Pat Harrington, Frank Hyers, Phyllis Brooks, Joan Carroll, June Allyson
OPENED: 10/30/40        THEATER: 46th Street        PERFORMANCES: 501

*Panama Hattie* had the longest run of all the five shows in which Ethel Merman was spotlighted singing the songs of Cole Porter. It was also the first musical in which she was starred with her name alone above the title. In the story, Ethel played Hattie Maloney, a flashy nightclub owner in Panama City, who gets engaged to divorcé Nick Bullett (James Dunn), a Philadelphia Main Liner. In order for the couple to marry, however, Hattie must first win the approval of Nick's snotty eight-year old daughter (Joan Carroll), which is accomplished—with Cole Porter's help—when Hattie sings "Let's Be Buddies." The cast was filled with stars of the future, including Betty Hutton and her understudy, June Allyson. For the 1942 MGM screen version, the leads were taken by Ann Sothern and Red Skelton, and the director was Norman Z. McLeod.

## PETER PAN

MUSIC: Mark Charlap  LYRICS: Carolyn Leigh;  Additional Music by Jule Styne;  Additional Lyrics by Betty Comden and Adolph Green
BOOK: James M. Barrie  PRODUCER: Richard Halliday  DIRECTOR: Jerome Robbins  CHOREOGRAPHER: Jerome Robbins
MAJOR PERFORMERS: Mary Martin, Cyril Ritchard, Kathy Nolan, Sondra Lee and Joe E. Marks
OPENED: 10/20/54        THEATER: Winter Garden        PERFORMANCES: 152

Although many actresses have portrayed *Peter Pan* in almost as many productions, Mary Martin and this version of the story are perhaps the best known and loved. In spite of a modest run on Broadway, this production found a vast new audience through numerous television broadcasts. Among the show's charms were Cyril Ritchard as the pirate Captain Hook and an evergreen score which included "I've Gotta Crow", "I Won't Grow Up" and "Never Never Land". The 1979 revival starring Sandy Duncan became the longest running *Peter Pan* ever on Broadway.

## THE PHANTOM OF THE OPERA

MUSIC: Andrew Lloyd Webber  LYRICS: Charles Hart, Richard Stilgoe
BOOK: Richard Stilgoe, Andrew Lloyd Webber  PRODUCER: Cameron Mackintosh & The Really Useful Theatre Co.
DIRECTOR: Harold Prince  CHOREOGRAPHER: Gillian Lynne
MAJOR PERFORMERS: Micahel Crawford, Sarah Brightman, Steve Barton, Judy Kaye, Cris Groenendaal, Nicholas Wyman, Leila Martin, David Romano, Elisa Heinsohn, George Lee Andrews
OPENED: 1/26/88        THEATER: Majestic Theatre        PERFORMANCES: over 3,800 (still running 6/1/97)

The most financially successful musical in history is based on the French novel *Le Fantôme de l'Opéra*, first published in 1911. The facially disfigured phantom lives in the forgotten bowels of the Paris Opera, and falls in love with Christine, for whom he is willing to do anything. He eliminates any rivals, and convinces her of his sincere affection. The production's most famous element is a chandelier that falls from above the audience and crashes onto the stage. The musical opened in London in 1986 prior to opening in New York. The show has had the most number of touring companies and the most successful road revenues in history. The standout melodies are "The Music of the Night," and "All I Ask of You."

## PICKWICK

MUSIC AND LYRICS: Cyril Ornadel and Leslie Bricusse  BOOK: Wolf Mankowitz
PRODUCER: David Merrick and Bernard Delfont  DIRECTOR: Peter Coe  CHOREOGRAPHER: Gillian Lynne
MAJOR PERFORMERS: Harry Secombe, Anton Rodgers, Roy Castle, Charlotte Rae, Elizabeth Parrish
OPENED: 10/4/65          THEATER: 46th Street          PERFORMANCES: 55

The solid success of the British musical, *Oliver!* based on *Oliver Twist*, inevitably sent writers scurrying to libraries in search of other adaptable Charles Dickens novels. The *Pickwick Papers* seemed an obvious choice, particularly with its collection of hearty good fellows who were forever getting into trouble, its colorful locales, and its many comic incidents. With rotund Harry Secombe as the bumbling Samuel Pickwick, the well-meaning but unworldly president of the Pickwick Club, the original London production of *Pickwick* opened at the Saville Theatre on July 4, 1963, where it was seen for 695 performances. Despite this impressive run, American producer David Merrick felt that much work still needed to be done for the Broadway facsimile, and, with Secombe again heading the cast, he kept the show on the road for six months before opening it in New York. This may not have helped *Pickwick* very much but it did help the song, "If I Ruled The World," to become a coast-to-coast favorite even before the official premiere.

## PINS AND NEEDLES

MUSIC AND LYRICS: Harold Rome
BOOK: Sketches by Charles Friedman, Arthur Arent, Marc Blitzstein, Emanuel Eisenberg, David Gregory
PRODUCER: I.L.G.W.U.  DIRECTOR: Charles Friedman  CHOREOGRAPHER: Gluck Sandor
MAJOR PERFORMERS: Members of the I.L.G.W.U.
OPENED: 11/27/37          THEATER: Labor Stage          PERFORMANCES: 1,108

*Pins and Needles* was one of Broadway's most surprising success stories. Initially presented as a satirical revue by and for the members of the International Ladies Garment Workers Union, it was not even covered by critics when it began its run at the tiny Labor Stage (formerly the Princess Theatre). But audiences soon began flocking to it in such droves that the show went on to achieve the record as Broadway's longest running musical (though the title would soon be relinquished to *Hellzapoppin*). The revue's barbs may have been aimed at militarists, bigots, reactionaries, Nazis, Fascists, Communists, and the Daughters of the American Revolution, but the tone was generally lighthearted, with even the demand "Sing Me A Song With Social Significance" done with tongue in cheek to keep up with the headlines, so much material had to be constantly changed that by 1939 the show was called *New Pins and Needles*.

## PIPE DREAM

MUSIC AND LYRICS: Richard Rodgers and Oscar Hammerstein II  BOOK: Oscar Hammerstein II
PRODUCER: Richard Rodgers and Oscar Hammerstein II  DIRECTOR: Harold Clurman  CHOREOGRAPHER: Boris Runanin
MAJOR PERFORMERS: Helen Traubel, Judy Tyler, Willam Johnson, G.D. Wallace, Mike Kellin
OPENED: 11/30/55          THEATER: Shubert          PERFORMANCES: 246

A leisurely paced musical with little conflict, *Pipe Dream* was adapted from John Steinbeck's novel, *Sweet Thursday*, and took a sympathetic look at the skid-row inhabitants of Cannery Row in California's Monterey peninsula. The plot is mostly about Doc, a marine biologist (William Johnson), whose romance with a pretty vagrant named Suzy (Judy Tyler) is abetted by Fauna, the warmhearted madam of a local bordello (played by former Metropolitan Opera diva Helen Traubel). The two most popular ballads to emerge from the score were "All At Once You Love Her" and "Everybody's Got A Home But Me."

## PLAIN AND FANCY

MUSIC AND LYRICS: Albert Hague and Arnold B. Horwitt  BOOK: Joseph Stein and Will Glickman
PRODUCER: Richard Kollmar and James W. Gardiner  DIRECTOR: Morton Da Costa  CHOREOGRAPHER: Helen Tamiris
MAJOR PERFORMERS: Richard Derr, Shirl Conway, Barbara Cook, David Daniels, Nancy Andrews, Gloria Marlowe
OPENED: 1/27/55          THEATER: Mark Hellinger          PERFORMANCES: 461

The setting of *Plain and Fancy* was Amish country in Pennsylvania, where two worldly New Yorkers (Richard Derr and Shirl Conway) have gone to sell a farm they had inherited—but not before they had a chance to meet the God-fearing people and appreciate their simple but unyielding way of living. The warm and atmospheric score, with its hit song "Young And Foolish" was composed by Albert Hague, familiar to television viewers as the bearded music teacher in the long-running series, *Fame*.

## PORGY AND BESS

MUSIC AND LYRICS: George Gershwin, DuBose Heyward and Ira Gershwin  BOOK: DuBose Heyward
PRODUCER: Theatre Guild  DIRECTOR: Rouben Mamoulian
MAJOR PERFORMERS: Todd Duncan, Anne Brown, John W. Bubbles, Georgette Harvey, Edward Matthews, Helen Dowdy,
Ford L. Buck, J. Rosamond Johnson
OPENED: 10/10/35        THEATER: Alvin         PERFORMANCES: 124

Universally recognized as the most esteemed and popular opera written by an American composer, *Porgy and Bess* began life in 1925 as a novel called *Porgy* by DuBose Heyward. Heyward's setting of Catfish Row in Charleston, South Carolina, and his emotional story of the crippled beggar Porgy, the seductive Bess, the menacing Crown, and the slinky cocaine dealer, Sportin' Life, fired Gershwin's imagination even before Heyward and his wife, Dorothy, transformed the book into a play two years later. After many delays, Gershwin, with Heyward and the composer's brother, Ira, began writing the opera late in 1933, and completed it—including orchestrations—in twenty months. The initial Broadway Production, with Todd Duncan and Anne Brown in the title roles. was not a commercial success, though many of the solos and duets—"Summertime," "Bess, You Is My Woman Now." "I Got Plenty O' Nuttin'," "It Ain't Necessarily So" for example—quickly caught on. Four major revivals of *Porgy And Bess* have been mounted on Broadway since the first engagement. In 1942, again with Todd Duncan and Anne Brown, it ran 286 performances in a somewhat trimmed down version. In 1952, as part of a four-year international tour, it returned with William Warfield and Leontyne Price and ran for 305 performances. An acclaimed production in 1976 by the Houston Grand Opera Company featured Donnie Ray Albert as Porgy and Clamma Dale as Bess. and had a 122-performance run on Broadway. The Metropolitan Opera first produced *Porgy and Bess* in 1985.


## PRESENT ARMS

MUSIC: Richard Rodgers  LYRICS: Lorenz Hart  BOOK: Herbert Fields
PRODUCER: Lew Fields  DIRECTOR: Alexander Leftwich  CHOREOGRAPHER: Bub Berkeley
MAJOR PERFORMERS: Charles King, Robert Spencer, Fuller Melish Jr., Flora Le Breton, Anthony Knilling, Sydney Smith
OPENED: 4/26/28        THEATER: Lew Fields' Mansfield Theater        PERFORMANCES: 155

One of the milder hits of Rodgers and Hart from the 1920s, best remembered for the song "You Took Advantage of Me." A marine stationed at Pearl Harbor falls in love with a member of the English aristocracy residing on the island. His buddies aid him in his pursuit of her, and outwit the rival suitor, Herr Ludwig Von Richter. The show was in the breezy spirit of *Good News* or *Hit the Deck*.


## PRIVATE LIVES

MUSIC AND LYRICS: Noel Coward BOOK: Play by Noel Coward
PRODUCER: Charles B. Cochran  DIRECTOR: Noel Coward
MAJOR PERFORMERS: Gertrude Lawrence, Noel Coward, Laurence Olivier, Jill Esmond
OPENED: 117/31        THEATER: Times Square        PERFORMANCES: 256

Noel Coward's brittle comedy, first presented at the Phoenix theatre, London, in 1930. was a light-hearted romp involving Amanda Prynne (Gertrude Lawrence) and Elyot Chase (Mr. Coward), a formerly married couple who meet again in France while on separate honeymoons—and fall in love again. The single song in the play, "Someday I'll Find You," was introduced as a tune they hear being performed by a hotel dance band and which they recall from their own honeymoon. In 1931, MGM made a film version of *Private Lives* starring Norma Shearer and Robert Montgomery, with Sidney Franklin directing.


## RED, HOT AND BLUE!

MUSIC AND LYRICS: Cole Porter  BOOK: Howard Lindsay and Russel Crouse
PRODUCER: Vinton Freedley  DIRECTOR: Howard Lindsay  CHOREOGRAPHER: George Hale
MAJOR PERFORMERS: Ethel Merman, Jimmy Durante, Bob Hope, Polly Walters, Paul and Grace Hartman, Vivian Vance
OPENED: 10/29/36        THEATER: Alvin        PERFORMANCES: 183

Anxious to repeat the success of *Anything Goes*, a 1934 Broadway smash involving Ethel Merman, William Gaxton and Victor Moore and writers Cole Porter, Howard Lindsay and Russel Crouse, producer Vinton Freedley engaged them all for his next musical, a political satire called *Red, Hot and Blue!* But after overhearing Freedley promise Miss Merman that hers would be the most important part, Gaxton and Moore quickly bowed out of the project. Replacing them were Bob Hope, as the lady's love interest, and Jimmy Durante, playing a convict who is released from prison to help Merman and Hope set up a national lottery. Though the show had only a modest run, at least three songs, "It's DeLovely," "Down In The Depths," and "Ridin' High." became acknowledged standards. For whatever reason, however, Paramount's 1949 movie version—starring Betty Hutton and Victor Mature and directed by John Farrow—substituted an entirely new score by Frank Loesser.


## RENT

MUSIC, LYRICS & BOOK: Jonathan Larson
PRODUCER: Jeffrey Seller, Kevin McCollum, Allan S. Gordon, New York Theatre Workshop DIRECTOR: Michael Greif
CHOREOGRAPHER: Marls Yearby
MAJOR PERFORMERS: Gilles Chaisson, Taye Diggs, Wilson Jermaine Heredia, Rodney Hicks, Kristen Lee Kelly, Jesse L. Martin, Idina Menzel, Aiko Nakasone, Timothy Britten Parker, Adam Pascal, Anthony Rapp, Daphne Rubin-Vega, Gwen Stewart, Byron Utley, Fredi Walker
OPENED: 4/29/96        THEATER: Nederlander        PERFORMANCES: (still running 6/1/97)

*Rent* received great acclaim, winning the Pulitzer Prize for Drama, a Tony award for Best Musical, and other awards. Tragically, composer/author Jonathan Larson died suddenly the night of the final dress rehearsal before the Off-Broadway opening. The story is loosely based on *La bohème*, set in the East Village of present day New York. The characters are a mix of various types of contemporary artists (a filmmaker, an HIV-positive musician, a drug-addicted dancer, a drag queen). Despite struggles, the group of friends remain devoted to one another. The compelling rock score has a gritty realism.

## REX

MUSIC AND LYRICS: Richard Rodgers and Sheldon Harnick  BOOK: Sherman Yellen
PRODUCER: Richard Adler  DIRECTOR: Edwin Sherin  CHOREOGRAPHER: Diana Krupska
MAJOR PERFORMERS: Nicol Williamson, Penny Fuller, Tom Aldredge, Glenn Close, April Shawhan, Barbara Andres
OPENED: 4/25/76          THEATER: Lunt-Fontanne          PERFORMANCES: 49

Richard Rodgers' 39th and penultimate Broadway musical was the only one on which he collaborated with lyricist Sheldon Harnick (whose credits include *Fiorello!* and *Fiddler on the Roof*). The richly mounted production, with a forceful performance by Nicol Williamson as King Henry VIII, covers a thirty-year period from Henry's marriage to Katharine of Aragon to his death. In the story the king is shown principally as husband and father, with special emphasis on his relationship with his strong-willed daughter, the future Elizabeth I.


## RIGHT THIS WAY

MUSIC AND LYRICS: Sammy Fain and Irving Kahal; Bradford Greene and Marianne Brown Waters
BOOK: Marianne Brown Waters, Parke Levy, and Allen Lipscott  PRODUCER: Alice Alexander
DIRECTOR: Bertrand Robinson  CHOREOGRAPHER: Marjery Fielding
MAJOR PERFORMERS: Guy Robertson, Tamara, Joe E. Lewis, Blanche Ring
OPENED: 1/4/38          THEATER: 46th Street          PERFORMANCES: 15

In *Right This Way*, a young couple meet and fall in love in Paris, split up in Boston, and reconcile back in Paris. So much for the plot. The musical, however, was not entirely without virtues, among them the gravelly humor of night club comedian Joe E. Lewis, the nostalgic appeal of old-timer Blanche Ring, and two songs by Sammy Fain and Irving Kahal, "I'll Be Seeing You" and "I Can Dream, Can't I?," which quickly won public favor. The first ballad, in fact, had special meaning during World War II when it became a hit all over again.


## THE ROAR OF THE GREASEPAINT—THE SMELL OF THE CROWD

MUSIC AND LYRICS: Leslie Bricusse and Anthony Newley  BOOK: Leslie Bricusse and Anthony Newley
PRODUCER: David Merrick with Bernard Delfont  DIRECTOR: Anthony Newley  CHOREOGRAPHER: Gillian Lynne
MAJOR PERFORMERS: Cyril Ritchard, Anthony Newley
OPENED: 5/16/65          THEATER: Shubert          PERFORMANCES: 232

This British musical was something of a follow-up to the previous Leslie Bricusse-Anthony Newley collaboration, *Stop the World—I Want to Get Off*. Presented as an allegory, the "haves" represented by Sir (Cyril Ritchard), confront the "have nots" in the person of Cocky (played by Anthony Newley). The show's rich score contained 14 songs, many of which became standards including "The Joker," "Feeling Good," "Nothing Can Stop Me Now," "Who Can I Turn To (When Nobody Needs Me)," and "A Wonderful Day Like Today."


## ROBERTA

MUSIC: Jerome Kern  LYRICS & BOOK: Otto Harbach
PRODUCER: Max Gordon    DIRECTOR: Hassard Short, uncredited
CHOREOGRAPHER: José Limon (John Lonergan, uncredited)
MAJOR PERFORMERS: Lyda Roberti, Bob Hope, Fay Templeton, Tamara, George Murphy, Sydney Greenstreet, Ray Middleton, Fred MacMurray
OPENED: 11/18/33          THEATER: New Amsterdam          PERFORMANCES: 295

The show was based on the novel *Gowns by Roberta* by Alice Duer Miller, and it moves in the world of fashion. Like *The Cat and the Fiddle* and *Music in the Air*, Roberta is set in present day Europe and is in an updated operetta style of writing.  It's best known for producing two great Kern-Harbach standards: "Yesterdays" and "Smoke Gets in Your Eyes."  The cast is also noteworthy, including Bob Hope in his first major Broadway role.  The 1935 RKO film starred Irene Dunne, Ginger Rogers and Fred Astaire.  MGM did another film adaptation of the musical in the 1950s.


## ST. LOUIS WOMAN

MUSIC AND LYRICS: Harold Arlen and Johnny Mercer
BOOK: Arna Bontemps and Countee Cullen  PRODUCER: Edward Gross
DIRECTOR: Rouben Mamoulian  CHOREOGRAPHER: Charles Walters
MAJOR PERFORMERS: Harold Nicholas, Pearl Bailey, Ruby Hill, Rex Ingram, Fayard Nicholas, June Hawkins, Juanita Hall
OPENED: 3/30/46          THEATER: Martin Beck          PERFORMANCES: 113

*St. Louis Woman*, based on Arna Bontemps' novel, *God Sends Sunday*, was something of a non-operatic *Porgy And Bess*. Set in 1898, it tells of a fickle St. Louis Woman, Della Green (Ruby Hill), who is first the girlfriend of saloon-keeper Biglow Brown (Rex Ingram), then falls for Li'l Augie (Harold Nicholas), a jockey with an incredible winning streak. Before Brown is killed by a rejected lover, he puts a curse on Li'l Augie which ends the winning streak and cools Della's affection. The lovers are, however, reunited for the final singing of their impassioned duet, "Come Rain Or Come Shine." In 1959, a revised version of *St. Louis Woman*, relocated in New Orleans and retitled Free And Easy, was performed in Amsterdam and Paris.

## SALLY

MUSIC: Jerome Kern  LYRICS: Clifford Grey and others  BOOK: Guy Bolton
PRODUCER: Florenz Ziegfeld  DIRECTOR-CHOREOGRAPHER: Edward Royce
MAJOR PERFORMERS: Marilyn Miller, Leon Errol, Walter Catlett, Irving Fisher, Mary Hay, Stanley Ridges
OPENED: 12/21/20          THEATER: New Amsterdam          PERFORMANCES: 570

This was the first starring role for Broadway legend Marilyn Miller. Ziegfeld initiated the musical from the team of Kern-Wodehouse-Bolton, but Wodehouse withdrew from the project. It's a rags to riches story, with Sally rising from a dishwasher to become a ballerina. One of the biggest hits of the 1920s, today the show is remembered for "Look for the Silver Lining." A movie was made, with Miller in the lead, in 1929.


## SALVATION

MUSIC AND LYRICS: Peter Link and C.C. Courtney  BOOK: Peter Link and C.C. Courtney
PRODUCER: David Black  DIRECTOR: Paul Aaron  CHOREOGRAPHER: Kathryn Posin
MAJOR PERFORMERS: Peter Link, C.C. Courtney, Yolande Bavan, Joe Morton, Chapman Roberts, Marta Heflin
OPENED: 9/24/69          THEATER: Jan Hus          PERFORMANCES: 239

Satirizing a variety of targets, mostly religious, *Salvation* followed in the path of *Hair* in its attempt to capitalize on the rock sound as the voice of protest. The show was presented as a series of songs and skits through which feelings were expressed about such topics as the Vietnam war, people who interpret the bible literally, and the ecumenical movement. During the run, Bette Midler replaced Marta Heflin.


## SARATOGA

MUSIC AND LYRICS: Music by Harold Arlen Lyrics by Johnny Mercer
BOOK: Morton DaCosta (based on the novel *Saratoga Trunk* by Edna Ferber)
PRODUCER: Robert Fryer  DIRECTOR: Morton DaCosta  CHOREOGRAPHER: Ralph Beaumont
MAJOR PERFORMERS: Howard Keel, Carol Lawrence, Odette Myrtil, Edith King, and Carol Brice
OPENED: 12/7/59          THEATER: Winter Garden          PERFORMANCES: 80

Set in late nineteenth-century New Orleans and Saratoga, the story concerns Clint Maroon and Clio Dulaine, fortune hunters who join forces out of necessity and unintentionally come to care for each other. Cecil Beaton's sets and costumes received well-deserved praise, but Harold Arlen's charming score was overshadowed by problems in the dramatization of Edna Ferber's atmospheric novel.


## SAY, DARLING

MUSIC AND LYRICS: Jule Styne, Betty Comden and Adolph Green  BOOK: Richard Bissell, Abe Burrows and Marian Bissell
PRODUCER: Jule Styne and Lester Osterman  DIRECTOR: Abe Burrows  CHOREOGRAPHER: Matt Mattox
MAJOR PERFORMERS: David Wayne, Vivian Blaine, Johnny Desmond, Jerome Cowan, Robert Morse, Matt Mattox
OPENED: 4/3/58          THEATER: ANTA          PERFORMANCES: 332

Billed as "A Comedy About a Musical," *Say, Darling* was, in fact, based on Richard Bissell's novel prompted by his experiences in adapting a previous novel, *7 1/2 Cents*, into the long-running hit, *The Pajama Game*. Of course, this kind of musical-comedy inbreeding was particularly enjoyed by the theatre crowd which recognized David Wayne's smalltown author as Bissell himself, Robert Morse's youthful producer as Harold Prince, Jerome Cowan's experienced director as George Abbott, and Johnny Desmond's egotistical composer-lyricist as a composite of Richard Adler and Jerry Ross.


## SEVEN LIVELY ARTS

MUSIC AND LYRICS: Cole Porter  BOOK: Sketches by Moss Hart, Ben Hecht, George S. Kaufman, and Charles Sherman
PRODUCER: Billy Rose  DIRECTOR: Hassard Short  CHOREOGRAPHER: Jack Donohue
MAJOR PERFORMERS: Beatrice Lillie, Bert Lahr, Benny Goodman, Alicia Markova, Anton Dolin, Doc Rockwell, Nan Wynn, Jere McMahon, Paula Bane, Billie Worth, Bill Tabbert, Dolores Gray, Mary Roche, Albert Carroll, Dennie Moore, Teddy Wilson, Red Norvo
OPENED: 12/7/44          THEATER: Ziegfeld          PERFORMANCES: 183

In an attempt to revive the glamorous days of the *Ziegfeld Follies*, showman Billy Rose opened his newly refurbished Ziegfeld Theatre with an excessively lavish star-filled revue that cost opening night patrons the steep price of $24 per seat (though this did include a champagne reception). The seven arts deemed lively—movies, opera, ballet, jazz, theatre, concert, and radio—served as framework for a succession of comic and musical turns that were highlighted by the buffonery of two super clowns, Beatrice Lillie and Bert Lahr, the swinging beat of Benny Goodman's Quintet, and the airy grace of ballet luminaries Alicia Markova and Anton Dolin, dancing to excerpts from Stravinsky's newly composed *Scene de Ballet*.

## 70, GIRLS, 70

MUSIC AND LYRICS: John Kander and Fred Ebb  BOOK: Fred Ebb and Norman L. Martin  PRODUCER: Arthur Whitelaw
DIRECTOR: Paul Aaron and Stanley Prager  CHOREOGRAPHER: Onna White
MAJOR PERFORMERS: Mildred Natwick, Hans Conried, Lillian Roth, Gil Lamb, Joey Faye, Lillian Hayman
OPENED: 4/15/71          THEATER: Broadhurst          PERFORMANCES: 36

*70, Girls, 70* was based on a play called *Breath of Spring* by Peter Coke and a 1960 British film version known as *Make Mine Mink*.
Appropriately, except for one juvenile, the entire cast was made up of veteran actors whose average age was seventy. Presented as a show within a
show, the musical was involved with a group of antic senior citizens living in a seedy Manhattan apartment house who embark on a career of
stealing fur coats from department stores. During the Philadelphia tryout, actor David Burns suffered a fatal heart attack on stage and was
replaced by Hans Conried.


## SHENANDOAH

MUSIC AND LYRICS: Music by Gary Geld Lyrics by Peter Udell
BOOK: James Lee Barrett, Peter Udell & Philip Rose (based on the screenplay by James Lee Barrett)
PRODUCER: Philip Rose, Gloria & Louis K. Sher  DIRECTOR: Philip Rose  CHOREOGRAPHER: Robert Tucker
MAJOR PERFORMERS: John Cullum, Donna Theodore, Penelope Milford, Joel Higgins, Ted Agress and Gordon Halliday
OPENED: 1/7/75          THEATER: Alvin          PERFORMANCES: 1,050

*Shenandoah* is a traditional musical concerned with a strong-willed Virginia widower and his determination to prevent his family from becoming
involved in the Civil War. John Cullum's robust performance and the play's old-fashioned morality found favor with Broadway audiences for
well over two years.


## SHOW BOAT

MUSIC: Jerome Kern  LYRICS & BOOK: Oscar Hammerstein II
PRODUCER: Florenz Ziegfeld  DIRECTOR: Zeke Colvan (Oscar Hammerstein II, uncredited)
CHOREOGRAPHER: Sammy Lee
MAJOR PERFORMERS: Charles Winninger, Norma Terris, Howard Marsh, Helen Morgan, Jules Bledsoe, Edna May Oliver, Eva Puck,
Sammy White, Tess Gardella, Charles Ellis, Francis X. Mahoney
OPENED: 12/27/27          THEATER: Ziegfeld          PERFORMANCES: 572

On anyone's list, *Show Boat* would have to be considered one of the pivotal accomplishments in American musical theater. Based on a popular
novel by Edna Ferber, this lavish Ziegfeld production boasted one of the first "grown-up" musical plays, with a mixture of comedy and tragedy.
An epic story, set from the 1880s to 1927, the show boat Cotton Blossom is run by Cap'n Andy Hawks, with his irritable wife Parthy and their
ingenuous daughter Magnolia. The boat is also populated with black servants, and the roles of Queenie and Joe are prominent. The leading
actress in the show, Julie, is discovered to be of mixed parentage, and this being Mississippi, she and her white husband are run out of town by the
sheriff. Magnolia steps into Julie's parts, and a river gambler, Ravenal, steps in for Julie's husband Steve in the romantic leading roles. Magnolia
and Ravenal marry and move to Chicago, where a lack of work combined with his gambling habits leave them in dire straights. Distraught and
ashamed, he leaves her. By chance Magnolia gets a job singing in a music hall, and Julie, now a disillusioned drunk, also works there. Julie gives
up her job for Magnolia. At the end of the show Ravenal and Magnolia meet once again, after many years, and watch their daughter Kim
perform in a show. The score is full of familiar standards: "Make Believe," "You Are Love," "Bill," "Life Upon the Wicked Stage," "Ol' Man
River," "Can't Help Lovin' Dat Man," "Why Do I Love You?" Kern also interpolated some period pieces (such as "After the Ball") by other writers
to help create authenticity. The show toured extensively (with the future movie star Irene Dunne taking on the role of Magnolia), and was
brought back to Broadway in 1932, this time with Paul Robeson in the role of Joe (which had been written for him anyway). A 1946 revival on
Broadway was successful, and the show was given a prominent production in the 1960s at Lincoln Center. Houston Grand Opera mounted an
important production in 1983. At this writing a new production is expected on Broadway with the year . There have been three movie
adaptations of the musical, in 1929 (part talkie, with Laura LaPlante and Joseph Schildkraut), in 1936 (with much of the New York cast,
including Irene Dunne, Helen Morgan, Charles Winninger, and Paul Robeson), and in 1951 (with Howard Keel, Kathryn Grayson, Ava Gardner,
and William Warfield). The recording released by John McGlinn in 1987 is considered definitive by many devotees of musical theater. A lavish
new production opened on Broadway in 1994.


## THE SHOW IS ON

MUSIC AND LYRICS: Vernon Duke and Ted Fetter; George and Ira Gershwin;
Hoagy Carmichael and Stanley Adams, etc.  BOOK: Sketches by David Freedman and Moss Hart
PRODUCER: Messrs. Shubert  DIRECTOR: Vincente Minnelli and Edward Clarke Lilley  CHOREOGRAPHER: Robert Alton
MAJOR PERFORMERS: Beatrice Lillie, Bert Lahr, Reginald Gardiner, Mitzi Mayfair, Paul Haakon, Gracie Barrie, Charles Walters
OPENED: 12/25/36          THEATER: Winter Garden          PERFORMANCES: 237

One of the brightest, funniest, most tuneful revues of the mid-Thirties, *The Show Is On* took a generally satirical look at various examples of
musical and nonmusical entertainment—from scat singing to burlesque shows, from *Hamlet* to Viennese waltzes (in the Gershwin brothers' "By
Strauss"), from concert arias to old-fashioned tent shows. Two brilliant comedians, Beatrice Lillie and Bert Lahr, headed the cast. The score was
made up of songs by most of the outstanding talent of the day, though only one number, "Little Old Lady," by Hoagy Carmichael and Stanley
Adams, became a popular hit.

## SILK STOCKINGS

MUSIC AND LYRICS: Cole Porter  BOOK: George S. Kaufman, Leueen McGrath and Abe Burrows
PRODUCER: Cy Feurer and Ernest H. Martin  DIRECTOR: Cy Feuer  CHOREOGRAPHER: Eugene Loring
MAJOR PERFORMERS: Hildegarde Neff, Don Ameche, Gretchen Wyler, George Tobias, Leon Belasco, Henry Lascoe, David Opatoshu
OPENED: 2/24/55          THEATER: Imperial          PERFORMANCES: 478

Cole Porter's last Broadway musical was based on the popular MGM film, *Ninotchka*, in which Greta Garbo was seen as a stern-faced Russian official who succumbs to the charms of both Paris and a French count, played by Melvyn Douglas. In the musical, *Ninotchka* (Hildegarde Neff) is again seduced by the city and a man, though this time he is an American talent agent (Don Ameche) involved in getting a Russian composer to write the score for a movie version of *War And Peace*. MGM made the screen version of *Silk Stockings* in 1957, with Fred Astaire and Cyd Charisse in the leads, and Rouben Mamoulian directing. "Fated To Be Mated" was one of the two songs Porter added for the film.


## SIMPLE SIMON

MUSIC: Richard Rodgers  LYRICS: Lorenz Hart  BOOK: Ed Wynn and Guy Bolton
PRODUCER: Florenz Ziegfeld  DIRECTOR: Zeke Colvan  CHOREOGRAPHER: Seymour Felix
MAJOR PERFORMERS: Ed Wynn,m Doree Leslie, Paul Stanton, Ruth Etting,
OPENED: 2/18/30          THEATER: Ziegfeld          PERFORMANCES: 135

Ed Wynn played Simon, who runs a newsstand in Coney Island, but Simon prefers fairytales. He dreams of Cindrella and two kingdoms, one good and one bad. Cinderella is saved by her Prince Charming who uses a Trojan Horse for the rescue. Like other Rogers and Hart shows of the period, the musical produced an essential standard in the field of theater song: "Ten Cents a Dance." "Dancing on the Ceiling" and "He Was too Good to Me" were cut from the show, but later showed up in subsequent shows.


## SINBAD

MUSIC: Sigmund Romberg and others  LYRICS: Harold Atteridge and others  BOOK: Harold Atteridge
PRODUCERS: Messrs. Shubert  DIRECTOR: J. C. Huffman  CHOREOGRAPHERS: Jack Mason, Alexis Kosloff
MAJOR PERFORMERS: Al Jolson, Kitty Doner, Mabel Withee, Forrest Huff, Grace Washburn, Alexis Kosloff
OPENED: 2/14/18          THEATER: Winter Garden          PERFORMANCES: 388

An Al Jolson show if there ever was one. The entire musical was built around him, despite a large cast, and Jolson's trademark was to improvise the script and to throw in new numbers as they suited him. This was one of Jolson's black-face roles. Besides the song "Rock-a-Bye Your Baby with a Dixie Melody," the show was the vehicle Jolson used for introducing George Gershwin's first hit, "Swanee" (on tour).


## SMOKEY JOE'S CAFE

MUSIC & LYRICS: Jerry Lieber & Mike Stoller  ORIGINAL CONCEPT: Stephen Helper & Jack Viertel; co-conceived, with additional musical staging by Otis Sallid  PRODUCER: Richard Frankel, Thomas Viertel, Steven Baruch, Jujamcyn Theaters, Jack Viertel, Rick Steiner, Frederic H. Mayerson, Center Theatre Group, Ahmanson Theatre, Gordon Davidson
MUSICAL STAGING: Joel McKneely  DIRECTOR: Jerry Zaks
MAJOR PERFORMERS: Ken Ard, Adrian Bailey, Brenda Braxton, Victor Trent Cook, B.J. Crosby, Pattie Darcy Jones, DeLee Lively, Frederick B. Owens, Michael Park
OPENED: 3/2/95          THEATER: Virginia          PERFORMANCES: (still running 6/1/97)

This show is a revue of the songs of Lieber & Stoller, which include many hits from the late 1950s and early 1960s. The songs include "Hound Dog," "Jailhouse Rock," "Kansas City," "On Broadway," "Stand by Me."


## SNOOPY

MUSIC AND LYRICS: Larry Grossman and Hal Hackaday
BOOK: Warren Lockhart, Arthur Whitelaw, Michael L. Grace, and Charles M. Schulz Creative Associates
PRODUCER: Gene Persson  DIRECTOR: Arthur Whitelaw  CHOREOGRAPHER: Marc Breaux
MAJOR PERFORMERS: David Garrison, Vicki Lewis, Kay Cole, Terry Kirvin
OPENED: 12/20/82          THEATER: Lambs          PERFORMANCES: 152

The success of *You're a Good Man, Charlie Brown*, a musical based on Charles M. Schulz's comic strip, "Peanuts," prompted another Off Broadway entertainment called *Snoopy*, which also involved the same characters in a variety of youthful attitudes and experiences. Here, though, the emphasis was placed on the activities of Charlie Brown's pet beagle (played by David Garrison). The show was first seen at the Little Fox Theatre, San Francisco, on December 9, 1975, and ran for seven months. At that time it had an entirely different cast and there were three exclamation marks after the title.

## SOMETHING FOR THE BOYS

MUSIC AND LYRICS: Cole Porter  BOOK: Herbert and Dorothy Fields
PRODUCER: Michael Todd  DIRECTOR: Hassard Short and Herbert Fields  CHOREOGRAPHER: Jack Cole
MAJOR PERFORMERS: Ethel Merman, Bill Johnson, Betty Garrett, Paula Laurence, Allen Jenkins, Betty Bruce, Anita Alvarez, Jed Prouty, Frances Mercer, Bill Callahan
OPENED: 1/7/43          THEATER: Alvin          PERFORMANCES: 422

Though it has seldom been heard from since, *Something For the Boys* was a big wartime hit, with Ethel Merman the chief attraction belting out Cole Porter songs. Vinton Freedley, who had discovered Miss Merman and produced three of her best-remembered shows, was to have been the sponsor, but he lost interest in the venture and the show came to Broadway under the banner of a brash young Broadway showman named Michael Todd. The musical, which originally had the title *Jenny Get Your Gun*, concerns Blossom Hart, a night-club entertainer turned defense worker, who is one of three cousins to inherit a ranch in Texas located right next to Kelly Field. After a series of misadventures, Blossom becomes a hero when she helps rescue an airplane in distress by picking up radio signals in the carborundum of her teeth fillings. 20th Century-Fox made a movie version in 1944, directed by Lewis Seiler, with Carmen Miranda, Perry Como, and Phil Silvers. None of the Cole Porter songs were retained.

## SOMETHING'S AFOOT

MUSIC AND LYRICS: James McDonald, David Vos and Robert Gerlach  BOOK: James McDonald, David Vos and Robert Gerlach
PRODUCER: Emanuel Azenberg, Dasha Epstein  DIRECTOR: Tony Tanner and John Mason Kirby
MAJOR PERFORMERS: Tessie O'Shea, Gary Beach, Neva Small, Marc Jordan
OPENED: 5/27/76          THEATER: Lyceum          PERFORMANCES: 61

Billed as a "Murder Mystery Musical," *Something's Afoot* was a spoof of whodunnits, particularly of the Agatha Christie stripe. Set in Rancour's Retreat, the country estate of Lord Dudley Rancour, the show had a cast of characters consisting entirely of British stereotypes, such as the birdbrained ingenue, the dissolute nephew, the pompous retired colonel, the haughty grande-dame, the formal butler, and the tweedy amateur detective (with Tessie O' Shea playing Miss Tweed). At the end of *Something's Afoot* no one remained alive—not even Miss Tweed—and the biggest laughs came from the ingenious stage devices used to do away with each character.

## SONG AND DANCE

MUSIC: Andrew Lloyd Webber  LYRICS: Don Black, Richard Maltby, Jr.
ADAPTATION: Richard Maltby, Jr.  PRODUCERS: Cameron Mackintosh, Shubert Organization, FWM Producing Group
DIRECTOR: Richard Maltby, Jr.  CHOREOGRAPHER: Peter Martins
MAJOR PERFORMERS: Bernadette Peters, Christopher d'Amboise, Gregg Burge, Charlotte d'Amboise, Cynthia Onrubia, Scott Wise
OPENED: 9/18/85          THEATER: Royale          PERFORMANCES: 474

The piece has a patchwork history of origin. In 1979 Lloyd Webber composed the set of variations of the A minor Cappriccio of Paganini, which became the act 2 or "dance" part of the show. In 1980 the composer wrote a television musical for one woman actor/singer entitled *Tell Me on a Sunday*. After some rewriting, they were presented first in London, then in New York as a full evening, with the story of an English girl who comes to New York, detours through Los Angeles, connects up with several men, wins her Green Card and some business success, and after much heartache, comes round to her true love. Act I was a virtuoso performance by Bernadette Peters on Broadway, who, alone on stage, created the presence of several other characters and situations, and with no spoken dialogue. The stand-out songs of the show have proven to be "Tell Me on a Sunday" and "Unexpected Song."

## SONG OF NORWAY

MUSIC AND LYRICS: Robert Wright and George Forrest based on music by Edvard Grieg  BOOK: Milton Lazarus
PRODUCER: Edwin Lester  DIRECTOR: Edwin Lester and Charles K Freeman  CHOREOGRAPHER: George Balanchine
MAJOR PERFORMERS: Irra Petina, Lawrence Brooks, Robert Shafer, Helena Bliss, Sig Arno, Frederic Franklin, Alexandra Danilova
OPENED: 8/21/44          THEATER: Imperial          PERFORMANCES: 860

*Song of Norway* was first presented in July 1944 by Edwin Lester's Los Angeles and San Francisco Light Opera Company. Its success prompted the move to Broadway. The operetta-type musical, with its lush score based on melodies by Edvard Grieg, spun a romanticized tale of the early years of the composer (played by Lawrence Brooks) who, with his friend, the poet Rikard Nordraak (Robert Shafer), are anxious to bring new artistic stature to Norway. Temporarily thwarted from this noble aim by his dalliance in Rome with an Italian prima donna (Irra Petina), Grieg eventually returns to his country and his patient wife (Helena Bliss) and composes the A-minor Piano Concerto. A film version of the musical was made by Cinerama in 1970, with Andrew Stone directing. Florence Henderson, Toralv Maustad, and Edward G. Robinson were in the cast.

## SOPHISTICATED LADIES

MUSIC: Duke Ellington  LYRICS: Various  CONCEPTION: Donald McKayle
PRODUCERS: Roger Berlind, Manheim Fox, Sondra Gilman, Burton Litwin, Louise Westergaard
DIRECTOR: Michael Smuin  CHOREOGRAPHERS: Donald McKayle, Michael Smuni, Henry LeTang
MAJOR PERFORMERS: Gregory Hines, Judith Jamison, Phyllis Hyman, P. J. Benjamin, Hinton Battle, Gregg Burge, Mercedes Ellington, Priscilla Baskerville.
OPENED: 3/1/81          THEATER: Lunt-Fontanne          PERFORMANCES: 767

A lavishly produced revue of Duke Ellington songs, following on the heels of *Ain't Misbehavin'* and *Eubie!* The 21-piece orchestra, led by the Duke's son Mercer, was on stage the entire time, and a festive nightclub atmosphere gave the show plenty of punch. It was a hit, despite a shaky beginning during the pre-Broadway tour. During the run Gregory Hines was succeeded by his brother, Maurice. Two road companies toured for years.

## THE SOUND OF MUSIC

MUSIC AND LYRICS: Richard Rodgers and Oscar Hammerstein II  BOOK: Howard Lindsay and Russel Crouse
PRODUCER: Leland Hayward, Richard Halliday  DIRECTOR: Vincent J. Donehue Richard Rodgers and Oscar Hammerstein II
CHOREOGRAPHER: Joe Layton
MAJOR PERFORMERS: Mary Martin, Theodore Bikel, Kurt Kasznar, Marion Marlowe, Patricia Neway
OPENED: 11/16/59          THEATER: Lunt-Fontanne          PERFORMANCES: 1,443

Rodgers and Hammerstein's final collaboration became their third longest running Broadway production. The story of *The Sound of Music* was adapted from Maria Von Trapp's autobiographical *The Trapp Family Singers* and the German film version, which Mary Martin was convinced would provide her with an ideal stage vehicle. Her husband, Richard Halliday, and producer Leland Hayward secured the rights and, initially, they planned to use only the music associated with the famed singing family plus one additional song by Rodgers and Hammerstein. Eventually, the songwriters were asked to contribute the entire score, and they also joined Halliday and Hayward as producers. The play is set in Austria in 1938. Maria Rainier (Miss Martin), a free-spirited postulant at Nonnburg Abbey, takes a position as governess to the seven children of the widowed and autocratic Capt. Georg Von Trapp (Theodore Bikel). After Maria and the captain fall in love and marry, their happiness is quickly shattered by the Nazi invasion which forces the family to flee over the Alps to Switzerland. The 1965 film version, presented by 20th Century-Fox and directed by Robert Wise, starred Julie Andrews and Christopher Plummer. According to *Variety*, from 1966 through 1969, *The Sound of Music* was the All-Time Box-Office Champion in rentals received in the U.S.-Canadian Market.


## SOUTH PACIFIC

MUSIC AND LYRICS: Richard Rodgers and Oscar Hammerstein II  BOOK: Oscar Hammerstein II and Joshua Logan
PRODUCER: Richard Rodgers and Oscar Hammerstein II, Joshua Logan and Leland Hayward  DIRECTOR: Joshua Logan
MAJOR PERFORMERS: Mary Martin, Ezio Pinza, Myron McCormick, William Tabbert, Juanita Hall, Betta St. John
OPENED: 4/7/49          THEATER: Majestic          PERFORMANCES: 1,925

*South Pacific* had the second longest Broadway run of the nine musicals with songs by Richard Rodgers and Oscar Hammerstein II. Director Joshua Logan first urged the partners to adapt a short story. "Fo' Dolla," contained in James Michener's book about World War II, *Tales of the South Pacific*. Rodgers and Hammerstein, however, felt that the story—about Lt. Joe Cable's tender romance with Liat, a Polynesian girl—was a bit too much like *Madame Butterfly*, and they suggested that another story in the collection, "Our Heroine," should provide the main plot. This one was about the unlikely attraction between Nellie Forbush, a naive Navy nurse from Little Rock, and Emile de Becque, a sophisticated French planter living on a Pacific island. Both tales were combined by having Cable and de Becque go on a dangerous mission together behind Japanese lines. This production was the first of two musicals (the other was The Sound of Music) in which Mary Martin, who played Nellie, was seen as a Rodgers and Hammerstein heroine, and it marked the Broadway debut of famed Metropolitan Opera basso, Ezio Pinza, who played de Becque. It was also the second musical to be awarded the prestigious Pulitzer Prize in drama. 20th Century-Fox co-starred Mitzi Gaynor and Rossano Brazzi in a film version in 1958. It too was directed by Joshua Logan.


## SPRING IS HERE

MUSIC: Richard Rodgers  LYRICS: Lorenz Hart  BOOK: Owen Davis
PRODUCER: Alex A. Aarons and Vinton Freedley  DIRECTOR: Alexander Leftwich  CHOREOGRAPHY: Bobby Connolly
MAJOR PERFORMERS: Glenn Hunter, Lillian Taiz, John Hundley, Charles Ruggles, Inez Courtney, Thelma White
OPENED: 3/11/29          THEATER: Alvin          PERFORMANCES: 104

The musical was adapted by Owen Davis from his play *Shotgun Wedding*. Terry loves Betty. Betty falls for Stacy, and they attempt to elope, but are stopped by her father. Terry flirts with other girls to make Betty jealous. It works, and she comes back to him for the happy ending. A pretty minor Rodgers & Hart musical, but it did produce two important songs in "With a Song in My Heart" and "Spring Is Here."


## STARLIGHT EXPRESS

MUSIC: Andrew Lloyd Webber  LYRICS: Richard Stilgoe
PRODUCER: Martin Starger & Lord Grade  DIRECTOR: Trevor Nunn  CHOREOGRAPHER: Arlene Phillips
MAJOR PERFORMERS; Ken Ard, Jamie Beth Chandler, Steve Fowler, Jane Krakowski, Ardea McArdle, Greg Mowry, Reva Rice, Robert Torti
OPENED: 3/15/87          THEATER: Gershwin          PERFORMANCES: 761

The $8 million production was a whirling, speeding, ramp-riding roller derby of a musical. The story concerns Rusty, a little steam engine, and the story of the show is basically that Rusty finds out that he could, as in "the little engine that...." The renovation of the Gershwin Theater cost $2.5 million. This flashy show has found a natural longterm home in Las Vegas (running at this writing), with a revised score.


## STARS ON ICE

MUSIC AND LYRICS: Paul McGrane and Al Stillman  PRODUCER: Sonja Henie and Arthur M. Wirtz
DIRECTOR: William H. Burke  CHOREOGRAPHER: Catherine Littlefield
MAJOR PERFORMERS: Carol Lynne, Skippy Baxter, Twinkle Watts, Freddie Trenkler, Vivienne Allen, Paul Castle
OPENED: 7/2/42          THEATER: Center          PERFORMANCES: 827

With dazzling costumes and spectacle, clowns and tumblers, speed skaters and ballet skaters, *Stars On Ice* proved a highly popular attraction at the Radio City Music Hall's big little brother across the street, the Center Theatre (later gutted to make room for office space). Among the impressive musical production numbers were a fox hunt, a South American Carnival, and a scene devoted to the lively doings prompted by the sounds emanating from a juke box on Saturday night. *Stars On Ice* was the second of six ice revues sponsored by Sonja Henie and Arthur Wirtz that played the Center Theatre between 1940 and 1949.

## STATE FAIR

MUSIC AND LYRICS: Richard Rodgers and Oscar Hammerstein II
BOOK: Tom Briggs & Louis Mattioli, based on the screenplay by Hammerstein
PRODUCERS: Phillip Langner, Robert Franz, Natalie Lloyd, Jonathan C. Herzog, Meredith Blair, Gordon Smith,
in association with Mark N. Sirangelo and The PGI Entertainment Company
DIRECTORS: James Hammerstein and Randy Skinner   CHOREOGRAPHER: Randy Skinner
MAJOR PERFORMERS: Donna McKechnie, Andrea McArdle, Kathryn Crosby, John Davidson, Scott Wise, Ben Wright
OPENED: 3/27/96          THEATER: Music Box          PERFORMANCES: 111

The only screen musical for which Broadway's Rodgers and Hammerstein collaborated on an original score, *State Fair* spun a simple tale of an Iowa farm family, the Frakes, and their adventures at the state fair. Fox had previously filmed the story, originally a novel by Phil Stong, without songs in 1933. Will Rogers, Louise Dresser, Janet Gaynor, and Norman Foster played members of the Frake family and Lew Ayres and Sally Eilers were the people they meet at the fair. In 1962, with Jose Ferrer directing, the studio remade the musical, but moved the action to Texas. It had virtually the same score plus five new songs—including "The Little Things In Texas," "Never Say 'No,'" and "Willing And Eager"—for which Rodgers supplied both words and music. The screen musical was adapted to the stage, using not only the songs from the two film versions, but also Rodgers and Hammerstein material cut from other shows.

## STOP! LOOK! LISTEN!

MUSIC & LYRICS: Irving Berlin   BOOK: Harry B. Smith
PRODUCER: Charles Dillingham   DIRECTOR: R.H. Burnside
MAJOR PERFORMERS; Gaby Deslys, Harry Fox,  Blossom Seeley, Marion Sunshine, Joseph Santley
OPENED; 12/25/15          THEATER: Globe          PERFORMANCES: 80

Attempting to follow up the success of 1914's *Watch Your Step*, producer Dillingham put together the same team, including a new score by Irving Berlin. The production was plagued with controversy, and there were several squabbles among the cast. But Berlin once again scored a success in his score. He himself always considered "I Love a Piano" his best popular song. The number was given an elaborate production, with a keyboard sweeping the width of the stage, and 3 pianists at grand pianos in front of it. The other notable number form the show was "The Girl on the Magazine Cover."

## STOP THE WORLD—I WANT TO GET OFF

MUSIC AND LYRICS: Leslie Bricusse and Anthony Newley   BOOK: Leslie Bricusse and Anthony Newley
PRODUCER: David Merrick with Bernard Delfont   DIRECTOR: Anthony Newley   CHOREOGRAPHER: Virginia Mason
MAJOR PERFORMERS: Anthony Newley, Anna Quayle
OPENED: 10/3/62          THEATER: Shubert          PERFORMANCES: 555

Anthony Newley, who also directed and starred in the original London production (Queen's Theatre, July 20, 1961), played the lead on Broadway in this colorful and imaginative allegorical musical. Littlechap, a clown version of Everyman, married the boss' daughter (Anna Quayle). As his life progresses and he becomes successful in business and politics, he begins having affairs with girls of various foreign nationalities (all played by Anna Quayle). Singing "What Kind of Fool Am I?", he ends his life reflecting on the absurdity of his ambitions. The 1966 Warner Bros. screen version, directed by Philip Saville, featured Tony Tanner and Millicent Martin. The stage production, somewhat revised, came back to Broadway in 1978 starring Sammy Davis Jr. The same year Davis also appeared in a film version of this revival entitled *Sammy Stops the World*, which was directed by Mel Shapiro.

## STREET SCENE

MUSIC AND LYRICS: Kurt Weill and Langston Hughs   BOOK: Elmer Rice
PRODUCER: Dwight Deere Wiman and The Playwrights' Company
DIRECTOR: Charles Friedman   CHOREOGRAPHER: Anna Sokolow
MAJOR PERFORMERS: Norman Cordon, Anne Jeffreys, Polyna Stoska, Brian Sullivan, Hope Emerson, Irving Kaufman, Don Saxon,
Sheila Bond, Danny Daniels, Juanita Hall
OPENED: 1/9/47          THEATER: Adelphi          PERFORMANCES: 148

Kurt Weill persuaded Elmer Rice to write the libretto based on his own Pulitzer Prize winning play with poet Langston Hughes supplying the powerful and imaginative lyrics. Billed as "a dramatic musical," the blending of drama and music was very close to genuine opera. In fact, the play went on in 1966 to become part of the repertory of the New York City Opera Company. The story deals principally with the brief, star-crossed romance of Sam Kaplan (Brian Sullivan) and Rose Maurrant (Anne Jeffreys) and the tragic consequences of the infidelity of Rose's mother (Polyna Stoska). This plot loosely frames a series of vignettes, each depicting one of the colorful characters inhabiting the seedy tenement of the setting.

## SUBWAYS ARE FOR SLEEPING

MUSIC AND LYRICS: Jule Styne, Betty Comden and Adolph Green  BOOK: Betty Comden and Adolph Green
PRODUCER: David Merrick  DIRECTOR: Michael Kidd  CHOREOGRAPHER: Michael Kidd
MAJOR PERFORMERS: Sydney Chaplin, Carol Lawrence, Orson Bean, Phyllis Newman
OPENED: 12/27/61        THEATER: St. James        PERFORMANCES: 205

With its book derived from Edmund Love's popular novel, *Subways Are for Sleeping* was a happy-go-lucky tribute to the kooky people and diverse pleasures to be found on the island of Manhattan. The story was mainly concerned with two love affairs: one was about Tom Bailey (Sydney Chaplin), a former successful businessman who now sleeps in subways, and Angie McKay (Carol Lawrence), a magazine writer; the other was about Martha Vail (Phyllis Newman), a beauty-contest winner from the south who spends most of her time clad only in a towel, and Charlie Smith (Orson Bean), who is so poor he tries to make local telephone calls collect. Though the show received mixed reviews in the seven dailies then published in New York, this did not faze producer David Merrick. He simply found seven other men with the same names as the critics and ran a large ad in the *Herald Tribune* featuring their rave notices.

## SUNNY

MUSIC: Jerome Kern  LYRICS & BOOK: Otto Harbach & Oscar Hammerstein II
PRODUCER: Charles Dillingham  DIRECTOR: Hassard Short
CHOREOGRAPHERS: Julian Mitchell, David Bennett, Alexis Kosloff, John Tiller, Fred Astaire
MAJOR PERFORMERS: Marilyn Miller, Jack Donahue, Clifton Webb, Mary Hay, Joseph Cawthorn, Paul Frawley, Cliff Edwards
OPENED: 9/22/25        THEATER: New Amsterdam        PERFORMANCES: 517

Another hit for Kern in his hit rich 1920s. Sunny (Marilyn Miller) is a bareback rider in a circus in Southampton. She's fallen for an American tourist, Tom Warren, and stows away on a ship to follow her crush. To be allowed entry into the U.S. she marries Tom's friend Jim and quickly divorces him to be with Tom. The show was a light frolic, typical of musical comedy of its time, and produced the song "Who?" and the title song.

## SUNSET BOULEVARD

MUSIC: Andrew Lloyd Webber  LYRICS & BOOK: Don Black & Christopher Hampton
PRODUCER: The Really Useful Group  DIRECTOR: Trevor Nunn
MAJOR PERFORMERS: Glenn Close, Alan Campbell, George Hearn, Alice Ripley, Alan Oppenheimer, Vincent Tumeo
OPENED: 11/17/94        THEATER: Minskoff        PERFORMANCES: 977

*Sunset Boulevard* is based on the 1950 Billy Wilder film. The show first opened in London in 1993 with Patti LuPone as the former silent screen star Norma Desmond. After several lawsuits, the role went to Glenn Close, who had played the show in Los Angeles, for the Broadway opening. The story involves a young screenwriter who happens into Norma Desmond's life. She falls in love with him, he accepts her lavish attentions. Miss Desmond desperately wants to return to the screen in her script for Salome. She doesn't, and it drives her mad.

## SWEENEY TODD, THE DEMON BARBER OF FLEET STREET

MUSIC AND LYRICS: Stephen Sondheim  BOOK: Hugh Wheeler
PRODUCER: Richard Barr, Charles Woodward, Robert Fryer, Mary Lea Johnson, Martin Richards
DIRECTOR: Harold Prince  CHOREOGRAPHER: Larry Fuller
MAJOR PERFORMERS: Angela Lansbury, Len Cariou, Victor Garber, Sarah Rice, Edmund Lyndeck
OPENED: 3/1/79        THEATER: Uris        PERFORMANCES: 558

Despite the sordidness of its main plot—a half-mad, vengeance-obsessed barber in Victorian London slits the throats of his customers whose corpses are then turned into meat pies by his accomplice, Mrs. Lovett—this near-operatic musical is a bold and often brilliant depiction of the cannibalizing effects of the Industrial Revolution. *Sweeney Todd* first appeared on the London stage in 1842 in a play called *A String of Pearls, or The Fiend of Fleet Street*. Other versions followed, the most recent being Christopher Bond's *Sweeney Todd*, produced in 1973, which served as the basis for the musical, which has entered the repertory of several prominent opera companies.

## SWEET ADELINE

MUSIC: Jerome Kern  LYRICS & BOOK: Oscar Hammerstein  PRODUCER: Arthur Hammerstein
DIRECTOR; Reginal Hammerstein  CHOREOGRAPHER: Danny Dare
MAJOR PERFORMERS: Helen Morgan, Charles Butterworth, Irene Franklin, Robert Chisholm, Violet Carlson, Max Hoffman Jr.
OPENED: 9/3/29        THEATER: Hammerstein's        PERFORMANCES: 234

After Helen Morgan's poignant performance as Julie Laverne in *Show Boat*, Kern and Hammerstein wanted to write a show to feature her talents in a starring role. This nostalgic story, set around New York in 1898, is of Addie and her three suitors, in episodic succession, reminding one of a set of 3 one acts. Her first love goes off to fight in the Spanish-American war. She then becomes a Broadway star and falls in love with a member of high society, only to be rejected by his family. She winds up with a composer with lots of talent and no money, naturally, and they presumably live happily ever after. The 1935 film version of the play starred Irene Dunne.

## TENDERLOIN

MUSIC AND LYRICS: Jerry Bock and Sheldon Harnick  BOOK: George Abbott and Jerome Weidman
PRODUCER: Robert Griffith and Harold Prince  DIRECTOR: George Abbott  CHOREOGRAPHER: Joe Layton
MAJOR PERFORMERS: Maurice Evans, Ron Husmann, Wynne Miller, Eileen Rodgers, Lee Becker, Irene Kane, Margery Gray
OPENED: 10/17/60        THEATER: 46th Street        PERFORMANCES: 216

Following the success of *Fiorello!*, the same team responsible for that musical—writers Jerry Bock, Sheldon Harnick, George Abbott, and Jerome Weidman—were reunited for another tale dealing with corruption in New York. Adapted from Samuel Hopkins Adams' novel, the story was based on the actual late Nineteenth Century crusade that Rev. Charles Henry Parkhurst led against the rampant vice and venality in the neighborhood known as the Tenderloin. As the courageous minister (here renamed Rev. Brock), Maurice Evans had his first singing role since 1933 when he appeared in the London musical, *Ball At The Savoy*.


## THEY'RE PLAYING OUR SONG

MUSIC AND LYRICS: Marvin Hamlisch and Carole Bayer Sager  BOOK: Neil Simon  PRODUCER: Emanuel Azenberg
DIRECTOR: Robert Moore  CHOREOGRAPHER: Patricia Birch  MAJOR PERFORMERS: Robert Klein. Lucie Arnaz
OPENED: 2/11/79        THEATER: Imperial        PERFORMANCES: 1,082

*They're Playing Our Song* was based in part on composer Marvin Hamlisch's often tempestuous romance with lyricist Carole Bayer Sager. In the quasi-drame á clef musical, Vernon Gersch, a wise-cracking neurotic song writer, and Sonia Walsk, a wise-cracking, neurotic lyric writer, try to have both a professional and a personal relationship despite constant interruptions caused by telephone calls from Sonia's former lover. To tell their story, the authors hit upon the notion of having only two real characters in the musical, though each has three singing alter egos, and their songs (including "They're Playing My Song" and "Fill In The Words") express how they feel about their work as well as about each other.


## THIS YEAR OF GRACE

MUSIC AND LYRICS: Noel Coward  BOOK: Sketches by Noel Coward
PRODUCER: Arch Selwyn  DIRECTOR: Frank Collins  CHOREOGRAPHER: Max Rivers
MAJOR PERFORMERS: Beatrice Lillie, Noel Coward, Queenie Leonard, Florence Desmond, Madeline Gibson, Billy Milton, Moss and Fontana
OPENED: 11/7/28        THEATER: Selwyn        PERFORMANCES: 158

Noel Coward's revue, *This Year of Grace*, scored such a success at the London Pavilion, where it opened March 22, 1928 (and eventually gave 316 performances), that even during the run the author was persuaded to costar in a Broadway version with Beatrice Lillie. Miss Lillie made the most of the comedy scenes—including her classic pantomime routine playing a frazzled but haughty woman being shoved around in a bus queue—and Coward took care of most of the sentimental ballads—including "A Room With A View."


## TICKETS, PLEASE!

MUSIC AND LYRICS: Joan Edwards and Lyn Duddy; Clay Warnick, Mel Tolkin and Lucille Kallen
BOOK: Sketches by Harry Herrmann, Edmund Rice, Jack Roche, and Ted Luce
PRODUCER: Arthur Klein  DIRECTOR: Mervyn Nelson  CHOREOGRAPHER: Joan Mann
MAJOR PERFORMERS: Paul and Grace Hartman, Jack Albertson, Tommy Wonder, Roger Price, Larry Kert
OPENED: 4/27/50        THEATER: Coronet        PERFORMANCES: 245

During the 1947-48 season, the comic dance team of Paul and Grace Hartman starred in an intimate revue, *Angel In The Wings*, which enjoyed a successful nine-month run at the Coronet Theatre. About a year and a half later, the Hartmans tried again with *Tickets, Please!* another intimate revue also shown at the Coronet. Though the run was two months less than that of its predecessor, that was still enough for the clever, unpretentious show to end up in the hit class. Among subjects dealt with in songs and sketches were roller derbies, the ballet, a Senate investigation, and the departed days of vaudeville at the Palace.


## TOO MANY GIRLS

MUSIC AND LYRICS: Richard Rodgers and Lorenz Hart  BOOK: George Marion Jr.
PRODUCER: George Abbott  DIRECTOR: George Abbott  CHOREOGRAPHER: Robert Alton
MAIOR PERFORMERS: Marcy Wescott, Desi Arnaz, Hal LeRoy, Mary Jane Walsh, Diosa Costello, Richard Kollmar, Eddie Bracken
OPENED: 10/18/39        THEATER: Imperial        PERFORMANCES: 249

By 1939, a rah-rah college show about football was not the most innovative idea along Broadway, but blessed with songs by Rodgers and Hart and fast-paced direction by George Abbott, *Too Many Girls* won the approval of both critics and public. Set in Pottawatomie College, Stop Gap, New Mexico, the musical's All-American backfield was composed of Desi Arnaz, Hal LeRoy, Richard Kollmar (succeeded by Van Johnson for the tour), and Eddie Bracken, who also act as bodyguards for wealthy co-ed Marcy Wescott.

For the movie version, made by RKO Radio in 1940 and also directed by Abbott, a new Rodgers and Hart song, "You're Nearer," was added. The cast was headed by Lucille Ball, Desi Arnaz (that's when Lucy and Desi met), Richard Kollmar, Hal LeRoy, Eddie Bracken, and Ann Miller.

## TREEMONISHA

MUSIC AND LYRICS: Scott Joplin  BOOK: Scott Joplin  PRODUCER: Adela Holzer, James Nederlander
DIRECTOR: Frank Corsaro and Victor Lurie  CHOREOGRAPHER: Louis Johnson
MAJOR PERFORMERS: Carmen Balthrop, Betty Allen, Raymond Bazemore, Ben Harney, Willard White
OPENED: 10/21/75       THEATER: Uris          PERFORMANCES: 64

Early in the century, the celebrated ragtime composer Scott Joplin took the bold step of creating an opera, *Treemonisha*, but he didn't live to see it performed on the stage. Almost seventy years later, after arranger Gunther Schuller had recreated the score from fragments, the work was given its world premiere by the Houston Grand Opera, which was the same production later shown on Broadway. In the story, set in Arkansas soon after the Civil War, the well-educated Treemonisha (so-named because as a child she was found under a tree) is abducted by a voodoo conjurer to prevent her from enlightening her superstitious neighbors. Treemonisha is rescued, forgives her abductor, and becomes a leader of her people.

## TWO BY TWO

MUSIC AND LYRICS: Richard Rodgers and Martin Charnin  BOOK: Peter Stone
PRODUCER: Richard Rodgers  DIRECTOR: Joe Layton
MAJOR PERFORMERS: Danny Kaye, Harry Goz, Madeline Kahn, Joan Copeland, Marilyn Cooper, Tricia O'Neil
OPENED: 1/10/70       THEATER: Imperial        PERFORMANCES: 352

After an absence of almost thirty years, Danny Kaye returned to Broadway in a musical based on the legend of *Noah and the Ark*. Adapted from Clifford Odets' play, *The Flowering Peach*, *Two By Two* dealt primarily with Noah's rejuvenation and his relationship with his wife and family as he undertakes the formidable task that God has commanded. During the run, Kaye suffered a torn ligament in his left leg and was briefly hospitalized. He returned hobbling on a crutch with his leg in a cast, a situation he used as an excuse to depart from the script by cutting up and clowning around. For his third musical following Oscar Hammerstein's death, composer Richard Rodgers joined lyricist Martin Charnin (later to be responsible for *Annie*) to create a melodious score that included "I Do Not Know A Day I Did Not Love You."

## TWO FOR THE SHOW

MUSIC AND LYRICS: Morgan Lewis and Nancy Hamilton  BOOK: Sketches by Nancy Hamilton
PRODUCER: Gertrude Macy and Stanley Gilkey  DIRECTOR: John Murray Anderson, Joshua Logan
CHOREOGRAPHER: Robert Alton
MAJOR PERFORMERS: Eve Arden, Alfred Drake, Keenan Wynn, Brenda Forbes, Betty Hutton, Richard Haydn, Eunice Healey, Nadine Gae, Frances Comstock
OPENED: 2/8/40          THEATER: Booth         PERFORMANCES: 124

Originally conceived as something of an antidote to left-wing revues on the order of *Pins and Needles*, the trio of *One for the Money* (1939), *Two for the Show* (1940), and *Three To Make Ready* (1946) were smart, intimate, usually well-mannered entertainments all bearing the creative stamp of Nancy Hamilton and Morgan Lewis. *Two for the Show* had two distinctions: it marked the Broadway debut of an uninhibited hoyden named Betty Hutton, and it had in "How High The Moon" the only enduring song to emerge from any of these revues. Alfred Drake and Frances Comstock introduced the ballad against the background of a wartime blackout in London.

## TWO GENTLEMEN OF VERONA

MUSIC AND LYRICS: Galt MacDermot and John Guare  BOOK: John Guare and Mel Shapiro
PRODUCER: New York Shakespeare Festival  DIRECTOR: Mel Shapiro  CHOREOGRAPHER: Jean Erdman
MAJOR PERFORMERS: Raul Julia, Clifton Davis, Jonelle Allen, Diana Davila, John Bottoms, Alix Elias
OPENED: 12/1/71       THEATER: St. James        PERFORMANCES: 613

*Two Gentlemen of Verona*, loosely based on the Shakespeare hit of 1594, was originally presented by Joseph Papp as part of the New York Shakespeare free series of free productions offered at the Delacorte Theatre in Central Park. Because of overwhelming response, it was transferred to Broadway where its blend of modern colloquialisms, ethnic references and the Bard's own words (the song "Who Is Silvia" uses the original lines in a modern musical setting) was winningly captured by a racially mixed cast. The plot covers the journey of two friends, Proteus (Raul Julia) and Valentine (Clifton Davis) from Verona to Milan and their often stormy relationships with Julia (Diana Davila) and Silvia (Jonelle Allen).

## THE UNSINKABLE MOLLY BROWN

MUSIC AND LYRICS: Meredith Willson  BOOK: Richard Morris
PRODUCER: The Theatre Guild and Dore Schary  DIRECTOR: Dore Schary  CHOREOGRAPHER: Peter Gennaro
MAJOR PERFORMERS: Tammy Grimes, Harve Presnell, Cameron Prud'homme, Edith Meiser, Christopher Hewett,
OPENED: 11/3/60          THEATER: Winter Garden       PERFORMANCES: 532

*The Unsinkable Molly Brown*, which provided Tammy Grimes with her most rewarding role in the theatre, retold the saga of a near-legendary figure of the Colorado silver mines who pulled herself up from poverty by her unswerving determination and by marrying a lucky prospector named "Leadville" Johnny Brown. Despite her gaucheries, Molly eventually becomes a leading figure in society both in Monte Carlo and—following her heroism displayed during the sinking of the Titanic—in Denver. The rousing " I Ain't Down Yet" and the stirring declaration, "I'll Never Say No" were among the most appealing numbers in Meredith Willson's score. MGM released the film version in 1964, with Debbie Reynolds and Harve Presnell co-starring and Charles Walters directing.

## UP IN CENTRAL PARK

MUSIC AND LYRICS: Sigmund Romberg and Dorothy Fields  BOOK: Herbert and Dorothy Fields
PRODUCER: Michael Todd  DIRECTOR: John Kennedy  CHOREOGRAPHER: Helen Tamiris
MAJOR PERFORMERS: Wilbur Evans, Maureen Cannon, Noah Beery, Betty Bruce, Maurice Burke
OPENED: 1/27/45          THEATER: New Century          PERFORMANCES: 504

Celebrated for his lush scores for such operettas as *The Desert Song* and *The New Moon*, Sigmund Romberg joined with lyricist Dorothy Fields to recapture the pastoral, Currier and Ives charms found up in New York's Central Park in the 1870s. The story, a combination of fact and fiction, deals with the efforts of John Matthews (Wilbur Evans), a New York Times reporter, and Thomas Nast (Maurice Burke), a *Harper's Weekly* cartoonist, to expose Tammany boss William Marcy Tweed (Noah Beery) and the other grafters who are lining their pockets with funds designated for the building of the park. Romance is supplied when John falls in love with Rosie Moore (Maureen Cannon), the daughter of a Tweed crony, and they vow their everlasting love in the ardent duet, "Close As Pages In A Book." Universal's 1948 film version starred Deanna Durbin and Dick Haymes and was directed by William A. Seiter.

## THE VAGABOND KING

MUSIC: Rudolf Friml  LYRICS: Brian Hooker  BOOK: Brian Hooker, Russell Janney, W. H. Post
PRODUCER: Russell Janney  DIRECTOR: Max Figman  CHOREOGRAPHER: Julian Alfred
MAJOR PERFORMERS: Dennis King, Carlyn Thomson, Max Figman, Herbert Corthell
OPENED: 9/21/25          THEATER: Casino          PERFORMANCES: 511

One of the last of the major operettas, and one of the most successful. By the mid 1920s the operetta style was waning on Broadway, giving way to the contemporary sounds of the Gershwin Brothers, Rodgers & Hart, Irving Berlin, and others. But the old appeal of Friml, Herbert, Romberg, and their like was still strong enough that some major shows came out of this last heyday for the style. (It's not dissimilar to the last hurrah of movie musicals in the late 1960s.) *The Vagabond King* was based on the play *If I Were a King*, set in XI century France during the reign of Louis XI. A poet-vagabond is appointed king for a day, and saves his life and defends Paris against attack. The first film version was released in 1930 (starring Dennis King and Jeanette MacDonald); another was made in 1956 (starring Kathryn Grayson and Oreste).

## VERY WARM FOR MAY

MUSIC: Jerome Kern  LYRICS & BOOK: Oscar Hammerstein II
PRODUCER: Max Gordon  DIRECTOR: Vincente Minnelli, Oscar Hammerstein, Leighton Brill
CHOREOGRAPHER: Albertina Rasch, Harry Losee
MAJOR PERFORMERS: Grace McDonald, Donald Brian, Jack Whiting, Hiram Sherman, Eve Arden, Vera Ellen
OPENED: 11/17/39          THEATER: Alvin          PERFORMANCES: 59

May is a girl, not a month in this story. May Graham, over her actor father and playwright brother's objections, runs away from home to join a barn theater. Her family is distraught and searches for her, but by the time they find her she's a big success in the barn. The book was condemned by all, even later by Hammerstein himself., but the show's saving grace was the great standard "All the Things You Are."

## VICTOR/VICTORIA

MUSIC: Henry Mancini; additional musical material by Frank Wildhorn  LYRICS: Leslie Bricusse  BOOK: Blake Edwards
PRODUCERS: Blake Edwards, Tony Adams, John Scher, Endemol Theatre Productions, Inc., PolyGram Ventures, Inc.
DIRECTOR: Blake Edwards  CHOREOGRAPHER: Rob Marshall
MAJOR PERFORMERS: Julie Andrews, Tony Roberts, Michael Nouri, Rachel York, Robert B. Shull, Adam Heller, Michael Cripe, Gregory Jbara
OPENED: 10/25/95          THEATER: Marquis          PERFORMANCES: (still running 6/1/97)

The show is based on the 1982 Blake Edwards musical film, which starred Julie Andrews, Robert Preston and James Garner. The story is set in Paris of the 1930s. A woman entertainer, in desperation, follows the advice of an aging "drag-queen" and pretends to be Victor, a Polish count who is a female impersonator. A gangster from Chicago falls for Victor, and can't understand why until he discovers that he's a she. Henry Mancini died before the show went into production, and Frank Wildhorn was brought in for additional music written on the pre-Broadway tour.

## WAIT A MINIM!

MUSIC AND LYRICS: Arranged by Andrew Tracey  BOOK: Devised by Leon Gluckman
PRODUCER: Frank Productions, Inc.  DIRECTOR: Leon Gluckman  CHOREOGRAPHER: Frank Staff and Kendrew Lascelles
MAJOR PERFORMERS: Andrew Tracey, Paul Tracey, Kendrew Lascelles, Michael Martel, Nigel Pegram, April Olrich, Dana Valery & Sarah Atkinson
OPENED: 3/7/66          THEATER: John Golden Theatre          PERFORMANCES: 457

Folk instruments and folk material combined with social and political satire were the key components of this white African revue which played over a year on Broadway, following successful runs in Africa and England.

## WHERE'S CHARLEY?

MUSIC AND LYRICS: Frank Loesser  BOOK: Gerge Abbott
PRODUCER: Cy Feuer and Ernest Martin  DIRECTOR: George Abbott  CHOREOGRAPHER: George Balanchine
MAJOR PERFORMERS: Ray Bolger, Allyn McLerie, Byron Palmer, Doretta Morrow, Horace Cooper
OPENED: 10/11/48        THEATER: St. James        PERFORMANCES: 792

*Where's Charley?* was based on Brandon Thomas' 1892 London hit, *Charley's Aunt*, one of the most durable farces in the English language. The first Broadway production to have a score by Frank Loesser, the musical deals with transvestite misunderstanding: Oxford undergraduates Charley Wykeham (Ray Bolger) and Jack Chesney (Byron Palmer) wish to entertain their lady friends, Amy Spettigue (Allyn McLerie) and Kitty Verdun (Doretta Morrow), but to do so, Charley must play chaperon by disguising himself as his own aunt ("from Brazil, where the nuts come from"). Further complications arise when the girls' guardian, Mr. Spettigue (Horace Cooper), proposes marriage to the "aunt," and also when the real aunt makes an unexpected appearance.  The musical was a perfect vehicle for dancing star Ray Bolger, who nightly invited audiences to join with him in singing "Once In Love With Amy." Bolger also played Charley—and Allyn McLerie was again his Amy—in the 1952 Warner Bros. movie version, directed by David Butler.

## WHOOPEE!

MUSIC: Walter Donaldson  LYRICS: Gus Kahn  BOOK: William Anthony McGuire  PRODUCER: Florenz Ziegfeld
DIRECTOR: William Anthony McGuire  CHOREOGRAPHERS: Seymour Felix, Tamara Geva
MAJOR PERFORMERS: Eddie Cantor, Ruth Etting, Ethel Shutta, Oaul Gregory, Frances Upton, Tamara Geva, , Buddy Ebsen
OPENED: 12/4/28        THEATER: New Amsterdam        PERFORMANCES: 379

Pure, rollicking 20s silliness. Eddie Cantor was a star of the *Ziegfeld Follies* before being featured in this book musical. It's a story of mishaps and misunderstandings, with a twisted plot, based on the play *The Nervous Wreck*. The Cantor character, Henry Williams, goes to California for his health, unwittingly interrupts the marriage plans of the daughter of a ranch owne to the local sherriff.  Henry runs off to hide from the sherriff at an Indian reservation.  Comic twists continue.  The show  is best remembered for 2 songs: "Love Me or Leave Me" and "Makin' Whoopee." There was a 1930 movie made of the show.  A revival ran 204 performances on Broadway in 1979.

## WILDCAT

MUSIC AND LYRICS: Music by Cy Coleman Lyrics by Carolyn Leigh  BOOK: N. Richard Nash
PRODUCER: Michael Kidd and N. Richard Nash  DIRECTOR: Michael Kidd  CHOREOGRAPHER: Michael Kidd
MAJOR PERFORMERS: Lucille Ball, Keith Andes, Paula Stewart, Clifford David and Don Tompkins
OPENED: 12/16/60        THEATER: Alvin        PERFORMANCES: 172

The plot took second place to the presence of the enormously popular television star Lucille Ball, for whom the show was created. Miss Ball appeared as Wildcat Jackson who, hoping to strike it rich in oil, found herself with a gusher and a husband by the final curtain. The first full score by songwriters Cy Coleman and Carolyn Leigh included the hit song "Hey, Look Me Over," which established Miss Ball's boastful character early in the first act.

## WISH YOU WERE HERE

MUSIC AND LYRICS: Harold Rome  BOOK: Arthur Kober and Joshua Logan
PRODUCER: Leland Hayward and Joshua Logan  DIRECTOR: Joshua Logan  CHOREOGRAPHER: Joshua Logan
MAJOR PERFORMERS: Sheila Bond, Jack Cassidy, Patricia Marand, Sidney Armus, Paul Valentine, Harry Clark, Florence Henderson
OPENED: 6/25/52        THEATER: Imperial        PERFORMANCES: 598

It was known as the musical with the swimming pool, but *Wish You Were Here* had other things going for it, including a castful of ingratiating performers, a warm and witty score by Harold Rome, and a director who wouldn't stop making improvements even after the Broadway opening (among them were new dances choreographed by Jerome Robbins). The musical was adapted by Arthur Kober and Joshua Logan from Kober's own play, *Having a Wonderful Time*, and was concerned with a group of middle-class New Yorkers trying to make the most of a two-week vacation at an adult summer camp in the mountains.

## WOMAN OF THE YEAR

MUSIC AND LYRICS: John Kander and Fred Ebb  BOOK: Peter Stone
PRODUCER: Lawrence Kasha, David S. Landay,  James M. Nederlander, Warner Theatre Productions Inc./ Claire Nichtern, Carole Shorenstein, Stewart Lane  DIRECTOR: Robert Moore  CHOREOGRAPHER: Tony Charmoli
MAJOR PERFORMERS: Lauren Bacall, Harry Guardino, Roderick Cook, Marilyn Cooper
OPENED: 3/29/81        THEATER: Palace        PERFORMANCES: 770

*Woman of the Year* was an updated version of the celebrated 1942 Katharine Hepburn-Spencer Tracy movie, with Lauren Bacall playing the part of a Barbara Walters-type television interviewer and Harry Guardino as a Gary Trudeau-type cartoonist. The story of their mismatched romance made for a popular Broadway attraction, with Lauren winning new laurels in an energetic song-and dance role that included her show-stopping duet with Marilyn Cooper, "The Grass Is Always Greener." During the run of the musical, Miss Bacall was succeeded by Raquel Welch, Debbie Reynolds, and Louise Troy.

## WONDERFUL TOWN

MUSIC AND LYRICS: Leonard Bernstein, Betty Comden and Adolph Green  BOOK: Joseph Fields and Jerome Chodorov
PRODUCER: Robert Fryer  DIRECTOR: George Abbott  Jerome Robbins (uncredited)  CHOREOGRAPHER: Donald Saddler
MAJOR PERFORMERS: Rosalind Russell, George Gaynes, Edith Adams, Henry Lascoe, Dort Clark, Nathanial Frey, Dody Goodman
OPENED: 2/25/53      THEATER: Winter Garden      PERFORMANCES: 559

Something of a successor to the Broadway hit, *On the Town*, which also had a score by Leonard Bernstein, Betty Comden and Adolph Green, *Wonderful Town* was another fun-filled view of Manhattan as just about the liveliest, friendliest, most colorful place on earth. The musical was based on Ruth McKenney's *New Yorker* short stories about her life in Greenwich Village with her kid sister Eileen after they had arrived from Ohio seeking careers. Set in the Thirties, the book was concerned with Ruth's attempts to get her stories sold to magazines and Eileen's difficulties in warding off admirers. After some over-amorous, Brazilian naval officers cause a near-riot, Ruth ends up in jail but also with the man she loves. Rosalind Russell, who played Ruth and scored a triumph in her only major musical-comedy role, was succeeded during the Broadway run by Carol Channing.

## WORDS AND MUSIC

MUSIC AND LYRICS: Noel Coward  BOOK: Sketches by Noel Coward  PRODUCER: Charles B. Cochran
DIRECTOR: Noel Coward  CHOREOGRAPHER: Buddy Bradley
MAJOR PERFORMERS: Ivy St. Helier, Steffi Duna, Doris Hare, John Mills, Edward Underdown, Norah Howard, Romney Brent,
Joyce Barbour
OPENED: 9/16/32      THEATER: Adelphi, London      PERFORMANCES: 164

*Words and Music* was another witty and melodic intimate revue with words and music by Noel Coward. It was not, however, without mishaps during the West End run. As the author once recalled, "One terrible night I had to conduct the orchestra unexpectedly, never having done so before. I remember the breathless agony on the faces of Joyce Barbour and John Mills when I took the tempo of "Something To Do With Spring" so fast they couldn't fit their very complicated dance to it and finally staggered off the stage cursing and exhausted." Some years later Coward did a thorough revision of *Words And Music* as a star vehicle for comedienne Beatrice Lillie. Renamed *Set To Music*, it opened at the Music Box Theatre in New York on January 18, 1939, and remained for 124 performances. Seven numbers in the previous revue were retained in the new one, including "Mad About the Boy," in which a movie idol is seen through the eyes of a society lady, a streetwalker, a cockney, and a schoolgirl. Miss Lillie was the schoolgirl.

## WORKING

MUSIC AND LYRICS: Stephen Schwartz, Craig Carnelia, James Taylor, Mary Rodgers and Susan Birkenhead, Micki Grant
BOOK: Stephen Schwartz  PRODUCER: Stephen Friedman and Irwin Meyer
DIRECTOR: Stephen Schwartz  CHOREOGRAPHER: Onna White
MAJOR PERFORMERS: Susan Bigelow, Rex Everhart, Arny Freeman, Robin Lamont, Patti LuPone
OPENED: 5/14/78      THEATER: 46th Street      PERFORMANCES: 25

Adapted from Studs Terkel's book of interviews with a variety of working men and women, this revue-type musical offered a cross-section of attitudes about the kind of work people do and why they do it. As Terkel put it, "Its theme is about a search for daily meaning as well as daily bread, for recognition as well as cash." *Working* had a score made up of songs by an assortment of writers, with Micki Grant contributing "If I Could've Been" and "Lovin' Al." On April 14, 1982, a television version was first aired over the Public Broadcasting System network, with its cast including Eileen Brennan, Barry Bostwick, Rita Moreno, and Charles Durning.

## THE YEARLING

MUSIC AND LYRICS: Michael Leonard and Herbert Martin
BOOK: Herbert Martin and Lore Noto (based on the novel by Marjorie Kinnan Rawlings)
PRODUCER: Lore Noto  DIRECTOR: Lloyd Richards  CHOREOGRAPHER: Ralph Beaumont
MAJOR PERFORMERS: David Wayne, Dolores Wilson, Carmen Mathews and Carmen Alvarez
OPENED: 12/10/65      THEATER: Alvin      PERFORMANCES: 3

Although the popular novel concerns a boy's love for his pet fawn and the boy's passage into maturity, it did not make a smooth transition to the stage in its original Broadway production. Outstanding songs from the score include "Why Did I Choose You?" and "I'm All Smiles".

## YOU NEVER KNOW

MUSIC AND LYRICS: Cole Porter  BOOK: Rowland Leigh  PRODUCER: Messrs. Shubert and John Shubert
DIRECTOR: Rowland Leigh, George Abbott (uncredited)  CHOREOGRAPHER: Robert Alton
MAJOR PERFORMERS: Clifton Webb, Lupe Velez, Libby Holman, Paul and Grace Hartman, Toby Wing, Rex O'Malley, June Preisser
OPENED: 9/21/38      THEATER: Winter Garden      PERFORMANCES: 78

One of Cole Porter's least-known musicals, *You Never Know* contained the first songs the composer wrote following a near-fatal horseback-riding accident. The show was based on a Viennese musical, *Bei Kerzenlicht*, with music by Robert Katscher, which, in turn, had been adapted from a play by Siegfried Geyer (as *Candle Light* it was seen in New York in 1929 with Gertrude Lawrence and Leslie Howard). Originally, *You Never Know* was to have had the same score as the Viennese musical, but by the time it got to Broadway only two Katscher tunes had been retained. Other major changes were made during the lengthy tryout period. Singer Jane Pickens left the cast, director George Abbott was called in, and the dancing Hartmans and June Preisser were added to perform their specialties. All this work for a romance about a valet (Clifton Webb), masquerading as his master (Rex O'Malley), and a maid (Lupe Velez), masquerading as her mistress (Libby Holman).

## YOUR ARMS TOO SHORT TO BOX WITH GOD

MUSIC AND LYRICS: Alex Bradford: Micki Grant  BOOK: Conceived by Vinnette Carroll  PRODUCER: Frankie Hewitt and
DIRECTOR: Vinnette Carroll The Shubert Organization  CHOREOGRAPHER: Talley Beatty
MAJOR PERFORMERS: Salome Bey, Clinton Derricks-Carroll, Delores Hall, William Hardy Jr.
OPENED: 12/22/76        THEATER: Lyceum        PERFORMANCES: 429

Like *Jesus Christ Superstar* and *Godspell*, *Your Arms Too Short To Box With God* was a musical retelling of the last days of Christ, from Palm
Sunday through the Passion in the Garden, the Betrayal, the Trial, and up to the Crucifixion and the Resurrection. Like *Don't Bother Me, I Can't
Cope*, it was a gospel musical first performed as a workshop project by Vinnette Carroll's Urban Arts Corps Theatre. Under the sponsorship of
the Italian government, the stirring work was first presented in the summer of 1975 at the Spoleto Festival of Two Worlds in honor of the Holy
Year; later it had a six-month run at Ford's Theatre, Washington. Return engagements on Broadway took place in 1980 (for 149 performances)
and in 1982 (for 70).


## ZIEGFELD FOLLIES OF 1919

MUSIC & LYRICS: Irving Berlin and others  SKETCHES: Gene Buck, Rennold Wolf
PRODUCER: Florenz Ziegfeld  DIRECTOR-CHOREOGRAPHER: Ned Wayburn
MAJOR PERFORMERS: Marilyn Niller, Eddie Cantor, Bert Williwmas, Eddie Dowling, Ray Dooley, Johnny Dolley, Delyele Alda, John Steel,
Van & Schench, Mary Hay
OPENED: 6/16/19        THEATER: New Amsterdam        PERFORMANCES: 171

This is the edition of the *Ziegfeld Follies* that's known for producing hit songs, including what became the theme song of the series, "A Pretty
Girl Is Like a Melody." There were the usual bevy of showgirls, this time dressed up as components of a salad. The new and much derided
Prohibition gave subject matter to one of the sketches, with the girls dressed up as soft drinks such as Coca-Cola, Saarsparilla, Grape Juice,
Lemonade and Bevo. This lavish production cost what was then a steep $100,000.


## ZIEGFELD FOLLIES OF 1936

MUSIC AND LYRICS: Vernon Duke and Ira Gershwin  BOOK: Sketches by David Freedman
PRODUCER: Mrs. Florenz Ziegfeld and the Messrs. Shubert (uncredited)  DIRECTOR: John Murray Anderson
CHOREOGRAPHER: Robert Alton, George Balanchine
MAJOR PERFORMERS: Fanny Brice, Bob Hope, Gertrude Niesen, Josephine Baker, Hugh O'Connell, Harriet Hoctor, Eve Arden,
Judy Canova, Cherry and June Preisser, John Hoystradt, Nicholas Brothers, Stan Kavanaugh
OPENED: 1/30/36        THEATER: Winter Garden        PERFORMANCES: 115

From 1907 to 1931, impresario Florenz Ziegfeld presented twenty-three editions of his legendary, opulent, star-filled revues known as the
*Ziegfeld Follies*. After the producer died in 1932, mounting debts forced his widow, actress Billie Burke, to sell the rights to the *Follies* title to her
husband's rivals, the Shubert brothers, and she also agreed to be the show's titular sponsor. There were two Shubert editions, in 1934 and in
1936, both suitably extravagant and both featuring veteran *Ziefeld Follies* clown, Fanny Brice. Because of Miss Brice's illness, the initial run of
the 1936 production was cut short, but the comedienne recovered well enough to head the cast when the show reopened in the fall, running an
additional 112 performances. The song "I Can't Get Started" (which later became Bunny Berigan's theme song) was introduced in the 1936
Follies by Bob Hope, singing it to Eve Arden; for the resumed run, Bobby Clark sang it to Gypsy Rose Lee.


## ZORBA

MUSIC AND LYRICS: John Kander and Fred Ebb  BOOK: Joseph Stein
PRODUCER: Harold Prince  DIRECTOR: Harold Prince  CHOREOGRAPHER: Ron Field
MAJOR PERFORMERS: Herschel Bernardi, Maria Karnilova, John Cunningham, Carmen Alvarez, Lorraine Serabian
OPENED: 11/17/68        THEATER: Imperial        PERFORMANCES: 305

As something of an Aegean counterpart to *Fiddler on the Roof*, Zorba offered a larger-than-life hero and a stageful of earthy, ethnic types. It also
had the same producer and librettist, and its leading roles were taken by two *Fiddler* alumni, Herschel Bernardi and Maria Karnilova. The tale
involves Zorba with a young man named Nikos who has inherited an abandoned mine on the island of Crete. This sets off a series of tragic
events, including the closing of the reopened mine, the killing of a young widow by a jealous suitor, and the death of the coquettish French
cocotte Hortense. Nothing, however, can dampen Zorba's lust for life and his desire to live it to the fullest. The saga of Zorba was first a novel
by Nikos Kazantzakis, then a popular movie starring Anthony Quinn and Lila Kedrova. Quinn and Kedrova also headed the cast of a new
production of the musical that began its cross-country tour early in 1983 and opened in New York on October 16, 1983, at the Broadway
Theatre.


## THE ZULU AND THE ZAYDA

MUSIC AND LYRICS: Harold Rome  BOOK: Howard DaSilva and Felix Leon
PRODUCER: Theodore Mann and Dore Schary  DIRECTOR: Dore Schary
MAJOR PERFORMERS: Menasha Skulnik, Ossie Davis, Louis Gossett, Joe Silver
OPENED: 11/10/65        THEATER: Cort        PERFORMANCES: 179

More of a play with music than a musical play—though it did have eleven songs—*The Zulu and the Zayda* was taken from a short story by Dan
Jacobson about the friendship, in modern-day Johannesburg, that develops between a frisky Jewish grandfather called a zayda (Menasha
Skulnik) and the young Zulu (Louis Gossett) whom the old man's family has hired to keep him out of trouble. The play's message was no less
valid for being obvious: barriers based on age, religion, race and nationality are bound to fall once people get to know one another.

# As Thousands Cheer

## SUPPER TIME

Copyright 1933 by Irving Berlin
copyright Renewed

Words and Music by
IRVING BERLIN

# EASTER PARADE

© Copyright 1933 by Irving Berlin
Copyright Renewed

Words and Music by
IRVING BERLIN

# HEAT WAVE

Copyright 1933 by Irving Berlin
Copyright Renewed

Words and Music by
IRVING BERLIN

We're hav-ing a Heat Wave, a trop-i-cal Heat Wave. The temp'-ra-ture's ris - ing, it is-n't sur-pris - ing. She cer-tain-ly can can - can. She start-ed the Heat Wave by let-ting her seat wave. And in such a way that the cus-tom-ers say that she cer-tain-ly can can - can. Gee her a-na-to-my made the mer-cur-y jump to nine-ty three. Yes sir! We're hav-ing a Heat Wave, a trop-i-cal Heat Wave. The way that she moves that ther-mo-me-ter proves that she cer-tain-ly can can - can. We're can - can.

# "The Act"

## CITY LIGHTS

Copyright © 1978 by Unichappell Music, Inc. and Kander-Ebb Inc.
All rights administered by Unichappell Music, Inc.

Words by FRED EBB
Music by JOHN KANDER

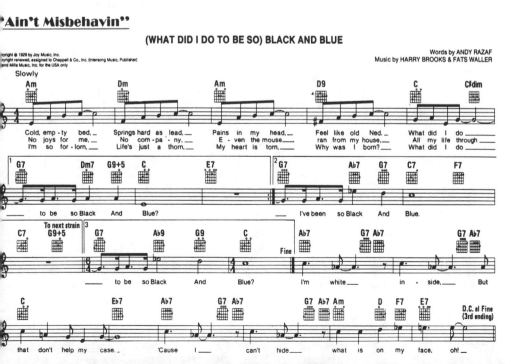

## AIN'T MISBEHAVIN'

Copyright © 1929 by Mills Music, Inc.
Copyright Renewed, Waller's Interest controlled by Chappell & Co., Inc. (Intersong Music, Publisher)
International Copyright Secured   ALL RIGHTS RESERVED

Words by ANDY RAZAF
Music by THOMAS WALLER & HARRY BROOKS

No one to talk with, all by my-self, No one to walk with, but I'm hap-py on __ the shelf, Ain't Mis-be-hav-in',

I'm sav-in' my love for you. ____ I know for cer-tain the one I love,

I'm thru with flir-tin', it's just you I'm think __ in' of. Ain't Mis-be-hav-in', I'm sav-in' my love for you. ____

__ Like Jack Horn-er in the cor-ner, don't go no-where, what do I care,

Your kiss-es are worth wait-in' for, be - lieve me I don't stay out late, don't care to go,

I'm home a-bout eight, just me and my ra - di - o, Ain't Mis-be hav-in' I'm sav-in' my love for you. ____

## LOOKIN' GOOD BUT FEELIN' BAD

Copyright © 1929 by Santley-Joy, Inc.
Copyright renewed, assigned to Chappell & Co., Inc. (Intersong Music, Publisher)

Words by A. SANTLEY
Music by FATS WALLER

Look-in' Good __ But Feel-in' Bad __ from griev-in' o - ver you, ____ Look-in' good __ to
Wea-ry days __ and lone-ly nights __ I'm wait-ing here for you, ____ Hop-in' that __ my
Look-in' Good __ But Feel-in' Bad __ is might-y hard to do, ____

hide those bit - ter blues. ____ (Blues.) love you won't re- ____ fuse. ____ Roh doh doh doh

doh doh doh. Roh doh doh doh doh. Roh doh __ doh doh __ doh doh doh. Bah bah bah bah bah

bah. ____ When I'm feel - in' blue and need-ing you.

## I'M GONNA SIT RIGHT DOWN AND WRITE MYSELF A LETTER

5 CHAPPELL & CO., INC.
wed 1963   RYTVOC, INC. and FRED AHLERT MUSIC CORP.

Words by JOE YOUNG
Music by FRED E. AHLERT

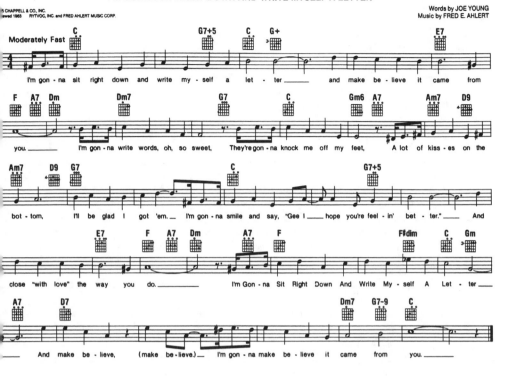

I'm gon-na sit right down and write my-self a let-ter _____ and make be-lieve it came from you. _____ I'm gon-na write words, oh, so sweet, They're gon-na knock me off my feet, A lot of kiss-es on the bot-tom, I'll be glad I got 'em. _____ I'm gon-na smile and say, "Gee I _____ hope you're feel-in' bet-ter." And close "with love" the way you do. _____ I'm Gon-na Sit Right Down And Write My-self A Let-ter _____ And make be-lieve, (make be-lieve.) _____ I'm gon-na make be-lieve it came from you.

## HANDFUL OF KEYS

opyright © 1930 and 1933 Joy Music, Inc.
yrights renewed, controlled in the USA by Chappell & Co., Inc. (Intersong Music, Publisher).

Words and Music by FATS WALLER

I like to tin-kle on an old pi-an-a.   I like to play it in a sub-tle man-nah.   I get a lot o' plea-sure
I like to sing a lit-tle tune that's mel-lah.   I like to vo-cal-ize, there's noth-ing swel-lah.   I love to have a sup-ple
I like to tin-kle on an old pi-an-a.   I like to play it in a sub-tle man-nah.   I know I'll al-ways be the

with a span-o' keys un-der-neath my fin-ger tips.   trick-lin' off _ o' my lips.   A
mel-o-dy just                                        trick-lin' off _ o' my lips.   A
top ba-na-na

hand-ful o' keys and a song to sing, _ now how could you ask for more? Than tick-lin' the i-vo-ry,

D.C. al Coda

sing-in' jive, _ I re-peat what I said be-fore. _   with a hand-ful o' keys.

## HONEYSUCKLE ROSE

Copyright © 1929 by Santly Bros., Inc.
Copyright Renewed, Waller's Interest controlled by Chappell & Co., Inc. (Intersong Music, Publisher)
International Copyright Secured    ALL RIGHTS RESERVED

Words by ANDY RAZAF
Music by THOMAS WALLER

## THE JOINT IS JUMPIN'

© 1938 PHILIP L. PONCE, INC.
© Renewed 1966 EDWIN H. MORRIS & COMPANY, A Division of MPL Communications, Inc.
and CHAPPELL & CO., INC. (INTERSONG MUSIC, Administrator)

Words by ANDY RAZAF & J.C. JOHNSON
Music by THOMAS "FATS" WALLER

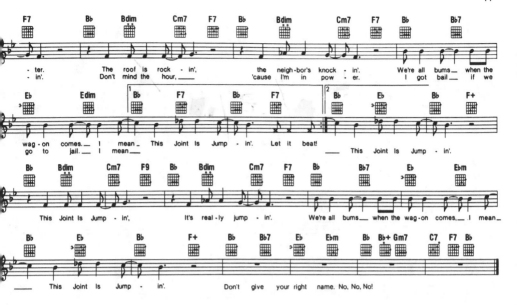

## "Allegro"

### A FELLOW NEEDS A GIRL

Copyright © 1947 by Richard Rodgers and Oscar Hammerstein II. Copyright Renewed.
Williamson Music Co., owner of publication and allied rights for all countries of the Western Hemisphere and Japan.
International Copyright Secured    ALL RIGHTS RESERVED

Words by OSCAR HAMMERSTEIN II
Music by RICHARD RODGERS

# SO FAR

Copyright © 1947 by Richard Rodgers and Oscar Hammerstein II
Copyright Renewed
WILLIAMSON MUSIC owner of publication and allied rights throughout the world

Lyrics by OSCAR HAMMERSTEIN II
Music by RICHARD RODGERS

**Gracefully and not fast**

We have noth-ing to re-mem-ber, So Far, So Far, So Far we have-n't walked by night and

shared the light of a star. So far, your heart has nev-er flut-tered so near, so near that my own

heart a-lone could hear it. We have-n't gone be-yond the ver-y be-gin-ning.

We've just be-gun to know how luck-y we are. So we have

noth-ing to re-mem-ber So Far, So Far. But now I'm face to face with you and now at last we've

met, And now we can look for-ward to the things we'll nev-er for-get!

# THE GENTLEMAN IS A DOPE

Copyright © 1947 by Richard Rodgers and Oscar Hammerstein II. Copyright Renewed.
Williamson Music Co., owner of publication and allied rights for all countries of the Western Hemisphere and Japan.
International Copyright Secured    ALL RIGHTS RESERVED

Words by OSCAR HAMMERSTEIN II
Music by RICHARD RODGERS

**Moderately**

The Gen-tle-man Is A Dope_ a man of man-y faults,. A clum-sy Joe who would-n't know a
Gen-tle man is-n't bright,. he does-'nt know the score,. A cake will come, He'll take a crumb and

Rhum-ba from a Waltz. The Gen-tle-man Is A Dope. and not my cup of tea._ (Why
nev-er ask for more. The gen-tle man's eyes are blue_ but lit-tle do they see_ (Why

do I get in a dith-er? He does-n't be-long_ to me!) The
Am I beat-ing my brains out? He does-n't be-long_ to me!)

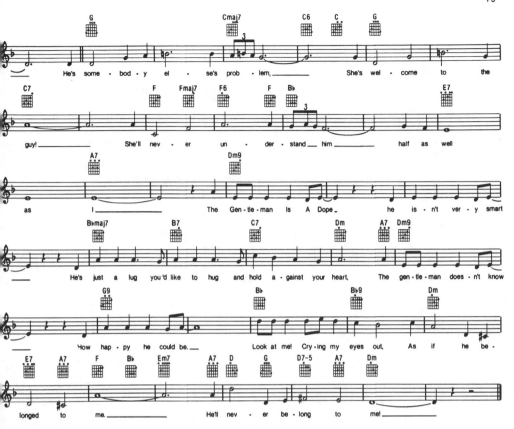

He's some·bod·y el·se's prob·lem, _____ She's wel·come to the guy! She'll nev·er un·der·stand _ him _____ half as well as I _____ The Gen·tle·man Is A Dope _ he is·n't ver·y smart _____ He's just a lug you'd like to hug and hold a·gainst your heart, The gen·tle·man does·n't know _____ How hap·py he could be. _____ Look at me! Cry·ing my eyes out, As if he be·longed to me. _____ He'll nev·er be·long to me!

## "Angel In The Wings"

### CIVILIZATION
(Bongo, Bongo, Bongo)

© 1947 EDWIN H. MORRIS & COMPANY, A Division of MPL Communications, Inc.
© Renewed 1975 EDWIN H. MORRIS & COMPANY, A Division of MPL Communications, Inc.

By BOB HILLIARD
& CARL SIGMAN

Bon·go, Bon·go, Bon·go, I don't want to leave the Con·go, Oh, no, no, no, no, no! _____ Bin·gle, ban·gle, bun·gle, I'm so hap·py in the jun·gle I re·fuse to go. _____ Don't want no bright lights, false teeth, door·bells, land·lords, I make it clear _____ That, no mat·ter how they coax me, I'll stay right here! _____ They have things like the a·tom bomb, _____ So, I think I'll stay where I 'om'. _ Civ·i·li·za·tion. _____ I'll stay right here!

# "Annie"

## EASY STREET

© 1977 EDWIN H. MORRIS & COMPANY,
A Division of MPL Communications, Inc. and CHARLES STROUSE

Lyric by MARTIN CHARNIN
Music by CHARLES STROUSE

Nice and mean

I re - mem - ber the way our saint - ed moth - er ___ would sit and croon us ___ her lul - la - by, she'd say "Kids, there's a place that's like

oth - er, ___ you got - ta get there ___ be - fore you die. You don't get there by play - in' from the rule book, ___ you stack the

a - ces, you load the dice!" Moth - er dear, oh I know you're Down There lis - t'nin', ___ we're gon - na fol - low ___ your sweet ad -

vice to { Eas - sy Street! Ea - sy Street! Where you sleep 'til noon, ___ (Yeah yeah
         { Ea - sy Street! Eas - sy Street! Where the rich folk play ___ (Play all

yeah!) She'd re - peat Ea - sy Street bet - ter get there soon. You don't
day!) Move them feet t' Ea - sy Street when you                                   get there, stay! ___

## LITTLE GIRLS

© 1977 EDWIN H. MORRIS & COMPANY,
A Division of MPL Communications, Inc. and CHARLES STROUSE

Lyric by MARTIN CHARNIN
Music by CHARLES STROUSE

Plain Mean

Lit - tle Girls, Lit - tle Girls, ev - 'ry - where I turn I can see them Lit - tle Girls, Lit - tle Girls, night and day I eat, sleep and

breathe 'em. I'm an or - di - nar - y wom - an with feel - ings, I'd like a man to nib - ble on my ear, but I ad -

mit no man has bit, so how come I'm the moth - er of the year? Lit - tle cheeks, lit - tle teeth, ev - 'ry - thing a - round me is
                                                                    How I hate lit - tle shoes, lit - tle socks and each lit - tle

lit - tle         If I wring lit - tle necks Sure - ly I will get an ac - quit - tal
bloom - er        I'd have cracked years a - go If it weren't for my sense of hu - mor

## IT'S THE HARD-KNOCK LIFE

© 1977 EDWIN H. MORRIS & COMPANY,
A Division of MPL Communications, Inc. and CHARLES STROUSE

Lyric by MARTIN CHARNIN
Music by CHARLES STROUSE

# MAYBE

© 1977 EDWIN H. MORRIS & COMPANY,
A Division of MPL Communications, Inc. and CHARLES STROUSE

Lyric by MARTIN CHARNIN
Music by CHARLES STROUSE

Maybe far a-way, Or May-be real near-by, He may be pour-ing her cof-fee, She may be straight-'ning his
Maybe in a house all hid-den by a hill, She's sit-ting play-ing pi-a-nah,

tie.
He's sit-ting pay-ing a bill. Bet-cha they're young,_ Bet-cha they're smart,_ Bet they col-lect_ things like

ash trays and art_ Bet-cha they're good_ why should-n't they be,_ Their one mis-take was giv-ing up me._ So
clos-et of clothes_ May-be they're strict_ As straight as a line,_ Don't real-ly care as long as they're mine._ So

May-be now it's time, and May-be when I wake They'll be there call-ing me "Ba-by," May-be.
May-be now this prayer's the last one of it's kind; Won't you please come get your ba-by,

May-be._

# N.Y.C.

© 1977 EDWIN H. MORRIS & COMPANY,
A Division of MPL Communications, Inc. and CHARLES STROUSE

Lyric by MARTIN CHARNIN
Music by CHARLES STROUSE

Gently

N. Y. C., What is it a-bout you? You're big, you're loud, you're tough.
N. Y. C., The Hud-son at sun-down, The roofs that scrape the sky.

N. Y. C., I go years with-out you, Then I can't get e-nough.
N. Y. C., The rich and the run-down, The big pa-rade goes by.

_ E-nough of cab driv-ers an-swer-ing back in lan-guage far from pure, E-nough of
Now, Fris-co does have an in-trest-ing bay, Kan-sas Cit-y has good steaks, Chi-ca-go's

frank-furt-ers an-swer-ing back... Broth-er you know you're in N. Y. C., Too bus-y, too
loop may be fun for a day._ New Or-leans real-ly shakes, but, N. Y. C., You make 'em all

cra-zy, too hot, too cold; Too late, I'm sold a-gain on N. Y. C.
post-cards. You snap. you fizz; The best there is is you, is N. Y. C.

# TOMORROW

© 1977 EDWIN H. MORRIS & COMPANY,
A Division of MPL Communications, Inc. and CHARLES STROUSE

Lyric by MARTIN CHARNIN
Music by CHARLES STROUSE

# YOU'RE NEVER FULLY DRESSED WITHOUT A SMILE

© 1977 EDWIN H. MORRIS & COMPANY,
A Division of MPL Communications, Inc. and CHARLES STROUSE

Lyric by MARTIN CHARNIN
Music by CHARLES STROUSE

# "Annie Get Your Gun"

© Copyright 1946 by Irving Berlin
Copyright Renewed

## ANYTHING YOU CAN DO

Words and Music by
IRVING BERLIN

## THERE'S NO BUSINESS LIKE SHOW BUSINESS

© Copyright 1946 by Irving Berlin
Copyright Renewed

Words and Music by
IRVING BERLIN

# THEY SAY IT'S WONDERFUL

© Copyright 1946 by Irving Berlin
Copyright Renewed

Words and Music by
IRVING BERLIN

# Aspects Of Love"

## LOVE CHANGES EVERYTHING

Copyright 1988 The Really Useful Group Ltd.
Rights for the US controlled by R&H Music Co.

Music by ANDREW LLOYD WEBBER
Lyrics by DON BLACK and CHARLES HART

**Drammatico**

Love, Love Chan-ges Ev-'ry-thing: hands and fac-es, earth and sky. Love, Love Chan-ges Ev-'ry-thing: how you
Love, Love Chan-ges Ev-'ry-thing: days are long-er, words mean more. Love, Love Chan-ges Ev-'ry-thing: pain is

live and how you die. Love can make the sum-mer fly or a night seem like a life-time. Yes
deep-er than be-fore. Love will turn your world a-round and that world will last for-ev-er. Yes

love, Love Chan-ges Ev-'ry-thing, now I trem-ble at your name.
love, Love Chan-ges Ev-'ry-thing, brings you glo-ry, brings you shame. Noth-ing in the world will ev-er be the

same. same.

Off in-to the world we go, plan-ning fu-tures, shap-ing years. Love bursts in and

sud-den-ly all our wis-dom dis-ap-pears. Love makes fools of ev-'ry-one: all the rules we make are

bro-ken. Yes love, love chan-ges ev-'ry-one. Live or per-ish in its flame. Love will nev-er, nev-er let you

be the same. Love will nev-er, nev-er let you be the same.

# OTHER PLEASURES

© Copyright 1989 The Really Useful Group Ltd.
All Rights for the US controlled by R&H Music Co.

Music by ANDREW LLOYD WEBBER
Lyrics by DON BLACK and CHARLES HART

# SEEING IS BELIEVING

Copyright 1989 The Really Useful Group Ltd.
All Rights for the US controlled by R&H Music Co.

Music by ANDREW LLOYD WEBBER
Lyrics by DON BLACK and CHARLES HART

ALEX: See-ing Is Be-liev-ing, and in my arms I see her: she's here, real-ly here, real-ly mine now she seems at home here...

See-ing Is Be-liev-ing. I dreamt that it would be her: at last life is full, life is fine now...

What-ev-er hap-pens, one thing is cer-tain: each time I see a train go by, I'll think of us, the night, the sky for-ev-

er... See-ing Is Be-liev-ing, my life is just be-gin-ning we touched and my head won't stop spin-ning _____ from

win - ning _____ your love!

ROSE: He's young, ver-y young, but ap-peal-ing
[MALE] Alternative: She's warm and she's wild and

I feel I know him... See-ing Is Be-liev-ing, and I like what I see here. I like where I am, what I'm feel-ing...
her

What are we do-ing? Can you be-lieve it? A starv-ing act-ress and a star struck boy oh well, I might as
who knows? Who cares? Let's

well en-joy the mo - ment...
just

BOTH: What-ev - er hap-pens, we have this mo-ment. Who needs to-mor-row, when we have to-day? To-

night we'll mean the things we say for-ev - er. See-ing Is Be-liev-ing! My life is just be-gin-ning! We

touched, and my head won't stop spin - ning _____ from win - ning _____ your love!

**LITTLE HANDS**
(Based on themes of S. Rachmaninoff)

© 1966 ROBERT WRIGHT and GEORGE FORREST
All Rights Throughout the Entire World Controlled by FRANK MUSIC CORP.

Music and Lyric by
ROBERT WRIGHT & GEORGE FORREST

Lit - tle Hands, Lit - tle fin - gers that steal in - to mine___ Seek - ing safe - ty and warmth, Bring - ing faith and trust in me.___ Lit - tle eyes With all of life a - shine,___ That turn my som - ber day to sun - light___ Lit - tle lips, Lit - tle se - crets they whis - per to me,___ In each dear lit - tle word It's the voice of Him I hear;___ Him to whom I bend my knee, Giv - ing thanks that He His gift of love has sent to me By Lit - tle Hands.___ Lit - tle Hands.___

**"Anyone Can Whistle"**

**ANYONE CAN WHISTLE**

Copyright © 1968 by Stephen Sondheim
Burthen Music, Co., Inc., Owner of publication and allied rights
Chappell & Co., Inc., Administrator

Words and Music by
STEPHEN SONDHEIM

An - y - one Can Whis - tle, that's what they say, eas - y.___ An - y - one Can Whis - tle, an - y old day, eas - y.___ It's all so sim - ple: Re - lax, let go, let fly! So some - one tell me why can't I?___ I can dance a tan - go, I can read Greek, eas - y.___

I can slay a drag-on an-y old week, eas-y! _____ What's hard is sim-ple, what's nat-u-ral comes hard.

May-be you could show me how to let go, low-er my guard, learn to be free, May-be if you whis-tle, whis-tle for me. _____

# "The Apple Tree"

Copyright © 1966 by Appletree Music Company
All rights administered by Hudson Bay Music, Inc.
Used by Permission

## BEAUTIFUL, BEAUTIFUL WORLD

Lyric by SHELDON HARNICK
Music by JERRY BOCK

I see an-i-mals and birds and flow-ers, Ev-'ry col-or, ev-'ry shape and size; Moss and peb-bles and a host of won-ders,
I hear chat-ter-ing and I hear chirp-ing, Whis-tling, mur-mur-ing and honks and snorts; When I sim-ply take the time to lis-ten,
Still it's pos-si-ble a day may come, When mo-men-tar-i-ly the world wears thin; If I wea-ry of the world out-side me,

Gleam-ing ev-'ry-where I aim my eyes. So if ev-er I'm at-tacked by bore-dom, I'll just o-pen up my eyes and see
I hear mu-sic of a thou-sand sorts. So if ev-er I would rest my eyes, My ears can eas-i-ly de-scribe to me
I can al-ways take a good look in. For a-long with ev-'ry cloud and cob-web, I'm em-phat-i-c'ly a mem-ber of

This di-ver-si-fied, cu-ri-ous, fas-ci-nat-ing boun-ti-ful, Beau-ti-ful, Beau-ti-ful

World. World. World, thank you ver-y much for

all I see, hear, taste and touch; Plus ev-'ry whiff I sniff. (Sniff)

Beau-ti-ful World I love. _____

## "Babes In Arms"

# I WISH I WERE IN LOVE AGAIN

Copyright © 1937 by Chappell & Co.
Copyright Renewed
The interest of Richard Rodgers for the extended term of copyright assigned to the
Rodgers Family Partnership (Administered by Williamson Music)
Rights on behalf of The Estate of Lorenz Hart administered by WB Music Corp.

Words by LORENZ HART
Music by RICHARD RODGERS

The sleep-less nights, The dai-ly fights, The quick to-bog-gan when you reach the heights; I miss the kiss-es and I
fur-tive sigh, The black-ened eye, The words "I'll love you till the day I die," The self de-cep-tion that be-

miss the bites, I Wish I Were In Love A-gain! The brok-en dates, The end-less waits, The love-ly lov-ing and the
lieves the lie, I Wish I Were In Love A-gain! When love con-geals It soon re-veals The faint a-ro-ma of per-

hate-ful hates, The con-ver-sa-tion with the fly-ing plates, I Wish I Were In Love A-gain! No more
form-ing seals, The dou-ble cross-ing of a pair of heels I Wish I Were In Love A-gain! No more

pain, No more strain, Now I'm sane, but I would rath-er be
care, No de-spair, I'm all there now, But I'd rath-er be

ga-ga! The pulled out fur of cat and cur, The fine mis-mat-ing of a him and her, I've
punch-drunk! Be-lieve me sir, I much pre-fer The clas-sic bat-tle of a him and her, I

learned my les-son, but I Wish I Were In Love A-gain! The
don't like qui-et and I Wish I Were In Love A-gain!

# JOHNNY ONE NOTE

Copyright © 1937 by Chappell & Co.
Copyright Renewed
The interest of Richard Rodgers for the extended term of copyright assigned to the
Rodgers Family Partnership (Administered by Williamson Music)
Rights on behalf of The Estate of Lorenz Hart administered by WB Music Corp.

Words by LORENZ HART
Music by RICHARD RODGERS

Poor John-ny One-Note. {Sang out with gus-to And just o-ver-lord-ed the
{Got in A-i-da. In-deed a great chance to be

place. Poor John-ny One-Note Yelled wil-ly-nil-ly, Un-til he was
brave. He took his one note Howled like the North Wind, Brought forth wind, that

93

Copyright © 1937 by Chappell & Co.
Copyright Renewed
The interest of Richard Rodgers for the extended term of copyright assigned to the
Rodgers Family Partnership (Administered by Williamson Music)
Rights on behalf of The Estate of Lorenz Hart administered by WB Music Corp.

# THE LADY IS A TRAMP

Words by LORENZ HART
Music by RICHARD RODGERS

I get too hun-gry for din-ner at eight,___ I like the thea-tre but
I don't like crap games With Bar-ons and Earls,___ Won't go to Har-lem In

nev-er come late.___ I nev-er both-er with peo-ple I hate.
er-mine and pearls,___ Won't dish the dirt with the rest of the girls.

That's why The La-dy Is A Tramp.___
That's why The La-dy Is A Tramp. I like the free fresh

wind in my hair,___ Life with-out care.___ I'm broke,___ it's oke,___ Hate Cal-i-

for-nia, It's cold and it's damp,___ That's why The La-dy Is A Tramp.

# WHERE OR WHEN

Copyright © 1937 by Chappell & Co.
Copyright Renewed
The interest of Richard Rodgers for the extended term of copyright assigned to the
Rodgers Family Partnership (Administered by Williamson Music)
Rights on behalf of The Estate of Lorenz Hart administered by WB Music Corp.

Words by LORENZ HART
Music by RICHARD RODGERS

It seems we stood and talked like this be-fore. We looked at each oth-er in the same way then, But I can't re-mem-ber Where Or

When.___ The clothes you're wear-ing are the clothes you wore. The smile you are smil-ing you were smil-ing then,

But I can't re-mem-ber Where Or When. Some things that hap-pen for the first time,

Seem to be hap-pen-ing a-gain.___ And so it seems that we have met be-fore, and

laughed be-fore, and loved be-fore, But who knows Where Or When!___

# MY FUNNY VALENTINE

Copyright © 1937 by Chappell & Co.
Copyright Renewed
The interest of Richard Rodgers for the extended term of copyright assigned to the
Rodgers Family Partnership (Administered by Williamson Music)
Rights on behalf of The Estate Of Lorenz Hart administered by WB Music Corp.

Words by LORENZ HART
Music by RICHARD RODGERS

My Fun-ny Val-en-tine, Sweet com-ic Val-en-tine, You make me smile with my heart. Your looks are laugh-a-ble, Un-pho-to-graph-a-ble, Yet, you're my fav-'rite work of art. Is your fig-ure less than Greek; Is your mouth a lit-tle weak, when you o-pen it to speak, Are you smart? But don't change a hair for me, Not if you care for me, Stay lit-tle Val-en-tine, stay! Each day is Val-en-tine's day.

## "Bajour"

### MUST IT BE LOVE?

© 1964 WALTER MARKS
All Rights Throughout the World Controlled by MPL COMMUNICATIONS, INC.

Music and Lyrics by
WALTER MARKS

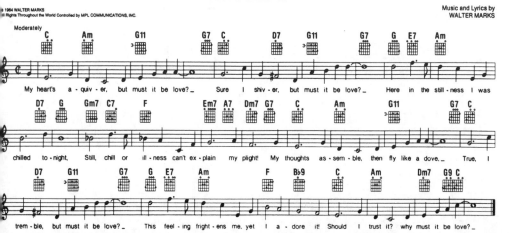

My heart's a-quiv-er, but must it be love?_ Sure I shiv-er, but must it be love?_ Here in the still-ness I was chilled to-night, Still, chill or ill-ness can't ex-plain my plight! My thoughts as-sem-ble, then fly like a dove._ True, I trem-ble, but must it be love?_ This feel-ing fright-ens me, yet I a-dore it! Should I trust it? why must it be love?_

# "Beauty And The Beast: A New Musical"

## IF I CAN'T LOVE HER

© 1994 Wonderland Music Company, Inc., Menken Music, Trunksong Music Ltd. and Walt Disney Music Company

Music by ALAN MENKEN
Lyrics by TIM RICE

# BEAUTY AND THE BEAST

© 1991 Walt Disney Music Company and Wonderland Music Company, Inc.

Lyrics by HOWARD ASHMAN
Music by ALAN MENKEN

"Betsy"

# BLUE SKIES

© Copyright 1927 by Irving Berlin
Copyright Renewed

Words and Music by
IRVING BERLIN

**Moderately**

| | | | | | | | |
|---|---|---|---|---|---|---|---|
| Em | B+/D♯ | B7/D♯ | G/D | C♯m7♭5 | Cm6/E♭ | G/D | |

Blue Skies _____ smil - ing at me. _____ Noth - ing but Blue Skies _____

| C9 | D+ | G | | Em | B+/D♯ | B7/D♯ | G/D |

_____ do I see. _____ Blue - birds _____ sing - ing a song; _____

| C♯m7♭5 | Cm6/E♭ | G/D | C9 | D+ | G | | |

_____ noth - ing but blue - birds _____ all day long. _____ Nev - er saw the sun

| Cm/G | G | Cm/G | G | Cm/G | G | | Cm/G | G |

shin - ing so bright. Nev - er saw things go - ing so right. No - tic - ing the days hur - ry - ing by;

| Cm/G | G | D7 | G | B+ | Em | B+/D♯ | B7/D♯ | G/D | C♯m7♭5 | Cm6/E♭ |

when you're in love, my how they fly. Blue days, _____ all of them gone. _____ Noth - ing but

| G/D | | C9 | D+ | | **1** G | | **2** G | D | G |

Blue Skies _____ from now on. _____

# BELLS ARE RINGING

Copyright © 1956 by Betty Comden, Adolph Green and Jule Styne
Copyright Renewed
Stratford Music Corporation, owner of publication and allied rights throughout the world
Chappell & Co., Administrator

Words by BETTY COMDEN and ADOLPH GREEN
Music by JULE STYNE

# THE PARTY'S OVER

Copyright © 1956 by Betty Comden, Adolph Green and Jule Styne
Copyright Renewed
Stratford Music Corporation, owner of publication and allied rights throughout the world
Chappell & Co., Administrator

Words by BETTY COMDEN and ADOLPH GREEN
Music by JULE STYNE

_____ The can - dles flick - er and dim._____ You danced and dreamed through the night, It seemed to be right just be - ing with him. _____

_____ Now you must wake up._____ All dreams must end._____ Take off your make - up. _____

_____ The Par - ty's O - ver,_____ It's all o - ver_____ my friend.

## JUST IN TIME

Copyright © 1956 by Betty Comden, Adolph Green and Jule Styne
Copyright Renewed
Stratford Music Corporation, owner of publication and allied rights throughout the world
Chappell & Co., Administrator

Words by BETTY COMDEN and ADOLPH GREEN
Music by JULE STYNE

Just In Time_____ I found you Just In Time_____ Be - fore you came, my time_____ was run - ning

low._____ I was lost,_____ The los - ing dice were tossed,_____ My bridg - es all were crossed,_____

_____ no - where to go._____ Now you're here_____ and now I know just where I'm go - ing, no more

doubt or fear,_____ I've found my way._____ For love came Just In Time._____ You found me Just In Time

and changed my lone - ly life, that love - ly day._____ day._____

# LONG BEFORE I KNEW YOU

Copyright © 1959, 1960 by Betty Comden, Adolph Green and Jule Styne
Copyright Renewed
Stratford Music Corp., owner, and Chappell & Co., Administrator
of publication and allied rights for the Western Hemisphere

Words by BETTY COMDEN and ADOLPH GREE
Music by JULE STYN

Long Be-fore I Knew You.___ Long be-fore I met you,___ I was sure I'd find you___ some-day some

how.___ I pic-tured some-one who'd walk and talk and smile as you do, And make me feel a

you do right now.___ All that was long be-fore I held you,___ Long be-fore I kissed you,___

Long be-fore I touched you___ and felt this glow.___ But now you real-ly are here and

now at last I know That Long Be-fore I Knew You___ I loved you so.___

## "Ben Franklin In Paris"

### HOW LAUGHABLE IT IS

© 1984 MARK SANDRICH, JR. and SIDNEY MICHAELS
All Rights Throughout the World Controlled by MORLEY MUSIC CO.

Lyric by SIDNEY MICHAE
Music by MARK SANDRICH,

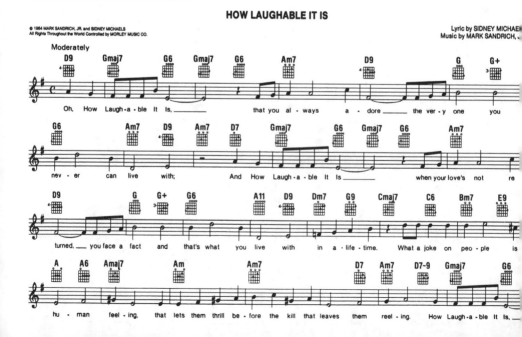

Oh, How Laugh-a-ble It Is,___ that you al-ways a-dore___ the ver-y one you

nev-er can live with; And How Laugh-a-ble It Is___ when your love's not re

turned,___ you face a fact and that's what you live with in a life-time. What a joke on peo-ple is

hu-man feel-ing, that lets them thrill be-fore the kill that leaves them reel-ing. How Laugh-a-ble It Is,

that my heart runs to hug___ the ver-y love that nev-er can ev-er be. I have

ev-'ry-thing my life re-quires, ex-cept the thing my heart de-sires; ___ some-one who can make me de-

pend-ent and free; ___ laugh-a-ble it is and the laugh is on me. ___

## LOOK FOR SMALL PLEASURES

1963, 1964 MARK SANDRICH, JR. and SIDNEY MICHAELS
Rights Throughout the World Controlled by MORLEY MUSIC CO.

Lyric by SIDNEY MICHAELS
Music by MARK SANDRICH, JR.

Moderately, with feeling

Look For Small Pleas-ures that hap-pen ev-'ry day; And not for for-tune or fame. ___

In-fi-nite treas-ures lie all a-long the way, As do can-dles wait-ing for flame. ___ How

sim-ple the joys at our fin-ger-tips, ___ This plain air we share is cham-pagne one sips.

Look For Small Pleas-ures up-on this ball of clay And not for light-ning to tame.

___ And one day there's some-one, Just a friend-ly some-one, Who'll be hus-band or wife to you, Be the

love of all your life to you; And you'll find how great small pleas-ures can prove. prove. ___

## "Best Foot Forward"

### BUCKLE DOWN, WINSOCKI

Copyright © 1941 by Chappell & Co., Inc.
Copyright Renewed
International Copyright Secured   ALL RIGHTS RESERVED

Words and Music by
HUGH MARTIN & RALPH BLANE

## "Between The Devil"

### BY MYSELF

Copyright © 1937 by DeSylva, Brown & Henderson, Inc.
Copyright Renewed, Assigned to Chappell & Co., Inc.
International Copyright Secured   ALL RIGHTS RESERVED

Words by HOWARD DIETZ
Music by ARTHUR SCHWARTZ

**TRIPLETS**

Words by HOWARD DIETZ
Music by ARTHUR SCHWARTZ

Copyright © 1937 by DeSylva, Brown & Henderson, Inc.
Copyright Renewed, assigned to Chappell & Co., Inc.

*Comically*

We do ev - 'ry-thing a - like ____ We look a - like, we dress a - like, we walk a - like, we talk a - like, and what is more we

hate each oth - er ver - y much. ____ We hate our folks, we're sick of jokes, on what an art it is to tell us a - part.

*If We*

one of us gets the meas - les, an - oth-er one gets the meas - les, then all of us gets the meas - les and mumps and croup. ____

eat the same kind of vit - tels, we drink the same kind of bot - tles, we sit in the same kind of high chair (hi - chair, hi - chair).

How I wish I had a gun, ____ a lit - tle gun, it would be fun to shoot the oth - er two and be on - ly one. ____ one. ____

# I SEE YOUR FACE BEFORE ME

Copyright © 1937 by DeSylva, Brown & Henderson, Inc.
Copyright Renewed, Assigned to Chappell & Co., Inc.
International Copyright Secured    ALL RIGHTS RESERVED

Words by HOWARD DIETZ
Music by ARTHUR SCHWARTZ

Moderately Slow

I See Your Face Be-fore Me Crowd-ing my ev' - ry dream, There is your face be-

fore me, You are my on-ly theme. It does-n't mat - ter where you are I can see how

fair you are I close my eyes and there you are, Al - ways. If you could share the

mag - ic If you could see me too There would be noth - ing trag - ic

In all my dreams of you. Would that my love could haunt you so; Know - ing I

want you so, I can't e-rase your beau-ti-ful face be-fore me.

# Big River"

## RIVER IN THE RAIN

Copyright © 1985 Tree Publishing Co., Inc. and Roger Miller Music, 8 Music Square West, Nashville, TN 37203
Rights administered by Tree International

Music and Lyrics by
ROGER MILLER

# MUDDY WATER

Copyright © 1966 Tree Publishing Co., Inc. and Roger Miller Music, 8 Music Square West, Nashville, TN 37203
All rights administered by Tree International

Music and Lyrics
ROGER MILLER

hide some-place to find my-self a-gain. Look out for me, oh, Mud-dy Wa-ter, your mys-ter-ies are deep and wide. And I got a need for go-in' some-place, and I got a need to climb up-on your back and ride.

## WAITIN' FOR THE LIGHT TO SHINE

Copyright © 1985 Tree Publishing Co., Inc. and Roger Miller Music, 8 Music Square West, Nashville, TN 37203
All rights administered by Tree International

Music and Lyrics by
ROGER MILLER

Slowly (in a folk style)

HUCK:

I have lived in the dark-ness for so long, I'm Wait-in' For The Light To Shine.

Far be-yond hor-i-zons I have seen, be-yond the things I've been, be-yond the dreams I've dreamed are the things I've done. In fact, each and ev-'ry one are the way that I was taught to run. I am wait-ing for the light to shine, I am wait-ing for the light to shine. I have lived in the dark-ness for so long, I'm wait-ing for the light to shine.

Tacet

# WORLDS APART

Copyright © 1985 by Tree Publishing Co., Inc. and Roger Miller Music, 8 Music Square West, Nashville, TN 37203
All rights administered by Tree International

Music and Lyrics
ROGER MILLER

part. To - geth - er, but Worlds___ A - part. And a mock - ing - bird

sings in an ole yon - der tree, twad - dle - ee ah dee dee dah dee dee dee.___

# "Blackbirds Of 1928"

## I CAN'T GIVE YOU ANYTHING BUT LOVE

Copyright © 1928 ALDI MUSIC and IRENEADELE MUSIC
Copyright Renewed
Pursuant to Sections 304© and 401(b) of the U.S. Copyright Law.

Words by DOROTHY FIELDS
Music by JIMMY McHUGH

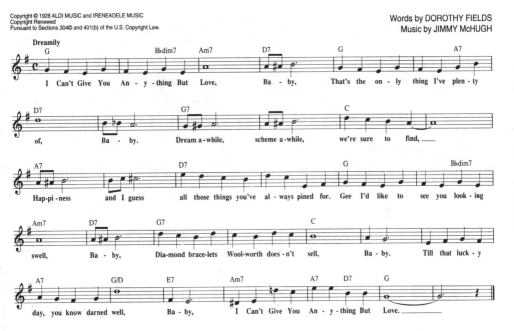

I Can't Give You An - y - thing But Love, Ba - by, That's the on - ly thing I've plen - ty

of, Ba - by. Dream a - while, scheme a - while, we're sure to find, ___

Hap - pi - ness and I guess all those things you've al - ways pined for. Gee I'd like to see you look - ing

swell, Ba - by, Dia - mond brace - lets Wool - worth does - n't sell, Ba - by. Till that luck - y

day, you know darned well, Ba - by, I Can't Give You An - y - thing But Love. ___

# "Bloomer Girl"

## EVELINA

Copyright © 1944 by Chappell & Co., Inc.
Copyright renewed

Words by E.Y. HARBURG
Music by HAROLD ARLEN

Slowly with rhythm

E - ve - li - na, won't ya ev - er take a shine to that moon? _____ E - ve - li - na, ain't ya

both - ered by the bo - bo - link's tune? _____ Tell me, tell me how long _____ ya gon - na

keep de - lay - in' the day. Don't_ ya reck - on it's wrong_ Tri - flin' with A - pril this

way? E - ve - li - na, won't ya pay a lit - tle mind to me soon? _____

Wake up! Wake up! The earth is fair, the fruit is fine _____ But what's the use o' smel - lin' wa - ter - mel - on

cling - in' to an - oth - er fel - la's vine? E - ve - li - na, won't ya roll off that vine an' be mine? _____

# RIGHT AS THE RAIN

Words by E.Y. HARBURG
Music by HAROLD ARLEN

opyright © 1944 by Chappell & Co., Inc.
opyright renewed

Right As The Rain that falls from a-bove; So real, so right, Is our love. It came like the spring that breaks thru the snow. I can't say what it may bring I on-ly know, I on-ly know it's right to be-lieve whatev-er gave your eyes this glow What-ev-er gave my heart this song can't be wrong. It's Right As The Rain that falls from a-bove and fills the world with the bloom of our love. love. As rain must fall and day must dawn, This love, this love must go on.

## "Bow Bells"

### YOU'RE BLASÉ

Copyright © 1931 by Chappell & Co., Ltd.
Copyright renewed, published in the USA by Chappell & Co., Inc.

Words by BRUCE SIEVIER
Music by ORD HAMILTON

Moderately Slow

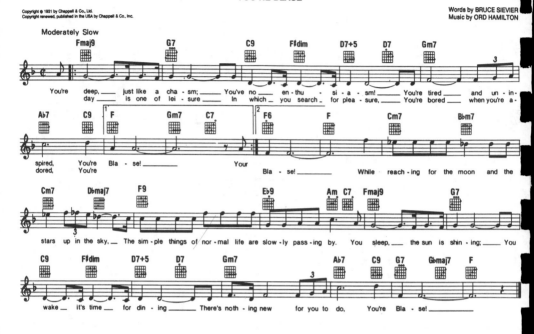

You're deep, _____ just like a cha-sm; You've no _____ en-thu-si-a-sm! _____ You're tired _____ and un-in-
day _____ is one of lei-sure In which _ you search _ for plea-sure, _____ You're bored _____ when you're a-

spired, You're Bla-se! _____ Your
dored, You're Bla-se! _____ While reach-ing for the moon and the

stars up in the sky, _____ The sim-ple things of nor-mal life are slow-ly pass-ing by. You sleep, _____ the sun is shin-ing; _____ You

wake _____ it's time _____ for din-ing _____ There's noth-ing new for you to do, You're Bla-se! _____

## "The Boys From Syracuse"

### SING FOR YOUR SUPPER

Copyright © 1938 by Chappell & Co.
Copyright Renewed
Rights on behalf of The Estate of Lorenz Hart administered by WB Music Corp.

Words by LORENZ HART
Music by RICHARD RODGERS

Moderately

Sing For Your Sup-per And you'll get break-fast, Song-birds al-ways eat If their song is sweet to hear. _____

Sing for your lunch-eon And you'll get din-ner, Dine with wine of choice If ro-mance is in your

voice. _____ I heard _____ from a wise ca-na-ry, Trill-ing makes a fel-low will-ing; So, _____ lit-tle

swal-low, swal-low now. Now is the time to Sing For Your Sup-per And you'll get break-fast, Song-birds are not dumb.

They don't buy a crumb of bread. It's said. So sing and you'll be fed. _____

# FALLING IN LOVE WITH LOVE

Copyright © 1938 by Chappell & Co.
Copyright Renewed
Rights on behalf of The Estate of Lorenz Hart administered by WB Music Corp.

Words by LORENZ HART
Music by RICHARD RODGERS

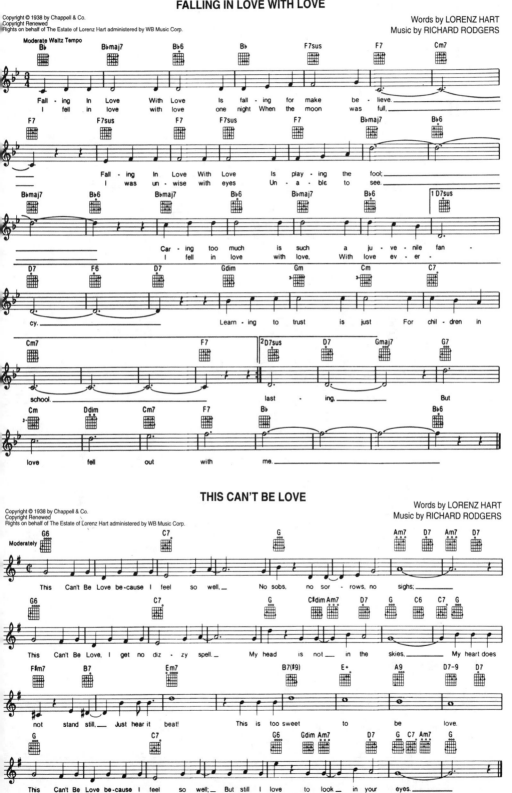

# THIS CAN'T BE LOVE

Copyright © 1938 by Chappell & Co.
Copyright Renewed
Rights on behalf of The Estate of Lorenz Hart administered by WB Music Corp.

Words by LORENZ HART
Music by RICHARD RODGERS

# "Bravo Giovanni"

## IF I WERE THE MAN

© 1962 RONNY GRAHAM and MILTON SCHAFER
All Rights Throughout the World Controlled by EDWIN H. MORRIS & COMPANY,
A Division of MPL Communications, Inc. and GIOVANNI MUSIC, INC.

Lyric by RONNIE GRAHAM
Music by MILTON SCHAFER

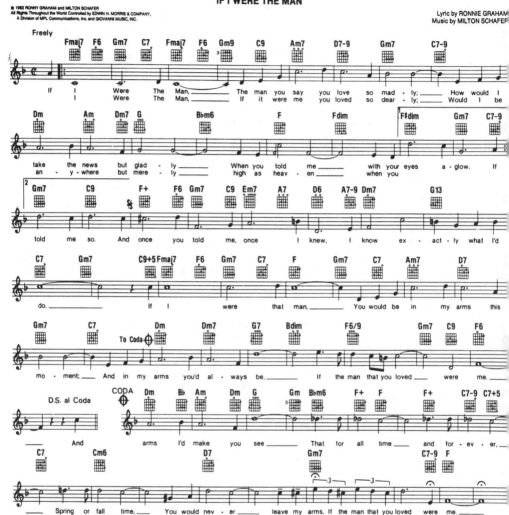

# "By The Beautiful Sea"

## ALONE TOO LONG

© 1954 ARTHUR SCHWARTZ and DOROTHY FIELDS
© Renewed 1982 ARTHUR SCHWARTZ and DOROTHY FIELDS
All Rights Controlled by EDWIN H. MORRIS & COMPANY, A Division of MPL Communications, Inc. and RUGBY MUSIC CORP.
By Arrangement with CHAPPELL & Co., Inc.

Words by DOROTHY FIELDS
Music by ARTHUR SCHWARTZ

**"By Jupiter"**

### EV'RYTHING I'VE GOT

Copyright © 1942 by Chappell & Co., Inc.
Copyright Renewed
International Copyright Secured    ALL RIGHTS RESERVED

Words by LORENZ HART
Music by RICHARD RODGERS

# WAIT TILL YOU SEE HER

Copyright © 1942 by Chappell & Co., Inc.
Copyright Renewed
International Copyright Secured    ALL RIGHTS RESERVED

Words by LORENZ HART
Music by RICHARD RODGERS

## "Bye Bye Birdie"

### THE TELEPHONE HOUR

© 1960, 1963 LEE ADAMS and CHARLES STROUSE
All Rights Throughout the World Controlled by EDWIN H. MORRIS & COMPANY,
A Division of MPL Communications, Inc.

Words by LEE ADAMS
Music by CHARLES STROUSE

# KIDS!

© 1960 LEE ADAMS and CHARLES STROUSE
All Rights Throughout the World Controlled by EDWIN H. MORRIS & COMPANY, A Division of MPL Communications, Inc.

Words by LEE ADAMS
Music by CHARLES STROUSE

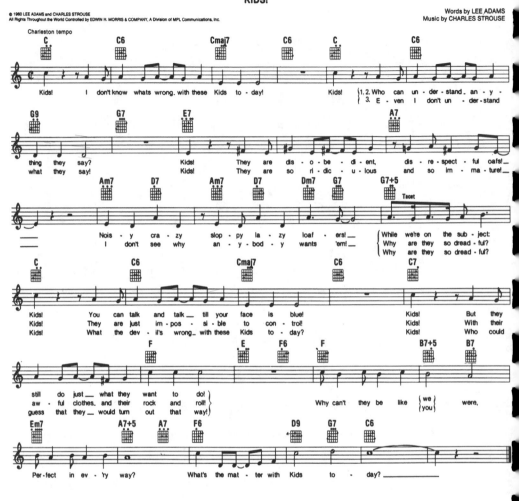

# A LOT OF LIVIN' TO DO

© 1960 LEE ADAMS and CHARLES STROUSE
All Rights Throughout the World Controlled by EDWIN H. MORRIS & COMPANY,
A Division of MPL Communications, Inc.

Lyric by LEE ADAMS
Music by CHARLES STROUSE

There's such A Lot Of Liv-in'___ To Do! There's mu-sic to play___ plac-es to go!___ Peo-ple to see!___

Ev-'ry-thing ___ for you and me! Life's a ball, if on-ly you know it! And it's all

just wait-in' for you! You're a-live, so come on and show it! ___ There's such A Lot Of Liv-in'___ To Do!

There are Liv-in', ___ Such A Lot Of Liv-in' ___ What A ___ Lot Of ___ Liv-in' ___ To Do!

## ONE BOY

© 1960 LEE ADAMS and CHARLES STROUSE
All Rights Throughout the World Controlled by EDWIN H. MORRIS & COMPANY,
A Division of MPL Communications, Inc.

Words by LEE ADAMS
Music by CHARLES STROUSE

One Boy, one spe-cial boy, One Boy to go with, to talk with and walk with; One Boy, ___ That's the way it should
(Girl), (girl), (Girl) (Girl,)

be. ___ One Boy, one cer-tain boy, One Boy to laugh with, to joke with, have coke with;
(That's the way it should be.) (Girl,) (Girl,) (Girl)

One Boy, ___ not two, or three.. ___ One day you find out, This is what life is all a-bout;
(Girl,)

You need some-one who is liv-ing just for you. ___ One Boy, one stead-y boy, One Boy to be with for-
(Girl,) (girl,) (Girl)

ev-er and ev-er; One Boy, That's the way it should be. ___ That's the way it should be. ___
(Girl,)

# PUT ON A HAPPY FACE

© 1960 LEE ADAMS and CHARLES STROUSE
All Rights Throughout the World Controlled by EDWIN H. MORRIS & COMPANY,
A Division of MPL Communications, Inc.

Words by LEE ADAMS
Music by CHARLES STROUSE

Gray skies are gon-na clear up, ___ Put On A Hap-py Face, Brush off the clouds and cheer up, ___ Put On A Hap-py Face. Take off the gloom-y mask of trag-e-dy, It's not your style; You'll look so good that you'll be glad ya' de-cid-ed to smile!. Pick out a pleas-ant out-look, ___ Stick out that no-ble chin; Wipe off that "full of doubt" look, ___ Slap on a hap-py grin! And spread sun-shine all o-ver the place, Just Put On A Hap-py Face!

# ROSIE

© 1960 LEE ADAMS and CHARLES STROUSE
All Rights Throughout the World Controlled by EDWIN H. MORRIS & COMPANY,
A Division of MPL Communications, Inc.

Words by LEE ADAMS
Music by CHARLES STROUSE

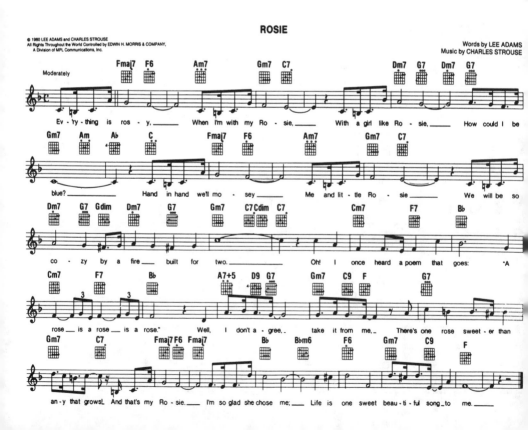

Ev-'ry-thing is ros-y, ___ When I'm with my Ro-sie, ___ With a girl like Ro-sie, ___ How could I be blue? ___ Hand in hand we'll mo-sey ___ Me and lit-tle Ro-sie ___ We will be so co-zy by a fire ___ built for two. ___ Oh! I once heard a poem that goes: "A rose ___ is a rose ___ is a rose." Well, I don't a-gree, take it from me, There's one rose sweet-er than an-y that grows! And that's my Ro-sie. ___ I'm so glad she chose me; ___ Life is one sweet beau-ti-ful song to me. ___

"Cabaret"

# CABARET

Copyright © 1966 by Alley Music Corp. and Trio Music Co., Inc.
All rights administered by Hudson Bay Music, Inc.
Used by Permission

Lyrics by FRED EBB
Music by JOHN KANDER

What good is sit-ting a-lone in your room?__ Come hear the mu - sic
Put down the knit-ting the book and the broom, To wipe ev - 'ry smile a -
No use per-mit-ting some proph-et of doom,

play;_____ } Life is a Cab - a - ret, old chum,__
day;_____ 
way;_____ 

Come to the Cab - a - ret._____ ret. Come taste the wine,

Come hear the band, Come blow the horn, start cel-e-brat-ing, Right this way, your ta-ble's wait-ing.

CODA

ret, old chum,__ Come to the Cab - a - ret.__

# MARRIED
(HEIRATEN)

Copyright © 1966 by Alley Music Corp. and Trio Music Co., Inc.
All rights administered by Hudson Bay Music, Inc.
Used by Permission

Lyrics by FRED EBB
Music by JOHN KANDER

How the world can change, it can change like that. Due to one lit-tle word: "Mar-ried."__ see a pal - ace

rise from a two room flat, Due to one lit-tle word: "Mar-ried."__ And the old de-spair that was

of-ten there, Sud-den-ly ceas-es to be.__ For you wake one day, look a-round and

say: "Some-bod-y won-der-ful Mar - ried me." How the me."

# TOMORROW BELONGS TO ME

Copyright © 1972 by Alley Music Corp. and Trio Music Co., Inc.
All rights administered by Hudson Bay Music, Inc.
Used by Permission

Lyrics by FRED EBB
Music by JOHN KANDER

The sun on the mead-ow is sum-mer-y warm, The stag in the for-est runs
branch of the lin-den is leaf-y and green, The rage has de-sert-ed the

free; _____ The heart as a shel-ter de-fies the storm,
sea; _____ The world holds a prom-ise that shines un-seen, To-mor-row Be-

longs To Me. _____ The
Me.

_____ The babe in his cra-dle is sound-ly a-sleep, The blos-som em-

brac-es the bee; _____ And love, like a val-ley, lies wide and deep, To-

mor-row Be-longs To Me, To-mor-row Be-longs To Me. _____

# TWO LADIES

Copyright © 1966 by Alley Music Corp. and Trio Music Co., Inc.
All rights administered by Hudson Bay Music, Inc.
Used by Permission

Lyrics by FRED EBB
Music by JOHN KANDER

Bee-dle-dee dee deedee, Two la-dies. Bee-dle-dee dee deedee, Two la-dies. Bee-dle-dee dee deedee

and I'm the on-ly man, ja! Bee-dle-dee dee deedee. I like it.

Bee-dle-dee dee deedee, they like it. Bee-dle-dee dee deedee This two for one.

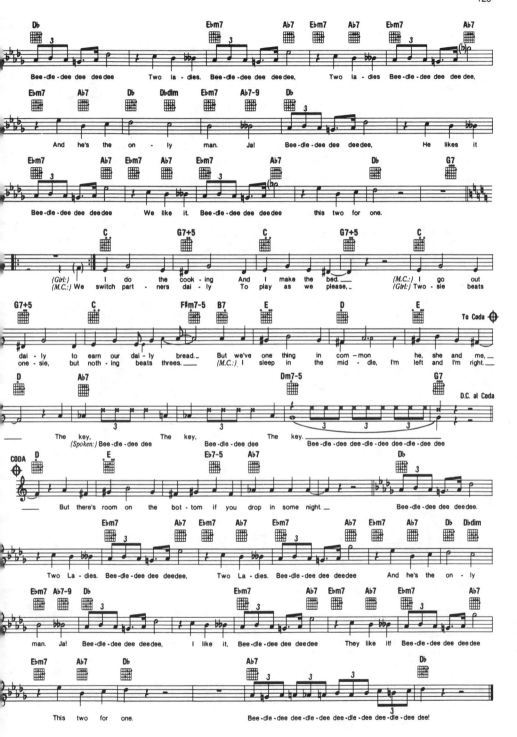

# IF YOU COULD SEE HER

Copyright © 1966 by Alley Music Corp. and Trio Music Co., Inc.
All rights administered by Hudson Bay Music, Inc.
Used by Permission

Lyrics by FRED EBB
Music by JOHN KANDER

If You Could See __ Her thru my eyes, You would-n't won-der at all. If You Could See __ Her thru
How can I speak __ of her vir-tues? I don't know where __ to be-gin. She's clev-er, she's sweet, __ she reads

my eyes, I guar-an-tee __ you would fall. (like I did) When we're in pub-lic to-geth-er,
mu-sic, She does-n't smoke __ or drink gin. (like I do) Yet when we're walk-ing to-geth-er, They

I hear so-ci-e-ty moan, But if they could see __ her thru my eyes, May-be they'd leave __ us a-
sneer if I'm hold-ing her hand, If they could see __ her thru my eyes, May-be they'd all __ un-der-

lone. stand. I un-der-stand __ your ob-jec-tion, I grant you my prob-lem's not

small; But If You Could See __ Her thru my eyes, She is-n't a mees-kite at all.

# MEIN HERR

Copyright © 1972 by Alley Music Corp. and Trio Music Co., Inc.
All rights administered by Hudson Bay Music, Inc.
Used by Permission

Lyrics by FRED EBB
Music by JOHN KANDER

ad lib.

You have to un-der-stand the way I am, Mein Herr. A ti-ger is a ti-ger, not a lamb, Mein Herr. You'll
con-ti-nent of Eu-rope is so wide, Mein Herr. Not on-ly up and down, but side to side, Mein Herr. I

nev-er turn the vin-e-gar to jam, Mein Herr. So I do what I do. When I'm through then I'm through and I'm through. Too-dle oo! Bye bye mein
could-n't ev-er cross it if I tried, Mein Herr. But I do what I can, inch by inch, step by step, mile by mile, man by man.

Tempo (Slowly at first, then gradually faster)

lie-ber Herr, Fare-well mein lie-ber Herr. __ It was a fine af-fair, but now it's o-ver.
eye, Mein Herr, __ or won-der why, Mein Herr. __ I've al-ways said that I __ was a rov-er.

To Coda

And though I used to care, __ I need the o-pen air __ You're bet-ter off with-out __ me, Mein
You must-n't knit your brow, __ you should have known by now You've ev-'ry cause to doubt __ me, Mein

## WILLKOMMEN

Copyright © 1966 by Alley Music Corp. and Trio Music Co., Inc.
All rights administered by Hudson Bay Music, Inc.
Used by Permission

Lyrics by FRED EBB
Music by JOHN KANDER

# "Call Me Madam"

### (I WONDER WHY?)
## YOU'RE JUST IN LOVE

© Copyright 1950 by Irving Berlin
Copyright Renewed

Words and Music by
IRVING BERLIN

## IT'S A LOVELY DAY TODAY

Copyright 1950 by Irving Berlin
Copyright Renewed

Words and Music by
IRVING BERLIN

Moderately

**Bb**
It's A Love - ly Day To - day.___ So what - ev - er you've got to do,___

**Bb7**   **Eb**   **Ebm**   **Bb/D**   **Dbdim**   **Cm7**   **F7**
___ you've got a love - ly day to do it in, ___ that's true. ___ And I

**Bb**   **Cm7**   **F7**   **Bb**   **Bdim**   **Cm**   **F7**
hope what - ev - er you've got to do is some - thing that can be done by two.

**Bb**   **F#dim**   **Gm**   **C7sus**   **C7**   **F7sus**   **F9**   **F7b9**   **Bb**
For I'd real - ly like to stay. ___ It's A Love - ly Day To - day. ___

**Bb7**   **Eb**   **Ebm**   **Bb/D**   **Dbdim**
___ And what - ev - er you've got to do___ I'd be so hap - py to be do - ing it ___ with

**Cm7**   **F7**   **Bb**   **Cm7**   **F7**   **Bb**   **Bdim**
you. ___ But if you've got some - thing that must be done, and it can on - ly be

**Cm**   **F7**   **Bb**   **F#dim**   **Gm**   **Am7**   **Ab7b5**   **G7sus**   **G7**
done by one, there is noth - ing more to say ___ ex -

| 1 | 2 |
| **Bb Dbdim Cm7 F7b9** | **Bb** |

**Eb**   **Ebm**   **Bb**   **C9**   **F7**
cept it's a love - ly day for say - ing it's a love - ly day. It's A day.

# "Camelot"

## CAMELOT

Copyright © 1960 & 1961 by Alan Jay Lerner & Frederick Loewe
Chappell & Co., Inc., owner of publication and allied rights throughout the World
International Copyright Secured    ALL RIGHTS RESERVED

Words by ALAN JAY LERN(
Music by FREDERICK LOE(

# I LOVED YOU ONCE IN SILENCE

Words and Music by
ALAN JAY LERNER & FREDERICK LOEWE

Copyright © 1960 by Alan Jay Lerner & Frederick Loewe
Chappell & Co., Inc., owner of publication and allied rights throughout the world

I Loved You Once In Si lence And mis-'ry was all I
loved me in lone-some si-lence; Your heart filled with dark de-

knew. Try-ing so to keep my love from show-ing, All the while not know-ing
spair. Think-ing love would flame in you for-ev-er, And I'd nev-er,

you loved me too. Yes, nev-er know the flame was there. Then one

day we cast a-way our se-cret long-ing; The rag-ing tide we held in-side would hold no

more. The si-lence at last was bro-ken! We

flung wide our pris-on door. Ev-'ry joy-ous word of love was

spo-ken. And now there's twice as much grief, Twice the strain for us; Twice the de-spair, Twice the pain for us

As we had known be-fore.

## HOW TO HANDLE A WOMAN

Copyright © 1960 & 1961 by Alan Jay Lerner & Frederick Loewe
Chappell & Co., Inc., owner of publication and allied rights throughout the World

Words by ALAN JAY LERNER
Music by FREDERICK LOEWE

## THE SIMPLE JOYS OF MAIDENHOOD

Copyright © 1960 & 1961 by Alan Jay Lerner & Frederick Loewe
Chappell & Co., Inc., owner of publication and allied rights throughout the world

Words by ALAN JAY LERNER
Music by FREDERICK LOEWE

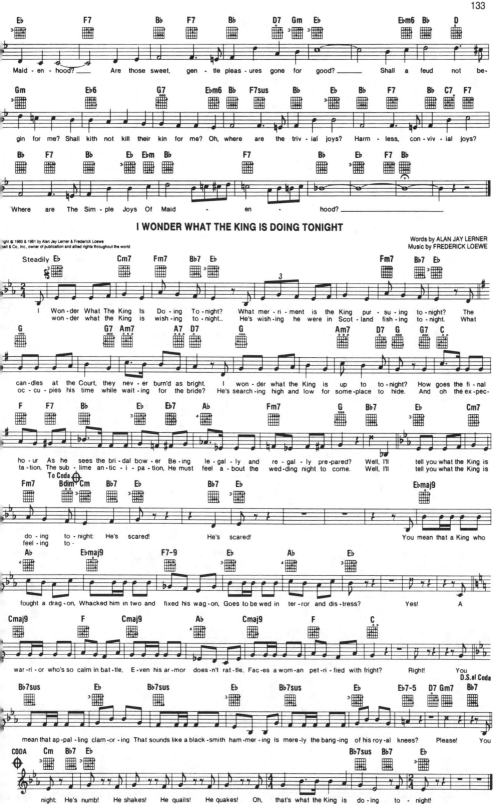

## I WONDER WHAT THE KING IS DOING TONIGHT

Words by ALAN JAY LERNER
Music by FREDERICK LOEWE

# THE LUSTY MONTH OF MAY

Words by ALAN JAY LERNER
Music by FREDERICK LOEWE

Copyright © 1960 & 1961 by Alan Jay Lerner & Frederick Loewe
Chappell & Co., Inc., owner of publication and allied rights throughout the world

# IF EVER I WOULD LEAVE YOU

Words by ALAN JAY LERNER
Music by FREDERICK LOEWE

Copyright © 1960 by Alan Jay Lerner & Frederick Loewe
Chappell & Co., Inc., owner of publication and allied rights throughout the World

**FOLLOW ME**

Copyright © 1960 & 1967 by Alan Jay Lerner & Frederick Loewe
Chappell & Co., Inc., owner of publication and allied rights throughout the World
International Copyright Secured    ALL RIGHTS RESERVED

Words by ALAN JAY LERNER
Music by FREDERICK LOEWE

# "Can-Can"

## I LOVE PARIS

Copyright © 1953 by Cole Porter
Chappell & Co., Inc., owner of publication and allied rights throughout the World.
International Copyright Secured    ALL RIGHTS RESERVED

Words and Music by
COLE PORTER

Copyright © 1953 by Cole Porter
Chappell & Co., Inc., owner of publication and allied rights throughout the World.
International Copyright Secured    ALL RIGHTS RESERVED

## IT'S ALL RIGHT WITH ME

Words and Music by
COLE PORTER

There's some-one I'm try-ing so hard to for-get, Don't you want to for-get some-one too? It's the wrong game with the wrong chips, tho' your lips are tempt-ing, they're the wrong lips, They're not her/his lips, but they're such tempt-ing lips that if some night you're free, dear, it's all right, It's All Right With Me.

## ALLEZ-VOUS-EN, GO AWAY

Copyright © 1953 by Cole Porter
Chappell & Co., Inc., owner of publication and allied rights throughout the World.

Words and Music by
COLE PORTER

Slowly

Al-lez-vous-en, al-lez-vous-en, Mam'-selle,/M'-sieur, Al-lez-vous-en, go a-way, Al-lez-vous-en, al-lez-vous-en, Mam'-selle,/M'-sieur, I have no time for you to-day, Do be a dear, just dis-ap-pear Mam'-selle,/M'-sieur, Bid me good-bye, do, do, do, Al-lez-vous-en, please go a-way, Mam'-selle,/M'-sieur, or I may go a-way with you. Al-lez-vous- or I may go a-way with you.

# C'EST MAGNIFIQUE

Copyright © 1953 by Cole Porter
Chappell & Co., Inc., owner of publication and allied rights throughout the World.
International Copyright Secured    ALL RIGHTS RESERVED

Words and Music by
COLE PORTER

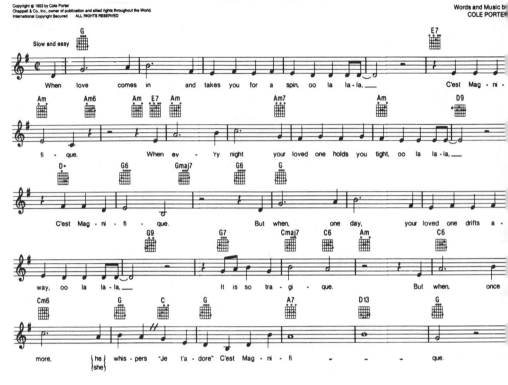

Slow and easy

When love comes in and takes you for a spin, oo la la-la, ___ C'est Mag-ni-fi-que. When ev-'ry night your loved one holds you tight, oo la la-la, ___ C'est Mag-ni-fi-que. But when, one day, your loved one drifts a-way, oo la la-la, ___ It is so tra-gi-que. But when, once more, {he} {she} whis-pers "Je t'a-dore" C'est Mag-ni-fi-que.

# I AM IN LOVE

Copyright © 1953 by Cole Porter
Copyright Renewed, Assigned to Robert H. Montgomery, Trustee of the
Cole Porter Musical and Literary Property Trusts
Chappell & Co. owner of publication and allied rights throughout the world

Words and Music by
COLE PORTER

Moderately

I am de-ject-ed, I am de-pressed, Yet res-ur-rect-ed and sail-ing the crest. Why this e-la-tion ___ mixed with de-fla-tion? What ex-pla-na-tion? ___ I ___ am in love! Such con-flict-ing ques-tions ride a-round in my brain. Should I or-der cy-a-nide or or-der cham-pagne? Oh, what is this sud-den jolt? ___ I feel like a fright-ened colt ___ just hit by a thun-der-bolt; ___ I ___ am in love! I knew the odds were a-gainst me be-fore,

I had no flare for flam-ing de-sire, But since the gods gave me you to a-dore, I may lose, but I re-fuse to fight the fire! So, come and en-light-en my days and nev-er de-part. You on-ly can bright-en the blaze that burns in my heart, For I am wild-ly in love with you and so in need of __ a stam-pede of __ love! __ I am de-pede of __ love! __

"Carousel"

## IF I LOVED YOU

Copyright © 1945 by WILLIAMSON MUSIC
Copyright Renewed

Lyrics by OSCAR HAMMERSTEIN II
Music by RICHARD RODGERS

If I Loved You Time and a-gain I would try to say All I'd want you to know. ___ If I Loved You, Words would-n't come in an eas-y way, 'Round in cir-cles I'd go. ___ Long-in' to tell you but a-fraid and shy, I'd let my gold-en chan-ces pass me by! Soon you'd leave me, Off you would go in the mist of day, Nev-er nev-er to know ___ How I loved you, If I Loved You. ___

# YOU'LL NEVER WALK ALONE

Copyright © 1945 by WILLIAMSON MUSIC
Copyright Renewed

Lyrics by OSCAR HAMMERSTEIN II
Music by RICHARD RODGERS

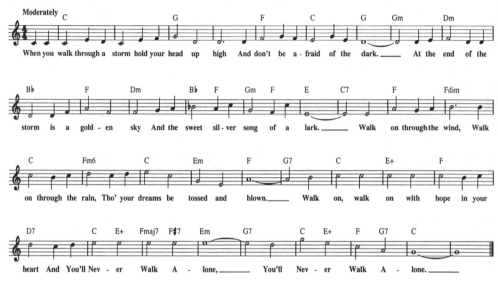

# JUNE IS BUSTIN' OUT ALL OVER

Copyright © 1945 by WILLIAMSON MUSIC
Copyright Renewed

Lyrics by OSCAR HAMMERSTEIN II
Music by RICHARD RODGERS

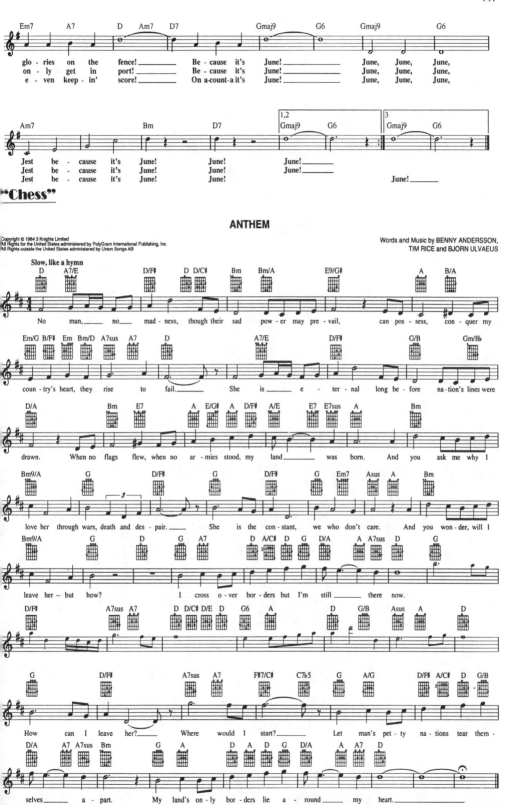

"Chess"

## ANTHEM

Copyright © 1984 3 Knights Limited
All Rights for the United States administered by PolyGram International Publishing, Inc.
All Rights outside the United States administered by Union Songs AB

Words and Music by BENNY ANDERSSON,
TIM RICE and BJORN ULVAEUS

# I KNOW HIM SO WELL

Copyright © 1984 3 Knights Limited
All Rights for the United States administered by PolyGram International Publishing, Inc.
All Rights outside the United States administered by Union Songs AB

Words and Music by BENNY ANDERSSON,
TIM RICE and BJORN ULVAEUS

# ONE NIGHT IN BANGKOK

Copyright © 1984 3 Knights Limited
All Rights for the United States administered by PolyGram International Publishing, Inc.
All Rights outside the United States administered by Union Songs AB

Words and Music by BENNY ANDERSSON
TIM RICE & BJORN ULVAEUS

The American

Get Thai'd: You're talk-ing to a tour-ist whose ev-ery move's a-mong the pur-est. I get my kicks a-

bove the waist-line, sun-shine! One night in Bang-kok makes a hard man humble, not much be-tween

de-spair and ec-sta-sy. One night in Bang-kok and the tough guys tum-ble, can't be too care-

ful with your com-pa-ny. I can feel the dev-il walk-ing next to me.

Flute solo on scale

D.S. al Coda

CODA

clois-ter, a lit-tle flesh, a lit-tle his-to-ry.

I can feel an an-gel slid-ing up to me. One night in Bang-kok makes a hard man

hum-ble, not much be-tween de-spair and ec-sta-sy. One night in Bang-kok and the tough guys

tum-ble, can't be too care-ful with your com-pa-ny. I can feel the dev-il walk-ing next to me.

# PITY THE CHILD

Copyright © 1984 3 Knights Limited
All Rights for the United States administered by PolyGram International Publishing, Inc.
All Rights outside the United States administered by Union Songs AB

Words and Music by BENNY ANDERSSON
TIM RICE and BJORN ULVAEUS

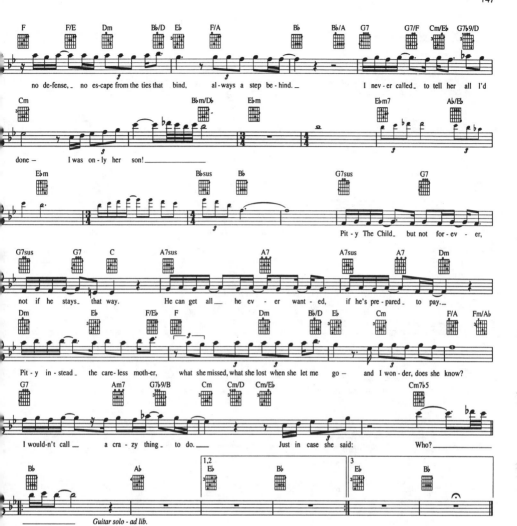

no de-fense, __ no es-cape from the ties that bind, al-ways a step be-hind. __ I nev-er called __ to tell her all I'd

done — I was on-ly her son! _____

Pit-y The Child __ but not for-ev - er,

not if he stays __ that way. He can get all __ he ev - er want-ed, if he's pre-pared __ to pay. __

Pit-y in-stead __ the care-less moth-er, what she missed, what she lost when she let me go — and I won-der, does she know?

I would-n't call __ a cra-zy thing __ to do. __ Just in case she said: Who? _____

*Guitar solo - ad lib.*

# YOU AND I

Copyright © 1984 3 Knights Limited
All Rights for the United States administered by PolyGram International Publishing, Inc.
All Rights outside the United States administered by Union Songs AB

Words and Music by BENNY ANDERSSON,
TIM RICE and BJORN ULVAEUS

# SOMEONE ELSE'S STORY

Copyright © 1984 3 Knights Limited
All Rights for the United States Administered by PolyGram International Publishing, Inc.
All Rights Outside the United States Administered by Union Songs AB

Words and Music by BENNY ANDERSSON,
TIM RICE and BJORN ULVAEUS

# HEAVEN HELP MY HEART

Copyright © 1984 3 Knights Limited
All Rights for the United States administered by PolyGram International Publishing, Inc.
All Rights outside the United States administered by Union Songs AB

Words and Music by BENNY ANDERSSON,
TIM RICE and BJORN ULVAEUS

If it were love I would give that love_ ev-ery sec-ond I had, and I __ do.___ Did I know where he'd lead me

to? Did __ I plan do-ing all of this for the love of a man?_ Well, I let it hap-pen an-y-how, and

what I'm feel-ing now has no eas-y ex-pla-na - tion. Rea-son plays_ no__ part, Heav - en, Help My __ Heart.__

I love him too much. What if he saw_ my whole ex-ist-ence turn-ing a-round_ a word, a

smile, a touch?__

One of these days, and it won't be long, he'll know more a-bout_ me__ than he __ should.___ All my dreams will be un-der -

stood, no__ sur - prise, noth-in'-more to learn from the look in my eyes. Don't you know that time is not my friend, I'll

fight it to the end,_ hop-ing to keep_ that best of mo - ments when the pas - sions___ start.

Heav - en, Help My _ Heart ____ the day that I find __ sud-den-ly I've_ run out _ of se-crets,

sud-den-ly I'm not al-ways on his__ mind. May-be it's best_ to love_ a stran-ger, well,

that's what I've done. Heav-en, Help My____ Heart.___ Heav-en, __ Help_ My__ Heart. ___

**"Cats"**

# THE AD-DRESSING OF CATS

© Copyright 1981 The Really Useful Group Ltd. and Faber and Faber Ltd.
All Rights for The Really Useful Group Ltd. for the United States and
Canada Administered by Songs Of PolyGram International, Inc.

Music by ANDREW LLOYD WEBBER
Text by T.S. ELIOT

Admirable March

You've heard of sev-eral kinds of cat. And my op-in-ion now is that you should need no _ in-ter-pre-ter to

un-der-stand our char-ac-ter. You've learned e-nough to take the view that cats are ver-y much like you. You've seen us both _ at _

work and games, and learn a-bout _ our _ prop-er names, Our hab-its and _ our _ hab-i-tat: But how would you ad-

dress a cat? So first, your mem-o-ry I'll jog, and _ say; a cat is

not a dog. So first, your mem-o-ry I'll jog, and _ say; a cat is not a

dog. With cats some say one rule is true: Don't speak 'til you are

spok-en to, My-self, I do not hold with that. I say, you should ad-dress a cat. But al-ways bear in

mind that he re-sents fam-il-i-ar-i-ty. You bow and tak-ing off your hat, ad-dress him

in this form: O Cat. Be-fore a cat will con-des-cend to treat you as a trust-ed friend. Some

lit-tle to-ken _ of es-teem is need-ed, like a dish of cream. And you might now and then sup-ply some Ca-vi-ar or

Strass-burg Pie, some Pot-ted Grouse_ or_ Sal-mon Paste: He's sure to have_ his_ per-son-al taste. And so in time_ you_ reach your aim, and

call him by his name. A cat's en-tit-led to ex-pect the e-vi-den-ces of res-pect. So

this is this, and that is that: And_ there's how you ad-dress a cat. A cat.____

# OLD DEUTERONOMY

Copyright 1980 The Really Useful Group Ltd. and Faber and Faber Ltd.
Rights for The Really Useful Group Ltd. for the United States and Canada
dministered by Songs Of PolyGram International, Inc.

Music by ANDREW LLOYD WEBBER
Text by T.S. ELIOT

**Slowly**
Tacet

I be-lieve it is Old Deu-ter-on-o-my well of all things; Can it be real-ly! No, Yes, Ho! Hi! Oh my eye!___ My

mind may be wan-der-ing but I con-fess, I be-lieve it is Old Deu-te-ro-no-my._____

Old Deu-te-ro-no-my's lived a long time: He's a cat who has lived man-y lives in suc-ces-sion. He was fa-mous in pro-verb and fa-mous in rhyme A
Old Deu-te-ro-no-my's bu-ried nine wives And more I am tempt-ed to say, nine-ty nine. And his nu-mer-ous pro-gen-y pros-pers and thrives, The

long while be-fore Queen Vic - to-ria's ac-ces-sion.
vil-lage is proud of him in his de-cline. At the sight of that pla-cid and bland phy-si-og-no-my, when he sits in the sun on the

vi-ca-rage wall; The Old-est In-hab-i-tant croaks: Well of All things Can it be real-ly! No! Yes! Ho! Hi! Oh my
All things Can it be real-ly! No! Yes! Ho! Hi! Oh my

eye! My mind may be wan-der-ing but I con-fess, I be-lieve it is Old Deu-te-ro-no-my. Well of
eye! My legs may be tot-ter-y, I must go slow And be care-ful of Old Deu-te ro-no-my.

# BUSTOPHER JONES: THE CAT ABOUT TOWN

© Copyright 1980 The Really Useful Group Ltd. and Faber and Faber Ltd.
All Rights for The Really Useful Group Ltd. for the United States and
Canada Administered by Songs Of PolyGram International, Inc.

Music by ANDREW LLOYD WEBBER
Text by T.S. ELIOT

**THE JOURNEY TO THE HEAVYSIDE LAYER**

Music by ANDREW LLOYD WEBBER

Text by T.S. ELIOT

© Copyright 1980 The Really Useful Group Ltd. and Faber and Faber Ltd.
All Rights for The Really Useful Group Ltd. for the United States and Canada
Administered by Songs Of PolyGram International, Inc.

# MEMORY

© Copyright 1981 The Really Useful Group Ltd. and Faber and Faber Ltd.
All Rights for The Really Useful Group Ltd. for the United States and Canada
Administered by Songs Of PolyGram International, Inc.

Music by ANDREW LLOYD WEBBER
Text by TREVOR NUNN after T.S. ELIOT

# MR. MISTOFFELEES

© Copyright 1980 The Really Useful Group Ltd. and Faber and Faber Ltd.
All Rights for The Really Useful Group Ltd. for the United States and Canada
Administered by Songs Of PolyGram International, Inc.

Music by ANDREW LLOYD WEBBER
Text by T.S. ELIOT

# THE OLD GUMBIE CAT

© Copyright 1981 The Really Useful Group Ltd. and Faber and Faber Ltd.
All Rights for The Really Useful Group Ltd. for the United States and Canada
Administered by Songs Of PolyGram International, Inc.

Music by ANDREW LLOYD WEBBER
Text by T.S. ELIOT

# "Cinderella"

Copyright © 1943 by WILLIAMSON MUSIC
Copyright Renewed

## BOYS AND GIRLS LIKE YOU AND ME

Lyrics by OSCAR HAMMERSTEIN II
Music by RICHARD RODGERS

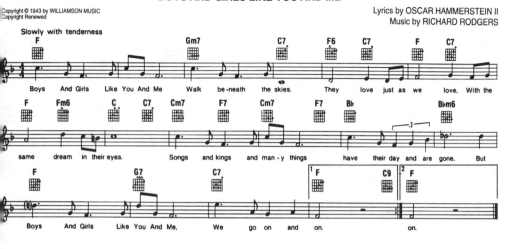

Slowly with tenderness

Boys And Girls Like You And Me Walk be-neath the skies. They love just as we love, With the

same dream in their eyes. Songs and kings and man-y things have their day and are gone, But

Boys And Girls Like You And Me, We go on and on. on.

## IN MY OWN LITTLE CORNER

Copyright © 1957 by Richard Rodgers and Oscar Hammerstein II
Copyright Renewed
WILLIAMSON MUSIC owner of publication and allied rights throughout the world

Lyrics by OSCAR HAMMERSTEIN II
Music by RICHARD RODGERS

Simply and not fast

In My Own Lit - tle Cor - ner, in my own lit - tle chair, I can be what - ev - er I want to
wing of my fan - cy I can fly an - y - where And the world will o - pen its arms to

be. _____ On the me. _____ I'm a young Nor - we - gian prin - cess or a milk - maid _____

_____ I'm the great - est pri - ma don - na in Mi - lan. _____ I'm an heir - ess who has al - ways had her

silk made _____ By her own flock of silk - worms in Ja - pan. _____ I'm a girl men go

mad for, love's a game I can play with a cool and con - fi - dent kind of air. Just as

long as I stay In My Own Lit - tle Cor - ner. _____ All a - lone in my own lit - tle chair.

# DO I LOVE YOU BECAUSE YOU'RE BEAUTIFUL?

Copyright © 1957 by Richard Rodgers and Oscar Hammerstein II
Copyright Renewed
WILLIAMSON MUSIC owner of publication and allied rights throughout the world

Lyrics by OSCAR HAMMERSTEIN II
Music by RICHARD RODGERS

## IMPOSSIBLE

Copyright © 1957 by Richard Rodgers and Oscar Hammerstein II
Copyright Renewed
WILLIAMSON MUSIC owner of publication and allied rights throughout the world

Lyrics by OSCAR HAMMERSTEIN II
Music by RICHARD RODGERS

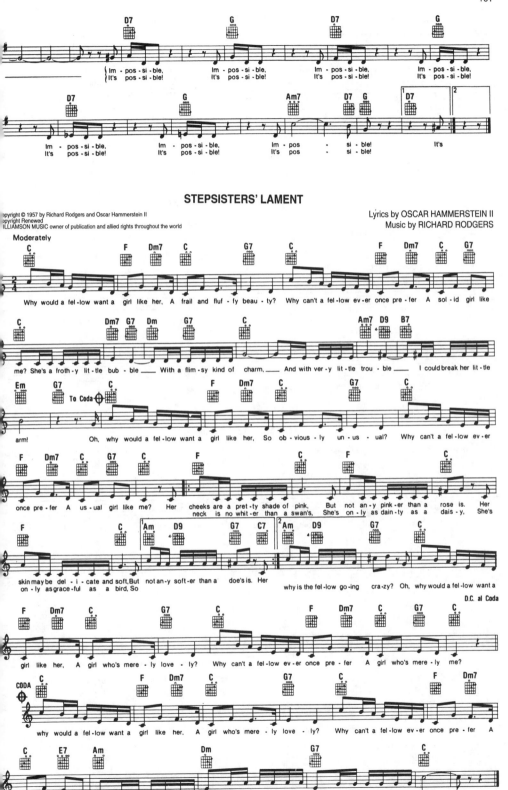

## STEPSISTERS' LAMENT

Copyright © 1957 by Richard Rodgers and Oscar Hammerstein II
Copyright Renewed
WILLIAMSON MUSIC owner of publication and allied rights throughout the world

Lyrics by OSCAR HAMMERSTEIN II
Music by RICHARD RODGERS

# A LOVELY NIGHT

Copyright © 1957 by Richard Rodgers and Oscar Hammerstein II
Copyright Renewed
WILLIAMSON MUSIC owner of publication and allied rights throughout the world

Lyrics by OSCAR HAMMERSTEIN
Music by RICHARD RODGERS

# TEN MINUTES AGO

Copyright © 1957 by Richard Rodgers and Oscar Hammerstein II
Copyright Renewed
WILLIAMSON MUSIC owner of publication and allied rights throughout the world

Lyrics by OSCAR HAMMERSTEIN II
Music by RICHARD RODGERS

We are danc - ing, we are fly - ing ___ And she's tak - ing me back to the skies. In the
arms of my love, I'm fly - ing ___ o - ver moun - tain and mea - dow and glen ___ And I like it so
well, that for all I can tell, I may nev - er come down a - gain! ___ I may nev - er come down to
earth a - gain. ___ Ten gain. ___

## "Company"

### SORRY — GRATEFUL

Copyright © 1970 by The Herald Square Music Company and Rilting Music, Inc.
Used by Permission

Music and Lyrics by
STEPHEN SONDHEIM

You're al - ways sor - ry, _ you're al - ways grate - ful, - { You're al - ways won - d'ring ___ what might have been, _ Then she walks in. ___
You hold her, think - ing, "I'm not a - lone." _ You're still a - lone. ___ }

And still you're sor - ry, and still you're grate - ful, And still you won - der, and still you doubt, ___ and
You don't live for ___ her, you do live with ___ her, You're scared she's start - ing to drift a - way. ___ and

she goes out. ___ { Ev - 'ry - thing's dif - f'rent, noth - ing's changed, ___ On - ly may - be slight - ly re - ar - ranged. } You're
scared she'll stay. ___ { Good things get bet - ter, bad gets worse, ___ Wait, I think I meant that in re - verse. }

Sor - ry Grate - ful, re - gret - ful hap - py. Why look for an - swers where none oc - cur? { You al - ways are ___
You'll al - ways be ___ } what you al - ways were, _ Which has

noth - ing to do with, All to do with her. her. ___

# ANOTHER HUNDRED PEOPLE

Copyright © 1970 by The Herald Square Music Company and Rilting Music, Inc.
Used by Permission

Music and Lyrics by
STEPHEN SONDHEIM

# SIDE BY SIDE BY SIDE

Copyright © 1970 by The Herald Square Music Company and Rilting Music, Inc.
Used by Permission

Music and Lyrics by
STEPHEN SONDHEIM

# BEING ALIVE

Copyright © 1970 by The Herald Square Music Company and Rilting Music, Inc.
Used by Permission

Music and Lyrics by
STEPHEN SONDHEIM

# COMPANY

Copyright © 1970 by The Herald Square Music Company and Rilting Music, Inc.
Used by Permission

Music and Lyrics by
STEPHEN SONDHEIM

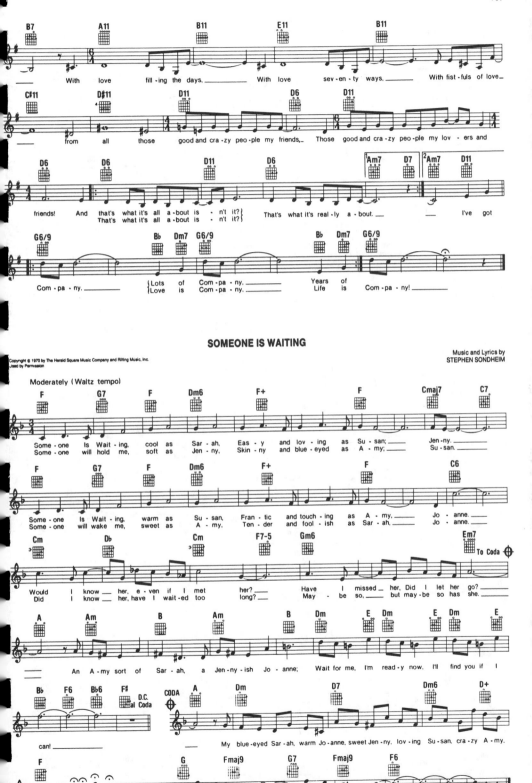

SOMEONE IS WAITING

Copyright © 1970 by The Herald Square Music Company and Rilting Music, Inc.
Used by Permission

Music and Lyrics by
STEPHEN SONDHEIM

# YOU COULD DRIVE A PERSON CRAZY

Copyright © 1970 by The Herald Square Music Company and Rilting Music, Inc.
Used by Permission

Music and Lyrics by
STEPHEN SONDHEIM

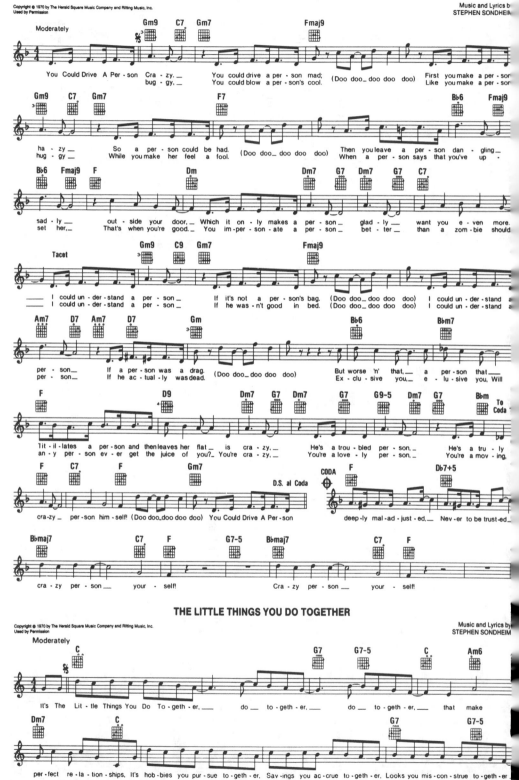

# THE LITTLE THINGS YOU DO TOGETHER

Copyright © 1970 by The Herald Square Music Company and Rilting Music, Inc.
Used by Permission

Music and Lyrics by
STEPHEN SONDHEIM

# "Chicago"

## MY OWN BEST FRIEND

Copyright © 1973, 1975 by Kander-Ebb, Inc., & Unichappell Music, Inc.
All Rights Administered by Unichappell Music, Inc.

Words by FRED EBB
Music by JOHN KANDER

# RAZZLE DAZZLE

opyright © 1974, 1975 by Kander-Ebb, Inc., & Unichappell Music, Inc.
Rights Administered by Unichappell Music, Inc.

Words by FRED EBB
Music by JOHN KANDER

# AND ALL THAT JAZZ

Copyright © 1973, 1974 by Kander-Ebb, Inc., & Unichappell Music, Inc.
All Rights Administered by Unichappell Music, Inc.

Words by FRED EBB
Music by JOHN KANDER

Come on, babe, __ why don't we paint the town, __ And All That Jazz! I'm gon-na rouge my knees __ and roll my stock-ings down __ And All That Jazz! __ Start the car, __ I know a whoop-ee spot __ where the gin is cold __ but the pi-an-o's hot. __ It's just a nois-y hall __ where there's a night-ly brawl __ And All That Jazz! Slick your hair __ and wear your buck-le shoes __ And All That Jazz! I hear that Fa-ther Dip __ is gon-na blow the blues __ And All That Jazz! Hold on, hon, we're gon-na bun-ny hug. __ I bought some as-pi-rin __ down at U-nit-ed Drug __ In case we shake a-part __ and want a brand new start __ to do that jazz! __ Oh, __ I'm gon-na see my She-ba shim-my shake. __ (And All That Jazz!) __ Oh, __ she's gon-na shim-my till her gar-ters break. __ (And All That Jazz!) __ Show __ her where to park her gir-dle, Oh, __ her moth-er's blood-'d cur-dle if she'd hear __ her ba-by's queer __ for all that jazz! __ Find a flask, __ we're play-ing fast and loose __ And All That Jazz! And

All That Jazz!__ Right up here_is where I store the juice,__ And All That Jazz!_. And All That Jazz!_. Come on, babe,_we're gon-na

brush the sky.__ I bet-cha luck-y Lin-dy nev-er flew so high, 'Cause in the stra-to-sphere__ how could he lend an ear_ to

all that jazz!

No, I'm no-one's wife,__ but oh, I love my life__ And All

That_____ Jazz!_____ That jazz!

## "A Chorus Line"

### AT THE BALLET

© 1975 MARVIN HAMLISCH and EDWARD KLEBAN
All Rights Controlled by WREN MUSIC CO. and AMERICAN COMPASS MUSIC CORP.

Lyric by EDWARD KLEBAN
Music by MARVIN HAMLISCH

Intense, emotional, driving

Dad-dy al-ways thought that he mar-ried be-neath__ him. That's what he said, that's what he said.
Moth-er al-ways said I'd be ver-y at-trac-tive when I grew up, when I grew up.

When he pro-posed he in-formed my moth-er he was prob-a-bly her ver-y_____ last chance. And
"Dif-f'rent," she said, "With a spe-cial some-thing and a ver-y ver-y person-al_____ flair." And

though she was twen-ty-two,__ though she was twen-ty-two.__ though she was twen-ty-two,__ she mar-ried him. And
though I was eight or nine,__ though I was eight or nine,__ though I was eight or nine,_____ I hat-ed her.__

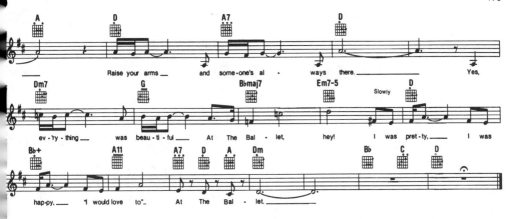

## I CAN DO THAT

Lyric by EDWARD KLEBAN
Music by MARVIN HAMLISCH

© 1975 MARVIN HAMLISCH and EDWARD KLEBAN
All Rights Controlled by WREN MUSIC CO. and AMERICAN COMPASS MUSIC CORP.

© 1975 MARVIN HAMLISCH and EDWARD KLEBAN
All Rights Controlled by WREN MUSIC CO. and AMERICAN COMPASS MUSIC CORP.

# DANCE: TEN; LOOKS: THREE

Lyric by EDWARD KLEBAN
Music by MARVIN HAMLISCH

# WHAT I DID FOR LOVE

© 1975 MARVIN HAMLISCH and EDWARD KLEBAN
All Rights Controlled by WREN MUSIC CO. and AMERICAN COMPASS MUSIC CORP.

Lyric by EDWARD KLEBAN
Music by MARVIN HAMLISCH

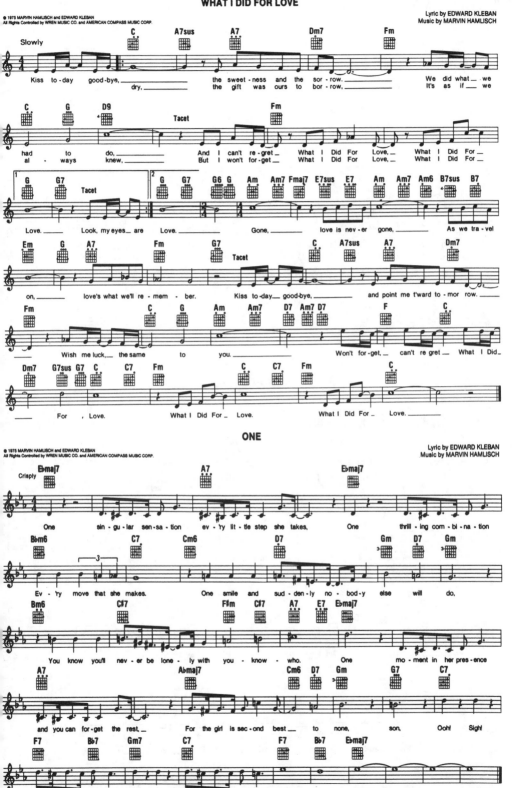

# ONE

© 1975 MARVIN HAMLISCH and EDWARD KLEBAN
All Rights Controlled by WREN MUSIC CO. and AMERICAN COMPASS MUSIC CORP.

Lyric by EDWARD KLEBAN
Music by MARVIN HAMLISCH

# "A Connecticut Yankee"

## MY HEART STOOD STILL

© 1927 WARNER BROS. INC. (Renewed)
Rights for the Extended Renewal Term in the United States Controlled by
MARLIN ENTERPRISES and THE ESTATE OF LORENZ HART
All Rights on behalf of MARLIN ENTERPRISES Administered by WILLIAMSON MUSIC
All Rights on behalf of THE ESTATE OF LORENZ HART Administered by WB MUSIC CORP.

Words by LORENZ HART
Music by RICHARD RODGERS

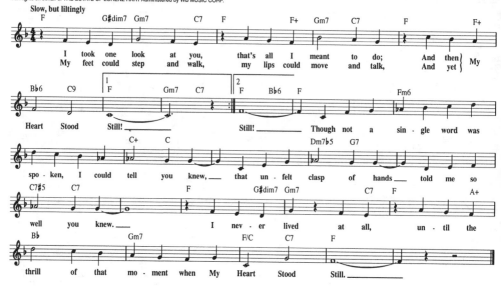

## THOU SWELL

© 1927 WARNER BROS. INC. (Renewed)
Rights for the Extended Renewal Term in the United States Controlled by
MARLIN ENTERPRISES and THE ESTATE OF LORENZ HART
All Rights on behalf of MARLIN ENTERPRISES Administered by WILLIAMSON MUSIC
All Rights on behalf of THE ESTATE OF LORENZ HART Administered by WB MUSIC CORP.

Words by LORENZ HART
Music by RICHARD RODGERS

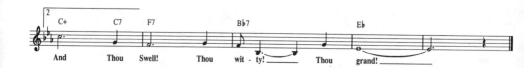

# "Drat! The Cat!"

## SHE (HE) TOUCHED ME

Lyric by IRA LEVIN
Music by MILTON SCHAFER

© 1965 EDWIN H. MORRIS & COMPANY, A Division of MPL Communications, Inc.

She Touched Me.___ she put her hand near mine and then She Touched Me.___ I felt a sud-den tin-gle when She

knew it,___ it was-n't ac-ci-tal, No she knew it,___ She smiled and seemed to tell me so all

Touched Me, ___ A spar-kle.___ a glow! _____ She

through it, ___ she knew it, ___ I

know. _____ She's real ___ and the world is a-live and shin-ing. ___

_____ I feel such a won-der-ful drive toward val-en-tin-ing. She Touched Me ___ I

sim-ply have to face the fact, She Touched Me, ___ Con-trol my-self and try to act as if I re-mem-ber my name. ___ But She

Touched Me, ___ She Touched Me. ___ And sud-den-ly noth-ing is ___ the same! ___

## "Conversation Piece"

### I'LL FOLLOW MY SECRET HEART

Copyright © 1934 by Chappell & Co., Ltd., London    Copyright Renewed
Published in the U.S.A. by Chappell & Co., Inc.

Words and Music by
NOEL COWARD

I'll Fol-low My Se-cret Heart my whole life through, I'll keep all my dreams a-part till one comes true. No mat-ter what price is paid, What stars may fade a-bove, I'll Fol-low My Se-cret Heart till I find love. love.

## "Dance Me A Song"

### MY LITTLE DOG HAS EGO

Copyright © 1950 by Chappell & Co., Inc.
Copyright renewed

Words and Music by
HERMAN HUPFELD

Don't like e-go-tis-ti-cal peo-ple, Why do they have to be? But My Lit-tle Dog Has E-go, And that's all right by me. With great e-go-tis-ti-cal peo-ple, I sim-ply can't a-gree, Yet, My Lit-tle Dog Has E-go, Makes per-fect com-pan-y. He A-thinks he's pret-ty swell each time the post-man rings the bell, He runs and fetch-es me the pa-pers and the mail, Does round his neigh-bor-hood, he makes it clear-ly un-der-stood, That he's a dog who thinks he has a ped-i-gree, He ev-'ry-thing but state, "Oh mas-ter don't you think I'm great?" then wags his tail, He's the boss, I'm at loss to know just why I seem to swag-gers and he struts, But nev-er min-gles with the muts a-round a tree, stays a-loof, Is it proof per-haps I don't ap-pre-ci-shun, E-go-tis-ti-cal peo-ple. Yet an-y-one can see, That My Lit-tle Dog Has E-go, And ate, E-go-tis-ti-cal peo-ple. I is-sue this de-cree, That My Lit-tle Dog Has E-go, And

## "A Day In Hollywood/A Night In The Ukraine"

### JUST GO TO THE MOVIES

© 1980 JERRY HERMAN
All Rights Controlled by JERRYCO MUSIC CO.
Exclusive Agent: EDWIN H. MORRIS & COMPANY, A Division of MPL Communications, Inc.

Music and Lyric by
JERRY HERMAN

## "Dear World"

© 1968 JERRY HERMAN
All Rights Controlled by JERRYCO MUSIC CO.
Exclusive Agent: EDWIN H. MORRIS & COMPANY, A Division of MPL Communications, Inc.

**DEAR WORLD**

Music and Lyric by
JERRY HERMAN

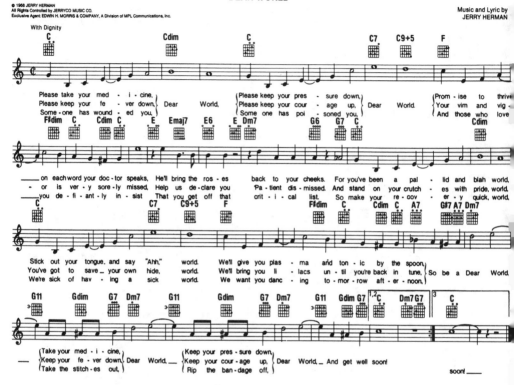

Please take your med - i - cine,
Please keep your fe - ver down, Dear World,
Some - one has wound - ed you,

(Please keep your pres - sure down,)
(Please keep your cour - age up,) Dear World.
(Some one has poi - soned you,)

(Prom - ise to thrive
(Your vim and vig -
And those who love

—— on each word your doc - tor speaks, He'll bring the ros - es back to your cheeks. For you've been a pal - lid and blah world.
— or is ver - y sore - ly missed, Help us de - clare you 'Pa - tient dis - missed. And stand on your crutch - es with pride, world.
—— you de - fi - ant - ly in - sist That you get off that crit - i - cal list. So make your re - cov - er - y quick, world.

Stick out your tongue, and say "Ahh," world. We'll give you plas - ma and ton - ic by the spoon,
You've got to save - your own hide, world. We'll bring your li - lacs un - til you're back in tune, So be a Dear World,
We're sick of hav - ing a sick world. We want you danc - ing to - mor - row aft - er - noon,

(Take your med - i - cine,)
Keep your fe - ver down, Dear World, ___
(Take the stitch - es out,)

(Keep your pres - sure down,)
Keep your cour - age up, Dear World, ___ And get well soon!
(Rip the ban - dage off,)

soon! ___

## I DON'T WANT TO KNOW

© 1968, 1969 JERRY HERMAN
All Rights Controlled by JERRYCO MUSIC CO.
Exclusive Agent: EDWIN H. MORRIS & COMPANY, A Division of MPL Communications, Inc.

Music and Lyric by
JERRY HERMAN

Waltz Tempo

If mu - sic is no long - er love - ly, If laugh - ter is no long - er lilt - ing, If lov - ers

are no long - er lov - ing. Then I Don't Want To Know. If sum - mer is

no long - er care - free, If chil - dren are no long - er sing - ing, If peo - ple are no long - er

hap - py, Then I Don't Want To Know. Let me hide ev - 'ry truth from my eyes with the back

of my hand, _____ Let me live in a world full of lies with my head _____ in the sand.

For my mem - o - ries all are ex - cit - ing. My mem - o - ries all are en - chant - ed, My

mem - o - ries burn in my head with a stead - y glow; _____ So if, my

**Repeat and Fade**

friends, if love is dead, I Don't Want _____ To _____ Know. _____

## KISS HER NOW

© 1968 JERRY HERMAN
All Rights Controlled by JERRYCO MUSIC CO.
Exclusive Agent: EDWIN H. MORRIS & COMPANY, A Division of MPL Communications, Inc.

Music and Lyric by
JERRY HERMAN

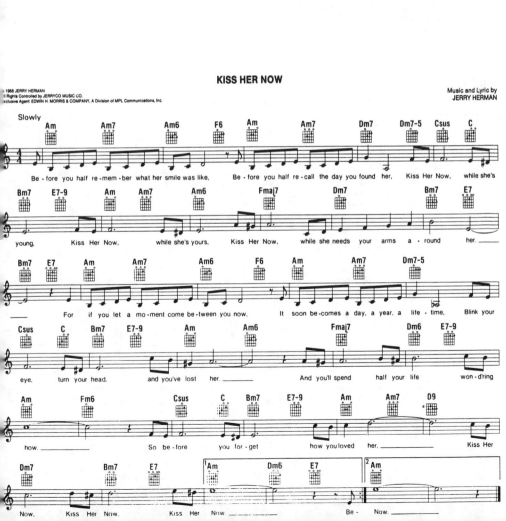

Slowly

Be - fore you half re - mem - ber what her smile was like, Be - fore you half re - call the day you found her, Kiss Her Now, while she's

young, Kiss Her Now, while she's yours, Kiss Her Now, while she needs your arms a - round her. _____

For if you let a mo - ment come be - tween you now, It soon be - comes a day, a year, a life - time, Blink your

eye, turn your head. and you've lost her. _____ And you'll spend half your life won - d'ring

how. _____ So be - fore you for - get how you loved her. _____ Kiss Her

Now, Kiss Her Now, Kiss Her Now. _____ Be - Now. _____

## "Destry Rides Again"

### ANYONE WOULD LOVE YOU

Copyright © 1959 by Harold Rome
Chappell & Co., Inc. owner of publication and allied rights throughout the world.

Words and Music by
HAROLD ROME

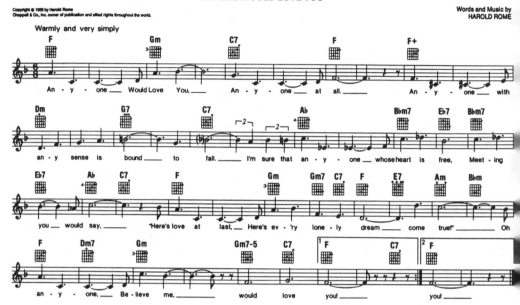

## "Do I Hear A Waltz?"

### DO I HEAR A WALTZ?

Copyright © 1965 by Richard Rodgers & Stephen Sondheim
Williamson Music Co., & Burthen Music Co., owner of publication and allied rights throughout the world.
All rights controlled by Chappell & Co., Inc.   International Copyright Secured   ALL RIGHTS RESERVED

Lyrics by STEPHEN SONDHEIM
Music By RICHARD RODGERS

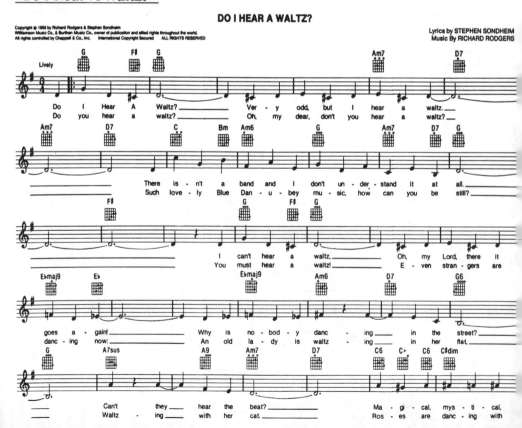

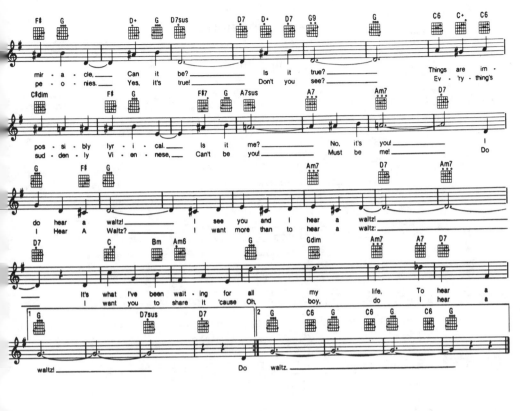

## SOMEONE LIKE YOU

Copyright © 1965 by Richard Rodgers and Stephen Sondheim
Williamson Music Co. and Burthen Music Co., Inc., owners of publication and allied rights
Chappell & Co., Inc., Administrator

Words by STEPHEN SONDHEIM
Music by RICHARD RODGERS

## "Do Re Mi"

### MAKE SOMEONE HAPPY

Copyright © 1960 by Betty Comden, Adolph Green & Jule Styne
Stratford Music Corp., owner, Chappell & Co., Inc., Administrator of publication and allied rights for the Western Hemisphere
International Copyright Secured   ALL RIGHTS RESERVED

Words by BETTY COMDEN & ADOLPH GREEN
Music by JULE STYNE

## "Don't Bother Me, I Can't Cope"

### THANK HEAVEN FOR YOU

© 1971, 1972 FIDDLEBACK MUSIC PUBLISHING CO., INC.
A Tommy Valando Publication

Words and Music by
MICKI GRANT

## IT TAKES A WHOLE LOT OF HUMAN FEELING

©1971, 1972 FIDDLEBACK MUSIC PUBLISHING CO., INC.
A Tommy Valando Publication

Words and Music by
MICKI GRANT

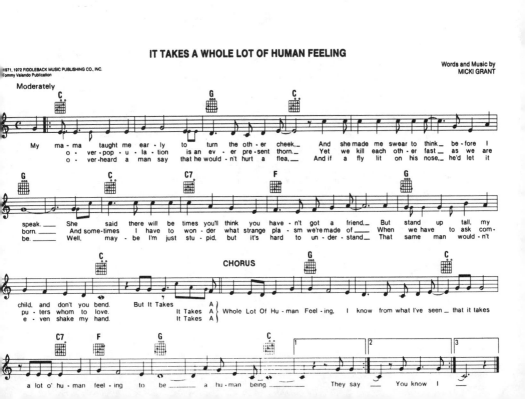

# "Five Guys Named Moe"

## IS YOU IS, OR IS YOU AIN'T
### (MA' BABY)

© Copyright 1943, 1944 MCA MUSIC PUBLISHING, A Division of MCA INC.
Copyright Renewed

Words and Music by BILLY AUSTIN
and LOUIS JORDAN

# "DuBarry Was A Lady"

## IT WAS WRITTEN IN THE STARS

Copyright © 1939 by Chappell & Co., Inc.
Copyright renewed, assigned to John F. Wharton, Trustee of the Cole Porter Musical & Literary Property Trusts
Chappell & Co., Inc. Publisher

Words and Music by
COLE PORTER

# WELL, DID YOU EVAH?

Copyright © 1940 & 1946 by Chappell & Co., Inc.
Copyrights Renewed, Assigned to John F. Wharton, Trustee of the Cole Porter Musical & Literary Property Trusts
Chappell & Co., Inc, owner of publication and allied rights throughout the World.
International Copyright Secured    ALL RIGHTS RESERVED

Words and Music by
COLE PORTER

Have you heard? The Coast of Maine Just got hit by a hur-ri-cane?} Well, Did You E-vah! What a
Have you heard? Pro-fes-sor Munch Ate his wife and di-vorced his lunch} 

swell par-ty this is! {Have you heard that poor dear Blanche Got run down by an a-va-lanche?} Well, Did Yo
{Mis-sus Smith in her new Hup Crossed the bridge when the bridge was up.}

E-vah! What a swell par-ty this is! What Dai-quir-is! What Sher-ry, please! What Bur-gun-

dy! What great Pom-mer-y! What bran-dy, wow! What whis-key, here's how! What

gin and what beer! Will you so-ber up my dear?    Well Did You E-vah! What a swell par-ty this is!

---

# FRIENDSHIP

Copyright © 1939 by Chappell & Co., Inc.
Copyright Renewed, Assigned to John F. Wharton, Trustee of the Cole Porter Musical & Literary Property Trusts
Chappell & Co., Inc, owner of publication and allied rights throughout the World.
International Copyright Secured    ALL RIGHTS RESERVED

Words and Music by
COLE PORTER

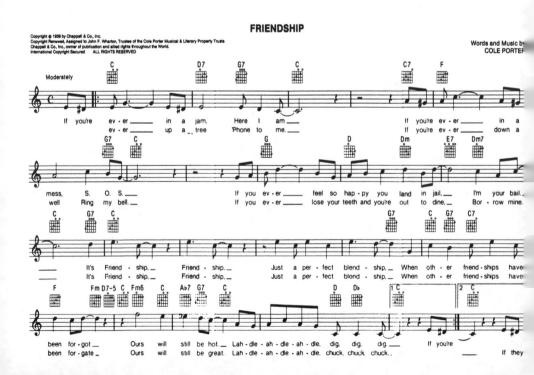

If you're ev-er in a jam, Here I am. If you're ev-er in a
ev-er up a tree 'Phone to me. If you're ev-er down a

mess, S. O. S. If you ev-er feel so hap-py you land in jail, I'm your bail.
well Ring my bell. If you ev-er lose your teeth and you're out to dine, Bor-row mine.

It's Friend-ship, Friend-ship, Just a per-fect blend-ship. When oth-er friend-ships have
It's Friend-ship, Friend-ship, Just a per-fect blend-ship. When oth-er friend-ships have

been for-got Ours will still be hot. Lah-dle-ah-dle-ah-dle, dig. dig. dig. If you're
been for-gate Ours will still be great. Lah-dle-ah-dle-ah-dle. chuck, chuck, chuck.. If they

ev - er _____ black your eyes, Put me wise. _ If they ev - er _____ cook your goose, Turn me loose.

_____ If they ev - er _____ put a bul - let through your br - ain. _ I'll com - plain. _ It's

Friend - ship. _ Friend - ship. _ Just a per - fect blend - ship. When oth - er friend - ships have been for - git _

Ours will still be it, Lah - dle - ah - dle - ah - dle, hep, hep, hep. _ If they

"Evita"

Copyright 1977 EVITA MUSIC LTD.
All Rights for the USA and Canada Controlled and Administered by
ON BACKSTREET MUSIC, INC., an MCA company

## BUENOS AIRES

Words by TIM RICE
Music by ANDREW LLOYD WEBBER

Fast 4

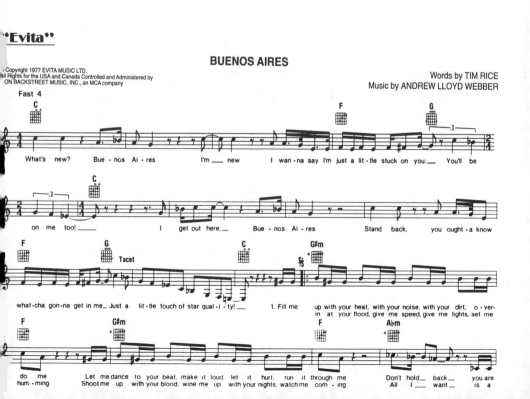

What's new? Bue - nos Ai - res I'm _ new I wan - na say I'm just a lit - tle stuck on you: _ You'll be

on me too! _____ I get out here, _ Bue - nos Ai - res Stand back, you ought - a know

Tacet

what - cha gon - na get in me _ Just a lit - tle touch of star qual - i - ty! _ 1. Fill me up with your heat, with your noise, with your dirt, o - ver -
in at your flood, give me speed, give me lights, set me

do me Let me dance to your beat, make it loud, let it hurt, run it through me Don't hold _ back _ you are
hum - ming Shoot me up with your blood, wine me up with your nights, watch me com - ing All I want _ is a

cer - tain to im - press___ Tell the dri - ver this is where I'm stay - ing    Hel - lo    Bue - nos Ai - res
whole lot of ex - cess___ Tell the sing - er this is where I'm play - ing    Stand back    Bue - nos Ai - res
                                                                              (3)Ri - o    de la

Get this___ just look at me dressed up some-where to go:    We'll put    on    a    show! ___ 2.Take me
Be - cause___ you ought-a know

what-cha gon-na get in me___ Just a lit - tle touch of star qual - i - ty!___    And _____ if ev - er I
                                                                                     And _____ if I need a

go too far _____ it's be - cause of the things___ you are ___ beau - ti - ful town___ I love ___ you
mo - ment's rest _____ give your lov - er the ver - y best___ real ei - der down___ and si -

- lence 3.You're a    Pla - ta!    Flo - ri - da!    Cor - ri - en - tes! Neu - ve de Ju - li - o!___ All I want to know

___ Stand back___ Bue - nos Ai - res    Be - cause    you ought-a know what 'cha gon-na get in me:___ Just

lit - tle touch of, Just___ a lit - tle touch of, Just___ a lit - tle touch of star qual - i - ty!_____

3. You're a tramp, you're a treat, you will shine to the death, you are shoddy;
   But you're flesh, you are meat, you shall have every breath in my body:
   Put me down for a lifetime of success
   Give me credit—I'll find ways of paying:

# DON'T CRY FOR ME ARGENTINA

Copyright 1976, 1977 EVITA MUSIC LTD.
All Rights for the USA and Canada Controlled and Administered by
ON BACKSTREET MUSIC, INC., an MCA company

Words by TIM RICE
Music by ANDREW LLOYD WEBBER

## ANOTHER SUITCASE IN ANOTHER HALL

© Copyright 1977 by EVITA MUSIC LTD.
All Rights for the USA and Canada Controlled and Administered by
ON BACKSTREET MUSIC, INC., an MCA company

Words by TIM RICE
Music by ANDREW LLOYD WEBBER

I don't ex-pect my love af-fairs to last for long; Nev-er fool my-self that my dreams will come true: Be-ing used to trou-ble I an-

ti-ci-pate it, but all the same I hate it, would-n't you? So what hap-pens now So what hap-pens now where am I go-ing to? Where am I

go-ing to? go-ing to?

Addtional Lyrics

2. Time and time again I've said that I don't care;
That I'm immune to gloom, that I'm hard through and through:
But every time it matters all my words desert me;
So anyone can hurt me and they do.
So what happens now?. . . etc., as above.

3. Call in three months' time and I'll be fine I know;
Well maybe not that fine, but I'll survive anyhow:
I won't recall the names and places of this sad occasion;
But that's no consolation, here and now.
So what's happens now?. . .etc., as above.

## "Face The Music"

## LET'S HAVE ANOTHER CUP O' COFFEE

© Copyright 1932 by Irving Berlin
Copyright Renewed

Words and Music by
IRVING BERLIN

Just a-round the cor-ner, there's a rain-bow in the sky. So Let's Have An-oth-er Cup O'

Cof-fee and let's have an-oth-er piece o' pie! Trou-ble's just a bub-ble, and the

clouds will soon roll by. So Let's Have An-oth-er Cup O' Cof-fee and let's have an-oth-er piece o'

pie. Let a smile be your um-brel-la, for it's just an A-pril show'r. E-ven John D. Rock-e-

fel-ler is look-ing for the sil-ver lin-ing. Mis-ter Her-bert Hoov-er says that now's the time to

buy. So Let's Have An-oth-er Cup O' Cof-fee and let's have an-oth-er piece o' pie! pie!

## "Fanny"

**FANNY**

Copyright © 1954 by Harold Rome
Chappell & Co., Inc., owner of publication and allied rights throughout the World
International Copyright Secured    ALL RIGHTS RESERVED

Words and Music by
HAROLD ROME

On - ly you, long as I may live, Fan - ny, Fan - ny, Fan - ny.
heart is - n't mine to give, Fan - ny, Fan - ny, Fan - ny.

You, long as I may live, Fan - ny, If I could love, That's what I would
No, no not mine to give, Fan - ny, For it is gone, giv - en long a-

say. But my way To the sea. my one love in her gray green

clothes, deep with won - ders be - yond the shore; To the isles 'neath the winds where the

spice wood grows. I must know them all, or sleep no more! Here's a boy with no

heart to give, Fan - ny Fan - ny, Fan - ny. Not worth one tear you'll cry,

Fan - ny, Oh, Fan - ny, good - bye!

## BE KIND TO YOUR PARENTS

Copyright © 1954 and 1955 by Harold Rome
Chappell & Co., Inc., owner of publication and allied rights throughout the world

Words and Music by
HAROLD ROME

## I HAVE TO TELL YOU

Copyright © 1954 by Harold Rome
Copyright renewed, assigned to Chappell & Co., Inc.

Words and Music by
HAROLD ROME

# "The Fantastics"

## PLANT A RADISH

Copyright © 1960 by Tom Jones and Harvey Schmidt
Chappell & Co., Inc., owner of publication and allied rights

Words by TOM JONES
Music by HARVEY SCHMIDT

With Spirit

Plant a rad-ish, get a rad-ish, Nev-er an-y doubt. That's why I love veg-'ta-bles; You know what you're a-bout!
Plant a bean-stalk, get a bean-stalk, Just the same as Jack. Then if you don't like it you can al-ways take it back. But

Plant a tur-nip, get a tur-nip, May-be you'll get two. That's why I love veg-'ta-bles, You know that they'll come true! They're de-
if your is-sue does-n't kiss you then I wish you luck. For once you've plant-ed chil-de-ren you're ab-so-lute-ly stuck. Ev-'ry

pend-a-ble! They're be-friend-a-ble! They're the best pal a par-ent's ev-er known. While with
tur-nip green ev-'ry kid-ney bean Ev-'ry plant grows ac-cord-ing to the plot. While with

chil-de-ren it's be-wil-der-in', You don't know un-til the seed is near-ly grown, Just what you've sown. So
prog-e-ny it's hodge-podge-e-nee, For as soon as you think you know what kind you've got, It's what they're not. So

plant a car-rot; get a car-rot, Not a brus-sel sprout. That's why I love veg-'ta-bles, You know what you're a-bout!
plant a cab-bage; get a cab-bage, Not a sau-er-kraut. That's why I love veg-'ta-bles, You know what you're a-bout!

Life is mer-ry if it's ver-y veg-e-tar-i-an. A man who plants a gar-den is a ver-y hap-py man!
Life is mer-ry if it's ver-y veg-e-tar-i-an. A man who plants a gar-den is a ver-y hap-py

man! A veg-e-tar-i-ver-y

mer-ry veg-e-tar-i-an.

198

# TRY TO REMEMBER

Copyright © 1960 by Tom Jones & Harvey Schmidt
Chappell & Co., Inc, owner of publication and allied rights throughout the World
International Copyright Secured    ALL RIGHTS RESERVED

Words by TOM JONES
Music by HARVEY SCHMIDT

# SOON IT'S GONNA RAIN

Copyright © 1960 by Tom Jones and Harvey Schmidt
Chappell & Co., Inc, Owner of publications and allied rights throughout the world
International Copyright Secured    ALL RIGHTS RESERVED

Words by TOM JONES
Music by HARVEY SCHMIDT

## THEY WERE YOU

Words by TOM JONES
Music by HARVEY SCHMIDT

...right © 1960 by Tom Jones and Harvey Schmidt
...pell & Co., Inc., owner of publication and allied rights

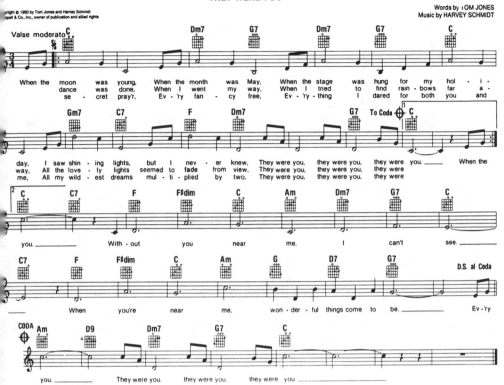

When the moon was young, When the month was May, When the stage was hung for my hol - i -
dance was done, When I went my way, When I tried to find rain - bows far a -
se - cret pray'r, Ev - 'ry fan - cy free, Ev - 'ry - thing I dared for both you and

day, I saw shin - ing lights, but I nev - er knew, They were you, they were you, they were you. _____ When the
way, All the love - ly lights seemed to fade from view, They were you, they were you, they were
me, All my wild - est dreams mul - ti - plied by two. They were you, they were you, they were

you. _____ With - out you near me, I can't see. _____

When you're near me, won - der - ful things come to be. _____ Ev - 'ry

D.S. al Coda

**CODA**

you. _____ They were you. they were you. they were you. _____

# "Fiddler On The Roof"

### DO YOU LOVE ME?

Copyright © 1964 by Alley Music Corp. and Trio Music Co., Inc.
All Rights Administered by Hudson Bay Music, Inc.
Used by Permission

Lyrics by SHELDON HARNICK
Music by JERRY BOCK

# FIDDLER ON THE ROOF

Copyright © 1964 by Alley Music Corp. and Trio Music Co., Inc.
All Rights Administered by Hudson Bay Music, Inc.
Used by Permission

Lyrics by SHELDON HARNICK
Music by JERRY BOCK

# IF I WERE A RICH MAN

Copyright © 1964 by Alley Music Corp. and Trio Music Co., Inc.
All Rights Administered by Hudson Bay Music, Inc.
Used by Permission

Lyrics by SHELDON HARNICK
Music by JERRY BOCK

# ANATEVKA

Copyright © 1964 by Alley Music Corp. and Trio Music Co., Inc.
All Rights Administered by Hudson Bay Music, Inc.
Used by Permission

Lyrics by SHELDON HARNICK
Music by JERRY BOCK

# FAR FROM THE HOME I LOVE

Copyright © 1964 by Alley Music Corp. and Trio Music Co., Inc.
All Rights Administered by Hudson Bay Music, Inc.
Used by Permission

Lyrics by SHELDON HARNICK
Music by JERRY BOCK

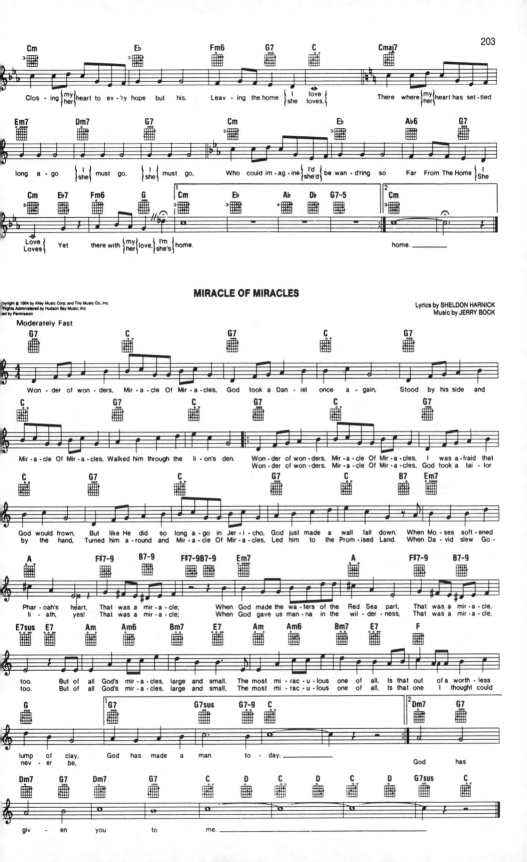

# SUNRISE, SUNSET

Copyright © 1964 by Alley Music Corp. and Trio Music Co., Inc.
All Rights Administered by Hudson Bay Music, Inc.
Used by Permission

Lyrics by SHELDON HARNICK
Music by JERRY BOCK

Is this the lit-tle girl I car-ried? Is this the lit-tle boy at play?
When did she get to be a beau-ty? When did he grow to be so tall?

I don't re-mem-ber grow-ing old-er, When did they? _____
Was-n't it yes-ter-day when they were small.

Sun-rise, ___ Sun-set, Sun-rise, ___ Sun-set, Swift-ly flow the
Sun-rise, ___ Sun-set, Sun-rise, ___ Sun-set, Swift-ly ___ fly the

days; _____ Seed-lings turn o-ver-night to sun-flow'rs, Blos-som-ing e-ven as we gaze.
years; _____

One sea-son fol-low-ing an-oth-er, La-den with hap-pi-ness and tears. _____

# TRADITION

Copyright © 1964 by Alley Music Corp. and Trio Music Co., Inc.
All Rights Administered by Hudson Bay Music, Inc.
Used by Permission

Lyrics by SHELDON HARNICK
Music by JERRY BOCK

(Poppas:) Who day and night must scram-ble for a liv-ing, Feed a wife and chil-dren, Say his dai-ly prayers: And who has the right, as

mas-ter of his house, To have the fi-nal word at home. The pop-pa. _____ the pop-pa,

(duet) Tra-di-tion, The pop-pa. _____ the pop-pa, Tra-di-tion.

Mommas: Who must know the way to make a prop-er home, A qui-et home, a ko-sher home; Who must raise a fam-i-ly and

run the home. So pop-pa's free to read the Ho-ly Book The mom-ma. _____ the mom-ma.

Tra - di - tion, The mom - ma, the mom - ma, Tra - di - tion.

Sons:
At three I start - ed He - brew school, At ten I learned a trade; I hear they picked a bride for me, I

All:
hope she's pret - ty. The sons, the sons, Tra - di - tion. The sons,

Daughters:
the sons, Tra - di - tion. And who does mom - ma teach To

mend and tend and fix, Pre - par - ing me to mar - ry Who - ev - er pop - pa picks. The daugh - ters,

the daugh - ters, Tra - di - tion, The daugh - ters, the daugh - ters, Tra - di - tion.

## MATCHMAKER

Copyright © 1964 by Alley Music Corp. and Trio Music Co., Inc.
All Rights Administered by Hudson Bay Music, Inc.
Used by Permission

Lyrics by SHELDON HARNICK
Music by JERRY BOCK

Slowly, with much sentiment

Match - mak - er, Match - mak - er, make me a match, Fine me a find, catch me a catch;
Match - mak - er, Match - mak - er, I'll bring the veil, You bring the groom, slen - der and pale;
Match - mak - er, Match - mak - er, make me a match, Fine me a find, catch me a catch;

To Coda

Match - mak - er, Match - mak - er, look through your book and make me a per - fect match.
Bring me a ring, for I'm long - ing to be the en - vy of all I
Night af - ter night in the dark all a - lone. So

see. For pop - pa, make him a schol - ar, For mom - ma, make him

rich as a king; For me, well, I would - n't hol - er if he were as hand - some as

D.C. al Coda

an - y - thing.

CODA

make me a match of my own.

## SABBATH PRAYER

Copyright © 1964 by Alley Music Corp. and Trio Music Co., Inc.
All Rights Administered by Hudson Bay Music, Inc.
Used by Permission

Lyrics by SHELDON HARNICK
Music by JERRY BOCK

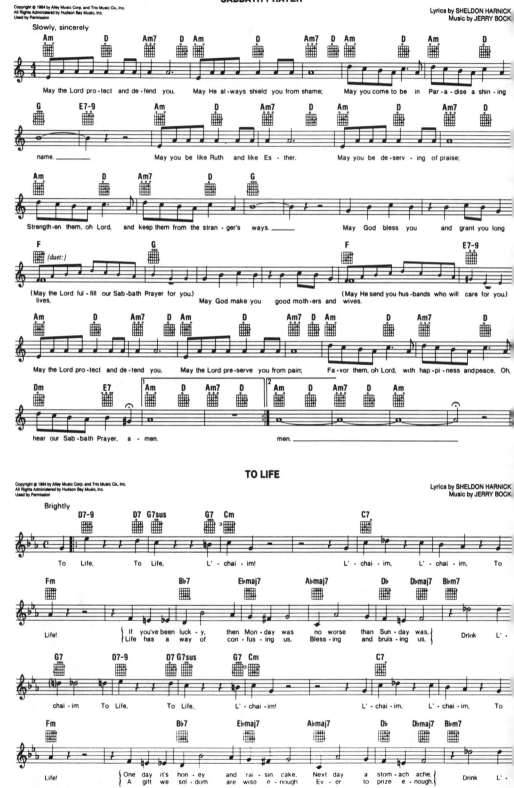

## TO LIFE

Copyright © 1964 by Alley Music Corp. and Trio Music Co., Inc.
All Rights Administered by Hudson Bay Music, Inc.
Used by Permission

Lyrics by SHELDON HARNICK
Music by JERRY BOCK

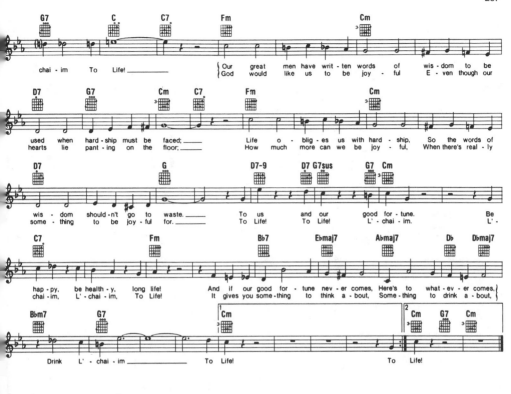

Copyright © 1946 by Chappell & Co. Inc.
Copyright Renewed
International Copyright Secured    ALL RIGHTS RESERVED

## "Finian's Rainbow"

### OLD DEVIL MOON

Words by E.Y. HARBURG
Music by BURTON LANE

# IF THIS ISN'T LOVE

Copyright © 1946 by The Players Music Corp.
Copyright Renewed, Assigned to Chappell & Co., Inc.
International Copyright Secured    ALL RIGHTS RESERVED

Words by E.Y. HARBURG
Music by BURTON LANE

# LOOK TO THE RAINBOW

Copyright © 1946 & 1947 by Chappell & Co., Inc.
Copyrights renewed
International Copyright Secured    ALL RIGHTS RESERVED

Words by E.Y. HARBURG
Music by BURTON LANE

Ab | Eb | Cm | Fm7 | Bb7 | Ebmaj7 | Eb6

**REFRAIN**

ev - er the world falls a - part.) Look, look, Look To The Rain - bow.
sing - in' be - yond the next hill.}

Fm7 | Bb7 | Eb | Ab | Cm6 | Bb7 | Eb | Cm | Fm7 | Bb7

Fol - low it o - ver the hill____ and stream. Look, look, Look To The

Eb | Ab | Bb7 | Eb | Ab | Eb

Rain - bow, Fol - low the fel - low who fol - lows a dream. Fol - low the fel - low.

Fm7 | Bb7 | Eb | Ab | Ebmaj7 | Bb7 | 1 Eb | 2 Eb

Fol - low the fel - low. Fol - low the fel - low who fol - lows a dream. 'Twas a dream.

## WHEN I'M NOT NEAR THE GIRL I LOVE

Copyright © 1946 by The Players Music Corp.
Copyright Renewed, Chappell & Co., Inc., sole selling agent
International Copyright Secured   ALL RIGHTS RESERVED

Words by E.Y. HARBURG
Music by BURTON LANE

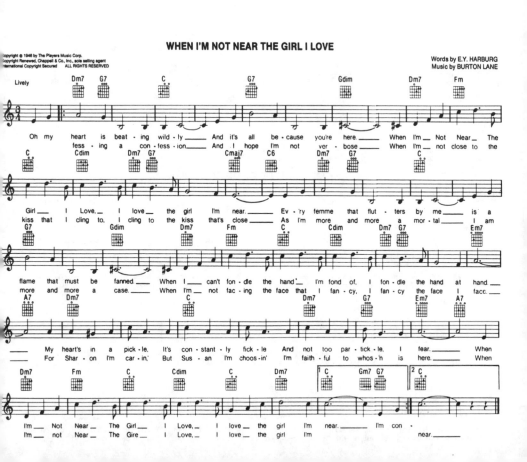

**Lively**   Dm7 | G7 | C | G7 | Gdim | Dm7 | Fm

Oh my heart is beat - ing wild - ly____ And it's all be - cause you're here.____ When I'm__ Not Near__ The
fess - ing a con - fess - ion. And I hope I'm not ver - bose____ When I'm__ not close to the

C | Cdim | Dm7 G7 | Cmaj7 | C6 | Dm7 | G7 | C

Girl____ I Love,__ I love__ the girl I'm near.____ Ev - 'ry femme that flut - ters by me____ is a
kiss that I cling to, I cling to the kiss that's close____ As I'm more and more a mor - tal____ I am

G7 | Gdim | Dm7 | Fm | C | Cdim | Dm7 G7 | Em7

flame that must be fanned.____ When I__ can't fon - dle the hand'__ I'm fond of, I fon - dle the hand at hand.____
more and more a case.____ When I'm__ not fac - ing the face that I fan - cy, I fan - cy the face I face.____

A7 | Dm7 | C | Dm7 | G7 | Em7 | A7

____ My heart's in a pick - le. It's con - stant - ly fick - le And not too par - tick - le, I fear.____ When
For Shar - on I'm car - in', But Sus - an I'm choos - in' I'm faith - ful to whos - 'n is here.____ When

Dm7 | Fm | C | Cdim | C | Dm7 | 1 C Gm7 G7 | 2 C

I'm__ Not Near__ The Girl____ I Love,__ I love__ the girl I'm near.____ I'm con -
I'm__ not Near__ The Gire____ I Love,__ I love__ the girl I'm____ near.____

# HOW ARE THINGS IN GLOCCA MORRA

Copyright © 1946 by The Players Music Corp.
Copyright Renewed, Assigned to Chappell & Co., Inc.
International Copyright Secured    ALL RIGHTS RESERVED

Words by E.Y. HARBURG
Music by BURTON LANE

## SOMETHING SORT OF GRANDISH

Copyright © 1946 by Chappell & Co., Inc.
Copyright Renewed

Words by E. Y. HARBURG
Music by BURTON LANE

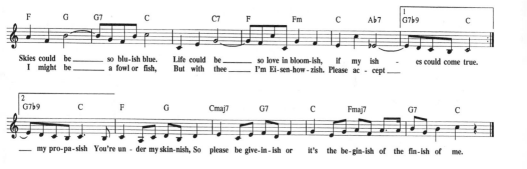

Skies could be _____ so blu-ish blue. Life could be _____ so love in bloom-ish, if my ish - es could come true.
I might be _____ a fowl or fish, But with thee _____ I'm Ei-sen-how-zish. Please ac - cept _____

_____ my pro-pa-sish You're un - der my skin-nish, So please be give-in-ish or it's the be-gin-ish of the fin-ish of me.

# THAT GREAT COME AND GET IT DAY

Copyright © 1946 by Chappell & Co., Inc.
Copyright Renewed
International Copyright Secured   ALL RIGHTS RESERVED

Words by E.Y. HARBURG
Music by BURTON LANE

On That Great Come - And - Get - It Day, _____ Won't it be fun when wor-ry is done and mon-ey is hay. _____

That's the time things - 'll come your way _____ On That Great, Great Come - And - It Day. _____

I'll get my gal _____ that cal-i-co gown. _____ I'll get my mule _____ that a-cre of groun'.
My gown will be _____ a cal-i-co gown. My shoes will dance _____ all o-ver the town. _____

'Cause word has come _____ from Ga-bri-el's horn _____ the earth be-neath your plow is a - bud-din' and now it's yourn.

Glo-ry times' com-in' for to stay _____ On That Great,_ Great,_ Come - And - Get - It

Day. _____ On That And keep it, and share it, great._ great._ "Come and get it" day! _____

## "Fiorello!"

### WHERE DO I GO FROM HERE

Copyright © 1959 by Alley Music Corp. and Trio Music Co., Inc.
All Rights Administered by Hudson Bay Music, Inc.
Used by Permission

Lyrics by SHELDON HARNICK
Music by JERRY BOCK

She does-n't love me I know it's true, the signs are all too clear, But lov-ing
The time is com-ing the mo-ment when she'll know how much I care, But once she

her the way I do, } Where Do I Go _____ From Here. _____
knows what hap-pens then,

go _____ from there _____ Must I play a wait-ing game as each ir-re-place-a-ble

day goes by She may nev-er feel the same as I _____ I'll take my chan-ces

And come what may I'll be where she is near And there I'll stay

un-til I know where I must go _____ from here. _____

### POLITICS AND POKER

Copyright © 1959 by Alley Music Corp. and Trio Music Inc.
All Rights Administered by Hudson Bay Music, Inc.
Used by Permission

Lyrics by SHELDON HARNICK
Music by JERRY BOCK

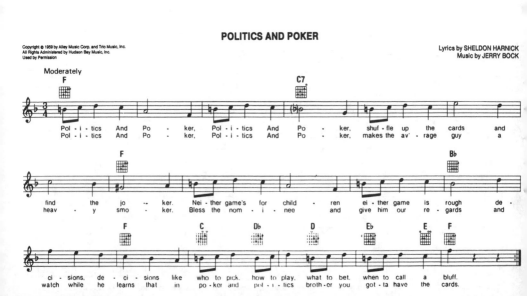

Pol-i-tics And Po-ker, Pol-i-tics And Po-ker, shuf-fle up the cards and
Pol-i-tics And Po-ker, Pol-i-tics And Po-ker, makes the av-'rage guy a

find the jo-ker. Nei-ther game's for child-ren ei-ther game is rough de-
heav-y smo-ker. Bless the nom-i-nee and give him our re-gards and

ci-sions, de-ci-sions like who to pick, how to play, what to bet, when to call a bluff.
watch while he learns that in po-ker and pol-i-tics broth-er you got-ta have the cards.

# GENTLEMAN JIMMY

Copyright © 1959 by Alley Music Corp. and Trio Music Co., Inc.
All Rights Administered by Hudson Bay Music, Inc.
Used by Permission

Lyrics by SHELDON HARNICK
Music by JERRY BOCK

# 'TIL TOMORROW

Copyright © 1959 by Alley Music Corp. and Trio Music Co., Inc.
All Rights Administered by Hudson Bay Music, Inc.
Used by Permission

Lyrics by SHELDON HARNICK
Music by JERRY BOCK

## WHEN DID I FALL IN LOVE

Copyright © 1959 by Alley Music Corp. and Trio Music Co., Inc.
All Rights Administered by Hudson Bay Music, Inc.
Used by Permission

Lyrics by SHELDON HARNICK
Music by JERRY BOCK

## "Fashion"

### A LIFE WITHOUT HER

© 1974 STEVE BROWN and DON PIPPIN
All Rights Throughout the World Controlled by WREN MUSIC CO.

Lyric by STEVE BROWN
Music by DON PIPPIN

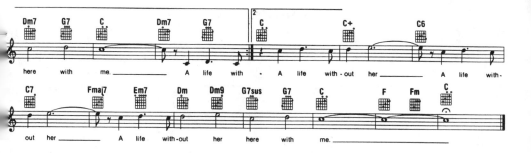

## 'Firebrand Of Florence'

### SING ME NOT A BALLAD

TRO - © Copyright 1945 and renewed 1973 Hampshire House Publishing Corp.
and Chappell & Co., Inc., New York, N.Y.

Words by IRA GERSHWIN
Music by KURT WEILL

## "Flower Drum Song"

### LOVE, LOOK AWAY

Copyright © 1958 by Richard Rodgers and Oscar Hammerstein II
Copyright Renewed
WILLIAMSON MUSIC owner of publication and allied rights throughout the world

Lyrics by OSCAR HAMMERSTEIN II
Music by RICHARD RODGERS

### A HUNDRED MILLION MIRACLES

Copyright © 1958 by Richard Rodgers and Oscar Hammerstein II
Copyright Renewed
WILLIAMSON MUSIC owner of publication and allied rights throughout the world

Lyrics by OSCAR HAMMERSTEIN II
Music by RICHARD RODGERS

# SUNDAY

Copyright © 1958 by Richard Rodgers and Oscar Hammerstein II
Copyright Renewed
WILLIAMSON MUSIC owner of publication and allied rights throughout the world

Lyrics by OSCAR HAMMERSTEIN II
Music by RICHARD RODGERS

# DON'T MARRY ME

Copyright © 1958 by Richard Rodgers and Oscar Hammerstein II
Copyright Renewed
WILLIAMSON MUSIC owner of publication and allied rights throughout the world.

Lyrics by OSCAR HAMMERSTEIN II
Music by RICHARD RODGERS

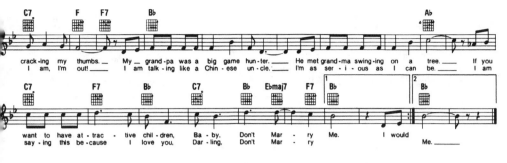

crack - ing my thumbs. ___ My ___ grand - pa was a big game hun - ter. He met grand - ma swing - ing on a tree. ___ If you
I am, I'm out! ___ I am talk - ing like a Chin - ese un - cle. ___ I'm as ser - i - ous as I can be. ___ I am

want to have at - trac - tive chil - dren, Ba - by, Don't Mar - ry Me. I would
say - ing this be - cause I love you, Dar - ling, Don't Mar - ry Me. ___

## I ENJOY BEING A GIRL

Copyright © 1958 by Richard Rodgers and Oscar Hammerstein II
Copyright Renewed
WILLIAMSON MUSIC owner of publication and allied rights throughout the world

Lyrics by OSCAR HAMMERSTEIN II
Music by RICHARD RODGERS

When I have a brand new hair - do ___ With my eye - lash - es all in curl. ___
men say I'm cute and fun - ny ___ And my teeth are - n't teeth but pearl.

___ I float as the clouds on air do, ___ I En - joy Be - ing A
I just lap it up like hon - ey, ___ I En - joy Be - ing A

Girl! ___ When Girl! ___ I flip when a fel - low sends me flow - ers,

I drool o - ver dress - es made of lace, ___ I talk on the tel - e - phone for

ho - urs ___ With a pound and a half of cream up - on my face! I'm

strict - ly a fe - male fe - male ___ And my fu - ture I hope will be ___

___ In the home of a brave and free male Who'll en - joy be - ing a

guy hav - ing a girl ___ like ___ me.

# YOU ARE BEAUTIFUL

Copyright © 1958 by Richard Rodgers and Oscar Hammerstein II
Copyright Renewed
WILLIAMSON MUSIC owner of publication and allied rights throughout the world

Lyrics by OSCAR HAMMERSTEIN
Music by RICHARD RODGERS

You Are Beau - ti - ful, small and shy. You are the girl whose eyes met mine

Just as your boat sailed by. This I know of you, noth - ing more,

You are the girl whose eyes met mine Pass - ing the riv - er shore. You are the girl whose laugh I heard,

Sil - ver and soft and bright; Soft as the fall of lo - tus leaves Brush - ing the air of night.

While your flow - er boat sailed a - way, Gen - tly your eyes looked back on mine,

Clear - ly you heard me say: "You are the girl I will love some day." ____

## "Follies"

### AH, PARIS!

Copyright © 1971 by The Herald Square Music Company and Rilting Music, Inc. and Burthen Music Company, Inc.
Used by Permission

Music and Lyrics by
STEPHEN SONDHEIM

I have trav - eled o - ver this earth, ____ From Bom - bay to Ven - ice to
I have seen the ru - ins of Rome, ____ I've been in the ig - loos of

Perth. ____ I've been down to Ri - o and up to Brest. ____ To East and West ____ and to all the rest. ____ I have
Nome. ____ I have gone to Mos - cow. It's ver - y gay. ____ Well, an - y - way, on the first of May! ____ I have

seen the gar - dens of Kew ____ And I've been to Tim - buk - tu, too. ____ But when I've re - turned ____ The
seen Ran - goon ____ and So - ho. ____ And I like them more than so - so. ____ But when there's a moon, ____ Good -

**Cdim** **Dm7** **G7**

thing I've learned__ is what I al - ways knew: _____
bye Ran - goon, __ Hel - lo, Mont - marte, hel - lo! _____

**G7** **C** **C+** **C#dim** **G9** **Dm**

___ New York has ne - on, Ber - lin has bars.__ But Ah, Pa - ris! Shang - hai has silk __ and Ma -
Pe - king has rick - shaws, New Or - leans jazz, __ But Ah, Pa - ris! Bei - rut has sun - shine, That's

**C#dim** **G9** **C6** **C+** **C11**

drid gui - tars, __ But Ah, Pa - ris! In Cai - ro you __ find bi - zarre ba - zaars, __ In Lon - don pip! pip!
all it has, __ But Ah, Pa - ris! Con - stan - ti - no - ple has Turk - ish baths, And Ath - ens that love -

**F** **Fmaj7** **G11** **Cmaj7** **C#dim** **Dm** **Ebdim** **C6**

___ you sip tea. But when it comes _ to love, None of the __ a - bove com - pares, com - pris? So Carls -
- ly de - bris. Carls - bad may have __ a spa, But for ooh - la - la, you come with me! Carls -

**F6** **A7** **Dm** **G7** **C**

if it's mak - ing love that you're think - ing of Ah ah ah __ ah ah, Ah ah ah __ Ah Pa - ris! _____
bad is where _ you're cured af - ter you __ have toured Ah ah ah __ ah ah, Ah ah ah __ Ah Pa - ris! _____

## IN BUDDY'S EYES
### (Buddy's There)

Copyright © 1971 by The Herald Square Music Company and Rilting Music, Inc. and Burthen Music Company, Inc.
Used by Permission

Music and Lyrics by
STEPHEN SONDHEIM

**Moderately**

**Abmaj9** **Eb7** **Abmaj9** **Db**

In Bud - dy's Eyes, _____ I'm young, I'm beau - ti - ful. ___ In Bud - dy's Eyes, _____ I can't get old - er.

**Abmaj9** **Bb** **Absus** **Abmaj9**

___ I'm still the prin - cess, ___ Still the prize. ___ In Bud - dy's Eyes, _____ I'm

**Eb7** **Abmaj9** **Db** **Abmaj7** **Ab**

young, I'm beau - ti - ful. ___ In Bud - dy's arms, _____ On Bud - dy's shoul - der, I won't get old - er.

**Db** **Absus** **Abmaj9** **Absus**

___ Noth - ing dies. ___ And all I ev - er _ dreamed I'd be, The best I ev - er thought of

**Abmaj9** **Ab** **B** **Ebm9** **Ab7sus** **Ab6**

me. is ev - 'ry min - ute there to see ____ In Bud - dy's Eyes, ____

# TOO MANY MORNINGS

Copyright © 1971 by The Herald Square Music Company and Rilting Music, Inc. and Burthen Music Company, Inc.
Used by Permission

Music and Lyrics by
STEPHEN SONDHEIM

Lyrics:

Too Many Mornings, waking and pretending I reach for you, Thousands of mornings, dreaming of my {girl. / boy.} All that time wasted, merely passing through.

Time I could have spent, so content, wasting time with you. Too Many Mornings, wishing that the room might be filled with you, Morning to morning, Turning into days. All the days that I thought would never end, All the nights with another day to spend,

Too Many Mornings, wasted in pretending I reach for you, How many mornings Are there still to come? How much time can we hope that there will be? Not much time, but it's time enough for me,

All those times I'd look up to see {Someone standing at the door, Someone moving to the

If there's time To look up and see

bed, Someone resting in my arms with {her / his} head against my head. head.

# BROADWAY BABY

Copyright © 1971 by The Herald Square Music Company and Rilting Music, Inc. and Burthen Music Company, Inc.
Used by Permission

Music and Lyrics by
STEPHEN SONDHEIM

I'm just a Broadway Baby, walking off my tired feet. Pounding Forty Second Street
Broadway Baby, slaving at the five and ten. Dreaming of the great day when

to be in a show. Broadway Baby. Learning how to sing and dance,
I'll be in a show. Broadway Baby. Making rounds all afternoon,

# WAITING FOR THE GIRLS UPSTAIRS

Copyright © 1971 by The Herald Square Music Company and Rilting Music, Inc. and Burthen Music Company, Inc.
Used by Permission

Music and Lyrics by
STEPHEN SONDHEIM

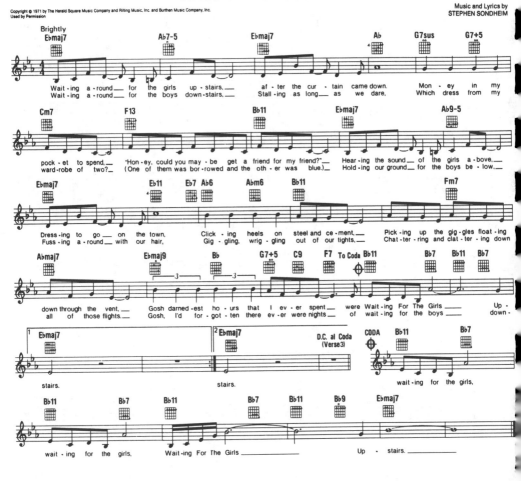

Brightly

Wait-ing a-round\_\_\_ for the girls up-stairs,\_\_\_ af-ter the cur-tain came down. Mon-ey in my
Wait-ing a-round\_\_\_ for the boys down-stairs, Stall-ing as long\_\_\_ as we dare, Which dress from my

pock-et to spend,\_\_\_ "Hon-ey, could you may-be get a friend for my friend?"\_\_\_ Hear-ing the sound\_\_\_ of the girls a-bove,\_\_\_
ward-robe of two?\_\_\_ (One of them was bor-rowed and the oth-er was blue.)\_\_\_ Hold-ing our ground\_\_\_ for the boys be-low,\_\_\_

Dress-ing to go\_\_\_ on the town, Click-ing heels on steel and ce-ment,\_\_\_ Pick-ing up the gig-gles float-ing
Fuss-ing a-round\_\_\_ with our hair, Gig-gling, wrig-gling out of our tights, Chat-ter-ring and clat-ter-ing down

down through the vent.\_\_\_ Gosh darned-est ho-urs that I ev-er spent\_\_\_ were Wait-ing For The Girls \_\_\_ Up-
all of those flights.\_\_\_ Gosh, I'd for-got-ten there ev-er were nights\_\_\_ of wait-ing for the boys \_\_\_ down-

1 Eb maj7
stairs.

2 Eb maj7
stairs.

D.C. al Coda
(Verse 3)

CODA
wait-ing for the girls,

wait-ing for the girls, Wait-ing For The Girls \_\_\_\_ Up - stairs. \_\_\_\_

3. Waiting around for the girls upstairs
Weren't we chuckle-heads then
Very young and very old hat
Everybody has to go through stages like that
Waiting around for the girls upstairs
Thank you but never again

Life was fun, but oh, so intense
Everything was possible and nothing made sense
Back there when one of the major events was
Waiting for the girls, waiting for the girls,
Waiting for the girls upstairs.

# THE GOD-WHY-DON'T-YOU-LOVE-ME BLUES

Copyright © 1971 by The Herald Square Music Company and Rilting Music, Inc. and Burthen Music Company, Inc.
Used by Permission

Music and Lyrics by
STEPHEN SONDHEIM

Quickly

I've got those "God. Why don't you love me, oh you do I'll see you la-ter" Blues. \_\_\_\_ That
"Whis-per how I'm bet-ter than I think, but what do you know?" Blues \_\_\_\_ That

"long as you ig-nore me, you're the on-ly thing that mat-ters" feel-ing \_\_\_\_ That "if I'm good e-nough for you, you'r
"Why do you keep tell-ing me I stink when I a-dore you?" feel-ing \_\_\_\_ That "say I'm all the world to you, you'r

## COULD I LEAVE YOU

Copyright © 1971 by The Herald Square Music Company and Rilting Music, Inc. and Burthen Music Company, Inc.
...d by Permission

Music and Lyrics by
STEPHEN SONDHEIM

226

# WHO'S THAT WOMAN?
### (The Mirror Song)

Copyright © 1971 by The Herald Square Music Company and Rilting Music, Inc. and Burthen Music Company, Inc.
By Permission

Music and Lyrics by
STEPHEN SONDHEIM

# I'M STILL HERE

Copyright © 1971 by The Herald Square Music Company and Rilting Music, Inc. and Burthen Music Company, Inc.
Used by Permission

Music and Lyrics by
STEPHEN SONDHEIM

# LOSING MY MIND

Copyright © 1971 by The Herald Square Music Company and Rilting Music, Inc. and Burthen Music Company, Inc.
Used by Permission

Music and Lyrics
STEPHEN SONDHE

The sun __ comes up, I think __ a-bout you. The cof-fee cup, I think __ a-bout you. I want you so,
the morn-ing ends, I think __ a-bout you, I talk to friends, I think __ a-bout you, And do __ they know

__ It's like I'm Los-ing My Mind. __
__ It's like I'm Los-ing My Mind.__

All af-ter-noon, do-ing

ev-'ry lit-tle chore, The thought of you stays bright. Some-times I stand in the mid-dle of the floor,

Not go-ing left, Not go-ing right. I dim __ the lights and think __ a-bout you, Spend sleep-less nights to think __ a-bout

you. You said __ you loved me, or were you just be-ing kind?__ Or am I Los-ing My Mind? __

# ONE MORE KISS

Copyright © 1971 by The Herald Square Music Company and Rilting Music, Inc. and Burthen Music Company, Inc.
Used by Permission

Music and Lyrics
STEPHEN SONDHE

One More Kiss be-fore we part, __ One More Kiss and fare-well. __ Nev-er __ shall we meet a
One More Kiss to melt the heart, __ One more glimpse of the past, __ One more sou-ven-ir o

gain __ just a kiss and then we break the spell. __
bliss, __ know-ing well that this one must be the last. __

Dreams __ are a sweet mis-take. __ All dream-ers must a-wake. __ On then with the

dance, No back-ward glance __ or my heart will break. Nev-er look back. Nev-er look back. __

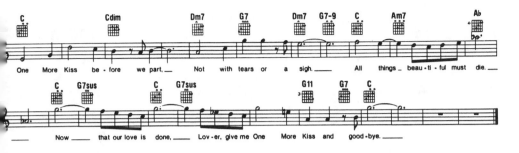

One More Kiss be-fore we part,__ Not with tears or a sigh.__ All things __ beau-ti-ful must die.__

__ Now __ that our love is done,__ Lov-er, give me One More Kiss and good-bye.

## PROLOGUE
### (Beautiful Girls)

Copyright © 1971 by The Herald Square Music Company and Rilting Music, Inc. and Burthen Music Company, Inc.
Used by Permission

Music and Lyrics by
STEPHEN SONDHEIM

Hats off, here they come, those beau-ti-ful girls. That's what you've been wait-ing for. ____
Care-ful, here's the home of beau-ti-ful girls. Where your rea-son is un-done. ____

Na-ture nev-er fash-ioned a flow-er so fair. No rose__ can com-pare,
Beau-ty can't be hin-dered from tak-ing its toll. You may__ lose con-trol.

Noth-ing re-spect-a-ble half so de-lec-ta-ble. Cheer them in their glo-ry, Dia-monds and pearls,
Faced with these Lo-re-leis, what man can mor-al-ize? Cau-tion, on your guard with beau-ti-ful girls,

Daz-zling jew-els by the score. ____ This is what beau-ty can be.
Flaw-less charm-ers ev-'ry-one. ____ This is how Sam-son was shorn;

Beau-ty ce-les-tial, the best, you'll a-gree. All for you, these beau-ti-ful girls!
Each in her style a De-li-lah re-born, Each a gem, a beau-ti-ful

di-a-dem of beau-ti-ful, wel-come them, the beau-ti-ful girls!

## "Follow Thru"

### BUTTON UP YOUR OVERCOAT

Copyright © 1928 by DeSylva, Brown & Henderson, Inc.
Copyright Renewed, Assigned to Chappell & Co., Inc.
International Copyright Secured    ALL RIGHTS RESERVED

Words and Music by B.G. DESYLVA
LEW BROWN and RAY HENDERSON

## "For The Love Of Mike"

### GOT A DATE WITH AN ANGEL

Copyright © 1931 by Chappell & Co., Ltd. London
Copyright © 1932 by Chappell & Co. Inc.
Copyrights Renewed, Chappell & Co., Inc., Publisher
International Copyright Secured    ALL RIGHTS RESERVED

Words by CLIFFORD GREY & SONNIE MILLER
Music by JACK WALLER & JOSEPH TURNBRIDGE

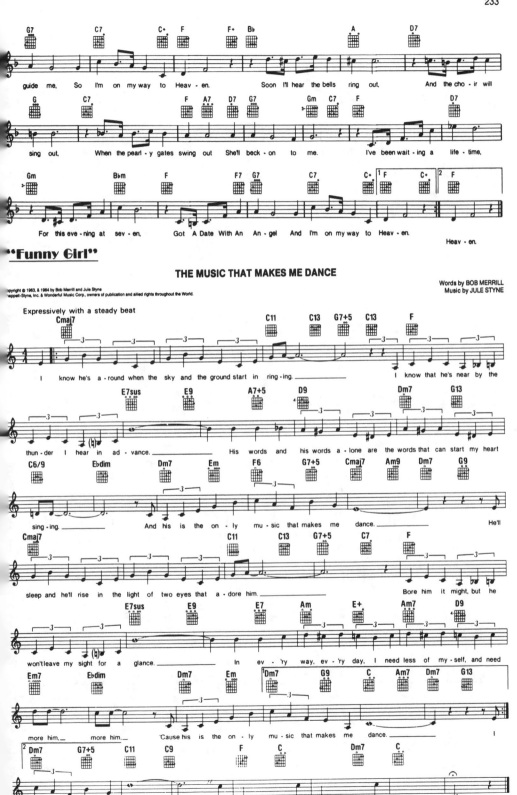

"Funny Girl"

## THE MUSIC THAT MAKES ME DANCE

Words by BOB MERRILL
Music by JULE STYNE

Copyright © 1963, & 1964 by Bob Merrill and Jule Styne
Chappell-Styne, Inc. & Wonderful Music Corp., owners of publication and allied rights throughout the World.

# DON'T RAIN ON MY PARADE

Copyright © 1963, & 1964 by Bob Merrill and Jule Styne
Chappell-Styne, Inc. and Wonderful Music Corp., owners of publication and allied rights throughout the World
Chappell & Co., Inc., sole and exclusive agent
International Copyright Secured    ALL RIGHTS RESERVED

Words by BOB MERRILL
Music by JULE STYNE

bam! Hey, world, here I am! _____ Get rea - dy for me,.

____ love, 'cause I'm a "com - er." I sim - ply got - ta ___ march, my heart's a drum - mer. No - bod - y, no.

no - bod - y Is gon - na rain on my pa - rade. _____

## SADIE, SADIE

right © 1964 by Bob Merrill and Jule Styne
pell-Styne, Inc. and Wonderful Music, Corp., owners of publication and allied rights throughout the World
ational Copyright Secured    ALL RIGHTS RESERVED

Words by BOB MERRILL
Music by JULE STYNE

Sa - die, Sa - die, mar - ried la - dy, See what's on my hand. There's noth - ing quite as
Sa - die, Sa - die, mar - ried la - dy, Meet a mort - ga - gee! The own - er of an

touch - ing as ___ A sim - ple wed - ding band. ___ Oh, how that mar - riage li - cense works. On cham - ber maids and
ice - box With a ten year guar - an - tee. ___ Oh, sit me in the soft - est seat. _____ Quick! A cush - ion

ho - tel clerks. The Hon - ey - moon was such de - light That we got mar - ried that same night. I'm
for my feet. _____ Do for me, buy for me, lift me, carry me. Fin - 'lly got a guy to marry me!!

Sa - die, Sa - die, mar - ried la - dy. Still in bed at noon. Wrack - ing my brain de - cid - ing Be - tween
do my nails, read up on sales, All day the re - cords play. ___ Then he comes home, I tell him, "Oy! What a

or - ange juice and prune! He says noth - ing is too good for me,__ And who am I not to a - gree?. I'm
day I had to - day!" I swear I'll do my wife - ly job.__ Just sit at home be - come a slob __ I'm

Sa - die, Sa - die, mar - ried la - dy, that's me!
Sa - die, Sa - die, mar - ried la - dy, that's me! _____

# IF A GIRL ISN'T PRETTY

Copyright © 1963, & 1964 by Bob Merrill and Jule Styne
Chappell-Styne, Inc. & Wonderful Music Corp., owners of publication and allied rights throughout the World.

Words by BOB MERRILL
Music by JULE STYNE

If A Girl Isn't Pretty Like a Miss Atlantic City, All she gets from life is pity and a pat. Is a nose with deviation Such a crime against the nation? Should I throw her into jail Or drown the cat? She must shine in ev'ry detail, Like a ring you're buying retail; A standard size that fits a standard dress. When a girl's incidentals Are no bigger than two lentils, Then to me it doesn't spell success! Ricky-Ticky If A Girl Isn't Pretty, Like a Miss Atlantic City. She should dump the stage And try another route. Any guy who pays a quarter For a seat just feels he oughter See a figger that his wife can't substitute! Kid, my heart ain't made of marble. But your rhythm's really horrible And that map of yours just ain't no valentine. Ev'ry thing you got's about right, But the damn thing don't come out right... for get it, kid, And just re sign!

237

**YOU ARE WOMAN, I AM MAN**

Copyright © 1963, & 1964 by Bob Merrill and Jule Styne
Chappell-Styne, Inc. & Wonderful Music Corp., owners of publication and allied rights throughout the World
Chappell & Co., Inc., sole selling agent
International Copyright Secured    ALL RIGHTS RESERVED

Words by BOB MERRILL
Music by JULE STYNE

# I'M THE GREATEST STAR

Copyright © 1963, & 1964 by Bob Merrill and Jule Styne
Chappell-Styne, Inc. & Wonderful Music Corp., owners of publication and allied rights throughout the World.

Words by BOB MERRILL
Music by JULE STYNE

## PEOPLE

Copyright © 1963, & 1964 by Bob Merrill and Jule Styne
Chappell-Styne, Inc. and Wonderful Music, Corp, owners of publication and allied rights throughout the World
Chappell & Co, Inc, sole selling agent
International Copyright Secured    ALL RIGHTS RESERVED

Words by BOB MERRILL
Music by JULE STYNE

luck - i - est peo - ple____ in the world.____ With one per - son,____ One ver - y spe - cial

per - son,____ A feel - ing deep in your soul____ Says: you were half, now you're whole.____

No more hun - ger and thirst, But first, be a per - son who needs peo - ple. Peo - ple who need

peo - ple____ Are the luck - i - est peo - ple in the world.____

# "A Funny Thing Happened On The Way To Forum"

## COMEDY TONIGHT

Copyright © 1962 by Stephen Sondheim
Burthen Music Co., Inc. owner of publication and allied right throughout the World
Chappell & Co., Inc., sole selling agent
International Copyright Secured     ALL RIGHTS RESERVED

Words and Music by
STEPHEN SONDHEIM

Some - thing fa - mil - iar, some - thing pe - cul - iar, Some - thing for ev - 'ry - one, a Com - e - dy To -
Some - thing con - vul - sive, some - thing re - pul - sive, Some - thing for ev - 'ry - one, a Com - e - dy To -

night! Some - thing ap - peal - ing, some - thing ap - pal - ling, Some - thing for ev - 'ry - one, a
night! Some - thing es - thet - ic, some - thing fre - net - ic, Some - thing for ev - 'ry - one, a

Com - e - dy To - night! Noth - ing with kings, noth - ing with crowns. Bring on the
Com - e - dy To - night! Noth - ing of Gods, noth - ing of Fate. Weigh - ty af -

lov - ers, li - ars and clowns!____ Old sit - u - a - tions, new com - pli - ca - tions,
fairs will just have to wait.____ Noth - ing that's for - mal, noth - ing that's nor - mal,

Noth - ing por - ten - tous or po - lite:____ Trag - e - dy to - mor - row. Com - e - dy To - night!
No re - ci - ta - tions to re - cite!____ O - pen up the cur - tains,

Com - e - dy____ To - night!____

# LOVELY

Copyright © 1962 by Stephen Sondheim
Burthen Music Co., Inc., owner of publication and allied rights
Chappell & Co., Inc., Administrator

Words and Music
STEPHEN SONDHE[IM]

# "Guys And Dolls"

## A BUSHEL AND A PECK

© 1950 FRANK MUSIC CORP.
© Renewed 1978 FRANK MUSIC CORP.

By FRANK LOESSER

I love you A Bu-shel And A Peck A Bu-shel And A Peck and a hug a-round the neck Hug a-round the neck and a barrel and a heap
I love you A Bu-shel And A Peck A Bu-shel And A Peck tho' you make my heart a wreck Make my heart a wreck and you make my life a mess

Bar-rel and a heap and I'm talk-in' in my sleep a-bout you a-bout you 'Cause I love you A Bu-shel And A Peck y'
Make my life a mess yes a mess of hap-pi-ness a-bout

bet your pur-ty neck I do Doo-dle oo-dle Doo-dle doo-dle oo-dle oo-dle doo-dle oo-dle oo-dle ooo.

## LUCK BE A LADY

© 1950 FRANK MUSIC CORP.
© Renewed 1978 FRANK MUSIC CORP.

By FRANK LOESSER

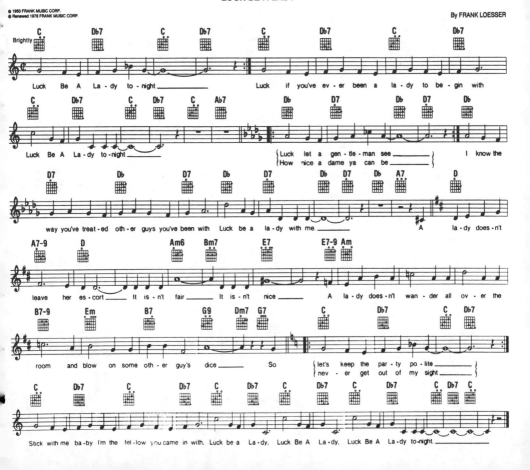

Luck Be A La-dy to-night Luck if you've ev-er been a la-dy to be-gin with

Luck Be A La-dy to-night Luck let a gen-tle-man see I know the
How nice a dame ya can be

way you've treat-ed oth-er guys you've been with Luck be a la-dy with me. A la-dy does-n't

leave her es-cort It isn't fair It isn't nice A la-dy does-n't wan-der all ov-er the

room and blow on some oth-er guy's dice So let's keep the par-ty po-lite
nev-er get out of my sight

Stick with me ba-by I'm the fel-low you came in with, Luck be a La-dy. Luck Be A La-dy. Luck Be A La-dy to-night.

# GUYS AND DOLLS

© 1950 FRANK MUSIC CORP.
© Renewed 1978 FRANK MUSIC CORP.

By FRANK LOESSER

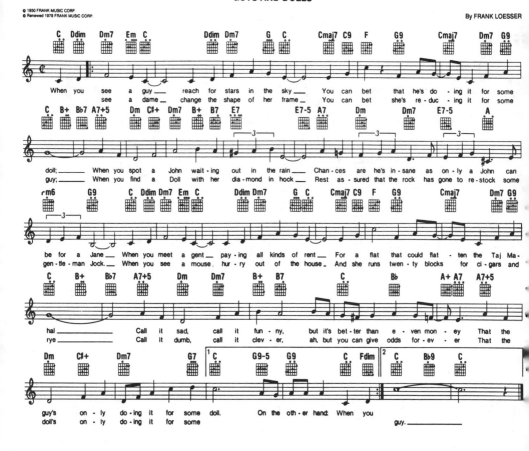

# ADELAIDE'S LAMENT

© 1950 FRANK MUSIC CORP.
© Renewed 1978 FRANK MUSIC CORP.

By FRANK LOESSER

## I'LL KNOW

© 1950 FRANK MUSIC CORP.
© Renewed 1978 FRANK MUSIC CORP.

By FRANK LOESSER

## I'VE NEVER BEEN IN LOVE BEFORE

© 1950 FRANK MUSIC CORP.
© Renewed 1978 FRANK MUSIC CORP.

By FRANK LOESSER

## IF I WERE A BELL

© 1950 FRANK MUSIC CORP.
© Renewed 1978 FRANK MUSIC CORP.

By FRANK LOESSER

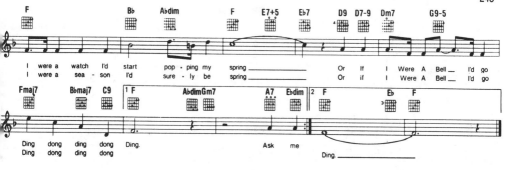

## SIT DOWN YOU'RE ROCKIN' THE BOAT

© 1950 FRANK MUSIC CORP.
© Renewed 1978 FRANK MUSIC CORP.

By FRANK LOESSER

# FUGUE FOR TINHORNS

© 1950 FRANK MUSIC CORP.
© Renewed 1978 FRANK MUSIC CORP.

By FRANK LOESSER

# MORE I CANNOT WISH YOU

© 1949, 1950 FRANK MUSIC CORP.
© Renewed 1977, 1978 FRANK MUSIC CORP.

By FRANK LOESSER

calling cards upon a silver tray ____ But more I cannot wish you than to wish you find your love, ____ Your own true love, ____ this day. ____ Standing there ____ gazing at you ____ Full of the bloom of youth ____ Standing there ____ gazing at you ____ with the sheep's eye ____ And the lick-er-ish tooth ____

CODA

day ____ With the sheep's eye ____ And the lick-er-ish tooth ____ And the strong arms to car-ry you a-way.

## TAKE BACK YOUR MINK

©1950 FRANK MUSIC CORP.
Renewed 1978 FRANK MUSIC CORP.

By FRANK LOESSER

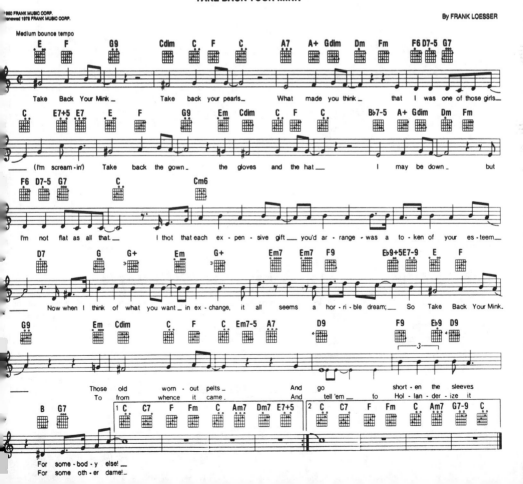

Take Back Your Mink ____ Take back your pearls ____ What made you think ____ that I was one of those girls ____ (I'm scream-in') Take back the gown ____ the gloves and the hat ____ I may be down ____ but I'm not flat as all that. ____ I thot that each ex-pen-sive gift ____ you'd ar-range ____ was a to-ken of your es-teem ____ Now when I think of what you want ____ in ex-change, it all seems a hor-ri-ble dream; ____ So Take Back Your Mink. ____

Those old worn-out pelts ____ And go short-en the sleeves
To from whence it came ____ And tell 'em to Hol-lan-der-ize it

For some-bod-y else! ____
For some oth-er dame! ____

# "Garrick Gaieties"

## MOUNTAIN GREENERY

Words by LORENZ HART
Music by RICHARD RODGERS

© 1926 WARNER BROS. INC. (Renewed)
Rights for the Extended Renewal Term in the United States controlled by
MARLIN ENTERPRISES and THE ESTATE OF LORENZ HART
All Rights on behalf of MARLIN ENTERPRISES Administered by WILLIAMSON MUSIC
All Rights on behalf of THE ESTATE OF LORENZ HART Administered by WB MUSIC CORP.

Moderato

**C Am Dm7 G7 C Am Dm7 G7 C F**

In a Moun-tain Green-er-y, where God paints the scen-er-y, just two

**D7 G Am7 Bbdim7 G/B C Am Dm7 G7**

cra-zy peo-ple to-geth-er; _____
While you love your lov-er, let
How we love se-ques-ter-ing

**C Am Dm7 G7 C F D7**

blue skies be your cov-er-let, when it rains, we'll laugh at the
where no pests are pest-er-ing, no, dear, ma-ma holds_ us in

**G Am7 Bbdim7 G/B C7#5 F6 C7**

weath-er. _____ And if you're good _____ I'll search for wood;
teth-er! _____ Mos-qui-tos here _____ won't bite you, dear;

**F6 Fm6 Em7 D7 Dm7/G G7**

_____ so you can cook _____ while I stand look-ing.
I'll let them sting _____ me on the fin-ger.

**C Am Dm7 G7 C Am Dm7 G7**

Beans could get no keen-er re-cep-tion in a bean-er-y,
We could find no clean-er re-treat from life's ma-chin-er-y,

**C Am Dm7 G7** | **1 C Dm7 G7** | **2 C**

bless our Moun-tain Green-er-y home! _____
than our Moun-tain Green-er-y home! _____

## SENTIMENTAL ME

Words by LORENZ HART
Music by RICHARD RODGERS

Copyright © 1925 by Edward B. Marks Music Company
Copyright Renewed

Moderately

**Cm7 F7 Bb F7#5 Bb F7**

Sen-ti-men-tal Me _____ guess I'll al-ways be _____ so in love with you, don't know what to

**F9 Bb Bdim7 F7 Cm7 F7 Bb F7#5**

do, Sen-ti-men-tal Me _____ Dream-ing while I live. _____ Liv-ing just to give _____

**Bb F7 F9 Bb Ebm6 Bb D7**

_____ all my love to you, no one else will do, Sen-ti-men-tal Me _____ Reach-ing for the moon _____

**Gm Em7 A7 ⌐3⌐ Dm A/C#**

_____ and wish-ing on a star. _____ On my hon-ey-moon _____ I want to be where you

# MANHATTAN

Copyright © 1925 by Edward B. Marks Music Company
Copyright Renewed

Words by LORENZ HART
Music by RICHARD RODGERS

250

## "George M!"

### HARRIGAN

Copyright © 1968 by George M. Cohan Music Publishing Company
Used by Permission

Words and Music by
GEORGE M. COHAN

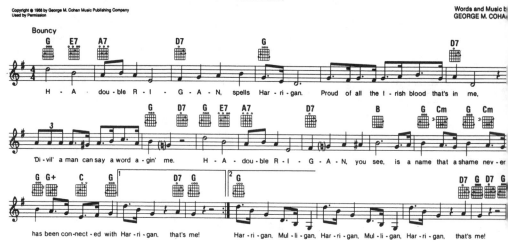

H - A - dou-ble R - I - G - A - N, spells Har-ri-gan. Proud of all the I-rish blood that's in me, 'Di-vil' a man can say a word a-gin' me. H - A - dou-ble R - I - G - A - N, you see, is a name that a shame nev-er has been con-nect-ed with Har-ri-gan, that's me! Har-ri-gan, Mul-li-gan, Har-ri-gan, Mul-li-gan, Har-ri-gan, that's me!

### MARY'S A GRAND OLD NAME

Copyright © 1968 by George M. Cohan Music Publishing Company
Used by Permission

Words and Music by
GEORGE M. COHAN

For it is Ma - ry, Ma - ry, plain as an-y name can be: But with pro-pri-et-y, so-ci-e-ty will say Ma-rie. But it was Ma-ry, Ma-ry, long be-fore the fash-ions came; And there is some-thing there that sounds so fair, it's a grand old name! For it is name!

### GIVE MY REGARDS TO BROADWAY

Copyright © 1968 by George M. Cohan Music Publishing Company
Used by Permission

Words and Music by
GEORGE M. COHAN

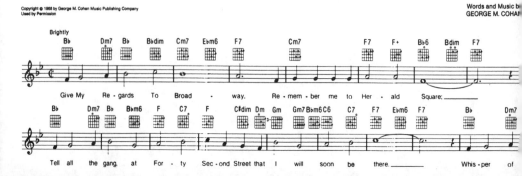

Give My Re-gards To Broad - way, Re-mem-ber me to Her - ald Square: Tell all the gang at For-ty Sec-ond Street that I will soon be there. Whis-per of

## (I'M A) YANKEE DOODLE DANDY

Words and Music by
GEORGE M. COHAN

## YOU'RE A GRAND OLD FLAG

Words and Music by
GEORGE M. COHAN

# FORTY-FIVE MINUTES FROM BROADWAY

Copyright © 1906 by George M. Cohan Music Publishing Company
Used by Permission

Words and Music by GEORGE M. COHAN
Revisions by MARY COHAN

## "George White's Scandals (1931 Edition)"

### LIFE IS JUST A BOWL OF CHERRIES

Copyright © 1931 by DeSylva, Brown & Henderson, Inc.
Copyright Renewed, Assigned to Chappell & Co. Inc.
International Copyright Secured    ALL RIGHTS RESERVED

Words and Music by
LEW BROWN & RAY HENDERSON

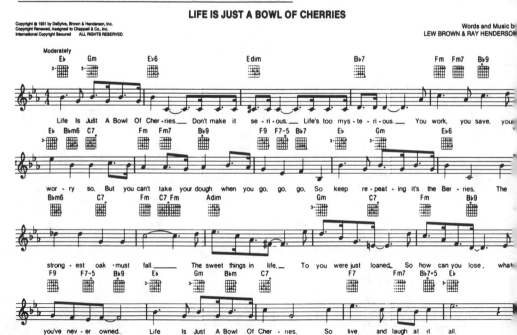

# THE THRILL IS GONE

Copyright © 1922 by DeSylva, Brown & Henderson, Inc.
Copyright Renewed, Assigned to Chappell & Co., Inc.
International Copyright Secured     ALL RIGHTS RESERVED

Words and Music by
LEW BROWN & RAY HENDERSON

## '"George White's Scandals (1939 Edition)'"

# ARE YOU HAVIN' ANY FUN?

Copyright © 1917 by DeSylva, Brown & Henderson, Inc.
Copyright Renewed, Assigned to Chappell & Co., Inc.
International Copyright Secured     ALL RIGHTS RESERVED

Words by JACK YELLEN
Music by SAMMY FAIN

## "Gigi"

### GIGI

Copyright © 1957 & 1958 by Chappell & Co., Inc.
International Copyright Secured    ALL RIGHTS RESERVED

Words by ALAN JAY LERNER
Music by FREDERICK LOEWE

### I REMEMBER IT WELL

Copyright © 1957 & 1958 by Chappell & Co., Inc.
International Copyright Secured    ALL RIGHTS RESERVED

Words by ALAN JAY LERNER
Music by FREDERICK LOEWE

The Night They Invented Champagne — section:

# THE NIGHT THEY INVENTED CHAMPAGNE

Words by ALAN JAY LERNER
Music by FREDERICK LOEWE

Copyright © 1957 & 1958 by Chappell & Co., Inc.
International Copyright Secured    ALL RIGHTS RESERVED

# THANK HEAVEN FOR LITTLE GIRLS

Copyright © 1957 & 1958 by Chappell & Co., Inc.
International Copyright Secured    ALL RIGHTS RESERVED

Words by ALAN JAY LERNER
Music by FREDERICK LOEWE

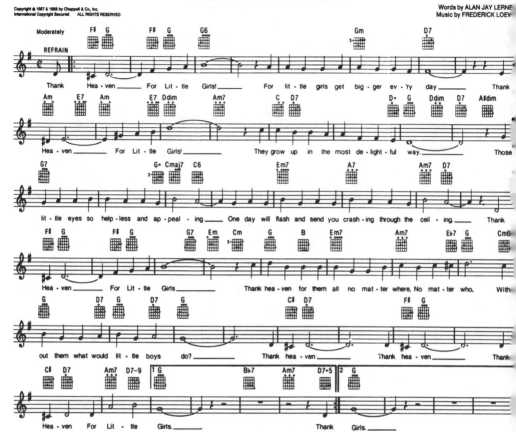

# I'M GLAD I'M NOT YOUNG ANYMORE

Copyright © 1957 & 1958 by Chappell & Co., Inc.

Words by ALAN JAY LERNER
Music by FREDERICK LOEWE

lu - sion ___ That when you're tell - ing those lies, She is - n't wise. And e - ven if love comes thru the door; The
va - tion ___ Just one re - luc - tant re - ply. "La - dy, good - bye." The foun - tain of youth is dull as paint, Me -

kind that goes on for - ev - er - more; For - ev - er - more is short - er than be - fore. ___ Oh, I'm so
thu - se - lah is my pa - tron saint; I've nev - er been so com - fort - a - ble be - fore.

glad ___ that I'm ___ not young ___ an - y - more. ___ The

Oh, I'm so glad ___ that I'm ___ not young ___ an - y - more.

## "The Girl From Utah"

### THEY DIDN'T BELIEVE ME

Copyright © 1994 by HAL LEONARD CORPORATION

Moderately

And when I told them ___ how beau - ti - ful you are ___ They Did - n't Be - lieve Me. ___ They Did - n't Be -

lieve Me! ___ Your lips your eyes, your cheeks, your hair Are in a class be - yond com - pare, you're the

love - li - est girl ___ that one could see! ___ And when I tell them ___ And I cert - n'ly am goin' to tell them, ___

That I'm the man whose wife one day you'll be ___ They'll nev - er be - lieve me. ___

They'll nev - er be - lieve me ___ That from this great big world you've cho - sen me!

## "The Girl Friend"

### THE BLUE ROOM

© 1926 WARNER BROS. INC. (Renewed)
Rights for the Extended Renewal Term in the United States Controlled by
MARLIN ENTERPRISES and THE ESTATE OF LORENZ HART
All Rights on behalf of MARLIN ENTERPRISES Administered by WILLIAMSON MUSIC
All Rights on behalf of THE ESTATE OF LORENZ HART Administered by WB MUSIC CORP.

Words by LORENZ HART
Music by RICHARD RODGERS

## "Glad To See You"

### GUESS I'LL HANG MY TEARS OUT TO DRY

Copyright © 1944 by Sammy Cahn and Jule Styne. Copyright Renewed.
Stratford Music Corporation, Publisher and owner of publications and allied rights
throughout the word. Sole selling agent: Chappell & Co., Inc.

Words by SAMMY CAHN
Music by JULE STYNE

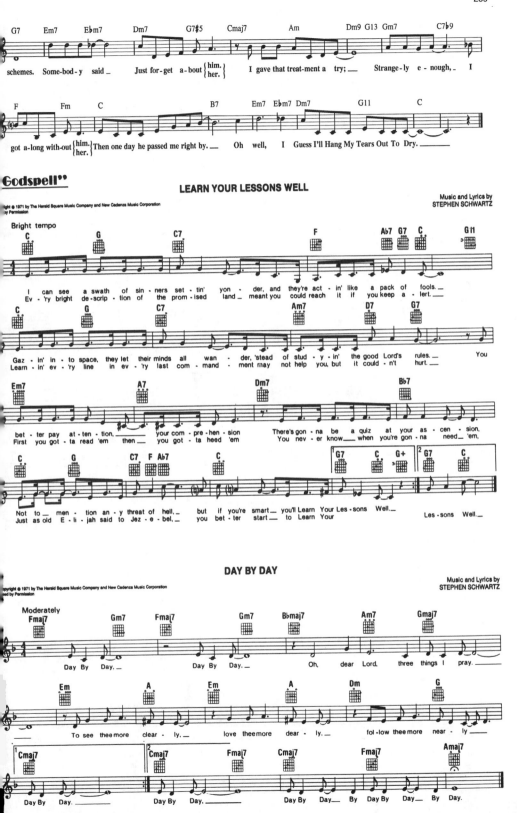

**Godspell**

## LEARN YOUR LESSONS WELL

Music and Lyrics by
STEPHEN SCHWARTZ

Copyright © 1971 by The Herald Square Music Company and New Cadenza Music Corporation
Used by Permission

## DAY BY DAY

Music and Lyrics by
STEPHEN SCHWARTZ

Copyright © 1971 by The Herald Square Music Company and New Cadenza Music Corporation
Used by Permission

## SAVE THE PEOPLE

Copyright © 1971 by The Herald Square Music Company and New Cadenza Music Corporation
Used by Permission

Music and Lyrics
STEPHEN SCHWARTZ

When wilt thou save the peo - ple, Oh, God of mer - cy when?_ Not kings and lord
Shall crime bring crime for - ev - er, Strength aid - ing still the strong? Is it Thy will
When wilt thou save the peo - ple, Oh, God of mer - cy when?_ The peo - ple, Lord

but na - tions, Not thrones and crowns, but men? Flowers of _ Thy
oh Fa - ther, that man shall toil for wrong? No, say _ Thy
the peo - ple, Not thrones and crowns, but men? God save the _ Thy

heart. Oh, God, _ are they. Let them _ not pass _ like weeds _ a -
moun - tains, No, say _ Thy skies, Man's cloud - ed sun _ shall bright - ly
peo - ple For Thine _ they are, Thy child - ren, as _ Thy an - gels

way, their her - i - tage of sun - less days, God
rise, and sngs be heard in - stead of sighs.
fair, save the peo - ple from des - pair.

save the peo - ple. God save the peo - ple.

God save the peo - ple. God save the peo - ple.

## ALL FOR THE BEST

Copyright © 1971 by The Herald Square Music Company and New Cadenza Music Corporation
Used by Permission

Music and Lyrics
STEPHEN SCHWARTZ

When you feel sad or un - der a curse, Your life is bad, Your pros - pects are

worse, Your wife is sigh - ing cry - ing. and your ol - ive tree is dy - ing. Tem - ples are grey - ing and

teeth are de - cay - ing and cre - di - tors weigh - ing your purse! Your mood and your robe are both _ a deep blue. You'd bet th

Job had noth - ing on you. Don't for - get that when you go to heav - en you'll be

# O BLESS THE LORD, MY SOUL

Copyright © 1971 by The Herald Square Music Company and New Cadenza Music Corporation
Used by Permission

Music and Lyrics
STEPHEN SCHWARTZ

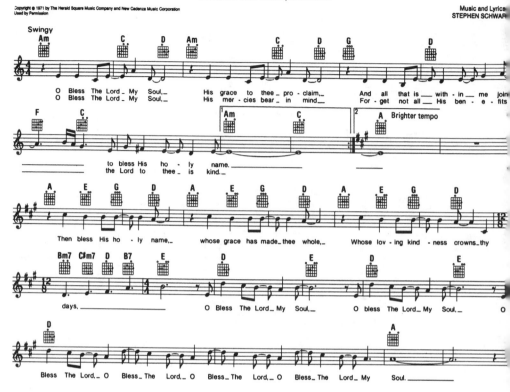

O Bless The Lord _ My Soul, _ His grace to thee _ pro-claim, _ And all that is _ with-in me join
O Bless The Lord _ My Soul, _ His mer-cies bear _ in mind _ For-get not all _ His ben-e-fits

_ to bless His ho-ly name.
the Lord to thee _ is kind. _

Brighter tempo

Then bless His ho-ly name, _ whose grace has made _ thee whole, _ Whose lov-ing kind-ness crowns _ thy

days, _ O Bless The Lord _ My Soul, _ O bless The Lord _ My Soul, _ O

Bless The Lord, _ O Bless _ The Lord, _ O Bless _ The Lord, _ O Bless _ The Lord _ My Soul. _

# ALL GOOD GIFTS

Copyright © 1971 by The Herald Square Music Company and New Cadenza Music Corporation
Used by Permission

Music and Lyrics
STEPHEN SCHWARTZ

We plow the fields _ and scat-ter the good seed on _ the land, But it is fed _ and wa-tered by
thank thee then, _ oh Fa-ther, for all things bright _ and good, The seed time and _ the har-vest, our

God's al-might-y hand. _ He sends the snow _ in win-ter, the warmth to swell _ the grain, The bree-zes and _ the
life, our health, our food. _ No gifts have we _ to of-fer for all thy love _ im-parts, But that which Thou _ de

sun-shine and soft re-fresh-ing rain. _ All Good Gifts a-round _ us
sir-est our hum-ble, thank-ful hearts. _

are sent from heav-en a-bove _ So thank the Lord, oh thank _ the Lord,

| D | D7 | C | A11 | A11 |

for all his love. _____ We I real-ly want to thank you, Lord.__

| D | Gmaj7 | Cmaj7 | Fmaj7 | D | Gmaj7 | Cmaj7 | Fmaj7 |

I want to thank you, Lord,__ Thank you for all __ of your love. _____ Oh,

| D | Gmaj7 | Cmaj7 | Fmaj7 | D | Am |

thank you, Lord. __ I want to thank you, Lord, _____ thank __ you, Lord.

| C | G | D | E | Gm | D |

## ON THE WILLOWS

Copyright © 1971 by The Herald Square Music Company and New Cadenza Music Corporation
Used by Permission

Music and Lyrics by
STEPHEN SCHWARTZ

Moderately

| A | B | Bm7 | E11 |

On the wil-lows__ there, we hung up our__ lives for our cap-tors__ there re - quired__ of us songs

| Bm7 | E9 | Amaj9 | A |

and our tor - men - tors' __ mirth. _____ On the wil-lows__ there, we hung up our__ lives

| B | Bm7 | E11 | Bm7 | E11 | A |

for our cap-tors__ there re - quired__ of us songs and our tor-men-tors' __ mirth, _____

| E F#m | Gmaj7 | C° | A | E F#m | Gmaj7 | C6 |

_____ say-ing: "Sing us one of the songs of Zi - on. __ sing us one of the songs of Zi - on,

| A | E F#m | Gmaj7 | F#m7 |

sing us one of the songs of Zi - on. _____ But how shall __ we sing. sing the Lord's song in a for-eign

| Em | A | C#m | A |

land? On the wil-lows__ there. we hung up our__ lives. _____

# LIGHT OF THE WORLD

Copyright © 1971 by The Herald Square Music Company and New Cadenza Music Corporation
Used by Permission

Music and Lyrics by
STEPHEN SCHWARTZ

# BY MY SIDE

Copyright © 1971 by The Herald Square Music Company and New Cadenza Music Corporation
Used by Permission

Lyrics by JAY HAMBURGER
Music by PEGGY GORDON

**C**

Far be - yond ___ where the hor - i - zon lies ___ where the hor - i - zon

**D**         **C**         **D7**

lies, and the land sinks in - to mel - low blue - ness, oh, ___ please ___ take me with you.

**D**    **C**         **D**         **C**         **D**

___ Let me skip the road with ___ you, I can dare my - self, I can dare my -

**C**         **D**         **C**         **D**

self. ___ I'll put a peb - ble in my shoe ___ and watch me walk, ___ I can walk and

**Dm**         **C**     **Am**    **Dm**

walk. I shall call the peb - ble dare. ___ We will walk to - geth - er a - bout

**C**    **Am**         **Dm**         **C**         **Am**

walk - ing. ___ dare shall be car - ried, and when we both ___ have had e - nough, ___ I will

**Dm**         **C**     **Am**         **Dm**

take him from my shoe, sing - ing, "Meet your new road." ___ Then I'll take ___ your ___

**C**     **Am**         **Dm**

hand ___ fin - al - ly glad ___ that you are here ___ By My Side. (By My

**C**     **Am**     **Dm**         **C**    **Am**

Side) ___ By My Side (By My Side) ___ By My

**Dm**         **C**     **Am**

Side (that you are here) ___ By My Side. ___

## PREPARE YE
### (The Way Of The Lord)

Copyright © 1971 by The Herald Square Music Company and New Cadenza Music Corporation
Used by Permission

Music and Lyrics by
STEPHEN SCHWARTZ

Moderately

**Bb**    **Cm**    **Dm**    **Eb**   **F**    **Bb**         **Cm**         **Dm7**   **Eb**    **F**   **Bb**

Pre - pare ye ___ the way of ___ the lord. Pre - pare ye ___ the way of ___ the lord.

# WE BESEECH THEE

Copyright © 1971 by The Herald Square Music Company and New Cadenza Music Corporation
Used by Permission

Music and Lyrics by
STEPHEN SCHWARTZ

3. By the gracious saving call,
Spoken tenderly to all
Who have shared man's guilt and Fall,
We beseech Thee, hear us.

By the love that longs to bless,
Pitying our sure distress,
Leading us to holiness,
We Beseech Thee, (To Coda)

# TURN BACK, O MAN

Copyright © 1971 by The Herald Square Music Company and New Cadenza Music Corporation
Used by Permission

Music and Lyrics by
STEPHEN SCHWARTZ

# "The Golden Apple"

Copyright © 1953 & 1954 by John Latouche & Jerome Moross
Chappell & Co., Inc., owner of publication and allied rights
International Copyright Secured    ALL RIGHTS RESERVED

## LAZY AFTERNOON

Words by JOHN LaTOUCHE
Music by JEROME MOROSS

It's a La - zy Af - ter - noon And the bee - tle bugs are zoom - in' And the tu - lip trees are bloom - in' And there's not an - oth - er hu - man in view _____ but us two. It's a La - zy Af - ter - noon And the farm - er leaves his reap - in,' In the mea - dow cows are sleep - in' And the speck - led trout stop leap - in' up - stream _____ as we dream. _____ A fat pink cloud hangs o - ver the hill, un - fold - in' like a rose. If you hold my hand and sit real still You can hear the grass as it grows. _____ It's a ha - zy af - ter - noon And I know a place that's qui - et 'cept for dais - ies run - ning ri - ot And there's no one pass - ing by it to see. Come spend this La - zy Af - ter - noon with me. _____

# "Good News"

Copyright © 1927 by DeSylva, Brown & Henderson, Inc.
Copyright Renewed, Assigned to Chappell & Co., Inc.
International Copyright Secured    ALL RIGHTS RESERVED

## THE BEST THINGS IN LIFE ARE FREE

Words & Music by B.G. DESYLVA,
LEW BROWN & RAY HENDERSON

The moon be - longs to ev - 'ry - one, _____ The Best Things In Life Are Free. _____ The stars be - long to ev - 'ry - one _____ They gleam there for you and me. _____ The flow - ers in Spring, _____ The rob - ins that sing. _____ The sun - beams that shine _____ They're your's, They're mine! And love can come to ev - 'ry - one. _____ The Best Things In Life Are Free. _____

## TOGETHER

Copyright © 1928 by DESYLVA, BROWN & HENDERSON, INC.
Copyright Renewed, Assigned to Chappell & Co., Inc.
International Copyright Secured   ALL RIGHTS RESERVED

Words & Music by B.G. DESYLVA,
LEW BROWN & RAY HENDERSON

Moderately slow

We strolled the lane, To - geth - er_____ Laughed at the rain. To - geth - er_____ Sang love's re -

frain, To - geth - er._____
{ And we'd both pre - tend it would nev - er end. One day we
{ We knew long a - go that our love would grow. Through storm and

cried To - geth - er,_____ Cast love a - side To - geth - er._____ You're gone from me, But in
sun To - geth - er._____ Our hearts as one To - geth - er._____

my mem - o - ry We al - ways will be To - geth - er. geth - er.____

## LUCKY IN LOVE

Copyright © 1927 by DeSylva, Brown & Henderson, Inc.
Copyright Renewed, Assigned to Chappell & Co., Inc.
International Copyright Secured   ALL RIGHTS RESERVED

Words & Music by B.G. DESYLVA,
LEW BROWN & RAY HENDERSON

Moderately

Luck - y In Love! Luck - y In Love! What else mat - ters, if you're Luck - y In

Love? Good breaks are few, Few skies are blue.____ But bad luck scat - ters, ev - 'ry

time I'm with you. { I don't mind that at po - ker I'm green _ If I stand ace
{ I won't mind that at po - ker I'm green _ If my King of

high with a beau - ti - ful Queen! _ I'll say I'm Luck - y In Love If you take me,
hearts on - ly takes in his Queen! _

that - 'll make me Oh, so Luck - y In Love _

# GOOD NEWS

Copyright © 1927 by DeSylva, Brown & Henderson, Inc.
Copyright Renewed, Assigned to Chappell & Co., Inc.
International Copyright Secured    ALL RIGHTS RESERVED

Words & Music by B.G. DESYLVA,
LEW BROWN & RAY HENDERSON

# PASS THAT PEACE PIPE

Copyright © 1943 & 1947 by Robbins Music, Corp./Copyrights Renewed
Publication and Mechanical Rights for the World owned by Chappell & Co., Inc.
International Copyright Secured    ALL RIGHTS RESERVED

Words & Music by ROGER EDENS,
HUGH MARTIN & RALPH BLANE

crank - y, ___ Try to use a lit - tle re - straint. Fold ___ that hank - y, An' wipe off all a - that
ears in, ___ Try to use a lit - tle con - trol. When ___ all clear's in, ___ You'll be top man on the

war - paint ___ And if you find your - self in a fu - ry, Be your own judge and your own ju - ry:
totem pole. ___ So if you wan - na be ___ an all - right guy, Not a long faced "Blues in the Night" guy,

Pass That Peace Pipe an' bur - y that hat - chet like the Choc - taws, Chick - a - saws, Chat - ta - hoo - chies, Chip - pe - was do. ___

___ Write that a - pol - o - gy and dis - patch it. When you've quar - relled it's grand to patch it. Pass That Peace Pipe an'

bur - y that hat - chet like the Choc - taws, Chick - a - saws, Cahat - ta - hoo - chies, Chip - pe - was And those Chi - chi - mecs, Che - ro - kees, Che - pul - te - pecs

And those Chi - cu - ti - mees, Che - pe - chets and Chic - a - pees, Cho - cho's Chang - o's, Chat - ta - noog - as, Cheec - ar - ows do. ___

# SUNNY SIDE UP

Copyright © 1929 by DeSylva, Brown & Henderson, Inc.
Copyright Renewed, Assigned to Chappell & Co., Inc.
International Copyright Secured   ALL RIGHTS RESERVED

By B.G. DESYLVA, LEW BROWN
& RAY HENDERSON

Keep your Sun - ny Side Up. Up! Hide the side ___ that gets blue. ___

If you have nine sons in a row. ___ Base - ball teams make mon - ey, you know! ___

Keep your fun - ny side up. up! Let your laugh - ter come thru. do!

Stand up - on ___ your legs, Be like two ___ fried eggs. Keep your Sun - ny Side Up!

# THE VARSITY DRAG

Copyright © 1927 by DeSylva, Brown & Henderson, Inc.
Copyright Renewed, Assigned to Chappell & Co., Inc.
International Copyright Secured    ALL RIGHTS RESERVED

Words & Music by B.G. DESYLV
LEW BROWN & RAY HENDERSO

Here is the Drag, See how it goes; Down on the heels, up on the toes. That's the way to do the Var-si-ty Drag.___

Hot-ter than hot, New-er than new! Mean-er than mean, Blu-er than blue, Gets as much ap-plause as wav-ing the Flag!

You can pass man-y a class, wheth-er you're dumb or wise. If you all an-swer the call, when your pro-fess-or cries: "Ev-'ry-bo-dy

down on the heels, up on the toes, Stay af-ter school, Learn how it goes; Ev-'ry-bo-dy do the Var-si-ty Drag."___

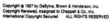

# WE GO TOGETHER

© 1971, 1972 WARREN CASEY & JIM JACOBS
All Rights Throughout the World Controlled by EDWIN H. MORRIS & COMPANY,
A Division of MPL Communications, Inc.

Lyric & Music
WARREN CASEY & JIM JACO

We Go To-geth-er, like ra-ma la-ma la-ma ka ding-a da ding-dong, Re-mem-bered for
We're one of a kind like dip da dip___ da dip doo wop-a doo-bee doo, our___ names are

ev- er as shoo- bop- sha -wad-da wad-da yip-pi-ty boom de-boom
signed boog-e-dy boog-e-dy booge-dy booge-dy shoo-by doo wop___ she bop

chang chang ah chang-it-ty chang - shoo bop, that's the way it should be,___ wha
chang chang ah chang-it-ty chang - shoo bop, we'll al-ways bee-ee like

oooh, yeah! one. Wa-wa-wa-waaah.___ When we go out at night,

**BEAUTY SCHOOL DROPOUT**

Lyric & Music by
WARREN CASEY & JIM JACOBS

© 1971, 1972 WARREN CASEY & JIM JACOBS
All Rights Throughout the World Controlled by EDWIN H. MORRIS & COMPANY,
A Division of MPL Communications, Inc.

# SUMMER NIGHTS

© 1972 WARREN CASEY & JIM JACOBS
All Rights Throughout the World Controlled by EDWIN H. MORRIS & COMPANY,
A Division of MPL Communications, Inc.

Lyric & Music by
WARREN CASEY & JIM JACOBS

## THERE ARE WORSE THINGS I COULD DO

© 1971, 1972 WARREN CASEY & JIM JACOBS
All Rights Throughout the World Controlled by EDWIN H. MORRIS & COMPANY,
A Division of MPL Communications, Inc.

Lyric & Music by
WARREN CASEY & JIM JACOBS

## "Greenwillow"

### NEVER WILL I MARRY

© 1959, 1960 FRANK MUSIC CORP.

By FRANK LOESSER

Nev - er, Nev-er __ Will I Mar-ry, __ Nev - er, nev-er __ will I wed.

Born to wan - der sol - i - tar-y, __ Wide my world, nar-row my bed. Nev - er,

nev - er, Nev-er __ Will I Mar-ry, Born to wan - der 'til I'm dead. __ No bur-dens

to bear, __ No con - science nor care. __ No mem - 'ries to mourn, __ No turn - ing, For I was

### THE MUSIC OF HOME

© 1959, 1960 FRANK MUSIC CORP.

By FRANK LOESSER

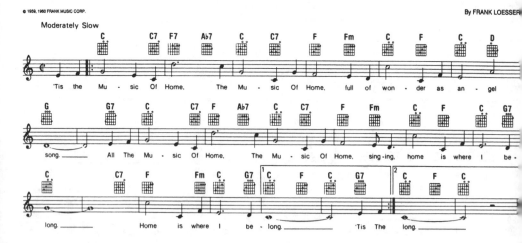

'Tis the Mu - sic Of Home, The Mu - sic Of Home, full of won - der as an - gel

song. __ All The Mu - sic Of Home, The Mu - sic Of Home, sing-ing, home is where I be -

long. __ Home is where I be - long. __ 'Tis The long. __

## SUMMERTIME LOVE

© 1959, 1960 FRANK MUSIC CORP.

By FRANK LOESSER

**"Gypsy"**

Copyright © 1959 by Norbeth Productions, Inc. and Stephen Sondheim
Copyright Renewed
All Rights Administered by Chappell & Co.

## ALL I NEED IS THE GIRL

Words by STEPHEN SONDHEIM
Music by JULE STYNE

## EVERYTHING'S COMING UP ROSES

Copyright © 1959 by Norbeth Productions, Inc. and Stephen Sondheim
Copyright Renewed
All Rights Administered by Chappell & Co.

Words by STEPHEN SONDHEIM
Music by JULE STYNE

## YOU'LL NEVER GET AWAY FROM ME

Copyright © 1959 by Norbeth Productions, Inc. and Stephen Sondheim
Copyright Renewed
All Rights Administered by Chappell & Co.

Words by STEPHEN SONDHEIM
Music by JULE STYNE

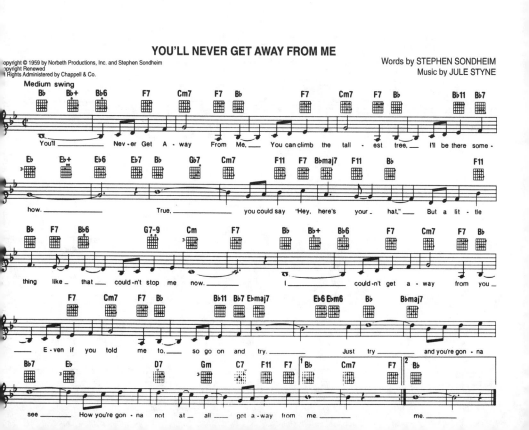

# LET ME ENTERTAIN YOU

Copyright © 1959 by Norbeth Productions, Inc. and Stephen Sondheim
Copyright Renewed
All Rights Administered by Chappell & Co.

Words by STEPHEN SONDHEIM
Music by JULE STYNE

# SOME PEOPLE

Copyright © 1959 by Norbeth Productions, Inc. and Stephen Sondheim
Copyright Renewed
All Rights Administered by Chappell & Co.

Words by STEPHEN SONDHEIM
Music by JULE STYNE

## LITTLE LAMB

Copyright © 1959 by Norbeth Productions, Inc. and Stephen Sondheim
Copyright Renewed
All Rights Administered by Chappell & Co.

Words by STEPHEN SONDHEIM
Music by JULE STYNE

# SMALL WORLD

Copyright © 1959 by Norbeth Productions, Inc. and Stephen Sondheim
Copyright Renewed
All Rights Administered by Chappell & Co.

Words by STEPHEN SONDHEIM
Music by JULE STYNE

Fun - ny, __ you're a stran - ger who's come here, Come from an - oth - er town. Fun - ny, __ I'm a stran - ger my - self here.

Small World, is - n't it? Fun - ny, __ you're a {girl/man} who goes trav' - ling, Rath - er than set - tling down.

Fun - ny, __ 'cause I'd love to go trav' - ling. Small World, is - n't it? We have so much in com - mon

It's a phe - nom - e - non. We could pool our re - sourc - es by join - ing forc - es

from now on. __ Luck - y, __ you're a {man/girl} who likes chil - dren, That's an im - por - tant sign.

Luck - y, __ 'cause I'd love to have chil - dren. Small World, is - n't it? Fun - ny, is - n't it?

Small and fun - y and fine. _____ fine. _____

# TOGETHER WHEREVER WE GO

Copyright © 1959 by Norbeth Productions, Inc. and Stephen Sondheim
Copyright Renewed
All Rights Administered by Chappell & Co.

Words by STEPHEN SONDHEIM
Music by JULE STYNE

Wher - ev - er we go, __ What - ev - er we do, __ We're gon - na go through __ it to -

geth - er. _____ We may not go far, __ But sure as a star, __ Wher - ev - er we are, __

_____ it's to - geth - er. __ Wher - ev - er I go. __ I know he goes. __ Wher -

## "Half A Sixpence"

### HALF A SIXPENCE

Copyright © 1963 by Britannia Music Company Ltd. London
Chappell & Co. Inc. owner of publication and allied rights for the Western Hemisphere
International Copyright Secured    ALL RIGHTS RESERVED

Words & Music by
DAVID HENEKER

## "Happy Hunting"

### MUTUAL ADMIRATION SOCIETY

Copyright © 1955 by Matt Dubey & Harold Karr
Chappell & Co. Inc. Publisher
International Copyright Secured    ALL RIGHTS RESERVED

Words by MATT DUBEY
Music by HAROLD KARR

We be-long to a Mu-tu-al Ad-mi-ra-tion So-ci-e-ty, My ba-by and me. We be-long to a Mu-tu-a____l Ad-mi-ra-tion So-ci-e-ty! She thinks I'm hand-some and I'm smart, I think that she's a work of art.__ She says that / She says, "Oh, you're the sweet-est one."__ I say, "No, you're the sweet-est one." She claims that I'm the great-est man,__ and like-wise, I'm her big-gest fan.__ I say her kiss-es are like wine, she says they're / I'm a na-t'ral wit,__ I say it's just the op-po-site. The on-ly fight-in' that we do is just who not as good as mine,__ And that's the way we pass the time of day! My ba-by and me, Oh / loves who more than who,__ And we go on like that from night 'til dawn! My ba-by and me, Oh

## "The Happy Time"

### WITHOUT ME

Copyright © 1967 by Alley Music Corporation and Trio Music Company, Inc.
All rights administered by Hudson Bay Music, Inc.

Music by JOHN KANDER
Words by FRED EBB

With-out Me, With-out Me, how could he con-sid-er go-ing an-y-where? Look-ing for his right / Me, With-out Me, you would hear him rav-ing like a lu-na-tic, be-ing a cam-er-a / Me, With-out Me, could he hope to win an-oth-er lov-ing cup, know-ing he can't be-arm he'd find it was-n't there With-out Me. With-out Me, With-out / a whose shut-ter could-n't click With-out Me. With-out Me, With-out / gin to know which end is up With-out Me. With-out Me, With-out Me. His ex-ist-ence de-pends on my in-val-u-able as-sist-ance. If

**THE HAPPY TIME**

Copyright © 1967 by Alley Music Corporation and Trio Music Company, Inc.
All rights administered by Hudson Bay Music, Inc.

Music by JOHN KANDER
Words by FRED EBB

# SEEING THINGS

Copyright © 1967 by Alley Music Corporation and Trio Music Company, Inc.
All rights administered by Hudson Bay Music, Inc.

Music by JOHN KANDER
Words by FRED EBB

Moderately

See - ing Things, \_\_\_ there's a way of See - ing Things, \_\_\_ a cer-tain way of See - ing Things \_\_\_ that makes the dif - fer - ence. I need more than love, \_\_\_ I need some-one I'm cer - tain of; \_\_\_ and when I reach for her, she must be there. You and I \_\_\_ have a way of See - ing Things, \_\_\_ a dif - f'rent way of See - ing Things \_\_\_ I'd say. One is truth and one's il - lu - sion, \_\_\_ please con - sid - er See - ing Things \_\_\_ my way.

## "Hazel Flagg"

# HOW DO YOU SPEAK TO AN ANGEL?

Copyright © 1952 by Jule Styne and Bob Hilliard
Copyright Renewed
All rights Administered by Chappell & Co.

Words by BOB HILLIARD
Music by JULE STYNE

Slowly, with expression

How Do You Speak To An An - gel? \_\_\_ I'm com-plete-ly in the dark. \_\_\_ When you know that you've just met an an - gel Is there a pro - per re - mark? \_\_\_ We were a - lone for a mo - ment. Why was I lost in a cloud? \_\_\_ Do you speak to an an - gel in a whis - per? \_\_\_ Or do you just say "I love you" \_\_\_ out loud? \_\_\_ loud? \_\_\_

"Hello, Dolly!"

# HELLO, DOLLY!

© 1963 JERRY HERMAN
All Rights Throughout the World Controlled by EDWIN H. MORRIS & COMPANY,
A Division of MPL Communications, Inc.

Music & Lyric by
JERRY HERMAN

Medium Strut tempo

| Bb | Gm | Bbmaj7 | Bbdim | Cm7 | F7 |

Hel - lo, Dol - ly, well, Hel - lo, Dol - ly, It's so nice to have you back where you be - long. You're look - ing

| Cm | Cm7 | Ab | Cm7 | F7 | Bb6 Bbdim | F7 |

swell, Dol - ly, we can tell, Dol - ly, You're still glow - in', you're still crow - in', you're still go - in' strong. We feel the

| Bb | Gm | Fm7 | Bb7 | Fm7 | Bb7 | Ebmaj7 | Eb6 | Cm6 | D7 |

room sway - in', for the band's play - in' one of your old fa - v'rite songs from 'way back when. So

| Gm | Dm | Gm | Dm | C9 | C9+5 | Cm7 | F9 | Bb | Bdim Cm7 | F7 |

{take her wrap, fel - las, Find her an emp - ty lap, fel - las,}
{gol - ly gee, fel - las, Find her a va - cant knee, fel - las,} Dol - ly - 'll nev - er go a - way a - gain! Hel -

| Cm7 | F9 | C9 | C9+5 | Cm7 | F9 | C9 | C9+5 | Cm7 | F9 | Bb | F7 Bb |

go a - way, Dol - ly - 'll nev - er go a - way, Dol - ly - 'll nev - er go a - way a - gain!

# RIBBONS DOWN MY BACK

© 1963 JERRY HERMAN
All Rights Throughout the World Controlled by EDWIN H. MORRIS & COMPANY,
A Division of MPL Communications, Inc.

Music & Lyric by
JERRY HERMAN

Slowly

| Dm | Gm6 | A7 | D6 | Dmaj7 | Dm |

I'll be wear - ing, Rib - bons Down My Back ___ this sum - mer, ___ Blue and green and
he might smile and take me by the hand ___ this sum - mer, ___ Mak - ing me re -

| Gm7 | C7 | Fmaj7 | A7 | Dm | Gm6 | A7 |

To Coda

stream - ing in the yel - low sky; ___ So, if some - one spe - cial comes my way ___ this
call how love - ly love ___ can

| D6 | Adim | Em | A7-9 | Dmaj7 | Ebdim | Em | Em7 | A7 |

sum - mer, ___ He might no - tice me ___ pass - ing by. And so I'll try to make it eas - i - er to find me in the

| Dmaj7 | Ebdim | Em | Em7 | A7 | Dmaj7 | Bm | Em7 | A7 |

D.C. al Coda

still - ness of Ju - ly, Be - cause a breeze might stir a rain - bow up be - hind me, That might hap - pen to catch the gen - tle - man's eye. And

CODA

| Cm6 | D7 | Gm7 | C7 | Cm6 | D7 | Gm | Gm7 C7 | Fmaj7 |

be. ___ And so I will proud - ly wear ___ Rib - bons Down My Back ___ Shin - ing in my hair, ___ That he might no - tice me!

# BEFORE THE PARADE PASSES BY

© 1984 JERRY HERMAN
All Rights Throughout the World Controlled by EDWIN H. MORRIS & COMPANY,
A Division of MPL Communications, Inc.

Music & Lyric by
JERRY HERMAN

# IT ONLY TAKES A MOMENT

© 1963 JERRY HERMAN
All Rights Throughout the World Controlled by EDWIN H. MORRIS & COMPANY,
A Division of MPL Communications, Inc.

Music & Lyric by
JERRY HERMAN

Bb  Gm  Cm7-5      Bb  Gm  Cm7  F7  Bb          INTERLUDE  Bbmaj7      Bb6          Cm7          F7

To Coda

Mo - ment, __ To be loved a whole life long. I've heard it said __ that love must grow, __ That to be

Bbmaj7  Bb6      Cm7  F7      Bbmaj7          Gm7                  Cm7-5

sure, __ you must be slow. I saw you smile __ and now I know, I'll lis-ten to just my heart, __ That smile made me

F7-9      D.S. al Coda with Repeat      CODA      Bb          Bbmaj7  Bb6      Cm7  F7      Bbmaj7  Gm7

trust my heart. __ For It          long, And that is all __ that love's a - bout And we'll re - call __ when time runs

C9  Cm7-5      Bb  Gm  Cm7-5      Bb  Gm  Cm7-5      Bb  Gm  Cm7  F7  Bbmaj7      Bb6

out __ That it on - ly took a mo - ment __ To be loved a whole life long. __

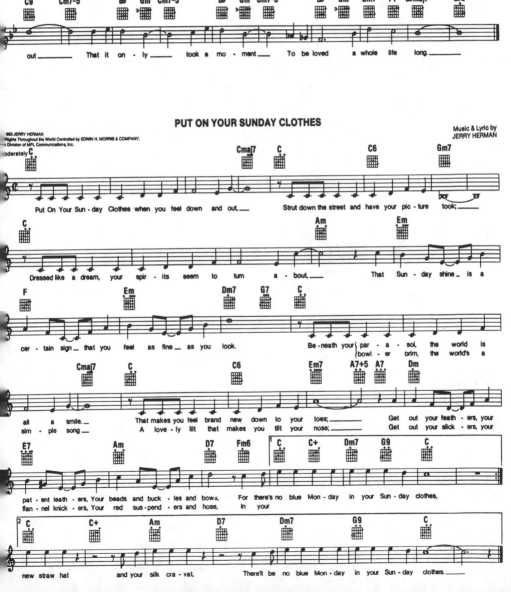

## PUT ON YOUR SUNDAY CLOTHES

1963 JERRY HERMAN
Rights Throughout the World Controlled by EDWIN H. MORRIS & COMPANY,
A Division of MPL Communications, Inc.

Music & Lyric by
JERRY HERMAN

Moderately  C          Cmaj7      C          C6          Gm7

Put On Your Sun - day Clothes when you feel down and out, __ Strut down the street and have your pic - ture took; __

C          Am          Em

Dressed like a dream, your spir - its seem to turn a - bout, __ That Sun - day shine __ is a

F          Em      Dm7  G7  C

cer - tain sign, that you feel as fine __ as you look. Be - neath your par - a - sol, the world is
(bowl - er brim, the world's a

Cmaj7      C          C6          Em7  A7+5  A7  Dm

all a smile. __ That makes you feel brand new down to your toes; __ Get out your feath - ers, your
sim - ple song. __ A love - ly lilt that makes you tilt your nose! __ Get out your slick - ers, your

E7      Am          D7  Fm6      1 C  C+  Dm7  G9  C

pat - ent leath - ers, Your beads and buck - les and bows, For there's no blue Mon - day in your Sun - day clothes;
flan - nel knick - ers, Your red sus - pend - ers and hose, In your

2 C      C+      Am      D7      Dm7      G9      C

new straw hat      and your silk cra - vat,      There'll be no blue Mon - day in your Sun - day clothes. __

# "Here's Love"

## MY WISH

© 1963 (Renewed) FRANK MUSIC CORP. and MEREDITH WILLSON MUSIC

Words and Music by
MEREDITH WILLSON

## LOVE, COME TAKE ME AGAIN

© 1963 (Renewed) FRANK MUSIC CORP. and MEREDITH WILLSON MUSIC

Words and Music by
MEREDITH WILLSON

## PINE CONES AND HOLLY BERRIES

1963 (Renewed) FRANK MUSIC CORP. and MEREDITH WILLSON MUSIC

Words and Music by
MEREDITH WILLSON

## "High Button Shoes"

### CAN'T YOU JUST SEE YOURSELF?

© 1947 EDWIN H. MORRIS & COMPANY. A Division of MPL Communications, Inc.
© Renewed 1975 EDWIN H. MORRIS & COMPANY. A Division of MPL Communications, Inc.

Lyric by SAMMY CAHN
Music by JULE STYNE

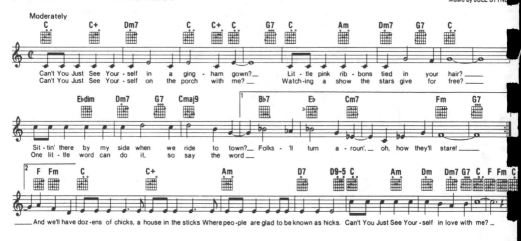

Can't You Just See Your-self in a ging - ham gown?__ Lit - tle pink rib - bons tied in your hair? _____
Can't You Just See Your-self on the porch with me? __ Watch-ing a show the stars give for free? _____

Sit - tin' there by my side when we ride to town? Folks - 'll turn a - roun', _ oh, how they'll stare!
One lit - tle word can do it, so say the word

_____ And we'll have doz -ens of chicks, a house in the sticks Where peo -ple are glad to be known as hicks. Can't You Just See Your -self in love with me? _

### I STILL GET JEALOUS

© 1947 MORLEY MUSIC CO.
© Renewed 1975 MORLEY MUSIC CO.

Lyric by SAMMY CAHN
Music by JULE STYNE

I Still Get Jeal - ous when they look at you. _____ I may not show it, but I do. _____
Jeal - ous when we kiss good - night _____ Un - less you hold me ex - tra tight. _____

_____ It's more than I can bear when they start to stare. Guess they think you're too good to be true. _
And, dear, I know a

I Still Get se - cret you did - n't know I knew. I Still Get Jeal - ous 'cause it pleas -es you. _____

# High Spirits°°

## IF I GAVE YOU...

Words & Music by
HUGH MARTIN & TIMOTHY GRAY

IO · © Copyright 1964 Cromwell Music, Inc., New York, N.Y.

## FOREVER AND A DAY

TRO - © Copyright 1964 Cromwell Music, Inc., New York, N.Y.

Words & Music
HUGH MARTIN & TIMOTHY GR

## YOU'D BETTER LOVE ME

TRO - © Copyright 1964 Cromwell Music, Inc., New York, N.Y.

Words & Music
HUGH MARTIN & TIMOTHY GR

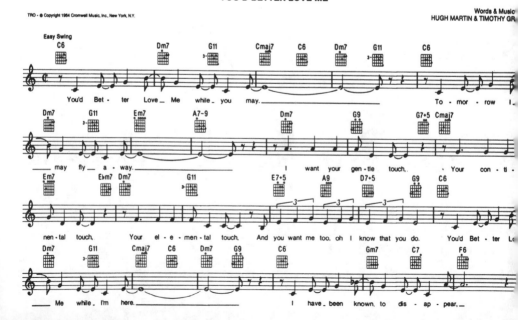

**"Higher And Higher"**

### IT NEVER ENTERED MY MIND

Words by LORENZ HART
Music by RICHARD RODGERS

Copyright © 1940 by Chappell & Co., Inc.
Copyright Renewed
International Copyright Secured    ALL RIGHTS RESERVED

## "Hold Everything"

### YOU'RE THE CREAM IN MY COFFEE

By B.G. DeSYLVA,
LEW BROWN & RAY HENDERSON

Copyright © 1928 by DeSylva, Brown & Henderson, Inc.
Copyright Renewed, Assigned to Chappell & Co., Inc.
International Copyright Secured    ALL RIGHTS RESERVED

## "Hold On To Your Hats"

### THERE'S A GREAT DAY COMING MAÑANA

Words by E.Y. HARBURG
Music by BURTON LANE

Copyright © 1940 by Chappell & Co., Inc.
Copyright renewed

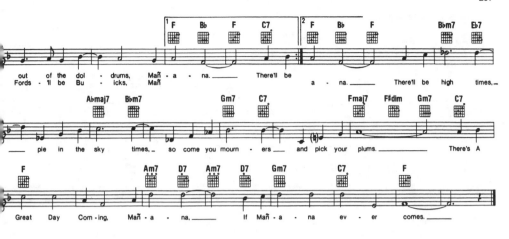

**"Hooray For What"**

### DOWN WITH LOVE

Words by E.Y. HARBURG
Music by HAROLD ARLEN

Copyright © 1937 by Chappell & Co., Inc.
Copyright renewed

# "House Of Flowers"

## DON'T LIKE GOODBYES

© 1954, 1963 HAROLD ARLEN and TRUMAN CAPOTE
© Renewed 1982 HAROLD ARLEN and TRUMAN CAPOTE
All Rights Throughout the World Controlled by HARWIN MUSIC CO.

Lyric by TRUMAN CAPOTE & HAROLD ARLEN
Music by HAROLD ARLEN

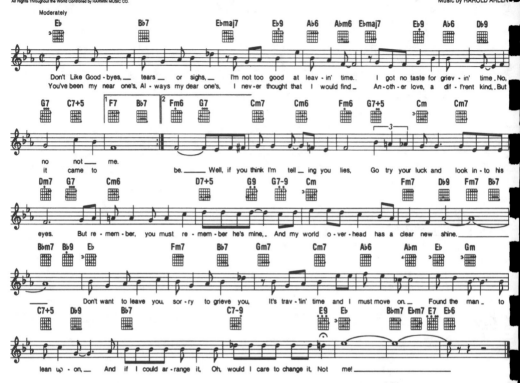

Don't Like Good-byes,_ tears_ or sighs,_ I'm not too good at leav-in' time.. I got no taste for griev-in' time.. No,
You've been my near one's, Al-ways my dear one's, I nev-er thought that I would find An-oth-er love, a dif-f'rent kind,. But

no not_ me.
it came to be._ Well, if you think I'm tell-ing you lies, Go try your luck and look in-to his

eyes. But re-mem-ber, you must re-mem-ber he's mine,. And my world o-ver-head has a clear new shine.__

Don't want to leave you, sor-ry to grieve you, It's trav-lin' time and I must move on._ Found the man to

lean up-on,_ And if I could ar-range it, Oh, would I care to change it, Not me!__

## HOUSE OF FLOWERS

© 1954 HAROLD ARLEN and TRUMAN CAPOTE
© Renewed 1982 HAROLD ARLEN and TRUMAN CAPOTE
All Rights Throughout the World Controlled by HARWIN MUSIC CO.

Lyric by TRUMAN CAPOTE & HAROLD ARLEN
Music by HAROLD ARLEN

My house is made of flow-ers,_ the warm winds car-pet the floor._ When-ev-er there's spring
frog, the toad, the tur-tle,__ Make my home their home.__ My cur-tains are crepe

show-ers_ I o-pen a rain-bow door_ The
myr-tle,_ and the fire-flies fly 'neath my dome. I've nev-er had mon-ey and I'll

nev-er need none, the moon is my lamp and my clock is the sun. My home's a home for all those things

## A SLEEPIN' BEE

Lyric by TRUMAN CAPOTE & HAROLD ARLEN
Music by HAROLD ARLEN

# "How To Succeed In Business Without Really Trying"

## BROTHERHOOD OF MAN

By FRANK LOESSER

© 1961 FRANK MUSIC CORP.

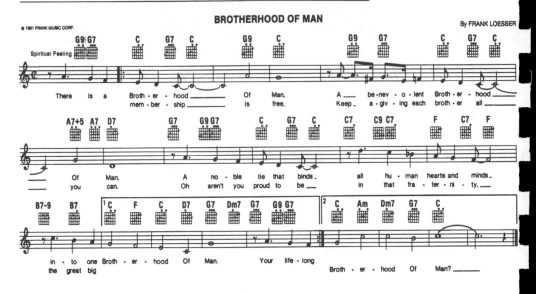

There is a Broth-er-hood _____ Of Man, A ____ be-nev-o-lent Broth-er-hood ____
mem-ber-ship _____ is free, Keep a-giv-ing each broth-er all

____ Of Man, A no-ble tie that binds_ all hu-man hearts and minds__
____ you can. Oh aren't you proud to be __ in that fra-ter-ni-ty, __

in-to one Broth-er-hood Of Man. Your life-long
the great big Broth-er-hood Of Man? _____

## A SECRETARY IS NOT A TOY

By FRANK LOESSER

© 1961, 1962 FRANK MUSIC CORP.

A Sec-re-tar-y Is Not A Toy, no, my boy; Not a toy to

fon-dle and dan-dle and play-ful-ly han-dle in search of some pu-er-ile joy. No, a sec-re-

tar-y is not def-i-nite-ly not a toy. A Sec-re-tar-y Is Not A Toy,

no, my boy, not a toy; So do not go jump-ing for joy, boy. A sec-re-tar-y is not, a sec-re-tar-y is not, A

Sec-re-tar-y Is Not A Toy. A sec-re-tar-y is not to be

# I BELIEVE IN YOU

© 1961 FRANK MUSIC CORP.

By FRANK LOESSER

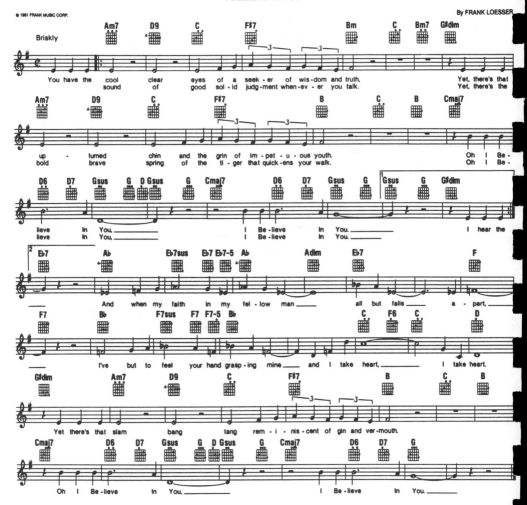

## "I Can Get It For You Wholesale"

### MISS MARMELSTEIN

Copyright © 1962 Chappell & Co., Inc.

Words & Music by
HAROLD ROME

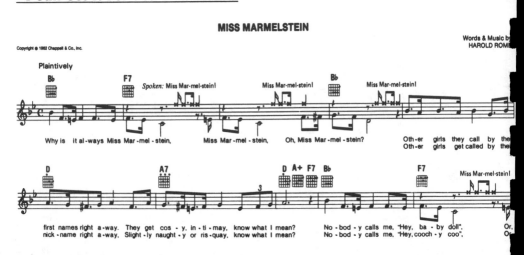

# "I Do! I Do!"

## MY CUP RUNNETH OVER

Copyright © 1966 by Tom Jones and Harvey Schmidt
Portfolio Music, Inc., owner, Chappel & Co., Inc., Administrator of publication and allied rights throughout the World
International Copyright Secured    ALL RIGHTS RESERVED

Words by TOM JONES
Music by HARVEY SCHMIDT

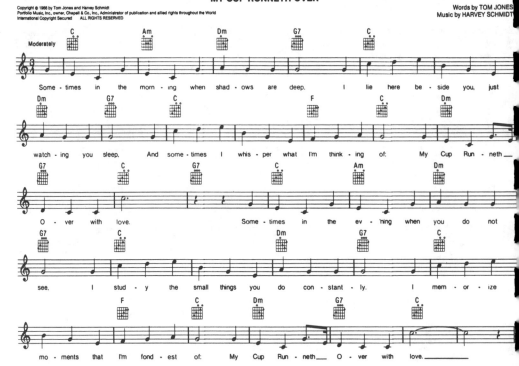

Some-times in the morn-ing when shad-ows are deep, I lie here be-side you, just watch-ing you sleep. And some-times I whis-per what I'm think-ing of: My Cup Run-neth O-ver with love. Some-times in the ev-'ning when you do not see, I stud-y the small things you do con-stant-ly. I mem-or-ize mo-ments that I'm fond-est of: My Cup Run-neth O-ver with love.

## I LOVE MY WIFE

Copyright © 1966 by Tom Jones and Harvey Schmidt
Chappell & Co., Inc., owner of publication and allied rights

Words by TOM JONES
Music by HARVEY SCHMIDT

I Love My Wife. What should I do? I've been to see a spe-cial-ist, But when he was thru He told me it's hope-less. I'm strick-en for life. "My son," he said. "Get back to bed. You hap-pen to love your wife!" Oth-er men love mov-ie stars,

but not I. The sort you wor-ship from a-far, And I try.

Oth-er men love Femme Fa-tales,__ Svelte-ly dressed; But when I'm with those femme fa-tales__ I

get de-pressed; 'cause I Love My Wife.__ How will it end? I

love her as a lov-er and not just as a friend. It may be ab-nor-mal; With

dra-ma it's rife, But ne-ver-the-less, I con-fess, I Love My Wife!

Wife! I a-dore my wife! I Love My Wife!

## TOGETHER FOREVER

Copyright © 1986 by Tom Jones and Harvey Schmidt
Chappell & Co., Inc., owner of publication and allied rights

Words by TOM JONES
Music by HARVEY SCHMIDT

A man and a wom-an are meant for each oth-er, Are meant for each oth-er As hus-band and wife. From this mo-ment
(To) hon-or and cher-ish, For-sak-ing all oth-ers, For-sak-ing all oth-ers, I of-fer my heart. For rich-er, For

for-ward, I pro-mise to love thee, I pro-mise to love thee the rest of my life. To-geth-er For-ev-er, For-
poor-er, To love and to com-fort, To love and to com-fort Till death do us part.

ev-er to-geth-er, For this is the pro-mise you give.__ To-geth-er For-ev-er, For-ev-er to-geth-er, Through

all of the sor-row and hap-pi-ness,__ To-geth-er as long as you live.__ To live.__

# "I Had A Ball"

© 1964 LARSTON, INC. and STAN FREEMAN
All Rights Throughout the World Controlled by MPL COMMUNICATIONS, INC.

## ALMOST

Lyric & Music by
JACK LAWRENCE & STAN FREEMAN

Moderately

Al - most we made it, But Al - most, that's all; Now it ends, what's more, be - fore it starts.

Yes, Al - most we had it, I Al - most re - call Yes - ter - day the

look that shook our hearts. ___ Some fools want so much, But some fools don't

know much, Hold one dream a - bove life, Well, that's the sto - ry of my love life. Al - most means

nev - er, we're so far a - part, I laugh to think we Al - most let it start; ___

___ And there's the joke that Al - most broke my heart. ___

## I HAD A BALL

© 1964 LARSTON, INC. and STAN FREEMAN
All Rights Throughout the World Controlled by MPL COMMUNICATIONS, INC.

Lyric & Music by
JACK LAWRENCE & STAN FREEMAN

Lightly swinging

Love was hid - ing a - round the cor - ner, This lone - ly mourn - er heard the call; ___

___ Then love found me and put her arms a - round me, So beat the drum, ___ sound the brass,

What a groove, ___ what a gas, ___ Here I come, ___ let me pass. ___ Cot - tage small, a wall to wall en - chant - ed

bliss - ville in old new kiss - ville, The green - est, grand - est, great - est state__ of 'em all. ___ If it

lasts for - ev - er, I'll love ___ it, ___ If it's just a life - time, what

of ___ it? ___ One short life - time is long e - nough for sing - in', Lis - ten,

love, I Had A Ball! Ball! ___

## "I'd Rather Be Right"

### I'D RATHER BE RIGHT

Copyright © 1937 by Chappell & Co.
Copyright Renewed
The interest of Richard Rodgers for the extended term of copyright assigned to the
Rodgers Family Partnership (Administered by Williamson Music)
Rights on behalf of The Estate Of Lorenz Hart administered by WB Music Corp.

Words by LORENZ HART
Music by RICHARD RODGERS

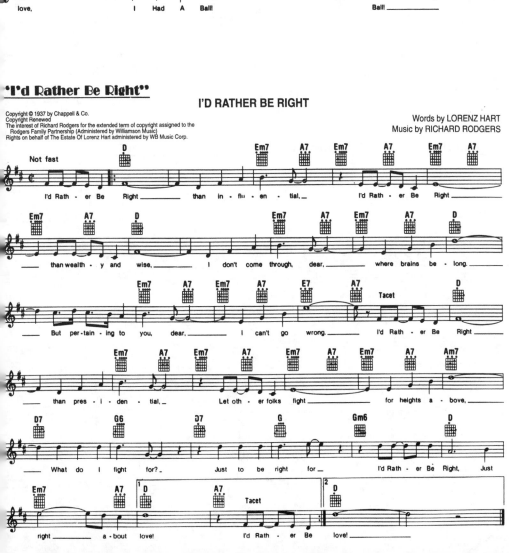

Not fast

I'd Rath - er Be Right ___ than in - flu - en - tial, ___ I'd Rath - er Be Right ___

___ than wealth - y and wise, ___ I don't come through, dear, where brains be - long. ___

___ But per - tain - ing to you, dear, ___ I can't go wrong. ___ I'd Rath - er Be Right ___

___ than pres - i - den - tial, ___ Let oth - er folks fight ___ for heights a - bove,

___ What do I fight for? _ Just to be right for _ I'd Rath - er Be Right, Just

right ___ a - bout love! I'd Rath - er Be love!

# HAVE YOU MET MISS JONES?

Copyright © 1937 by Chappell & Co.
Copyright Renewed
The interest of Richard Rodgers for the extended term of copyright assigned to the
Rodgers Family Partnership (Administered by Williamson Music)
Rights on behalf of The Estate of Lorenz Hart administered by WB Music Corp.

Words by LORENZ HART
Music by RICHARD RODGERS

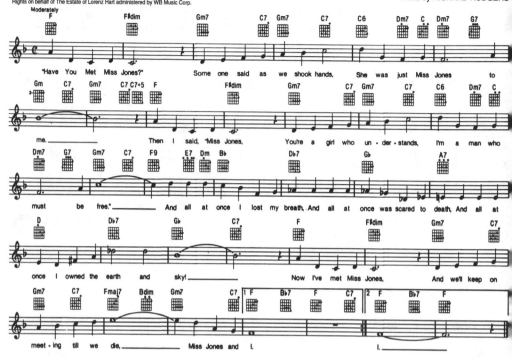

## "I'm Getting My Act Together And Taking It On The Road"

### OLD FRIEND

© 1976 FIDDLEBACK MUSIC PUBLISHING CO., INC.
A Tommy Valando Publication

Lyric by GRETCHEN CRYER
Music by NANCY FORD

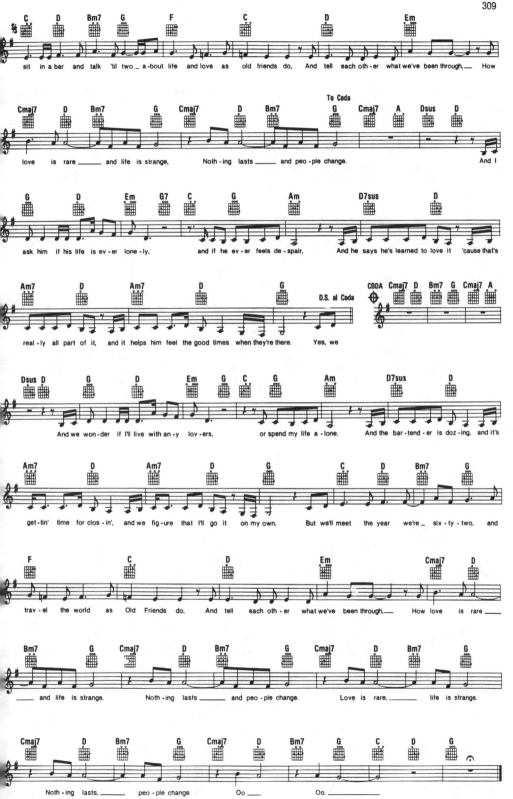

# IN A SIMPLE WAY I LOVE YOU

© 1976 FIDDLEBACK MUSIC PUBLISHING CO., INC.
A Tommy Valando Publication

Lyric by GRETCHEN CRYER
Music by NANCY FORD

## "Inside U.S.A."

### HAUNTED HEART

Copyright © 1948 by Chappell & Co., Inc. Copyright Renewed.

Words by HOWARD DIETZ
Music by ARTHUR SCHWARTZ

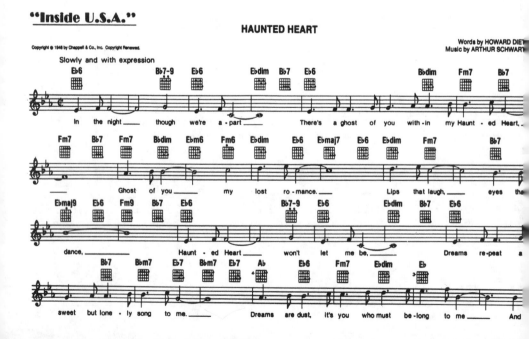

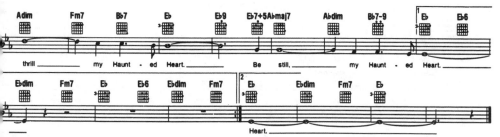

thrill _____ my Haunt - ed Heart. _____ Be still, _____ my Haunt - ed Heart. _____

_____ Heart. _____

## RHODE ISLAND IS FAMOUS FOR YOU

right © 1948 by Howard Dietz and Arthur Schwartz
right renewed, Chappell & Co., Inc., owner of publication and allied rights

Words by HOWARD DIETZ
Music by ARTHUR SCHWARTZ

Brightly

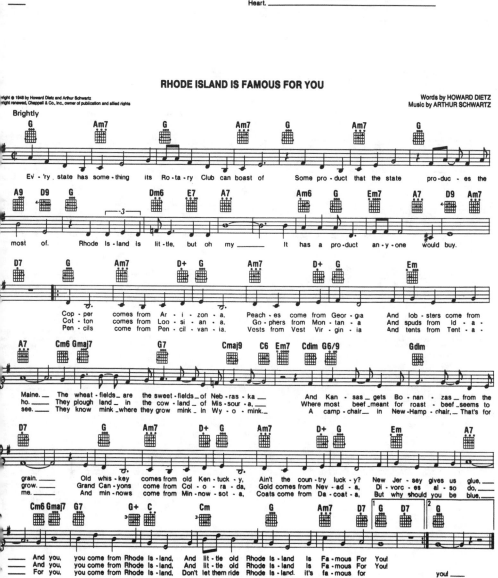

Ev - 'ry state has some-thing its Ro-ta-ry Club can boast of Some pro-duct that the state pro-duc-es the

most of. Rhode Is-land is lit-tle, but oh my _____ It has a pro-duct an-y-one would buy.

Cop - per comes from Ar - i - zon - a. Peach - es come from Geor - gia And lob - sters come from
Cot - ton comes from Loo - si - an - a. Go - phers from Mon - tan - a And spuds from Id - a -
Pen - cils come from Pen - cil - van - ia. Vests from Vest Vir - gin - ia And tents from Tent - a -

Maine. _____ The wheat - fields_ are the sweet - fields_of Neb - ras - ka _____ And Kan - sas_ gets Bo - nan - zas_ from the
ho. _____ They plough land_ in the cow - land_ of Mis - sour - a, _____ Where most beef_meant for roast - beef_seems to
see. _____ They know mink_where they grow mink_ in Wy - o - mink._ A camp - chair_ in New-Hamp - chair, _ That's for

grain. _____ Old whis - key comes from old Ken - tuck - y, Ain't the coun - try luck - y? New Jer - sey gives us glue, _____
grow. _____ Grand Can - yons come from Col - o - ra - da, Gold comes from Nev - ad - a, Di - vorc - es al - so do, _____
me. _____ And min - nows come from Min - now - sot - a, Coats come from Da - coat - a, But why should you be blue, _____

_____ And you, you come from Rhode Is - land, And lit - tle old Rhode Is - land is Fa - mous For You!
_____ And you, you come from Rhode Is - land, And lit - tle old Rhode Is - land is Fa - mous For You!
For you. you come from Rhode Is - land, Don't let them ride Rhode Is - land. It's fa - mous for

you! _____

# "Irma La Douce"

## OUR LANGUAGE OF LOVE

Original French Lyrics by ALEXANDER BREFFORT
English Words by JULIAN MORE
DAVID HENEKER and MONTY NORMAN
Music by MARGUERITE MONNOT

Copyright © 1958 by Editions Micro, Paris
Copyright © 1958 by Trafalgar Music, Ltd., London for All English speaking countries of the World
Chappell & Co., Inc., owner of publication and allied rights for the U.S.A. and Canada.
International Copyright Secured    ALL RIGHTS RESERVED

Slowly

No need to speak, No need to sing When just a glance means ev - 'ry - thing. Not a word need be spo - ken In Our Lan - guage Of Love, I'll touch your cheek, You'll hold my hand And on - ly we will un - der - stand That the si - lence is bro - ken By Our Lan - guage Of Love. It's clear to you. It's clear to me This pre - cious mo - ment had to be, Oth - er mo - ments out class - ing Guard - ian an - gels are pass - ing No words will do, No lips can say The ten - der mean - ing we con - vey, "I love you" is un - spo - ken, In Our Lan - guage Of Love.

## IRMA LA DOUCE

English Words by JULIAN MORE
DAVID HENEKER & MONTY NORMAN
Music by MARGUERITE MONNOT

Copyright © 1958 by Editions Micro
Copyright © 1958 by Trafalgar Music, Ltd. for All English-speaking countries
Chappell & Co., Inc., owner of publication and allied rights for the U.S.A. and Canada.

Moderately

What's the use of try - ing? Noth - ing mat - ters an - y - more. Why this bit - ter feel - ing that I nev - er felt be - fore? Sud - den - ly my
What the use of mem - o - ries that on - ly bring you pain? Gone the mag - ic spell of wed - dings at La - Mad - e - leine. What's the use of

Par - is is a cit - y full of lies. Par - is is a stran - ger in a cyn - i - cal dis - guise. Be - hind the gay fa
pray - ing when there's noth - ing to be - lieve? When I build a dream world it's my - self that I de - ceive. But ne - on paint - ed
Still he's ev - 'ry

cade, The streets are cold and hard, The shut - ters locked and barred, Ir - ma La
face, A mean ing - less em - brace, A love that leaves no trace, Ir - ma La
where, The light of my des - pair, Whose love I long to share, Ir - ma La

To Coda

1. Douce no more. A
Douce no
2. Douce the more.

D.C. al Coda

CODA

fool. Just sup - pose a mir - a - cle coul

"Jamaica"

## PUSH DE BUTTON

© 1956, 1957 HAROLD ARLEN and E.Y. HARBURG
All Rights Throughout the World Controlled by HARWIN MUSIC CO.

Lyric by E.Y. HARBURG
Music by HAROLD ARLEN

# COCOANUT SWEET

© 1957 HAROLD ARLEN and E.Y. HARBURG
All Rights Throughout the World Controlled by HARWIN MUSIC CO.

Lyric by E.Y. HARBURG
Music by HAROLD ARLEN

Catch me the smile you smile and I'll make this big world my ti - ny is - land, Shin - ing with spice and su - gar plum.

Cage me the laugh you laugh and I will make this ti - ny, shi - ny is - land my lit - tle slice of King - dom

Come. The wind may blow the hur - ri - cane whip up the sky. The vine go bare, the leaf go

dry _____ but when you smile for me _____ Spring tum - ble out of the tree, the peach is ripe, the lime is green, the

air is touched with tan - ger - ine and Co - coa - nut Sweet hon - ey - dew new Ev - 'ry - thing dear that wants to cheer the

near - ness of you _____ How it all come true _____ wher - ev - er we meet _____ The

mag - ic of cher - ry and ber - ry and Co - coa - nut Sweet. _____

# "Jesus Christ Superstar"

© Copyright 1969 LEEDS MUSIC LTD.
All Rights for the USA and Canada Controlled and Administered by
ON BACKSTREET MUSIC, INC., an MCA company

## SUPERSTAR

Words by TIM RICE
Music by ANDREW LLOYD WEBBER

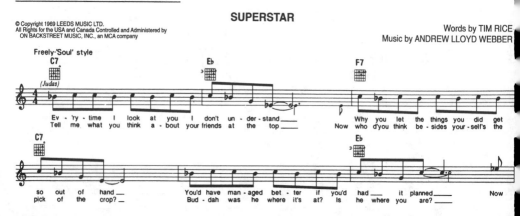

Freely-'Soul' style

(Judas)

Ev - 'ry - time I look at you I don't un - der - stand _____ Why you let the things you did get
Tell me what you think a - bout your friends at the top _____ Now who d'you think be - sides your - self's the

so out of hand _____ You'd have man - aged bet - ter if you'd had _____ it planned _____ Now
pick of the crop? _____ Bud - dah was he where it's at? Is he where you are? _____ Now

# I ONLY WANT TO SAY (GETHSEMANE)

Words by TIM RICE
Music by ANDREW LLOYD WEBBER

© Copyright 1970 LEEDS MUSIC LTD.
All Rights for the USA and Canada Controlled and Administered by
ON BACKSTREET MUSIC, INC., an MCA company

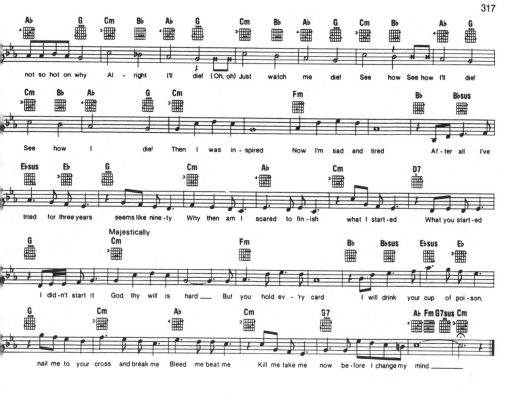

Copyright 1970 LEEDS MUSIC LTD.
Rights for the USA and Canada Controlled and Administered by
ON BACKSTREET MUSIC, INC., an MCA company

## PILATE'S DREAM

Words by TIM RICE
Music by ANDREW LLOYD WEBBER

# EVERYTHING'S ALRIGHT

© Copyright 1970 LEEDS MUSIC LTD.
All Rights for the USA and Canada Controlled and Administered by
ON BACKSTREET MUSIC, INC., an MCA company

Words by TIM RICE
Music by ANDREW LLOYD WEBBER

## I DON'T KNOW HOW TO LOVE HIM

© Copyright 1970 LEEDS MUSIC LTD.
ll Rights for the USA and Canada Controlled and Administered by
ON BACKSTREET MUSIC, INC., an MCA company

Words by TIM RICE
Music by ANDREW LLOYD WEBBER

# HOSANNA

© Copyright 1970 LEEDS MUSIC LTD.
All Rights for the USA and Canada Controlled and Administered by
ON BACKSTREET MUSIC, INC., an MCA company

Words by TIM RICE
Music by ANDREW LLOYD WEBBER

# KING HEROD'S SONG

Copyright © 1971 by Norrie Paramor Music Ltd.
All Rights Administered by Chappell & Co.

Words by TIM RICE
Music by ANDREW LLOYD WEBBER

# "Joseph And The Amazing Technicolor® Dreamcoat"

## ANY DREAM WILL DO

© Copyright 1969 The Really Useful Group Ltd.
All Rights for North America Controlled by Williamson Music Co.

Lyrics by TIM RICE
Music by ANDREW LLOYD WEBBER

## THOSE CANAAN DAYS

© Copyright 1975 The Really Useful Group Ltd.
All Rights for North America Controlled by Williamson Music Co.

Lyrics by TIM RICE
Music by ANDREW LLOYD WEBBER

## CLOSE EVERY DOOR

© Copyright 1969 The Really Useful Group Ltd.
All Rights for North America Controlled by Williamson Music Co.

Lyrics by TIM RICE
Music by ANDREW LLOYD WEBBER

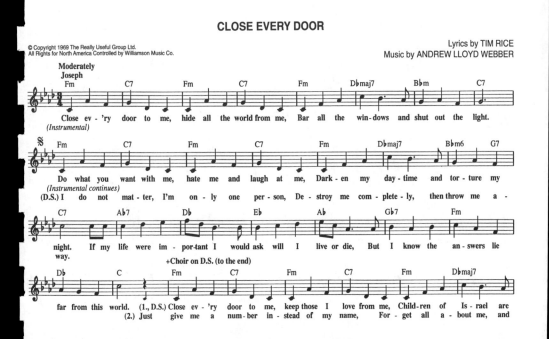

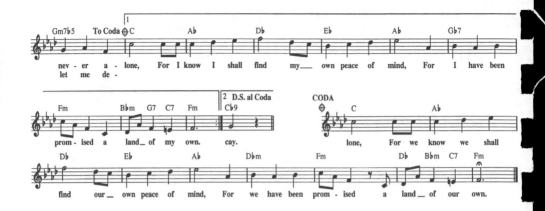

## "Jumbo"

## THE MOST BEAUTIFUL GIRL IN THE WORLD

Copyright © 1935 PolyGram International Publishing, Inc.
Copyright Renewed
The interest of Richard Rodgers for the extended term of copyright assigned to the
Rodgers Family Partnership (Administered by Williamson Music)
Rights on behalf of the Estate of Lorenz Hart administered by WB Music Corp.

Words by LORENZ HART
Music by RICHARD RODGERS

# LITTLE GIRL BLUE

Copyright © 1935 PolyGram International Publishing, Inc.
Copyright Renewed
The interest of Richard Rodgers for the extended term of copyright assigned to the
Rodgers Family Partnership (Administered by Williamson Music)
Rights on behalf of the Estate of Lorenz Hart administered by WB Music Corp.

Words by LORENZ HART
Music by RICHARD RODGERS

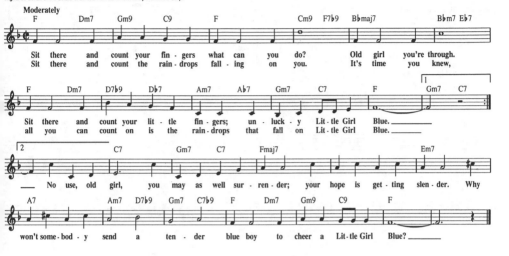

# MY ROMANCE

Copyright © 1935 PolyGram International Publishing, Inc.
Copyright Renewed
The interest of Richard Rodgers for the extended term of copyright assigned to the
Rodgers Family Partnership (Administered by Williamson Music)
Rights on behalf of the Estate of Lorenz Hart administered by WB Music Corp.

Words by LORENZ HART
Music by RICHARD RODGERS

# "Kean"

## SWEET DANGER

© 1961 ROBERT WRIGHT and GEORGE FORREST
All Rights Throughout the World Controlled by FRANK MUSIC CORP.

Lyric & Music b
ROBERT WRIGHT & GEORGE FORRES

Slowly and Expressively

There is dan-ger in my lov-ing you, Dan-ger in your let-ting me, Dan-ger in your
not in-stant-ly a-ban-don-ing and for-get-ting me. Sweet Dan-ger! Sweet Dan-ger, When we know we can share
Un-bound-ed beau-ty if we dare.___ We were des-tined for di-vid-ed paths,
Fat-ed to be far a-part, And there's dan-ger in de-fy-ing fate with a fool-hard-y heart! ___
Sweet Dan-ger! Sweet Dan-ger, So, why should we be-ware? Come, o-pen with your kiss
Our door to se-cret bliss, And though there's dan-ger wait-ing there, ___
We'll be in love and we won't care! ___ There is love and we won't care! ___

# "Kill That Story"

## TWO CIGARETTES IN THE DARK

Copyright © 1934 by DeSylva, Brown & Henderson, Inc.
Copyright Renewed, Assigned to Chappell & Co., Inc.
International Copyright Secured    ALL RIGHTS RESERVED

Words by PAUL FRANCIS WEBSTE
Music by LEW POLLACI

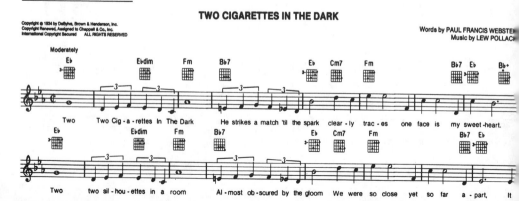

Moderately

Two Two Cig-a-rettes In The Dark He strikes a match 'til the spark clear-ly trac-es one face is my sweet-heart.
Two two sil-hou-ettes in a room Al-most ob-scured by the gloom We were so close yet so far a-part, It

hap-pened that I stum-bled in Up - on their ren-dez - vous. I heard my sweet-heart whis-per-ing "I love you I love you, you know that I do."

Two Two Cig-a-rettes In The Dark, Gone is the flame and the spark Leav-ing just re-grets And Two Cig-a-rettes In The Dark.

# "The King And I"

## HELLO, YOUNG LOVERS

Copyright © 1951 by Richard Rodgers and Oscar Hammerstein II. Copyright Renewed.
Williamson Music Co., owner of publication and allied rights for all countries of the Western Hemisphere and Japan.
International Copyright Secured   ALL RIGHTS RESERVED

Words by OSCAR HAMMERSTEIN II
Music by RICHARD RODGERS

Hel - lo Young Lov - ers, Who - ev - er you are, I hope your trou - bles are few

brave young lov - ers and fol - low your star, Be brave and faith - ful and true.

All my good wish - es go with you to - night, I've been in love like

Cling ver - y close to each oth - er to - night I've been in love like

you. Be you. I know how it feels to have wings on your heels, And to

fly down a street in a trance. You fly down a street on a chance that you'll

meet And you meet not real - ly by chance. Don't cry, young lov - ers, what -

ev - er you do, Don't cry be - cause I'm a - lone. All of my mem - 'ries are

hap - py to - night, I've had a love of my own. I've had a

love of my own like yours, I've had a love of my own.

# SOMETHING WONDERFUL

Copyright © 1951 by Richard Rodgers and Oscar Hammerstein II. Copyright Renewed.
Williamson Music Co., owner of publication and allied rights for all countries of the Western Hemisphere and Japan.
International Copyright Secured   ALL RIGHTS RESERVED

Words by OSCAR HAMMERSTEIN
Music by RICHARD RODGER

He will not al - ways say what you would have him say, But, now and then, he'll say Some - thing
The thought - less things he'll do will hurt and wor - ry you Then, all at once, he'll do

Won - der - ful. Some - thing Won - der - ful. He has a thou - sand dreams that won't come true. You

know that he be - lieves in them and that's e - nough for · you. You'll al - ways go a - long, De - fend him

when he's wrong And tell him when he's strong, He is won - der - ful. He'll al - ways need your love

and so he'll get your love. A man who needs your love can be won - der - ful. _____

# THE MARCH OF THE SIAMESE CHILDREN

Copyright © 1951 by Richard Rodgers and Oscar Hammerstein II. Copyright Renewed.
International Copyright Secured   ALL RIGHTS RESERVED

By RICHARD RODGER

# I HAVE DREAMED

Copyright © 1951 by Richard Rodgers and Oscar Hammerstein II. Copyright Renewed.
Williamson Music Co., owner of publication and allied rights for all countries of the Western Hemisphere and Japan.
International Copyright Secured   ALL RIGHTS RESERVED

Words by OSCAR HAMMERSTEIN II
Music by RICHARD RODGERS

# SHALL WE DANCE?

Copyright © 1951 by Richard Rodgers and Oscar Hammerstein II. Copyright Renewed.
Williamson Music Co., owner of publication and allied rights for all countries of the Western Hemisphere and Japan.
International Copyright Secured   ALL RIGHTS RESERVED

Words by OSCAR HAMMERSTEIN II
Music by RICHARD RODGERS

## I WHISTLE A HAPPY TUNE

Copyright © 1951 by Richard Rodgers and Oscar Hammerstein II. Copyright Renewed.
Williamson Music Co., owner of publication and allied rights for all countries of the Western Hemisphere and Japan.
International Copyright Secured    ALL RIGHTS RESERVED

Words by OSCAR HAMMERSTEIN II
Music by RICHARD RODGERS

## WE KISS IN A SHADOW

Copyright © 1951 by Richard Rodgers and Oscar Hammerstein II. Copyright Renewed.
Williamson Music Co., owner of publication and allied rights for all countries of the Western Hemisphere and Japan.
International Copyright Secured    ALL RIGHTS RESERVED

Words by OSCAR HAMMERSTEIN II
Music by RICHARD RODGERS

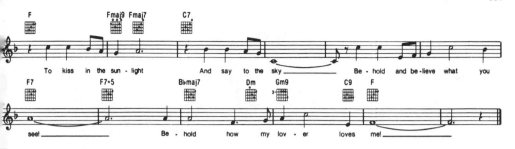

To kiss in the sun-light   And say to the sky _____ Be-hold and be-lieve what you

see! _____ Be-hold how my lov-er loves me!

## GETTING TO KNOW YOU

Copyright © 1951 by Richard Rodgers and Oscar Hammerstein II. Copyright Renewed.
Williamson Music Co., owner of publication and allied rights for all countries of the Western Hemisphere and Japan.
International Copyright Secured    ALL RIGHTS RESERVED

Words by OSCAR HAMMERSTEIN II
Music by RICHARD RODGERS

Get-ting To Know You,   get-ting to know all   a-bout you   Get-ting to like you,

get-ting to hope you   like me. _____ Get-ting To Know   You,   Put-ting it my way, but nice-ly _____

You are pre-cise-ly _____ My cup of tea! _____ Get-ting To Know   You,

get-ting to feel free   and eas-y _____ When I am with you,   get-ting to know what   to say.

_____ Have-n't you no-ticed?   Sud-den-ly I'm bright and breez-y _____ Be-cause of all the

beau-ti-ful and new   things I'm   learn-ing a-bout you   day   by   day. _____

# "Kismet"

HE'S IN LOVE

(From "Kismet" — Based on themes of A. Borodin)

Copyright © 1953 Frank Music Corp.
Copyright renewed and assigned to Scheffel Music Corp., New York, NY
Used by arrangement with Scheffel Music Corp.

Words & Music by
ROBERT WRIGHT & GEORGE FORREST

# "Johnny Johnson"

## MON AMI, MY FRIEND

TRO - © Copyright 1936 and renewed 1964 Hampshire House Publishing Corp.
and Chappell & Co., Inc., New York, N.Y.

Words by PAUL GREEN
Music by KURT WEILL

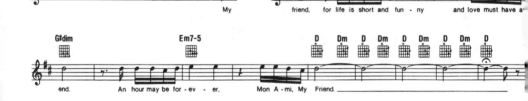

My Mad-elon of Pa - ree _ she'll laugh and dance and sing _ to cheer the wea -ry sol - dier at his home-com-ing. _ A lit-tle
Mad-elon of Pa - ree, _ She does not sit and grieve But sings a - way her sor - row to cheer the sol - diers' leave. For life is

room to-geth - er, An hour of love to spend Comme Ca your arm a - round me, oh, mon a - mi, my friend. But she ah she re-
short and fun - ny And love must have an end An hour may be for - ev - er Oh, mon a - mi, my

mem - bers that oth - er love and joy, the _ first, the _ best, the _ dear - est _ tir - ed sol - dier _ boy; A nar - row

room a - lone now, rain on the roof a - bove, And he will sleep for - ev - er oh, mon a - mi, my love.

My

**CODA**

friend, for life is short and fun - ny and love must have a-

end. An hour may be for - ev - er, Mon A - mi, My Friend.

# "Kiss Me, Kate"

## WHY CAN'T YOU BEHAVE

Copyright © 1948 by Cole Porter
Copyright Renewed, Assigned to John F. Wharton, Trustee of the Cole Porter Musical & Literary Property Trusts
Chappell & Co., Inc, owner of publication and allied rights throughout the World

Words & Music by
COLE PORTER

Why Can't You Be - have? _____ Oh, Why Can't You Be - have? _____

_____ Af - ter all the things you told me And the prom - is - es that you gave, Oh, Why Can't You Be -

have? _____ Why can't you be good? _____ And do just as you

should? _____ Won't you turn that new leaf o - ver, So your ba - by can be your slave? Oh, Why

Can't You Be - have? _____ There's a farm I know near my old home town _____ Where we

two can go and try set - tlin' down, _____ There I'll care for you for - ev - er, 'Cause you're all in the world I

crave, But Why Can't You Be - have? _____ have? _____

336

# BRUSH UP YOUR SHAKESPEARE

Copyright © 1949 by Cole Porter
Copyright Renewed, Assigned to John F. Wharton, Trustee of the Cole Porter Musical & Literary Property Trusts
Chappell & Co., Inc., owner of publication and allied rights throughout the World

Words & Music by
COLE PORTER

Brush Up Your Shake-speare, Start quot-ing him now ___ Brush Up Your

Shake-speare And the wo-men you will wow.

Just de-claim a few lines from O-thel-la And they'll
If your goil is a Wash-ing-ton Heights dream, Treat the
If you can't be a ham and do Ham-let They will

think you're a heck-uv-a fel-la, If your blonde won't re-spond, when you flat-ter 'er Tell her what To-ny told Cle-o-
kid to A Mid-sum-mer Night's Dream, With the wife of the Brit-ish em-bes-si-da Try a crack out of Troi-lus and
not give a damn or a damn-let. Just re-cite an oc-ca-sion-al son-net, And your lap-'ll have Hon-ey up-

pa-ter-er. And if still to be shocked she pre-tends, well, Just re-mind her that "All's Well That Ends Well," Brush Up Your
Cres-si-da, If she says she won't buy it or tike it, Make her tike it, what's more, As You Like It.
on it. When your ba-by is plead-ing for plea-sure Let her sam-ple your "Mea-sure for Mea-sure."

Shake-speare And they'll all kow-tow! ___ tow! ___

# ANOTHER OP'NIN', ANOTHER SHOW

Copyright © 1949 by Cole Porter Music
Copyright Renewed, Assigned to John F. Wharton, Trustee of the Cole Porter Musical & Literary Property Trusts
Chappell & Co., Inc., owner of publication and allied rights throughout the World
International Copyright Secured   ALL RIGHTS RESERVED

Words & Music by
COLE PORTER

An-oth-er Op'-nin', An-oth-er Show ___ In Phil-ly, Bos-ton or
oth-er job ___ that you hope, at last, will make your fu-ture for-

Balt-i-moe, ___ A chance for stage-folks to say "hel-lo" ___ An-oth-er Op'-
get your past ___ An-oth-er pain ___ where the ul-cers grow ___ An-oth-er Op'-

nin' of An-oth-er Show An-
nin' of An-oth-er Show! Four weeks, you re-

hearse and re-hearse, ___ Three weeks ___ and it could-n't be worse ___

**I HATE MEN**

Copyright © 1948 by Cole Porter
Copyright Renewed, Assigned to John F. Wharton, Trustee of the Cole Porter Musical & Literary Property Trusts
Chappell & Co., Inc., owner of publication and allied rights throughout the World

Words & Music by
COLE PORTER

Verse 3 I hate men
Though roosters they
I will not play the hen
If you espouse an older man through girlish optimisim
He'll always stay at home at night and make no criticism
Though you may call it "love" the doctors call it "rheumatism,"

Oh I hate men
From all I've read, alone in bed, from A to Zed about 'em
Since love is blind, then from the mind, all woman-kind should rout 'em
But ladies, you must answer too, what would we do without 'em,
Still I hate men

# SO IN LOVE

Copyright © 1948 by Cole Porter
Copyright Renewed, Assigned to John F. Wharton, Trustee of the Cole Porter Musical & Literary Property Trusts
Chappell & Co., Inc., owner of publication and allied rights throughout the World
International Copyright Secured    ALL RIGHTS RESERVED

Words & Music by
COLE PORTER

# ALWAYS TRUE TO YOU IN MY FASHION

Copyright © 1948 by Cole Porter
Copyright Renewed, Assigned to John F. Wharton, Trustee of the Cole Porter Musical & Literary Property Trusts
Chappell & Co., Inc., owner of publication and allied rights throughout the World

Words & Music by
COLE PORTER

{ I've been asked to have a meal_ By a big ty-coon in steel._ If the meal in-cludes a deal,_
{ From Mil-wau-kee, Mis-ter Fritz_ Oft-en dines me at the Ritz,_ Mis-ter Fritz in-vent-ed Schlitz

_ ac-cept I may,_ But I'm Al-ways True To You,_ dar-lin', in my fash-ion, Yes, I'm
_ And Schlitz must pay!_ Al-ways True To You,_ dar-lin', in my way._

{ There's an oil man known as "Tex" Who is keen to give me
{ Mis-ter Har-ris, plu-to-crat, Wants to give my cheek a

checks And his checks, I fear,_mean that "Tex" is here_to stay!_ But I'm Al-ways True To You,_ dar-lin', in my fash-ion,
pat, If the Har-ris pat_means a Pa-ris hat,_ Bé-bé! 

Yes, I'm Al-ways True To You,_ dar-lin', in my way! From O-

## WUNDERBAR

Copyright © 1948 by Cole Porter
Copyright Renewed, Assigned to John F. Wharton, Trustee of the Cole Porter Musical & Literary Property Trusts
Chappell & Co., Inc., owner of publication and allied rights throughout the World
International Copyright Secured     ALL RIGHTS RESERVED

Words & Music by
COLE PORTER

Wun-der-bar,_ Wun-der-bar!_ What a per-fect night for love,_ Here am I,
bar,_ Wun-der-bar!_ We're a-lone and hand in glove,_ Not a cloud

here you are,_ Why, it's tru-ly Wun-der-bar!_ Wun-der
near or far,_ Why, it's more than Wun-der-bar!_ _ Oh I care, dear,_ for you

mad-ly,_ And I long, dear._ For your kiss. I would die, dear,_ for you glad-ly._ You're di-

vine, dear!_ And you're mine, dear!_ Wun-der-bar, _ Wun-der-bar!_ There's our fav'-rite star a-

bove,_ What a bright shin-ing star,_ Like our love, it's Wun-der-bar!_

## TOO DARN HOT

Copyright © 1949 by Cole Porter
Copyright Renewed, Assigned to John F. Wharton, Trustee of the Cole Porter Musical & Literary Property Trusts
Chappell & Co, Inc, owner of publication and allied rights throughout the World
International Copyright Secured     ALL RIGHTS RESERVED

Words & Music by
COLE PORTER

Moderately Fast

It's Too Darn Hot, It's Too Darn Hot, I'd like to sup ____ with my ba-by to-night,
Too Darn Hot, It's Too Darn Hot, I'd like to stop ____ for my ba-by to-night,

And play the pup ____ with my ba-by to-night. ____ I'd
And blow my top ____ with my ba-by to-night. ____ I'd

like to sup ____ with my ba-by to-night, ____ And play the pup ____ with my ba-by to-night, ____ But
like to stop ____ for my ba-by to-night, ____ And blow my top ____ with my ba-by to-night, ____ But I'd

I ain't up ____ to my ba-by to-night ____ 'Cause it's Too Darn Hot. ____ It's
be a flop ____ with my ba-by to-night ____ 'Cause it's Too Darn Hot. ____

Hot.

## I SING OF LOVE

Copyright © 1948 by Cole Porter
Copyright Renewed, Assigned to John F. Wharton, Trustee of the Cole Porter Musical & Literary Property Trusts
Chappell & Co, Inc, owner of publication and allied rights throughout the World

Words & Music by
COLE PORTER

Quick with Vigor

We sing ____ of love, we sing ____ on-ly of love ____

Ye gods ____ a - bove, May we nev-er sing of an-y-thing but love. ____

For love is the joy ____ of ev-'ry girl and boy. ____ As love, lat-er on, keeps 'em go-ing 'til they're gone. Yes,

love is the theme ____ of all peo-ple who dream. So love, let's con-fess, ____ is ev-'ry-bod-y's bus - i - ness.

To Coda

Oh, ye gods ____ a - bove. ____ May we nev-er sing of an-y-thing but love, sweet ____

love. I won't sing a song a-bout bat-tle. I won't sing of ba-bies who prat-tle. I

get no glee from songs a-bout the sea, or cow-boy songs a-bout cat-tle. I won't waste a note of my pat-ters On

so-cial-ly sig-ni-fi-cant mat-ters. We sing of one thing And we a-dore it, Thank heav-en for it! We

love, sweet love.

## "Knickerbocker Holiday"

### IT NEVER WAS YOU

Words by MAXWELL ANDERSON
Music by KURT WEILL

RO - © Copyright 1938 and renewed 1966 Hampshire House Publishing
Corp. and Chappell & Co., Inc., New York, N.Y.

Moderately

But It Nev-er Was You,___ It nev-er was an-y-where you. An oc-ca-sion-al sun-set re-mind-ed me Or a

flower hang-ing high on a tu-lip-tree, Or one red star hung low in the west, Or a heart-break call from the mea-dow-lark's nest made me

think for a mo-ment: "May-be it's true___ I've found her in the star, in the call, in the

blue!" But It Nev-er Was You.___ It nev-er was an-y-where you. an-y-where.

an-y-where you.___ But It an-y-where, an-y-where you.___

# SEPTEMBER SONG

TRO - © Copyright 1938 and renewed 1966 HAMPSHIRE HOUSE PUBLISHING CORP. and CHAPPELL & CO. INC., New York, N.Y.

Words by MAXWELL ANDERSON
Music by KURT WEILL

## 'La Cage Aux Folles''

### THE BEST OF TIMES

© 1983 JERRY HERMAN/All Rights Controlled by JERRYCO MUSIC CO.
Exclusive Agent: EDWIN H. MORRIS & COMPANY, A Division of MPL Communications, Inc.

Words & Music by
JERRY HERMAN

# LA CAGE AUX FOLLES

© 1983 JERRY HERMAN/All Rights Controlled by JERRYCO MUSIC CO.
Exclusive Agent: EDWIN H. MORRIS & COMPANY, A Division of MPL Communications, Inc.

Words & Music
JERRY HERMAN

It's rath-er gaud-y but it's al-so rath-er grand,___ and while the wait-er pads your check, he'll kiss you
It's slight-ly "for-ties" and a lit-tle bit "new wave,"___ you may be danc-ing with a girl who needs a

hand.___ The clev-er gi-go-los ro-mance the wealth-y ma-trons at La Cage Aux
shave.___ Where both the riff-raff and the roy-al-ty are pa-trons at La

Folles___ Cage Aux Folles.___ La Cage Aux

Folles,___ the mai-tre d' is dash-ing, Cage Aux Folles,___ the hat-check girl is flash-ing

We im-port the drinks that you buy.___ (So the Per-ri-er is Can-a-da Dry!)___

Ec-cen-tric coup-les al-ways punc-tu-ate the scene;___ A pair of eu-nuchs and a nun with a Ma-

rine To feel a-live you get a lim-ou-sine to drive you to La Cage Aux

Folles ___

It's bad and beau-ti-ful, it's
Go for the mys-ter-y, the

bawd-y, and bi-zarre. I know a duch-ess who got preg-nant at the bar. Just who is
mag-ic, and the mood. A-void the hus-tlers, and the men's-room, and the food. For you get

who, and what is what, is quite the ques-tion at La Cage Aux Folles ___
glam-our and ro-mance, and in-di-ges-tion at La

# SONG ON THE SAND
### (La Da Da Da)

© 1983 JERRY HERMAN/All Rights Controlled by JERRYCO MUSIC CO.
Exclusive Agent: EDWIN H. MORRIS & COMPANY, A Division of MPL Communications, Inc.

Words & Music by
JERRY HERMAN

## "Ladies First"

# THE REAL AMERICAN FOLK SONG (IS A RAG)

Copyright © 1959 by Gershwin Publishing Corporation
Copyright assigned to Chappell & Co., Inc.

Words by IRA GERSHWIN
Music by GEORGE GERSHWIN

# "Lady In The Dark"

## MY SHIP

TRO - © Copyright 1941 and renewed 1969 HAMPSHIRE HOUSE PUBLISHING CORP.
& CHAPPELL & CO. INC, New York, N.Y.

Words by IRA GERSHWIN
Music by KURT WEILL

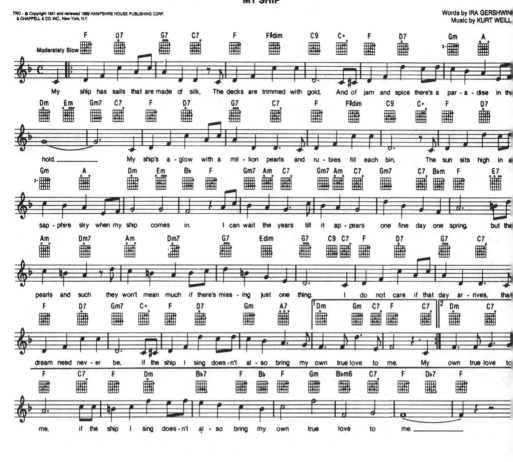

My ship has sails that are made of silk, The decks are trimmed with gold, And of jam and spice there's a par-a-dise in the hold. _____ My ship's a-glow with a mil-lion pearls and ru-bies fill each bin, The sun sits high in a sap-phire sky when my ship comes in. I can wait the years till it ap-pears one fine day one spring, but the pearls and such they won't mean much if there's miss-ing just one thing. I do not care if that day ar-rives, that dream need nev-er be, if the ship I sing does-n't al-so bring my own true love to me. My own true love to me, if the ship I sing does-n't al-so bring my own true love to me. _____

## THE SAGA OF JENNY

TRO - © Copyright 1941 and renewed 1969 Hampshire House Publishing Corp.
and Chappell & Co, Inc, New York, N.Y.

Words by IRA GERSHWIN
Music by KURT WEILL

Jen-ny made her mind up when she was three,— She, her-self, was going to trim the Christ-mas tree;— Christ-mas
Jen-ny made her mind up when she was twelve,— That in-to for-eign lan-guag-es she would delve,— But at

Eve she lit the can-dles, tossed the ta-pers a-way._ Lit-tle Jen-ny was an or-phan on Christ-mas day._
sev-en-teen to Vas-sar it was quite_ a blow_ That in twen-ty sev-en lan-guag-es she could-n't say no.

Poor Jen-ny! Bright as a pen-ny! Her e-qual would be hard to find. _____ She
Poor Jen-ny! Bright as a pen-ny! Her e-qual would be hard to find. _____ To

lost one dad and moth-er, A sis-ter and a broth-er, But she would make up her mind.
Jen-ny I'm be-hold-en, Her heart was big and gold-en, But she would make up her mind.

6. Jen-ny made her mind up at sev-en-ty-five, __ She would live to be the old-est wom-an a-live, __ But

gin and rum and des-ti-ny play fun-ny tricks __ And poor Jen-ny kicked the buck-et at sev-en-ty-six. __

Jen-ny points a mor-al, With which you can-not quar-rel, Makes a lot of com-mon sense. __ Jen-ny and her sa-ga,

Prove that you are ga-ga, If you don't keep sit-ting on the fence. __ Jen-ny and her sto-ry Point the way to glo-ry,

To all men and wom-an kind. __ An-y-one with vi-sion, Comes to this de-ci-sion, Don't make up, you should-n't make up, You

must-n't make up, oh nev-er make up An-y-one with vi-sion, Comes to this de-ci-sion, Don't __ make __

up __ your __ mind! __

3. Jenny made her mind up at twenty-two,
   To get herself a husband was the thing to do,
   She got herself all dolled up in her satins and furs,
   And she got herself a husband, but he wasn't hers.
   Poor Jenny! Bright as a penny! Her equal would be hard to find.
   Deserved a bed of roses, But history discloses,
   That she would make up her mind.

4. Jenny made up her mind at thirty-nine,
   She would take a trip to the Argentine!
   She was only on vacation, but the Latins agree,
   Jenny was the one who started the Good Neighbor Policy.
   Poor Jenny! Bright as a penny! Her equal would be hard to find.
   Oh passion doesn't vanish, In Portugese or Spanish,
   But she would make up her mind.

5. Jenny made up her mind at fifty-one,
   She would write her memmoirs before she was done,
   The very day her book was published hist'ry relates
   There were wives who shot their husbands in some thirty-three states.
   Poor Jenny! Bright as a penny! Her equal would be hard to find.
   She could give cards and spadeies, To many other ladies,
   But she would make up her mind.

# THIS IS NEW

TRO - © Copyright 1941 and renewed 1969 HAMPSHIRE HOUSE PUBLISHING CORP.
& CHAPPELL & CO. INC., New York, N.Y.

Words by IRA GERSHWIN
Music by KURT WEILL

# "Leave It To Me"

## MY HEART BELONGS TO DADDY

Copyright © 1938 by Chappell & Co., Inc.
Copyright Renewed, Assigned to John F. Wharton, Trustee of the Cole Porter Musical & Literary Property Trusts
Chappell & Co., Inc., owner of publication and allied rights throughout the World
International Copyright Secured    ALL RIGHTS RESERVED

Words & Music by
COLE PORTER

Dad - dy, Da - da, da - da - da, da - da - da - ad! So I want to warn you, lad - die, Tho' I know you're per - fect - ly

swell, That My Heart Be - longs To Dad - dy 'Cause my Dad - dy, he treats it so well.

## GET OUT OF TOWN

Copyright © 1938 by Chappell & Co., Inc.
Copyright Renewed, Assigned to John F. Wharton, Trustee of the Cole Porter Musical & Literary Property Trusts
Chappell & Co., Inc., owner of publication and allied rights throughout the World
International Copyright Secured    ALL RIGHTS RESERVED

Words & Music by
COLE PORTER

Slowly

Get Out Of Town. Be - fore it's too late, my love, Get Out Of Town, Be good to me, please.

Why wish me harm? Why not re - tire to a farm And be con - tent - ed to charm The birds off the

trees? Just dis - ap - pear, I care for you much too much, And when you are near,

Close to me, dear, We touch too much. The thrill when we meet Is so bit - ter sweet That, dar - ling, it's get - ting me down.

So on your mark, get set, Get Out Of Town. Town.

# "Les Misérables"

## I DREAMED A DREAM

Music and Lyrics Copyright © 1980 by Editions Musicales Alain Boublil
English Lyrics Copyright © 1986 by Alain Boublil Music Ltd. (ASCAP)
Mechanical and Publication Rights for the USA Administered by Alain Boublil Music Ltd.
(ASCAP) c/o Stephen Tenenbaum & Co., Inc., 605 Third Ave., New York, NY 10158
Tel. (212) 922-0625, Fax (212) 922-0626

Music by CLAUDE-MICHEL SCHÖNBERG
Lyrics by HERBERT KRETZMER
Original Text by ALAIN BOUBLIL and JEAN-MARC NATEL

Moderately slow

FANTINE:

I Dreamed A Dream in days gone by when hope was high and life worth liv - ing.__ I dreamed that love would nev - er

die. I dreamed that God would be for - giv - ing. Then I was young and un - a - fraid and dreams were made and used and

wast - ed.__ There was no ran - som to be paid, no song un - sung no wine un - tast - ed. But the ti - gers come at

night with their voic - es soft as thun - der. As they tear your hope a - part, as they turn your dream to

shame.__ He slept a sum - mer by my side. He filled my days with end - less

won - der. He took my child - hood in his stride. But he was gone when au - tumn came.

And still I dreamed he'd come to me, that we would live the years to - geth - er. But there are dreams that can - not be,

and there are storms we can - not weath - er.__ I had a dream my life would be

so dif - f'rent from this hell I'm liv - ing, so dif - f'rent now from what it seemed. Now life has killed the dream I

dreamed.

# CASTLE ON A CLOUD

Music by CLAUDE-MICHEL SCHÖNBERG
Lyrics by HERBERT KRETZMER
Original Text by ALAIN BOUBLIL and JEAN-MARC NATEL

...c and Lyrics Copyright © 1980 by Editions Musicales Alain Boublil
...ish Lyrics Copyright © 1986 by Alain Boublil Music Ltd. (ASCAP)
...hanical and Publication Rights for the USA Administered by Alain Boublil Music Ltd.
...SCAP) c/o Stephen Tenenbaum & Co., Inc., 605 Third Ave., New York, NY 10158
... (212) 922-0625, Fax (212) 922-0626

**COSETTE:**

There is a Cas - tle On A Cloud. I like to go there in my sleep.
There is a room that's full of toys. There are a hun - dred boys and girls.

Aren't an - y floors for me to sweep, not in my Cas - tle On A Cloud.
No - bod - y shouts or talks too loud, not in my Cas - tle On A Cloud.

There is a la - dy all in white, holds me and sings a lul - la - by. She's nice to see and she's soft to touch. She

says, "Co - sette, I love you ver - y much." I know a place where no - one's lost. I know a place where no - one

cries. Cry - ing at all is not al - lowed, not in my Cas - tle On A Cloud.

# DRINK WITH ME (TO DAYS GONE BY)

Music by CLAUDE-MICHEL SCHÖNBERG
Lyrics by HERBERT KRETZMER and ALAIN BOUBLIL

Music and Lyrics Copyright © 1986 by Alain Boublil Music Ltd. (ASCAP)
...echanical and Publication Rights for the USA Administered by Alain Boublil Music Ltd.
...(ASCAP) c/o Stephen Tenenbaum & Co., Inc., 605 Third Ave., New York, NY 10158
Tel. (212) 922-0625, Fax (212) 922-0626

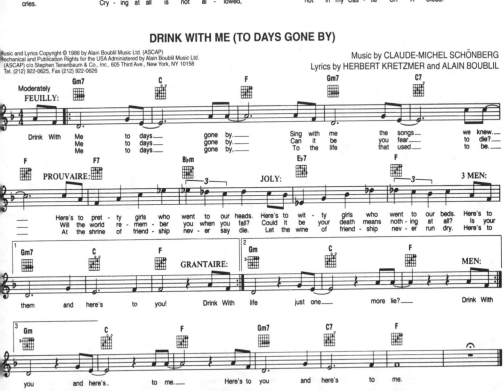

**FEUILLY:**

Drink With Me to days gone by. Sing with me the songs we knew.
Me to days gone by, Can it be you fear to die?
Me to days gone by, To the life that used to be.

**PROUVAIRE:** **JOLY:** **3 MEN:**

Here's to pret - ty girls who went to our heads. Here's to wit - ty girls who went to our beds. Here's to
Will the world re - mem - ber you when you fall? Could it be your death means noth - ing at all? Is your
At the shrine of friend - ship nev - er say die. Let the wine of friend - ship nev - er run dry. Here's to

**GRANTAIRE:** **MEN:**

them and here's to you! Drink With life just one more lie? Drink With

you and here's to me. Here's to you and here's to me.

# BRING HIM HOME

Music and Lyrics Copyright © 1986 by Alain Boublil Music Ltd. (ASCAP)
Mechanical and Publication Rights for the USA Administered by Alain Boublil Music Ltd.
(ASCAP) c/o Stephen Tenenbaum & Co., Inc., 605 Third Ave., New York, NY 10158
Tel. (212) 922-0625, Fax (212) 922-0626

Music by CLAUDE-MICHEL SCHÖNBERG
Lyrics by HERBERT KRETZMER and ALAIN BOUBLIL

# IN MY LIFE

Music and Lyrics Copyright © 1980 by Editions Musicales Alain Boublil
English Lyrics Copyright © 1986 by Alain Boublil Music Ltd. (ASCAP)
Mechanical and Publication Rights for the USA Administered by Alain Boublil Music Ltd.
(ASCAP) c/o Stephen Tenenbaum & Co., Inc., 605 Third Ave., New York, NY 10158
Tel. (212) 922-0625, Fax (212) 922-0626

Music by CLAUDE-MICHEL SCHÖNBERG
Lyrics by HERBERT KRETZMER
Original Text by ALAIN BOUBLIL and JEAN-MARC NATEL

# DO YOU HEAR THE PEOPLE SING?

Music and Lyrics Copyright © 1980 by Editions Musicales Alain Boublil
English Lyrics Copyright © 1986 by Alain Boublil Music Ltd. (ASCAP)
Mechanical and Publication Rights for the USA Administered by Alain Boublil Music Ltd.
(ASCAP) c/o Stephen Tenenbaum & Co., Inc., 605 Third Ave., New York, NY 10158
Tel. (212) 922-0625, Fax (212) 922-0626

Music by CLAUDE-MICHEL SCHÖNBER
Lyrics by HERBERT KRETZME
Original Text by ALAIN BOUBLIL and JEAN-MARC NAT

**March**

ENJOLRAS:

Do You Hear The Peo- ple Sing, sing-ing the song of an- gry men? It is the mu- sic of a peo- ple who will not be slaves a-gain! When th

COMBEFERRE:

beat- ing of your heart ech-oes the beat- ing of the drums, there is a life a-bout to start when to- mor- row comes. Will you

COURFEYRA

join in our cru- sade? Who will be strong and stand with me? Be- yond the bar- ri- cade is there a world you long to see? Th
give all you can give so that our ban- ner may ad- vance? Some will fall and some will live. Will you stand up and take your chance?

CHORUS:

join in the fight that will give you the right to be free! } Do You Hear The Peo- ple Sing, sing-ing the song of an- gry men? It is the
blood of the mar- tyrs will wa- ter the mea- dows of France! }

mu- sic of a peo- ple who will not be slaves a- gain! When the beat- ing of your heart ech-oes the beat- ing of the drums, there is a

1. life a- bout to start when to- mor- row comes! Will you

FEUILLY:

2. life a- bout to start when to- mor- row comes!

---

# MASTER OF THE HOUSE

Music and Lyrics Copyright © 1980 by Editions Musicales Alain Boublil
English Lyrics Copyright © 1986 by Alain Boublil Music Ltd. (ASCAP)
Mechanical and Publication Rights for the USA Administered by Alain Boublil Music Ltd.
(ASCAP) c/o Stephen Tenenbaum & Co., Inc., 605 Third Ave., New York, NY 10158
Tel. (212) 922-0625, Fax (212) 922-0626

Music by CLAUDE-MICHEL SCHÖNBER
Lyrics by HERBERT KRETZME
Original Text by ALAIN BOUBLIL and JEAN-MARC NATE

THERNARDIER:

Wel- come M' sieur. Sit your- self down and meet the best inn- keep- er in town. As for the rest,
En- ter, M' sieur. Lay down your load, un- lace your boots and rest from the road. This weighs a ton.

all of them crooks, rook- ing the guests and cook- ing the books. Sel- dom do you see hon- est men like
Trav- el's a curse. But here we strive to light- en your purse. Here the goose is cooked. Here the fat is

me. A gent of good in- tent who's con- tent to be... Mas- ter Of The House, dol- ing out the charm,
fried. And noth- ing's o- ver- looked till I'm sa- tis- fied... Food be- yond com- pare, food be- yond be- lief,

**B7**

read-y with a hand-shake and an o-pen palm. tells a sau-cy tale, makes a lit-tle stir, cus-tom-ers ap-pre-ci-ate a bon vi-veur.
mix it in a min-cer and pre-tend it's beef. Kid-ney of a horse, liv-er of a cat, fill-ing up the sau-sag-es with this and that.

**E**

Glad to do a friend a fa - vor. Does-n't cost me to be nice.__ But noth-ing gets you noth-ing, ev - 'ry-thing has got a lit-tle
Res - i - dents are more than wel - come. Bri - dal suite is oc - cu - pied.__ Rea - son - a - ble char - ges plus__ some lit - tle ex-tras on the

**A**

price.__ Mas - ter Of The House, keep-er of the zoo, rea-dy to re-lieve them of a sou or two. Wa - ter-ing the wine,
side.__ Charge 'em for the lice, ex - tra for the mice, two per-cent for look-ing in the mir-ror twice. Here a lit - tle slice,

**B7**    **E**    **C#**

mak-ing up the weight, pick-ing up their knick-knacks when they can't see straight. Ev - 'ry-bod - y loves a land - lord. Ev - 'ry-bod-y's bos - om friend.__
there a lit-tle cut, three per cent for sleep-ing with the win-dow shut. When it comes to fix-ing pric - es, there are lots of tricks he knows.__

**1**    **F#m**    **D**    **E7**    **A**    To next strain  **2**  **F#m**    **D**

__ I do what-ev - er pleas - es, Je - sus, don't I bleed 'em in the end! __ How it all in-creas - es, all __

**E7**    **A**    **CHORUS**    **A**

__ them bits and piec - es, Je - sus, it's a-maz-ing how it grows! Mas - ter Of The House, quick to catch your eye, nev - er wants a pas-ser - by to
Mas - ter Of The House, mas - ter and a half, com - for - ter, phi - los - o - pher. Don't

**B7**    **E**    To Coda

pass him by. Ser-vant to the poor, but-ler to the great, com-for-ter, phi-los-o-pher and life-long mate. Ev-'ry-bod-y's boon com-pan - ion.
make me laugh! Ser-vant to the poor, but-ler to the great. Hyp-o-crite and toad-y and in-e - bri-ate! Ev-'ry-bod-y bless our land-

**C#/E#**    **F#m**    **D**    **E7**    **1**  **A**    **Am(add9)**

**THERNARDIER:**

Ev - 'ry-bod-y's chap - er-one.__ But lock up your va-lis - es. Je - sus, won't I skin you to the bone!
Give 'em ev - 'ry-thing I've got. Dir - ty bunch of geez - ers, Je - sus what a sor - ry lit - tle

**2**  **A**    **Em**    **MADAME**    **Am6**    **B**
                 **THERNARDIER:**

lot! I used to dream that I__ would meet a prince. But, God Al-might - y have you seen what's hap-pened since?__

**E**

Mas - ter Of The House? Is-n't worth my spit! Com-for-ter phi-los-o-pher and life-long shit! Cun-ning lit-tle brain, reg-u-lar Vol-taire. Thinks she's quite a lover but there's

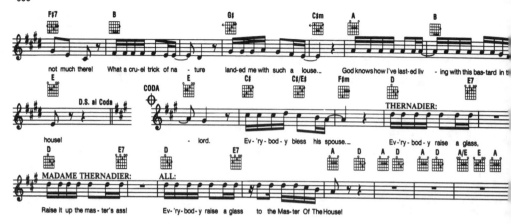

not much there! What a cru-el trick of na-ture land-ed me with such a louse.. God knows how I've last-ed liv-ing with this bas-tard in ti

D.S. al Coda    CODA    THERNADIER:

house!                – lord.    Ev-'ry-bod-y bless his spouse..    Ev-'ry-bod-y raise a glass,

MADAME THERNADIER:    ALL:

Raise it up the mas-ter's ass!    Ev-'ry-bod-y raise a glass    to the Mas-ter Of The House!

Music and Lyrics Copyright © 1980 by Editions Musicales Alain Boublil
English Lyrics Copyright © 1986 by Alain Boublil Music Ltd. (ASCAP)
Mechanical and Publication Rights for the USA Administered by Alain Boublil Music Ltd.
(ASCAP) c/o Stephen Tenenbaum & Co., Inc., 605 Third Ave., New York, NY 10158,
Tel. (212) 922-0625, Fax (212) 922-0626

## WHO AM I?

Music by CLAUDE-MICHEL SCHÖNBERG
Lyrics by HERBERT KRETZMER
Original Text by ALAIN BOUBLIL and JEAN-MARC NATEL

Moderately slow

VALJEAN:
Who Am I?    Can I con-demn this man to slav-er-y, pretend I do not see his ag-o-ny? Thi

in-no-cent who wears my face who goes to judge-ment in my place. Who Am I?__ Can I con-ceal my-self for-ev-er more, pre-tend I'm not the man

was be-fore?    And must my name un-til I die be no more than an al-i-bi? Must I lie?__ How can I ev-er face m

fel-low men? How can I ev-er face my-self a-gain? My soul be-longs to God, I know, I made that bar-gain long a-go. H

gave me hope when hope was gone. He gave me strength to jour-ney on. Who Am I? Who Am I? I'm Jean Val-jean! A

so, Ja-vert, you see it's true. That man bears no more guilt than you. Who Am I? Two, Four, Six, Oh, One!

# EMPTY CHAIRS AT EMPTY TABLES

and Lyrics Copyright © 1986 by Alain Boublil Music Ltd. (ASCAP)
nical and Publication Rights for the USA Administered by Alain Boublil Music Ltd.
AP) c/o Stephen Tenenbaum & Co., Inc., 605 Third Ave., New York, NY 10158
212) 922-0625, Fax (212) 922-0626

Music by CLAUDE-MICHEL SCHÖNBERG
Lyrics by HERBERT KRETZMER and ALAIN BOUBLIL

# A LITTLE FALL OF RAIN

Music and Lyrics Copyright © 1980 by Editions Musicales Alain Boublil
English Lyrics Copyright © 1986 by Alain Boublil Music Ltd. (ASCAP)
Mechanical and Publication Rights for the USA Administered by Alain Boublil Music Ltd.
(ASCAP) c/o Stephen Tenenbaum & Co., Inc., 605 Third Ave., New York, NY 10158
Tel. (212) 922-0625, Fax (212) 922-0626

Music by CLAUDE-MICHEL SCHÖNBERG
Lyrics by HERBERT KRETZME
Original Text by ALAIN BOUBLIL and JEAN-MARC NATE

# ON MY OWN

Music and Lyrics Copyright © 1980 by Editions Musicales Alain Boublil
English Lyrics Copyright © 1986 by Alain Boublil Music Ltd. (ASCAP)
Mechanical and Publication Rights for the USA Administered by Alain Boublil Music Ltd.
(ASCAP) c/o Stephen Tenenbaum & Co., Inc., 605 Third Ave., New York, NY 10158
Tel. (212) 922-0625, Fax (212) 922-0626

Music by CLAUDE-MICHEL SCHÖNBERG
Lyrics by HERBERT KRETZMER, JOHN CAIRD and TREVOR NUNN
Original Text by ALAIN BOUBLIL and JEAN-MARC NATEL

# "Let's Face It"

## LET'S NOT TALK ABOUT LOVE

Copyright © 1941 by Chappell & Co., Inc.
Copyright Renewed, assigned to John F. Wharton, Trustee of the Cole Porter Musical & Literary Property Trusts/Chappell & Co., Inc., Publisher

Words & Music by
COLE PORTER

# ACE IN THE HOLE

Copyright © 1941 by Chappell & Co., Inc.
Copyright Renewed, assigned to John F. Wharton, Trustee of the Cole Porter Musical & Literary Property Trusts/Chappell & Co., Inc., Publisher

Words & Music by
COLE PORTER

## "The First"

### WILL WE EVER KNOW EACH OTHER

Lyric by MARTIN CHARNIN
Music by BOB BRUSH

© 1981, 1982 MPL COMMUNICATIONS, INC.

# "Little Mary Sunshine"

LITTLE MARY SUNSHINE

Copyright © 1980 by Alley Music Corp. and Trio Music Co., Inc.
All rights administered by Hudson Bay Music, Inc.
Used by Permission

Words & Music by
RICK BESOYAN

Brightly

You've got to hand it to Lit-tle Ma-ry Sun-shine, _ Lit-tle Ma-ry is the sun-shine of the sun. _ You've got to hand it to Lit-tle Ma-ry Sun-shine, _ Lit-tle Ma-ry has a smile for ev-'ry-one. _ She may be a bit old fash-ioned it's true, _ When you lock your heart sub-lime. _ You've got to hand it to Lit-tle Ma-ry Sun-shine. _ For she's ve-ry mer-ry all the time. _

ONCE IN A BLUE MOON

Copyright © 1980 by Alley Music Corp. and Trio Music Co., Inc.
All rights administered by Hudson Bay Music, Inc.
Used by Permission

Words & Music by
RICK BESOYAN

Moderato (with a lilt)

(Boy:) Once In A Blue Moon I think you love me (Girl:) I of-ten think I'd like to love you Once In A Blue Moon I think you don't It's rath-er pleas-ing to be so teas-ing Once In A Blue Moon I think you hate me I on-ly hate you cause I love you Once In A Blue Moon I think you won't I'm un-de-cid-ed and must be guid-ed Once In A Blue Moon you want to leave me I can't i-ma-gine why I'd leave you Once In A Blue Moon you're in a whirl You set me reel-ing with such a feel-ing Why this con-fus-ion? Why this con-fus-ion? Here's the con-clu-sion Here's the con-clu-sion You are my Once In A Blue Moon girl. girl.

## "Little Me"

### I'VE GOT YOUR NUMBER

©1962 CAROLYN LEIGH and CY COLEMAN
Rights Throughout the World Controlled by EDWIN H. MORRIS & COMPANY,
A Division of MPL Communications, Inc.

Lyric by CAROLYN LEIGH
Music by CY COLEMAN

### REAL LIVE GIRL

©1960 CAROLYN LEIGH and CY COLEMAN
Rights Throughout the World Controlled by EDWIN H. MORRIS & COMPANY,
A Division of MPL Communications, Inc.

Lyric by CAROLYN LEIGH
Music by CY COLEMAN

# ON THE OTHER SIDE OF THE TRACKS

© 1962 CAROLYN LEIGH and CY COLEMAN
All Rights Throughout the World Controlled by EDWIN H. MORRIS & COMPANY,
A Division of MPL Communications, Inc.

Lyric by CAROLYN LEIGH
Music by CY COLEMAN

Deliberately

Gmaj7 Am7 Gmaj7 Am7 Gmaj7 G6 Bm7 E9 Am

On The Oth-er Side_ Of The Tracks_ That is where I'm go-in' to be;_ On the oth-er side_ of that

G#+ Am7 D9 Dm7 G7 Cmaj9 C6

great di-vide,_ Be-tween fame and for-tune and me! Gon-na put my shad-ows be-hind me._ Give my

Em7 A9 Dmaj7 Dm7 G7 Cmaj7 Bm7 Am7 D9

in-hi-bi-tions the axe; And to-mor-row morn-ing you'll find me, On The Oth-er Side_ Of The

G6 D9 Gmaj7 Am7 Bm7 Am7 Gmaj7 G6 Bm7 E9

Tracks. On the oth-er side_ of that line,_ Where the life is fan-cy and free,_ Gon-na

Amaj7 Bm7 Amaj9 Bm7 Amaj7 A6 C#m7 F#7 F#m7 B7

sit and fan_ on my fat di-van,_ While the but-ler but-tles the tea! But for now I'm fac-in' the

Emaj7 Em7 A7 Dmaj7 D7 Dm7 G7 Cmaj7 Bm7

fenc-es And I can't af-ford_ to re-lax; When the whole ka-boo-dle com-menc-es, On The

Am7 D9 G6 Gmaj7 C#m7 F#7 C#m7 F#7 Bmaj9 B6 Bmaj9

Oth-er Side_ Of The Tracks. So I'm off and run-nin' o-ver the rail, I'm go'n' gun-nin' aft-

B6 Dm7 G7 Dm7 G7 Cmaj7 F7

-er the quail! Off and run-nin', send_ me the mail, To the great big world on the oth-er side,_ The

Em7 A9 Am7 G6 Cmaj7 D11 G

great big world on the far-ther side,_ The great big world On The Oth-er Side_ Of The Tracks!_

# "A Little Night Music"

## A LITTLE NIGHT MUSIC

1973 REVELATION MUSIC PUBLISHING CORP. & RILTING MUSIC, INC.
Tommy Valando Publication

By STEPHEN SONDHEIM

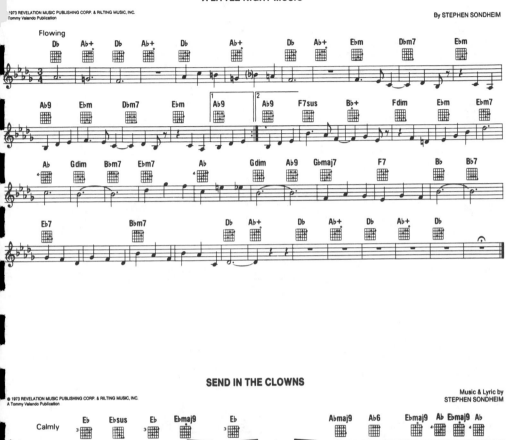

## SEND IN THE CLOWNS

© 1973 REVELATION MUSIC PUBLISHING CORP. & RILTING MUSIC, INC.
A Tommy Valando Publication

Music & Lyric by
STEPHEN SONDHEIM

## REMEMBER?

© 1973 REVELATION MUSIC PUBLISHING CORP. & RILTING MUSIC, INC.
A Tommy Valando Publication

Music & Lyric by
STEPHEN SONDHEIM

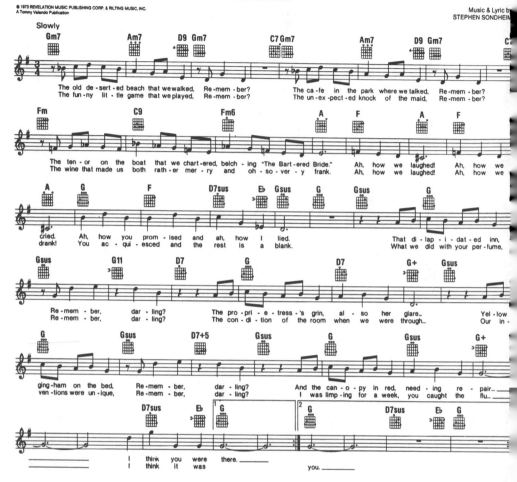

The old de-sert-ed beach that we walked, Re-mem-ber? The ca-fe in the park where we talked, Re-mem-ber?
The fun-ny lit-tle game that we played, Re-mem-ber? The un-ex-pect-ed knock of the maid, Re-mem-ber?

The ten-or on the boat that we chart-ered, belch-ing "The Bart-ered Bride." Ah, how we laughed! Ah, how we
The wine that made us both rath-er mer-ry and oh-so-ver-y frank. Ah, how we laughed! Ah, how we

cried. Ah, how you prom-ised and ah, how I lied. That di-lap-i-dat-ed inn,
drank! You ac-qui-esced and the rest is a blank. What we did with your per-fume,

Re-mem-ber, dar-ling? The pro-pri-e-tress-'s grin, al-so her glare... Yel-low
Re-mem-ber, dar-ling? The con-di-tion of the room when we were through... Our in-

ging-ham on the bed, Re-mem-ber, dar-ling? And the can-o-py in red, need-ing re-pair...
ven-tions were un-ique, Re-mem-ber, dar-ling? I was limp-ing for a week, you caught the flu...

I think you were there.
I think it was you.

## "Lost In The Stars"

### LOST IN THE STARS

TRO - © Copyright 1944 (renewed 1972) & 1946 (renewed 1974) HAMPSHIRE
HOUSE PUBLISHING CORP. & CHAPPELL & CO., INC, New York, N.Y.

Words by MAXWELL ANDERSON
Music by KURT WEILL

Be-fore Lord God made the sea and the land, He held all the stars in the palm of His hand, And they ran through His fin-gers li

grains of sand, And one lit-tle star fell a-lone. Then the Lord God hunt-ed through the

wide night air For the lit-tle dark star on the wind down there And he stat-ed and prom-ised he'd

take spec - ial care So it would - n't get lost a - gain. Now a man don't mind if the stars grow dim And the

clouds blow o - ver and dark - en him, So long as the Lord God's watch - ing o - ver them, Keep - ing track how it all goes

on. But I've been walk - ing through the night and the day Till my eyes get wear - y and my head turns gray, And

some - times it seems may - be God's gone a - way, For - get - ting the prom - ise that we heard him say And we're lost out

here in the stars, Lit - tle stars, big stars, blow - ing through the night, And we're lost out here in the stars,

Lit - tle stars, big stars, blow - ing through the night, And we're lost out here in the stars.

# "Love Life"

## GREEN-UP TIME

Copyright © 1948 by Chappell & Co. Inc.
Copyright renewed, Chappell & Co., Inc., and Hampshire House Publishing, owners of publication and allied rights

Words by ALAN JAY LERNER
Music by KURT WEILL

Gaily, but not too fast

Yes - ter - day morn - ing I did see blos - soms on the ap - ple tree, I took a breath and thought, could it be, it's
Then I be - gan to look a - round And in ev - 'ry field I found greens were a push - ing up through the ground for

green - up time? green - up time! And sure e - nough the blue - bells tink - led

A - pril in the glen, And sure e - nough I fell in love with love a - gain! Then I start - ed feel - ing

aw - ful bright, Had a thought that hit me right. I'll have my hon - ey dance me to - night and have a time to

wel - come in the green - up time! time!

# HERE I'LL STAY

TRO - © Copyright 1948 and renewed 1976 HAMPSHIRE HOUSE PUBLISHING CORP. and CHAPPELL & CO. INC., New York, N.Y.

Words by ALAN JAY LERNER
Music by KURT WEILL

There's a far land, I'm told, Where I'll find a field of gold, But Here I'll Stay with you. And they say there's an isle deep with clo-ver Where your heart wears a smile all day through. But I know well they're wrong and I know where I be-long, And Here I'll Stay with you. For that land is a sand-y il-lu-sion; It's the theme of a dream gone a-stray, And the world oth-ers woo I can find lov-ing you. And so Here I'll Stay!

# "Man Of La Mancha"

## DULCINEA

Copyright © 1965 Andrew Scott, Inc. and Helena Music Corp.

Music by MITCH LEIGH
Lyric by JOE DARION

# THE IMPOSSIBLE DREAM
## (THE QUEST)

Copyright © 1965 Andrew Scott, Inc. and Helena Music Corp.

Music by MITCH LEIGH
Lyric by JOE DARION

Bolero

To dream ___ The Im - pos - si - ble Dream, ___ to fight ___ the un - beat - a - ble foe, ___ to
right ___ the un - right - a - ble wrong, ___ to love ___ pure and chaste from a - far, ___ to

bear ___ with un - bear - a - ble sor - row, ___ to run ___ where the brave dare not go. ___ To
try ___ when your arms are too wea - ry, ___ to reach ___ the un - reach - a - ble

star! This is my quest, ___ to fol - low that star, ___ no mat - ter how hope-less ___ no mat - ter how far: ___ to fight for the

right ___ with - out ques-tion or pause, ___ to be will - ing to march in - to hell for a heav - en - ly cause! And I

know, ___ if I'll on - ly be true ___ to this glo - ri - ous quest, ___ that my heart ___ will lie peace - ful and calm, ___ when I'm laid to my

rest. And the world ___ will be bet - ter for this; ___ that one man, ___ scorned and cov - ered with scars, ___ still

strove ___ with his last ounce of cour - age, ___ to reach ___ the un - reach - a - ble stars. ___

# MAN OF LA MANCHA
## (I, DON QUIXOTE)

Copyright © 1965 Andrew Scott, Inc. and Helena Music Corp.

Music by MITCH LEIGH
Lyric by JOE DARION

Paso Doble

Hear me now, oh thou bleak and un-bear-a-ble world, thou art base and de-bauched as can be.
heath-ens and wiz-ards and ser-pents of sin, all your das-tard-ly do-ings are past.

And a knight with his ban-ners all brave-ly un-furled now hurls down his gaunt-let to
For a ho-ly en-deav-or is now to be-gin, and vir-tue shall tri-umph at

thee! I am I, Don Qui-xo-te, the Lord of La Man-cha, de-stroy-er of
last! I am I, Don Qui-xo-te, the Lord of La Man-cha, my des-ti-ny

e-vil am I. I will march to the sound of the trum-pets of glo-ry for-
calls and I go. And the wild winds of for-tune will car-ry me on-ward oh

ev-er to con-quer or die! Hear me,
whith-er so-

ev-er they blow.

Whith-er so-ev-er they blow, on-ward to glo-ry I go!

# "Mack And Mabel"

## I WON'T SEND ROSES

© 1974 JERRY HERMAN
All Rights Controlled by JERRYCO MUSIC CO.
Exclusive Agent: EDWIN H. MORRIS & COMPANY, A Division of MPL Communications, Inc.

Music & Lyric by
JERRY HERMAN

## TIME HEALS EVERYTHING

© 1974 JERRY HERMAN
All Rights Controlled by JERRYCO MUSIC CO.
Exclusive Agent: EDWIN H. MORRIS & COMPANY, A Division of MPL Communications, Inc.

Music & Lyric by
JERRY HERMAN

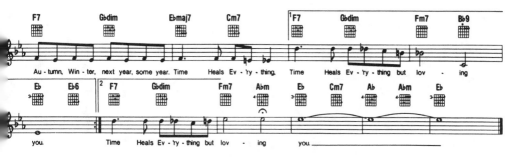

## "Mame"

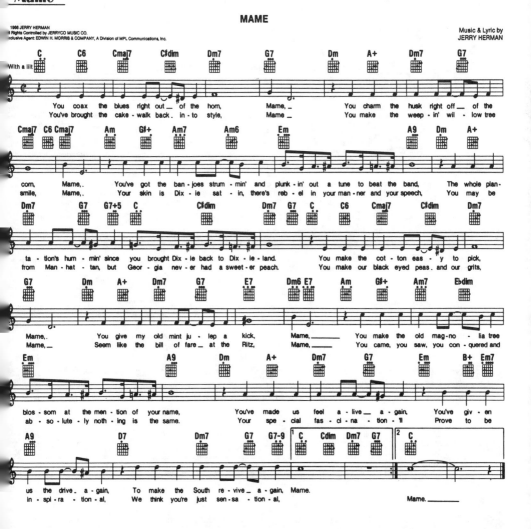

# IF HE WALKED INTO MY LIFE

© 1966 JERRY HERMAN
All Rights Controlled by JERRYCO MUSIC CO.
Exclusive Agent: EDWIN H. MORRIS & COMPANY, A Division of MPL Communications, Inc.

Music & Lyric by
JERRY HERMAN

VERSE (ad lib)

Abmaj7  Abdim  Ebmaj7  Fm7  Bb7sus  Bb7-9  Ebmaj7  Gm9  C7-9

Girl: Where's that boy with the bu - gle? My lit - tle love who was al - ways my big ro - mance; Where's that boy with the
Boy: Where's that girl with the prom - ise? The girl who tried to show me what love could be; Where's that girl with the

Fmaj7  F6  Gm7  C7sus  C7-9  F6

CHORUS  Slowly
Tacet

bu - gle? And why did I ev - er buy him those damn long pants? Did {he/she} need a strong - er hand?
prom - ise? And why do I feel the some - one to blame is me? fast.

Fmaj7  F7  Am7  D7  G9  G9+5  G7  G9  G9+5  Gm7  C9  C9+5  Fmaj7

Did he need a light - er touch? Was I soft or was I tough? Did I give e - nough? Did I give too much?
Was his world a lit - tle free? Was there too much of a crowd? All too lush and loud and not e - nough of me.

Cm6  D7-9  Gm  Gm7  Bbm6  Am7  Fdim

At the mo - ment that {he/she} need - ed me, Did I ev - er turn a - way? Would I be there when {he/she}
Though I'll ask my - self my whole life long, What went wrong a - long the way; Would I make the same mis-

Gm7  G9  C7sus  C7-9  Fmaj9  C7  F6  Fmaj7  F7  Am7

To Coda
Tacet

called, If He Walked In - to My Life to - day. {Were his days a lit - tle dull? Were his nights a lit - tle wild?
takes {Did she mind the lone - ly nights? Did she count the emp - ty days?

D7  G9  G9+5  G7  G9  G9+5  Gm7  C9  C9+5  Fmaj7  Cm6  D7-9  Gm  Gm7

Did I o - ver - state my plan? Did I stress the man? And for - get the child. {And there must have been a mil - lion things.
Was I si - lent, was I cold? Was I quick to scold? Was I slow to praise?

Bbm6  Am7  Fdim  Gm7  G9  C7sus  C7-9  F

That my heart for - got to say. Would I think of one or two, If {He/She} Walked In - to My Life to - day.

Db  Db6  Dbmaj7  Db6  Ebm7  Ab7  Db  Db6

Tacet

Should I blame the times I pam - pered {him,/her,} Or blame the times I bossed {him;/her,} What a shame I nev - er real - ly found the

Dbmaj7  Db6  Gm7  C7  Fdim  C7sus  C7-9

CODA

D.S. al Coda

{boy,/girl,} Be - fore I lost {him./her.} Were the years a lit - tle  Life to -

Am7  D7  G9  Bbm6  C7-9  Fmaj7  Ab6  Fmaj7

day? If that {boy/girl} with the {bu - gle/prom - ise} Walked in - to my life to - day.

## MY BEST GIRL (MY BEST BEAU)

1966 JERRY HERMAN
Rights Controlled by JERRYCO MUSIC CO.
lusive Agent: EDWIN H. MORRIS & COMPANY, A Division of MPL Communications, Inc.

Music & Lyric by
JERRY HERMAN

You're My Best Girl and noth-ing you do is wrong, I'm proud you be-long to me;
My Best Beau, you're hand-some and brave and strong, There's noth-ing we two can't face;

And if a day is rough for me, Hav-ing you there's e - nough for me. And if some -
If you're with me, what-ev - er comes, We'll see that trou - ble nev - er comes. And if some -

day an-oth-er girl comes a - long, It won't take her long to see, That I'll still be found
day when ev-'ry-thing turns out wrong, You're through with the hu - man race, Come run-ning to me,

just hang-in' a - round My Best Girl. You're Girl.
For you'll al-ways be My Best Beau.

## WE NEED A LITTLE CHRISTMAS

1966 JERRY HERMAN
Rights Controlled by JERRYCO MUSIC CO.
lusive Agent: EDWIN H. MORRIS & COMPANY, A Division of MPL Communications, Inc.

Music & Lyric by
JERRY HERMAN

Haul out the hol - ly, Put up the tree be - fore my spir - it falls a - gain;
climb down the chim - ney, Turn on the bright - est string of lights I've ev - er seen;

Fill up the stock - ing, I may be rush - ing things, but deck the halls a - gain.
Slice up the fruit - cake, It's time we hung some tin - sel on the ev - er - green

now. For We Need A Lit - tle Christ - mas, Right this ver - y min - ute,
bough. For I've grown a lit - tle lean - er, Grown a lit - tle cold - er,

Can - dles in the win - dow, Car - ols at the spin - et. Yes, We Need A Lit - tle Christ - mas, Right this ver - y min - ute, It
Grown a lit - tle sad - der, Grown a lit - tle old - er. And I need a lit - tle an - gel, Sit - ting on my shoul - der, And

has - n't snowed a sin - gle flur - ry, But San - ta, dear, we're in a hur - ry. So Need a lit - tle Christ - mas now!

# "Mata Hari"

## MAMAN

© 1967, 1988 MARTIN CHARNIN and EDWARD THOMAS
All Rights Controlled by MPL COMMUNICATIONS, INC.

Lyric by MARTIN CHARNIN
Music by EDWARD THOMAS

## "Me And Juliet"

Copyright © 1953 by Richard Rodgers and Oscar Hammerstein II
Copyright Renewed
WILLIAMSON MUSIC owner of publication and allied rights throughout the world

# MARRIAGE TYPE LOVE

Lyrics by OSCAR HAMMERSTEIN II
Music by RICHARD RODGERS

# NO OTHER LOVE

Copyright © 1953 by Richard Rodgers and Oscar Hammerstein II
Copyright Renewed
WILLIAMSON MUSIC owner of publication and allied rights throughout the world

Lyrics by OSCAR HAMMERSTEIN II
Music by RICHARD RODGERS

# "Me And My Girl"

## LAMBETH WALK

Copyright © 1937 Richard Armitage Ltd.
Copyright Renewed
All Rights Managed in the United States by PolyGram International Publishing, Inc.

Words by DOUGLAS FURBER
Music by NOEL GAY

# LEANING ON A LAMP-POST

Copyright © 1937 Richard Armitage Ltd.
Copyright Renewed
All Rights Managed in the United States by PolyGram International Publishing, Inc.

Words and Music by
NOEL GAY

# LOVE MAKES THE WORLD GO ROUND

Copyright © 1937 Richard Armitage Ltd.
Copyright Renewed
All Rights Managed in the United States by PolyGram International Publishing, Inc.

Words and Music by
NOEL GAY

# ME AND MY GIRL

Copyright © 1937 Richard Armitage Ltd.
Copyright Renewed
All Rights Managed in the United States by PolyGram International Publishing, Inc.

Words by DOUGLAS FURBER
Music by NOEL GAY

# ONCE YOU LOSE YOUR HEART

Copyright © 1953 Richard Armitage Ltd.
Copyright Renewed
All Rights Managed in the United States by PolyGram International Publishing, Inc.

Words and Music by
NOEL GAY

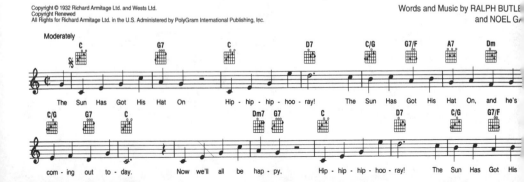

### THE SUN HAS GOT HIS HAT ON
#### (HE'S COMING OUT TODAY)

Copyright © 1932 Richard Armitage Ltd. and Wests Ltd.
Copyright Renewed
All Rights for Richard Armitage Ltd. in the U.S. Administered by PolyGram International Publishing, Inc.

Words and Music by RALPH BUTLER
and NOEL GAY

Hat On, and he's com-ing out to - day. He's been roast-ing pea-nuts out in Tim-buc-too

Now he's com-ing back to do the same for you. So jump in - to your sun-bath Hip-hip-hip-hoo -

ray! The Sun Has Got His Hat On, and he's com-ing out to - day. Joy bells are ring - ing, the

song birds are sing - ing, And ev-'ry-one's hap - py and gay. Dull days are o-

- ver, we'll soon be in clo - ver, So chase all your trou - bles a - way. The

All the lit - tle boys ex - cit - ed, All the lit - tle girls de - light - ed, What a lot of fun for

ev - ery - one, Sit - ting in the sun all day. skil - li - a - ta - da - da dit - ty bum! skil - li - a - ta - da - da

til - ly pum! What a lot of fun for ev - ery - one, sit - ting in the sun all day. So jump in - to your

sun - bath Hip - hip - hip - hoo - ray! The Sun Has Got His Hat On, and he's com - ing out to - day.

# "The Me Nobody Knows"

## BLACK

Copyright © 1970 by Alley Music Corp. and Trio Music Co., Inc.
All rights administered by Hudson Bay Music, Inc.
Used by Permission

Words by WILL HOL
Music by GARY WILLIAM FRIEDMA

# DREAM BABIES

Copyright © 1970 by Alley Music Corp. and Trio Music Co., Inc.
All rights administered by Hudson Bay Music, Inc.
Used by Permission

Lyric by HERB SCHAPIRO
Music by GARY WILLIAM FRIEDMAN

# LET ME COME IN

Copyright © 1970 by Alley Music Corp. and Trio Music Co., Inc.
All rights administered by Hudson Bay Music, Inc.
Used by Permission

Words by WILL HOLT
Music by GARY WILLIAM FRIEDMAN

# LIGHT SINGS

Copyright © 1970 by Alley Music Corp. and Trio Music Co., Inc.
All rights administered by Hudson Bay Music, Inc.
Used by Permission

Words by WILL HOL
Music by GARY WILLIAM FRIEDMA

# HOW I FEEL

Copyright © 1970 by Alley Music Corp. and Trio Music Co., Inc.
Rights administered by Hudson Bay Music, Inc.
Used by Permission

Words by WILL HOLT
Music by GARY WILLIAM FRIEDMAN

Plaintively

Hard to tell you How I Feel ____ Ev - 'ry - thing is so un - real __ Lord, but

life is a hard thing to get to ____ Saw my shad - ow on the wall ____

Saw my love no - where at all __ Saw my life as a hard thing to get through. ____

When you're born they car - ry you __ When you're gone they bur - y you __ In be - tween, __ you're on your own. __ Hard to stand __ there

all ____ a - lone. ____ Some - one's cry - ing down the hall ____ Dy - ing cries they tell it all,

Lord, this life is a hard thing to live ____ And hard - er still to leave. ____

## "Merlin"

### I CAN MAKE IT HAPPEN

Copyright © 1983 Dick James Music Ltd.
All Rights Administered by Songs Of PolyGram International Publishing, Inc.

Lyrics by DON BLAC
Music by ELMER BERNSTEI

## HE WHO KNOWS THE WAY

Copyright © 1983 Dick James Music Ltd.
All Rights Administered by Songs Of PolyGram International Publishing, Inc.

Lyrics by DON BLACK
Music by ELMER BERNSTEIN

# SATAN RULES

Copyright © 1983 Dick James Music Ltd.
All Rights Administered by Songs Of PolyGram International Publishing, Inc.

Lyrics by DON BLAC
Music by ELMER BERNSTE

**With a Fiery Driving Rhythm**

Gm  Ebmaj7  D7  Gm  Ebmaj7  Am7-5  Cm7

Sa - tan Rules,___ we both know it. You're a fool _ and I'll show it. All of your talk a - bout love and peace
You are wrong,___ I can prove it. Hate is strong,___ you can't move it. You can - not stop all the peo - ple's sins,
Sa - tan Rules,___ we both know it. You're a fool _ and I'll show it. While you are play - ing your ho - ly games,

D11  Ebmaj7  Gm

has - n't made kill - ing and hun - ger cease, not a bit!
seems ev - 'ry bat - tle the dev - il wins. Look at it!
mil - lion of souls will go down in flames, lov - ing it!

Cm6  Ebmaj7  Cm6  Ebmaj7  Cm6

Look at this world you ro - manc - ers, life is a curse for you danc - ers. Sa - tan gets

Ebmaj7  D7sus

all of the an - swers right. _____

Bb  C7  C11  Bb  C7

Right - eous is rub - bish, the good won't in - her - it much; kneel - ing and pray - ing won't save you at
Tri - umph's de - li - cious, I drool at the taste of it; sav - or - ing con - quest is what I love

Fmaj7 Cmaj9 Fmaj7 Cmaj9  Gm7  Am7  Gm7  Am7

all. This world could do with less dream - ers, fac - ing the truth is much hard - er. Come
best. Did - n't I say I could do it? Now the whole world bet - ter lis - ten. Come,

G  Bb  G  Bb  C  Am7  D

out of your twi - light shell. Face the world as it is, smile and say: "Hel - lo Hell!" _____
fol - low - ers, fol - low me. If you don't, then you won't ev - er know vic - to - ry! _____

To Coda

Cm7  Dm7  Cm7  Dm7  Am7-5

Don't hide your eyes from the fire ___ that's not the way that a fire ___ dies. ___
Don't ev - er doubt what I tell you, next time I swear I won't tell you

D7sus  D7  CODA  Am7-5  D7sus  D7

D.S. al Coda  twice. ___

Gm  Ebmaj7  D7sus  Gm  Ebmaj7  Am7-5  Cm7

Sa - tan Rules,___ look a - bout you. He will win ___ with or with - out you E - vil de - pends on which side you're on;

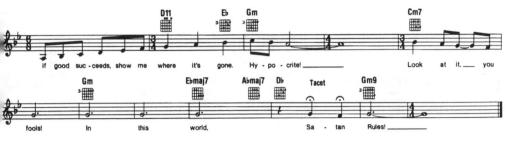

if good suc-ceeds, show me where it's gone. Hy-po-crite! _____ Look at it, _____ you

fools! In this world, Sa-tan Rules! _____

# BEYOND MY WILDEST DREAMS

Copyright © 1983 Dick James Music Ltd.
All Rights Administered by Songs Of PolyGram International Publishing, Inc.

Lyrics by DON BLACK
Music by ELMER BERNSTEIN

Be-yond My Wild-est Dreams, I can't be-lieve I'm here. I've nev-er been this far be-fore, I've

nev-er been this near. Feel as though I want to leap in-to the sky, I can't keep still. Feel so good I want to

soar, I think I will. _____ Be-yond My Wild-est Dreams, what-ev-er road I take, I

can't be-lieve I'm stand-ing here, I can't be-lieve that I'm a-wake. _____ Now I've tast-ed this

life, I don't_want to lose it. _____ If I could_choose one life, then I'd_choose to choose it. _____

This may be_my one chance and I_mean to use it. _____ Be-ware, _____ your world_now has me there. _____

_____ Be-yond My Wild-est Dreams, I'll make sure I stay free. He'll find me ir-re-sis-ta-ble. He's bound to fall in

love with me. _____

# SOMETHING MORE

Copyright © 1983 Dick James Music Ltd.
All Rights Administered by Songs Of PolyGram International Publishing, Inc.

Lyrics by DON BLACK
Music by ELMER BERNSTEIN

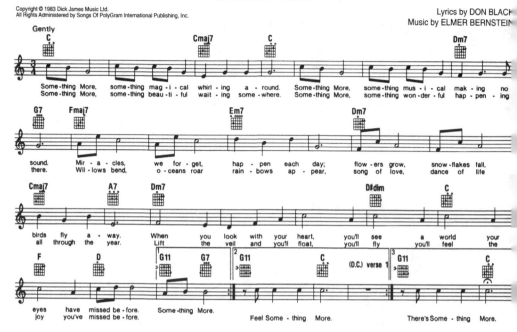

Gently

C / Cmaj7 / C / Dm7

Some-thing More, some-thing mag-i-cal whirl-ing a-round. Some-thing More, some-thing mus-i-cal mak-ing no
Some-thing More, some-thing beau-ti-ful wait-ing some-where. Some-thing More, some-thing won-der-ful hap-pen-ing

G7 / Fmaj7 / Em7 / Dm7

sound. Mir-a-cles, we for-get, hap-pen each day; flow-ers grow, snow-flakes fall,
there. Wil-lows bend, o-ceans roar rain-bows ap-pear, song of love, dance of life

Cmaj7 / A7 / Dm7 / D#dim / C

birds fly a-way. When you look with your heart, you'll see a world your
all through the year. Lift the veil and you'll float, you'll fly you'll feel the

F / D / G11 / G7 / G11 / C / (D.C.) verse 1 / G11 / C

eyes have missed be-fore. Some-thing More.
joy you've missed be-fore. Feel Some-thing More. There's Some-thing More.

# WE HAVEN'T FOUGHT A BATTLE IN YEARS

Copyright © 1983 Dick James Music Ltd.
All Rights Administered by Songs Of PolyGram International Publishing, Inc.

Lyrics by DON BLACK
Music by ELMER BERNSTEIN

Moderately

Cm / Cm7 / Bbmaj9 / Ab / Cmaj7

*Prince:* What a lot of luck-y men you are, it is bliss to die in a war. You've a lot to thank me for, so dig out your dag-gers and
pects to lose a limb or two, lots of blood is bound to be spilled. You'll be he-roes when you've killed, so march to your mak-er, my

F / G7sus / C Cm / C Cm Dm7-5

sharp-en your spears. We Have-n't Fought A Bat-tle In Years! One ex-
brave vol-un-teers. We Have-n't Fought A Bat-tle In Years! Con-quer-ing __ as you pull your bows

G7 / Cm

not a soul __ will be spared! Slit-ting throats __ of your wick-ed foes, *Men:* Oh my God, __ we're so scared! We'd pre

Cm7 / F / Ab / Cmaj7

fer to wipe the dun-geons sir, than to wipe the blood from our blades. *Prince:* Quick! Be-fore the foe in-vades. Be proud that I've chos-en you. Wha *Men:*

G11 / Cm7 / Bbmaj9 / Ab

*Prince:* harm did we ev-er do. Off you go, my val-iant men. *Men:* Don't think you'll see us a-gain. *Prince:* When you're breath-ing your last breath,

## "Merrily We Roll Along"

### GOOD THING GOING

© 1981 REVELATION MUSIC PUBLISHING CORP. & RILTING MUSIC, INC.
Tommy Valando Publication

Music and Lyric by
STEPHEN SONDHEIM

# NOT A DAY GOES BY

© 1981 REVELATION MUSIC PUBLISHING CORP. & RILTING MUSIC, INC.
A Tommy Valando Publication

Music and Lyric by
STEPHEN SONDHEIM

# "The Merry Widow"

## VILIA

Copyright © 1907 by Chappell & Co., Ltd.
Copyright renewed, published in the USA by Chappell & Co., Inc.

Music BY FRANZ LEHAR
Words by ADRIAN ROSS

"Vil - ia, O Vil - ia! the witch of the wood! Would I not die for you, dear, if I could! Vil - ia, O Vil - ia, my love and my bride!"

Soft - ly and sad - ly he sigh'd. __ "Vil - ia, O Vil - ia, the witch of the wood! Would I not die for you, dear, if I could! Vil - ia, O

Vil - ia, my love and my bride!" Soft - ly and sad - ly he sigh'd. __ sigh'd, Sad - ly he sigh'd, Vil - ia. ____

# "Mexican Hayride"

## I LOVE YOU

Copyright © 1943 Chappell & Co., Inc.
Copyright Renewed
International Copyright Secured    ALL RIGHTS RESERVED

Words & Music by
COLE PORTER

"I Love You" ___ Hums the A - pril breeze ___ "I Love You" ___ ech - o the

hills. ___ "I Love You" ___ the gold - en dawn a - grees ___ As once

more she sees daf - fo - dils ___ It's spring a - gain ___ And birds on the wing a - gain ___

start to sing a - gain ___ The old mel - o - die ___ "I Love You" ___ That's the

song of songs, ___ And it all be - longs to you and me. ___ "I me

And it all be - longs to __ you and me. ____

# "Milk And Honey"

## MILK AND HONEY

© 1961 JERRY HERMAN
All Rights Controlled by JERRYCO MUSIC CO.
Exclusive Agent EDWIN H. MORRIS & COMPANY, A Division of MPL Communications, Inc.

Lyric and Music by
JERRY HERMAN

This is the land of Milk And Hon-ey This is the land of sun and song, and This is a world of
What if the earth is dry and bar-ren What if the morn-ing sun is mean to us for This is a state of

good and plen-ty Hum-ble and proud and young and strong. and This is the place where the
mind we live in We want it green and so it's green to us for When you have won-der-ful

hopes of the home-less and the dreams of the lost com-bine This is the land that heav-en blessed and
plans for to-mor-row some-how e-ven to-day looks fine so what if it's rock and dust and sand, For

This love-ly land is mine
this love-ly land is mine
mine This love-ly land is mine

## SHALOM

© 1961 JERRY HERMAN
All Rights Throughout the World Controlled by JERRYCO MUSIC CO.
Exclusive Agent EDWIN H. MORRIS & COMPANY, A Division of MPL Communications, Inc.

Music and Lyric by
JERRY HERMAN

Sha - lom, The nic - est greet - ing I know; Sha - lom,

Means twice as much as hel - lo. It means a mil - lion love - ly things, like

peace be yours, wel - come home And e - ven when you say good - bye, If your voice has I don't want to

go in it, Say good-bye with a lit-tle "hel-lo" in it And say good - bye with Sha - lom.

# "Minnie's Boys"

## BE HAPPY

Copyright © 1969, 1970 by Alley Music Corp. and Trio Music Co., Inc.
All rights administered by Hudson Bay Music, Inc.
Used by Permission

Lyric by HAL HACKADY
Music by LARRY GROSSMAN

Life's a beau-ti-ful mess, but live and nev-er-the-less Be Hap - py!
Life's the bat of an eye, you're born, you live and you die, Be Hap - py!

Life is full of re-grets, but let's for-get 'em and let's Be Hap - py!
Look, you nev-er can tell, so while you're here, might as well Be Hap - py!

Life's a joke, but you know the laugh's on all of us, so Be Hap - py, hap - py.
If life is a mis-take, it's one we're all going to make, Be Hap - py, hap - py.

You can like it or not, a life - time's all that you got to live.
Life has lit - tle to spare so find your hap - pi - ness where you can.

## MAMA, A RAINBOW

Copyright © 1969, 1970 by Alley Music Corp. and Trio Music Co., Inc.
All rights administered by Hudson Bay Music, Inc.
Used by Permission

Lyric by HAL HACKADY
Music by LARRY GROSSMAN

Ma-ma, A Rain-bow, Ma-ma, a sun-rise, Ma-ma, the moon to wear. That's not good_ e-nough,
Ma-ma, a pal-ace, Dia-monds like door-knobs, Moun-tains of gold to spare. That's not rich_ e-nough,

No, not good_ e-nough, Not for Ma-ma. Ma-ma, a life-time, crowd-ed with laugh-ter,
No, not rich_ e-nough,

That's not long_ e-nough, Not half long_ e-nough. What can I give you that I can give you? What will your pres-ent be?

Ma-ma, young_ and beau-ti-ful, Al-ways young_ and beau-ti-ful, That's the Ma-ma

I'll al-ways see, That's for Ma-ma with love_ from me.

# "Miss Saigon"

## THE LAST NIGHT OF THE WORLD

Music and Lyrics Copyright © 1987 by Alain Boublil Music Ltd. (ASCAP)
English Lyrics Copyright © 1988 by Alain Boublil Music Ltd. (ASCAP)
Additional Music and English Lyrics Copyright © 1989 and 1991 by Alain Boublil Music Ltd. (ASCAP)
Mechanical and Publication Rights for the U.S.A. Administered by Alain Boublil Music Ltd. (ASCAP)
c/o Stephen Tenenbaum & Co., Inc., 605 Third Ave., New York, NY 10158
Tel. (212) 922-0625 Fax (212) 922-0626

Music by CLAUDE-MICHEL SCHÖNBERG
Lyrics by RICHARD MALTBY JR. and ALAIN BOUBLIL
Adapted from original French Lyrics by ALAIN BOUBLIL

# WHY GOD WHY?

Music and Lyrics Copyright © 1987 by Alain Boublil Music Ltd. (ASCAP)
English Lyrics Copyright © 1988 by Alain Boublil Music Ltd. (ASCAP)
Additional Music and English Lyrics Copyright © 1989 and 1991 by Alain Boublil Music Ltd. (ASCAP)
Mechanical and Publication Rights for the U.S.A. Administered by Alain Boublil Music Ltd. (ASCAP)
c/o Stephen Tenenbaum & Co., Inc., 605 Third Ave., New York, NY 10158
Tel. (212) 922-0625  Fax (212) 922-0626

Music by CLAUDE-MICHEL SCHÖNBERG
Lyrics by RICHARD MALTBY JR. and ALAIN BOUBLIL
Adapted from original French Lyrics by ALAIN BOUBLIL

When I went home be - fore ___ no one talked of the war. ___ What they knew from T. V. ___ did -n't have a thing to do with me. ___ I went back and re - upped. ___

___ Sure Sai - gon is cor - rupt. ___ It felt bet - ter to be ___ here driv - ing for the Em - bas - sy. ___

'Cause here ___ if you can pull a string a guy ___ like me lives like a king, just as long as you

don't be - lieve an - y - thing. Why, God?

Why this face? ___ Why such beau - ty in this place? ___ I liked my mem - 'ries as they were ___ but now i'll leave ___ re-mem-b'ring

her, just her. _____

# SUN AND MOON

Music and Lyrics Copyright © 1987 by Alain Boublil Music Ltd. (ASCAP)
English Lyrics Copyright © 1988 by Alain Boublil Music Ltd. (ASCAP)
Additional Music and English Lyrics Copyright © 1989 and 1991 by Alain Boublil Music Ltd. (ASCAP)
Mechanical and Publication Rights for the U.S.A. Administered by Alain Boublil Music Ltd. (ASCAP)
c/o Stephen Tenenbaum & Co., Inc., 605 Third Ave., New York, NY 10158
Tel. (212) 922-0625 Fax (212) 922-0626

Music by CLAUDE-MICHEL SCHÖNBERG
Lyrics by RICHARD MALTBY JR. and ALAIN BOUBLIL
Adapted from original French Lyrics by ALAIN BOUBLIL

# "Mr. Wonderful"

## MR. WONDERFUL

Copyright © 1956 by Herald Square Music, Inc.
Used by Permission

Words and Music by JERRY BOCK,
LARRY HOLOFCENER & GEORGE WEISS

# JACQUES D'IRAQUE

Copyright © 1956 by Herald Square Music, Inc.
Used by Permission

Words and Music by JERRY BOCK,
LARRY HOLOFCENER & GEORGE WEISS

# TOO CLOSE FOR COMFORT

Copyright © 1956 by Herald Square Music, Inc.
Used by Permission

Words and Music by JERRY BOCK,
LARRY HOLOFCENER & GEORGE WEISS

## "Music Box Revue Of 1924"

### WHAT'LL I DO?

© Copyright 1924 by Irving Berlin
© Arrangement Copyright 1947 by Irving Berlin
Copyright Renewed

Words and Music by
IRVING BERLIN

# "The Most Happy Fella"

## BIG D

© 1956 FRANK MUSIC CORP.

By FRANK LOESSER

## JOEY, JOEY, JOEY

© 1956 FRANK MUSIC CORP.

By FRANK LOESSER

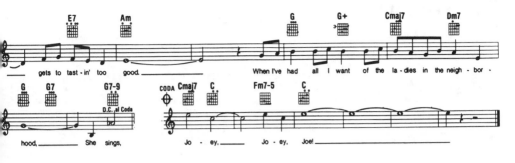

gets to tast-in' too good. _____ When I've had all I want of the la-dies in the neigh-bor-

hood, _____ She sings, _____ Jo-ey, _____ Jo-ey, Joe! _____

## STANDING ON THE CORNER

© 1956 FRANK MUSIC CORP.

By FRANK LOESSER

Stand-ing On The Corn-er watch-ing all the girls go by,
Stand-ing On The Corn-er
Stand-ing On The Corn-er
Stand-ing On The Corn-er

watch-ing all the girls go by
giv-ing all the girls the eye
un-der-neath a spring-time sky

Broth-er you don't know a nic-er oc-cu-pa-tion, Mat-ter of
Broth-er if you've got a rich i-mag-i-na-tion, give it a
Broth-er you can't go to jail for what you're think-ing, Or for the

fact    neith-er do I.    than
whirl,    give it a try.    Try    Stand-ing On The Corn-er watch-ing all the girls, watch-ing all the girls, watch-ing all the
"woooooo"    look in your eye.    You're only

1, To next strain; 2, To next strain    3

girls    go by. _____    by. _____    FINE    I'm the cat    that got the cream,
Sat-ur-day    and I'm so broke,

Have-n't got a girl, ___ But I can dream, Have-n't got a girl, ___ But I can wish, so I
Could-n't buy a girl, ___ a nick-el coke, Still I'm liv-ing like ___ A mil-lion-aire, when I

Last time
D.C. al Fine

take me down to Main Street And that's where I se-lect my i-mag-i-na-ry dish!
take me down to Main Street And I re-view the ha-rem pa-rad-ing for me here.

# "Music In The Air"

### THE SONG IS YOU

Copyright © 1932 PolyGram International Publishing, Inc.
Copyright Renewed

Lyrics by OSCAR HAMMERSTEIN II
Music by JEROME KERN

Meredith Willson's

# "The Music Man"

### SEVENTY SIX TROMBONES

© 1957 (Renewed) FRANK MUSIC CORP. and MEREDITH WILLSON MUSIC

By MEREDITH WILLSON

Thun-der-ing, thun-der-ing, all a-long the way. Dou-ble bell eu-pho-ni-ums and big bas-soons,
Thun-der-ing, thun-der-ing loud-er than be-fore Clar-i-nets of ev-'ry size and

Each bas-soon hav-ing his big fat say. There were trum-pet-ers who'd im-pro-vise a full oc-tave

high-er than the score. Sev-en-ty

Six Trom-bones led the big pa-rade, When the or-der to march rang out loud and clear. Start-ing off with a
Six Trom-bones hit the coun-ter-point, While a hun-dred and ten cor-nets played the air. Then I mod-est-ly

big bang bong on a Chi-nese gong, By a big bang bong-er at the rear. Sev-en-ty
took my place as the

one and on-ly bass, And I oom-pahed up and down the square.

## GOODNIGHT MY SOMEONE

© 1957 (Renewed) FRANK MUSIC CORP. and MEREDITH WILLSON MUSIC

Words and Music by
MEREDITH WILLSON

Good-night, My Some-one, Good-night, my love. Sleep tight, my some-one, sleep tight, my love. Our
dreams be yours, dear, if dreams there be: Sweet dreams to car-ry you close to me. I

star is shin-ing its bright-est light For good-night, my love for good-night. Sweet
wish they may and I wish they might. Now Good-

night, My Some-one, Good-night. good-night, good-night, good-night.

# LIDA ROSE

© 1957 (Renewed) FRANK MUSIC CORP. and MEREDITH WILLSON MUSIC

By MEREDITH WILLSON

Li - da Rose, I'm home a - gain, Rose,_ to get the sun back in my sky. Li - da Rose, I'm home a - gain, Rose_ a - bout a thou - sand kiss - es shy. Ding, dong, ding! I can hear the chap - el bell chime. Ding, dong, ding! At the least sug - ges - tion I'll pop the ques - tion. Li - da Rose, I'm home a - gain, Rose,_ without a sweet - heart to my name. Li - da Rose, now ev - 'ry - one knows. that I am hop - ing you're the same._ So here is my love song, Not fan - cy or fine, Li - da Rose, Oh won't you be mine!_____ mine!

# TILL THERE WAS YOU

© 1950, 1957 (Renewed) FRANK MUSIC CORP. and MEREDITH WILLSON MUSIC

By MEREDITH WILLSON

There were bells on the hill, but I nev - er heard them ring - ing, No, I nev - er heard them at all Till There Was birds in the sky, but I nev - er saw them wing - ing No I nev - er saw them at all Till There Was You._ There were You._ And there was mu - sic and there were won - der - ful ros - es, they tell me in sweet fra - grant mea - dows of dawn, and dew, There was love all a - round, but I nev - er heard it sing - ing, No, I nev - er heard it at all Till There Was You._

# YA GOT TROUBLE

© 1957, 1958, 1966 (Renewed) FRANK MUSIC CORP. and MEREDITH WILLSON MUSIC

Words and Music by
MEREDITH WILLSON

# THE WELLS FARGO WAGON

© 1957, 1959 (Renewed) FRANK MUSIC CORP. and MEREDITH WILLSON MUSIC

By MEREDITH WILLSON

Walking Horse Tempo

O-ho the Wells Far-go Wag-on is a - com-in' down the street, oh please let it be for me.____ O-ho the
Wells Far-go Wag-on is a - com-in' down the street, oh don't let him pass my door.____ O-ho the

Wells Far-go Wag-on is a - com-in' down the street, I wish, I wish I knew what it could be.____ I got some
Wells Far-go Wag-on is a - com-in' down the street, I wish I knew what he was com-in' for.____ I got some

box of ma-ple su-gar on my birth-day.____ In March I got a grey mack - i - naw. And
sal-mon from Se-at-tle last Sep-tem-ber.____ And I ex-pect a new rock - in' chair. I

once I got some grape-fruit from Tam-pa.____ Mont-gom-'ry Ward sent me a bath-tub and a cross-cut saw. O-ho, the
hope I get my rais-ins from Fres-no.____ The D. A. R. have sent a can-non for the court-house square. O-ho, the

Wells Far-go Wag-on is a - com-in' now. Is it a pre-paid sur-prise or C. O. D.? It could be
Wells Far-go Wag-on is a - com-in' now, I don't know how I can ev-er wait to see. It could be

cur-tains, or dish-es, or a dou-ble boil-er, Or it could be__some-thin' spe-cial just for me.____ O-ho the
some-thin' from some-one who is no re-la-tion, but it could be__some-thin' spe-cial just for

me.

*Whole song twice*

## "My Fair Lady"

### GET ME TO THE CHURCH ON TIME

Copyright © 1956 by Alan Jay Lerner & Frederick Loewe
Chappell & Co., Inc., owner of publication and allied rights throughout the World
International Copyright Secured    ALL RIGHTS RESERVED

Words by ALAN JAY LERNER
Music by FREDERICK LOEWE

Moderately Fast

I'm get - ting mar - ried in the morn - ing____ Ding! dong! the bells are gon - na
I got - ta be there in the morn - ing____ Spruced up and look - ing in my

chime.____ Pull out the stop - per; Let's have a whop - per; But Get Me To The
prime.____ Girls, come and kiss me; Show how you'll miss me, But Get Me To The

**I'VE GROWN ACCUSTOMED TO HER FACE**

Copyright © 1956 by Alan Jay Lerner & Frederick Loewe
Chappell & Co., Inc., owner of publication and allied rights throughout the world
International Copyright Secured   ALL RIGHTS RESERVED

Words by ALAN JAY LERNER
Music by FREDERICK LOEWE

# I COULD HAVE DANCED ALL NIGHT

Copyright © 1956 by Alan Jay Lerner & Frederick Loewe
Chappell & Co., Inc, owner of publication and allied rights throughout the World
International Copyright Secured    ALL RIGHTS RESERVED

Words by ALAN JAY LERNER
Music by FREDERICK LOEWE

Lyrics:
I Could Have Danced ___ All Night! ___ I Could Have Danced ___ All Night! ___ And still ___ have begged ___ for more. ___ I could have spread ___ my wings ___ And done a thou - sand things ___ I've nev - er done be - fore. ___ I'll never know ___ what made it so ___ ex - cit - ing, ___ Why all at once ___ my heart took flight. ___ I on - ly know ___ when he ___ be - gan to dance ___ with me, ___ I could have danced, danced, danced, ___ All night. ___

# JUST YOU WAIT

Copyright © 1956 by Alan Jay Lerner & Frederick Loewe
Chappell & Co., Inc, owner of publication and allied rights throughout the world

Words by ALAN JAY LERNER
Music by FREDERICK LOEWE

Lyrics:
Just You Wait, 'en - ry 'ig - gins, Just You Wait! ___ You'll be sor - ry, but your tears - 'll be too late! ___ You'll be broke and I'll have mon - ey; Will I help you? Don't be fun - ny! Just You Wait, 'en - ry 'ig - gins, Just You Wait! ___ Just You Wait, 'en - ry 'ig - gins, till you're

# THE RAIN IN SPAIN

Copyright © 1956 by Alan Jay Lerner & Frederick Loewe
Chappell & Co., Inc., owner of publication and allied rights throughout the World
International Copyright Secured    ALL RIGHTS RESERVED

Words by ALAN JAY LERNER
Music by FREDERICK LOEWE

The Rain In Spain stays main - ly in the plain! ___ The Rain In Spain stays main - ly in the plain! ___

Now once a - gain, where does it rain? ___ On the plain! On the plain! And where's that blast - ed plain? ___ In Spain! In

Spain! ___ The Rain In Spain stays main - ly in the plain! ___ The rain In Spain stays main - ly in the plain! ___

# WITH A LITTLE BIT OF LUCK

Copyright © 1956 by Alan Jay Lerner & Frederick Loewe
Chappell & Co., Inc., owner of publication and allied rights throughout the World
International Copyright Secured    ALL RIGHTS RESERVED

Words by ALAN JAY LERNER
Music by FREDERICK LOEWE

The Lord a - bove gave man an arm of i - ron ___ So he could do his job and ne - ver shirk. ___ The Lord a - bove gave
bove made man to help his neigh - bor ___ No mat - ter where, on land or sea and foam. ___ The Lord a - bove made

man an arm of i - ron.) But    With A Lit - tle Bit Of Luck, With A Lit - tle Bit Of Luck, {Some - one else - 'll do the
man to help his neigh - bor.}                                                              {When he comes a - round you

blink - in' work. ___ With a lit - tle bit, With a lit - tle bit, With A Lit - tle Bit Of Luck you'll nev - er work.
won't be home. ___                                                                             you won't be home.

The Lord a -    Oh, you can walk the straight and nar - row, ___ But With A Lit - tle Bit Of Luck you'll run a - mok.    The gen - tle

sex was made for man to mar - ry; ___ To tend his needs and see his food is cooked. ___ The gen - tle sex was

made for man to mar - ry, But    With A Lit - tle Bit Of Luck, With A Lit - tle Bit Of Luck, You can

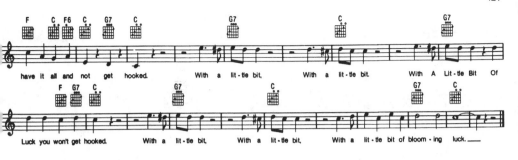

have it all and not get hooked. With a lit-tle bit, With a lit-tle bit. With A Lit-tle Bit Of

Luck you won't get hooked. With a lit-tle bit, With a lit-tle bit, With a lit-tle bit of bloom-ing luck. ___

## WITHOUT YOU

Copyright © 1956 by Alan Jay Lerner & Frederick Loewe
Chappell & Co., Inc., owner of publication and allied rights throughout the World

Lyrics by ALAN JAY LERNER
Music by FREDERICK LOEWE

There'll be spring ev-'ry year with-out you. Eng-land still will be here with-out you. There'll be fruit on the tree; And a
mu-sic will thrive with-out you. Some-how Keats will sur-vive with-out you. And there still will be rain on that

shore by the sea; There'll be crum-pets and tea with-out you. Art and
plain down in Spain, E-ven that will re-main with-out you. I can do ___ with-out you.

You, dear friend, who talk so well, You can go to Hart-ford, Her-es-ford and Hamp-shire.___ They can

still rule the land With-out You.___ Wind-sor Cas-tle will stand With-out You.___ And with-out much a-do We can all mud-dle through With-out

You. With-out You pull-ing it, the tide comes in; With-out your twirl-ing it, the earth can spin. With-

out your push-ing them the clouds roll by. If they can do With-out You, duck-y, so can I! I shall not feel a-lone With-out You. I can

stand on my own With-out You.___ So go back in your shell. I can do blood-y well With-out You!___

# WHY CAN'T THE ENGLISH?

Copyright © 1956 by Alan Jay Lerner & Frederick Loewe
Chappell & Co., Inc., owner of publication and allied rights throughout the world

Words by ALAN JAY LERNER
Music by FREDERICK LOEWE

**Moderately Fast**

Look at her, a pris-'ner of the gut-ters; con-demned by ev-'ry syl-la-ble she ut-ters. By right she should be tak-en out and

hung *Spoken:* For the cold blooded murder of the english tongue! *Sung:* This is what the Brit-ish pop-u-la-tion calls an el-e-men-t'ry ed-u-ca-tion.

Hear them down in So-ho Square, drop-ping aitch-es ev-'ry-where, speak-ing En-glish an-y way they like. _ You, Sir, did you go to school?

What-ya tike me fer, a fool? No one taught him "take" in-stead of "tike". _ Hear a York-shire-man, or worse, hear a Cor-nish-man con-verse. I'd

rath-er hear a cho-ir sing-ing flat! Chick-ens cack-ling in a barn, just like this one. It's "Aooow" and "Garn" that keep her in her

place, _ not her wretch-ed clothes and dirt-y face. Why Can't The En-glish teach their chil-dren how to speak? This ver-bal class dis-

tinc-tion by now should be an-tique. If you spoke as she does, Sir, in-stead of the way you do, why you might be sell-ing flow-ers too. An

En-glish-man's way of speak-ing ab-so-lute-ly clas-si-fies him. The mo-ment he talks he makes some oth-er En-glish-man de-

spise him. One com-mon lan-guage, I'm a-fraid we'll nev-er get. Oh, Why Can't The En-glish learn

to set a good ex-am-ple to peo-ple whose En-glish is pain-ful to your ears? _ The

Scotch and the I-rish leave you close to tears. _ There e-ven are plac-es where En-glish com-plete-ly dis-ap

pears. \_\_\_ Why Can't The En-glish, teach their chil-dren how to speak? Nor-we-gians learn Nor-we-gian; the Greeks are taught their Greek. In France ev-'ry French-man knows his lan-guage from "A" to "Zed". A- ra-bi- ans learn A- ra-bian with the speed of sum-mer light-ning; the He-brews learn it back-wards, which is ab-so-lute-ly fright-'ning. But use prop- er En- glish, You're re-gard-ed as a freak. Why Can't The En- glish, Why Can't The En- glish learn to speak?

## WOULDN'T IT BE LOVERLY

Copyright © 1956 by Alan Jay Lerner & Frederick Loewe
Chappell & Co., Inc, owner of publication and allied rights throughout the World
International Copyright Secured    ALL RIGHTS RESERVED

Words by ALAN JAY LERNER
Music by FREDERICK LOEWE

All I want is a room some-where, Far a-way from the cold night air, With one e- nor-mous chair; Oh, Would -n't It Be Lov- er-ly? Lots of choc'- late for me to eat; Lots of coal mak- in' lots of heat; Warm face, warm hands, warm feet, Oh, Would -n't It Be Lov- er-ly? Oh, so lov- er-ly sit- tin' ab-so-bloom- in'-lute- ly still! I would nev-er budge 'til spring crept o- ver the win-dow sill. Some-one's head rest- in' on my knee; Warm and ten-der as he can be; Who takes good care of me. Oh, Would -n't It Be Lov- er-ly? Lov- er-ly! Lov- er-ly! Lov- er-ly! Lov- er-ly! \_\_\_

# ON THE STREET WHERE YOU LIVE

Copyright © 1956 by Alan Jay Lerner & Frederick Loewe
Chappell & Co., Inc., owner of publication and allied rights throughout the world
International Copyright Secured    ALL RIGHTS RESERVED

Words by ALAN JAY LERNER
Music by FREDERICK LOEWE

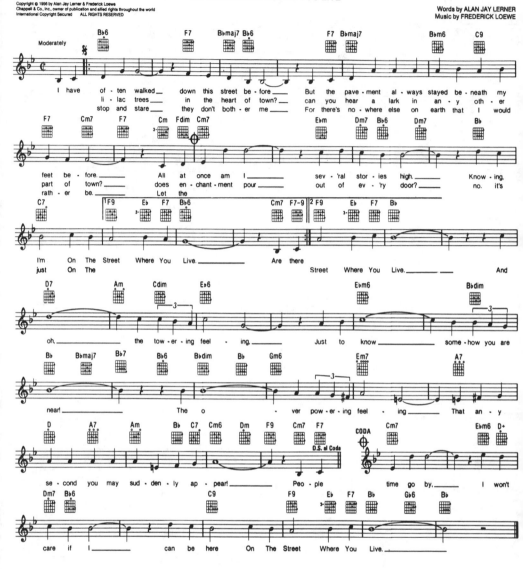

I have of-ten walked down this street be-fore But the pave-ment al-ways stayed be-neath my
li-lac trees in the heart of town? can you hear a lark in an-y oth-er
stop and stare they don't both-er me For there's no-where else on earth that I would

feet be-fore. All at once am I sev-'ral stor-ies high. Know-ing,
part of town? does en-chant-ment pour out of ev-'ry door? no, it's
rath-er be. Let the

I'm On The Street Where You Live. Are there
just On The Street Where You Live. And

oh, the tow-er-ing feel-ing. Just to know some-how you are

near! The o-ver-pow-er-ing feel-ing That an-y

se-cond you may sud-den-ly ap-pear! Peo-ple time go by, I won't

care if I can be here On The Street Where You Live.

# SHOW ME

Copyright © 1956 by Alan Jay Lerner & Frederick Loewe
Chappell & Co., Inc., owner of publication and allied rights throughout the World
International Copyright Secured    ALL RIGHTS RESERVED

Words by ALAN JAY LERNER
Music by FREDERICK LOEWE

Don't talk of stars burn-ing a-bove. If you're in love, Show Me! Tell me no dreams

filled with de-sire. If you're on fire, Show Me! Here we are to-geth-er in the mid-dle of the

night! Don't talk of spring! Just hold me tight!____ An-y-one who's ev-er been in love 'll tell you

that this is no time for a chat!____ Have-n't your lips longed for my touch?

Don't say how much; Show Me!____ Show Me!____ Don't talk of love last-ing through time.

Make me no un-dy-ing vow.____ Show _____ Me now! _____

## "New Faces Of 1936"

### YOU BETTER GO NOW

Copyright © 1936 by Chappell & Co., Inc.
Copyright Renewed
International Copyright Secured   ALL RIGHTS RESERVED

Words by BICKLEY REICHNER
Music by ROBERT GRAHAM

Slowly

You Bet-ter Go Now,____ Be-cause I like you much too much, You have a way with you.____ You ought to

know now,____ Just why I like you ver-y much. The night was gay with you.____ There's the moon a-

bove And it gives my heart a lot of swing. In your eyes there's love,

And the way I feel it must be spring. I want you so now.____ You have the lips I love to touch; You Bet-ter

Go Now,____ You bet-ter go, be-cause I like you much too much.____

# "The Nervous Set"

## THE BALLAD OF THE SAD YOUNG MEN

Copyright © 1959 by FRANK MUSIC CORP.
Copyright Reassigned to WOLFLAND, 7949 Belton Dr., Los Angeles, CA 90045

Lyric by FRAN LANDESMAN
Music by TOMMY WOLF

# "Nine"

## GETTING TALL

Copyright © 1962, 1983 by Yeston Music, Ltd. (BMI)
Worldwide rights administered by Cherry River Music (BMI)

Lyrics and Music by
MAURY YESTON

Scrap-ing knees, ty-ing shoes, start-ing school, pay-ing dues, find-ing there's no way we can spend a life-time play-ing ball part of Get-ting Tall. Learn-ing more, know-ing less, sim-ple words, ten-der-ness part of Get-ting Tall. Gui-do, you're not cra-zy, you're all right. Ev-'ry-one wants ev-'ry-one in sight... But, know-ing you have no one if you try to have them all is part of ty-ing shoes, part of start-ing school, part of scrap-ing knees if we should fall part of Get-ting Tall.

# SIMPLE

Copyright © 1982 by Yeston Music, Ltd. (BMI)
Worldwide rights administered by Cherry River Music (BMI)

Lyrics and Music by
MAURY YESTON

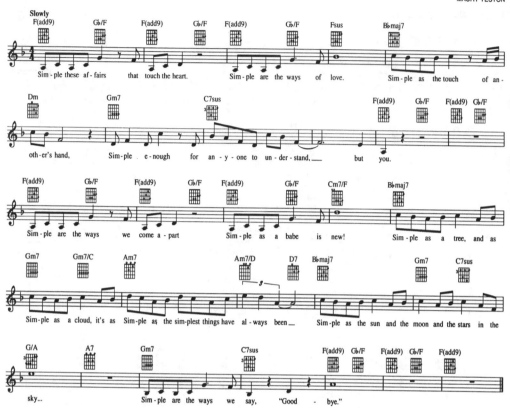

Sim - ple these af - fairs that touch the heart. Sim - ple are the ways of love. Sim - ple as the touch of an -

oth - er's hand, Sim - ple e - nough for an - y - one to un - der - stand, ___ but you.

Sim - ple are the ways we come a - part Sim - ple as a babe is new! Sim - ple as a tree, and as

Sim - ple as a cloud, it's as Sim - ple as the sim - plest things have al - ways been ___ Sim - ple as the sun and the moon and the stars in the

sky... Sim - ple are the ways we say, "Good - bye."

# UNUSUAL WAY
## (IN A VERY UNUSUAL WAY)

Copyright © 1982 by Yeston Music, Ltd.
Worldwide rights administered by Cherry River Music (BMI)

Lyrics and Music by
MAURY YESTON

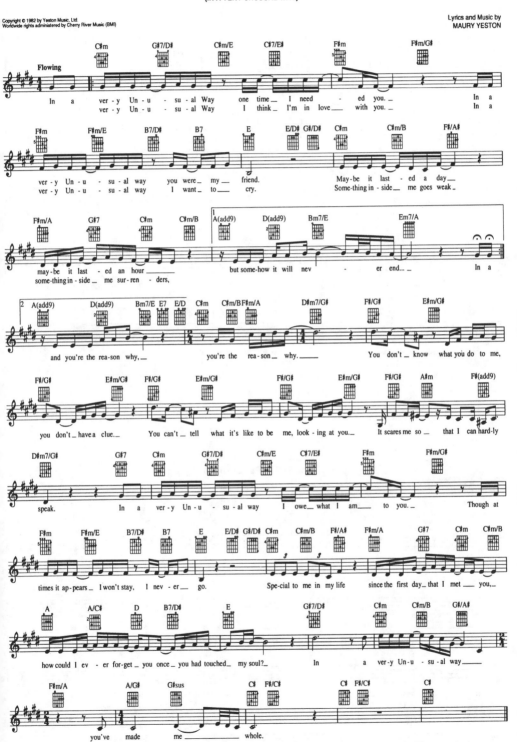

"No Strings"

# NO STRINGS

Copyright © 1962 by RICHARD RODGERS
Williamson Music Co., owner of publication and allied rights for all countries of the Western Hemisphere and Japan.
International Copyright Secured    ALL RIGHTS RESERVED

Music and Lyrics by
RICHARD RODGERS

# THE SWEETEST SOUNDS

Copyright © 1962 by RICHARD RODGERS
Williamson Music Co., owner of publication and allied rights for all countries of the Western Hemisphere and Japan.
International Copyright Secured    ALL RIGHTS RESERVED

Words and Music by
RICHARD RODGERS

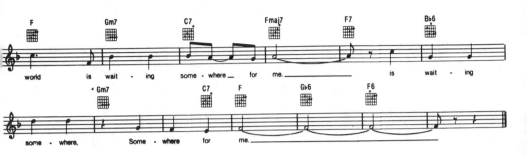

| F | Gm7 | C7 | Fmaj7 | F7 | Bb6 |
|---|---|---|---|---|---|

world      is   wait - ing   some - where __ for   me. _____ is   wait - ing

| Gm7 | C7 | F | Gb6 | F6 |
|---|---|---|---|---|

some - where,    Some - where   for   me. _____

## "Oh Boy!"

### TILL THE CLOUDS ROLL BY

Copyright © 1994 by HAL LEONARD CORPORATION

Words by P.G. WODEHOUSE
Music by JEROME KERN

**Moderately**

Eb    Bb7      Eb       Bb7

Oh, the   rain _____ comes a pit - ter,   pat - ter, _____ And I'd   like _____ to be safe in

Eb     Eb7   Ab      Bb9   Eb      Fm

bed. _____ Skies are weep - ing, _____ while the world is   sleep - ing, _____ Trou-ble heap - ing   on

F9    Bb7       Eb    Bb7       Eb

our   head. _____ It   is   vain _____ to re-main and chat - ter, _____ And to

Bb7      Eb       Eb7   Ab      Bb9    Eb   Bbm/Db

wait _____ for a clear - er   sky, _____ Hel - ter   skel - ter _____ I must fly for shel - ter ____

C7      Fm9      Bb7      | 1. Eb     Bb7     | 2. Eb

__ Till   The   Clouds    Roll     By.      Oh, the   By.

# "Oklahoma!"

## ALL ER NOTHIN'

Copyright © 1943 by WILLIAMSON MUSIC
Copyright Renewed

Lyrics by OSCAR HAMMERSTEIN II
Music by RICHARD RODGERS

## I CAIN'T SAY NO!

Copyright © 1943 by Williamson Music Co. Copyright Renewed.
International Copyright Secured    ALL RIGHTS RESERVED

Words by OSCAR HAMMERSTEIN II
Music by RICHARD RODGERS

**OUT OF MY DREAMS**

Copyright © 1943 by WILLIAMSON MUSIC
Copyright Renewed

Lyrics by OSCAR HAMMERSTEIN II
Music by RICHARD RODGERS

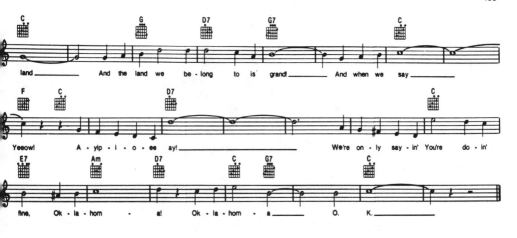

land _____ And the land we be-long to is grand! _____ And when we say _____

Yeeow! A - yip - i - o - ee ay! _____ We're on - ly say - in' You're do - in'

fine, Ok - la - hom - a! Ok - la - hom - a _____ O. K. _____

## PEOPLE WILL SAY WE'RE IN LOVE

Copyright © 1943 by WILLIAMSON MUSIC
Copyright Renewed

Lyrics by OSCAR HAMMERSTEIN II
Music by RICHARD RODGERS

Don't throw _____ bou - quets at me, _____ Don't please _____ my folks too much. _____

Don't laugh _____ at my jokes too much, _____ Peo - ple Will Say We're In

Love! _____ Don't sigh _____ and gaze at me, _____ Your sighs _____

_____ are so like mine. _____ Your eyes _____ must - n't glow like mine, _____

Peo - ple Will Say We're In Love! _____ Don't start _____ col - lect - ing things,

Give me my rose and my glove. _____ Sweet - heart, _____ they're sus -

-pect - ing things. _____ Peo - ple Will Say We're In Love. _____

# MANY A NEW DAY

Copyright © 1943 by WILLIAMSON MUSIC
Copyright Renewed

Lyrics by OSCAR HAMMERSTEIN II
Music by RICHARD RODGERS

# OH, WHAT A BEAUTIFUL MORNIN'

Copyright © 1943 by WILLIAMSON MUSIC
Copyright Renewed

Lyrics by OSCAR HAMMERSTEIN II
Music by RICHARD RODGERS

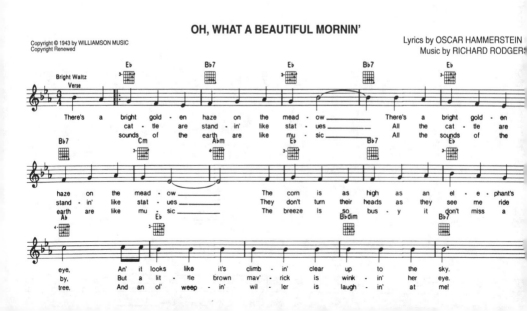

## THE SURREY WITH THE FRINGE ON TOP

Copyright © 1943 by WILLIAMSON MUSIC
Copyright Renewed

Lyrics by OSCAR HAMMERSTEIN II
Music by RICHARD RODGERS

# THE FARMER AND THE COWMAN

Lyrics by OSCAR HAMMERSTEIN II
Music by RICHARD RODGERS

Copyright © 1943 by WILLIAMSON MUSIC
Copyright Renewed

**Brightly**

The Farm-er And The Cow-man should be friends,_ Oh, The Farm-er And The Cow-man should be friends. _ One man likes to
Farm-er And The Cow-man should be friends,_ Oh, The Farm-er And The Cow-man should be friends. _ The cow-man ropes a

push a plough, the oth-er likes to chase a cow, But that's no rea-son why they cain't be friends._ Ter-ri-to-ry folks should stick to-geth-er,
cow with ease, the farm-er steals her but-ter and cheese, But that's no rea-son why they cain't be friends._ Ter-ri-to-ry folks should stick to-geth-er,

Ter-ri-to-ry folks should all be pals. Cow-boys dance with the farm-ers' daugh-ters, Farm-ers dance with the ranch-ers gals. _
Ter-ri-to-ry folks should all be pals. Cow-boys dance with the farm-ers' daugh-ters, Farm-ers dance with the ranch-ers gals. _

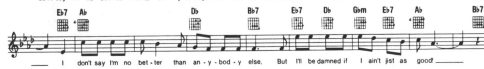

I'd like to say a word for the farm-er, _ He come out west and made a lot of chang-es _ He
I'd like to teach you all a lit-tle say-in' _ And learn the words by heart the way you should _ I

come out west and built a lot of fenc-es, _ And built 'em right a-crost our cat-tle rang-es. _ The
don't say I'm no bet-ter than_ an-y-bod-y else. But I'll be damned if I ain't just as good!

_ I don't say I'm no bet-ter than an-y-bod-y else. But I'll be damned if I ain't jist as good! _

Ter-ri-to-ry folks should stick to-geth-er, Ter-ri-to-ry folks should all be pals, Cow-boys dance with the farm-ers' daugh-ters, Farm-ers dance with the ranch-ers gals!

**"Oliver!"**

## I'D DO ANYTHING

Copyright 1960 Lakeview Music Co. Ltd., London, England
RO - HOLLIS MUSIC, INC., New York, controls all publication rights for the U.S.A., Canada and South America

Words & Music by
LIONEL BART

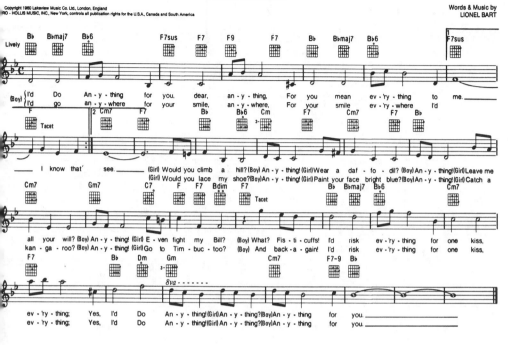

## WHERE IS LOVE?

Copyright 1960 Lakeview Music Co. Ltd., London, England
O - HOLLIS MUSIC, INC., New York, controls all publication rights for the U.S.A., Canada and South America

Words & Music by
LIONEL BART

# AS LONG AS HE NEEDS ME

© Copyright 1980 Lakeview Music Co. Ltd., London, England
TRO - HOLLIS MUSIC, INC., New York, controls all publication rights for the U.S.A., Canada and South America

Words & Music by
LIONEL BART

Lyrics:
As Long As He Needs Me I know where I must be. I'll cling on stead-fast-ly, As Long As He Needs Me. As long as life is long, I'll love him, right or wrong; And some-how I'll be strong As long As He Needs Me. If you are lone-ly then you will know When some-one needs you 'you love them so. I won't be-tray his trust, Tho' peo-ple say I must. I've got to stay true, just As Long As He Needs Me. As Long As He Needs Me.

(whole song)
2 twice

# CONSIDER YOURSELF

© Copyright 1980 Lakeview Music Co. Ltd., London, England
TRO - HOLLIS MUSIC, INC., New York, controls all publication rights for the U.S.A., Canada and South America

Words & Music by
LIONEL BART

Lyrics:
Con-sid-er Your-self at home, Con-sid-er Your-self one of the
Con-sid-er Your-self well in: Con-sid-er your-self part of the
fam-i-ly We've tak-en to you so strong, It's who
fur-ni-ture There is-n't a lot to spare; who
clear we're go-ing to get a-long! Con- share! If it should chance to be
cares? What ev-er we've got we
we should see some hard-er days, Emp-ty lard-er days, why grouse?

**WHO WILL BUY?**

Copyright 1960 and 1968, Lakeview Music Co. Ltd., London, England
— HOLLIS MUSIC, INC., New York, controls all publication rights for the U.S.A., Canada and South America

Words & Music by
LIONEL BART

# "On A Clear Day You Can See Forever"

**WHAT DID I HAVE THAT I DON'T HAVE?**

Copyright © 1965 by Alan Jay Lerner & Frederick Loewe
ppell & Co., Inc., owner of publication and allied rights throughout the World
rnational Copyright Secured   ALL RIGHTS RESERVED

Words by ALAN JAY LERNER
Music by BURTON LANE

Slowly

# "On Your Toes"

## SLAUGHTER ON TENTH AVENUE

Copyright © 1936 by Chappell & Co.
Copyright Renewed
The interest of Richard Rodgers for the extended term of copyright assigned to the
Rodgers Family Partnership (Administered by Williamson Music)

By RICHARD RODGERS

Copyright © 1936 by Chappell & Co.
Copyright Renewed
The interest of Richard Rodgers for the extended term of copyright assigned to the
Rodgers Family Partnership (Administered by Williamson Music)
Rights on behalf of The Estate Of Lorenz Hart administered by WB Music Corp.

## ON YOUR TOES

Words by LORENZ HART
Music by RICHARD RODGERS

See the pret - ty ap - ple top of the tree!_ The high - er up the sweet - er it grows. Pick - ing fruit you've
See the pret - ty pent -house top of the roof!_ The high - er up the high - er rent goes. Get that dough, don't

got to be __ up On Your Toes.
be a goof _ up On Your Toes, they climb the clouds, _____ To come through with

air - mail. _____ The danc - ing crowds _____ Look up to some rare male, like that A - staire male,

See the pret - ty la - dy, top of the crop!_ You want to know the way the wind blows! Then, my boy, you'd

bet - ter hop _ up On Your Toes, up On Your Toes! _____

## QUIET NIGHT

Copyright © 1936 by Chappell & Co.
Copyright Renewed
The interest of Richard Rodgers for the extended term of copyright assigned to the
Rodgers Family Partnership (Administered by Williamson Music)
Rights on behalf of The Estate Of Lorenz Hart administered by WB Music Corp.

Words by LORENZ HART
Music by RICHARD RODGERS

Qui - et Night, and all a - round the calm and balm - y weath - er.

_____ Qui - et Night, no oth - er sound but hearts that beat to -

geth - er. _____ You can al - most hear the things I'm think - ing, _____ You can al - most see my

heart take flight. _____ Whis - per low, but don't say

no, It's such a Qui - et Night! Night! _____

# GLAD TO BE UNHAPPY

Copyright © 1936 by Chappell & Co.
Copyright Renewed
...e interest of Richard Rodgers for the extended term of copyright assigned to the
...odgers Family Partnership (Administered by Williamson Music)
...ts on behalf of The Estate of Lorenz Hart administered by WB Music Corp.

Words by LORENZ HART
Music by RICHARD RODGERS

Gracefully

Fools rush in, so here I am Ver-y Glad To Be Un-hap-py;___ I can't win, but here I am,

More than Glad To Be Un-hap-py. ___ Un-re-qui-ted love's a bore. And I've got it pret-ty bad,

But for some-one you a-dore, It's a pleas-ure to be sad. Like a stray-ing ba-by lamb, With no mam-my and no

pap-py. ___ I'm so un-hap-py. ___ But oh, so glad! glad! ___

# THERE'S A SMALL HOTEL

Copyright © 1936 by Chappell & Co.
Copyright Renewed
...e interest of Richard Rodgers for the extended term of copyright assigned to the
...odgers Family Partnership (Administered by Williamson Music)
...ts on behalf of The Estate of Lorenz Hart administered by WB Music Corp.

Words by LORENZ HART
Music by RICHARD RODGERS

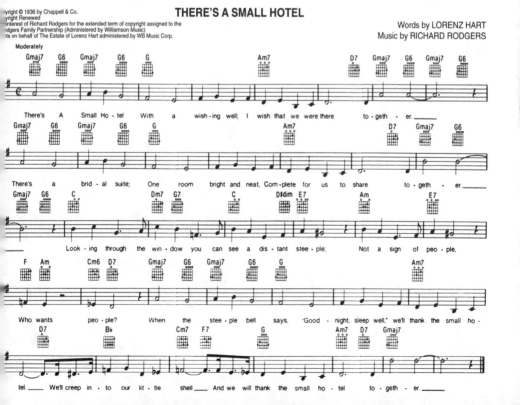

Moderately

There's A Small Ho-tel With a wish-ing well; I wish that we were there to-geth-er.

There's a brid-al suite; One room bright and neat, Com-plete for us to share to-geth-er. ___

___ Look-ing through the win-dow you can see a dis-tant stee-ple; Not a sign of peo-ple,

Who wants peo-ple? When the stee-ple bell says, "Good-night, sleep well," we'll thank the small ho-

tel. ___ We'll creep in-to our lit-tle shell ___ And we will thank the small ho-tel to-geth-er. ___

# "110 In The Shade"

## SIMPLE LITTLE THINGS

Words by TOM JONES
Music by HARVEY SCHMIDT

Copyright © 1963 by Tom Jones and Harvey Schmidt
Copyright Renewed
Portfolio Music, Inc., owner, and Chappell & Co., administrator, of publication and
allied rights throughout the world

# "One Mo' Time"

## MY MAN BLUES

Words and Music
BESSIE SMI

© 1926, 1974 FRANK MUSIC CORP.
© Renewed 1954 FRANK MUSIC CORP.

## AFTER YOU'VE GONE

© 1918 EDWIN H. MORRIS & COMPANY, A Division of MPL Communications, Inc.
© Renewed 1946 MORLEY MUSIC CO.

By CREAMER & LAYTON

# "One Touch Of Venus"

## SPEAK LOW

Words by OGDEN NASH
Music by KURT WEILL

TRO © Copyright 1943 and renewed 1971 HAMPSHIRE HOUSE PUBLISHING CORP. & CHAPPELL & CO., INC., New York, N.Y.

# "Out Of This World"

### FROM THIS MOMENT ON

Copyright © 1950 by Cole Porter
Copyright Renewed, Assigned to John F. Wharton, Trustee of the Cole Porter Musical & Literary Property Trusts
Chappell & Co., Inc., owner of publication and allied rights throughout the World.
International Copyright Secured    ALL RIGHTS RESERVED

Words & Music by
COLE PORTER

# I AM LOVED

Copyright © 1950 by Cole Porter
Copyright renewed, assigned to Robert H. Montgomery, Trustee of the Cole Porter Musical and Literary Property Trusts
Chappell & Co., Inc., Publisher

Words and Music by
COLE PORTER

# CHERRY PIES OUGHT TO BE YOU

Copyright © 1950 by Cole Porter
Copyright renewed, assigned to Robert H. Montgomery, Trustee of the Cole Porter Musical and Literary Property Trusts
Chappell & Co., Inc., Publisher

Words and Music by
COLE PORTER

Chords: Am, D9, Gm, D7, Gm, Gm7, C7

You are just the ic-ing to put on my cake,

start-ing to shake. To con-tin-ue,

Chords: F, Gm7, C7, F, Gm7, C7, F

Heav-en too ought to be you,

Heav-en's blue ought to be you, Ev-'ry-thing su-per-do

Chords: G7, C7, F, F7, Bb, Bbm6, F, Fdim, Bbm6

Ought to be you, Ought to be you, Ought to be you.

ought to be you, Ought to be you, Ought to be you.

Chords: F, Fdim, Gm7, C7, [1. F, Gm7, C7], [2. F]

Ought to be you, Ought to be you! you!

Ought to be you, Ought to be you! you!

## "Over Here!"

### THE BIG BEAT

Copyright © 1974 by Alley Music Corp. and Trio Music Co., Inc. and Sherbro Music Co.
All rights administered by Hudson Bay Music, Inc.
Used by Permission

Words and Music by
RICHARD M. SHERMAN & ROBERT B. SHERMAN

Moderate Swing

Chords: C, G7

The Big Beat goes stomp-in' on __ Dig the cra-zy rhy-thm and your cares are gone__ The Big Beat Keeps

Beat is loud and strong__ Dig the cra-zy rhy-thm as you move a-long__ The Big Beat

Chords: Ab9, G9, [1. Ab9, G7sus, C, G7+5], [2. Ab9, G7sus, C]

romp-in' on __ All a-round the U. S. A __ The Big

All a-round the U. S. A __

# MY DREAM FOR TOMORROW

Copyright © 1974 by Alley Music Corp. and Trio Music Co., Inc. and Sherbro Music Co.
All rights administered by Hudson Bay Music, Inc.
Used by Permission

Words and Music by
RICHARD M. SHERMAN & ROBERT B. SHERMAN

**CHARLIE'S PLACE**

Copyright © 1974 by Alley Music Corp. and Trio Music Co., Inc. and Sherbro Music Co.
All rights administered by Hudson Bay Music, Inc.
Used by Permission

Words and Music by
RICHARD M. SHERMAN & ROBERT B. SHERMAN

# OVER HERE!

Copyright © 1974 by Alley Music Corp. and Trio Music Co., Inc. and Sherbro Music Co.
All rights administered by Hudson Bay Music, Inc.
Used by Permission

Words and Music by
RICHARD M. SHERMAN & ROBERT B. SHERMAN

'Cause O-ver Here (toot toot-tle-ee-toot)__ we'll do the thing that we start-ed to do. ___ 'Cause O-ver
Here (toot toot-tle-ee toot)__ we'll do the thing that we start-ed to do. ___ Right O-ver

Here (toot toot-tle-ee toot)__ we're gon-na sing for the red, white and blue; __ while the ser-geants do the train-in' we'll
Here (toot toot-tle-ee toot)__ we're gon-na keep a-groov-in' O-ver Here. (toot toot, too-tle-ee toot.)__} To-geth-er __ work-in' on the team to-

do the en-ter-tain-in' O-ver Here. (toot toot, too-tle-ee toot.)__}
gon-na keep a-groov-in' O-ver Here. (toot toot, too-tle-ee toot.)__}

geth-er, __ get-tin' up the steam to-geth-er, __ giv-in' all our all __ (On the beam and right on the ball. Right O-ver
(Oh de-Paul's you're right on the ball. We're gon-na

look a-live and jam and jive O-ver Here; ___ We're gon-na spread some joy for ev-'ry boy__ we come near.

___ While the ser-geants do the train-in' we'll do the en-ter-tain-in' O-ver Here! (toot toot, too-tle-ee toot.)

# SINCE YOU'RE NOT AROUND

Copyright © 1974 by Alley Music Corp. and Trio Music Co., Inc. and Sherbro Music Co.
All rights administered by Hudson Bay Music, Inc.
Used by Permission

Words and Music by
RICHARD M. SHERMAN & ROBERT B. SHERMAN

When I walked with you how the morn-ing dew spar-kled on the ground; Fun-ny how the ma-gic's

gone now, since you're not a-round. Songs we used to know, not so long a-go

have a lone-some sound; Noth-ing is the same. my dar-ling. Since You're Not A-

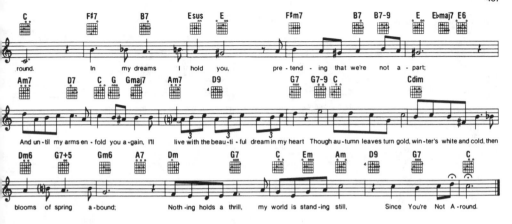

round. In my dreams I hold you, pre-tend-ing that we're not a-part;

And un-til my arms en-fold you a-gain, I'll live with the beau-ti-ful dream in my heart Though au-tumn leaves turn gold, win-ter's white and cold, then

blooms of spring a-bound; Noth-ing holds a thrill, my world is stand-ing still, Since You're Not A-round.

## WHERE DID THE GOOD TIMES GO?

Copyright © 1974 by Alley Music Corp. and Trio Music Co., Inc. and Sherbro Music Co.
All rights administered by Hudson Bay Music, Inc.
Used by Permission

Words and Music by
RICHARD M. SHERMAN & ROBERT B. SHERMAN

What fun we had, then laugh-ter turned sad, Oh, Where Did The Good Times

Go? _____ Our hopes and plans slipped right through our hands, Oh, where, Where____

____ Did The Good Times Go? Some-place some-where, in-stead of de-spair is the

love _____ we used to know; _____ Why can't we re-turn? _____ Won't we

ev-er learn? Oh, Where Did The Good Times Go? _____

## NO GOODBYES

Copyright © 1974 by Alley Music Corp. and Trio Music Co., Inc. and Sherbro Music Co.
All rights administered by Hudson Bay Music, Inc.
Used by Permission

Words and Music by
RICHARD M. SHERMAN & ROBERT B. SHERMAN

# "Paint Your Wagon"

Copyright © 1951 by Alan Jay Lerner & Frederick Loewe
Chappell & Co., Inc., owner of publication and allied rights throughout the World
Copyright Renewed
International Copyright Secured    ALL RIGHTS RESERVED

## I TALK TO THE TREES

Words by ALAN JAY LERNER
Music by FREDERICK LOEWE

see them ___ come true. ___ I can see us on an true. ___

A - pril night, ___ Look-in' out a-cross a roll-in' farm. ___ Hav-in' sup-per in the can - dle-light, ___

___ Walk-in' la - ter arm in arm. ___ Then I'll tell you how I passed the day. ___ Think-in' main-ly how the

night would be. ___ And I'll try to find the words to say, ___ All the things you mean to me. ___ I Talk To The

## WAND'RIN' STAR

Copyright © 1951 by Alan Jay Lerner & Frederick Loewe
Chappell & Co., Inc, owner of publication and allied rights throughout the World
Copyright Renewed
International Copyright Secured    ALL RIGHTS RESERVED

Words by ALAN JAY LERNER
Music by FREDERICK LOEWE

I was born ___ un - der a Wand' - rin' Star. Mud can make you pris' - ner and the plains can make you dry.

Snow can burn your eyes but on-ly peo-ple make you cry. Home is made for com-in' from, for dreams of go-in' to Which, with an-y luck will nev-er come

true. I was born ___ un - der a Wand' - rin' Star. I was born ___ un - der a

Wand' - rin' Star. When I get to heav-en ___ tie me to a tree, Or I'll be-gin to roam, And soon you know where I will be.

I was born ___ un - der a Wand' - rin' Star, A Wand' - rin', Wand' - rin' Star. ___

# I STILL SEE ELISA

Copyright © 1951 by Alan Jay Lerner & Frederick Loewe
Copyright Renewed. Chappell & Co., Inc. owner of publication and allied rights throughout the world
International Copyright Secured    ALL RIGHTS RESERVED

Words and Music by
ALAN JAY LERNER & FREDERICK LOEWE

I Still See E-li-sa She keeps on re-turn-ing as breath-less and young as ev-er I still hear E-li-sa, And still feel a yearn-ing to hold her a-gainst me a-gain. Her heart was made of hol-i-days, Her smile was made of dawn. Her laugh-ter was an A-pril song, That ech-oes on and on. Since I saw E-li-sa, The shad-ows are fall-ing and win-ter is call-ing a-bove. But I Still See E-li-sa when-ev-er I dream of love. I love.

# THEY CALL THE WIND MARIA

Copyright © 1951 by Alan Jay Lerner & Frederick Loewe
Copyright Renewed Chappell & Co. Inc. owner of publication and allied rights throughout the world
International Copyright Secured    ALL RIGHTS RESERVED

Words by ALAN JAY LERNER
Music by FREDERICK LOEWE

A-way out here they got a name for wind, and rain and fi-re. The rain is Tess, the fire is Joe, And They
fore I knew Ma-ri-a's name And heard her wail and whin-in.' I had a girl, and she had me, And the

Call The Wind Ma-ri-a. Ma-ri-a blows the stars a-round, And sends the clouds a fly-in. Ma-
sun was al-ways shin-in.' But then one day I left my girl, I left her far be-hind me. And

ri - a makes the moun - tain sound Like folks were up there dy - in.'
now I'm lost, so gol - durn lost, Not e - ven God can find me.

Ma - ri - a!_____ Ma-

ri - a!_____ They call the wind Ma - ri - a!_____ Be - ri - a!_____ Ma-

ri - a!_____ Ma - ri - a!_____ Blow my love to me!

## "Pal Joey"

### BEWITCHED

Copyright © 1941 by Chappell & Co., Inc.
Copyright Renewed
International Copyright Secured     ALL RIGHTS RESERVED

Words by LORENZ HART
Music by RICHARD RODGERS

Moderately Slow

I'm wild a - gain, Be - guiled a - gain, A sim - per - ing, whim - per - ing child a - gain, Be - witched, both - ered and be -

wild - ered am I._____ Could -n't sleep, And would -n't sleep, When love came and told me I

should -n't sleep, Be - witched, both - ered and be - wild - ered am I._____ Lost my heart, but what

of it? He is cold I a - gree, He can laugh, but I love it, Al - though the laugh's on

me. I'll sing to him, Each spring to him, And long for the day when I'll cling to him, Be -

witched, both - ered and be - wild - ered am I. I'm I._____

## I COULD WRITE A BOOK

Copyright © 1940 by Chappell & Co., Inc.
Copyright Renewed
International Copyright Secured    ALL RIGHTS RESERVED

Words by LORENZ HART
Music by RICHARD RODGERS

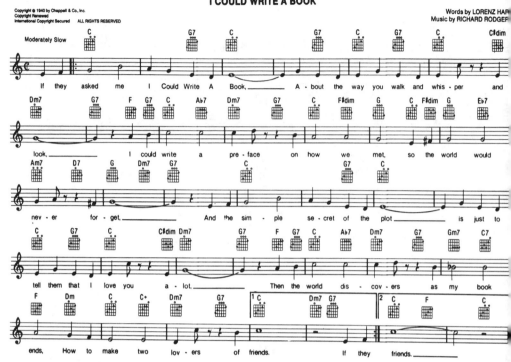

## YOU MUSTN'T KICK IT AROUND

Copyright © 1940 by Chappell & Co., Inc.
Copyright renewed

Words by LORENZ HART
Music by RICHARD RODGERS

Ab / Eb7 / Abmaj7 Ab6 / Eb7 / Abmaj7 Ab6 / F7

E - ven though I'm mild and meek_ When we have a brawl,_ If I turn the

Bbmaj7 Bb6 Bb7 / Eb7 Ab / Abm7 Eb7 / Ab / Eb7 Ab7

oth - er cheek_ You must - n't kick it at all._ When I try to ring the bell._ You nev - er care for the sound._ The

Db / Dbm / Eb7 / Ab

next guy may not do as well,_ You Must - n't Kick_ It A - round.

## ZIP

Words by LORENZ HART
Music by RICHARD RODGERS

Copyright © 1951 by Chappell & Co., Inc.
Copyright renewed

Lively

G

Bb D7

Zip! Walt - er Lipp - man was - n't bril - liant to - day._ Zip! Will Sar - y - an ev - er
Zip! I con - sid - er Dal - i's paint - ing pas - se._ Zip! Can they make the Met - ro -
Zip! Tos - ca - ni - ni leads the great - est of bands._ Zip! Jer - gens Lo - tion does the

G

Bb D7

write a great play?_ Zip! I was read - ing Scho - pen - hau - er last night._ Zip! And I
pol - i - tan pay?_ Zip! En - glish peo - ple don't say clerk, they say clark._ Zip! An - y -
trick for his hands._ Zip! Rip Van Win - kle on the screen would be smart._ Zip! Ty - rone

C Fmaj7 B

think that Scho - pen - hau - er was right._ I don't want to see Zor - i - na, I don't want to meet Cob - i - na. Zip! I'm an
bod - y who says clark is a jark!_ I have read the great Ca - ba - la. And I sim - ply wor - ship Al - lah. Zip! I am
Pow - er will be cast in the part._ I a - dore the great Con - fu - cius. And the lines of lus - cious Lu - cius. Zip! I am

C Fmaj7 G E Am D7 G

in - tel - lec - tual. I don't like a deep con - tral - to, Or a man who's voice is al - to. Zip! I'm a het - ero - sex - ual. Zip! It took
just a mys - tic. I don't care for Whist - ler's moth - er. Char - lie's aunt. or Shu - bert's bro - ther. Zip! I'm mis - o - gyn - is - tic. Zip! My in -
so ec - lec - tic. I don't care for ei - ther Mick - ey Mouse and Roon - ey make me sick - y! Zip! I'm a lit - tle hec - tic. Zip! My ar -

Bb D7 1,2 G D7 3 G

in - tel - lect to mas - ter my art._ Zip! Who the hell is Mar - gie Hart?_
tel - li - gence is guid - ing my hand._ Zip! Who the hell is Sal - ly Rand?_
tis - tic taste is clas - sic and dear._ Zip! Who the hell is Li - li St. Cyr?_

# "Panama Hattie"

## LET'S BE BUDDIES

Copyright © 1940 by Cole Porter
Copyright renewed, assigned to John F. Wharton, Trustee of the Cole Porter Musical and Literary Property Trusts
Chappell & Co., Inc., Publisher

Words and Music by
COLE PORTER

## MY MOTHER WOULD LOVE YOU

Copyright © 1940 by Cole Porter
Copyright renewed, assigned to John F. Wharton, Trustee of the Cole Porter Musical and Literary Property Trusts
Chappell & Co., Inc., Publisher

Words and Music by
COLE PORTER

**Peter Pan''**

1954 CAROLYN LEIGH and MARK CHARLAP
Renewed 1982 CAROLYN LEIGH and MARK CHARLAP
Rights Throughout the World Controlled by EDWIN H. MORRIS & COMPANY, A Division of MPL Communications, Inc.

## I'M FLYING

Lyric by CAROLYN LEIGH
Music by MARK CHARLAP

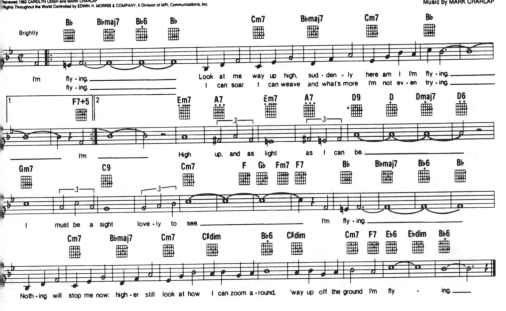

## NEVER NEVER LAND

1954 BETTY COMDEN, ADOLPH GREEN and JULE STYNE
Renewed 1982 BETTY COMDEN, ADOLPH GREEN and JULE STYNE
Rights Throughout the World Controlled by EDWIN H. MORRIS & COMPANY, A Division of MPL Communications, Inc.

Lyric by BETTY COMDEN & ADOLPH GREEN
Music by JULE STYNE

# I'VE GOTTA CROW

© 1964 CAROLYN LEIGH and MARK CHARLAP
© Renewed 1992 CAROLYN LEIGH and MARK CHARLAP
All Rights Throughout the World Controlled by EDWIN H. MORRIS & COMPANY, A Division of MPL Communications, Inc.

Lyric by CAROLYN LEIGH
Music by MARK CHARLAP

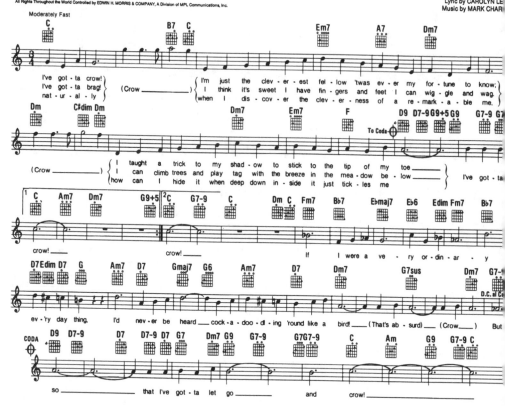

# I WON'T GROW UP

© 1964 CAROLYN LEIGH and MARK CHARLAP
© Renewed 1992 CAROLYN LEIGH and MARK CHARLAP
All Rights Throughout the World Controlled by EDWIN H. MORRIS & COMPANY, A Division of MPL Communications, Inc.

Lyric by CAROLYN LEIGH
Music by MARK CHARLAP

and make me. An-y-one who wants to try ___ and make me turn in-to a man, catch me if you can. I

won't grow up. ___ Not a pen-ny will I pinch. ___ I will nev-er grow a mus-tache, ___ or a

frac-tion of an inch. ___ 'Cause grow-ing up is aw-ful-er than all the aw-ful things that ev-er were. I'll

nev-er grow up, nev-er grow up, nev-er grow u-up, no sir, not I, not me, I won't, no sir!

# The Phantom Of The Opera"

## THE MUSIC OF THE NIGHT

Music by ANDREW LLOYD WEBBER
Lyrics by CHARLES HART
Additional Lyrics by RICHARD STILGOE

Copyright 1986 The Really Useful Group Ltd.
Rights for the United States and Canada Administered by PolyGram International Publishing, Inc.

Moderately slow

PHANTOM

Night time sharp-ens, height-ens each sen-sa-tion; dark-ness stirs and wakes im-ag-i-na-tion. Si-lent-ly the sen-ses a-

ban-don their de-fen-ces. Slow-ly, gent-ly.

night un-furls its splen-dour; grasp it, sense it, trem-u-lous and ten-der. Turn your face a-way from the gar-ish light of day, turn your

thoughts a-way from cold, un-feel-ing light and lis-ten to The Mu-sic Of The Night. Close your eyes and sur-ren-der to y

dark-est dreams! Purge your thoughts of the life you knew be - fore! Close your eyes let your spir-it start to soar and you

live as you've nev-er lived be-fore. Soft-ly, deft-ly, mu-sic shall ca-ress you. Hear it, feel it,

se-cret-ly pos-sess you. O-pen up your mind let your fan-ta-sies un-wind in this dark-ness which you know you can-not fight, the

dark-ness of The Mu-sic Of The Night. Let your mind start a jour-ney through a strange, new world; leave all thoughts of the world you know be -

fore. Let your soul take you where you long to be! On-ly then can you be-long to me.

Float-ing, fall-ing, sweet in-tox-i-ca-tion. Touch me, trust me, sa-vour each sen-sa-tion. Let the dream be-gin, let your

dark-er side give in to the pow-er of the mu-sic that I write, the pow-er of The Mu-sic Of The Night.

You a-lone can make my song take flight, help me make The Mu-sic Of The Night._____

## ALL I ASK OF YOU

© Copyright 1986 The Really Useful Group Ltd.
All Rights for the United States and Canada Administered by PolyGram International Publishing, Inc.

Music by ANDREW LLOYD WEBBE
Lyrics by CHARLES HAM
Additional Lyrics by RICHARD STILGO

Moderately slow

RAOUL

No more talk of dark-ness, for - get these wide-eyed fears; I'm here, noth-ing can harm you, my words will warm and calm you.

469

# THE PHANTOM OF THE OPERA

Music by ANDREW LLOYD WEBBER
Lyrics by CHARLES HART
Additional Lyrics by RICHARD STILGOE and MIKE BATT

© Copyright 1986 The Really Useful Group Ltd.
All Rights for the United States and Canada Administered by PolyGram International Publishing, Inc.

# ANGEL OF MUSIC

© Copyright 1986 The Really Useful Group Ltd.
All Rights for the United States and Canada Administered by PolyGram International Publishing, Inc.

Music by ANDREW LLOYD WEBBE[R]
Lyrics by CHARLES HA[RT]
Additional Lyrics by RICHARD STILG[OE]

## THE POINT OF NO RETURN

Music by ANDREW LLOYD WEBBER
Lyrics by CHARLES HART
Additional Lyrics by RICHARD STILGOE

Copyright 1986 The Really Useful Group Ltd.
Rights for the United States and Canada Administered by PolyGram International Publishing, Inc.

474

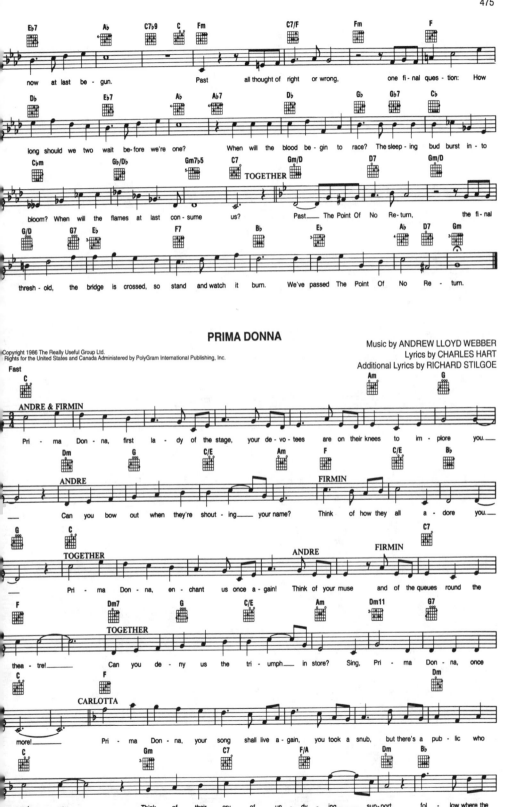

## PRIMA DONNA

Copyright 1986 The Really Useful Group Ltd.
Rights for the United States and Canada Administered by PolyGram International Publishing, Inc.

Music by ANDREW LLOYD WEBBER
Lyrics by CHARLES HART
Additional Lyrics by RICHARD STILGOE

# WISHING YOU WERE SOMEHOW HERE AGAIN

Copyright 1986 The Really Useful Group Ltd.
Rights for the United States and Canada Administered by PolyGram International Publishing, Inc.

Music by ANDREW LLOYD WEBBER
Lyrics by CHARLES HART
Additional Lyrics by RICHARD STILGOE

# MASQUERADE

© Copyright 1986 The Really Useful Group Ltd.
All Rights for the United States and Canada Administered by PolyGram International Publishing, Inc.

Music by ANDREW LLOYD WEBBER
Lyrics by CHARLES HART
Additional Lyrics by RICHARD STILGOE

479

# THINK OF ME

© Copyright 1986 The Really Useful Group Ltd.
All Rights for the United States and Canada Administered by PolyGram International Publishing, Inc.

Music by ANDREW LLOYD WEBBE
Lyrics by CHARLES HAF
Additional Lyrics by RICHARD STILG(

## I'LL NEVER BE LONELY AGAIN

Words and Music by
LESLIE BRICUSSE

# IF I RULED THE WORLD

Copyright © 1963 by Chappell & Co., Ltd./Published by Delfont Music, Ltd., London
Chappell & Co., Inc., owner of publication and allied rights for the Western Hemisphere
International Copyright Secured    ALL RIGHTS RESERVED

Words by LESLIE BRICUSSE
Music by CYRIL ORNADEL

# "Red, Hot And Blue!"

## DOWN IN THE DEPTHS
(On The Ninetieth Floor)

Copyright © 1936 by Chappell & Co., Inc.
Copyright renewed, assigned to John F. Wharton, Trustee of the Cole Porter Musical and Literary Property Trusts
Chappell & Co., Inc., Publisher

Words and Music by
COLE PORTER

Strict slow foxtrot tempo

With a mil-lion ne-on rain-bows burn-ing be-low me, ___ And a mil-lion blaz-ing tax-is rais-ing a roar, ___ Here I sit a-bove the town, ___ In my pet pail-let-ted gown, Down In The Depths ___ on the nine-ti-eth floor, ___

{ While the crowds in all the night-clubs pun-ish the par-quet, ___ And the bars are packed with coup-les call-ing for more, ___ }
{ While the crowds at El Ma-roc-co pun-ish the par-quet, ___ And at Twen-ty One the coup-les cla-mor for more, ___ }

I'm de-sert-ed and de-pressed __ In my reg-al ea-gle nest, Down In The Depths, __ on the nine-ti-eth floor, When the on-ly one you want-ed wants an-oth-er, ___ What's the use of swank and cash in the bank ga-lore?

{ Why ev-en the jan-i-tor's wife Has a per-fect-ly good love-life, And here am I, ___ }
{ Why ev-en the jan-i-tor's wife Has some sen-ti-ment in her life, And here am I, ___ }

fac-ing to-mor-row, ___ A-lone with my sor-row, ___ Down In The Depths, ___ on the nine-ti-eth floor. ___ With a floor. ___

# IT'S DE-LOVELY

Copyright © 1936 by Chappell & Co., Inc.
Copyright Renewed
International Copyright Secured    ALL RIGHTS RESERVED

Words and Music by
COLE PORTER

# YOU'VE GOT SOMETHING

Copyright © 1936 by Chappell & Co., Inc.
Copyright renewed, assigned to John F. Wharton, Trustee of the Cole Porter Musical and Literary Property Trusts
Chappell & Co., Inc., Publisher

Words and Music by
COLE PORTER

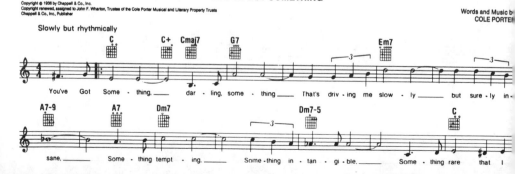

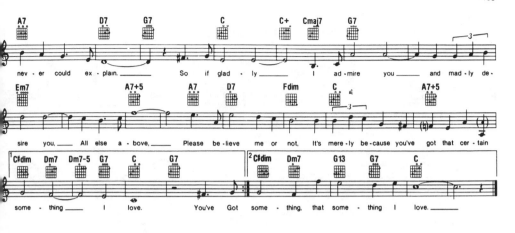

A7 | D7 | G7 | C | C+ | Cmaj7 | G7

nev-er could ex-plain. So if glad-ly ____ I ad-mire you ____ and mad-ly de-

Em7 | A7+5 | A7 | D7 | Fdim | C | A7+5

sire you, ____ All else a-bove, ____ Please be-lieve me or not, It's mere-ly be-cause you've got that cer-tain

1. C#dim Dm7 Dm7-5 G7 | C | G7 | 2. C#dim Dm7 | G13 | G7 | C

some-thing ____ I love. You've Got some-thing, that some-thing I love. ____

Copyright © 1936 by Chappell & Co., Inc.
Copyright renewed, Assigned to John F. Wharton, Trustee of the Cole Porter Musical & Literary Property Trusts
Chappell & Co., Inc., owner of publication and allied rights throughout the World
International Copyright Secured ALL RIGHTS RESERVED

# RIDIN' HIGH

Words and Music by
COLE PORTER

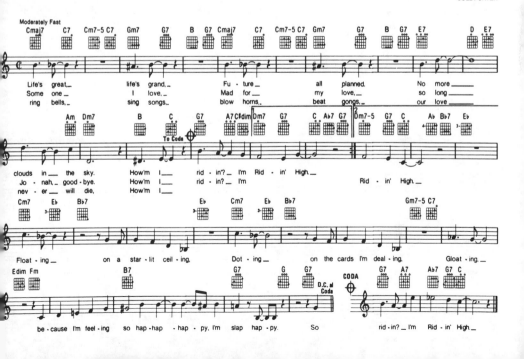

Moderately Fast

Cmaj7 | C7 | Cm7-5 C7 | Gm7 | G7 | B G7 Cmaj7 | C7 | Cm7-5 C7 | Gm7 | G7 | B G7 E7 | D E7

Life's great, ____ life's grand, ____ Fu-ture ____ all planned. No more ____
Some one ____ I love, ____ Mad for ____ my love, ____ so long ____
ring bells, ____ sing songs, ____ blow horns, ____ beat gongs, ____ our love

Am Dm7 | B | C G7 | A7 C#dim Dm7 | G7 | C Ab7 G7 | 2. Dm7-5 G7 C | Ab Bb7 Eb

clouds in ____ the sky. How'm I ____ rid-in'? I'm Rid-in' High. ____
Jo-nah, good-bye. How'm I ____ rid-in'? I'm Rid-in' High. ____
nev-er will die, How'm I ____

Cm7 | Eb | Bb7 | Eb | Cm7 | Eb | Bb7 | Gm7-5 C7

Float-ing ____ on a star-lit ceil-ing. Dot-ing ____ on the cards I'm deal-ing. Gloat-ing ____

Edim Fm | B7 | G7 | G G7 | CODA | G7 A7 Ab7 G7 C

be-cause I'm feel-ing so hap-hap ____ hap-py, I'm slap hap-py. So rid-in'? ____ I'm Rid-in' High. ____

## "Pins And Needles"

Copyright © 1937 by Chappell & Co., Inc.
Copyright renewed

### SING ME A SONG WITH SOCIAL SIGNIFICANCE

Words and Music by HAROLD ROME

Sing Me A Song With So-cial Sig-nif-i-cance all oth-er tunes are ta-boo I want a dit-ty with
Sing Me A Song With So-cial Sig-nif-i-cance all oth-er tunes are ta-boo I want a song that's sa-

heat in it, Ap-peal-ing with feel-ing andmeat in it! Sing Me A Song With So-cial Sig-nif-i-cance
tir-i-cal, And put-ting the mere in-to mir-a-cle Sing Me A Song With So-cial Sig-nif-i-cance

or you can sing till you're blue___ Let mean-ing shine from ev-'ry line or I won't love you
or you can sing till you're blue___ It must be packed with so-cial fact or I won't love you

Sing me of wars and sing me of bread-lines Tell me of front page news Sing me of strikes and last min-ute head-lines
Sing me of kings and con-f'ren-ces mar-tial Tell me of mills and mines Sing me of courts that are-n't im-par-tial

dress your ob-ser-va-tion in syn-co-pa-tion! Sing Me A Song With So-cial Sig-nif-i-cance there's noth-ing else that will
what's to be done with 'em tell me in rhy-thm! Sing Me A Song With So-cial Sig-nif-i-cance there's noth-ing else that will

do___ It must get hot with what is what or I won't love you.
do___ It must be tense with com-mon sense or I won't love you.___

## "Pipe Dream"

Copyright © 1955 by Richard Rodgers and Oscar Hammerstein II
Williamson Music Co., owner of publication and allied rights for all countries of the Western Hemisphere and Japan.
International Copyright Secured    ALL RIGHTS RESERVED

### ALL AT ONCE YOU LOVE HER

Words by OSCAR HAMMERSTEIN II
Music by RICHARD RODGERS

You start too light her cig-a-rette And All At Once You

Love Her. You've scarce-ly talked, you've scarce-ly met,

But All At Once You Love Her You like her eyes, you tell her

so. She thinks you're wise and clev — er. You kiss good-night and then you know You'll kiss good-night for ev — er. You won-der where, your heart can go Then all at once you know.

## EVERYBODY'S GOT A HOME BUT ME

Copyright © 1955 by Richard Rodgers and Oscar Hammerstein II
Williamson Music Co., owner of publication and allied rights for all countries of the Western Hemisphere and Japan.
International Copyright Secured     ALL RIGHTS RESERVED

Words by OSCAR HAMMERSTEIN II
Music by RICHARD RODGERS

Slowly, with expression

I rode by a house with the win-dows light-ed up Look-in' bright-er than a Christ-mas
rode by a house where the moon was on the porch And a girl was on her fel-ler's

tree. And I said to my-self as I rode by my-self, Ev-'ry-bod-y's Got A
knee.

Home But Me. I Home But Me. I am free and I'm

hap-py to be free, To be free in the way I want to be. But

once in a while when the road is kind-a dark And the end is kind-a hard to see,

I look up and I cry to a cloud go-in by: "Won't there ev-er be a

home for me, some-where? Ev-'ry-bod-y's Got A Home But Me."

# "Plain And Fancy"

### YOUNG AND FOOLISH

Copyright © 1954 by Chappell & Co., Inc.
International Copyright Secured     ALL RIGHTS RESERVED

Words by ARNOLD B. HORWIT
Music by ALBERT HAGUE

Young And Fool-ish, Why is it wrong to be Young And Fool-ish?

We have-n't long to be. Soon e-nough the care-free days, the sun-lit days go by.

Soon e-nough the blue-bird has to fly. ___ We were fool-ish, One day we

fell in love. Now we won-der what we were dream-ing of? Smil-ing in the sun-light,

Laugh-ing in the rain, I wish that we were Young And Fool-ish a-gain! ___

# "Porgy And Bess"

### I LOVES YOU PORGY

Copyright © 1935 by Gershwin Publishing Corporation
Copyright Renewed, Assigned to Chappell & Co., Inc.

Words by IRA GERSHWIN & DuBOSE HEYWARD
Music by GEORGE GERSHWIN

I wants to stay here, but I ain't wor-thy. You is too de-cent to un-der-stan', for when I see him he hyp-no-

tize me, when he take hol' of me with his hot han'. Some-day, I know he's com-in' back to call me, he's goin' to han-dle me an'

hol' me so. It's goin' to be like dy-in', Por-gy, deep in-side me. But when he calls, I know I have to go.

I Loves You,

If dere warn't no Crown, Bess, if dere was on-ly just you an' Por-gy, what den? ___

# BESS, YOU IS MY WOMAN

Copyright © 1935 Gershwin Publishing Corporation
Copyright Renewed, Assigned to Chappell & Co., Inc.

Words by DuBOSE HEYWARD & IRA GERSHWIN
Music by GEORGE GERSHWIN

# IT AIN'T NECESSARILY SO

Copyright © 1935 by Gershwin Publishing Corporation
Copyright Renewed, Assigned to Chappell & Co., Inc.
International Copyright Secured   ALL RIGHTS RESERVED

Words by IRA GERSHWIN
Music by GEORGE GERSHWIN

ever it's pos'-ble, But wid a grain of salt. Me - thus' - lah lived nine hun - dred years. Me-

thus - lah lived nine hun - dred years, But who calls dat liv - in' When no gal 'll give in To no man what's nine - hun - dred

years? I'm preach - in' dis ser - mon to show, It ain't nes - sa, ain't nes - sa,

ain't nes - sa, ain't nes - sa, ain't nes - ces - sa - ri - ly so.

## SUMMERTIME

Copyright © 1935 by Gershwin Publishing Corporation
Copyright Renewed, Assigned to Chappell & Co., Inc.
International Copyright Secured   ALL RIGHTS RESERVED

Words by DuBOSE HEYWARD
Music by GEORGE GERSHWIN

Sum - mer time an' the liv - in' is eas - y, Fish are jump - in';

an' the cot - ton is high. Oh, yo' dad - dy's rich, An' yo' ma is good - look - in'

So hush, lit - tle ba - by, don' you cry.

One of these morn - in's you goin' to rise up sing - in', Then ou'll spread yo' wings.

an' you'll take the sky. But till that morn - in' there's noth - in' can harm you With

Dad - dy an' Mam - my stand - in' by.

# I GOT PLENTY O' NUTTIN'

Copyright © 1935 by Gershwin Publishing Corporation
Copyright Renewed, Assigned to Chappell & Co., Inc.
International Copyright Secured   ALL RIGHTS RESERVED

Words by IRA GERSHWIN
Music by GEORGE GERSHWIN

**THERE'S A BOAT DAT'S LEAVIN' SOON FOR NEW YORK**

Copyright © 1935 by Gershwin Publishing Corporation
Copyright Renewed, Assigned to Chappell & Co., Inc.

Words by DuBOSE HEYWARD
Music by GEORGE GERSHWIN

me, _____ dere you can't go wrong, sis-ter. _____ I'll buy you de swell-est man-sion up on

up-per Fi'th Av-en-ue. An' through Har-lem we'll go strut-tin', we'll go a-strut-tin' an' dere'll be nut-tin' too good for

you. I'll dress you in silks and sat-ins in de lat-est Pa-ris styles. All de

blues you'll be for-get-tin', you'll be for-get-tin', there'll be no fret-tin', jes' noth-in' but smiles. _____ Come a-

long wid me, _ dat's de place, _____ don't be a fool, _ come a-long. come a-long. _____ There's A

Boat Dat's Leav-in' Soon_ For New York. _____ Come wid me, _____ dat's where we be-

long, _____ sis-ter, _____ dat's where we be-long. _____

# A WOMAN IS A SOMETIME THING

Copyright © 1935 by Gershwin Publishing Corporation
Copyright Renewed, Assigned to Chappell & Co., Inc.

Words by DuBOSE HEYWARD
Music by GEORGE GERSHWIN

# MY MAN'S GONE NOW

Copyright © 1935 by Gershwin Publishing Corporation
Copyright Renewed, Assigned to Chappell & Co., Inc.

Words by DuBOSE HEYWARD
Music by GEORGE GERSHWIN

# "Present Arms"

## YOU TOOK ADVANTAGE OF ME

© 1928 WARNER BROS. INC. (Renewed)
Rights for the Extended Renewal Term in the United States Controlled by
MARLIN ENTERPRISES and THE ESTATE OF LORENZ HART
All Rights on behalf of MARLIN ENTERPRISES Administered by WILLIAMSON MUSIC
All Rights on behalf of THE ESTATE OF LORENZ HART Administered by WB MUSIC CORP.   ORP.

Words by LORENZ HART
Music by RICHARD RODGERS

I'm a sent-i-ment-al sap, that's all.__ What's the use of try-ing not to fall?__ I
I'm just like an ap-ple on a bough__ And you're gon-na shake me down some-how,__ So

have no will,__ You've made your kill 'Cause You Took Ad-vant-age Of Me!
what's the use, you've cooked my goose__ 'Cause You Took Ad-vant-age Of

Me! I'm so hot and both-ered that I don't know__ My el-bow from__ my

ear; I suf-fer some-thing aw-ful each time you go__ And much worse when__ you're near.

Here am I with all my bridg-es burned,__ Just a babe in arms where you're con-cerned,__ So

lock the doors__ and call me yours__ 'Cause You Took Ad-van-tage Of Me!

# "Private Lives"

## SOMEDAY I'LL FIND YOU

Copyright © 1931 by Chappell & Co., Ltd.
Published in the U.S.A. by Chappell & Co., Inc.
International Copyright Secured    ALL RIGHTS RESERVED

Words & Music by
NOEL COWARD

Some-day I'll Find You, Moon-light be-hind you, True to the dream I am dream - ing.

As I draw near you You'll smile a lit-tle smile; For a lit-tle while We shall stand Hand in hand. I'll leave you

nev-er, Love you for ev-er. All our past sor-row re-deem - ing. Make it all come

true, Make me love you too, Some-day I'll Find You a-gain. gain.__

**"Simple Simon"**

## DANCING ON THE CEILING

Words by LORENZ HART
Music by RICHARD RODGERS

© 1931 WARNER BROS. INC. (Renewed)
Rights for the Extended Renewal Term in the United States Controlled by
MARLIN ENTERPRISES and the ESTATE OF LORENZ HART
All Rights on behalf of MARLIN ENTERPRISES Administered by WILLIAMSON MUSIC
All Rights on behalf of THE ESTATE OF LORENZ HART Administered by WB MUSIC CORP.

## TEN CENTS A DANCE

Words by LORENZ HART
Music by RICHARD RODGERS

© 1930 WARNER BROS. INC. (Renewed)
Rights for the Extended Renewal Term in the United States Controlled by
MARLIN ENTERPRISES and THE ESTATE OF LORENZ HART
Rights on behalf of MARLIN ENTERPRISES Administered by WILLIAMSON MUSIC
Rights on behalf of THE ESTATE OF LORENZ HART Administered by WB MUSIC CORP.

## "Rex"

### AS ONCE I LOVED YOU

Copyright © 1976 by Richard Rodgers and Mayerling Productions, Ltd.
WILLIAMSON MUSIC owner of publication and allied rights of Richard Rodgers throughout the world

Words by SHELDON HARNICK
Music by RICHARD RODGERS

As Once I Loved You, I love you now. As once I need-ed you, I need you
Once I Loved You, I want you now. As once I ran to you, I need you

now. What peo-ple told you is all un-true. In your heart, you must know this,
now. A world of car-ing was ours be-fore And it waits to be shared once

too. _____ As once you trust-ed me, be-lieve me now. I could not
more. _____ The price-less tap-es-try we wove as one That crowd-ed

leave you, I don't know how. As once our days be-gan and end-ed with a kiss.
can-vas re-mains half done. Don't bid me say good-bye to you, I won't know

Don't let it end, not like this. _____ As how. As Once I

Loved You, I love you now. _____

## "Right This Way"

### I CAN DREAM, CAN'T I?

Copyright © 1937 by Chappell & Co., Inc.
Copyright Renewed
International Copyright Secured    ALL RIGHTS RESERVED

Words by IRVING KAHAL
Music by SAMMY FAIN

Slowly

I can see, ___ no mat-ter how near you'll be, ___ You'll nev-er be-long to me ___ But I Can

Dream, Can't I? Can't I pre-tend that I'm locked in the bend of your em-brace? _ For dreams are

just like wine, And I am drunk with mine. I'm a - ware my heart is a sad af - fair.

There's much dis - il - lu - sion there, But I Can Dream, Can't I? Can't I a - dore you al -

though we are o - ceans a - part? I can't make you o - pen your heart, But I Can Dream, Can't I? Can't I?

# I'LL BE SEEING YOU

Copyright © 1938 by Williamson Music Co.
Copyright Renewed, Administered by Chappell & Co., Inc.
International Copyright Secured   ALL RIGHTS RESERVED

Words and Music by
IRVING KAHAL & SAMMY FAIN

I'll Be See - ing You In all the old fa - mil - iar plac - es That this heart of mine em - brac - es all day thru:

In that small ca - fe, The park a - cross the way, The chil - dren's ca - rou - sel, The

chest - nut trees, the wish - ing well. I'll Be See - ing You In ev - 'ry love - ly sum - mer's day, In ev - 'ry - thing that's

light and gay, I'll al - ways think of you that way I'll find you in the morn - ing sun; And when the night is

new, I'll be look - ing at the moon But I'll Be See - ing You! You!

# "The Roar Of The Greasepaint — The Smell Of The Crowd"

## FEELING GOOD

© Copyright 1964 Concord Music Ltd., London, England
TRO - MUSICAL COMEDY PRODUCTIONS, INC, New York, controls all publication rights for the U.S.A. & Canada

Words and Music by
LESLIE BRICUSSE & ANTHONY NEWLEY

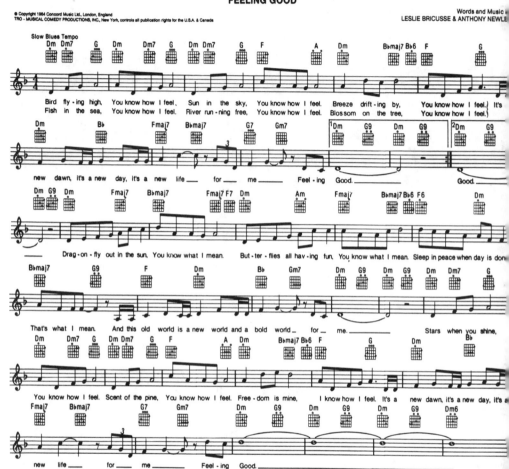

Bird fly-ing high, You know how I feel. Sun in the sky, You know how I feel. Breeze drift-ing by, You know how I feel. It's a
Fish in the sea, You know how I feel. River run-ning free, You know how I feel. Blos-som on the tree, You know how I feel.

new dawn, it's a new day, it's a new life_ for _ me _ Feel-ing Good. _ Good.

_ Drag-on-fly out in the sun, You know what I mean. But-ter-flies all hav-ing fun, You know what I mean. Sleep in peace when day is done,

That's what I mean. And this old world is a new world and a bold world_ for _ me. _ Stars when you shine,

You know how I feel. Scent of the pine, You know how I feel. Free-dom is mine, I know how I feel. It's a new dawn, it's a new day, it's a

new life _ for _ me _ Feel-ing Good. _

## THE JOKER

© Copyright 1964 Concord Music Ltd., London, England
TRO - MUSICAL COMEDY PRODUCTIONS, INC, New York, controls all publication rights for the U.S.A. & Canada

Words and Music by
LESLIE BRICUSSE & ANTHONY NEWLEY

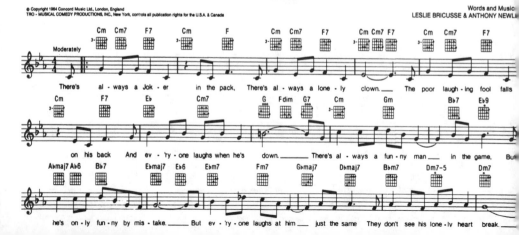

There's al-ways a Jok-er in the pack, There's al-ways a lone-ly clown. _ The poor laugh-ing fool falls

on his back And ev-'ry-one laughs when he's down. _ There's al-ways a fun-ny man_ in the game, But

he's on-ly fun-ny by mis-take. _ But ev-'ry-one laughs at him _ just the same They don't see his lone-ly heart break.

They don't care as long as there is a jest-er, just a fool, As fool-ish as he can be.__ There's al-ways a Jok-er that's a rule But fate deals a hand and I see__ The Jok-er is__ me. There's me.__ The Jok-er is__ me.__ The Jok-er is__ me.

## A WONDERFUL DAY LIKE TODAY

Copyright 1964 Concord Music Ltd., London, England
O - MUSICAL COMEDY PRODUCTIONS, INC., New York, controls all publication rights for the U.S.A. & Canada

Words and Music by
LESLIE BRICUSSE & ANTHONY NEWLEY

Brightly

On A Won-der-ful Day__ Like To-day__ I de-fy an-y cloud__
won-der-ful morn-ing like this__ When the sun is as big__
take this oc-ca-sion to say__ That the whole hu-man race__

to ap-pear in the sky.__ Dare an-y rain-drop to plop in my eye.__
as a yel-low bal-loon.__ E-ven the spar-rows are sing-ing in tune.__
should go down on its knees,__ Show that we're grate-ful for morn-ings like these__

On A Won-der-ful Day__ Like To-day.__ On a -ing like this.__
On a won-der-ful morn-
for the

On a morn-ing like this__ I could kiss ev-'ry-bod-y I'm so full of love

and good-will.__ Let me say fur-ther-more__ I'd a-dore ev-'ry-

bod-y to come and dine. The plea-sure's, mine And I will pay the bill. May I
world's in a won-

D.S. al Coda    CODA

-der-ful way.__ On A Won-der-ful Day__ Like To-day.__

## WHO CAN I TURN TO
### (When Nobody Needs Me)

© Copyright 1964 Concord Music Ltd., London, England
TRO - MUSICAL COMEDY PRODUCTIONS, INC., New York, controls all publication rights for the U.S.A. & Canada

Words and Music by
LESLIE BRICUSSE & ANTHONY NEWLEY

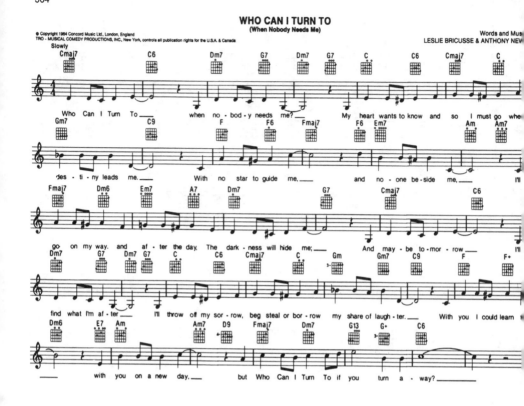

## NOTHING CAN STOP ME NOW!

© Copyright 1965 Concord Music Ltd., London, England
TRO - MUSICAL COMEDY PRODUCTIONS, INC., New York, controls all publication rights for the U.S.A. & Canada

Words and Music by
LESLIE BRICUSSE & ANTHONY NEWLEY

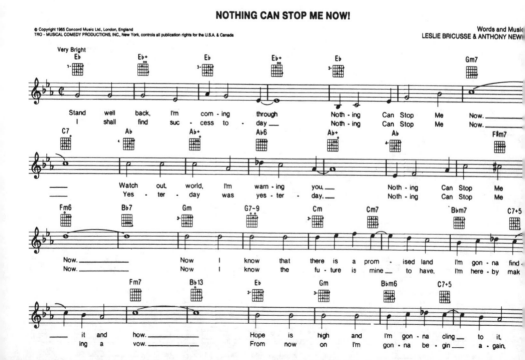

Tie ev - 'ry string ___ to it, Give ev - 'ry - thing ___ to it. I'll make all my
Stick out my chin ___ a - gain Go in and win ___ a - gain. Get you gone, you

dreams come true ___ Be - fore my fi - nal bow. ___ How I'll
sky of grey ___ Fare - well you fur - rowed brow. ___ Now my

do it, who can say? ___ But I know I will some day. ___
fu - ture's crys - tal clear. ___ No more woe for me to fear. ___ I'm gonna

Watch out, world, I'm on my way, ___ Noth - ing Can Stop ___ Me Now.
stand this world up - on its ear, ___ And I'll suc - ceed ___ some -

how. ___ Noth - ing Can Stop ___ Me Now. ___

506

## "Roberta"

## SMOKE GETS IN YOUR EYES

Copyright © 1933 PolyGram International Publishing, Inc.
Copyright Renewed

Words by OTTO HARBACH
Music by JEROME KERN

## YESTERDAYS

Copyright © 1933 PolyGram International Publishing, Inc.
Copyright Renewed

Words by OTTO HARBACH
Music by JEROME KERN

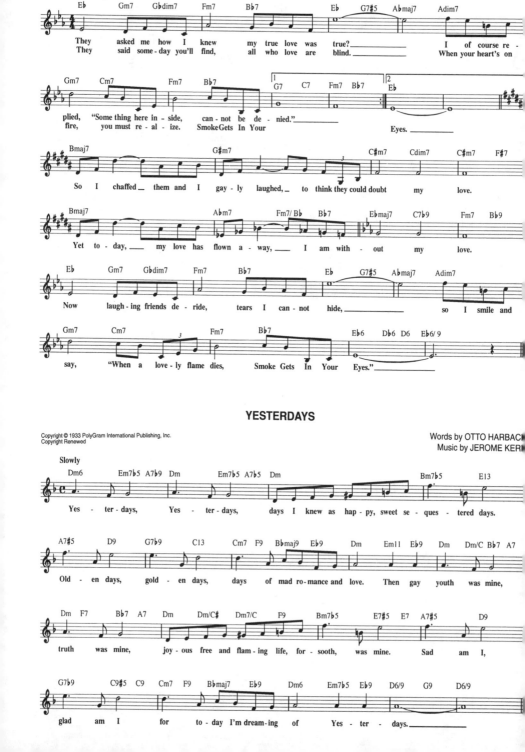

"Song & Dance"

# TELL ME ON A SUNDAY

yright © 1980 The Really Useful Group Ltd. and Dick James Music Ltd.
ghts for the United States and Canada Administered by PolyGram International Publishing, Inc.
d Songs Of PolyGram International, Inc.

Music by ANDREW LLOYD WEBBER
Lyrics by DON BLACK

# CAPPED TEETH AND CAESAR SALAD

Copyright © 1980 The Really Useful Group Ltd. and Dick James Music Ltd.
All Rights for the United States and Canada Administered by
PolyGram International Publishing, Inc. and Songs Of PolyGram International, Inc.

Music by ANDREW LLOYD WEBB
Lyrics by DON BLA

**Additional Lyrics**

**Verse 2** Capped Teeth And Caesar Salad
Spotless Beverly Hills
If someone takes a walk
All the neighbours talk
Ev'ry man and beast
Came from out east
Earthquakes and English muffins
Ulcers poppin' away
The films are being hyped
Before the scripts are typed
I'll call you back and have a nice day.

**Verse 3** Instrumental
(Telephone voice over second half)
"Hello. . .Mr. Bloom's office."
(Hello! Can I speak to Sheldon, please?)
"No, I am afraid Mr. Bloom's at a screening.
If you would like to leave word,"
(Oh, yes.) "We'll get right back to you."
(But I wanted to. . .)
"Thank you for calling
Have a nice day, too. . .
And a nice swim!

**Verse 4** Capped Teeth And Caesar Salad
Cozy Beverly Hills
Out here a woman shops
Until her chauffer drops
When her bosoms droop
Fifty surgeons swoop
Don't work — sit and look pretty
Keep your boredom at bay
Out here the rainbow ends
In your Mercedes Benz
I'll call you back and have a nice day.

# COME BACK WITH THE SAME LOOK IN YOUR EYES

Copyright © 1985 The Really Useful Group Ltd. and Dick James Music Ltd.
All Rights for the United States and Canada Administered by
PolyGram International Publishing, Inc. and Songs Of PolyGram International, Inc.

Music by ANDREW LLOYD WEBBE
Lyrics by DON BLAC

Moderate Rock

I will see you in a week or two___ it's late, you bet-ter get go - ing___
know you've got your work to do,___ and I know how much you love___ me,___

# UNEXPECTED SONG

Copyright © 1982 The Really Useful Group Ltd. and Steam Power Music Ltd.
All Rights for the United States and Canada Administered by PolyGram International Publishing, Inc.
and Songs Of PolyGram International, Inc.

Music by ANDREW LLOYD WEBBER
Lyrics by DON BLACK

# SO MUCH TO DO IN NEW YORK

ht © 1985 The Really Useful Group Ltd. and Dick James Music Ltd.
ts for the United States and Canada Administered by PolyGram International Publishing, Inc.
ongs Of PolyGram International, Inc.

Music by ANDREW LLOYD WEBBER
Lyrics by DON BLACK
Additional Lyrics by RICHARD MALTBY, JR.

With smooth motion

I guess that's one way to have an ar - riv - al, first night here___ out on my ear. New York's first les - son they say is sur - viv - al. Well, all right,___ look at this night. First I must get my green card, I don't dare take a chance. For if I'm caught work - ing they'll sim - ply de - port me, and no one will see all the fab - u - lous hats that I make. Need one break. So Much To Do in New York when you're sin - gle.___ Where to start, bal - let or art? So Much To Do In New York with no mon - ey; thou - sand pounds,___ less than it sounds. I'm mak - ing plans, but I've no___ place to live, It's three A. M. Good - bye Chuck. Hel - lo Viv.___

## "Sinbad"

# ROCK-A-BYE YOUR BABY WITH A DIXIE MELODY

Copyright © 1994 by HAL LEONARD CORPORATION

Words by SAM M. LEWIS and JOE YOUN
Music by JEAN SCHWART

## "Something For The Boys"

### SOMETHING FOR THE BOYS

Copyright © 1942 by Chappell & Co. Inc.
Copyright renewed

Words and Mus
COLE PO

# "Something's Afoot"

## YOU FELL OUT OF THE SKY

Copyright © 1971, 1975 by Alley Music Corp. and Trio Music Co., Inc.
All rights administered by Hudson Bay Music, Inc.
Used by Permission

Music & Lyrics by JAMES McDONALD,
DAVID VOS & ROBERT GERLACH
Additional Music by ED LINDERMAN

# "Snoopy"

## JUST ONE PERSON

Copyright © 1976 and 1978 by Unichappell Music, Inc.

Words by HAL HACKADY
Music by LENNY GROSSMAN

Slowly, with expression

If Just One Per-son be-lieves in you,__ deep e-nough and strong e-nough be-lieves in you,__
two whole peo-ple be-lieve in you__ deep e-nough and strong e-nough be-lieve in you.__

hard e-nough and long e-nough, be-fore you knew it, some-one else would think: "If he can do it, I can do it"
hard e-nough and long e-nough, there's bound to be some-

Mak-ing it two.__ Two whole peo-ple who be-lieve in you.__ And if

oth-er per-son who be-lieves in mak-ing it a three-some. Mak-ing it three,__

Peo-ple you can say __ be-lieve in me.__ And if three whole peo-ple,__ why not four? And if

four whole peo-ple,__ why not more __ and more and more?__ And when

all those peo-ple be-lieve in you,__ deep e-nough and strong e-nough be-lieve in you,__ hard e-nough and long e-nough.

it stands to rea-son you your-self would start to see what ev-'ry-bod-y sees in you,__ And

Rubato

may-be ev-en you can be-lieve in you too.__

## "Salvation"

### IF YOU LET ME MAKE LOVE TO YOU THEN WHY CAN'T I TOUCH YOU?

Words and Music by
C.C. COURTNEY & PETER LINK

Copyright © 1969 by Chappell & Co., Inc.

Moderately, deliberately

# TOMORROW IS THE FIRST DAY OF THE REST OF MY LIFE

Words and Music by
C.C. COURTNEY & PETER LINK

Copyright © 1969 by Chappell & Co., Inc.

**"Sally"**

# LOOK FOR THE SILVER LINING

Copyright © 1920 PolyGram International Publishing, Inc. and Stephen Ballentine Publishing
Copyright Renewed

Words by BUDDY DeSYLVA
Music by JEROME KERN

**"Say, Darling"**

### DANCE ONLY WITH ME

Copyright © 1958 by Betty Comden and Adolph Green
Stratford Music Corporation, Publisher and owner of publication and allied rights throughout the world.
Sole selling agent: Chappell & Co., Inc.

Words by BETTY COMDEN and ADOLPH GREEN
Music by JULE STYNE

518

## "Saratoga"

### YOU FOR ME

© 1959, 1963 HAROLD ARLEN and JOHNNY MERCER
All Rights Throughout the World Controlled by HARWIN MUSIC CO.

Lyric by JOHNNY MERCER
Music by HAROLD ARLEN

## "Seven Lively Arts"

### EV'RY TIME WE SAY GOODBYE

Copyright © 1944 by Chappell & Co.
Copyright Renewed
International Copyright Secured   ALL RIGHTS RESERVED

Words and Music by
COLE PORTER

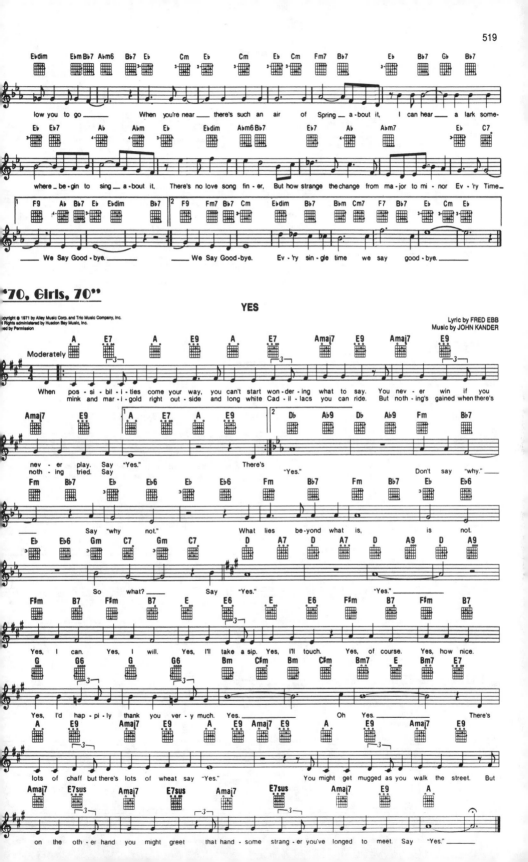

**"70, Girls, 70"**

YES

Copyright © 1971 by Alley Music Corp. and Trio Music Company, Inc.
All Rights administered by Husdon Bay Music, Inc.
Used by Permission

Lyric by FRED EBB
Music by JOHN KANDER

## WE MAKE A BEAUTIFUL PAIR

© 1974, 1975 GARY GELD and PETER UDELL
All Rights Throughout the World Controlled by EDWIN H. MORRIS & COMPANY, A Division of MPL Communications, Inc.

Lyric by PETER UDELL
Music by GARY GELD

# VIOLETS AND SILVERBELLS

© 1974, 1975 GARY GELD and PETER UDELL
All Rights Throughout the World Controlled by EDWIN H. MORRIS & COMPANY, A Division of MPL Communications, Inc.

Lyric by PETER UDEL
Music by GARY GEL

Vi - lets And Sil - ver - bells, ___ grapes on the vine. ___ Love, like a vine - yard grows del - i - cate
wine. ___ Sug - ar 'n' cin - na - mon, pep - per and spice, ___ Love is the re - ci - pe that
fla - vors a life. ___ Sure as the bri - er and bram - ble en - twine ___ So it will
al - ways be {your dreams and mine. } to cherish till death do us part According to God's Holy ordinance
{your love and mine. }
And there to I plight thee my troth. (Reverend:) In the name of the Father and the Son and the Holy Ghost, I now pronounce you man and wife.
Amen. Dai - sies and mar - i - gold, ros - es that climb, Love, like a gar - den, grows
sweet - er with time, ___ So will our gar - den grow sweet - er with time.
(Group:) Hum under dialogue
(Bride:) For richer, for poorer, In sickness, in health, To love and
sweet - er with time. ___

## "Show Boat"

### BILL

Copyright © 1927 PolyGram International Publishing, Inc.
Copyright Renewed

Lyrics by P.G. WODEHOUSE and OSCAR HAMMERSTEIN II
Music by JEROME KERN

But a - long came Bill, who's not the type at all. You'd meet him on the street and nev - er no - tice him ___ His
just my Bill, an or - di - nar - y boy. He has - n't got a thing that I can brag a - bout. ___ And
form and face, his man - ly grace Are not the kind that you would find in a sta - tue. And I
yet to be up - on his knee so com - fy and room - y feels nat - u - ral to me. And I

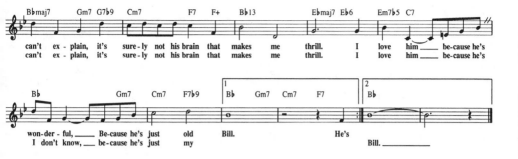

can't ex-plain, it's sure-ly not his brain that makes me thrill. I love him____ be-cause he's
can't ex-plain, it's sure-ly not his brain that makes me thrill. I love him____ be-cause he's

won-der-ful, ____ Be-cause he's just old Bill. He's
I don't know, ___ be-cause he's just my Bill. _____

# CAN'T HELP LOVIN' DAT MAN

Copyright © 1927 PolyGram International Publishing, Inc.
Copyright Renewed

Lyrics by OSCAR HAMMERSTEIN II
Music by JEROME KERN

Fish got to swim ___ and birds got to fly ___ I got to love ___ one man till I die ___ Can't Help

Lov-in' Dat Man ___ of mine. Tell me he's la-zy tell me he's slow. ___

Tell me I'm cra-zy may-be I know. Can't Help Lov-in' Dat Man ___ of mine.

When he goes a-way ___ Dat's a rain-y. day ___ And when he comes back dat day is

fine, ____ The sun will shine He can come home ___ as late as can be. ___ Home with-out him ___ ain't

no home to me ___ Can't Help Lov-in' Dat Man ___ of mine. _____

# MAKE BELIEVE

Copyright © 1927 PolyGram International Publishing, Inc.
Copyright Renewed

Lyrics by OSCAR HAMMERSTEIN II
Music by JEROME KERN

We could Make Be - lieve I love you, on - ly Make Be - lieve that you love me. Oth - ers find peace of mind in pre - tend - ing. Could - n't you, could - n't I? Could - n't we Make Be - lieve our lips are blend - ing in a phan - tom kiss or two or three? Might as well Make Be - lieve I love you, for to tell the truth I do.

# OL' MAN RIVER

Copyright © 1927 PolyGram International Publishing, Inc.
Copyright Renewed

Lyrics by OSCAR HAMMERSTEIN II
Music by JEROME KERN

Ol' Man Riv-er, dat Ol' Man Riv-er, He must know sump-in', but don't say noth-in', He jus' keeps roll-in', He keeps on roll-in' a - long. He don't plant 'ta-ters, he don't plant cot-ton, An' dem dat plants 'em is soon for-got-ten; But Ol' Man Riv-er, he jus' keeps roll-in' a - long. You an' me, we sweat an' strain, Bod-y all ach-in' an' racked wid pain. "Tote dat barge!" "Lift dat bale," Git a lit-tle drunk an' you land in jail. Ah gits wea-ry an' sick of try-in', Ah'm tired of liv-in' An' skeered of dy-in', But Ol' Man Riv-er, he jus' keeps roll-in' a - long. long.

# WHY DO I LOVE YOU?

Copyright © 1927 PolyGram International Publishing, Inc.
Copyright Renewed

Lyrics by OSCAR HAMMERSTEIN II
Music by JEROME KERN

## "The Show Is On"

## BY STRAUSS

Copyright © 1936 by Chappell & Co., Inc.
Copyright Renewed
International Copyright Secured    ALL RIGHTS RESERVED

Words by IRA GERSHWIN
Music by GEORGE GERSHWIN

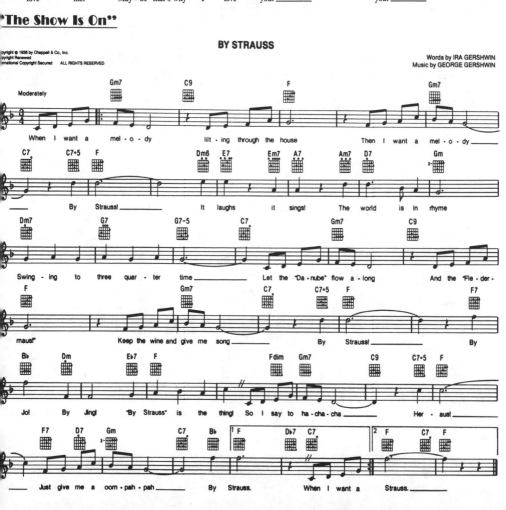

# LITTLE OLD LADY

Copyright © 1936 by Chappell & Co., Inc.
Copyright Renewed

Words and Music by
STANLEY ADAMS and HOAGY CHARMICHAEL

Slowly and Gracefully

Lit - tle Old La - dy pass-ing by, Catch-ing ev - 'ry-one's eye, You have such a charm-ing man-ner, sweet and

La - dy so pe - tite, Ask the cop on the beat, He'll be glad to help you when you cross the

shy. Lit - tle old bon - net set in place, And a smile on your face, You're a per - fect pic - ture in your

street. Lit - tle Old La - dy where's your shawl? It's so late in the fall, You might start to sneeze, and my! That

lav - en - der and lace. Lit - tle bit of busi - ness here, Lit - tle bit of busi - ness there,

would - n't do at all. Lit - tle lav-el - ier of jet, Lit - tle things you can't for - get,

Bet that you've been win - dow shop-ping all a - round the square. Lit - tle Old La - dy time for tea, Here's a kiss, two or

Bet you were the reign-ing belle at ev - 'ry min - u - et. Lit - tle Old la - dy so po - lite, Close your eyes, that's all

three, You're just like that Lit - tle Old La - dy. I hold dear to me. Lit - tle Old

right, You de - serve a sweet bou-quet of pleas-ant dreams to night.

---

**"Silk Stockings"**

## ALL OF YOU

Copyright © 1954 by Cole Porter
Chappell & Co., Inc., owner of publication and allied rights throughout the world.
International Copyright Secured    ALL RIGHTS RESERVED

Words and Music
COLE PORTER

Moderately

I love the looks of you, the lure of you, The sweet of you, the

pure of you, The eyes, the arms, the mouth of you, The East, West, North and the

South of you.___ I'd love to gain com - plete con - trol of you, And han - dle

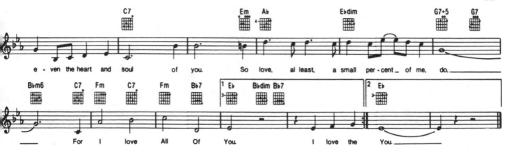

e-ven the heart and soul of you. So love, at least, a small per-cent of me, do,

For I love All Of You. I love the You.

## FATED TO BE MATED

Copyright © 1957 by Buxton Hill Music Corporation
nappell & Co., Inc., owner of publication and allied rights throughout the World.

Words and Music by
COLE PORTER

Foxtrot

We were Fat-ed To Be Mat-ed, We were slat-ed to be tied.

Me as the burn-ing bride-groom, You as the yearn-ing bride.

We were spot-ted to be knot-ted And al-lot-ted

a glor-i-ous life. Me as the won-der hus-band,

You as the won-der-ful wife. So why not have a fling with a wed-ding ring

Trust-ing ev'-ry-thing to the gods a-bove? For we were Fat-ed To Be

Mat-ed And for-ev-er and ev-er in love. We were love.

# PARIS LOVES LOVERS

Copyright © 1954 Cole Porter
Copyright renewed, Chappell & Co., Inc., owner of publication and allied rights throughout the world

Words and Music by
COLE PORTER

Pa - ris Loves Lov - ers, For lov - ers it's heav - en a - bove.

Pa - ris tells lov - ers "Love is su - preme, wake up your dream and make love!"

On - ly in Pa - ris one dis - cov - ers The urge to merge with the splurge of the spring.

Pa - ris Loves Lov - ers. For lov - ers know that love is ev - 'ry - thing.

love is ev - 'ry - thing.

## "Song Of Norway"

# I LOVE YOU
(Song Of Norway)

Copyright © 1944 by Chappell & Co., Inc.
Copyright Renewed
International Copyright Secured    ALL RIGHTS RESERVED

Words & Music Adaptation (Based on
EDWARD GREIG Music) arr. by ALBERT SIRMAY
Words by ROBERT WRIGHT & GEORGE FORREST

I hear you ask if I am yours for keep - ing, Shame, that a doubt should ev - er pass your lips.

I say it wak - ing, shall I say it sleep - ing? I love your lips, I love your laugh, I love the tear that dims your

danc - ing eyes, I love You, dear, and there your an - swer lies. And should you ask if time has dulled my long - ing, Say, has the

North-ern star gone cours-ing South? If me you doubt, 'Tis on-ly you you're wrong-ing, I loved you then, I love you now, I'll love you when the world grows old and dies I Love You, dear, and here your an-swer lies.

## STRANGE MUSIC
(Based on "Nocturne" & "Wedding Day in Troldhaugen" by Edward Grieg)

Musical Adaptation by
ROBERT WRIGHT & GEORGE FORREST

Copyright © 1944 by Chappell & Co., Inc.
Copyright Renewed
International Copyright Secured    ALL RIGHTS RESERVED

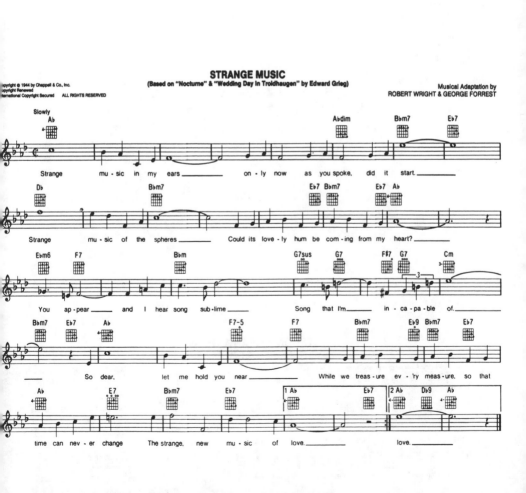

Strange mu-sic in my ears ____ on-ly now as you spoke, did it start. ____

Strange mu-sic of the spheres ____ Could its love-ly hum be com-ing from my heart? ____

You ap-pear ____ and I hear song sub-lime Song that I'm ____ in-ca-pa-ble of.

____ So dear, let me hold you near ____ While we treas-ure ev-'ry meas-ure, so that

time can nev-er change The strange, new mu-sic of love. ____ love. ____

## "Sophisticated Ladies"

## CARAVAN

Copyright © 1937 (Renewed 1965) and Assigned to Famous Music Corporation and
EMI Mills Music Inc. in the U.S.A.
Rights for the world outside the U.S.A. Controlled by EMI Mills Music Inc. and CPP/Belwin, Inc.

Words and Music by DUKE ELLINGTON,
IRVING MILLS and JUAN TIZOL

Night _____ and stars a - bove that shine so bright _____ the mys - t'ry
Sleep _____ up - on my shoul - der as we creep _____ a - cross the
you, _____ be - side me here be - neath the blue _____ my dream of

of their fad - ing light _____ that shines up - on our Car - a -
sands so I may keep _____ this mem - 'ry of our Car - a -
love is com - ing true _____ with - in our des - ert Car - a -

van. _____ This _____ is so ex - cit - ing
van. _____
van. _____

you _____ are so in - vit - ing rest - ing in my

arms as I thrill to _____ the mag - ic charms _____ of

## IT DON'T MEAN A THING
### (IF IT AIN'T GOT THAT SWING)

Copyright © 1932 (Renewed 1959) and Assigned to Famous Music Corporation and
EMI Mills Music Inc. in the U.S.A.
Rights for the world outside the U.S.A. Controlled by EMI Mills Music Inc. and CPP/Belwin, Inc.

Words and Music by DUKE ELLINGTON
and IRVING MILLS

It Don't Mean A Thing, if it ain't got that swing, _ (doo wah, _ doo wah,

doo wah, doo wah, doo wah, _ doo wah, doo wah, doo wah,) It Don't Mean A Thing, _ all you

got to do is sing, (doo wah,_ doo wah, doo wah, doo wah, doo wah,_ doo wah, doo wah, doo wah,) It makes no diff-'rence if _ it's sweet or hot, _____ Just give that rhy-thm ev-'ry-thing you got, Oh, It Don't Mean A Thing, if it ain't got that swing, _ (doo wah,_ doo wah, doo wah, doo wah, doo wah,_ doo wah, doo wah, doo wah.) It wah.)

## MOOD INDIGO

Copyright © 1931 (Renewed 1958) and Assigned to Famous Music Corporation,
EMI Mills Music Inc. and Indigo Mood Music c/o The Songwriters Guild Of America in the U.S.A.
Rights for the world outside the U.S.A. Controlled by EMI Mills Music Inc. and CPP/Belwin, Inc.

Words and Music by DUKE ELLINGTON,
IRVING MILLS and ALBANY BIGARD

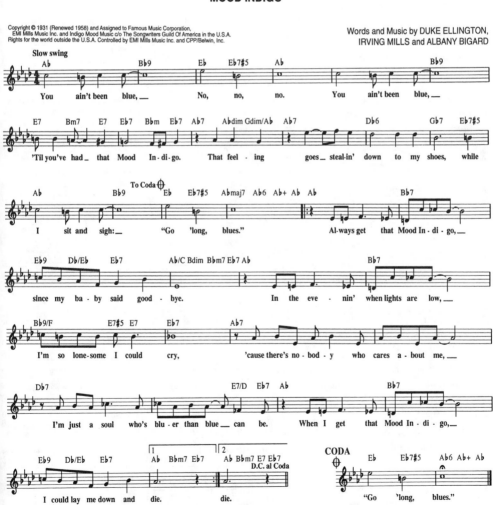

**Slow swing**

You ain't been blue, _ No, no, no. You ain't been blue, _ 'Til you've had _ that Mood In - di - go. That feel - ing goes _ steal-in' down to my shoes, while I sit and sigh: _ "Go 'long, blues." Al-ways get that Mood In - di - go, _ since my ba - by said good - bye. In the eve - nin' when lights are low, _ I'm so lone - some I could cry, 'cause there's no - bod - y who cares a - bout me, _ I'm just a soul who's blu - er than blue _ can be. When I get that Mood In - di - go, _ I could lay me down and die. die. "Go 'long, blues."

**To Coda**

**D.C. al Coda**

**CODA**

# SATIN DOLL

Copyright © 1958 (Renewed 1986) and Assigned to Famous Music Corporation,
WB Music Corp. and Tempo Music, Inc. c/o Music Sales Corporation in the U.S.A.
Rights for the world outside the U.S.A. Controlled by EMI Robbins Music Ltd. and CPP/Belwin, Inc.

Words by JOHNNY MERCER
Music by BILLY STRAYHORN and DUKE ELLINGTON

# SOPHISTICATED LADY

Copyright © 1933 (Renewed 1960) and Assigned to Famous Music Corporation and
EMI Mills Music Inc. in the U.S.A.
Rights for the world outside the U.S.A. Controlled by EMI Mills Music Inc. and CPP/Belwin, Inc.

Words and Music by DUKE ELLINGTON,
IRVING MILLS and MITCHELL PARISH

# The Sound Of Music"

## AN ORDINARY COUPLE

right © 1959 by Richard Rodgers and Oscar Hammerstein II
right Renewed
AMSON MUSIC owner of publication and allied rights throughout the world

Lyrics by OSCAR HAMMERSTEIN II
Music by RICHARD RODGERS

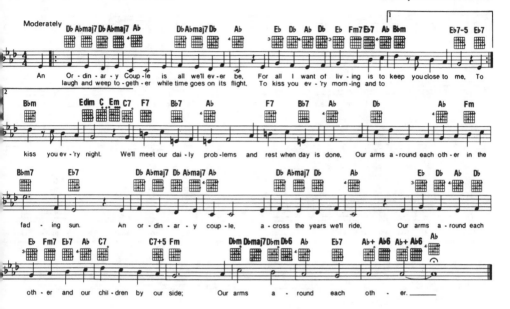

An Or - din - ar - y Coup - le is all we'll ev - er be, For all I want of liv - ing is to keep you close to me, To
laugh and weep to - geth - er while time goes on its flight. To kiss you ev - 'ry morn - ing and to

kiss you ev - 'ry night. We'll meet our dai - ly prob - lems and rest when day is done, Our arms a - round each oth - er in the

fad - ing sun. An or - din - a - ry coup - le, a - cross the years we'll ride, Our arms a - round each

oth - er and our chil - dren by our side; Our arms a - round each oth - er.

## CLIMB EV'RY MOUNTAIN

opyright © 1959 by Richard Rodgers and Oscar Hammerstein II
opyright Renewed
LLIAMSON MUSIC owner of publication and allied rights throughout the world

Lyrics by OSCAR HAMMERSTEIN II
Music by RICHARD RODGERS

Climb Ev - 'ry Moun - tain, search high and low. Fol - low ev - 'ry by - way, ev - 'ry path you

know. Climb Ev - 'ry Moun - tain, ford ev - 'ry stream, Fol - low ev - 'ry rain - bow,

till you find your dream! A dream that will need all the love you can give. Ev - 'ry

day of your life for as long as you live. Climb Ev - 'ry Moun - tain, ford ev - 'ry

stream. Fol - low ev - 'ry rain - bow till you find your dream!

# DO-RE-MI

Copyright © 1959 by Richard Rodgers and Oscar Hammerstein II
Copyright Renewed
WILLIAMSON MUSIC owner of publication and allied rights throughout the world

Lyrics by OSCAR HAMMERSTEIN
Music by RICHARD RODGERS

Doe a deer, a fe-male deer, Ray a drop of gol-den sun,

Me a name I call my-self, Far a long, long way to run.

Sew a nee-dle pull-ing thread,____ La a note to fol-low sew,

Tea a drink with jam and bread____ That will bring us back to do—oh—

oh—oh! do! Do-re-mi-fa-so-la-ti-do!____

# HOW CAN LOVE SURVIVE

Copyright © 1959 by Richard Rodgers and Oscar Hammerstein II
Copyright Renewed
WILLIAMSON MUSIC owner of publication and allied rights throughout the world

Lyrics by OSCAR HAMMERSTEIN
Music by RICHARD RODGERS

No lit-tle shack do you share with me,__ We do not flee from a mort-ga-gee,__ Nar-y a
No lit-tle cold wa-ter flat have we,__ Warmed by the glow of in-sol-ven-cy,__ Up to your

care in the world have we: How can love sur-vive? You're fond of bonds and you
necks in' se-cur-i-ty.____ How can love sur-vive? How can I show what I

own a lot.__ I have a plane and a die-sel yacht,__ Plen-ty of noth-ing you have-n't got
feel for you?_ I can-not go out and steal for you,__ I can-not die like Ca-mille for you,__ are too

____ How can love sur-vive?____ No rides for us on the top of a bus in the
____ How can love sur-vive? You mil-lion-aires with fi-nan-cial af-fairs are too

face of the freez-ing breez-es. ___ You reach your goals in your com-fy old Rolls or in one of your
bus-y for sim-ple plea-sure. When you are poor it is tou-jours l'a-mour, For l'a-mour all the

Mer-ce-des-es! ___ Far, ver-y far off the beam are we, ___ Quaint and bi-zarre as a
poor have lei-sure! ___ Caught in our gold plat-ed chains are we, ___ Lost in our wealth-y do-

team are we, ___ Two mil-lion-aires with a dream are we, ___ We're keep-ing ro-mance a-live. ___
mains are we, ___ Trapped by our cap-i-tal gains are we, ___ But we'll keep ro-mance a-live. ___

___ Two mil-lion-aires with a dream are we, We'll make our love ___
___ Trapped by your cap-i-tal gains are you, We'll/You'll make our/your love ___

sur - vive.

sur - vive!

## MARIA

Copyright © 1959 by Richard Rodgers and Oscar Hammerstein II
Copyright Renewed
WILLIAMSON MUSIC owner of publication and allied rights throughout the world

Lyrics by OSCAR HAMMERSTEIN II
Music by RICHARD RODGERS

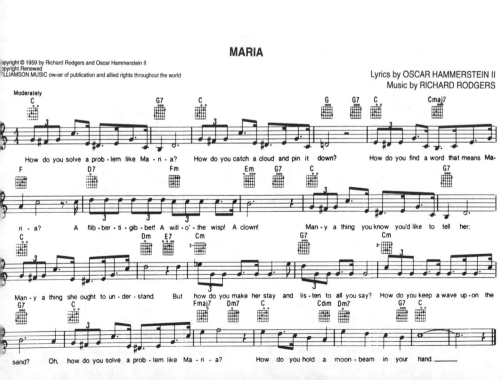

How do you solve a prob-lem like Ma-ri-a? How do you catch a cloud and pin it down? How do you find a word that means Ma-

ri-a? A flib-ber-ti-gib-bet! A will-o'-the wisp! A clown! Man-y a thing you know you'd like to tell her;

Man-y a thing she ought to un-der-stand. But how do you make her stay and lis-ten to all you say? How do you keep a wave up-on the

sand? Oh, how do you solve a prob-lem like Ma-ri-a? How do you hold a moon-beam in your hand. ___

# THE LONELY GOATHERD

Copyright © 1959 by Richard Rodgers and Oscar Hammerstein II
Copyright Renewed
WILLIAMSON MUSIC owner of publication and allied rights throughout the world

Lyrics by OSCAR HAMMERSTEIN
Music by RICHARD RODGERS

# MY FAVORITE THINGS

Copyright © 1959 by Richard Rodgers and Oscar Hammerstein II
Copyright Renewed
WILLIAMSON MUSIC owner of publication and allied rights throughout the world

Lyrics by OSCAR HAMMERSTEIN
Music by RICHARD RODGERS

warm wool-en mit-tens, Brown pa-per pack-ag-es tied up with string,
schnitz-el with noo-dles Wild gese that fly with the moon on their wings,
These are a few of My Fa-vor-ite Things. Girls in white
dress-es with blue sat-in sash-es, Snow-flakes that stay on my nose and eye-lash-es,
Sil-ver white win-ters that melt in-to springs. These are a few of my
Fa-vor-ite Things. When the dog bites, When the bee stings, When I'm
feel-ing sad, I sim-ply re-mem-ber My Fa-vor-ite Things and
then I don't feel so bad.

## EDELWEISS

Copyright © 1959 by Richard Rodgers and Oscar Hammerstein II
Copyright Renewed
WILLIAMSON MUSIC owner of publication and allied rights throughout the world

Lyrics by OSCAR HAMMERSTEIN II
Music by RICHARD RODGERS

Slowly, with expression

E - del - weiss, E - del - weiss, Ev - 'ry morn - ing you greet me.

Small and white, Clean and bright, You look hap - py to meet me.

Blos - som of snow, may you bloom and grow, Bloom and grow for - ev - er.

E - del - weiss, E - del - weiss, Bless my home - land for - ev - er.

# SIXTEEN GOING ON SEVENTEEN

Copyright © 1959 by Richard Rodgers and Oscar Hammerstein II
Copyright Renewed
WILLIAMSON MUSIC owner of publication and allied rights throughout the world

Lyrics by OSCAR HAMMERSTEIN
Music by RICHARD RODGE

# SO LONG, FAREWELL

Copyright © 1959, 1960 by Richard Rodgers and Oscar Hammerstein II
Copyright Renewed
WILLIAMSON MUSIC owner of publication and allied rights throughout the world

Lyrics by OSCAR HAMMERSTEIN
Music by RICHARD RODGE

## THE SOUND OF MUSIC

Copyright © 1959 by Richard Rodgers and Oscar Hammerstein II
Copyright Renewed
WILLIAMSON MUSIC owner of publication and allied rights throughout the world

Lyrics by OSCAR HAMMERSTEIN II
Music by RICHARD RODGERS

# "South Pacific"

## BALI HA'I

Copyright © 1949 by Richard Rodgers and Oscar Hammerstein II
Copyright Renewed
WILLIAMSON MUSIC owner of publication and allied rights throughout the world

Lyrics by OSCAR HAMMERSTEIN
Music by RICHARD RODGER

Ba - li Ha'i may call you an - y night, an - y day. In your heart____ you'll hear it

call you: "Come a - way, come a - way." Ba - li Ha'i will whis - per In the wind of the

sea: "Here am I,____ Your spe - cial is - land! Come to me, come to me!" Your own spe - cial

hopes, Your own spe - cial dreams, Bloom on the hill - side and shine in the

streams. If you try, You'll find me where the sky Meets the sea. Here am I____ Your spe - cial

is - land! Come to me, come to me!" Ba - li Ha'i, Ba - li Ha'i Ba - li Ha'i!____

# BLOODY MARY

Copyright © 1949 by Richard Rodgers and Oscar Hammerstein II
Copyright Renewed
WILLIAMSON MUSIC owner of publication and allied rights throughout the world

Lyrics by OSCAR HAMMERSTEIN II
Music by RICHARD RODGERS

Blood-y Ma-ry is the girl I love. Blood-y Ma-ry is the girl I love. Blood-y
Her skin is ten-der as Di-Mag-gio's glove. Her skin is

Ma-ry is the girl I love. Now ain't that too damn bad!
ten-der as Di-Mag-gio's glove. Now ain't that too damn bad!

Blood-y Ma-ry's chew-ing be-tel nuts, She is al-ways chew-ing be-tel nuts, Blood-y Ma-ry's chew-ing

be-tel nuts, And she don't use Pep-so-dent! Now ain't that too damn bad!

# TWIN SOLILOQUIES
## (THIS IS HOW IT FEELS)

Copyright © 1949 by Richard Rodgers and Oscar Hammerstein II
Copyright Renewed
WILLIAMSON MUSIC owner of publication and allied rights throughout the world

Lyrics by OSCAR HAMMERSTEIN II
Music by RICHARD RODGERS

Won-der how I'd feel Liv-ing on a hill-side, Look-ing on an o-cean, Beau-ti-ful and still.

This is what I need, This is what I've longed for, Some-one young and smil-ing Climb-ing up my hill!

We are not a-like. Prob-a-bly I'd bore him. He's a cul-tured French-man, I'm a lit-tle hick.

Young-er men than I, Off-i-cers and doc-tors, Prob-a-bly pur-sue her, she could have her pick.

Won-der why I feel Jit-ter-y and jump-y! I am like a school-girl, Wait-ing for a dance. Can I ask her

now? I am like a school-boy! What will be her an-swer? Do I have a chance?

# DITES-MOI (TELL ME WHY)

Copyright © 1949 by Richard Rodgers and Oscar Hammerstein II
Copyright Renewed
WILLIAMSON MUSIC owner of publication and allied rights throughout the world

Lyrics by OSCAR HAMMERSTEIN
Music by RICHARD RODGERS

Di - tes - moi _____ Pour - quoi _____ La vie est bel - le, Di - tes - moi _____
Tell me why _____ The sky is filled with mu - sic, Tell me why _____

_____ Pour - quoi _____ La vie est gai? Di - tes - moi _____ Pour - quoi, _____ Chere ma - d'm'
_____ We fly _____ on clouds a - bove Can it be that we Can fly to

sel - le, Est - ce - que Par - ce - que vous m'ai - mez? mez?
mu - sic Just be - cause, Just be - cause we're in love? love?

# A COCK-EYED OPTIMIST

Copyright © 1949 by Richard Rodgers and Oscar Hammerstein II
Copyright Renewed
WILLIAMSON MUSIC owner of publication and allied rights throughout the world

Lyrics by OSCAR HAMMERSTEIN
Music by RICHARD RODGERS

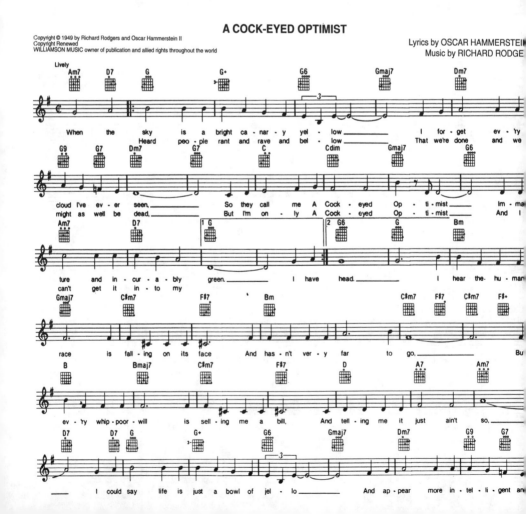

When the sky is a bright ca - nar - y yel - low _____ I for - get ev - 'ry
Heard peo - ple rant and rave and bel - low _____ That we're done and we

cloud I've ev - er seen, _____ So they call me A Cock - eyed Op - ti - mist _____ Im - ma
might as well be dead, _____ But I'm on - ly A Cock - eyed Op - ti - mist _____ And I

ture and in - cur - a - bly green. I have head. _____ I hear the hu - man
can't get it in - to my

race is fall - ing on its face And has - n't very far to go. _____ Bu

ev - 'ry whip - poor - will is sell - ing me a bill, And tell - ing me it just ain't so. _____

_____ I could say life is just a bowl of jel - lo _____ And ap - pear more in - tel - i - gent an

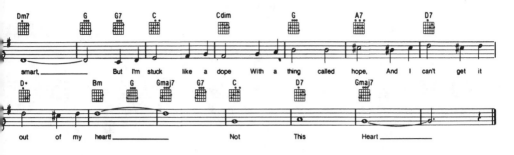

**smart, _____ But I'm stuck like a dope With a thing called hope, And I can't get it**

**out of my heart! _____ Not This Heart _____**

## A WONDERFUL GUY

Copyright © 1949 by Richard Rodgers and Oscar Hammerstein II
Copyright Renewed
WILLIAMSON MUSIC owner of publication and allied rights throughout the world

Lyrics by OSCAR HAMMERSTEIN II
Music by RICHARD RODGERS

**Moderately Bright**

I'm as corn-y as Kan-sas in Au-gust, I'm as nor-mal as
I am in a con-ven-tion-al dith-er, With a con-ven-tion-al

blue-ber-ry pie. No more a smart lit-tle girl with no heart, I have
star in my eye. And you will note there's a lump in my throat when I

found me A Won-der-ful Guy! _____
speak of that won-der-ful guy! _____ I'm as

trite and as gay as a dai-sy in May, A cli-ché com-ing true!

I'm bro-mid-ic and bright as a moon hap-py night Pour-ing light on the dew! _____

I'm as corn-y as Kan-sas in Au-gust, High as a flag on the

Fourth of Ju-ly! If you'll ex-cuse an ex-pres-sion I use, I'm in love, I'm in

love, I'm in love, I'm in love, I'm in love with A Won-der-ful Guy! _____

# HAPPY TALK

Copyright © 1949 by Richard Rodgers and Oscar Hammerstein II
Copyright Renewed
WILLIAMSON MUSIC owner of publication and allied rights throughout the world

Lyrics by OSCAR HAMMERSTEIN
Music by RICHARD RODGERS

Hap - py Talk, keep talk - in' Hap - py Talk,_____ Talk a - bout things you'd like to do._____

You got - ta have a dream. If you don't have a dream. How you gon - na

have a dream come true?_____ true?_____ Talk a - bout a moon

Float - in' in de sky Look - in' like a lil - y on a lake;_____ Talk a - bout a

bird Learn - in' how to fly, Mak - in' all de mu - sic he can make._____

# THERE IS NOTHIN' LIKE A DAME

Copyright © 1949 by Richard Rodgers and Oscar Hammerstein II
Copyright Renewed
WILLIAMSON MUSIC owner of publication and allied rights throughout the world

Lyrics by OSCAR HAMMERSTEIN
Music by RICHARD RODGERS

1. We got sun - light on the sand, We got moon - light on the sea, We got man - goes and ba - na - nas You can

pick right off a tree, We got vol - ley ball and ping pong and a lot of dan - dy games! What ain't

got? We ain't got dames!_____ 2. We get There Is Noth - in' Like A

Dame,_____ Noth - in'____ in the____ world,_____ There is noth - in' you can

name That is an - y - thin' like a dame! 3. We feel dame! There are no

books like a dame, ____ And noth - in' looks like a dame. ____ There are no

drinks like a dame, ____ And noth - in' thinks like a dame, ____ And noth - in'

acts like a dame, ____ Or at - tracts like a dame. There ain't a

thing that's wrong with an - y man here That can't be cured by put - tin' him

near A girl - y, wom - an - ly, fe - male, fem - i - nine dame!

VERSE 2
We get packages from home,
We get movies, we get shows,
We get speeches from our skipper
And advice from Tokyo Rose,
We get letters doused with perfume
We get dizzy from the smell!
What don't we get?
You know darn well!
(Recitation - ad lib:)
We got nothin' to put on a clean
    white suit for
We got nothin' to look masculine
    and cute for!
CHORUS

VERSE 3
We feel lonely and we long
For the fair and gentle sex,
We would like to feel the feeling
Of some arms around our necks.
We feel hungry as the wolf felt
When he met Red Riding Hood.
What don't we feel?
We don't feel good!
(Recitation - ad lib:)
Lots of things in life are beautiful,
    but brother,
There is one particular thing that is
    nothin' whatsoever in any way,
    shape or form like any other.
CHORUS

## YOU'VE GOT TO BE CAREFULLY TAUGHT

Lyrics by OSCAR HAMMERSTEIN II
Music by RICHARD RODGERS

Copyright © 1949 by Richard Rodgers and Oscar Hammerstein II
Copyright Renewed
WILLIAMSON MUSIC owner of publication and allied rights throughout the world

Lively

You've got to be taught to hate and fear, You've got to be taught from year to year, It's
got to be taught to be a - fraid of peo - ple whose eyes are odd - ly made, And

got to be drummed in your dear lit - tle ear You've Got To Be Care - ful - ly Taught. ____ You've
peo - ple whose skin is a dif - f'rent shade You've Got To Be Care - ful - ly

Taught. ____ You've got to be taught be - fore it's too late Be - fore you are six or sev - en or eight, To hate all the

peo - ple your rel - a - tives hate You've Got To Be Care - ful - ly Taught! ____ You've Got To Be Care - ful - ly Taught!

# YOUNGER THAN SPRINGTIME

Copyright © 1949 by Richard Rodgers and Oscar Hammerstein II
Copyright Renewed
WILLIAMSON MUSIC owner of publication and allied rights throughout the world

Lyrics by OSCAR HAMMERSTEIN
Music by RICHARD RODGER

# I'M GONNA WASH THAT MAN RIGHT OUTA MY HAIR

Copyright © 1949 by Richard Rodgers and Oscar Hammerstein II
Copyright Renewed
WILLIAMSON MUSIC owner of publication and allied rights throughout the world

Lyrics by OSCAR HAMMERSTEIN
Music by RICHARD RODGERS

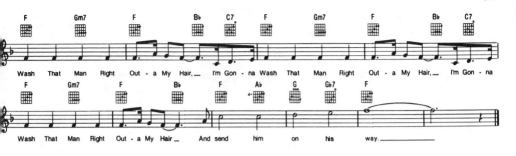

## THIS NEARLY WAS MINE

Copyright © 1949 by Richard Rodgers and Oscar Hammerstein II
Copyright Renewed
WILLIAMSON MUSIC owner of publication and allied rights throughout the world

Lyrics by OSCAR HAMMERSTEIN II
Music by RICHARD RODGERS

# HONEY BUN

Copyright © 1949 by Richard Rodgers and Oscar Hammerstein II
Copyright Renewed
WILLIAMSON MUSIC owner of publication and allied rights throughout the world

Lyrics by OSCAR HAMMERSTEIN II
Music by RICHARD RODGERS

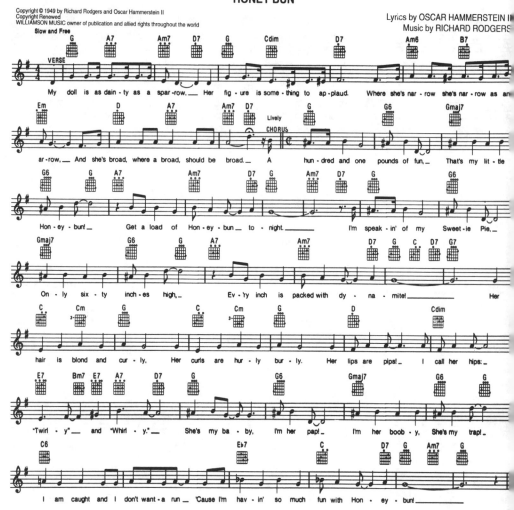

# SOME ENCHANTED EVENING

Copyright © 1949 by Richard Rodgers and Oscar Hammerstein II
Copyright Renewed
WILLIAMSON MUSIC owner of publication and allied rights throughout the world

Lyrics by OSCAR HAMMERSTEIN II
Music by RICHARD RODGERS

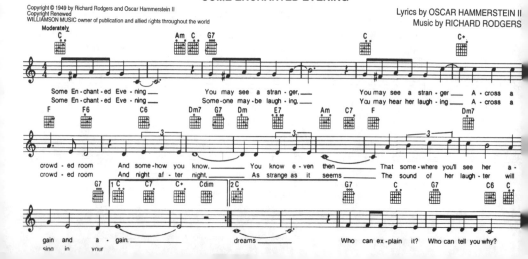

Fools give you rea-sons, Wise men nev-er try._____ Some en-chant-ed eve-ning_____ When you find your true love,_____ When you feel her call you____ A-cross a crowd-ed room, Then fly to her side_____ And make her your own_____ Or all through your life you may dream all a-lone. Once you have found her, Nev-er let her go. Once you have found her, Nev-er let her go!

## "St. Louis Woman"

### ANY PLACE I HANG MY HAT IS HOME

Copyright © 1946 by A-M Music
Copyright renewed, all rights controlled by Chappell & Co., Inc.

Words by JOHNNY MERCER
Music by HAROLD ARLEN

Slowly, with a steady rock

Free _ an' ea-sy that's my style_ How - dy do me watch me smile,_ Fare _ thee well me af - ter - while _
Sweet - nin' wa-ter cher-ry wine,_ Thank _ you kind -ly, suits me fine _ Kan - sas Ci - ty, Ca-ro - line _

'Cause I got - ta roam _____ An' An - y Place I Hang My Hat Is Home!
That's my hon - ey comb. _____ 'cause An - y Place I Hang My Hat Is Home.

Birds roost - in' in the tree pick up an' go An' the go - in' proves That's how it ought to be, I pick up too When the spir - it moves me. Cross _ the riv - er round the bend, _ How - dy stran - ger, so long friend,_ There's a voice in the lone - some win' _ that keeps whis - per - in' roam! I'm go - in' where a wel - come mat is. No mat - ter where that is 'Cause An - y Place I Hang My Hat Is Home.

# COME RAIN OR COME SHINE

Copyright © 1946 by A-M Music Corp.
Copyright Renewed, Chappell & Co., Inc., sole selling agent
International Copyright Secured   ALL RIGHTS RESERVED

Words by JOHNNY MERCER
Music by HAROLD ARLEN

## "Spring Is Here"

# WITH A SONG IN MY HEART

© 1929 WARNER BROS. INC. (Renewed)
Rights for the Extended Renewal Term in the United States Controlled by
MARLIN ENTERPRISES and THE ESTATE OF LORENZ HART
All Rights on behalf of MARLIN ENTERPRISES Administered by WILLIAMSON MUSIC
All Rights on behalf of THE ESTATE OF LORENZ HART Administered by WB MUSIC CORP.

Words by LORENZ HART
Music by RICHARD RODGERS

# "Starlight Express"

## MAKE UP MY HEART

Copyright © 1987 The Really Useful Group Ltd.
Rights for the United States and Canada Administered by PolyGram International Publishing, Inc.

Lyrics by RICHARD STILGOE
Music by ANDREW LLOYD WEBBER

Moderately

It's time I chose be-tween the two of them.__ I'd bet-ter make a start.
You'd think two lov-ers would be twice the fun.__ It's tear-ing me a-part.
Some-one help me Make Up My Heart.__

Tell me how to Make Up My Heart.__ One of them is strong, one of them is

good. Both could turn out wrong, so who gets the part? Make up my mind, Make Up My Heart.

I don't want one to win and one to lose,__ can't tell them "yes" or "no".
You'd think two lov-ers would be twice the fun.__ It's tear-ing me a-part.
It's time I chose be-tween the two of them.__ I'd bet-ter make a start.

Choos-ing one means let-ting one go.__ Can't face let-ting one of them know.__ Some-one help me Make Up My Heart.__

To Next Strain

Some-one help me Make Up My Heart.__ Tell me how to Make Up My Heart.__ One can make me

laugh, one can make me sigh. Why tear my-self in half? So who gets the part? Make up my mind, please, Make Up My Heart.

To Coda

Instrumental
One can make me laugh, one can make me sigh. Why tear my-self in

CODA
D.S. al Coda

half? So who gets the part? Make Up My Heart.

# ENGINE OF LOVE

Copyright © 1984 The Really Useful Group Ltd.
All Rights for the United States and Canada Administered by PolyGram International Publishing, Inc.

Lyrics by RICHARD STILGOE
Music by ANDREW LLOYD WEBBER

**Bright Rock**

No-bod-y can do it like a steam train.

No-bod-y can do it like a steam train. Woo,— woo,— steam. Woo,— woo,—

steam pow-er. Woo,— woo,— steam. Woo,— woo,— steam. {Work in the yard burn-ing
{Head-in' for the coast, ain't no-

all of my day - light. work-ing till it's time to play,— watch-ing the clock till my time is my own_ now.
bod-y can catch_ me. Won't stop un - til I reach the sea. Noth-ing else will do, got to be_ with you_ now.

Tacet
Watch me I'm a run - a - way. } En - gine Of Love,_ take me with you, {ba - by._ } I'll
Come and take a ride with me. } {ba by }

take you a - long_ right a - long the line._ 'cause you're my En - gine Of Love_ {and I'll thrill you with e -
{I'll thrill you with e -

To Coda
mo - tion._ } If you'll fol - low me_ your love can be mine.
mo - tion._

Your love can be mine._ Steam woo,— woo, oo,— oo, oo.

D.S. al Coda
Steam,_ steam pow - er. Oo,— oo, oo. No-bod-y can do it like a woo,— woo.

CODA
Your love can be

mine._ 'cause you're my En - gine Of Love._ {Take me with you, ba - by._ } I'll take you a - long,_ take your right a - long_ that
{Take me with you, ba - by._ }

line._____ Hey,___ your love can be mine._____ 'cause you're my En - gine Of Love.___ I'll thrill you with e -

mo - tion._____ If you'll fol - low me_____ your love can be mine._____ I wan - na be your

# LIGHT AT THE END OF THE TUNNEL

Copyright © 1984 The Really Useful Group Ltd.
All Rights for the United States and Canada Administered by PolyGram International Publishing, Inc.

Lyrics by RICHARD STILGOE
Music by ANDREW LLOYD WEBBER

Die - sel is for un - be - liev - ers. E - lec - tric - i - ty is wrong. Steam has got the pow - er that will pull us a - long.___ There's a

Light At The End Of The Tun - nel. There's a Light At The End Of The Tun - nel. The in - side might__ be as

black as the night,__ but there's a Light At The End Of The Tun - nel. There's a Light At The End Of The Tun - nel. The

in - side might__ be as black as the night,__ but at the end of the tun - nel there's a light. It's the pow'r of James Watt, the

steam - ing Scot,__ the man who watched the pot and said, Hey,__ I've got a bril - liant plot.__ When the steam is hot,__ it

seems to make a lot__ of pow'r. It could turn a wheel,__ lots of pow - er. It could drive it down a track, click - e - ty

clack click - e - ty clack. It could drive it with a beat, choo__ choo choo, with e - nough left o - ver for a woo woo. He saw the

Light At The End Of The Tun - nel. He saw the Light At The End Of The Tun - nel. Well, thanks James Watt for

# ONLY YOU

Copyright © 1984 The Really Useful Group Ltd.
All Rights for the United States and Canada Administered by PolyGram International Publishing, Inc.

Words by RICHARD STILGOE
Music by ANDREW LLOYD WEBBER

## STARLIGHT EXPRESS

Copyright © 1984 by The Really Useful Group Ltd.
All Rights for the United States and Canada Administered by PolyGram International Publishing, Inc.

Lyrics by RICHARD STILGOE
Music by ANDREW LLOYD WEBBER

# I AM THE STARLIGHT

Lyrics by RICHARD STILGOE
Music by ANDREW LLOYD WEBBER

Copyright © 1984 The Really Useful Group Ltd.
All Rights for the United States and Canada Administered by PolyGram International Publishing, Inc.

Look in your mind, I'm there. Noth - ing's new. The Star - light Ex - press is no more nor less_ than you, Rus - ty._ I am you._ I'm you and on - ly you. I Am The Star - light._ RUSTY: STARLIGHT: Have the pow - er_ with - in_ _ you._ I can a - chieve_ Just be - lieve in your - self. The sea will part be - fore you, stop the rain_ and turn the tide. All the things I did - n't be - lieve I could do. On - ly you I Am The Star - light. use the pow - er_ with - in _ you, I can see_ it through._ Need_ n't beg the world_ to turn a - round and help_ you,_ if you beg the world_ to turn a - round and help_ you,_ if you draw on what is deep in - side._ draw on what is deep in - side._

## "Stars On Ice"

### JUKE BOX SATURDAY NIGHT

Copyright © 1942 by Chappell & Co., Inc.
Copyright Renewed
International Copyright Secured     ALL RIGHTS RESERVED

Words by AL STILLMAN
Music by PAUL McGRANE

Moderately
F

Mop - pin' up so - da pop rick - eys_ To our heart's de - light Danc - in' to swing - er - oo quick - ies,_ Juke Box Sat - ur - day Night._ Good - man and Ky - ser and Mil - ler_ Help to make things bright, Mix - in' hot licks_ with va - nil - la._ Juke Box Sat - ur - day Night._

They put noth - in' past us,. Me and hon - ey lamb,— Mak - ing one — coke last us —

Till it's time to scram;. Mon - ey, we real - ly don't need — that,— We make out all

right, Let - tin' the oth - er guy feed — that — Juke Box Sat - ur - day Night. —

## "State Fair"

### IT'S A GRAND NIGHT FOR SINGING

Copyright © 1945 by Williamson Music Co., Copyright Renewed.
International Copyright Secured    ALL RIGHTS RESERVED

Words by OSCAR HAMMERSTEIN II
Music by RICHARD RODGERS

It's A Grand Night For Sing - ing! The moon is

fly - ing high. — And some - where a bird who is bound he'll be

heard, is throw - ing his heart at the sky. It's A Grand Night For

Sing - ing The stars are bright a - bove. — The earth is a -

glow and to add to the show, I think I am fall - ing in love, —

Fall - ing, fall - ing in love. —

# IT MIGHT AS WELL BE SPRING

Copyright © 1945 by Williamson Music Co., Copyright Renewed.
International Copyright Secured   ALL RIGHTS RESERVED

Words by OSCAR HAMMERSTEIN II
Music by RICHARD RODGERS

# "Stop The World - I Want To Get Off"

## GONNA BUILD A MOUNTAIN

© Copyright 1961 TRO Essex Music Ltd., London, England
TRO - LUDLOW MUSIC, INC., New York, controls all publication rights for the U.S.A. and Canada

Words and Music by
LESLIE BRICUSSE and ANTHONY NEWLEY

least I hope I will. Gon-na Build A Moun-tain _ Gon-na build it high.
up the moun-tain slope. Gon-na build a day-dream. Gon-na see it through.
and I know darn well. If I build my moun-tain with a lot of care.

I don't know how I'm gon-na do it on-ly know I'm gon-na try. 2. Gon-na build a
Gonna Build A Moun-tain and a day-dream gon-na make 'em both come true. 3. Gon-na build a
And take my day-dream up the moun-tain heav-en will be wait-ing

there.
4. When I've built that heav-en _ as I will some day And the Lord sends Ga-briel

Tacet

_ to take me a-way, Wan-na fine young son to take my place _

_ I'll leave a son in my heav-en on earth, With the Lord's good grace. With a fine young son

to take my place I'll leave a son in my heav-en on earth with the good Lord's grace. _

## ONCE IN A LIFETIME

Copyright 1981 TRO Essex Music Ltd., London, England
RO - LUDLOW MUSIC, INC., New York, controls all publication rights for the U.S.A. and Canada

Words and Music by
LESLIE BRICUSSE and ANTHONY NEWLEY

Slowly, with feeling

Just Once In A Life-time. _ A man knows a mo-ment _ One won-der-ful mo-ment _
Once In A Life-time, _ I feel like a gi-ant _ I soar like an ea-gle

_ When fate takes his hand. _ And this is my mo-ment _ My Once In A Life-time _
As tho' I had wings, _ For this is my mo-ment _ My des-ti-ny calls me,

_ When I can ex-plore a new and ex-cit-ing land. _ For
And

tho' it may be just Once In My Life-time I'm going to do great things. _

## SOMEONE NICE LIKE YOU

© Copyright 1961 TRO Essex Music Ltd., London, England
TRO - LUDLOW MUSIC, INC, New York, controls all publication rights for the U.S.A. and Canada

Words and Music
LESLIE BRICUSSE and ANTHONY NEWLEY

Why did Some-one Nice Like You sweet-heart, Have to love some-one like me?
You ask why did some-one nice like me Have to love some-one like you?

When I think of all the men you could have loved, the men you should have loved,
And you men-tion all the men I could have loved, the men I should have loved

who would have loved you. You're worth so much more than me sweet-heart, Be-lieve you
who would have loved me. May-be Sig-mund Freud could tell you why I'll love you

me sweet-heart, You know that's true And if we could live twice I'd make life par-a-dise
till I die, The way I do But who wants Freud's ad-vice I'm sure it works with mice

for some-one real-ly nice like you.
But not with Some-one Nice Like You.

## WHAT KIND OF FOOL AM I?

© Copyright 1961 TRO Essex Music Ltd., London, England
TRO - LUDLOW MUSIC, INC, New York, controls all publication rights for the U.S.A. and Canada

Words and Music
LESLIE BRICUSSE and ANTHONY NEWLEY

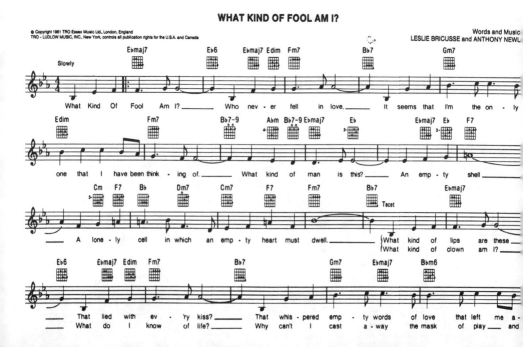

What Kind Of Fool Am I? Who nev-er fell in love, It seems that I'm the on-ly

one that I have been think-ing of. What kind of man is this? An emp-ty shell

A lone-ly cell in which an emp-ty heart must dwell. What kind of lips are these
What kind of clown am I?

That lied with ev-'ry kiss? That whis-pered emp-ty words of love that left me a-
What do I know of life? Why can't I cast a-way the mask of play and

lone like this \_\_\_\_ Why can't I fall in love \_\_\_\_ like an-y oth-er man \_\_\_\_ And may-be
live my life? \_\_\_\_ Why can't I fall in love \_\_\_\_ (like oth-er peo-ple can) \_\_\_\_ And may-be
till I don't give a damn \_\_\_\_

then I'll know what kind of fool I am. What Kind Of am. \_\_\_\_

## "Stop! Look! Listen!"

### I LOVE A PIANO

© Copyright 1915 by Irving Berlin
Copyright Renewed

Words and Music by
IRVING BERLIN

I Love A Pian-o, \_\_\_\_ I Love A Pian-o. \_\_\_\_ I love to hear some-bod-y play \_\_\_\_ up-on a

pian-o, \_\_\_\_ a grand pi-an-o. \_\_\_\_ It sim-ply car-ries me a - way.

I know a fine way to treat a Stein-way. I love to

run my fin-gers o'er the keys, \_\_ the i-vor-ies. And with the ped-al \_\_\_\_ I love to

med-dle. \_\_\_\_ Not on-ly mu-sic from Broad-way. \_\_\_\_ I'm so de-light-ed \_\_\_\_ if I'm in-

vit-ed \_\_\_\_ to hear a long haired gen-ius play. \_\_\_\_ So you can keep your fid-dle

and your bow. \_\_ Give me a p-i-an-o. Oh, oh, I love to stop right \_\_\_\_ be-side an

up-right, or a high toned ba-by grand. I Love A grand.

# "Street Scene"

## MOON-FACED, STARRY-EYED

Words by LANGSTON HUGHES
Music by KURT WEILL

TRO - © Copyright 1947 and renewed 1975 Hampshire House Publishing Corp. and Chappell & Co., Inc., New York, N.Y.

## WHAT GOOD WOULD THE MOON BE?

Words by LANGSTON HUGHES
Music by KURT WEILL

TRO - © Copyright 1946 and renewed 1974 Hampshire House Publishing Corp. and Chappell & Co., Inc., New York, N.Y.

low; Kiss me oh, dar-ling, kiss me ___ While eve-ning stars still glow. ___ No it won't be a prim-rose path for_ me, No it

won't be dia-monds and gold, But may-be it will be ___ Some-one who'll love me, ___ some-one who'll love just

me to have and to hold. What Good Would The love just me to have and to hold.

## "Sunny"

## WHO?

Copyright © 1925 PolyGram International Publishing, Inc.
Copyright Renewed

Lyrics by OTTO HARBACH and OSCAR HAMMERSTEIN II
Music by JEROME KERN

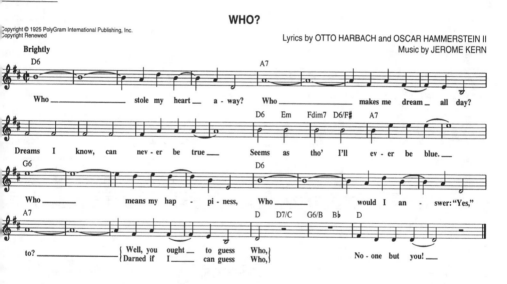

Who ___ stole my heart ___ a-way? Who ___ makes me dream ___ all day?

Dreams I know, can nev-er be true ___ Seems as tho' I'll ev-er be blue. ___

Who ___ means my hap-pi-ness, Who ___ would I an-swer: "Yes,"

to? ___ { Well, you ought ___ to guess Who, / Darned if I ___ can guess Who, } No-one but you! ___

## "Sweet Adeline"

## DON'T EVER LEAVE ME

Copyright © 1929 PolyGram International Publishing, Inc.
Copyright Renewed

Lyrics by OSCAR HAMMERSTEIN II
Music by JEROME KERN

Don't ev-er leave_ me, now that you're here! Here is where you_ be-long. Ev-'ry-thing seems_ so right when you're near,_

When you're a-way_ it's all wrong. I'm so de-pen-dent When I need com-fort I al-ways run_ to

you. Don't ev-er leave_ me! 'Cause if you do,_ I'll have no one_ to run to. to.__

# "Subways Are For Sleeping"

## BE A SANTA

Words by BETTY COMDEN & ADOLPH GREEN
Music by JULE STYNE

Copyright © 1961 by Betty Comden, Adolph Green and Jule Styne
Bradford Music Corp., owner, Chappell & Co., Inc., Administrator of publication and allied rights for the Western Hemisphere

# Sweeney Todd, The Demon Barber Of Fleet Street"

## NOT WHILE I'M AROUND

© REVELATION MUSIC PUBLISHING CORP. & RILTING MUSIC, INC.
my Valando Publication

Lyric and Music by
STEPHEN SONDHEIM

Noth-ing's gon-na harm you, Not while I'm a-round. ___ Noth-ing's gon-na

harm you, no sir, Not While I'm A-round. ___ De-mons are prowl-ing ev-'ry-where, Now-a-days. ___

I'll send 'em howl-ing, I don't care, I got ways. ___

No-one's gon-na hurt you, No-one's gon-na dare. ___ Oth-ers can de-

sert you, not to wor-ry, Whis-tle, I'll be there. ___ De-mons-'ll charm you with a smile

For a-while, But in time Noth-ing can harm you, Not While I'm A-round. ___

Noth-ing's gon-na harm you, Not While I'm A-round. ___

## THE BALLAD OF SWEENEY TODD

76 REVELATION MUSIC PUBLISHING CORP. & RILTING MUSIC, INC.
nmy Valando Publication

Lyric and Music by
STEPHEN SONDHEIM

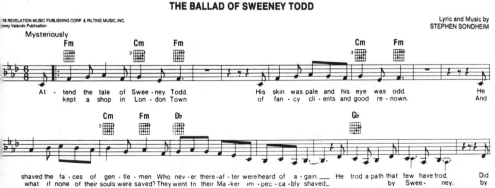

At-tend the tale of Swee-ney Todd. His skin was pale and his eye was odd. He
kept a shop in Lon-don Town of fan-cy cli-ents and good re-nown. And

shaved the fa-ces of gen-tle-men Who nev-er there-af-ter were heard of a-gain. ___ He trod a path that few have trod. Did
what if none of their souls were saved? They went to their Ma-ker im-pec-ca-bly shaved ___ by Swee-ney, by

## JOHANNA

Lyric and Music by
STEPHEN SONDHEIM

'76 REVELATION MUSIC PUBLISHING CORP. & RILTING MUSIC, INC.
mmy Valando Publication

Tranquilly

I feel you, Jo-han-na, I feel you. I was half con-vinced I'd wak-en,
steal you, Jo-han-na, I'll steal you. Do they think that walls can hide _ you?

Sat-is-fied e-nough to dream _ you. Hap-pi-ly, I was mis-tak - en, Jo-han-na! I'll
E-ven now I'm at your win - dow.

I am in the dark be-side _ you,

Bur-ied sweet-ly in your yel-low hair. _____

I feel you, Jo-

han - na, And one day I'll steal you.

Till I'm with you then I'm with you there,

Sweet-ly bur-ied in your yel-low hair. _____

## PRETTY WOMEN

Lyric and Music by
STEPHEN SONDHEIM

979 REVELATION MUSIC PUBLISHING CORP. & RILTING MUSIC, INC.
mmy Valando Publication

Languid but steady

Pret-ty Wom-en... _ fas-ci-nat-ing... _ sip-ping cof-fee, _ danc-ing. Pret-ty Wom-en, _ are a won-der. _
Pret-ty Wom-en... _ sil-hou-ett-ed... _ stay with in you, _ glanc-ing... stay for-ev-er, _ breath-ing light-ly... _

Pret-ty Wom-en! Sit-ting in the _ win-dow or stand-ing on the _ stair, Some-thing in them
Pret-ty Wom-en, _ Pret-ty Wom-en! Blow-ing out their can-dles or comb-ing out their hair, E-ven when they

cheers the air. _____ leave, _ they still _ are there. They're there. Ah, Pret-ty Wom-en, at their mir-rors, in their gar-dens,

let-ter-writ-ing, flow-er-pick-ing, weath-er-watch-ing, How they make a man sing! Proof of heav-en _ as you're liv-ing, _

Pret-ty Wom-en! _ Yes, Pret-ty Wom-en! Here's to Pret-ty Wom-en. Pret-ty Wom-en, Pret-ty Wom-en. Pret-ty Wom-en! _

570

# "Tenderloin"

## I WONDER WHAT IT'S LIKE

Copyright © 1960 by Alley Music Corp. and Trio Music Co., Inc.
All rights administered by Hudson Bay Music, Inc.
Used by Permission

Lyrics by SHELDON HARNICK
Music by JERRY BOCK

Slowly

I Won-der What It's Like, what it's real-ly like to be with a man. I won-der how it

feels, how it real-ly feels to be as close as two peo-ple can. I know I'll nev-er know, un-til I know I

would-n't dare un-til I know it is-n't right un-til you're mar-ried.

Of course, to be sure, to be sure of course how true! Quite true and still I Won-der What It's

Like I won-der how it feels to be _____ with a man. _____

## ARTIFICIAL FLOWERS

Copyright © 1960 by Alley Music Corp. and Trio Music Co., Inc.
All rights administered by Hudson Bay Music, Inc.
Used by Permission

Lyrics by SHELDON HARNICK
Music by JERRY BOCK

Sentimental

A - lone in the world was poor lit - tle Ann As sweet a young child as you'd find _____
pa - per and shears with wi - re and wax She fash - ioned each tu - lip and mum _____
found lit - tle Ann, all cov - ered with ice still clutch - ing her poor fro - zen shears

_____ Her par - ents had gone to their fin - al re - ward leav - ing their dar - ling be - hind
_____ As snow drift - ed in - to her ten - e - ment room her dear lit - tle fin - gers grew numb
_____ A - midst all the blos - soms she fash - ioned by hand and wat - ered with all her young tears

_____ This poor lit - tle child was but nine years of age when moth - er and dad _____ went a - way
_____ With pa - per and shears with wi - re and wax she lab - ored and nev - er com - plained
_____ There must be a heav - 'n where An - nie can play in heav - en - ly gar - dens and bow'rs

_____ But brave - ly she worked at the one thing she knew to earn her few pen - nies each day _____ She made
_____ 'Til cut - ting and fold - ing her health slipped a - way and wir - ing and wax - ing she waned - Mak - ing
_____ In - stead of a ha - lo she'll wear round her head a gar - land of gen - u - ine flow'rs No more

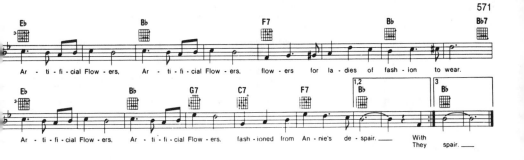

## MY MISS MARY

Copyright © 1960 by Alley Music Corp. and Trio Music Co., Inc.
Rights administered by Hudson Bay Music, Inc.
Used by Permission

Lyrics by SHELDON HARNICK
Music by JERRY BOCK

# "The Unsinkable Molly Brown"

## I'LL NEVER SAY NO

1960 (Renewed) FRANK MUSIC CORP. and MEREDITH WILLSON MUSIC

By MEREDITH WILLSON

# I AIN'T DOWN YET

© 1960, 1961 (Renewed) FRANK MUSIC CORP. and MEREDITH WILLSON MUSIC

Words and Music
MEREDITH WILLSON

I'm goan' to learn to read and write, I'm goan' to see what there is to see, ___ So if you go from no-where on the road to some-where and you meet an-y one you'll know it's me. I'm goan' to move from place to place to find a house with gold - en stair And if that house is red and has a big brass bed I'm liii - vin' there. ___

## "They're Playing Our Song"

### FALLIN'

Copyright © 1979 by Chappell & Co., Inc., Red Bullet Music, Unichappell Music, Inc. and Begonia Melodies, Inc.
Publication and allied rights administered by Chappell & Co., Inc., and Unichappell Music, Inc. throughout the world.

Lyrics by CAROLE BAYER SAGER
Music by MARVIN HAMLISCH

I'm a-fraid to fly, ___ and I don't know why I'm jeal-ous of ___ the peo-ple who ___ are not a-fraid to die. ___ It just that I ___ re-call, ___ back when I ___ was small, some-one prom-ised that they'd catch me, then they let me fall; and now I'm
Turn and walk a-way, ___ that's what I ___ should do. My head says go and find the door, my heart says I found you; and now I'm

Fall - in', Fall - in' fast a-gain. Why do I al-ways take a fall ___ when I fall ___ in love? You'd love. It al-ways turns out the same. Lov-ing some-one, los-ing my-self, on-ly got me to blame. Help me, I'm Fall - in'. Fall - in', catch me if you can. May-be this time I'll have it all, ___ may-be I'll make it af-ter all, ___ may-be this time I won't fall when I fall ___ in love. ___

# THEY'RE PLAYING MY SONG

right © 1979, 1980 by Chappell & Co., Inc., Red Bullet Music, Unichappell Music, Inc. and Begonia Melodies, Inc.
ation and allied rights administered by Chappell & Co., Inc. and Unichappell Music, Inc. throughout the World.
national Copyright Secured    ALL RIGHTS RESERVED

Lyrics by CAROLE BAYER SAGER
Music by MARVIN HAMLISCH

# I STILL BELIEVE IN LOVE

Copyright © 1979 by Chappell & Co., Inc., Red Bullet Music, Unichappell Music, Inc. and Begonia Melodies, Inc.
Publication and allied rights administered by Chappell & Co., Inc. and Unichappell Music, Inc. throughout the World.
International Copyright Secured    ALL RIGHTS RESERVED

Lyrics by CAROLE BAYER SA(
Music by MARVIN HAMLI(

**Moderate Rock Ballad**

Af - ter all the tears I cried, you'd think I would. give up on love,_ get off that line,_ but may - be I can get_ it right ti(

time. I was there as pas - sion turned to pain,_ sun - shine turned to rain - y days,. yet here I am_ read - y to be - gin_ once

gain. All my life ____ I've been a dream - er, dream - ing dreams that nev - er ___ quite come true; but

Still Be - lieve_ In Love and love be - liev - in' may - be you _ can make. my dreams come true. Here con - tent with who

am, I'm reach - in' out_ my hand to him_ (her) once a - gain;_ at least I know I made my - self a friend. All m(

life ____ I've been a dream - er, dream - ing dreams that al - ways. broke in two; but I still Be - lieve_ In Love

and love be - liev - in'; I'll keep on dream - in' be - cause I Still Be - lieve In Love,_

I Still Be - lieve In Love and me and you, I Still Be - lieve in love. _____

## JUST FOR TONIGHT

Copyright © 1979 by Chappell & Co., Inc., Red Bullet Music, Unichappell Music, Inc. and Begonia Melodies, Inc.
Publication and allied rights administered by Chappell & Co., Inc. and Unichappell Music, Inc. throughout the world.

Lyrics by CAROLE BAYER SA(
Music by MARVIN HAMLI(

**Slow Rock tempo**

Just for to - day let me love you. Just For To - night _ I'll close my eyes, and when I o - pen them my world will be
day_ I want to hold you. Just For To - night _ you'll be my dream. and when the morn - in' comes to wake me that's

right;_ it could - n't hurt an - y - one._ it would - n't hurt an - y - one._ Just for to
right;_ it could - n't hurt an - y - one, _____ it would - n't hurt an - y - one. Tak - in' just_ one mo - re c(

try-in' for some fun, __ Up to now __ my life's been too __ much said, too lit-tle done. Just for to-day __ I'll be my feel-ings, and I know they'll lead me home; and if we both come back a lit-tle wis-er it could-n't hurt an-y-one, __ it would-n't hurt an-y-one. ___ it should-n't hurt an-y-one _ Just For To - night. Just For To - night. _____

## IF YOU REALLY KNEW ME

Copyright © 1979 by Chappell & Co., Inc., Red Bullet Music, Unichappell Music, Inc. and Begonia Melodies, Inc.
Publication and allied rights administered by Chappell & Co. Inc. and Unichappell Music, Inc. throughout the world.

Lyrics by CAROLE BAYER SAGER
Music by MARVIN HAMLISCH

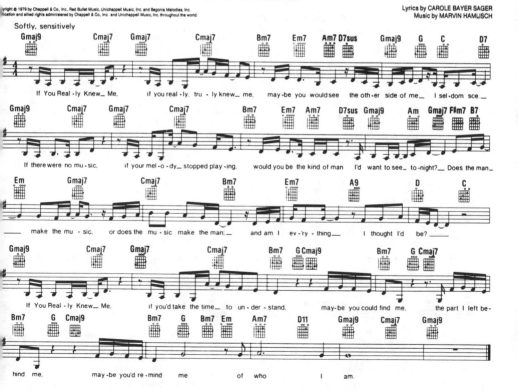

Softly, sensitively

If You Real-ly Knew __ Me, if you real-ly, tru-ly knew __ me, may-be you would see the oth-er side of me __ I sel-dom see. __

If there were no mu-sic, if your mel-o-dy __ stopped play-ing, would you be the kind of man I'd want to see __ to-night? __ Does the man __

__ make the mu-sic, or does the mu-sic make the man; __ and am I ev-'ry-thing __ I thought I'd be? _____

If You Real-ly Knew __ Me, if you'd take the time __ to un-der-stand, may-be you could find me, the part I left be-

hind me. may-be you'd re-mind me of who I am.

# "Tickets, Please!"

## DARN IT, BABY, THAT'S LOVE

Copyright © 1950 by Chappell & Co., Inc.
Copyright renewed

Words and Music
LYN DUDDY and JOAN EDWARDS

3. *She* Someday ya gonna develop gout.
   *He* All kinds of pills you can't do without.
   *She* I'll find you're gettin' a trifle stout.
   *He* You'll leave your teeth in a glass, no doubt.
   *She* Tho' you are falling apart, dear,
   You'll have the key to my heart, dear,
   *Both* Darn it! Baby that's love!

4. *He* Someday you're gonna have chins to spare.
   *She* Where are the muscles that once were there?
   *He* You'll sit and rock in your rockin' chair.
   *She* Gosh, dear, but we'll be a gruesome pair.
   *He* Tho' you may have indigestion,
   I'm glad that I popped the question,
   *Both* Darn it! Baby that's love!

## "Two Gentlemen Of Verona"

### WHO IS SILVIA?

Copyright © 1971 and 1972 by John Guare and Galt MacDermot
All rights administered by Chappell & Co., Inc.

Words by WILLIAM SHAKESPEARE
Music by GALT MacDERMOT

## "Too Many Girls"

### I DIDN'T KNOW WHAT TIME IT WAS

Copyright © 1939 by Chappell & Co., Inc.
Copyright Renewed
International Copyright Secured     ALL RIGHTS RESERVED

Words by LORENZ HART
Music by RICHARD RODGERS

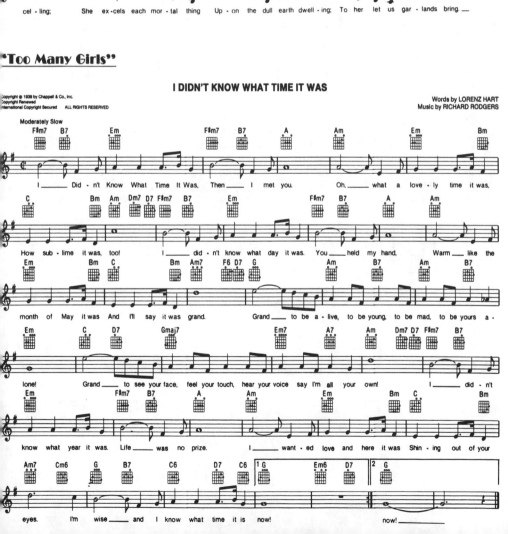

# "Treemonisha"

## A REAL SLOW DRAG

Copyright © 1975 by Many Wormley
Rights administered by Unichappell Music, Inc.

Words and Music by
SCOTT JOPLIN

Treemonisha:
Sa - lute your part - ner, do the drag, drag, drag. Stop and move back - ward, do the drag. All _____ of you stop. Look to your right _____ and do the drag, drag, drag. To _____ your left, to _____ your left, that's the way. _____

Treemonisha:
March - ing on - ward, march - ing on - ward, march - ing to _____ that love - ly tune; _____ March - ing on - ward,

Lucy:
March - ing on - ward, march - ing on - ward, march - ing to _____ that love - ly tune; _____ March - ing on - ward,

march - ing on - ward, hap - py as _____ a bird in June. Slid - ing on - ward, slid - ing on - ward,

march - ing on - ward, hap - py as _____ a bird in June. Slid - ing on - ward, slid - ing on - ward,

lis - ten to _____ that rag. Hop and skip, now do that slow, _____

lis - ten to _____ that rag. Hop and skip, now do that slow, _____

_____ do that slow drag. _____ Dance _____ slow - ly, prance _____ slow - ly,

_____ do that slow drag. _____ Dance _____ slow - ly, prance _____ slow - ly,

while you hear ____ that pret-ty rag. ___ Dance ____ slow-ly, prance ____ slow-ly,

while you hear _ that pret-ty rag. ___ Dance slow-ly, prance ____ slow-ly,

Now you do ___ The Real "Slow Drag" Walk ____ slow-ly, talk ____ low-ly,

Now you do ___ The Real "Slow Drag" Walk slow-ly, talk ____ low-ly,

Treemonisha:

Lis-ten to ____ that rag, Hop and skip, now do that slow, _____ O.

do that slow drag. _ Move a - long, don't stop, don't

stop danc-ing. Drag a - long. stop. Move a - long, don't

stop, don't stop danc-ing. Drag a - long, do-ing The Real Slow Drag. stop danc-ing, Drag a-

long, do-ing The Real Slow Drag. O do that slow drag. _ slow - - o - o - o.

# "Two By Two"

## I DO NOT KNOW A DAY I DID NOT LOVE YOU

Copyright © 1970 by Richard Rodgers and Beam One, Ltd.
Williamson Music Co., and Williamson Music, Ltd., owners of publication and allied rights of Richard Rodgers throughout the world
Edwin H. Morris & Co., Inc., owner of allied rights of Beam One, Ltd., throughout the world
Williamson Music Co., Sole Selling Agent

Words by MARTIN CHARNIN
Music by RICHARD RODGERS

I Do Not Know A Day I Did Not Love You. I can't re-mem-ber love not be-ing there;

The plant-ing, when the earth ran through your fin - gers; The har-vest, when the sun danced in your

hair. I do not know a day I did not need you For shar-ing ev-'ry

mo-ment that I spent. I need-ed you be-fore I ev-er knew you, Be-fore I

knew what need-ing some - one meant. And if we ev-er were to have to-mor - row,
as we face the prom-ise of to-mor - row,

One fact a-lone is full (and filled with song;) You will not know a day I do not

love you The way that I have loved you all a - long. I long.

# "Two For The Show"

## HOW HIGH THE MOON

Copyright © 1940 by Chappell & Co. Inc.
Copyright Renewed
International Copyright Secured    ALL RIGHTS RESERVED

Words by NANCY HAMILTON
Music by MORGAN LEWIS

Some - where there's mu - sic, How faint the tune! Some - where there's heav - en, How High The

Moon! There is no moon a - bove When love is far _ a-way too. Till _ it comes true

That you love me as I love you. Some - where there's mu - sic, It's where you are, Some - where there's

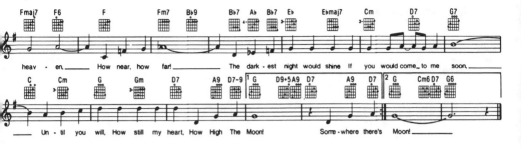

heav - en, _____ How near, how far! _____ The dark - est night would shine If you would come, to me soon, _____

_____ Un - til you will, How still my heart, How High The Moon! Some - where there's Moon! _____

## "This Year Of Grace"

### A ROOM WITH A VIEW

Copyright © 1928 by Chappell & Co., Ltd.
Copyright renewed published in the U.S.A. by Chappell & Co., Inc.

Words and Music by
NOEL COWARD

*Gracefully*

*He:* A Room _ With A View and you, And no one to wor - ry us, No one to hur - ry us through This

dream we've found. _____ We'll gaze _ at the sky and try To guess what it's all a - bout.

Then we will fig - ure out why the world is round. _____ *She:* We'll be as hap - py and con -

tent - ed As birds _ up - on _ a tree. High a - bove the moun - tains and sea.

*Both:* _____ We'll bill _ and we'll coo - oo - oo, And sor - row will nev - er come. Oh, will it ev - er come

true? _____ Our room _ with a view! A Room _ With A view! _____

# "Up In Central Park"

## CLOSE AS PAGES IN A BOOK

Copyright © 1944 by Williamson Music, Inc.
Copyright Renewed.
International Copyright Secured    ALL RIGHTS RESERVED

Words by DOROTHY FIELDS
Music by SIGMUND ROMBERG

We'll be Close As Pag-es In A Book, My love and I. So close we can share a sin-gle look,

Share ev-'ry sigh. So close that be-fore I hear your laugh, My laugh breaks through; And when a tear

starts to ap-pear, My eyes grow mist-y too ____ Our dreams won't come tumb-ling to the ground, We'll hold them

fast. Darl-ing, as the strong-est book is bound, We're bound to last. Your life is

my life and while life beats a-way in my heart ____ We'll be Close As Pag-es In A Book, nev-er to part.

## "The Vagabond King"

### ONLY A ROSE

Copyright © 1925 (Renewed 1952) by Famous Music Corporation

Words by BRIAN HOOKER
Music by RUDOLF FRIML

On-ly a rose I give you On-ly a song Dy-ing a-way, On-ly a smile To keep in mem-o-ry Un-til we meet An-oth-er day. On-ly a rose To whis-per Blush-ing as ros - es do, I'll bring a-long a smile or a song for an-y-one On-ly a rose for you.

## "Very Warm For May"

### ALL THE THINGS YOU ARE

Copyright © 1939 PolyGram International Publishing, Inc.
Copyright Renewed

Lyrics by OSCAR HAMMERSTEIN II
Music by JEROME KERN

You are the prom-ised kiss of spring-time That makes the lone-ly win-ter seem long. You are the breath-less hush of eve-ning That trem-bles on the brink of a love-ly song. You are the an-gel glow that lights a star. The dear-est things I know are what you are. Some day my hap-py arms will hold you, And some day I'll know that mo-ment di-vine. When All The Things You Are, are mine.

584

# "Wait A Minim!"

## I KNOW WHERE I'M GOING

© 1964, 1966 BURLINGTON MUSIC CO., Ltd., London, England
Published by FRANK MUSIC CORP.
By arrangement with BURLINGTON MUSIC CORP.

Adapted
ANDREW & PAUL TRACEY

## I GAVE MY LOVE A CHERRY

© 1964, 1966 BURLINGTON MUSIC CO., Ltd., London, England
Published by FRANK MUSIC CORP.
By arrangement with BURLINGTON MUSIC CORP.

Adapted b
ANDREW & PAUL TRACE

# "Where's Charley?"

## THE NEW ASHMOLEAN MARCHING SOCIETY AND STUDENTS CONSERVATORY BAND

© 1948, 1950 FRANK MUSIC CORP.
© Renewed 1976, 1978 FRANK MUSIC CORP.

By FRANK LOESSER

March Tempo

**VERSE**

Here they come with the sun-light on the trum-pets
march on-ly slight-ly out of tem-po

Here they come with the ban-ners fly-ing
Though they play just a tri-fle out of

high ___ In my throat I've a lump-y sort of feel-ing
tune ___ Though there's just a sug-ges-tion in the o-boe

And the bright gleam of
Of the sound of a

pride is in my eye. ___ Here they come with the clar-i-nets a-wail-ing
hound be-neath the moon. ___ Though the trom-bone's a lit-tle in-de-pend-ent

Here they
And the

come rath-er brave-ly up the square ___ And I know in a mo-ment I'll be cheer-ing
drum-mer is not ex-act-ly choice ___ Still the old col-lege spir-it is up-on me

**CHORUS**

And my fine Sun-day hat will be high in the air for The} New Ash-mo-le-an
And I shout ev-'ry time at the top of my voice for The}

March-ing So-ci-e-ty And Stu-dents Con-serv-a-to-ry Band. ___
Yes the New Ash-
If you're an a-

mo-le-an could have beat Na-po-le-on with all those dead-ly in-stru-ments in hand.
lyt-i-cal sen-si-tive or crit-i-cal you'll like it more the far-ther back you stand.

There are
But to

those who fa-vor the phil-har-mon-ic fla-vor but to me the fin-est in the land ___ is The} New Ash-
me it's bul-ly it sat-is-fies me ful-ly when I hear that thun-der close at hand ___ from The}

mo-le-an March-ing So-ci-e-ty And Stu-dents Con-serv-a-to-ry Band. ___
[1.] (To Verse) Though they
[2.] Band. ___

## MY DARLING, MY DARLING

© 1948 FRANK MUSIC CORP.
© Renewed 1976 FRANK MUSIC CORP.

By FRANK LOESSER

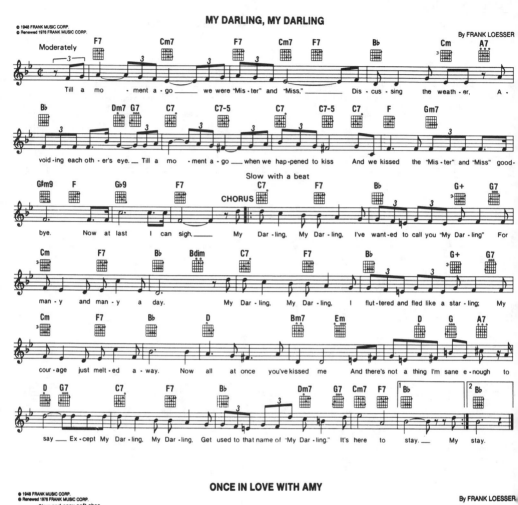

Till a mo - ment a - go ____ we were "Mis - ter" and "Miss," ____ Dis - cus - sing the weath - er, A-

void - ing each oth - er's eye.__ Till a mo - ment a - go ____ when we hap - pened to kiss And we kissed the "Mis - ter" and "Miss" good-

bye. Now at last I can sigh,____ My Dar - ling, My Dar - ling, I've want - ed to call you "My Dar - ling" For

man - y and man - y a day. My Dar - ling, My Dar - ling, I flut - tered and fled like a star - ling; My

cour - age just melt - ed a - way. Now all at once you've kissed me And there's not a thing I'm sane e - nough to

say __ Ex - cept My Dar - ling, My Dar - ling, Get used to that name of "My Dar - ling." It's here to stay.__ My stay.

## ONCE IN LOVE WITH AMY

© 1948 FRANK MUSIC CORP.
© Renewed 1976 FRANK MUSIC CORP.

By FRANK LOESSER

Once In Love With A - my, __ Al - ways in love with A - my. __ Ev - er and ev - er fas - cin - at - ed by 'er,

Sets your heart a - fire to stay. Once you're kissed by A - my, __ Tear up your list, it's A - my.

Ply her with bon - bons, po - et - ry and flow - ers, Moon a mil - lion hours __ a - way.__ You might be quite the fick - le - heart - ed

ro - ver, So care - free and bold _____ Who loves a girl and la - ter thinks it o - ver And

just quits cold, But Once In Love With A - my, __ Al - ways in love with

A - my. __ Ev - er and ev - er sweet - ly you'll ro - mance 'er. Trou - ble is, the an - swer will be _____ That

A - my'd rath - er stay in love with me. _____ me. _____

## LOVELIER THAN EVER

By FRANK LOESSER

© 1948 FRANK MUSIC CORP.
© Renewed 1976 FRANK MUSIC CORP.

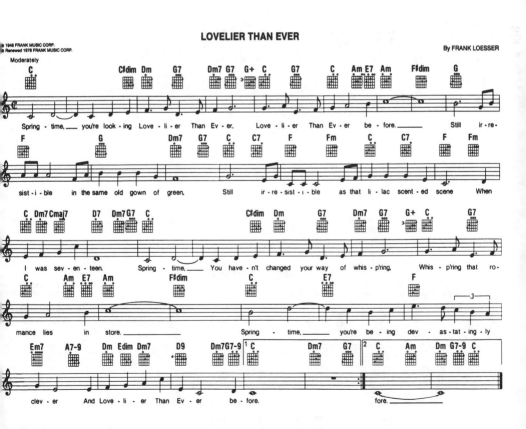

Spring - time, __ you're look - ing Love - li - er Than Ev - er, Love - li - er Than Ev - er be - fore. _____ Still ir - re -

sist - i - ble in the same old gown of green, Still ir - re - sist - i - ble as that li - lac scent - ed scene When

I was sev - en - teen. Spring - time, __ You have - n't changed your way of whis - p'ring, Whis - p'ring that ro -

mance lies in store. _____ Spring - time, _____ you're be - ing dev - as - tat - ing - ly

clev - er And Love - li - er Than Ev - er be - fore. fore. _____

## "Whoopee!"

### MAKIN' WHOOPEE!

Copyright © 1928 (Renewed) by Donaldson Publishing Co. and Gilbert Keyes Music Co.

Lyrics by GUS KAHN
Music by WALTER DONALDSON

## "Wildcat"

### HEY, LOOK ME OVER

© 1980 CAROLYN LEIGH and CY COLEMAN
All Rights Throughout the World Controlled by EDWIN H. MORRIS & COMPANY, A Division of MPL Communications, Inc.

Lyric by CAROLYN LEIGH
Music by CY COLEMAN

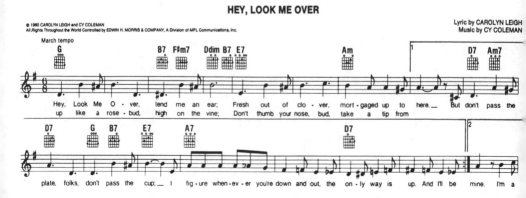

lit - tle bit short of the el - bow room, but let me get me some, (And look out) world, here I come.
(Hear me shout,)
come. _____

**INTERLUDE**

No - bod - y in the world was ev - er with - out a pray'r; How can you win the world, if no - bod - y knows you're there.

Kid, when you need the crowd, the tick - ets are hard to sell; Still you can lead the crowd, if you can get up and yell:

## YOU'VE COME HOME

© 1960, 1961 CAROLYN LEIGH and CY COLEMAN
All Rights Throughout the World Controlled by EDWIN H. MORRIS & COMPANY, A Division of MPL Communications, Inc.

Lyric by CAROLYN LEIGH
Music by CY COLEMAN

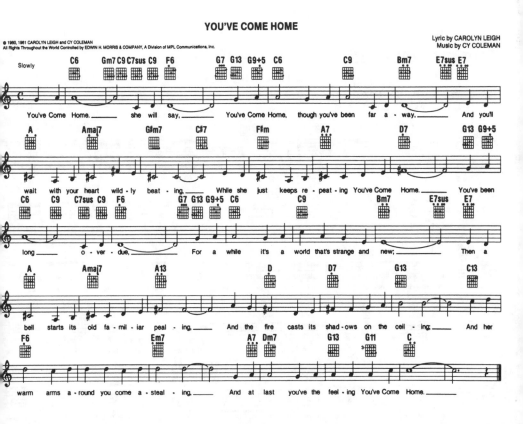

You've Come Home. _____ she will say, _____ You've Come Home, though you've been far a - way, _____ And you'll

wait with your heart wild - ly beat - ing, _____ While she just keeps re - peat - ing You've Come Home. _____ You've been

long _____ o - ver - due, _____ For a while it's a world that's strange and new; Then a

bell starts its old fa - mil - iar peal - ing, _____ And the fire casts its shad - ows on the ceil - ing; And her

warm arms a - round you come a - steal - ing, _____ And at last you've the feel - ing You've Come Home. _____

# "Wish You Were Here"

### WISH YOU WERE HERE

Copyright © 1952 by Harold Rome
Chappell & Co., Inc., owner of publication and allied rights throughout the World
International Copyright Secured   ALL RIGHTS RESERVED

Words and Music by
HAROLD ROME

They're not mak-ing the skies as blue this year. Wish You Were Here! As blue as they used to when you were near. Wish You Were Here! And

morn-ings don't seem as new, Brand new as they did with you. Wish You Were Here! Wish You Were Here! Wish You Were Here! __ Some-one's

paint-ing the leaves all wrong this year. Wish You Were Here! And why did the birds change their song this year? Wish You Were Here! They're no

shin-ing the stars as bright. They've stol-en the joy from the night! Wish You Were Here! Wish You Were Here! Wish You Were Here! __

# "Woman Of The Year"

### I WROTE THE BOOK

© 1981 FIDDLEBACK MUSIC PUBLISHING CO., INC. & KANDER & EBB, INC.
A Tommy Valando Publication

Lyric by FRED EBB
Music by JOHN KANDER

I Wrote The Book on how to be cool,__ I Wrote The Book on how to be strong__ I Wrote The Book on how to in-ter-

-pret the news__ and nev-er be wrong. _____ I Wrote The Book on how to be tough__ I Wrote The

Book on how to be terse._ I Wrote The Book on ev-'ry sub-tex- tu-al phrase__ in El-i-ot's verse.__

I Wrote The Book on how to have class.__ I Wrote The Book on how to have clout.__ I Wrote The

Book on read-ing gov-ern-ment pam-phlets and dop-ing them out.__ So, when it comes to los-ing a man,

© 1961 FIDDLEBACK MUSIC PUBLISHING CO., INC. & KANDER & EBB, INC.
A Tommy Valando Publication

# ONE OF THE GIRLS

Lyric by FRED EBB
Music by JOHN KANDER

Brightly

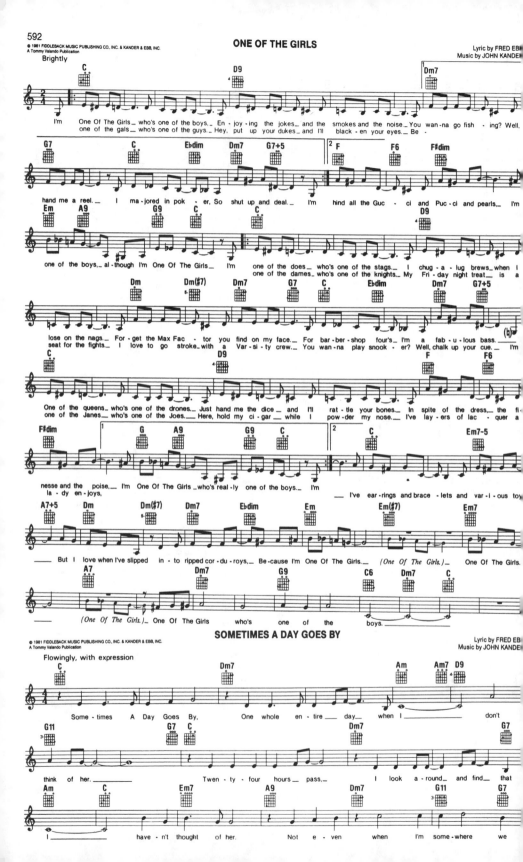

I'm One Of The Girls_ who's one of the boys._ En-joy-ing the jokes_ and the smokes and the noise. You wan-na go fish - ing? Well,
one of the gals_ who's one of the guys. Hey, put up your dukes_ and I'll black - en your eyes._ Be -

hand me a reel._ I ma-jored in pok - er, So shut up and deal._ I'm hind all the Guc - ci and Puc - ci and pearls,_ I'm

one of the boys,_ al - though I'm One Of The Girls._ I'm one of the does_ who's one of the stags._ I chug - a - lug brews_ when I
one of the dames_ who's one of the knights._ My Fri - day night treat_ is a

lose on the nags._ For - get the Max Fac - tor you find on my face._ For bar - ber - shop four's_ I'm a fab - u - lous bass._
seat for the fights._ I love to go stroke_ with a Var - si - ty crew._ You wan - na play snook - er? Well, chalk up your cue._ I'm

One of the queens_ who's one of the drones._ Just hand me the dice_ and I'll rat - tle your bones._ In spite of the dress,_ the fi -
one of the Janes_ who's one of the Joes._ Here, hold my ci - gar_ while I pow - der my nose._ I've lay - ers of lac - quer a -

nesse and the poise,_ I'm One Of The Girls_ who's real - ly one of the boys._ I'm
la - dy en - joys,

_ I've ear - rings and brace - lets and var - i - ous toy-

_ But I love when I've slipped in - to ripped cor - du - roys,_ Be - cause I'm One Of The Girls._ *(One Of The Girls.)_* One Of The Girls.

*(One Of The Girls.)_* One Of The Girls who's one of the boys.

# SOMETIMES A DAY GOES BY

© 1961 FIDDLEBACK MUSIC PUBLISHING CO., INC. & KANDER & EBB, INC.
A Tommy Valando Publication

Lyric by FRED EBB
Music by JOHN KANDER

Flowingly, with expression

Some - times A Day Goes By, One whole en - tire ___ day_ when I_ don't

think of her. ____ Twen - ty - four hours_ pass,_ I look a - round_ and find_ that

I _____ have - n't thought of her. Not e - ven when I'm some - where we

used to go, Not e - ven if that's some - one we used to know. _____

It's hard - ly ev - 'ry - day, _____ it's most un - u - su - al, _____ In fact, I can't re -

mem - ber when, But, _____ Some - times A Day Goes By when I don't think of her _____ 'til morn - ing

comes, And then _____ there she is a - gain.

## "Words And Music"

### SOMETHING TO DO WITH SPRING

Copyright © 1932 by Chappell & Co. Ltd.
Copyright renewed, published in the USA by Chappell & Co., Inc.

Words and Music by
NOEL COWARD

Moderately

The sun is shin - ing where clouds have been, _____ May - be it's Some - thing To Do With
The dew - drops glit - ter like dia - mond links, _____ May - be it's Some - thing To Do With

Spring. _____ I feel no old - er than sev - en - teen, _____
Spring. _____ They say that rab - bits have minds like sinks, _____

May - be it's Some - thing To Do With Spring. _____ A some - thing I can't ex - press, _____ A sort of
May - be it's Some - thing To Do With Spring _____ The way that the sows be - have _____ May seem de -

lilt in the air, _____ A ly - ri - cal love - li - ness seems ev - 'ry - where.
light - ful - ly quaint, _____ But why should the cows be - have _____ with no res - traint?

That sheep's be - ha - vior is most ob - scene, _____
I'd love to know what that don - key thinks, _____

May - be it's Some - thing To Do With Spring. _____
May - be it's Some - thing To Do With Spring. _____

# MAD ABOUT THE BOY

Copyright © 1932 by Chappell & Co., Ltd., London    Copyright Renewed
Published in the U.S.A. by Chappell & Co., Inc.

Words and Music
NOEL COWARD

## "Wonderful Town"

### THE WRONG NOTE RAG

Copyright © 1953 by Leonard Bernstein, Betty Comden and Adolph Green
Copyright renewed, Chappell & Co., Inc. and G. Schirmer, Inc., owners of publication
and allied rights throughout the world

Words by BETTY COMDEN & ADOLPH GREEN
Music by LEONARD BERNSTEIN

## OHIO

Copyright © 1953 by Leonard Bernstein, Betty Comden and Adolph Green
Copyright renewed, Chappell & Co., Inc., and G. Schirmer, Inc., owners of publication
and allied rights throughout the world

Words by BETTY COMDEN & ADOLPH GREEN
Music by LEONARD BERNSTEIN

# "Working"

## LOVIN' AL

© 1978 FIDDLEBACK MUSIC PUBLISHING CORP
A Tommy Valando Publication

Words and Music
MICKI GRANT

Moderate groove

Ask an-y-bod-y to tell you 'bout Lov-in' Al. You can ask an-y-bod-y and an-y-bod-y will tell you. There was a time when no-bod-y could beat me doin' what I do. I'd punch out a tick-et, slide un-der the wheel and, right off the bat, have it un-der con-trol. Us-in' one hand I'd spin 'er a-round and with out back-in' up, put 'er straight in the hole.

*Spoken:* Peo-ple won-der how I do it! Ain't noth-in' to it! *Sung:* 'Cause I'm Lov-in' Al the Wiz-ard. "One Swing Al," that's me! Lov-in' Al is a Wiz-ard. So don't be sur-prised at what you see. *Spoken:* One swing-in'! One swing out! Look out, there he goes. *Sung:* Why can't I be a rich man with some big bucks in my jeans? I'd buy me a brand new Cad-dy! And a fif-ty-cent ci-gar! 'Cause you

**IF I COULD'VE BEEN**

©1978 FIDDLEBACK MUSIC PUBLISHING CORP.
Tommy Valando Publication

Words and Music by
MICKI GRANT

"The Yearling"

I'M ALL SMILES

## WHY DID I CHOOSE YOU?

Lyric by HERBERT MARTIN
Music by MICHAEL LEONARD

© 1965 HERBERT MARTIN and MICHAEL LEONARD
Rights Throughout the World Controlled by EDWIN H. MORRIS & COMPANY,
A Division of MPL Communications, Inc., and EMANUEL MUSIC CORP.

# THE KIND OF MAN A WOMAN NEEDS

© 1966 HERBERT MARTIN and MICHAEL LEONARD
All Rights Throughout the World Controlled by EDWIN H. MORRIS & COMPANY,
A Division of MPL Communications, Inc., and EMANUEL MUSIC CORP.

Lyric by HERBERT MARTIN
Music by MICHAEL LEONARD

# "The Zulu And The Zayda"

## OUT OF THIS WORLD

Words and Music by
HAROLD ROME

Copyright © 1965 by Harold Rome
Chappell & Co., Inc., owner of publication and allied rights throughout the world

3. It could be the smell of bread that bakes,
   Or a hot bath when bones are aching,
   After work, a welcome glass of schnapps,
   Or an aching tooth when it fin'lly stops.

4. It could be a game of cards you win,
   A glass of seltzer after a big dinner,
   Biting on a ripe and juicy peach,
   Or someone to scratch where you cannot reach.

# "You Never Know"

## AT LONG LAST LOVE

Copyright © 1937 and 1938 by Chappell & Co., Inc.
Copyrights renewed

Words and Musi
COLE POR

# "Your Arms Too Short To Box With God"

## WE'RE GONNA HAVE A GOOD TIME

© 1977 FIDDLEBACK MUSIC PUBLISHING CO., INC.
A Tommy Valando Publication

Words and Music
MICKI GRA

Let's have a good time. But I'm gon-na do what the Lord said do.__ And have a good time.
Let's have a good time. That's what He meant 'cause the Lord don't lie.__ Let's have a good time.

We're Gon-na Have A

good time.__ We're Gon - na Have A Good Time.__ Come on in, __ sit right down.__ Let's have a good time.

## "Ziegfeld Follies - 1936"

Copyright © 1935 by Kay Duke Music and Ira Gershwin Music
Copyright Renewed
Rights for Kay Duke Music Administered by BMG Songs, Inc.
Rights for Ira Gershwin Music Administered by WB Music Corp.

# I CAN'T GET STARTED WITH YOU

Words by IRA GERSHWIN
Music by VERNON DUKE

Slowly

I've flown a - round the world in a plane; __ I've set - tled re - vo - lu - tions in Spain; The North Pole I have char - ted, But
hun - dred yards in ten flat; __ The Prince of Wales has cop - ied my hat; With queens I've a - la cart - ed, But

can't get start - ed with you. __ A - round a golf course I'm __ un - der par, __ And all the mov - ies want __ me to
can't get start - ed with you. __ The lead - ing tail - ors fol - low my styles. __ And tooth-paste ads all fea - ture my

star; I've got a house, a show place, But I get no __ place with you. You're so su - preme,
smiles; The As - tor - bilts I vis - it, But say, what Is __ it with you? When first we met,

lyr - ics I write __ of you, Scheme just for a sight __ of you, Dream both day and night __ of you And what
how you e - lat - ed me! Pet, you dev - as - tat - ed me! Yet, now you've de - flat - ed me Till you're

good does it do? In nine - teen twen - ty - nine __ I sold short, __ In Eng - land I'm pre - sen - ted at court, But you've got
my Wa - ter - loo. I've sold my kiss - es at __ a ba - zaar, And af - ter me they've named a ci - gar; But late - ly

me down - heart - ed 'Cause I Can't Get Start - ed With You.
how I've smart - ed, 'Cause I Can't Get Start - ed With

I do a

You. __

# "Zorba"

## ZORBA THEME
### (Life Is)

Copyright © 1968 by Alley Music Corp. and Trio Music Company, Inc.
All rights administered by Hudson Bay Music, Inc.
Used by Permission

Lyric by FRED EB
Music by JOHN KANDE

# HAPPY BIRTHDAY TO ME

Copyright © 1968 by Alley Music Corp. and Trio Music Company, Inc.
All rights administered by Hudson Bay Music, Inc.
Used by Permission

Lyric by FRED EBB
Music by JOHN KANDER

# ONLY LOVE

Copyright © 1968 by Alley Music Corp. and Trio Music Company, Inc.
All rights administered by Hudson Bay Music, Inc.
Used by Permission

Lyric by FRED EBB
Music by JOHN KANDER

# I AM FREE

Copyright © 1966 by Alley Music Corp. and Trio Music Company, Inc.
All rights administered by Hudson Bay Music, Inc.
Used by Permission

Lyric by FRED E
Music by JOHN KAND

I have noth-ing! I want noth-ing! I Am Free!____ I need noth-ing! I

owe noth-ing! I Am Free!____ If my feet say come this way I prob-ab-ly would

____ But if they say go that way, that way is just as good! I ask noth-ing! I

judge noth-ing! I Am Free!____ There's one Zor-ba! But that Zor-ba I must be!____

Heav-en waits for oth-er men but not for me.____ I fear noth-ing! I

hope for noth-ing! ____ I Am Free.____ One morn-ing in Sa-lon-i-ca I

nev-er will for-get. I was pass-ing by the old-est man that I had ev-er met. He was

kneel-ing in an or-chard when he turned and looked at me. And he said: "Come watch me, Son-ny, as I

plant this al-mond tree." Well I tell you boss that fel-la he was o-ver nine-ty-five. And I

think he had a week or may-be two to stay a-live. But he had to plant that al-mond tree and

when I asked him why He said: "I live ev-'ry min-ute as if I would nev-er die." For

that rea-son! Just that rea-son! I Am Free!____ I see some-where! I

go some-where! I Am Free! _____ Think of that when-ev-er you re-mem-ber me _____ I

fear noth-ing _____ I hope for noth-ing! _____ I Am Free.

# THE FIRST TIME

Lyric by FRED EBB
Music by JOHN KANDER

Copyright © 1968 by Alley Music Corp. and Trio Music Company, Inc.
All rights administered by Hudson Bay Music, Inc.
Used by Permission

Moderately

I hear a ba-zou-ki. You can't i-ma-gine how of-ten I've heard a ba-zou-ki, but each time

_____ is The First Time. I sniff at a wom-an. You can't i-

ma-gine how of-ten I've sniffed at a wom-an, but each time _____ is The First Time. _____ I

pound on a ta-ble. I jump on a chair. I crawl up a moun-tain to breathe in the air. By now I've stopped count-ing how of-ten I've been there, but

each time _____ is The First Time. _____ I look at a flow-er

I stick my nose in, or stare at, or sleep on a flow-er and each time is The First Time. I soar like a sea-gull,

stamp like a bull. I comb out my whis-kers for la-dies to pull. I chew on the mut-ton un-til my bel-ly's full and

each time, each time I talk to a stran-ger. You can't i-ma-gine how of-ten I've

talked to a stran-ger, but each time this time _____ is The First Time.

# "Ziegfeld Follies Of 1919"

© Copyright 1919 by Irving Berlin
Copyright Renewed

## A PRETTY GIRL IS LIKE A MELODY

Words and Music by
IRVING BERLIN

# "Jekyll & Hyde"

## SOMEONE LIKE YOU

Copyright © 1990, 1995 Stage & Screen Music, Inc. (BMI),
Cherry Lane Music Publishing Company, Inc. (ASCAP),
Scaramanga Music (ASCAP) and Les Etoiles De La Musique (ASCAP)
Rights for Stage & Screen Music, Inc. administered worldwide by Cherry River Music (BMI)

Lyrics by LESLIE BRICUSSE
Music by FRANK WILDHORN

# A NEW LIFE

Copyright © 1990 Stage & Screen Music, Inc. (BMI),
Cherry Lane Music Publishing Company, Inc. (ASCAP)
and Scaramanga Music (ASCAP)

Lyrics by LESLIE BRICUSSE
Music by FRANK WILDHORN

# TAKE ME AS I AM

Copyright © 1995 Stage & Screen Music Ltd. (BMI),
Cherry Lane Music Publishing Company, Inc.,
Scaramanga Music and Les Etoiles De La Musique (ASCAP)
Stage & Screen Music Ltd. administered worldwide by Cherry River Music (BMI)

Words by LESLIE BRICUSSE
Music by FRANK WILDHORN

# THIS IS THE MOMENT

Copyright © 1990, 1995 Stage & Screen Music, Inc. (BMI),
Cherry Lane Music Publishing Company, Inc. (ASCAP),
Scaramanga Music (ASCAP) and Les Etoiles De La Musique (ASCAP)
Rights for Stage & Screen Music, Inc. administered worldwide by Cherry River Music (BMI)

Words by LESLIE BRICUSSE
Music by FRANK WILDHORN

## "Martin Guerre"

# WHEN WILL SOMEONE HEAR?

Copyright © 1996 by Bouberg Music Ltd.
Administered for the U.S.A. by Alain Boublil Music Ltd. (ASCAP)
c/o Stephen Tenenbaum & Co., Inc., 1775 Broadway, Suite 708,
New York, NY 10019, Tel. (212) 246-7204, Fax (212) 246-7217

Music by CLAUDE-MICHEL SCHÖNBERG
Lyrics by ALAIN BOUBLIL and STEPHEN CLARK

**Andante**

**BERTRANDE:**

When Will Some-one Hear? _ All I know is fear. _ And now I see the lone - li - ness of

lo - sing all you trust. _ Day has turned to night, stone has turned to dust. And

now I need to find the words. _ When Will Some - one Hear? Love that once was close, _

faith that once was clear. _ Now all I've known and all I've loved is all I have to grieve.

All that I've be - gun, all that I be - lieve is just an - oth - er bro - ken dream. _ When Will Some - one

Hear? They seem so strong, they seem so sure. They'd take my soul and still want more.

No one here will lis - ten, it's not me they're fight - ing for. Now I know. Don't de - cide for me.

Now at last it's clear, and don't think I'm that lit - tle girl they want - ed me to be.

They don't know me now, fight - ing to be free. There's no one here to un - der - stand.

When Will Some - one Hear? I will car - ry on, till the fear has gone,

Till the day I find... there's some - one who will hear.

# HERE COMES THE MORNING

Music by CLAUDE-MICHEL SCHÖNBERG
Lyrics by ALAIN BOUBLIL, STEPHEN CLARK,
EDWARD HARDY and HERBERT KRETZMER

Copyright © 1996 by Bouberg Music Ltd.
Administered for the U.S.A. by Alain Boublil Music Ltd. (ASCAP)
c/o Stephen Tenenbaum & Co., Inc., 1775 Broadway, Suite 708,
New York, NY 10019, Tel. (212) 246-7204, Fax (212) 246-7217

# TELL ME TO GO

Copyright © 1996 by Bouberg Music Ltd.
Administered for the U.S.A. by Alain Boublil Music Ltd. (ASCAP)
c/o Stephen Tenenbaum & Co., Inc., 1775 Broadway, Suite 708,
New York, NY 10019, Tel. (212) 246-7204, Fax (212) 246-7217

Music by CLAUDE-MICHEL SCHÖNBERG
Lyrics by ALAIN BOUBLIL, EDWARD HARDY
and STEPHEN CLARK

# SOMEONE

Copyright © 1996 by Bouberg Music Ltd.
Administered for the U.S.A. by Alain Boublil Music Ltd. (ASCAP)
c/o Stephen Tenenbaum & Co., Inc., 1775 Broadway, Suite 708,
New York, NY 10019, Tel. (212) 246-7204, Fax (212) 246-7217

Music by CLAUDE-MICHEL SCHÖNBERG
Lyrics by ALAIN BOUBLIL, EDWARD HARDY
and STEPHEN CLARK

# "Smokey Joe's Cafe"

## JAILHOUSE ROCK

Words and Music by
JERRY LEIBER and MIKE STOLLER

© 1957 (Renewed) JERRY LEIBER MUSIC and MIKE STOLLER MUSIC

*Additional Lyrics*

2. Spider Murphy played the tenor saxophone
   Little Joe was blowin' on the slide trombone.
   The drummer boy from Illinois went crash, boom, bang;
   The whole rhythm section was the Purple Gang.
   *(Chorus)*

3. Number Forty-seven said to number Three:
   "You're the cutest jailbird I ever did see.
   I sure would be delighted with your company,
   Come on and do the Jailhouse Rock with me."
   *(Chorus)*

4. The sad sack was a-sittin' on a block of stone,
   Way over in the corner weeping all alone.
   The warden said: "Hey, Buddy, don't you be no square,
   If you can't find a partner, use a wooden chair!"
   *(Chorus)*

5. Shifty Henry said to Bugs: "For heaven's sake,
   No one's lookin', now's our chance to make a break."
   Bugsy turned to Shifty and he said: "Nix, nix;
   I wanna stick around a while and get my kicks."
   *(Chorus)*

# KANSAS CITY

© 1959 (Renewed) JERRY LEIBER MUSIC, MIKE STOLLER MUSIC
and NANCY NATHAN GOLDSTEIN

Words and Music by
JERRY LEIBER and MIKE STOLLER

# ON BROADWAY

© 1962, 1963 (Renewed 1990, 1991) SCREEN GEMS-EMI MUSIC INC.

Words and Music by BARRY MANN, CYNTHIA WEIL,
MIKE STOLLER and JERRY LEIBER

# LOVE POTION NUMBER 9

© 1959 (Renewed) JERRY LEIBER MUSIC and MIKE STOLLER MUSIC

Words and Music by
JERRY LEIBER and MIKE STOLLER

# "Sunset Boulevard"
## AS IF WE NEVER SAID GOODBYE

© Copyright 1993 The Really Useful Group Ltd.
All Rights for the United States Controlled by Famous Music Corporation

Music by ANDREW LLOYD WEBBER
Lyrics by DON BLACK and CHRISTOPHER HAMPTON
with contributions by AMY POWERS

coming out of make-up, the light's al-read-y burn-ing, _____ not long un-til _____ the cam-eras will _____ start turn-ing, _____ and the ear-ly morn-ing mad-ness, _____ and the mag-ic in the mak-ing, _____ yes, ev-ery-thing's as if we nev-er said good-bye. _____ I don't want to be a-lone, that's all in the past. This world's wait-ed long e-nough, _____ I've come home at last, and this time will be big-ger, _____ and bright-er than we knew it. _____ So watch me fly, we all know I _____ can do it. _____ Could I stop my hand from shak-ing? _____ Has there ev-er been a mo-ment with so much to live for? The whis-pered con-ver-sa-tions _____ in o-ver-crowd-ed hall-ways, _____ so much to say, not just to-day, _____ but al-ways. _____ We'll have ear-ly morn-ing mad-ness, _____ we'll have mag-ic in the mak-ing, _____ yes, ev-ery-thing's as if we nev-er said good-bye, _____ yes, ev-ery-thing's as if we nev-er said good-bye. _____ We taught the world new ways to dream.

# WITH ONE LOOK

© Copyright 1993 The Really Useful Group Ltd.
All Rights for the United States Controlled by Famous Music Corporation

Music by ANDREW LLOYD WEBBER
Lyrics by DON BLACK and CHRISTOPHER HAMPTON
with contributions by AMY POWERS

**Lento moderato**

NORMA: With one look I can break your heart, with one look I play ev - ery part.

I can make your sad heart sing. With one look you'll know all you need to know.

With one smile I'm the girl next door or the love that you've hun - gered for.

When I speak it's with my soul. I can play an - y role. No

words can tell the sto - ries my eyes tell. Watch me when I frown, you can't write that down. You

know I'm right, it's there in black and white. When I look your way you'll hear what I say. Yes,

with one look I put words to shame, just one look sets the screen a - flame.

Si - lent mu - sic starts to play. One tear in my eye makes the whole world cry.

With one look they'll for - give the past, they'll re - joice I've re - turned at last

to my peo - ple in the dark, still out there in the dark.

Si - lent mu - sic starts to play. With one look you'll know all you need to know.

With one look I'll ig - nite a blaze, I'll re - turn to my glo - ry days.

They'll say Nor-ma's back at last. This time I am stay - ing, I'm stay-ing for good, I'll be

back where I was born to be. With one look I'll be me.

# SURRENDER

© Copyright 1993 The Really Useful Group Ltd.
All Rights for the United States Controlled by Famous Music Corporation

Music by ANDREW LLOYD WEBBER
Lyrics by DON BLACK and CHRISTOPHER HAMPTON

NORMA

No more wars to fight, white flags fly to - night, you are out of dan - ger

now. Bat - tle field is still, wild pop - pies on the hill,

peace can on - ly come when you sur - ren - der. Here the tra - cers fly,

light - ing up the sky, but I'll fight on to the end.

Let them send their ar - mies, I will ne - ver bend, I won't see you now till I sur -

ren - der, I'll see you a - gain when I sur - ren - der.

# NEW WAYS TO DREAM

© Copyright 1993 The Really Useful Group Ltd.
All Rights for the United States Controlled by Famous Music Corporation

Music by ANDREW LLOYD WEBBER
Lyrics by DON BLACK and CHRISTOPHER HAMPTON

# LIVING IN THE SHADOWS

Copyright © 1995 Stage & Screen Music Ltd. (BMI), Bronx Flash Music, Inc.,
Sbocaj Publishing Inc. and Scaramanga Music (ASCAP)
Stage & Screen Music Ltd. administered worldwide by Cherry River Music (BMI)

Words by LESLIE BRICUSSE
Music by FRANK WILDHORN

# PARIS BY NIGHT

Copyright © 1995 Stage & Screen Music Ltd. (BMI) and Hollyweed Music (ASCAP)
Stage & Screen Music Ltd. administered worldwide by Cherry River Music (BMI)
Hollyweed Music administered by All Nations Music

Words by LESLIE BRICUSSE
Music by HENRY MANCINI

# IF I WERE A MAN

Copyright © 1995 Stage & Screen Music Ltd. (BMI) and Hollyweed Music (ASCAP)
Stage & Screen Music Ltd. administered worldwide by Cherry River Music (BMI)
Hollyweed Music administered by All Nations Music

Words by LESLIE BRICUSSE
Music by HENRY MANCINI

# ONE SONG GLORY

© 1995 FINSTER & LUCY MUSIC LTD. CO.
All Rights Controlled and Administered by EMI APRIL MUSIC INC.

Words and Music by
JONATHAN LARSON

# SEASONS OF LOVE

© 1995 FINSTER & LUCY MUSIC LTD. CO.
All Rights Controlled and Administered by EMI APRIL MUSIC INC.

Words and Music by
JONATHAN LARSON

# TAKE ME OR LEAVE ME

© 1995 FINSTER & LUCY MUSIC LTD. CO.
All Rights Controlled and Administered by EMI APRIL MUSIC INC.

Words and Music by
JONATHAN LARSON

# RENT

© 1995 FINSTER & LUCY MUSIC LTD. CO.
All Rights Controlled and Administered by EMI APRIL MUSIC INC.

Words and Music by
JONATHAN LARSON

# WITHOUT YOU

© 1995 FINSTER & LUCY MUSIC LTD. CO.
All Rights Controlled and Administered by EMI APRIL MUSIC INC.

Words and Music by
JONATHAN LARSON